THE
COLD WAR
DEBATED

THE COLD WAR DEBATED

David Carlton
Herbert M. Levine

McGRAW-HILL BOOK COMPANY

New York St. Louis San Francisco Auckland Bogotá
Hamburg London Madrid Mexico Milan Montreal New Delhi
Panama Paris São Paulo Singapore Sydney Tokyo Toronto

This book was set in Times Roman by the College Composition Unit
in cooperation with York Graphic Services, Inc.
The editor was James D. Anker;
the cover was designed by John Hite;
the production supervisor was Denise L. Puryear.
Project Supervision was done by The Total Book.
R. R. Donnelley & Sons Company was printer and binder.

THE COLD WAR DEBATED

1 2 3 4 5 6 7 8 9 0   DOCDOC   8 9 2 1 0 9 8 7

ISBN 0-07-027990-X

Library of Congress Cataloging-in-Publication Data

The Cold war debated.

  Bibliography: p.
  1. World politics, 1945–   . I. Carlton,
David (Date). II. Levine, Herbert M.
D843.F576 1988   327.73047   87-9296
ISBN 0-07-027990-X

CONTENTS

Editors   xi
List of Contributors   xiii
Preface   xvii

CHAPTER 1   Historical Issues   1

1   Has Franklin Roosevelt Been Unfairly Criticized for Yalta?   9

YES   Theodore Draper, "Neoconservative History"   10

NO   Paul Seabury, "Yalta and the Neoconservatives"   21

Questions for Discussion   25
Suggested Readings   25

2   Is It Likely That the U.S. Use of Atomic Bombs at Hiroshima and
Nagasaki Was Designed to Intimidate the Soviet Union?   26

YES   Gar Alperovitz, "More on Atomic Diplomacy"   27

NO   Geoffrey Warner, "To End a War: The Decision to Drop the Bomb"   34

Questions for Discussion   39
Suggested Readings   39

3   Was U.S. Intervention in Vietnam Immoral?   41

YES   Hendrik Hertzberg, "Why the War Was Immoral"   42

NO   David Horowitz, "My Vietnam Lessons"   46

Questions for Discussion   50
Suggested Readings   50

4   Was U.S. Acceptance of the Helsinki Accords a Mistake?   51

YES   Eric Breindel, "The Price of Helsinki"   52

NO   Leonard R. Sussman, "In Support of the Helsinki Process"   53

Questions for Discussion   58
Suggested Readings   58

5   Was Detente of Mutual Benefit to the United States and the Soviet
Union?   60

YES   Henry A. Kissinger, ["Detente"]   61

NO   George Meany, ["The Case against Detente"]   76

Questions for Discussion   88
Suggested Readings   89

6   Was the United States Primarily Responsible for the Cold War?   90

YES   D. F. Fleming, ["The Cold War: Origins and Developments"]   91

NO   Robert J. Maddox, "The Rise and Fall of Cold War Revisionism"   95

Questions for Discussion   104
Suggested Readings   104

CHAPTER 2   International System   105

7   Does the Coming to Power of Marxist Regimes in Central America
Inevitably Mean a Strengthening of the Soviet Union?   110

YES   Carl Gershman, "Soviet Power in Central America and the
Caribbean: The Growing Threat to American Security"   110

NO   Sol M. Linowitz, ["The United States and Central America"]   122

Questions for Discussion   127
Suggested Readings   128

8   Has U.S. Hegemony Declined Drastically over Recent Years?   129

YES   Kenneth A. Oye, "International Systems Structure and American
Foreign Policy"   130

NO   Bruce Russett, "The Mysterious Case of Vanishing Hegomony;
or Is Mark Twain Really Dead?"   137

Questions for Discussion   155
Suggested Readings   155

CHAPTER 3   Goals   157

9   Is U.S.–Soviet Competition Influenced Primarily by Ideological
Factors?   164

YES   Herbert J. Ellison, ''Soviet-American Intervention''   165

NO   Brian Thomas, ''Ideology and The Cold War''   172

Questions for Discussion   179
Suggested Readings   179

10   Was the Soviet Invasion of Afghanistan a Major Geopolitical
Challenge to the West?   180

YES   William E. Griffith, ''Super-Power Relations after Afghanistan''   181

NO   Geoffrey Stern, ''The Soviet Union, Afghanistan and East-West
Relations''   187

Questions for Discussion   196
Suggested Readings   196

11A   Does the Application of an Activist Human Rights Policy by the
United States against Its Allies Hurt U.S. Interests?   198

YES   Jeane Kirkpatrick, ''Dictatorships and Double Standards''   199

NO   Sidney Blumenthal, ''An Ideology That Didn't Match Reality''   215

11B   Are Developments in the Philippines That Resulted in the Toppling
of the Marcos Regime an Exception to the Validity of the Kirkpatrick
Thesis about the Use of Human Rights as a Goal of Foreign Policy?   219

YES   Jeane Kirkpatrick, ''Philippine Exception''   220

NO   Sidney Blumenthal, ''Kirkpatrick and Democracy''   221

Questions for Discussion   223
Suggested Readings   224

12   Should the Reagan Doctrine Be Implemented?   225

YES   Jack Wheeler, [''In Defense of the Reagan Doctrine'']   226

NO   Christopher Layne, ''The Real Conservative Agenda''   229

Questions for Discussion   240
Suggested Readings   240

CHAPTER 4   Instruments of Power   241

13   Can the United States Use Economic Inducements to Achieve
Political Concessions from the Soviet Union?   248

YES   Bruce W. Jentleson, "The Political Basis for Trade in U.S.–Soviet
Relations"   249

NO   Edward A. Hewett, ["Economic Leverage in U.S.–Soviet
Relations"]   266

Questions for Discussion   271
Suggested Readings   271

14   Do Most Terrorists Serve as Instruments of Soviet Foreign Policy?   272

YES   *Wall Street Journal*, "Bombing the West"   273

NO   Alexander Cockburn, "A Connected Terrorist under Every Bed"   274

Questions for Discussion   276
Suggested Readings   276

15   Is It a U.S. Interest to Develop and Deploy Ballistic Missile Defenses?   278

YES   John C. Toomay, "The Case for Ballistic Missile Defense"   279

NO   Jack Mendelsohn, "Five Fallacies of SDI"   290

Questions for Discussion   298
Suggested Readings   298

16   Are Superpower Nuclear Arms Control Agreements So Vital That the
United States Should Avoid Using the Negotiations to Introduce Linkages
to Other Issues?   299

YES   John A. Hamilton, "To Link or Not to Link"   300

NO   Richard Pipes, ["Linkage"]   309

Questions for Discussion   312
Suggested Readings   312

17   Is It Wise for the United States to Threaten Its NATO Allies with
Possible Reduction in U.S. troops in Europe If the Allies Do Not Live Up
to Their Alliance Commitments?   314

YES   Sam Nunn, ["The Nunn Amendment"]   315

NO   Richard Lugar, ["The Nunn Amendment"]   323

Questions for Discussion   326
Suggested Readings   326

CHAPTER 5 Formal Constraints on Conflict   328

18   Should the United States Acknowledge the Jurisdiction of the World
Court?   331

YES   Richard N. Gardner, ["The United States and the World Court"]   332

NO   Burton Yale Pines, "Should the United States Acknowledge the
Jurisdiction of the World Court?   336

Questions for Discussion   337
Suggested Readings   337

19   Do U.S.–Soviet Arms Control Agreements Enhance the Prospects for
Peace between the Superpowers?   339

YES   Wolfgang K. H. Panofsky, "Arms Control: Necessary Process"   340

NO   William A. Schwartz and Charles Derber, "Arms Control: Misplaced
Focus"   346

Questions for Discussion   354
Suggested Readings   355

EDITORS

DAVID CARLTON is Senior Lecturer in History at the Polytechnic of North London, Great Britain. He is author of *Anthony Eden: A Biography* (1981; reprinted by Unwin Paperbacks, 1986). Dr. Carlton is co-editor with Herbert M. Levine of *The Nuclear Arms Race Debated* (McGraw-Hill, 1986). He is also co-editor of nine volumes produced under the auspices of the Rome-based International School on Disarmament and Research on Conflicts.

HERBERT M. LEVINE is a political scientist who taught at the University of Southwestern Louisiana for twenty years. He has written and edited several textbooks in political science, including most recently *World Politics Debated: A Reader in Contemporary Issues* (McGraw-Hill, 1986), and *Political Issues Debated: An Introduction to Politics* (Prentice-Hall, 1987). He is currently a political writer.

LIST OF CONTRIBUTORS

GAR ALPEROVITZ, an historian and political economist, is the President of the National Center for Economic Alternatives in Washington, D.C. He is the author of *Atomic Diplomacy: Hiroshima and Potsdam: The Use of the Atomic Bomb and the American Confrontation with Soviet Power* (Penguin).

SIDNEY BLUMENTHAL is a staff writer for *The Washington Post*. He is the author of *The Rise of the Counter-Establishment: From Conservative Ideology to Political Power* (Times Books) and *The Permanent Campaign: Inside the World of Elite Political Operatives* (Beacon Press).

ERIC BREINDEL is a member of the editorial board of *The New York Daily News*.

ALEXANDER COCKBURN is a correspondent for *The Nation*. He is editor, with James Ridgeway, of *Political Ecology* (Times Books).

CHARLES DERBER is Associate Professor of Sociology at Boston College.

THEODORE DRAPER is the author of several books, including *Abuse of Power* (Viking) and *Present History: On Nuclear War, Detente, and Other Controversies* (Random House).

HERBERT J. ELLISON is Secretary of the Kennan Institute for Advanced Russian Studies at the Wilson Center and Professor of History and Chairman of the Russian and East European Studies at the University of Washington. He served as a trustee of the National Council for Soviet and East European Research.

D. F. FLEMING was Professor Emeritus of Political Science at Vanderbilt University. He was the author of several books, including *The Cold War and Its Origins* (Doubleday) and *The Origins and Legacies of World War I* (Doubleday).

RICHARD N. GARDNER is Henry L. Moses Professor of Law and International Organization at Columbia University. He served as U.S. Ambassador to Italy from 1977 to 1981.

CARL GERSHMAN is President of the National Endowment for Democracy. He served as a member of the U.S. Mission to the United Nations.

WILLIAM E. GRIFFITH is Ford Professor of Political Science at the Massachusetts Institute of Technology. He is the author of several books, including *The Sino-Soviet Rift* (MIT Press) and *The Superpowers and Regional Tensions: The USSR, the United States, and Europe* (Lexington Books).

JOHN A. HAMILTON, a Foreign Service Officer, served as the State Department's country officer for Tunisia.

HENDRIK HERTZBERG is a senior associate at the Press–Politics Center at Harvard University's John F. Kennedy School of Government.

EDWARD A. HEWETT is a Senior Fellow in the Foreign Studies Program at Brookings Institution. He is the author of *Energy, Economics, and Foreign Policy in the Soviet Union* (Brookings Institution).

DAVID HOROWITZ, a former editor of *Ramparts,* was an anti-Vietnam War activist. He is the author, with Peter Collier, of *The Kennedys: An American Drama* (Summit Books).

BRUCE W. JENTLESON is Assistant Professor of Political Science at the University of California at Davis. He is the author of *Pipeline Politics: The Complex Political Economy of East-West Energy Trade* (Cornell University Press).

JEANE KIRKPATRICK is Professor of Political Science at Georgetown University and a resident scholar at the American Enterprise Institute for Public Policy Research. She was the U.S. Permanent Representative to the United Nations from 1981 to 1985.

HENRY A. KISSINGER was Assistant to the President for National Security Affairs from 1969 to 1975, and Secretary of State from 1973 to 1977. He is the author of numerous books and articles on world politics.

CHRISTOPHER LAYNE, an attorney in Los Angeles, served in 1984 as NATO/Western Europe analyst at the U.S. Army's Arroyo Center think tank.

SOL M. LINOWITZ is a senior partner in the law firm of Coudert Brothers. He served as Ambassador to the Organization of American States from 1966 to 1969 and has held other diplomatic posts.

RICHARD LUGAR is a U.S. Senator from Indiana. A Republican, he is a member of the Senate Foreign Relations Committee.

ROBERT J. MADDOX is Professor of History at Pennsylvania State University. He is the author of *The New Left and the Origins of the Cold War* (Princeton University Press).

GEORGE MEANY was President of the American Federation of Labor–Congress of Industrial Organizations from 1955 to 1979.

JACK MENDELSOHN is Deputy Director of the Arms Control Association.

SAM NUNN is a U.S. Senator from Georgia. A Democrat, he is Chairman of the Senate Armed Services Committee.

KENNETH A. OYE is Assistant Professor of Politics at Princeton University and an editor of *World Politics.* He is a co-editor of *Eagle Defiant: United States Policy in the 1980s* (Little, Brown).

WOLFGANG K. H. PANOFSKY, director emeritus of the Stanford Linear Accelerator Center, chairs the National Academy of Sciences Committee on International Security and Arms Control.

BURTON YALE PINES is Vice President of the Heritage Foundation, a conservative research organization. He is the author of *Back to Basics: The Traditionalist Movement That Is Sweeping Grass Roots America* (Morrow).

RICHARD PIPES is Frank B. Baird Jr. Professor of History at Harvard University. He was director of East European and Soviet Affairs at the National Security Council from 1981 to 1982.

BRUCE RUSSETT is Professor of Political Science at Yale University. He is editor of *The Journal of Conflict Resolution* and author of several books on world politics and arms control.

WILLIAM A. SCHWARTZ is a doctoral student in the Sociology Department at Boston College.

PAUL SEABURY, Professor of Political Science at the University of California at Berkeley, is the author of *The Rise and Decline of the Cold War* (Basic Books) and *The United States in World Affairs* (McGraw-Hill).

GEOFFREY STERN is a Lecturer in the Department of International Relations at the London School of Economics.

LEONARD R. SUSSMAN is Executive Director of Freedom House. He is the author of *Glossary for International Communications* (Media Institute).

BRIAN THOMAS is Principal Lecturer in International Relations at the Polytechnic of North London. Formerly London correspondent of *Nowa Wies* (Warsaw), he has written a number of articles on the theme of East-West relations.

JOHN C. TOOMAY is a retired Major General of the U.S. Air Force. A member of the U.S. Air Force Scientific Advisory Board, he has worked extensively in research and development for U.S. strategic systems.

WALL STREET JOURNAL is a national newspaper.

GEOFFREY WARNER is Professor of European Humanities at the Open University in Great Britain. He has also taught at the universities of Reading, Hull, and Leicester in Great Britain; at the Australian National University, Canberra; and at the Bologna Center of the Johns Hopkins University. He has written extensively about the Cold War for *International Affairs* (London).

JACK WHEELER is Director of the Freedom Research Foundation in Malibu, California, and foreign policy consultant for Citizens for America in Washington, D.C.

PREFACE

In this book, we intend to examine the Cold War in terms of both its historical evolution and its contemporary manifestations. The subject poses certain organizational problems to which no wholly satisfactory solutions are on offer.

As editors, we had to ask ourselves first whether the Cold War is primarily to be seen as a struggle between the two present-day superpowers—the United States and the Soviet Union—or, alternatively, as a contest between communism in all its forms and its no less variegated adversaries. A case might be made for either approach, but in a somewhat arbitrary fashion, we have decided that we shall concentrate on the superpowers for the purposes of the present text. This decision means, for example, that China receives much less attention than would have been the case if we had made the other broad choice.

Another principal difficulty has been to decide on the period we should attempt to cover, for there is no consensus among political leaders and scholars about the date on which the Cold War began. Everyone knows, for example, that fighting in World War I began in August 1914 and ended in November 1918. But no such precision is possible in the matter of the rivalry between the United States and the Soviet Union. In analyzing the phenomenon known as the Cold War, some authorities would go back to 1917 when the Bolsheviks or Communists seized power in the city they renamed Leningrad—an event that provoked unsuccessful intervention by armed forces from several Western countries including the United States. Rivalry has arguably existed ever since and hence the Cold War might be said to have begun some seventy years ago. But most people, at least in the West, do not use the term ''Cold War'' to cover so long a period. They incline to see the U.S.-Soviet relationship during most of the interwar period as characterized more by mutual indifference than by acute hostility. And they see the U.S.-Soviet wartime alliance against Nazi Germany as sufficiently close to make categorizing it as deeply adversarial sheer nonsense. In other words the Cold War, according to this interpretation, did not begin in earnest until after V-E Day. This is the interpretation we have adopted as the basis for the present volume.

The Cold War Debated focuses on some of the most contentious issues that have marked U.S.-Soviet relations. It does not seek, however, to provide a comprehensive analysis of the Cold War. Each chapter begins with headnotes that place the issues in context. Each debate is followed by Questions for Discussion and Suggested Readings that can be used for further development in critical evaluation and research.

The book is organized into five chapters: (!) historical issues, (2) the international system, (3) goals, (4) instruments of power, and (5) formal constraints on conflict. The structure is based heavily on *World Politics Debated: A Reader in Contemporary Issues* (McGraw-Hill), edited by Herbert M. Levine and *The Cold War Debated* can be considered as a sequel to that book. *The Cold War Debated* thus can be used in courses in world politics. It can also, however, fit into courses in Soviet foreign policy, U.S. foreign policy, and twentieth-century history.

As editors we have sought to emphasize broad issues. And so, for example, a question dealing with arms control asks: "Do U.S.-Soviet arms control agreements enhance the prospects for peace between the superpowers?" rather than, more specifically: "Has the Partial Test Ban Treaty strengthened arms control?" At times, however, the meaning of specific historical events is appraised as in the debates on the Yalta Conference and the Helsinki Accords.

The perspectives of policy makers, scholars, and journalists are represented in this volume. Sources include congressional hearings, academic journals, magazines, and newspapers. In addition three articles have been expressly written for this book—those by Brian Thomas, Geoffrey Warner, and the second of two articles on human rights by Sidney Blumenthal.

The debate format is useful in stimulating critical thinking. For example, in analyzing each debate, students should consider whether the views of the contending authors may best be understood as stemming from differences over the facts, the consequences of certain actions, or in background and ideological orientation. A major weakness of the debate format, however, is that only two points of view are expressed. Students may want to consider other viewpoints and questions on each subject. In that regard, they may find chapter headnotes and the selections cited in Suggested Readings helpful.

We wish to express our appreciation to the many people who helped us in producing *The Cold War Debated*. We are grateful to these colleagues who reviewed the manuscript: Valerie J. Assetto, Colorado State University; Alberto R. Coll, Georgetown University; Larry Elowitz, Georgia College; Thomas Magstadt, Kearney State College and Donald Pienkos, University of Wisconsin-Milwaukee.

Our thanks also, to James D. Anker, our political science editor, Ann Hofstra Grogg, who was the copy editor, and to the McGraw-Hill production team.

David Carlton

Herbert M. Levine

THE
COLD WAR
DEBATED

CHAPTER 1

HISTORICAL ISSUES

In this chapter we shall examine the historical origins of the Cold War. As stated in the Preface, we had to make two arbitrary decisions. First, we concluded that by the Cold War we mean the adversarial relationship between the United States and the Soviet Union. Second, we assumed that the Cold War did not begin in earnest until after V-E Day.

There remain, however, further problems concerning the temporal limits of the Cold War, even for historians who accept that it has been a post-World War II development. There is no consensus, for example, about whether the decisive moves leading to unambiguous hostility between Moscow and Washington came in 1945, 1946, or 1947. Moreover, establishing an ending date, if any, for the Cold War is fraught with equally serious divisions. Some historians hold that the Cold War never ended and is with us still. Others believe that it had effectively terminated by the 1970s with the coming of the Strategic Arms Limitation Talks (SALT) Accords of 1972 and the mutual acceptance of détente. And at least one historian in this camp, Prof. Fred Halliday of the London School of Economics and Political Science, contends that the Cold War, having virtually ended, has now resumed as a result of the rise in the United States of the phenomenon known as Reaganism—hence the title of his important book, *The Making of the Second Cold War* (2d ed., London: Verso, 1986). For the purpose of the present text, however, we intend to avoid adopting a dogmatic line on the details of these disputes. Instead, we shall work on the assumption that what most people consider to be the Cold War began around the end of World War II and has continued, with varying degrees of intensity, until the present day. Hence we take as our starting point the meeting of President

Franklin Delano Roosevelt with Winston Churchill and Joseph Stalin at Yalta in the Crimea in February 1945. Subsequent controversies about the significance of the conference suggest that it was indeed a decisive turning point in U.S.-Soviet relations, the end of one era and the beginning of another.

THE YALTA CONTROVERSY

What was done and not done at the Yalta Conference has provoked a number of different debates. Among the most important is the question of what the Big Three really agreed to. Some writers in the West consider that the Soviets solemnly undertook in the so-called Yalta Declaration to permit free elections in the countries of East Central Europe which the Red Army had recently liberated; that Stalin was presumed by Roosevelt and Churchill to be sincere in giving this pledge; and that accordingly the subsequent Cold War was entirely the fault of the Soviet Union when it failed to live up to its promises. Other Western commentators— with the tacit support of their Soviet counterparts—contend that all parties actually understood that Europe was to be divided into spheres of influence and that whether free elections along Western lines would in practice be introduced into countries in the Soviet sphere was a matter for Stalin to determine. In short, the Yalta Declaration, according to this view, was tacitly understood by Roosevelt and Churchill to be mere window dressing.

Those who accept this latter interpretation of what really took place at Yalta divide into two broad categories, as illustrated in our first debate between Theodore Draper and Paul Seabury. One group holds that Roosevelt had no realistic alternative but to accept the division of Europe into two camps and that accordingly he was wise to avoid worsening relations with Moscow by futile name-calling. The Cold War, according to many who hold this view, actually arose as a result of the conduct of President Harry S. Truman, who succeeded Roosevelt on April 12, 1945. While in practice turning out to be no more willing than his predecessor to use force to eject the Soviets from East Central Europe, Truman saw fit to denounce them stridently for the ruthless way in which they imposed their will on the various countries concerned and to accuse them without real justification of not keeping faith with the solemn promises they had supposedly given to Roosevelt at Yalta. Truman's actions, in turn, may have led to increasing Soviet intransigence and reciprocal name-calling about the evils of "capitalism" and "imperialism."

Opposed to this school of thought are those like Seabury, who hold that Roosevelt was morally culpable for tacitly accepting the division of Europe into two spheres of influence. In this camp it is generally assumed that a strong diplomatic stand by Roosevelt would have led Stalin to exercise more restraint. Whether that would really have been the case is of course debatable, for, as Draper stresses, the Soviets occupied most of the relevant territory. And such skeptics ask whether it really was practical politics for the United States to contemplate, if necessary, the use or threat of armed force to evict them. On the other hand, Roosevelt may have made matters unnecessarily easy for Stalin by not even attempting to bring serious pressure to bear on him with respect to

Eastern European questions. In particular, Roosevelt's critics stress the alleged folly of his gratuitous announcement at Yalta that he expected the bulk of U.S. forces to be withdrawn from Europe within 2 years.

A subsidiary debate emerging from the Draper-Seabury encounter concerns the role of Churchill. Those who have been most prone to pillory Roosevelt over Yalta have tended to suggest that Churchill favored a more hard-line policy toward the Soviet Union but was ignored by the president. Draper offers some evidence that brings this interpretation into question. But it is arguable that, in common with most U.S. writers, he does not recognize the difficulties facing Great Britain at this juncture. The fact is that Great Britain and the Soviet Union knew that they would be the only European powers of any military significance in the immediate postwar years. Given that the United States was expected to withdraw from the scene, it was therefore entirely understandable that the British found it prudent to strike bargains with the Soviets—hence the Percentages Agreement of 1944 to which Draper refers. But had the United States been contemplating a more active future role in Europe, during the last year of Roosevelt's presidency British conduct would probably have taken a less "appeasing" form. It may therefore be an oversimplification to see Churchill as having the same basic outlook as Roosevelt—and indeed there is a good deal of evidence that in private the prime minister was severely critical of the president and greatly welcomed the somewhat more robust U.S. approach eventually adopted by Truman.

A final pedagogic point we would wish to stress is that the controversy about Yalta is many-sided. The debate in this book, however interesting, is not the only one we could have chosen. In short, despite the impression suggested by this book's format, there can indeed be more than two sides to a given controversy.

TRUMAN AND THE USE OF ATOMIC WEAPONS

Mention has already been made of the argument that President Truman approached relations with the Soviet Union in a spirit different from that of his predecessor. Soon after he took office, for example, Truman had an angry encounter in Washington with Vyasheslav Molotov, the Soviet foreign minister. In particular, the president stressed his disapproval of Soviet treatment of Poland. Molotov is said to have turned white at the dressing down. "I have never been talked to like that in my life," he said. "Carry out your agreements and you won't get talked to like that," Truman curtly replied.[1]

During most of the next 2 years Truman gradually allowed his disillusionment with the Soviet Union to become public knowledge. In the early months of 1947 he gave a clear indication that he was anxious to use U.S. economic strength to prevent any further spread of Soviet influence in Europe. In March 1947 he put forth the so-called Truman Doctrine, a strong denunciation of international communism that was to be the basis for congressional approval of funds to help friendly governments in Greece and Turkey defend themselves

[1]Quoted in Daniel Yergen, *Shattered Peace* (Boston: Houghton Mifflin, 1977), pp. 82–83.

against internal subversion. In June of the same year Truman's secretary of state, George Marshall, announced the famous plan associated with his name— a generous offer to assist the economic recovery of war-devastated Europe and thus to reduce the appeal of communism there. Countries under Soviet influence refused the assistance. This U.S. economic strategy inevitably worsened relations with the Soviet Union. But it must be stressed that, in the view of most historians in the West, the Cold War as it had already become known was not at this point generally thought likely to erupt into armed conflict in Europe, for the Americans had withdrawn from Europe most of their armed forces, apart from those needed to occupy the U.S. Zone of Germany. The Americans did not threaten to go to war to evict the Soviets from their satellite states; nor, on the other hand, do they seem to have expected a military attack by the Red Army on the countries outside the Soviet sphere of influence. It was only later, according to this interpretation, that the rivalry in Europe assumed a stark military aspect. Vital for this was the alarm caused by the Soviet blockade of West Berlin in 1948–1949 (successfully resisted by an airlift of essential supplies) and the attack on South Korea by North Korea in 1950. The result in the European theater was first the signing of the North Atlantic Treaty of 1949. Then in 1950 came the establishment of the North Atlantic Treaty Organization (NATO), under whose auspices large numbers of U.S. troops and weapons (including eventually those of the atomic type) were sent to Europe, and a distinguished American, Gen. Dwight D. Eisenhower, became Supreme Allied Commander Europe (SACEUR).

That the Cold War only assumed a serious military aspect between 1948 and 1950 is not, however, a universally accepted thesis. Some historians contend that Truman implicitly introduced a harsh note of threat into the U.S.-Soviet relationship as early as August 1945. They take this view because they are not convinced that the use of atomic bombs on Hiroshima and Nagasaki was in any way necessary given the evidence said to be available to Truman that the Japanese were on the verge of collapse. Lacking a clear military motive, Truman must have used the bombs, they contend, for the political purposes of intimidating the Soviets. But other historians are unconvinced by this argument. It is this issue that we have chosen for our next debate. Gar Alperovitz, a U.S. scholar, leans strongly toward the first view, whereas Prof. Geoffrey Warner of the British Open University remains skeptical of the idea that Truman, when he made the decision to drop the atomic bombs, was no longer worried about continued Japanese resistance and hence must have had the intimidation of Moscow in mind.

Whether the reader agrees with Alperovitz or Warner, two points remain to be made. First, neither historian claims to provide absolute proof for his thesis—a situation common in matters of controversy relating to the Cold War. Second, if Truman really did use atomic bombs on Japan in an effort to influence Soviet behavior, he must have been sorely disappointed at the result, for the Soviets appear to have become more, not less, brutal in their sphere of influence while simultaneously redoubling their efforts to obtain atomic weapons of their own (a goal they reached in 1949). It should be noted, moreover, that Truman, whatever his thoughts may have been in 1945, did not in these circumstances see fit to threaten the Soviets with atomic bombardment if they did not mend their ways. A final tantalizing question: Supposing the Soviets, not the Americans, had had an atomic monopoly from 1945 to 1949; would they have exercised a similar restraint?

THE VIETNAM WAR

The main theater for the early Cold War was Europe, and in some respects it has remained so. It is in Europe along the line of the Iron Curtain that the two principal military alliances confront each other, namely NATO and the Warsaw Pact, the latter founded in 1955 in response to the admission of the Federal Republic of Germany to NATO. Yet since the Berlin Blockade, which ended before either of the two armed camps was established in its present form, there has been no crisis in Europe sufficiently serious that war has seemed imminent. The main theaters in which armed encounters involving either the superpowers or their real or presumed proxies have occurred or threatened to occur have been in the Third World.

The most direct single superpower crisis arose in 1962 over the Soviet attempt to place missiles in Cuba—a crisis defused by a Soviet climb-down. But other crises have also occurred—not least in Asia. In the 1950s, in particular, the United States became deeply concerned over what it thought would be the consequences of the coming to power in China in 1949 of a communist regime (which remained unrecognized diplomatically by Washington and barred from entry to the United Nations until the presidency of Richard Nixon). From 1950 to 1953 the United States led United Nations' forces in successfully resisting North Korea's attempted conquest of South Korea—an act of aggression presumed, rightly or wrongly, to have been inspired by both the Soviet Union and China. Then in 1954 the United States, led by President Eisenhower and his fanatically anticommunist secretary of state, John Foster Dulles, came close to committing itself to giving military assistance to the French in their effort to prevent communist guerrillas from seizing power in Indochina. A compromise solution was engineered, however, at the Geneva Conference, and as a result North Vietnam was established under communist rule while the remainder of French Indochina was carved up into three independent noncommunist states, namely South Vietnam, Laos, and Cambodia.

When in the early 1960s this settlement was seriously undermined by North Vietnamese sponsorship of communist guerrilla activities in South Vietnam, successive Democratic administrations, led by John F. Kennedy and Lyndon B. Johnson, gradually found themselves drawn into fighting a major counter-guerrilla war in this remote corner of Asia. The underlying assumption on the part of most U.S. supporters of the war was that the guerrillas, known as the Vietcong, and the North Vietnamese were surrogates of either China or the Soviet Union or both. That the Soviet Union and China were by now on bad terms was of course well known. But the idea that communism was a global conspiracy had taken too deep a hold during the first postwar decade for most Americans to take a relaxed view of what was happening in Indochina. It is therefore arguable that the Vietnamese war was as much a reflection and a by-product of the U.S.-Soviet struggle as the Korean war had been—even though Soviet forces took no part in the fighting on either occasion.

For the United States to get out of Vietnam proved harder than to get in, but by 1968 significant elements at home, particularly the articulate young, had become convinced that the war was futile or immoral, or both. It thus became the mission of President Nixon and his secretary of state, Henry A. Kissinger, to extricate the United States from the quagmire with whatever honor they could muster. The result was the Paris Agreements of 1973, which in the final analysis left the South Vietnamese to fend for themselves—a task that proved beyond their strength, as the communist take-over in Saigon in 1975 proved.

For many Americans the controversy about Vietnam still arouses strong emotions—as our next debate illustrates. Hendrik Hertzberg, a relatively moderate opponent of the war, remains convinced that U.S. policy was inexpedient and, above all, totally immoral in its execution. David Horowitz was a more extreme opponent of the U.S. role in the Vietnamese war, a convert to a Marxist outlook that not only condemned U.S. policy but actually sympathized with the Vietcong. Today he holds a totally different view, believing that the United States was and is engaged in a "life and death struggle with its global totalitarian adversaries."

THE HELSINKI ACCORDS

The majority of American policy makers in the 1970s did not draw such clear-cut conclusions from the Vietnam experience as Horowitz now does. Instead, there was an increased willingness to reinforce withdrawal from Vietnam with a serious attempt to reach a modus vivendi with the other superpower both in the original theater of tension, namely Europe, and then more widely in the control of the arms race and the management of the international system as a whole. The aim of some Americans was thus to prevent the Cold War from becoming too intense and of others to bring it to an end.

So far as Europe was concerned, the United States followed a lead set by the Federal Republic of Germany. The Social Democrat chancellor, Willy Brandt, had launched in 1969 a policy known as *Ostpolitik,* which led to a series of agreements intended to solidify the status quo as it had emerged after World War II. The West Germans recognized the frontiers involving themselves, the German Democratic Republic (G.D.R.), and Poland; they agreed to mutual diplomatic recognition with the G.D.R.; and they reached an agreement concerning the status of Berlin. By 1975 the United States was ready to endorse all these various moves and accordingly signed the so-called Helsinki Final Act under which the superpowers, Canada, and all European states except Albania agreed that no existing frontiers on the European continent could be changed by force. Tacitly, too, the United States recognized the legitimacy of all the governments of East Central Europe, even those that had been established and sustained only by Soviet armed force. The hopes that Soviet power in East Central Europe might be "rolled back" had faded as the United States proved unable to assist the vain attempts of the Hungarians and the Czechoslovaks to escape from the Soviet sphere in 1956 and 1968, respectively. As for the division of Germany and the continuing anomaly of Berlin (symbolized by the building of the Berlin Wall by the communists in 1961), there had been a gradual acceptance in Washington that the postwar ad hoc arrangements might after all prove viable for a protracted period and could conceivably be the basis for stability in U.S.-Soviet relations in Europe. This approach was in sharp contrast to that of the immediate postwar years, when German unification was assumed in the West to be a sine qua non for reducing the risk of war. As Sir Michael Howard, Regius Professor of History at the University of Oxford, has written:

> A generation brought up to believe in the inevitability and the desirability of national self-determination, and which had fought two wars in favour of that principle, could not believe that the world would remain stable if the greatest of the European peoples, the Germans, remained artificially divided.[2]

The Helsinki Accords were not limited, however, to mutual recognition of the territorial status quo. The Soviets were persuaded in return to pay a price of a kind, namely to agree to seek various goals designed to improve East-West relations. Most dramatic among these were mutual pledges to enhance so-called human rights. But in the view of many Western critics, the totalitarian regimes of the Warsaw Pact have not lived up to their promises. Whether genuinely surprised or not at this failure, some Western commentators have accordingly demanded that the United States admit it was mistaken in forging the Helsinki Accords and forthwith repudiate them. This is the line taken in our next debate by Eric Breindel. He is opposed by Leonard R. Sussman. While not denying that the Warsaw Pact countries have failed to carry out the letter of their pledges, Sussman nevertheless believes that the existence of the Accords "places some limits even on *their* tyrannies."

DÉTENTE

The U.S. failure in Vietnam also prodded successive administrations to widen their understanding with the Soviets from the European theater to the entire global canvas. This quest was reinforced by the Soviet achievement in the late 1960s of approximate nuclear parity with the United States. Central to this effort to provide at least some ground rules for the conduct of the U.S.-Soviet competition was Kissinger—though President Jimmy Carter sought to conti-

---

[2]Michael Howard, intro. to Olav Riste (ed.), *Western Security: The Formative Years: European and Atlantic Defence, 1947–1953* (Oslo: Norwegian Univ. Press, 1985), pp. 12–13.

nue the process at least until the Soviet invasion of Afghanistan in 1979. At first the process was formally known as détente—though, for domestic political reasons, administration spokespersons usually saw fit to use some euphemism by the second half of the 1970s.

In our next debate the concept's original architect, Kissinger, offers an explanation, dating from 1974, of détente's scope and purpose. The design that emerges is in many respects relatively modest and unambitious. Yet as early as 1974 there were those who thought it doomed to failure because Soviet goals were not compatible with even these limited suggestions for promoting stability in the international system. One skeptic was George Meany, the president of the AFL-CIO, whose testimony to Congress we reproduce.

It is a matter of history that détente, however defined, had broken down by the end of the 1970s and has not been revived during Ronald Reagan's presidency. It is a matter for dispute, however, whether the breakdown arose from particular misdeeds by one or another of the superpowers or whether the whole concept was fatally flawed from the outset because it was based on a U.S. misreading of the extent of Soviet ambitions as a world power and an unreconstructed champion of an internationalist ideology.

THE REVISIONIST CONTROVERSY AMONG HISTORIANS

A consequence of the breakdown of consensus among Americans, symbolized by a decade of failure in Vietnam, was the emergence of an influential school of historians inclined to question the merits of the U.S. role in the earlier stages of the Cold War. Our final debate in this chapter reflects this development.

One of the pioneers of this revisionism was Prof. D. F. Fleming of Vanderbilt University, who summarized his views in the congressional testimony we reproduce here. Pitted against him is Prof. Robert J. Maddox of Pennsylvania State University. Maddox examines critically not only Fleming's views but those of a whole range of so-called revisionists, including William Appleman Williams, Gabriel Kolko, and Gar Alperovitz, who were by no means in full agreement with one another. But these multiple points of view need not surprise us, given that the Cold War itself is, as we have seen, too imprecise a phenomenon to command even a generally agreed-on definition.

1 Has Franklin Roosevelt been unfairly criticized for Yalta?

YES

Theodore Draper

Neoconservative History

NO

Paul Seabury

Yalta and the Neoconservatives

Neoconservative History

Theodore Draper

1

Myths are notoriously hardy. They can flourish, subside, and flourish again. One of the hardiest myths in modern American history is associated with the Yalta conference toward the end of World War II. It originally arose during the Truman administration, when Yalta was made into a code word for treason. The Republican party's platform of 1952 went so far as to denounce the Yalta agreements on the ground that they had secretly aided "Communist enslavements." That there was nothing secret about them after the full text was published in March 1947 and that they were intended to prevent Communist enslavements made no difference to the platform writers. The guilt for this treasonable sellout of Eastern Europe was attributed to one man, Franklin Delano Roosevelt, and through him to the Democratic party in particular and to liberals in general. The accusation envenomed American politics throughout the McCarthy period but seemed to be spent by the late 1950s.

Now it has returned. It has just been put forward in one form or another not once but three times by three different writers in the pages of the November 1985 issue of *Commentary,* its fortieth anniversary issue. A related version has also come to the surface in the recently published diaries of John Colville, Churchill's wartime private secretary and a contributor to the September 1985 issue of *Commentary.* I came across these reincarnations in casual reading; no doubt more intensive research would turn up others, but these are enough to indicate a resurgence of an ominous mythology.

Theodore Draper, "Neoconservative History," *New York Review of Books*, 32 (Jan. 16, 1986), pp. 5–6, 8, 10, 12, 14–15. Reprinted with permission of the author.

This phenomenon is worth examining for its own sake, because a nation should know its own past, and because Yalta-and-Roosevelt baiting is a form of retroactive politics that tells us something about the present.

The first specimen in the November 1985 *Commentary* was contributed by Lionel Abel, whose recent book was aptly entitled *The Intellectual Follies*. He based himself on a single article by Colville in the following way:

> And Roosevelt was personally responsible for terrible foreign-policy decisions (described in these pages only two months ago by John Colville in his article, "How the West Lost the Peace in 1945") which gave the Soviet Union control of Eastern Europe.

Colville in turn had placed the giveaway at Yalta in February 1945 and had specifically named Poland as the victim:

> After long discussions and much argument [at Yalta] it was agreed that some non-Communist Poles should be invited to join the [Polish] government—though they would be but a minority—and that "free and unfettered elections," in which all except the fascist parties should be allowed to put forward candidates, would be held within a few months. The British delegation was not content with the vagueness of the Soviet promises or the design of the proposed Polish government; but since the Soviets and Americans were in agreement, Churchill and Eden had to give way, though they knew there would be trouble in the House of Commons.

Here we have two enduring elements of the Yalta myth—that vague Soviet promises, rather than the breach of not-so-vague promises, were responsible for the subsequent fate of Poland, and that the Americans, not the British, bear the burden of guilt. Colville does not hold

Roosevelt "personally responsible" and does not use any such crass expression as that Roosevelt "gave the Soviet Union control of Eastern Europe." Abel's embellishment of Colville's version is a good example of how these stories can go from bad to worse in the telling.

The next appearance of another form of the myth comes from a more serious source, Ambassador and now again Professor Jeane J. Kirkpatrick. Yalta was where it was decided to give the Soviet Union three votes in the General Assembly of the future United Nations. In the November *Commentary* Kirkpatrick deals with it this way:

> Founding the UN also required falsifying the relations between the Soviet Union and those two "autonomous Soviet Socialist republics," the Ukraine and Byelorussia. The Charter required that members be independent states. The Ukraine and Byelorussia were neither autonomous nor republics. Why did the United States and its democratic allies accept this falsification? Presumably, the reason was that they could not bear to face the fact that even after this most recent, most terrible war, there remained a powerful, repressive, expansionist dictatorship to cope with.
>
> Nothing in the Soviet past justified optimism concerning its future behavior. Winston Churchill knew this, Franklin D. Roosevelt should have.

Kirkpatrick's sense of history here is—to be charitable—defective. The decision on the Ukraine and Byelorussia memberships was made before there was a U.N. and before it had a charter. The reason for the decision could not have had anything to do with whatever remained *after* "this most recent, most terrible war." The war was not yet over; fighting remained even against Germany; the last hard phase of the battle against Japan, with the possible entrance of the Soviet Union into the Far Eastern war, was still ahead; the atomic bomb had not even been tested; American military planners were still counting on a "most

terrible war" to come. One must try to put oneself back into the real world of Churchill and Roosevelt at the time of Yalta before judging either of them so loftily.

If Kirkpatrick's history is bad, her attribution of motives is worse. Her differentiation between Churchill and Roosevelt is, as we shall see, as wrongheaded as can be. The mystery is how a former U.N. ambassador could get the whole story topsy-turvy.

But she is not the only one who has the allocation of the three Soviet seats in the U.N. all wrong. Another is John Colville in his recently published book, *The Fringes of Power*, made up largely of his wartime diaries. Colville was not at Yalta; the British foreign secretary, Anthony Eden, was. In an entry dated February 19, 1945, Colville tells about a conversation with Eden:

> The PM had been very persuasive about the Dumbarton Oaks compromise (voting in the Security Council) and the Russians would have been quite happy to agree to none of their constituent states belonging to the Assembly, had not the Americans foolishly acquiesced. Finally the Americans had been very weak.[1]

Since this is apparently attributed to Eden, there is no telling what Colville knew. Nevertheless, Colville should have known—or learned—by the time his diaries were prepared for publication that there was no truth to this story. Colville's book has footnotes in which he frequently explains or comments on the text; he has no footnote on this one and this would lead the reader to believe that his source is trustworthy.

In any case, Kirkpatrick and Colville have put into circulation the same fable—that Churchill and the British opposed the allocation of Soviet seats in the United Nations, while Roosevelt and the Americans for reasons of undue optimism or weakness were responsible for it.

[1]John Colville, *The Fringes of Power: 10 Downing Street Diaries, 1939–1955* (Norton, 1985), p. 560.

Kirkpatrick writes so loosely that she first accuses "the United States and its democratic allies," which would include Great Britain, of accepting the falsification and then suggests that Churchill knew better than Roosevelt. Either way, she completely muddles what actually happened.

The third exhibit from *Commentary,* by Professor Robert Nisbet, shows how closely interwoven is the past and present in anti-Roosevelt, pro-Churchill retrospection. He does not mention Yalta specifically, but it would be the prime test of his indictment of Roosevelt. His starting point is in the past:

> The recently published correspondence between Churchill and Roosevelt must make for bitter reading in some quarters. All that we had known in a general sort of way about Roosevelt's strong disposition to trust Stalin, even over Churchill's cautionary advice, is detailed richly in these letters. Roosevelt's credulity toward Stalin and his sometimes rather pathetic ignorance of political history and geopolitics were joined unfortunately to a complacent certainty that Stalin wanted only one thing out of the war: world peace and democracy.

Nisbet then moves into the present:

> In many walks of life do we find alive and well the institutionalization of Roosevelt's unwavering faith in the Soviet Union.

There is nothing—I repeat *nothing*—in the recently published correspondence between Churchill and Roosevelt that shows Roosevelt's strong disposition to trust Stalin, or his credulity toward Stalin, or his complacent certainty about the only thing that Stalin wanted, or his unwavering faith in the Soviet Union, or that Churchill gave Roosevelt "cautionary advice" about not trusting Stalin. I have read and reread this correspondence without finding any of these things. All these charges against Roosevelt have been invented by Nisbet; they are not in the correspondence. Thus for the third time

in this little anti-Roosevelt anthology, Churchill is played off against Roosevelt in order to make Roosevelt appear to be an "unwavering" stooge of the Soviet Union.

If such misrepresentation is still possible in 1985, forty years after Yalta, it is time to set the record straight again. But there would be no urgent need for such an effort if history were not again being made to serve current political extremism. Did Roosevelt personally give the Soviet Union control of Eastern Europe? Why were three seats in the United Nations allotted to the Soviet Union? Did Churchill know so much better than Roosevelt? Before turning to the present political climate in which these questions have been raised, we need to clear up the past.

2

Franklin D. Roosevelt did not give the Soviet Union control of Eastern Europe; the Red Army did. By the time of Yalta, when the last diplomatic effort was made to stave off total control, the Red Army occupied most of Poland and Eastern Europe. But diplomacy can rarely save what is lost by force of arms. Both Churchill and Roosevelt failed not because they did not want to succeed but for lack of force at the right place at the right time. To accuse one of them, Roosevelt, of in effect doing whatever Stalin wanted him to do is grotesquely false.

If Stalin had any reason to believe that he could take Eastern Europe with impunity, he owed it in the first place to Churchill. Churchill had made a preliminary deal with Stalin in May 1944; they agreed that the Soviet Union would "take the lead" in Romania in return for letting the British "take the lead" in Greece.[2] At a

---

[2]*Churchill and Roosevelt: The Complete Correspondence,* edited with a commentary by Warren F. Kimball (Princeton University Press, 1985), Vol. III, pp. 137, 153. This arrangement was first opposed by Roosevelt, who later agreed to it for a three-month trial period after renewed pressure by Churchill (pp. 177, 181–182).

meeting in Moscow in October 1944, Churchill proposed a more far-reaching arrangement: a division of power in percentages—for the Soviets, 90 percent in Romania, 75 percent in Bulgaria, 50 percent in Hungary and Yugoslavia, in exchange for 90 percent for Great Britain in Greece. These figures implied that Churchill envisaged a Soviet sphere of influence in Eastern Europe in exchange for a British sphere of influence in the Mediterranean area. When Churchill had reported "the system of percentage" to his colleagues in London, he had tried to pass it off as a way for both the British and Soviet governments to "reveal their minds to each other." Stalin had revealed his mind by immediately accepting the deal.[3]

This was far more than a mind-revealing exercise. It is less well known that the two foreign ministers, Eden and Molotov, haggled over the percentages the following day. Molotov wanted 75 percent in Hungary, Bulgaria, and Yugoslavia, then 90 percent in Bulgaria and 50 percent in Yugoslavia. Eden agreed to 75 percent for the Soviets in Hungary, 80 percent in Bulgaria, 50 percent in Yugoslavia. The two haggled some more the next day. Churchill

described the percentages as a "guide" for the British and Soviet governments.[4] In fact, they guided Churchill's diplomacy right through and after Yalta. Churchill, as Eden's latest biographer has noted, "remained convinced that the British should try to hold the Soviets to the 'percentages' arrangements of the previous October even at the cost of condoning Stalin's breaches of the Yalta Declaration in the Soviet sphere-of-influence."[5]

There would be no need to rake up these old embarrassments if Churchill were not now being held up as the one who knew better what Roosevelt should have known. At this late stage of the war, Roosevelt had nothing to do with this open invitation to Stalin to take over most of Eastern Europe. No doubt Churchill had not counted on the brutality with which the Soviets would impose their "predominance"—another word that Churchill used—in Romania, Bulgaria, and Hungary. But then Churchill cannot be held up as a model for Roosevelt.

Poland was a special case, though it is hard to believe that it could have stayed out of the Soviet sphere if the rest of Eastern Europe went the way of the Churchill–Stalin deal. If Professor Nisbet were right, Roosevelt should have shown a "strong disposition to trust Stalin" and an "unwavering faith in the Soviet Union" precisely on the issue of Poland. Roosevelt did nothing of the kind.

The trouble in Poland was that the Soviets had already installed a puppet provisional government in Lublin, while the British and Americans had previously recognized another Polish provisional government in London. Roosevelt had tried before Yalta to get Stalin to postpone Soviet recognition of the Lublin Poles until they could meet and discuss the problem. Stalin refused.

---

[3]In his review of the Churchill–Roosevelt correspondence in *The New York Review of Books* (February 14, 1985), Martin Gilbert, Churchill's distinguished biographer, reversed the roles played by Churchill and Stalin in what Gilbert called the "notorious 'percentages agreement.'" He described it as "that piece of paper on which, at Churchill's suggestion, Stalin marked his 'percentages'" and which was "in fact Churchill's belated attempt to find out from Stalin just what degree of influence the Soviet leader imagined Russia would have in Eastern Europe, country by country. Stalin's jottings about the countries he expected to control revealed an ambitious tyrant, but a tyrant whose armies were gaining every day by military conquest the 'percentages' which he had so brazenly committed to paper." It has been known at least since the sixth and last volume of Churchill's memoirs that it was Churchill who had written the percentages "on a half-sheet of paper" and had "pushed this across to Stalin, who by then had heard the translation. There was a slight pause. Then he took his blue pencil and made a large tick on it, and passed it back to us" (*Triumph and Tragedy,* Houghton Mifflin, 1953, p. 227). Such are the tricks of memory in this seemingly treacherous field.

[4]Sir Llewellyn Woodward, *British Foreign Policy in the Second World War* (London: Her Majesty's Stationery Office, 1971), Vol. III, pp. 150–153.

[5]David Carlton, *Anthony Eden* (London: Allen Lane, 1981), p. 253. The reference here is to Romania.

Roosevelt replied that he was "disturbed and deeply disappointed" by Stalin's action.[6] So far, no trust and no faith.

The Polish issue took up more time than anything else at Yalta. At no point did Churchill or Roosevelt agree to the Soviet plan to put the "Lublin Government" in power. With the Red Army in most of Poland, they had few cards to play, the only one of consequence being their refusal to rubber-stamp the Soviet design. If words had counted, they did not do at all badly. They arrived at a declaration on Poland which, while not foolproof, would have been satisfactory if the Soviets had lived up to it. It provided for a "new government" to be formed by reorganizing the Soviet-sponsored provisional government "with the inclusion of democratic leaders from Poland itself and from Poles abroad." The new government was pledged "to the holding of free and unfettered elections as soon as possible on the basis of universal suffrage and secret ballot." Stalin had said that this election could be held in no more than a month, in which case the new provisional government would have been short-lived.[7]

On paper, neither side had its own way. Roosevelt was willing to fudge the issue of the new provisional government; Stalin was willing to concede the matter of early free elections. The combination might have extricated Poland if Stalin had seen it to be in his interests to make it work. In the end, words hardly mattered. The Soviets ignored both the promised reorganization of the provisional government and the commitment to free elections. Yalta was a

dividing line, not because of what happened at the meeting there but because of what happened after it. Brute power decided, not fair words. The trouble with the argument over Yalta is that it is too much about words and not enough about power.

After Yalta, however, a difference emerged between Churchill and Roosevelt. It is hard to tell what Nisbet has in mind, but if there were any truth in the story of Roosevelt's trust and faith in Stalin, it should have come out during their disagreement. Between February 23 and March 8, 1945, an Anglo-American-Soviet commission met to put the Polish agreement into effect. Only then did it become clear to Churchill that the Soviets were determined to have their own way in Poland, in violation of both the letter and the spirit of the agreement. On March 8, Churchill sent Roosevelt a message of alarm and proposed that both countries should send a protest to Stalin.

This cable has been described by Professor Warren F. Kimball, the editor of the Churchill–Roosevelt correspondence, as marking "a British reversal on Eastern Europe." It was a reversal in the sense that Churchill had publicly expressed more confidence in Stalin's good faith than Roosevelt had ever done.[8] Churchill, as Professor Kimball puts it, "was playing a tricky game" of pressing Roosevelt to protest over Poland, while Churchill himself was rebuking Eden for wanting to protest the Soviets' oppressive behavior in Romania.[9] Romania was

[6]*Stalin's Correspondence with Roosevelt and Truman, 1941–1945* (Capricorn Books, 1965), pp. 175, 182. This is a reprint of the edition originally published in Moscow by the Soviet publishing house in 1957. It is mystifying why this is the only extant version of the complete correspondence, even though some of the documents were available in the Soviet Union in Russian translation only and lack the original English texts.

[7]The full record is in *Foreign Relations of the United States: The Conferences at Malta and Yalta, 1945* (Government Printing Office, 1955).

[8]Winston Churchill, House of Commons, February 27, 1945:

The impression I brought back from the Crimea, and from all my other contacts, is that Marshal Stalin and the Soviet leaders wish to live in honourable friendship and equality with the Western democracies. I feel also that their word is their bond. I know of no Government which stands to its obligations, even in its own despite, more solidly than the Russian Soviet Government.

[9]*Churchill and Roosevelt: The Complete Correspondence,* Vol. III, pp. 545–547.

different, because Churchill's deal with Stalin had made British interests in Greece depend on giving the Soviets a free hand in Romania. One of the reasons Churchill resented being "defrauded" by Stalin on Poland was, as he informed Roosevelt, that he had "advised critics of the Yalta settlement to trust Stalin."[10] If Roosevelt had permitted himself to be "defrauded," Churchill could not claim to have been any the wiser. In effect, Churchill, having invited the Soviets to predominate in much of Eastern Europe, was appalled at the prospect as soon as the Red Army began to turn it into a reality.

Roosevelt held back. Now was the time, according to the myth makers, when Roosevelt should have shown his trust and faith in Stalin. But he disagreed with Churchill on altogether different grounds. On March 11, 1945, a month after Yalta, Roosevelt wrote to Churchill: "I can assure you that our objectives are identical, namely, to bring about a cessation on the part of the Lublin Poles of the measures directed against their political opponents in Poland." The difference between himself and Churchill was tactical. Roosevelt thought that they should recommend "a general political truce" between the Lublin Poles and their opponents instead of complaining immediately to the Soviet government. As Professor Kimball sums up the situation, "Roosevelt and his advisers avoided making an appeal to Stalin lest the Soviet Premier give the wrong answer and thus force a confrontation or a retreat."

That was the rub—the British and Americans had nothing more than words to back up a confrontation. Again and again Roosevelt assured Churchill that the difference was over tactics, not policy. With this view Churchill

agreed. In any case, the tactical difference was over by the end of March. Both Churchill and Roosevelt addressed strong, coordinated protests to Stalin, Roosevelt on April 1, 1945, Churchill immediately afterward.[11] Roosevelt died twelve days later.

During this entire period, when it was most likely to have happened, Churchill never cautioned Roosevelt not to trust Stalin. There is no such Churchillian "cautionary advice" in the entire correspondence. One begins to wonder whether Nisbet really read the correspondence as carefully as he pretends to have done.

The Western allies did not give away anything at Yalta that they actually had; they did get some promissory notes which they could not cash in once Stalin decided to stop payment. They still hoped against hope—Churchill as well as Roosevelt—to find some way to coexist peacefully, a hope that nourished illusions and compromises. But illusions and compromises were not born at Yalta; they had been fostered throughout the war in both liberal and conservative circles; they helped to sustain morale, when the British-American forces, even after the establishment of the second front on the Continent, were engaging only one third of the total German forces. Little or nothing would have changed if the break with the Soviet Union had come at Yalta instead of soon afterward; as long as the Western allies could not contest Soviet power on the ground in Eastern Europe, they could do no more than get paper promises and respond with paper protests. It is easy enough now to scoff at the Yalta illusions; it was not so easy to give them up then. The illusions,

---

[10]Churchill to Roosevelt (March 27, 1945), in *Churchill and Roosevelt: The Complete Correspondence,* Vol. III, p. 588.

[11]The entire sequence can be followed in *Churchill and Roosevelt: The Complete Correspondence,* Vol. III, pp. 545–602, after which Churchill wrote to Roosevelt: "I am delighted with our being in such perfect step."

moreover, were about the Soviet Union, not about the merit—at least as far as the plain-meaning of the words—of the Yalta agreements.[12]

If Roosevelt and Churchill were wrong to hope for postwar cooperation with the Soviet Union, they had a lot of company. How hard it was to give up wishful thinking can be seen from the case of John Foster Dulles, no liberal, no Democrat, no trusting soul. In a speech on March 17, 1945, at this very juncture, he said:

> Many do not like the sample of reality which Yalta produced. But that is because the collaborators are themselves imperfect. Their defects will not be removed by breaking up the collaboration. On the contrary, that would intensify the defects.[13]

At a press conference on November 24, 1953, he remarked that, at the end of the war, "those in charge of our foreign policy at the time seemed to have assumed—*many of us did*—that we were entering into an era of lasting peace and that the Soviet Union would not be a

threat" (emphasis added).[14] And toward the end of the 1950s, Dulles confided to Andrew H. Berding, then assistant secretary of state for public affairs:

> The general impression is that the Yalta agreement was a mistake. I don't feel so categorical about this. In 1945 we still had the hope that the Russians would cooperate with us. Furthermore, since the Russians were already in occupation of the Balkans, all we could hope for was their promise that the peoples of the Eastern European countries could have governments of their own choosing.[15]

Not so long ago, Professor Kirkpatrick herself defended the Yalta agreements from the charge of having sold out Eastern Europe and Poland.[16] When an old Republican like Dulles and a new Republican like Kirkpatrick could see the rationale of Roosevelt's actions at Yalta, the defamatory fury of others requires an extrahistorical explanation. The reason must have less to do with the past than with the present.

Ironically, Stalin succeeded in scoring a double triumph after Yalta. First, he took over

---

[12]The merit of the agreement on Poland was most recently recognized by a leader of the Solidarity movement, Jack Kuron, in an interview with Tamar Jacoby, deputy editor of the *New York Times* Op-Ed page, in an article in *The New Republic,* December 23, 1985:

> Kuron insists that what he wants is "not revising but renewing Yalta"—reviving at least some of the demands that the West put to Moscow in 1945. He admits that it might not be possible today to insist on free elections in Poland. But he believes that other demands, for economic reform and genuinely free trade unions, could now be made to stick because "there are political forces here within the country now that can fight for these conditions and defend them." What he envisions is nothing short of democratization, induced by the West, in the heart of Eastern Europe—and he apparently doesn't see much contradiction in either this or the original Yalta formulation, calling for free elections within the Soviet sphere of influence.

If Kuron's view prevails, Yalta may someday represent a historical weapon against the Soviet oppression of Poland, rather than the sellout it is supposed to have been.

[13]"From Yalta to San Francisco," delivered at the Foreign Policy Association in New York (typescript in the "Dulles Papers," Seeley G. Mudd Library, Princeton University).

[14]Typescript in "Dulles Papers."

[15]Andrew H. Berding, *Dulles on Diplomacy* (D. Van Nostrand, 1965), pp. 22–23. These sentiments did not prevent Dulles from helping to draft the 1952 Republican platform denouncing Yalta.

[16]In *The Reagan Phenomenon—and Other Speeches on Foreign Policy* (American Enterprise Institute, 1983), pp. 176–177:

> Today, in the shadow of the Soviet-ordered repression in Poland, it is easy to forget that Yalta reaffirmed the principles of the Atlantic Charter, recognizing "the right of all people to choose the form of government under which they will live," and, in the case of Poland specifically, pledged that "free and unfettered elections" would be held "as soon as possible on the basis of universal suffrage and secret ballot." Roosevelt and Churchill no doubt took these words very seriously. But Stalin, who once wrote that "good words are a mask for the concealment of bad deeds," clearly did not. A Soviet puppet regime was already in place in Warsaw. The Red Army had occupied all of Eastern Europe, with the exception of most of Czechoslovakia. Words and dreams could neither conceal nor change this reality.

Poland without a new, reorganized provisional government and without "free and unfettered elections as soon as possible on the basis of universal suffrage and secret ballot." Then he managed to get the blame shifted from himself to Franklin D. Roosevelt. For the second half of his triumph he needed the collaboration of Americans, some of whom knew no better and some of whom should by now know better.

3

There is something peculiarly shameful about the idea that Roosevelt gave away Eastern Europe. But putting the blame on him for the three Soviet seats in the United Nations is merely ludicrous. Again, it is Churchill who is being mistaken for Roosevelt.

The subject of membership in the future United Nations first came up at the Dumbarton Oaks conference in August 1944. The Soviets unexpectedly proposed that the sixteen individual Soviet "republics" be made full members of the U.N. The demand was not as outrageous as it may seem today. It was explained by Ambassador Charles E. Bohlen, the wartime interpreter and adviser: "The Soviets knew they would be virtually alone in the United Nations, that their ideological system provided little common ground with other countries." Times have changed; it is again necessary to try to put oneself back into a very different period. The Americans flatly opposed the Soviet request. "President Roosevelt went so far as to tell members of Congress that if the Russians persisted in this proposal, he would counter with a demand that the forty-eight states of the United States be members."[17]

The dispute was resolved at Yalta. The Soviets decided to cut down the number from sixteen to two or three, eventually two more, the Ukraine and Byelorussia. Roosevelt

initially objected even to this number. But Churchill for his own reasons made an eloquent plea in support of the Soviet request.[18] With some reluctance, Roosevelt went along with Stalin and Churchill, though he later regretted that the Soviet Union would get three votes in the General Assembly, Great Britain with its dominions six votes, and the United States only one. Roosevelt soon changed his mind and actually wrote Stalin and Churchill requesting three votes for the United States, to which they agreed. When the story was leaked to the papers, it was subjected to such ridicule that the idea was dropped. Since substantive decisions could only be made in the Security Council, in which each of the three powers had a veto, the votes in the General Assembly were not considered all that important.

Why was Churchill so willing to let the Soviets have their way? He explained the reason in a contemporary letter to Deputy Prime Minister Clement Attlee:

> For us to have four or five members, six if India is included, when Russia has only one is asking a

---

[17]Charles E. Bohlen, *Witness to History* (Norton, 1973), pp. 159–160.

[18]In *Foreign Relations of the United States: The Conferences at Malta and Yalta, 1945,* p. 714:

> This is why, Mr. President, the Prime Minister said, he had great sympathy with the Soviet request. His heart went out to mighty Russia which though bleeding was beating down the tyrants in her path. He said he could understand their point of view, as they were represented by only one voice in comparison with the British organization which had a smaller population, if only white people were considered.

Even so knowledgeable a historian as Professor Adam B. Ulam has perpetuated the myth that Churchill, "having very largely accepted Roosevelt's leadership when it came to dealing with Russia, felt constrained, even if groaning inwardly, to go along with the president" in acceding to Stalin's wish for three Soviet seats in the U.N. ("Forty Years After Yalta," *The New Republic,* February 11, 1985, p. 20). Professor Ulam is wrong here on two counts: Churchill was quite independent when it came to dealing with Russia, as the "percentages deal" and his disagreement with Roosevelt soon after the Yalta conference showed; and it was Roosevelt who in this case went along with the prime minister, even if groaning inwardly.

great deal of an Assembly of this kind. In view of other important concessions by them which are achieved or pending I should like to be able to make a friendly gesture to Russia in this matter. That they should have two besides their chief is not much to ask, and we will be in a strong position, in my judgment, because we shall not be the only multiple voter in the field.[19]

Thus Kirkpatrick and Colville have the whole story upside down. Churchill, not Roosevelt, made possible the deal that gave the Soviets three members in the United Nations. There was no "falsification" which the United States and its democratic allies accepted, as Kirkpatrick alleges. Above all, her presumption of why they were parties to a "falsification" is itself most presumptuous. The reason had nothing to do with their being unable to face the fact that there remained a powerful, repressive, expansionist dictatorship to cope with. It had nothing to do with whether Churchill knew and Roosevelt should have known that nothing in the Soviet past justified optimism concerning its future behavior. The reason had everything to do with a temporary coincidence of interests on the part of both Stalin and Churchill to get more than one vote in the nascent U.N.

We are now in a better position to assess the latter-day glorification of Churchill and denigration of Roosevelt. The wonder is not that they sometimes disagreed but that they worked together so well for so long, given the different traditions and interests of their countries. They were both giants in their time, whatever their shortcomings. I am inclined to think that Churchill was right about Roosevelt's "truce plan" in the period of their disagreement after Yalta, but the issue itself came up too late and would have changed too little to count for much. What is unforgivable is the ignorance and effrontery of those who now accuse one of them of virtual betrayal or outright falsification.

[19]*Triumph and Tragedy,* pp. 359–360.

4

What in the present has provoked this abuse of the past?

The main source, I suspect, is the influence of the so-called neoconservative ideology. The latest pronunciamento from that front on American foreign policy has made "liberal internationalism" the enemy. In this view, the era of liberal internationalism is fortunately coming to an end. No one represents this era more conspicuously than Franklin D. Roosevelt, who inaugurated it in our time. For this reason he is being belittled and his reputation besmirched.

"Global unilateralism" has been presented by Irving Kristol, the reputed "godfather" and "standard-bearer" of the new creed, as the neoconservative alternative to "liberal internationalism." His new order would require a total break with all our allies and the abandonment by the United States of NATO, the United Nations, and the Organization of American States. He wants to get rid of allies, because they are "very effective hindrances to American action."[20] This is another myth; the United States has not been hindered by NATO or the U.N. from doing anything it really wanted to do—not in Korea, not in Vietnam or Grenada or Central America or anywhere. Others have also had reservations about NATO's strategy and the U.N.'s behavior. There is no law that says these organizations may not be modified or reformed to reflect the conditions of today rather than those in existence immediately

[20]Irving Kristol, "Foreign Policy in an Age of Ideology," *The National Interest,* No. 1 (Fall 1985), pp. 6–15.

Kristol is uncharacteristically squeamish in his avowal of "global unilateralism." After demanding the dismantling of NATO, the U.N., and the OAS, as well as the virtually defunct Southeast Asia Treaty Organization, he coyly adds: "Whether the United States will then move all the way to what has been called 'global unilateralism' depends on the reaction among America's allies"—after he has just written them off as allies.

after World War II. But Kristol is engaged in a throw-out-the-baby-with-the-bath-water operation. It is so extreme that even his friend Jeane Kirkpatrick cannot go along with it.[21] If the Soviet Union has one governing objective in Europe it is the destruction of NATO. "Global unilateralism" is another way of doing it.

The world according to Kristol is a world in the grip of a "conflict of ideologies." The ideologies, however, do not seem to be in very good shape for a final conflict. They were in Kristol's view better off after 1945, when they were clearly identifiable as "liberal internationalism and Marxism-Leninism." But now both are said to be "floundering," each in its own way.

The "liberal internationalism" of the United States was allegedly "mortally wounded" in Vietnam. There is now, in Kristol's opinion, only "a tentative, fumbling search" for a new American ideology. Just what is taking its place is far from clear. Unfortunately, the "natural and instinctive attitude" of most Americans is said to be some version of isolationism. A liberal-capitalist ideology which aspires to be "universal" would seem to have the wrong people as its chosen instrument. But there is also better news. The same American people, in their post-Vietnam phase, wish the United States to "reassert its proprietary claim to the future." One might imagine from this that the future is a piece of property which should

belong exclusively to the United States. If so, the ideological conflict may be not only with the Soviet Union but with any country that is selfish enough to want a piece of the future for and by itself.

The Soviet ideology is supposedly floundering for a different reason. We are assured that Marxism-Leninism is dead in the Soviet Union and in every other communist nation. We are also told that the Soviet system "works" in foreign affairs only because it rests on Soviet military power and that this power alone legitimates the Soviet system abroad. Without such military power, "the Soviet leadership is under threat of being de-legitimated." Nevertheless, despite the internal bankruptcy of Marxism-Leninism and its total dependence abroad on military power, Soviet ideology is still "messianic."

How an ideology can be "messianic," if no one within the Soviet Union believes in it anymore, and it is carried abroad solely with guns, is a mystery that Kristol never clears up. A "messianic" ideology without true believers is something new under the sun. The present-day Soviet Union is far more imperialistic than messianic; the proportion of sheer imperialism has increased as the messianic veneer has worn thinner and thinner. It may well be that Marxism-Leninism or whatever passes for it in such advanced proletarian nations as Ethiopia and South Yemen possesses an attractiveness of its own for military dictatorships that wish to pass themselves off as "progressive" or "revolutionary," but Soviet messianism has little to do with it. Kristol seems to need a Soviet messianism in order to convert the United States to a corresponding capitalist messianism.

There surely are ideological elements in the Soviet-American conflict, but they are precisely those elements that could be pursued most peacefully. Kristol and cohorts have something more in mind. Their version of ideological conflict shades into a real, ordinary, bloodletting war—anything up to nuclear devastation, which is the only concession Kristol makes to stopping short of

---

[21]"NATO has been a great success. It remains one. It was never intended to be an all-purpose instrument. It should, therefore, not be criticized for failing to be one" (*The Reagan Phenomenon*, p. 181).

More useful advice: "The dynamics of the American political system precludes the successful practice of purist politics and guarantees chronic frustration to all persons whose public policy preferences deviate significantly from the status quo. That includes most of us some of the time and some of us most of the time. The Reagan administration is no more able than any other to escape the powerful moderating, aggregating, consensus-building pressures that the American system puts on our governors. And that, as always, is a good thing for the United States." (p. 218).

mutual catastrophe. We are instructed to be "not at all risk-averse." We are also assured that "in the years ahead, the United States will be far less inhibited in its use of military power." If the Soviet Union does not convert "its secular, political messianism into a stable orthodoxy," whatever the latter may mean, global conflict will likely be "political, economic, and military, though always short of nuclear war," as if an impenetrable barrier could be built between nuclear and other types of war. In any case Kristol's "war of ideology" is not likely to be purely ideological.

This neoconservatism is not merely a hopeless muddle; it is also misnamed. We are probably stuck with the term, but it has little or nothing to do with traditional conservatism, particularly in foreign policy; it is a new concoction, much closer to other types of political extremism. We have had isolationists; we have had interventionists; we have never had isolationists who were also interventionists. This abnormal crossbreeding of isolationism and interventionism has produced the new species of "global unilateralists." They are global in their interventionism and unilateral in the way they wish to go about it. In the past, isolationists did not want us to intervene and interventionists did not want us to be isolated.

Though the enemy is ostensibly communism and the Soviet Union, what really stirs the "neo" to a sort of holy wrath is anything that can be blamed on liberals. There is not much he can do about getting at the Soviet Union, but homegrown liberals are readily available as targets of his rancor. It is de rigueur for a "neo" who was formerly a liberal to be particularly unforgiving in his anathemas upon liberals. Against this enemy the "neo" goes into battle as if in a civil war, with more than a hint that those who differ are really serving the enemy. A disagreement over policy comes to resemble a quasi-religious war rather than a legitimate secular dispute. Indeed, Kristol wishes us to believe that "in our own era, the distinction between religious ideas and political ideas is blurred."

The remaking of history plays a large part in this apocalyptic drama of good and evil because the older "neo" has repented and recanted transgressions that he committed as a liberal or leftist. No one raises his blood pressure more than the liberal with whom he once shared the same views—about the Vietnam War, for example—but who has stubbornly refused to admit grievous error and recant publicly. The present frustrates "neos" because it resists their unconstrained adventurism; only in historical reinterpretations can they indulge themselves in ideological imperatives and infallible hindsights. Thus their treatment of history is peculiarly guilt ridden, with the guilt often displaced on to others.

Foreign policy is actually not the best place to distinguish between American liberals and conservatives. The line between them can be drawn more clearly in domestic policy—and then not always. In the past, there have been interventionist conservatives and interventionist liberals, isolationist conservatives and isolationist liberals. In foreign policy, presidents have not been liberal or conservative so much as isolationist or interventionist. Presidents have sacrificed their liberal domestic policies for the sake of foreign interventionism. Lyndon Johnson was such a case; he did not intervene in Vietnam on such a large scale because he was a liberal; liberals and Democrats were on both sides of the war. Johnson also knew that the Republicans would have pilloried him if he could have been accused of "giving away Vietnam," just as Truman and Acheson had been pilloried for "giving away China," and as Roosevelt even to this day is being pilloried for having "given away Eastern Europe."

The irony in all this is that, if it were not for "liberal internationalism," Nazi Germany would in all probability still be astride all of Europe, and the United States would now have no credible ideology for trying to prevent the Soviet Union from doing the same thing.

Yalta and the Neoconservatives

Paul Seabury

Last January, in an article in the *New York Review of Books* entitled "Neoconservative History," Theodore Draper delivered himself of a fevered attack on four pieces in *Commentary* which he accused of slandering Franklin D. Roosevelt and misrepresenting the role he played at the Yalta conference of 1945. Three of the pieces thus singled out for attack were the contributions of Lionel Abel, Jeane J. Kirkpatrick, and Robert Nisbet to the symposium, "How Has the United States Met Its Major Challenges Since 1945?" (November 1985). The fourth was an article by John Colville, "How the West Lost the Peace in 1945" (September 1985).

According to Draper, these writers severally and in concert have resurrected the "Yalta myth"—a myth invented by right-wing opponents of liberal internationalism in the early 1950's and intensified by McCarthyites. Today, says Draper, in the service of a new assault on the Rooseveltian heritage of liberal internationalism, the neoconservatives—and here his wrath turns upon Irving Kristol in particular—have not only brought the "myth" back but have done so by means of a deliberate falsification of history.

Contrary to the "myth," Draper maintains, Roosevelt and Churchill at Yalta did not sign away Poland and Eastern Europe to Stalin. The *fait accompli* already had happened: i.e., the Red Army already had the region in its clutches. At Yalta, the Western leaders signed an agreement with Stalin which, had the Soviet dictator lived up to it, "might have extricated Poland" from the Soviet grip. But, Draper writes, "words hardly mattered" at Yalta; what mattered was "brute

power." Thus, "Yalta was a dividing line, not because of what happened there, but because of what happened after it."

Yet if we are to understand what happened at Yalta, the main task surely is to ask not "what happened after it" but what happened *before* it. For here what is past really is prologue.

Specifically we must inquire—as Jeane Kirkpatrick and Nisbet do—into Roosevelt's mind-set in the four years before Yalta. In doing so, we must avoid either being vindictive or full of praise. Instead we simply must ask: what was Roosevelt's overriding strategic objective in World War II? Subordinate to that, what was his view of the Soviet element in the war after June 22, 1941?

Here we deal not with Roosevelt alone, but with a major component of an American strategic attitude. In the war, Roosevelt displayed both the best and the worst qualities of American attitudes toward war and peace. The clear merits of Roosevelt as wartime leader were that he wished to employ American force in the most concentrated fashion in order to gain battlefield victory quickly, rejecting doctrines, such as those of Liddell Hart and Churchill, which argued for a strategy of indirection that could have prolonged the war. Roosevelt instinctively sensed the impatience of the American public, which, hating war, despised protracted conflicts. He thus in effect abandoned politics and became Commander-in-Chief. (As he himself said in 1942, "Dr. Win-the-War" had replaced "Dr. New Deal.") Roosevelt also understood the need for Americans to have a sure and even simple principled base for going to war. Beyond defeating Hitler and Tojo, he therefore enunciated a high goal: the Four Freedoms, which he was able to sell to Churchill at the Atlantic Conference in 1941.

Paul Seabury, "Yalta and the Neoconservatives," *Commentary*, **82** (Aug. 1986), pp. 47–49. Reprinted from *Commentary*, August 1986, by permission; all rights reserved.

Such vague and principled aspirations were in themselves important; they were (and remain) consonant with a long American liberal tradition. But what of the serious "political goal," so crucial to seminal strategists like Clausewitz? Here we come to Roosevelt's defects which, like his merits, were also consonant with a long American tradition.

The great Spanish liberal historian, Salvador de Madariaga, once wrote a little book, *The Blowing Up of the Parthenon,* a commentary on the early years of the cold war and the wartime years which preceded it. Like Arthur Koestler and others, he described World War II as a triangular war, among the liberal democracies, the Nazi totalitarians, and the Leninist totalitarians.

But to be more precise than Madariaga, World War II as a triangular war consisted of phases and theaters. In phase one, 1939-41, Hitler and Stalin arrayed themselves against the West; in phase two, 1941-45, Churchill, Roosevelt, and Stalin arrayed themselves against Hitler. In the theaters, however, the triangular war continued uninterruptedly through both phases—as may be seen, for instance, in Yugoslavia and China, where battles raged among pro-Western, pro-Soviet, and Axis forces.

Another, somewhat different example—the terrifying episode of the Warsaw uprising in 1944, where Nazi and Soviet forces in taut concert eliminated the Polish pro-Western resistance—remains a hideous scar on the Western conscience. As the recently published Roosevelt-Churchill correspondence shows, the British leader vainly pleaded with Roosevelt to demand of Stalin that Anglo-American airborne assistance be permitted to reach the freedom fighters. Roosevelt procrastinated. As the Red Army stood by on the east bank of the Vistula, Hitler's forces exterminated the Poles.

I cite this unpleasant instance of triangularity not as a revelation derived from hindsight, but as one in which the actors at the time knew full well what was going on. Why was Roosevelt so loath to act? Because, surely, his overriding political objective was defeating the Axis; warwinning excluded or superseded all other considerations.

Moreover, while Churchill recognized the triangularity of the war, Roosevelt did not, seeing it rather as a sequential set of conflicts.

During the time of the Nazi-Soviet Pact, in a 1940 White House speech to the Communist-dominated American Youth Congress, Roosevelt gave a bitter, extemporaneous tongue-lashing to the Soviet Union and to American fellow-travelers. The U.S.S.R., he then said, was run by a dictatorship as absolute as any in the world, and was allied with another dictatorship. Scarcely two years later, Stalin, the absolute dictator, had to Roosevelt become "Uncle Joe." Was this transformation in Roosevelt's mind a consequence of a changed *Realpolitik* situation, or was it a result of genuine self-mesmerization?

This is no idle question. As to nuances of triangularity in the Roosevelt administration, Roosevelt, regardless of his own personal convictions, certainly harbored, among his advisers, individuals of known pro-Soviet persuasion. (There were, by contrast, no crypto-Nazis in Roosevelt's cabinet or on his staff at that or any other time.) One Soviet agent went with him to Yalta—Alger Hiss; others, like Harry Dexter White, played significant roles in shaping U.S. postwar policy in both China and in Central Europe.

But long before these events, in the 1930's, Roosevelt, cultivating Stalin before Hitler did, dispatched the notoriously pro-Soviet Joseph Davies as Ambassador to Moscow—an appointment which at the time almost caused the U.S. Moscow embassy staff to resign en masse.

In addition, in 1937, as George Kennan tells it in his *Memoirs,* the White House one day out of the blue ordered the State Department to dismantle its Division of East European Affairs (colloquially known as the Russian Division)—

a full-scale, sudden purge of talented Sovieto-logists, who then were banished to obscure posts like Teheran. The division's precious archives unceremoniously were removed to dark, obscure stacks in the Library of Congress; the State Department thus was blinded, as far as its knowledge of Soviet affairs was concerned. As Kennan comments:

> I never learned the real background of this curious purge. It was rumored that the Western European Division considered that we in the Russian Division "took Russia too seriously"—that we gave it attention that was out of proportion to that given by other divisions to other countries. I have no doubt there was something in this; but it surely was not the whole story. There is strong evidence that pressure was brought to bear from the White House. I was surprised, in later years, that the McCarthyites...never got hold of the incident and made capital of it; for here, if ever, was a point at which there was indeed the smell of Soviet influence...somewhere in the higher reaches of the government.

Small wonder, then, that Roosevelt in 1942 already wrote to Churchill that he, Roosevelt, should be the leader in wartime discussions with Stalin, since Stalin trusted him and distrusted Churchill's advisers as anti-Soviet! "I know you will not mind my being brutally frank with you when I tell you that I think I can handle Stalin better than your Foreign Office or my State Department. Stalin hates the guts of all your top people. He thinks he likes me better and I hope he will continue to do so." (Draper, in a subsequent exchange of letters in the *New York Review,* dismisses this statement as mere Rooseveltian boastfulness; it helps considerably, however, to understand the context for this boast, if boast it was and not simple candor.)

Whatever one makes of such speculations, it is undoubtedly true that from the moment of Pearl Harbor, Roosevelt gave his undivided attention to winning the war—this was the job to be done.

It is also true that he paid very little attention to Soviet wartime actions or their portents. Whatever worries others in his entourage may have had, Roosevelt simply does not appear to have been bothered about Stalin's possible betrayal of the Allied war effort. Instead, Roosevelt clearly defined the war in simple ways. He wished to smash the Axis. Also, he had two fronts to fight upon: the *American* front in the Pacific and the joint front in Europe. He thought it necessary to get Stalin's help, after V-E day, in winning against Japan, and he was willing to pay the price of Soviet domination of Eastern Europe for that.

Yet considering the combination of these obvious facts, we still must judge Roosevelt for the missing element in his equations—an absence of strategic reflection as to the likely contours of world politics *after* the Axis collapse and defeat. Despite Draper's tortured attempt to make it appear otherwise, again and again Churchill tried to remind Roosevelt of the *political* implications and side effects of battlefield operations, particularly the unpleasant ones. Again and again, as in the Warsaw uprising affair, Roosevelt showed little interest.

This Roosevelt mind-set, it must be emphasized, infected key subordinates and their battlefield decisions as well: *no* political considerations other than those related to the surrender of Nazi Germany were allowed to contaminate field operations. One logical consequence of this was to be seen in the spring of 1945, soon after Yalta, when Eisenhower—charged, as Allied Supreme Commander, with the pursuit and defeat of the *Reichswehr*—turned his forces southward toward a pitiful *Reichswehr* redoubt in Bavaria, and away from the momentous drive to Berlin. The decision may have been Eisenhower's alone, but it certainly was compatible with Roosevelt's overall strategy. In any event, it was the Soviet Red banner which was raised in triumph over the Reichstag in May 1945, and not the Stars and Stripes.

If Roosevelt correctly sized up the American temperament, then both as politician and warrior-leader he succeeded brilliantly. Americans got what they wanted—a quick solution. But as statesman he failed miserably. The eastern periphery of the Free World was thenceforward to lie to the west of Magdeburg, and Prague, which could easily have been taken by American forces, was to experience Red Army liberation instead. Roosevelt led his nation to victory, but at a price which his colleague Churchill clearly did not wish to share, and whose dangers many experienced and well-informed Americans on whom the White House could have drawn (such as Averell Harriman, George Kennan, and others) also sensed.

What happened at Yalta itself was the catastrophic consummation of these wartime strategic decisions. In fact, that consummation was foreshadowed by the very choice of Yalta as a site.

"Magneto" was the code word used by Roosevelt and Churchill in 1944 in correspondence to denote their upcoming summit meeting with Stalin in early 1945—as though the yet-to-be-determined site for it, had Stalin insisted, might have been in Magnetogorsk in far Siberia. The two Western leaders tried to lure Stalin ("U.J.," for "Uncle Joe," as they both by then called him) to various Mediterranean places. Stalin feigned ill health: such a long trip was impossible. So the ailing American President (who was soon to die) and his British partner (then recovering from a bout of pneumonia) ventured on a perilous long voyage to a disease-wracked and rubbled Soviet city.

The site agreement corresponded in one respect with previous summit locations, and with the one later to be held in Potsdam. During the war, Anglo-American leaders invariably went *east*. During the entire war, from 1939 to 1945, only twice did a major Soviet leader venture beyond the Red Army's pale to treat with the enemies of Stalin's enemies. This was Molotov,

who went to Berlin in December 1940 and then to London and Washington in 1942. The wartime Moscow, Teheran, Yalta, and Potsdam conference sites thus betokened a Western supplicant willingness to deal with the totalitarian partner on his own turf. So the chosen site was Yalta.

Draper tries to put a good face on Roosevelt's conduct there, but his sophistries cannot and do not explain the coy, flippant role the President assumed in the negotiations, posing as genial umpire between Churchill the British imperialist and Stalin the Russian socialist. Nor does Draper's perverse revisionism explain why Roosevelt should have abandoned a common front with Churchill, engaging in bilateral talks with Stalin in which he and the Soviet dictator discussed ways to overthrow the British Raj in India.

But as the title of his article indicates, Draper is not mainly interested in what happened at Yalta in 1945; he is interested in discrediting the neoconservative critique of the neutered internationalism of the Carter years. To accomplish this, indeed, he abruptly changes gears, and subject, in the last section of his article and launches an assault on "the so-called neoconservative ideology," which is supposedly typified by the foreign-policy writings of Irving Kristol.

Draper himself was once a very sharp critic of détente.[1] But like many other formerly hard-headed analysts of the Soviet-American conflict, he seems to have become so fearful of Soviet power that he is now trying to dissociate himself from his earlier ideas. He has every right to change his mind on these matters. But this gives him no license to warp the thoughts of others. While it is, for example, fair enough to say that Irving Kristol is against liberal internationalism and in favor of "global unilateral-

---

[1] See, for example, his article, "Détente," in the June 1974 *Commentary*.

ism,'' most other neoconservatives, including (as Draper himself is forced to acknowledge) Jeane Kirkpatrick, remain committed precisely to the liberal internationalist tradition which Roosevelt helped to shape but whose principles he himself then betrayed in appeasing Stalin at Yalta.

What is even worse than Draper's failure to distinguish among the varieties of neoconservative thought, however, is his near-hysterical defamation of those who are still trying to dispel the kinds of illusions about the Soviet Union that Franklin D. Roosevelt brought with him to Yalta, and that—thanks in part to people like Draper—now enjoy a dangerous revival.

QUESTIONS FOR DISCUSSION

1 Did Roosevelt at Yalta, either wittingly or unwittingly, hand over much of East Central Europe to long-term Soviet domination?
2 Was Churchill more anti-Soviet than Roosevelt?
3 With forceful diplomacy at Yalta, could the United States have persuaded the Soviet Union to behave with greater restraint in East Central Europe?
4 Did the United States have the military means at the time of Yalta to compel the Soviet Union to permit free elections and national independence for the states of East Central Europe?
5 Would U.S. public opinion in 1945 have supported a war against the Soviet Union for the sake of East Central Europe?
6 What were Stalin's short-term and long-term aims at the time of the Yalta Conference?

SUGGESTED READINGS

Brzezinski, Zbigniew. ''The Future of Yalta,'' *Foreign Affairs,* **63** (Winter 1984–85), pp. 279–302.

Buhite, Russell D. *Decisions at Yalta: An Appraisal of Summit Diplomacy.* Wilmington, Del.: Scholarly Resources, 1986.

Colville, John. ''How the West Lost the Peace in 1945,'' *Commentary,* **80** (Sept. 1985), pp. 41–47.

Dackiewicz, Miroslav. ''Undo Yalta? Who Has a Stake in This?'' *World Marxist Review,* **28** (May 1985), pp. 17–23.

Edmonds, Robin. ''Yalta and Potsdam: Forty Years Afterwards,'' *International Affairs* (London), **62** (Spring 1986), pp. 197–216.

Ford, Robert A. D. ''The Legacy of Yalta,'' *Maclean's* (Toronto), **98** (Feb. 11, 1985), pp. 16–17.

Luchsinger, Fred. ''Yalta: Legend and History,'' *Swiss Review of World Affairs* (Zurich), **35** (Apr. 1985), pp. 25–26.

Miller, Robert. ''At the Dawn of the Cold War,'' *Maclean's* (Toronto), **98** (Feb. 11, 1985), pp. 22–23.

Roberts, Sir Frank. ''Yalta Reviewed after Forty Years,'' *NATO Review,* **33** (Oct. 1985), pp. 18–23.

Theoharis, Athan G. *The Yalta Myths: An Issue in U.S. Politics, 1945–1955.* Columbia, Mo.: Univ. of Missouri Press, 1970.

Yergin, Daniel. *Shattered Peace: The Origins of the Cold War and the National Security State.* Boston: Houghton Mifflin, 1977.

2 Is it likely that the U.S. use of atomic bombs at Hiroshima and Nagasaki was designed to intimidate the Soviet Union?

YES

Gar Alperovitz

More on Atomic Diplomacy

NO

Geoffrey Warner

To End a War: The Decision to Drop the Bomb

More on Atomic Diplomacy

Gar Alperovitz

In the fortieth-anniversary issue of the *Bulletin,* Robert Messer usefully reviewed some of the contents of Harry S. Truman's most recently discovered diary, along with other materials concerning the president's personal viewpoint at the time of the Hiroshima and Nagasaki bombings. My aim here is to suggest additional implications of the new evidence and to indicate some of the limits of our present knowledge.

As Messer observes, the new information reveals that "contrary to his public justification of the bombings as the only way to end the war without a costly invasion of Japan, Truman had already concluded that Japan was about to capitulate." Beyond this crucial point the materials throw considerable light on two controversial historical questions:

- The first is whether there actually was anything like a "decision" to use the bombs. Some have argued that it is more accurate to say that Truman was simply carried along, on the basis of assumptions that he inherited, or by the momentum of events, or both.
- The second has to do with just how much of the decision, or assumption-decision, to use the bomb must be ascribed to political-diplomatic considerations related to the Soviet Union.

In recent years several historians, urging the assumption theory, have stressed the continuity between the Roosevelt and Truman periods.[1]

Since my own work helped initiate the case for an "assumption-based" theory, let me state now that the idea must be handled with considerable care.[2] Even if the theory is accepted, it is all too easy to ignore crucial elements of choice in connection with Hiroshima.

For instance, it is simply not true that the use of the atomic bomb was never challenged, as Secretary of War Henry L. Stimson later wrote. Several top leaders—General Dwight D. Eisenhower, Admiral William D. Leahy, Undersecretary of the Navy Ralph A. Bard, Assistant Secretary of War John J. McCloy, Acting Secretary of State Joseph E. Grew, and Stimson himself—at various points urged Truman not to use the bomb or to use other methods first.

There is also the matter of what assumptions Truman actually did inherit. There is no doubt that part of the legacy was a policy concerning international control of atomic weapons promulgated by Franklin D. Roosevelt and his top officials. This was to foster an American, and partially British, monopoly. Truman did not, however, inherit a clear policy on the use of the bomb. Rather, what evidence we have suggests that Roosevelt had doubts about using the bomb against Japan—and that in his last conversations on the subject he himself was raising the possibility of a "demonstration."

Truman, in any case, knew virtually nothing about Roosevelt's position. Moreover, while Stimson, General Leslie R. Groves, a number of scientists, and several other high officials

Gar Alperovitz, "More on Atomic Diplomacy," *Bulletin of the Atomic Scientists,* **41** (Dec. 1985), pp. 35–39. Reprinted by permission of the *Bulletin of the Atomic Scientists,* a magazine of science and world affairs. Copyright © 1985 by the Educational Foundation for Nuclear Science.

[1]See Martin J. Sherwin, *A World Destroyed: The Atomic Bomb and the Grand Alliance* (New York: Knopf, 1975); Barton J. Bernstein, "Roosevelt, Truman and the Atomic Bomb, 1941–1945: A Reinterpretation," in *Political Science Quarterly* (Spring 1975), pp. 23–69; Gregg Herken, *The Winning Weapon: The Atomic Bomb in the Cold War, 1945–1950* (New York: Knopf, 1980).

[2]Gar Alperovitz, *Atomic Diplomacy: Hiroshima and Potsdam* (New York: Simon and Schuster, 1965); *Cold War Essays* (New York: Doubleday, 1970). This work, which focuses primarily on 1945, picks up the assumptions as they existed at the beginning of the Truman Administration. The newer studies explore the earlier sources of the assumptions in the Roosevelt period.

associated with the Manhattan Project from the
Roosevelt period undoubtedly assumed early
on that the bomb would be used, Truman's
main policy adviser, Secretary of State James
F. Byrnes, was not part of that group. (And
Admiral William Leahy, the chief of staff whom
Truman inherited from Roosevelt and, simulta-
neously, presiding officer of the Joint Chiefs of
Staff, was against the bombing.)[3]

Finally, and far more important, are changes
which occurred throughout the summer of 1945.
Whatever assumptions Truman may have inherited, these changes presented decision-
makers with a new situation.

Here the new evidence is particularly illuminating. In reviewing the history of Hiroshima,
one must be extremely careful about statements
and judgments made at different times between
April 12, 1945, when Truman became president,
and the August 6 bombing. It is almost certainly
true, for instance, that American leaders assumed the bomb, like any weapon, would be
used against Japan in the early summer of
1945—up to, say, the end of June. I use the
qualifier "almost certainly" because there is
also evidence to the contrary: At the request of
the White House, Leo Szilard met with Truman's key adviser, James Byrnes, on May 28,
1945—two-and-a-half months before Hiroshima. According to Szilard, "Byrnes did not
argue that it was necessary to use the bomb
against the cities of Japan in order to win the
war....Mr. Byrnes's...view [was] that our
possessing and demonstrating the bomb would
make Russia more manageable." Admiral
Leahy was also convinced that the war was
essentially over by mid-June.

In any event, in the six weeks or so before
Hiroshima the situation in Japan changed dra-

matically. First, the intensity of Japanese peace
initiatives increased—in Switzerland, Sweden,
and, we now know, in Portugal. As early as
May 12, 1945, almost three months before Hiroshima, William Donovan, the head of the
Office of Strategic Services (OSS) personally
advised the president of indications that Japan
might surrender if the terms included a provision that the emperor (regarded as a deity)
would not be removed. Thereafter others—
including, most importantly, Acting Secretary
of State Joseph Grew and Stimson—urged such
a change at different times. And we know from
several sources that although Truman may have
preferred to make no change, he had no objection in principle to the provision—and, of
course, ultimately accepted it.

The United States had also, of course,
cracked the Japanese code early in the war. In
mid-June, and then very actively on into July,
the emperor became involved in attempting to
arrange a surrender, using Moscow as the negotiating channel. The evidence on this—and
U.S. leaders' knowledge of the emperor's initiative—is now well established. (Robert C.
Butow's *Japan's Decision to Surrender* is the
classic work.) The mere fact that the emperor,
traditionally aloof from politics, instigated the
diplomatic move was extraordinary. We also
know that Truman clearly understood what was
happening; afterwards he confirmed his awareness of the main cables. The new evidence from
the diaries adds to our sense of the president's
personal assessment; in these pages Truman
straightforwardly terms the most important intercepted message the "telegram from Jap Emperor asking for peace."

In a new edition of *Atomic Diplomacy*, I
have reviewed additional intelligence and other
information which helps clarify how U.S. officials understood what was happening, especially in the six or seven weeks before Hiroshima. It is enough to say here that many top
officials understood that Japan's situation had
changed drastically. The following (often ig-

---

[3]Unless otherwise specifically noted, documentation for
these and other points made in this article can be found in
the new edition of *Atomic Diplomacy: Hiroshima and
Potsdam* (New York: Penguin, 1985), especially the Introduction, Appendix V, and footnote references to both.

nored) illustrations help illuminate the shifting environment in which policy was being developed:

• Admiral Leahy's diary entry of June 18, 1945, just short of two months before Hiroshima: "It is my opinion at the present time that a surrender of Japan can be arranged with terms that can be accepted by Japan and that will make fully satisfactory provision for America's defense."

• After the war Leahy wrote: "The use of this barbarous weapon at Hiroshima and Nagasaki was of no material assistance in our war against Japan. The Japanese were already defeated and ready to surrender.... My own feeling is that in being the first to use it, we had adopted an ethical standard common to the barbarians of the Dark Ages.... I was not taught to make war in that fashion, and wars cannot be won by destroying women and children."

• General Dwight D. Eisenhower's report of his response when Stimson briefed him on the forthcoming use of the bomb:

> During his recitation of the relevant facts, I had been conscious of a feeling of depression and so I voiced to him my grave misgivings, first on the basis of my belief that Japan was already defeated and that dropping the bomb was completely unnecessary, and secondly because I thought that our country should avoid shocking world opinion by the use of a weapon whose employment was, I thought, no longer mandatory as a measure to save American lives....
>
> Japan was, at that very moment, seeking some way to surrender with a minimum loss of 'face'....It wasn't necessary to hit them with [that] awful thing.

Eisenhower met with Truman on July 20, 1945 and urged him not to use the bomb, a fact recently confirmed by the late General Omar N. Bradley, but rarely cited in studies of the period.

• Undersecretary of the Navy Ralph Bard also met with Truman, just before Potsdam, to advise another course. Bard, who resigned his official post on July 1, 1945, wrote a memo dated June 27, which included the following paragraphs:

> During recent weeks I have...had the feeling very definitely that the Japanese government may be searching for some opportunity which they could use as a medium of surrender....This country could contact representatives from Japan... and make representations with regard to Russia's position and...give them some information regarding the proposed use of atomic power, together with whatever assurances the President might care to make with regard to the Emperor of Japan....It seems quite possible to me that this presents the opportunity which the Japanese are looking for.
>
> I don't see that we have anything in particular to lose....The only way to find out is to try.

• The assistant to the Secretary of the Navy, Admiral Lewis L. Strauss (later chairman of the Atomic Energy Commission) proposed a demonstration of the new weapon over a Japanese redwood-like forest. "The war was very nearly over. The Japanese were nearly ready to capitulate."

Several other important military figures also illuminate the shifting appraisal of Japan's collapse. General Curtis LeMay, who has repeatedly declared that use of the atomic bomb was unnecessary, reportedly felt that Japan would have surrendered in two weeks. (The atomic bomb "had nothing to do with the end of the war.") Army Air Force Chief, General Henry "Hap" Arnold, demanded that a statement be entered into the record of the Joint Chiefs of Staff on July 16, 1945, indicating his view that the war could easily be ended by September or October 1945 without an invasion. General Douglas MacArthur was never asked about the atomic bomb; on several occasions after the war he indicated his view that it was unnecessary. The chief British military figure, General

Hastings Ismay, was filled with "revulsion" at the report that the atomic bomb had been successfully tested and could now be used: "For some time past it had been firmly fixed in my mind that the Japanese were tottering."

In many studies suggesting the near unanimity of support for using the bomb, such information is ignored or played down. Yet this information helps to clarify the way in which at least some key policy-makers viewed the situation; and, since several of them pressed their views in meetings with the president, it contributes to an assessment of what Truman must have understood. Such evidence also provides background for a consideration of other aspects of the newer materials.

The collapse of Japan during the summer of 1945—which challenged the initial assumption that the bomb would be used—must be understood in still another context: at the time, U.S. officials recognized that the Soviet Union's forthcoming declaration of war would almost certainly force Japan to surrender. The planned date for Soviet entry was August 8, 1945 (amended by one week at Potsdam). Hiroshima was destroyed on August 6, 1945; Nagasaki on August 9, 1945.

We now know that after the successful Alamogordo test U.S. leaders tried to stall Moscow's entry so that (as one official's diary put it) the Soviets would not get "so much in on the kill, thereby being in a position to press for claims against China." But that is not the first point to focus upon. Rather, it is that during the summer of 1945 Japan's situation deteriorated so rapidly that Truman had available an obvious option to end the war. All he really had to do was wait a week or so for the Soviet declaration to see whether his advisers were right.

In mid-June General Marshall pointed out that "the impact of Russian entry on the already hopeless Japanese may well be the decisive action levering them into capitulation at that time or shortly thereafter if we land in Japan."

With the situation in Japan worsening, a month later the Combined U.S.-U.K. Intelligence Staffs advised (as General Ismay summarized for Churchill): "If and when Russia came into the war against Japan, the Japanese would probably wish to get out on almost any terms short of the dethronement of the Emperor."

The new diary evidence confirms that Truman understood the advice he was receiving on the significance of the Soviet attack well before Hiroshima. On July 17, 1945, when Stalin told him personally that the Red Army would march, Truman's private diary shows him noting: "Fini Japs when that comes about."

And, of course, there was plenty of time. The full invasion of Japan was not scheduled until March 1946; even an initial landing on Kyushu was still three months in the future. Moreover, the invasion date could easily have been postponed. (According to Admiral Leahy, Truman told him that, should negotiations take longer, time was not a major consideration if this would avoid an invasion.)

Truman's order to drop the atomic bomb at a time when he knew the war was soon likely to be over is—as Messer observes—"devastating" to the orthodox case that he took the step only because he wished to avoid a costly invasion. However, the significance extends further.

Given Truman's awareness of the Japanese peace initiatives and his understanding of the power of a Soviet declaration of war, a key question is: Why did the initial assumption that the bomb would be used continue among some people and not among others?

The evidence had become increasingly clear by early July that, from a military point of view, Japan was finished. By mid-July it was exceedingly doubtful that Truman believed the war would end by invasion. Moreover, several top military figures clearly understood this reality—and were shocked that in these changed circumstances the bomb would still be used.

1945: Events Leading to Truman's Decision

April 12:	Truman becomes president.
May 12:	William Donovan, director of OSS, advises Truman that Japan might surrender if the United States promises not to depose the emperor.
May 28:	Manhattan Project scientist Leo Szilard meets with Secretary of State James Byrnes, who says the atomic bomb would "make Russia more manageable."
Mid-June through July:	The emperor of Japan tries to arrange a surrender, with the Soviets as negotiating channel.
June 18:	Admiral William Leahy writes in his diary of his belief in Japan's imminent surrender.
June 27:	Ralph Bard, undersecretary of the Navy, writes a memo to Truman stating that the Japanese are looking for a way to surrender.
July 6:	A memo from the Combined Chiefs of Staff states that the Japanese would be likely to accept U.S. terms of surrender.
July 16:	The New Mexico "Trinity" test of a nuclear explosive is successful; Army Air Force chief General Henry Arnold states that the war against Japan would be over in September or October without an invasion.
July 17:	Potsdam Conference begins. Stalin tells Truman that the Red Army would march into Manchuria; Truman writes in his diary, "Fini Japs when that comes about."
July 20:	General Dwight D. Eisenhower tells Truman not to use the bomb.
July 21:	Truman receives a full report of the Trinity test.
July 24:	Truman tells Stalin about "a new weapon of unusual force."
July 25:	Secretary of War Henry Stimson issues a formal order to use the atomic bomb in combat; an intercepted message reveals Tokyo's instructions to the Japanese ambassador in Moscow "to impress them with the sincerity of our desire" to terminate the war.
July 26:	Potsdam proclamation issued.
July 28:	Japanese premier issues *mokusatsu* ("ignore") response to Potsdam declaration.
August 2:	Donovan advises Truman that Japanese officials were trying to clarify their earlier response to the Potsdam proclamation.
August 6:	Hiroshima bombing.
August 8:	Original date for planned Soviet entry into war against Japan.
August 9:	Nagasaki bombing.
August 14:	Japanese surrender.

Who did not recognize the changed circumstances? Or, to put it another way, who refused to alter the early assumption? The military leaders went along with the president's decision, but they were not the source of initiative. It was Secretary of State Byrnes, Truman's chief adviser, and other officials most directly involved in diplomacy toward the Soviet Union who appeared to have been most unwilling or unable to alter their views.

Byrnes's general viewpoint is consistent and clear. He saw the atomic bomb as a way to impress the Soviets. The evidence is now massive on this point. A few of the numerous and by now well-known diary and other accounts will illustrate:

• From another report by Leo Szilard on his May 28, 1945 meeting with Byrnes:

Byrnes...was concerned about Russia's postwar behavior. Russian troops had moved into Hungary and Rumania; Byrnes thought it would be very difficult to persuade Russia to withdraw her troops from these countries, and that Russia might be more manageable if impressed by American military might. I shared Byrnes's concern about Russia's throwing around her weight in the postwar period, but I was completely flabbergasted by the assumption that rattling the bomb might make Russia more manageable.

• From Ambassador Joseph Davies's diary during the Potsdam Conferences: ''Byrnes' attitude that the atomic bomb assured ultimate success in negotiations disturbed me more than his description of its success amazed me....I told him the threat wouldn't work and might do irreparable harm.''

• From Secretary of the Navy James V. Forrestal's diary: "Byrnes said he was most anxious to get the Japanese affair over with before the Russians got in, with particular reference to [the Manchurian ports of] Dairen and Port Arthur.''

• From Secretary of War Stimson's diary after Potsdam: "I found that Byrnes was very much against any attempt to cooperate with Russia. His mind is full of his problems with the coming meeting of foreign ministers and he looks to having the presence of the bomb in his pocket, so to speak, as a great weapon to get through the thing.''

It is also now clear that, on the basis of advice (from Stimson and—though the record is less clear—probably from Byrnes) about the bomb's importance to diplomatic relations with Moscow, Truman postponed the Potsdam meeting with Stalin until after the atomic bomb had been proven. The president wanted to have what Stimson called his "master card" in hand before negotiating on Europe. The Alamogordo test took place on July 16, 1945; the Potsdam meeting began on July 17, 1945.

We do not know for sure whether Byrnes, like Leahy and Eisenhower, clearly recognized that Japan was already finished and that the bomb was therefore not needed—but that he wanted to use it anyway. Szilard's report suggests this view. A more generous interpretation is that he and the president simply got so caught up in the assumption that the bomb would be vital to their diplomacy that they blinded themselves to information which was evident to other high-ranking officials.

However, the new evidence also calls into question the whole assumption-based theory. Since Truman had the readily available option of simply waiting for the shock of the Soviet declaration of war, the evidence suggests that he appears knowingly to have rejected this choice in favor of using the bomb first. The explanation for this decision—and decision it was—appears to have been political, not military. As a plethora of diary and other evidence powerfully suggests, he and especially Byrnes wished to avoid the Red Army's entrance into Manchuria and northern China and the enhanced Soviet political influence this would bring.

Because so many documents make it so obvious that by the end of July top U.S. officials were deeply concerned about securing U.S. objectives in Manchuria and northern China, perhaps many have ignored the fact that in so doing they were consciously rejecting what seemed the easiest way to bring about surrender. If there is an unmistakable ongoing assumption, it is that, as Truman and Byrnes repeatedly stressed at Potsdam, U.S. economic and political interests in Manchuria and northern China—the "Open Door"—had to be maintained; thus, accordingly, Soviet influence had to be opposed.

Further doubts about "ongoing assumption" theories are raised by the fact that this was not a passive act; great efforts were made both to rush the atomic bomb project and to stall the Soviets.

Although a narrow focus on ending the war cannot be excluded as an important presidential motive, the new evidence suggests that at the decision-making level the decision or assumption that the bomb would be used appears to have been sustained—in July and early August—primarily by political considerations related to the Soviet Union. The "Soviet factor," in short, becomes central to any explanation of how the atomic bomb came to be used.

We still do not have the full story of Hiroshima. There are huge gaps, particularly in our understanding of what happened between the two key actors, Truman and Byrnes.

We do know that Truman relied heavily on the enormously prestigious Byrnes, a man who had been his senior and mentor in the Senate: that he spent the month leading up to Hiroshima with him, first on shipboard and then sharing a villa at Potsdam; that Byrnes kept other key advisers away from the President; that Truman had designated Byrnes as the lead man in connection with the bomb.

But there is much we do not know. For instance, the decision to postpone negotiations with Stalin until the bomb had been tested was a very important one. Yet we have almost no information on precisely what advice Byrnes (as opposed to Stimson) gave Truman in April and May. We do know, however, that it was Byrnes who was responsible for preparing the U.S. position for the meeting, and that he was also advising Truman about the bomb.

Throughout the summer we know that Truman and Byrnes met regularly in private, but we have almost no information on their discussions, even though the meetings between the two men both in Washington and subsequently—far more than the work of the Interim Committee, the scientists' efforts, or even top military meetings—were almost certainly where much real strategy was formulated.

Nor do we know much about the details of the many meetings between the president and his chief of staff, Admiral Leahy, who was very much against the bombing. As presiding officer of the Joint Chiefs of Staff, Leahy was in a key role, but only very sketchy and occasional diary entries exist. Allen Dulles, who was handling the Japanese negotiations through Switzerland for the OSS, was called to Potsdam, but we know little about precisely what happened there. It appears likely that, had the nuclear test failed at Alamogordo, Dulles would have been sent back to arrange a quick Japanese surrender as he had done with Italy.

It is also curious that while Eisenhower reported challenging Stimson on the decision, he never disclosed that he met with Truman and urged him not to use the bomb. Why? What considerations were expressed by the president? We do not know.

In fact, although we now know a great deal about the attitudes of many key actors during the summer of 1945, we actually know surprisingly little about how Truman himself viewed several points. The two most interesting periods—the weeks in April, May, and June which encompass the private talks with Byrnes while he was developing atomic policy for the president but before he was officially in office, and shipboard talks between Truman, Byrnes, and possibly Leahy on the way to Potsdam—are almost a complete blank. Were others as reluctant as Eisenhower to discuss very private and potentially embarrassing facts? (When doing the original research on *Atomic Diplomacy*, I interviewed Benjamin V. Cohen, the New Dealer who served as special assistant to Byrnes; he fell silent when asked about the relationship of Byrnes's diplomacy to the Hiroshima bombing. He said he "didn't remember" in response to numerous questions which other documents reveal were at the center of attention when he was assisting Byrnes.)

One final point: We know that the Japanese did not respond positively to the Potsdam proclamation; the usual version is that they rejected it. A number of historians have noted that the term they used—*mokusatsu*—can be translated in several ways: "ignore," "treat with silent contempt," "take no notice of," among others. It is sometimes argued that U.S. leaders unfortunately chose to interpret the term as a full rejection—and then went ahead with the bombing.

However, we now know that Truman was advised by OSS Director William Donovan on August 2, 1945, four days before Hiroshima, that Japanese officials in Switzerland tried to clarify the meaning of their government's response. Both the Japanese chief of staff and the foreign minister in Tokyo had replied to the reports of Japanese officials in touch with the OSS operation in Switzerland. The Japanese official in Switzerland emphasized to Dulles's go-between, Per Jacobsson, that he was hoping for a "real response" from Tokyo within a week unless resistance was too great. Meanwhile, the Allies should not take "too seriously" what was said on Tokyo Radio concerning the Potsdam proclamation as this was merely "propaganda to maintain morale." The "real reply" would be transmitted through some "official channel," possibly the minister himself or General Okamoto in Switzerland.[4]

Here, again, we do not have much information. We do not know how Truman and his chief advisers felt about Donovan's report. On the surface it clearly reinforced other evidence—especially the cables indicating the emperor's strong initiative—of Japan's willingness to surrender, evidence we know the president had at the time.

[4]Anthony Cave Brown, *The Last Hero: Wild Bill Donovan* (New York: Times Books, 1982), p. 774.

I cite such points because nonspecialists often believe historians know and have reported the full Hiroshima story, and because I believe further caution is advisable with respect to the "ongoing-assumption" theory of the bombing. The new evidence suggests that there may well have been full awareness that the bomb was not needed, and explicit consideration of it primarily in terms of its political role vis-à-vis the Soviet Union. And privately, between Truman and Byrnes, a conscious decision may have been taken.

A modified form of the ongoing-assumption theory can still be fitted to the presently known facts. But as one who put a version of it forward originally—with, I hope, adequate caveats—let me stress that it is no longer possible to rule out the likelihood that the president knew exactly what he was doing and made a clear decision with his closest adviser. Further historical discoveries may answer the remaining questions.

To End a War: The Decision to Drop the Bomb

Geoffrey Warner

The conclusion of Gar Alperovitz's 1965 book, *Atomic Diplomacy,* was straightforward enough.

> The evidence strongly suggests that the view which the President's personal representative offered to one of the atomic scientists [Leo Szilard] in May 1945 was an accurate statement of policy: "Mr. Byrnes did not argue that it was necessary to use the [atomic] bomb against the cities of Japan in order to win the war.... Mr. Byrnes's view [was] that our possessing and demonstrating the bomb would make Russia more manageable in Europe."

Geoffrey Warner, "To End a War: The Decision to Drop the Bomb," was written especially for *The Cold War Debated.*

More than twenty years later, and after the release of a great deal of relevant new documentation, Dr. Alperovitz concludes his article in the *Bulletin of the Atomic Scientists* as follows:

> The new evidence suggests that there may well have been full awareness that the bomb was not needed, and explicit consideration of it primarily in terms of its political role vis-à-vis the Soviet Union. And privately, between Truman and Byrnes, a conscious decision may have been taken.

One could be forgiven for thinking that the middle-aged Dr. Alperovitz of 1985 is taking a rather more cautious line than the angry young man of 1965, which is a little surprising, because if his original hypothesis had been correct, one would have expected it to have been confirmed and indeed strengthened by the new evidence. If it has not, then there may well have been something wrong with the hypothesis in the first place. Indeed, it is the thesis of the present article that the evidence—both new and old—provides more support for the traditional view that the principal reason for the use of the atomic bomb was to end the war against Japan than Dr. Alperovitz is prepared to allow.

Crucial to Dr. Alperovitz's case is the chain of argument he summarizes:

> The evidence had become increasingly clear by early July [1945] that, from a military point of view, Japan was finished. By mid-July it was exceedingly doubtful that Truman believed the war would end by invasion. Moreover, several top military figures clearly understood this reality—and were shocked that, in these changed circumstances the bomb would still be used.

The argument is crucial because if Japan was about to capitulate anyway, without the use of the atomic bomb, and if the Americans knew this, then they must have dropped the bombs for another reason, e.g., in order to intimidate the Soviet Union. Unfortunately, any chain is only as strong as its weakest link, and there are some very weak links in this particular chain.

Dr. Alperovitz quotes what looks at first sight to be an impressive list of witnesses who took the view in the summer of 1945 that Japan was on the verge of collapse and that the use of the atomic bomb was therefore both unnecessary and repugnant: Adm. William Leahy, Gen. Dwight D. Eisenhower, Ralph Bard, Adm. Lewis L. Strauss, Gen. Curtis LeMay, Gen. Henry Arnold, Gen. Douglas MacArthur, and Gen. Hastings Ismay. Upon closer examination, however, it turns out that much of this testimony—that of Eisenhower, LeMay, MacArthur, and Ismay—is not in fact contemporary, so that we cannot be sure how far it represents what those witnesses actually thought and said at the time, or how far it reflects what they had subsequently come to believe as a result of later developments, such as the release in July 1946 of the report of the U.S. Strategic Bombing Survey arguing that "in all probability" Japan would have surrendered before November 1, 1945, without the atomic bomb, without the Soviet declaration of war, and without an invasion. Any historian knows how hard it is to avoid such ex post facto "contamination" and will therefore not place much reliance upon later testimony unless it is firmly rooted in the contemporary record.

This leaves us with Leahy, Bard, Strauss, and Arnold. Leahy's contemporary diary entry must of course be accepted as an accurate reflection of his views at the time, although, as we shall see, the precise nature of the terms upon which Japan could have been induced to surrender without the use of the atomic bomb is a matter of some dispute. One is not obliged to give the same credence to Leahy's postwar expression of moral revulsion at the use of the bomb, however, especially when we know that, at the time, he had considerable doubts as to whether the weapon would even work.

Both Bard and Strauss were clearly opposed to the direct use of the atomic bomb, favoring, in the former's case, a warning to the Japanese, and in the latter's, some form of demonstration of its power. Many, including the present author, would argue that their opinions were greatly to their credit, but from the point of view of those who had to make the decision whether or not to drop the bomb, it is worth pointing out that the question of a demonstration had been considered by a special presidential advisory committee (the so-called Interim Committee) and that it was the scientists on that committee—not the politicians or the military men—who concluded that they could "propose no technical demonstration likely to bring an end to the war" and therefore saw "no acceptable alternative to direct military use." If a

demonstration would not bring about the desired result, a warning along the lines advocated
by Bard would presumably have been even less
effective.

General Arnold's testimony seems quite
unequivocal. According to Dr. Alperovitz, he
"demanded that a statement be entered into
the record of the Joint Chiefs of Staff on July
16, 1945, indicating his view that the war
could easily be ended by September or October 1945 without an invasion." But did he?
The updated edition of *Atomic Diplomacy,* to
which Dr. Alperovitz refers readers who wish
to check the documentation for some of his
statements, shows that he has not consulted
the original records of the Joint Chiefs of Staff
on this point. Moreover, the secondary
source upon which he does seem to be rely-
ing—Ray Cline's volume in the official U.S.
Army history of World War II—creates a
somewhat different impression. According to
Cline, Arnold "read into the record"—there
is no mention of his having "demanded"
anything—"a statement representing *the
most optimistic point of view,* that of the
Army Air Forces, on a date when the Japanese *might* be forced to surrender. General
Arnold foresaw *a possibility* of crushing Japan's resistance by a month before the invasion of Japan, that is, during October 1945"
[emphasis added]. There is no reference to
September.

Cline's account makes clear (1) that Arnold's
position was less categorical than Dr. Alperovitz suggests; and (2) that, in any case, it
represented an extremely optimistic assessment, which will not come as a surprise to
anyone acquainted with the effusions of air
power enthusiasts during the Second World
War. This view was not shared by the Joint
Chiefs of Staff as a whole. Indeed, as Cline
points out, they subscribed to a "conservative
logistic planning date of 15 November 1946 for
the end of organised Japanese resistance," a
date retained in the final report of the Combined

Chiefs of Staff to the president and the British
prime minister at Potsdam, after the successful
testing of the atomic bomb. No doubt the Chiefs
were playing exceedingly safe, but the evidence
does show that Dr. Alperovitz's picture of a
near-unanimous military consensus that Japan
was about to throw in the sponge is, to say the
least, somewhat misleading.

In support of his contention that U.S. policy
makers knew that there was no need for an
invasion of Japan, Dr. Alperovitz cites Gen.
George Marshall, the Combined U.S.-U.K. Intelligence Staffs, and President Truman himself
to the effect that Soviet entry into the war alone
would probably precipitate a Japanese collapse.
The citations are accurate, but these sources
are silent as to the precise timing of such a
collapse. If a Soviet declaration of war obviated
the need for an invasion, there is no evidence to
suggest that anyone thought it meant an immediate end to the fighting and hence no further
casualties. Moreover, by implying that because
"there was plenty of time" before the planned
invasion of the Japanese home islands, the
United States should not have used the atomic
bomb but waited to see what effect the Soviet
entry into the war would have, Dr. Alperovitz
conveniently ignores the fact that fighting was
already going on in various other parts of the
Pacific and on the mainland of Asia. For every
day that the war continued, casualties mounted
all over the Far East. By not employing the
atomic bomb as soon as it was ready, the
United States would have been gambling with
even more lives.

But surely, the skeptic will claim, all this
ignores the evidence, cited by Dr. Alperovitz
and many others, that the Japanese were in fact
already trying to get out of the war and that, as
a result both of direct soundings and their
deciphering of Japanese cable traffic, the Americans knew all about it long before they were
officially informed by Stalin at the Potsdam
Conference. If the Japanese were ready to
make peace anyway, why was there any need to

use the atomic bomb, unless of course its use was intended to serve a purpose other than that of ending the war?

The answer to this apparently plausible argument is that all the Japanese peace moves were predicated upon a negotiated settlement of the war and not upon the unconditional surrender that the United States (and its allies) demanded, just as they had done in the case of Nazi Germany. The Allied leaders went as far as they felt they could in the Potsdam Declaration of July 26, 1945. Why should they have entered into further and possibly protracted negotiations that would have involved a prolongation of the war when they believed they possessed a means of ending it more quickly on their own terms, i.e., the atomic bomb? Although, of course, he had his own reasons, it is interesting to note that Stalin himself urged the rejection of the Japanese peace feelers, a fact Dr. Alperovitz does not mention in his article.

Indeed, Dr. Alperovitz tries to suggest that unconditional surrender was some sort of red herring. The key issue, of course, was the fate of the Japanese emperor. If his position were safeguarded, surrender could have been more easily arranged. "And we know from several sources," writes Dr. Alperovitz, "that although Truman may have preferred to make no change, he had no objection in principle to the provision—and, of course, ultimately accepted it." He could have gone even further, for the draft of the Potsdam Declaration that the president took with him to Germany stated that the postwar Japanese government "could include a constitutional monarchy under the present dynasty if it be shown to the complete satisfaction of the world that such a government will never again aspire to aggression."

This passage was of course struck out of the final version of the Declaration issued on July 26, 1945. When we come to examine the reasons why, however, they offer little comfort to those who might be tempted cynically to argue that the passage was struck precisely to make it

easier to use the atomic bomb. The available documents show that two separate representations were made concerning the passage in question. The first came from the former secretary of state, Cordell Hull, who had been shown the draft declaration in Washington. He cabled Byrnes in Potsdam that while an undertaking to retain the imperial dynasty might be justified if it led to a shortening of the war and a reduction in Allied casualties, "no person knows how the proposal would work out. The militarists would try hard to interfere. Also should it fail the Japs would be encouraged while terrible political repercussions would follow in the U.S." Hull's advice was "to await the climax of allied bombing and Russia's entry into the war" before issuing any such undertaking. He did not know about the atomic bomb.

The second representation came from the Joint Chiefs of Staff. They argued that, as it stood, the passage ran the risk of antagonizing both conservatives and radicals in Japan—the former by implying that it was the Allies' intention "to depose or execute the present Emperor and install some other member of the Imperial family," and the latter by implying that it was "to continue the institution of the Emperor and Emperor worship." It would be better, the Chiefs maintained, to replace the passage by a more general statement to the effect that, subject to guarantees against renewed aggression, the Japanese would be free to choose their own form of government. The final formulation was indeed along these lines.

While historians and others are legitimately entitled to criticize Truman and his advisers for being unnecessarily rigid in their insistence upon unconditional surrender and, in particular, for their failure to issue some sort of pledge concerning the future of the emperor that could have facilitated a negotiated settlement, they must also recognize that there were reasons for their attitude and that these do not appear to have been connected with the need for an excuse to use the atomic bomb.

From hindsight we can supply another reason why the Japanese peace feelers should not necessarily be taken at their face value. Thus, we know from Japanese sources that although the emperor was involved in the approaches via the Soviet Union, these were deliberately kept secret from the military, to whom any suggestion of a compromise peace was anathema. The approaches did not therefore commit those who were actually doing the fighting and who would have to stop it. In other words, there was no guarantee that a negotiated settlement would have stuck. It could be argued, of course, that the emperor would have imposed his will, as he did on August 9–10, 1945, and again on August 14, but this was *after* both atomic bombs had been dropped and the Soviet Union had entered the war. He might not have been able or willing to do so in the absence of these developments. Given all the circumstances, therefore, it seems unlikely that the United States could have obtained the same terms of surrender from Japan in July 1945 as it did in August.

So far, as reconstructed here, Dr. Alperovitz's case has been a circumstantial one: there was no need to use the atomic bomb to end the war, so there must have been another reason for using it. That argument, for the reasons set out above, does not hold up. But what if Dr. Alperovitz can produce positive and direct evidence to show that the atomic bombs were indeed dropped to intimidate the Soviets? His case would then be virtually unassailable.

He cannot do it, of course, for no such evidence exists. But he does the next best thing. In a long section of his article he demonstrates that the "general viewpoint" of Truman's secretary of state, James F. Byrnes, was "consistent and clear. He saw the atomic bomb as a way to impress the Soviets." The evidence is indeed overwhelming—as far as Byrnes is concerned. What Dr. Alperovitz does not succeed in showing is that Byrnes's "general viewpoint" was that of the administration, and more particularly of President Truman.

Dr. Alperovitz is naturally at great pains to emphasize Byrnes's key role. "We do know that Truman relied heavily on the enormously prestigious Byrnes," he writes, "a man who had been his senior and mentor in the Senate: that he spent the month leading up to Hiroshima with him, first on shipboard and then sharing a villa at Potsdam; that Byrnes kept other key advisers away from the President; that Truman had designated Byrnes as the lead man in connection with the bomb."

What Truman actually thought of Byrnes can be found in the former's diary entry for July 7, 1945, when both men were en route for Potsdam. "Had a long talk with my able and conniving Secretary of State," wrote the president. "My but he has a keen mind! And he is an honest man. But all country politicians are alike. They are sure all other politicians are circuitous in their dealings. When they are told the straight truth, unvarnished, it is never believed—an asset *sometimes*." This is hardly the portrait of someone whose views the president would have been inclined to accept uncritically. Indeed, we know from the same source that Truman had already overruled Byrnes's opposition to the despatch of Harry Hopkins on a special mission to Moscow in May. Truman, in fact, had every reason to be wary of the South Carolinian. But for Roosevelt's backstabbing at the Democratic party convention in 1944, Byrnes would have been in the White House instead of Truman, and both men knew it. Byrnes was ambitious and inclined to play a lone hand, character traits that were soon to bring him into conflict with the president.

Toward the end of his article, Dr. Alperovitz admits that "although we now know a great deal about the attitudes of many key actors during the summer of 1945, we actually know surprisingly little about how Truman himself viewed several points." The truth of that statement depends, of course, upon the points in question. If we are concerned to discover how Truman felt about the atomic bomb and the ending of the war against Japan, it would seem that his views are fairly clear: he was anxious to bring about the defeat of Japan on acceptable terms as soon as possible with the minimum loss of American lives; and he was prepared to use whatever means seemed most likely to achieve that end.

The president's concern about casualties emerges very clearly from the record of his meeting with the Joint Chiefs of Staff on June 18, 1945, in which he "reiterated that his main reason for this conference...was his desire to know definitely how far we could afford to go in the Japanese campaign. He had hoped that there was a possibility of preventing an Okinawa from one end of Japan to the other." As long as the atomic bomb was untested, Soviet entry into the war seemed the best way of minimizing the loss of U.S. lives. This assumption accounts for Truman's steadfast determination to pin Stalin down on this at Potsdam, a determination that Dr. Alperovitz tended to play down in the first edition of *Atomic Diplomacy*. And Truman thought he had succeeded, writing to his wife on July 18, 1945: "I've gotten what I came for—Stalin goes to war on August 15 with no strings on it....I'll say that we'll end the war a year sooner now, and think of the kids who won't be killed! That is the important thing." At that very moment, however, news of the successful nuclear test at Alamogordo began to come in, and Truman realized that here was an even quicker way of ending the war. "Believe Japs will fold up before Russia comes in," he noted in his diary on that same July 18. "I am sure they will when Manhattan [i.e., the atomic bomb] appears over their homeland."

Nowhere in Truman's published diaries and letters is there any indication that he ordered the dropping of the atomic bombs on Japan in order to impress the Soviets or to limit their advance in Asia. Yet if that was indeed his purpose, the absence of any such indication is rather surprising, for the president was not a reticent man. His private papers are full of explosive outbursts of all kinds, including some extremely belligerent statements in the field of foreign policy. It is hard to believe that he could or would have exercised total self-restraint on this important issue. Surely the truth is much more likely to have been what he always maintained it was, and what his papers tend to confirm: that he saw the atomic bomb primarily as a means of bringing the war in the Pacific to a rapid conclusion.

Dr. Alperovitz and other revisionist historians are right to question the bland assumptions and explanations of the origins of the Cold War that by and large prevailed until their works began to appear in the 1960s. They have forced many of us to reconsider and revise our own interpretation of events, and the present author, for one, is grateful for the stimulus they have provided. There is, however, an air of the courtroom about much of their work, and, like all attorneys, they tell only one side of the story. There is also a case for the defense.

QUESTIONS FOR DISCUSSION

1 Was Truman's use of atomic bombs on Japan immoral?
2 Was the Japanese surrender caused by the use of U.S. atomic bombs, or was it about to happen anyway?
3 Did Truman's use of atomic weapons signify a reversal of Roosevelt's policy toward the Soviet Union?
4 Should Truman have threatened the Soviets with atomic attack if they did not change their policies in East Central Europe?
5 Would the course of Soviet-U.S. relations have been the same had the United States not used atomic bombs against Japan? Give reasons for your answer.

SUGGESTED READINGS

Alperovitz, Gar. *Atomic Diplomacy: Hiroshima and Potsdam: The Use of the Atomic Bomb and the American Confrontation with Soviet Power.* Rev.

ed. New York: Elisabeth Sifton Books/Penguin Books, 1985.

Bernstein, Barton J. "The Dropping of the A-Bomb," *Center Magazine,* **16** (Mar.–Apr. 1983), pp. 7–15.

Herken, Gregg. *The Winning Weapon: The Atomic Bomb in the Cold War, 1945–1950.* New York: Knopf, 1980.

Messer, Robert L. "New Evidence on Truman's Decision," *Bulletin of the Atomic Scientists,* **41** (Aug. 1985), pp. 50–56.

Meyerson, Adam. "Atoms for Peace: Truman Was Right to Drop the Bomb," *Policy Review,* no. 33 (Summer 1985), pp. 46–47.

Miles, Rufus E., Jr. "Hiroshima: The Strange Myth of Half a Million American Lives Saved," *International Security,* **10** (Fall 1985), pp. 121–140.

Ryerson, André. "The Cult of Hiroshima," *Commentary,* **80** (Oct. 1985), pp. 36–40.

Sherwin, Martin J. "Old Issues in New Editions," *Bulletin of the Atomic Scientists,* **41** (Dec. 1985), pp. 40–44.

———. *A World Destroyed: The Atomic Bomb and the Grand Alliance.* New York: Knopf, 1975.

Stimson, Henry L. "The Decision to Use the Atomic Bomb," *SAIS Review,* **5** (Summer–Fall 1985), pp. 1–15.

Truman, Harry S. *Year of Decisions.* Garden City, N.Y.: Doubleday, 1955.

3 Was U.S. intervention in Vietnam immoral?

YES

Hendrik Hertzberg

Why the War Was Immoral

NO

David Horowitz

My Vietnam Lessons

Why the War Was Immoral

Hendrik Hertzberg

Was the war in Vietnam wrong? Not just inadvisable, not just a costly mistake, but morally wrong? How one answers that depends partly, I guess, on how one experienced the war and the opposition to it. A few days ago, at the university where I'm spending a semester, I found myself deep in conversation with a tutor in the philosophy department, an intense, articulate man five or six years younger than I am. (I'm 41.) We were talking about our experiences in the antiwar movement—ten and 15 and nearly 20 years ago—and he said that when he looks back on that time he feels mostly a kind of angry regret. He had been a member of Students for a Democratic Society when SDS dropped its homegrown ideology of participatory democracy in favor of mindless Maoism; he had chanted, "Ho! Ho! Ho Chi Minh! NLF is gonna win!"; he had longed for the triumph of the forces of "liberation" not only in Vietnam but everywhere in the Third World and ultimately at home; he had spelled it Amerika and dismissed its political system—"bourgeois democracy"—as a hoax, a cover for racism and imperialism. When the war ended and Indochina vanished into blood-soaked totalitarianism (instead of the gentle egalitarianism he had expected), he was wrenchingly disillusioned. Gradually he discovered that the "revolutionary socialism" of the Third World is brutal, that the Soviet Union is armed and dangerous, that for all its flaws American democracy is the moral superior of any form of communism. "I was wrong, just totally wrong," he told me. Last year he voted for Reagan.

I was luckier. I happened to have been brought up in a political and moral atmosphere of left-wing anti-communism. Reared on Or-

Hendrik Hertzberg, "Why the War Was Immoral," *New Republic*, **192** (Apr. 29, 1985), pp. 13–16.

well, Gandhi, and Silone, it was no great trick for me to avoid the more blatant naïvetés of New Leftism, and thus also to avoid the subsequent disillusionments. I took my antiwar arguments from Theodore Draper, not Noam Chomsky; from *Commentary* (yes, *Commentary*) and *The New Republic,* not the *National Guardian* and *Monthly Review*. I was similarly lucky in my encounter with military service. Opposed to what was then still called the "Vietnam policy," yet not so fiercely opposed as to be willing to risk prison, and too straight to dodge the draft, I signed up at the end of 1966 for a three-year hitch in the Navy. I asked to be sent to Vietnam, figuring a desk job in Saigon would be interesting without being unduly risky, but was sent—catch-22—to a sleepy shore billet in New York instead. Two years later I *was* ordered to Vietnam (desk job in Da Nang); but by then my antiwar convictions had grown so strong I preferred jail to further military service, and I announced my intention to refuse the orders. I hoped for antiwar martyrdom; instead, quite by chance, a medical difficulty developed, and I was hastily mustered out. I'd managed to have it both ways: veteran (sort of), and resister (in a way). In the Navy and after, I campaigned for Bobby Kennedy and Allard Lowenstein and other antiwar politicians; went on all the marches; hung around the office of a lively little pacifist weekly, *Win*, whose editor had two stickers on the bumper of his Volkswagen: US OUT OF VIETNAM and RUSSIA OUT OF LATVIA. But I didn't join any of what the inimitable Norman Podhoretz calls (in *Why We Were in Vietnam*) "the three main currents of the 'antiwar' movement": pro-Communist, anti-anti-Communist, and anti-American. I guess that I (along with more prominent opponents of the war, such as Podhoretz himself) must have joined one of the non-main currents. Perhaps it was the current that cheered when Norman Thomas, whom I had been taught to revere and who never disappointed, advised the movement to wash the flag, not burn it.

It's no surprise that the differences over Vietnam, rooted as they are in such different experiences, persist in the form of different histories remembered, different lessons learned. The war turned my tutor friend into a "communist" and me into a pacifist. A decade later, neither of us is what we were. We are merely a Republican and a Democrat, passing the time in earnest conversation. And I still think the war was immoral. So when my tutor friend told me the story of his days in the movement, I readily agreed with him that he had been wrong. "It could have been worse, though," I added. "You could have *supported* the war."

There were always two main arguments in favor of the war, the geopolitical and the "moral." The war's aftermath has undermined the first argument, but has seemingly strengthened the second. For the aftermath proved to be at once worse than the war's opponents had predicted and better than its supporters had feared—worse for the Indochinese, better for everyone else.

The geopolitical argument took many forms, some of which lay in ruins long before the war ended. The notion that the war was needed to stop Sino-Soviet expansionism, for example, had become an embarrassment well before Nixon arrived in Peking. So had the notion that the war was needed to convince the Chinese to abandon revolution and follow the Soviet example of peaceful coexistence.

The most persistent form of the geopolitical argument was the domino theory. Some of the war's retrospective defenders maintain that the fall of Cambodia and Laos proves that the theory was correct. Not so. Cambodia and Laos were Vietnam battlefields long before the Americans arrived, and by the end the three

countries became one domino. Anyway, the domino theory always encompassed more than Indochina. Even in its most modest version it envisaged the loss of all Southeast Asia, which is to say Thailand, Burma, and Malaysia. And in its more grandiose form it predicted that Indonesia, India, Australia, and Hawaii would topple too. None of this has happened; on the contrary, the American position in Asia and the Pacific is stronger now than it was before 1975. Such troubles as do exist there, such as instability in the Philippines, cannot remotely be traced to the defeat in Vietnam.

A milder corollary to the domino theory was the argument from will: we needed to go on fighting in Vietnam in order to demonstrate our resolve and reliability. This argument implicitly recognized that the fate of Vietnam was, by itself, peripheral to the national security of the United States; it shifted the ground of discussion from the geopolitics of the map to the geopolitics of the soul. Yes, their will to rid their country of foreigners was stronger than our will to demonstrate our will; but by any reasonable standard, our resolve was strong. We did far, far more than enough to meet our treaty obligations, demonstrate our will, and prove our reliability. We financed a quarter of a century of war in Vietnam. We fought there in strength for ten years—longer than we fought in World War I, in World War II, or in Korea, longer than in all of them put together. Fifty-eight thousand American soldiers were killed. We said we would fight, therefore we must fight: at many a juncture along the way that logic seemed compelling. But it was not a compelling reason to fight forever. Our guarantees were not worthless. It was the war that was worthless.

The importance of the collapse of the domino theory to the debate over the war's morality is that the theory, if correct, could arguably have justified an enormous degree of suffering and death. What if it had really been true that the loss of Vietnam would doom Australia, India,

Hawaii, and the rest to war followed by Communist totalitarianism? A firm moral case can be made that preventing the certain devastation and enslavement of many countries can justify the destruction, even the total destruction, of one. "We had to destroy this village in order to save a hundred villages" is a defensible proposition. But "we had to destroy this village in order to save it" is a moral absurdity. When the domino theory fell, so, domino-like, did one of the moral props of the war.

We are left, then, with the "moral case," as Podhoretz calls it—the view that the war was moral because it was an attempt to save South Vietnam from Communism. My tutor friend, back in his SDS days, did not think this a moral aim, would not have thought it a moral aim even if it could have been achieved without cost. In thinking these things he made a moral error, and he is right to rue it. Even those of us who took the view that it did not make much difference to the South Vietnamese whether they lived under Communism or under the Saigon regime made a moral error. Take away the war and the Saigon regime, with all its noisy corruption and repressiveness, was morally preferable to the totalitarian silence that now rules, with scarcely less corruption, in Ho Chi Minh City. Except that you can't take away the war.

The overwhelming majority of those who opposed the war did not in any case reject the aim of saving South Vietnam from Communism. And to the extent that the war was fought for this aim it was fought for a moral aim. But this says no more than that the war was fought with good intentions rather than evil ones, which is saying very little. If good intentions were enough, there would be no neoconservatives.

In war the moral question is always the same: does the end justify the means? The calculations are necessarily ugly, but they are unavoidable. Ten years ago the choice was not between a Communist South Vietnam and a non-Communist one. It was between a Commu-

nist South Vietnam on the one hand, and the terrible cost of keeping South Vietnam non-Communist on the other. The aftermath of the war—the boat people, the "reeducation" camps, above all the unimaginable horror that engulfed Cambodia—has made the "moral case," the argument that the war was worth fighting solely for the sake of the people of Indochina, seem much more plausible than it did at the time. But for the "moral case" to be clinched, the war must be judged to have been winnable—winnable, moreover, at a lower cost in suffering and death than the cost of the Communist victory.

The retrospective defenders of the war must argue that the war could have been won, and their arguments mostly take the form of "if only." If only the bombers had hit "worthwhile targets" on their 1,000 sorties a day, says the military analyst Edward Luttwak in a current *Harper's* symposium, it "would have ended the war in a day." If only Lyndon Johnson had rallied the country behind the war as a moral imperative, writes Podhoretz in his Vietnam book, then the American people would have remained steadfast. If only the United States had followed a purposeful military strategy, argues Harry G. Summers in *On Strategy: A Critical Analysis of the Vietnam War,* then the conditions for a successful South Vietnamese war against the Vietcong might have been created. If only Congress hadn't voted down supplementary military aid to the Saigon government in 1975, contends Richard Nixon in his new book, *No More Vietnams,* then everything might have turned out fine.

All of these arguments rest on the assumption that there was a point at which North Vietnam, having calculated that the actual costs of war were exceeding the prospective benefits of victory, would have stopped fighting. It seems clearer than ever today that there was no such point. Some people understood this at the time. Ten years ago, this magazine published a special issue devoted to the end of the war. Richard Holbrooke, who had resigned in protest from the foreign service, and who later became an assistant secretary of state, began his essay with these words:

> For at least eight years it seemed reasonable to me to assume that sooner or later, no matter what we did in Vietnam, things would end badly for us. This feeling was not based on any desire to see us humiliated, or any feeling that the other side represented the forces of goodness and light; it Ajust seemed that the only way to stave off an eventual Communist victory was with an open-ended, and therefore endless, application of American firepower in support of the South Vietnamese regime. No matter how much force we were willing to use, this would not end the war, only prevent Saigon's defeat. And the human suffering would be bottomless. The war would go on until the North Vietnamese achieved their objectives.

Holbrooke's judgment has stood up well. "The essential reality of the struggle," wrote Stanley Karnow in *Vietnam: A History,* published in 1983, "was that the Communists, imbued with an almost fanatical sense of dedication to a reunified Vietnam under their control, saw the war against the United States and its South Vietnamese ally as the continuation of two thousand years of resistance to Chinese and later French rule. They were prepared to accept limitless casualties to attain their sacred objective. Ho Chi Minh, their leader, had made that calculation plain to the French as they braced for war in the late 1940s. 'You can kill ten of my men for every one I kill of yours,' he warned them, 'but even at those odds, you will lose and I will win.' " William Broyles Jr., who fought in Vietnam 15 years ago as a Marine officer, and who recently went back for a visit during which he talked to hundreds of his former enemies, has a similar assessment. Writing in the April *Atlantic,* he concludes, "Whatever the price of winning the war—twenty more

years of fighting, another million dead, the destruction of Hanoi—the North Vietnamese were willing to pay it."

If the North Vietnamese were willing to accept limitless casualties, if they were willing to pay any price, then the war could not have been won except by the physical destruction of North Vietnam and the killing of a large proportion of its people. A million? Three million? Six million? The shrill accusation of some in the antiwar movement that the war was "genocidal" was not entirely without justice. Of course no American wanted to kill everybody in North Vietnam. Americans are not monsters. But Americans are not losers, either. Americans are winners. But the logic of winning in Vietnam was inescapably the logic of genocide. We did not lose in Vietnam. We chose not to win. If our entry into the war had something to do with preserving our values, so did our exit from it.

Even Podhoretz, in his book on Vietnam, admits repeatedly that the war could not have been won. In the end, he writes, "The United States demonstrated that saving South Vietnam from Communism was not only beyond its reasonable military, political, and intellectual capabilities but that it was ultimately beyond its moral capabilities as well." Yes, it was beyond our moral capabilities—except that what he understands as a moral failure I understand as a moral success. It wasn't cowardice that finally impelled us to quit. It was conscience.

The old arguments for the war still walk among us, zombielike, in the form of the theory of the Vietnam syndrome, a term calculated to make the American people's desire to avoid another Vietnam sound pathological rather than prudent. Of course, if the war did result in a syndrome, if it did result in a paralysis of American will and so forth, that is hardly an argument that the war was a good idea. Nor do the follies of parts of the antiwar movement somehow vindicate the war. On the contrary, the antiwar movement was created by the war. Is it really so surprising that this unending, unwinnable war became a machine for producing irrationality, hysteria, and rage? The conservatives' anger at the antiwar movement is misplaced.

The actual consequences of this so-called syndrome are highly problematic. We "lost" Iran after Vietnam, but we "lost" Cuba before it. A more precise effect of the war upon the American political psyche was diagnosed in 1971 by Nathan Glazer, who wrote in a famous *Commentary* article titled "Vietnam: The Case for Immediate Withdrawal" that "the experience of Vietnam has turned the American people into haters of war." That seems exactly right. By August 1964, 300 Americans had been killed and 1,000 wounded in Vietnam. Yet there were only a half-dozen American correspondents reporting on the war. (Meanwhile President Johnson was running as the peace candi-

date, with the support of SDS.) Such relative public indifference to a war with American deaths running into the hundreds would be unthinkable today. It took years for any significant movement of protest to develop against the Vietnam War. The premises of U.S. involvement were scarcely questioned for the first 15 years. But if the Reagan administration launches an invasion of Nicaragua today, thousands of church people are ready to commit civil disobedience tomorrow. And before giving its support to the new war, the public would insist on a full and prompt discussion of its aims, purposes, and prospects—not out of cynicism or morbid suspicion, but out of a healthy, skeptical, democratic spirit of self-government. War can sometimes be a necessity, but is always to be abhorred. Yes, we were right to oppose the Vietnam War, all of us. Even my friend the Reagan-voting ex-SDSer. Even Norman Podhoretz.

My Vietnam Lessons
David Horowitz

When I see today's protestors, in the flush of youthful idealism, with their signs proclaiming "No Vietnams in Central America" a feeling of ineffable sadness overtakes me. For twenty years ago I was one of them. In 1962, as a student at Berkeley, I wrote the first book of New Left protest and helped to organize perhaps the first anti-war demonstration opposing President Kennedy's policies in Vietnam. In the mid-Sixties I went to England to work for Bertrand Russell and helped organize the International War Crimes Tribunal which brought American military actions under damning scrutiny but ignored analagous excesses by the North Vietnamese.

David Horowitz, "My Vietnam Lesson," *Policy Forum,* **2** (Oct. 1985), pp. 1–6. Reprinted with permission of the National Forum Foundation.

While in England I also wrote *The Free World Colossus,* which identified America as the aggressor in the cold war, and was used as a radical text in colleges and in the growing protest movement. At the end of the Sixties I returned to America and was an editor of *Ramparts,* the most widely read New Left magazine. Our most famous cover featured a photograph of the My Lai massacre with a sign superimposed and planted among the corpses saying "Re-Elect the President."

My political activities in these years were inspired in part by the belief that America was not living up to its democratic ideals at home or abroad. At the time, American blacks were still second class citizens, lacking basic political rights in many regions of the South, including the right to vote. (The civil rights struggle remains for me a historic triumph for American democracy and one in which radicals like myself played a strategic and honorable part.) Abroad, the United States supported many dictatorships, and opposed nationalist movements led by Communists like the one in Vietnam. I supported their "National Liberation Front" first of all because I believed they were struggling for self-determination. If they were Marxists, well Marxism to me implied economic development and power over one's national destiny—a basic ingredient of self-determination.

Like today's young radicals, my priorities reflected a double standard. I judged other countries and political movements by the futures I imagined they could have if only the United States and its allies would get out of their way. I judged America, however, by its *actual* performance, which I held up to a standard of high and even impossible ideals. Of course, if I had looked at the facts (or been able to) I would have seen that America was more tolerant, more democratic and more open to change than the countries and movements to whom I gave my support. But I was unable to do just that. I was—in the then fashionable term—"alienated" from what was near to me and unable to judge it objectively. Some of my alienation could be attributed to youth itself, the feeling that I and my peers could understand the world better and accomplish more than the older generation could.

But there was another dimension to my disaffection, an ideology that committed me to "truths" behind the common sense surfaces of things. I was a Marxist and a socialist. I believed in the "dialectic" of history and therefore, even though I knew that the societies calling themselves Marxist were ruled by ruthless dictatorships I believed that they would soon evolve into socialist democracies. I attributed their negative features to underdevelopment and to the capitalist pasts from which they had emerged. I believed that Marxist economic planning was the most rational solution to their underdevelopment and would soon bring them untold prosperity (an idea refuted as dramatically by the experience of the last twenty-five years as the parallel notion that private property is the source of all tyranny and that socialist states will soon become free). But at the time, I expected (as did most of my comrades in the New Left who gave any thought to the subject) that the de-Stalinization process begun by Khrushchev would continue until Russia and the Communist world generally became even more democratic than the United States.

On the other hand, the same Marxist analysis told me that America, however amenable to reform in the past, was now set on a course that would make it increasingly rigid, repressive, and ultimately fascist. The United States was the leviathan of a global imperialist system under attack at home and abroad. Its ruling class could not afford to retreat from this challenge; it could only grow more reactionary and repressive. This expectation (wrong, as events proved, in every respect) was not an idiosyncratic theory of mine, but was the linchpin of the New Left's political view of the world and its strategy of opposition to America's war in Vietnam. The New Left believed that in Vietnam America's corporate-liberal empire had reached a point of no return. As a result, electoral politics and reform were futile and counter-productive. The only way to alter America's imperial course was to take to the streets—first to organize resistance to the war, and then to "liberate" ourselves from the corporate capitalist system.

What happened to change my views? First of all [is] the very experience of being part of a radical protest movement in this country. As our opposition to the war grew more violent and our prophecies of impending fascism more strident, I observed how we were actually being treated by the system we reviled and condemned. By the decade's end we had deliberately crossed the line of legitimate dissent and abused every First Amendment privilege and right granted us as Americans. While American boys were dying overseas, we spat on the flag, broke the law, denigrated and disrupted the institutions of government and education, revealed classified secrets and gave comfort to the enemy. Some of us provided a protective propaganda shield for Hanoi's Communist regime while it tortured American fliers; others engaged in violent sabotage against the war effort. All the time I thought to myself: if we did this in any other country, the very least of our punishments would be long prison terms and the stigma of traitors. In any of the *socialist* countries we supported—from Cuba to North Vietnam— we would spend most of our lives in jail and more probably be shot.

And what actually happened to us in repressive capitalist America? Here and there our wrists were slapped (some of us went to trial, some spent months in jail) but the overwhelming national response to our assault was one of tolerance and eventually respect. We began as a peripheral minority, but gradually people joined us: first in thousands and then in tens of thousands, swelling our ranks until finally we reached what can only be called the conscience of the nation. America itself became troubled about its presence in Vietnam, about the justice and morality of the war it had gone there to fight. And because the nation became so troubled, it lost its will to continue the war, and withdrew.

Out the window went all our assumptions about the rigidity of American politics, about the controlled capitalist media (which in fact provided most of the information that fueled our attacks on the war) and about ruling class control of American foreign policy. That policy had shown itself in its most critical dimension responsive to the will of ordinary people, and to their sense of justice and morality. As a historian, I believe I am correct in saying that America's

withdrawal from the battlefield in Vietnam under such circumstances is unique in human history: there is no other case on record of a major power retreating from a war in response to the moral opposition of its own citizenry.

If America's political response to its test of fire gave me an entirely new regard for American institutions and for the culture of democracy which informs and supports them, the aftermath of America's military retreat gave me a new appreciation of the Communist side of the international power struggle.

In 1975, America not only withdrew its forces from Vietnam, as we on the left said it could never do, but from Laos and Cambodia, and ultimately from its role as guardian of the international status quo. Far from increasing the freedom and well-being of Third World nations, as we in the left had predicted, however, America's withdrawal resulted in an international power vacuum that was quickly filled by the armies of Russia, Cuba, and the mass murderers of the Khmer Rouge (not to mention the non-Communist but no less bloodthirsty fanatics of revolutionary Islam). In Afghanistan, the Soviet Union perpetrated the most naked aggression by a great power since World War II, killing a million people (three times the per capita death rate of Vietnamese in the Vietnam War) while making half the population refugees. In Africa, Cuban intervention propped up a bloody Ethiopian dictator whose officially designated "Red Terror" claimed 100,000 lives including, in one year, virtually the entire graduating class of the high schools of Addis Ababa, and whose Marxist economic programs produced a famine that still threatens the lives of millions. In Cambodia, America's withdrawal paved the way for a 20th Century nightmare— the genocidal destruction of two million Cambodians by the Khmer Rouge protégés of the North Vietnamese. All this bloodshed and misery was the direct result of America's post-Vietnam withdrawal, of the end of *Pax*

Americana, which we had ardently desired and helped to bring about.

In Vietnam itself, the war's aftermath showed beyond any doubt the struggle there was not ultimately to achieve or prevent self-determination but—as various Presidents said and we denied—a Communist conquest of the South. Today, the National Liberation Front of South Vietnam, whose cause we supported, no longer exists. Its leaders are dead, in exile, in detention camps, under house arrest or power-less in their own land. American forces left Vietnam ten years ago; but today Hanoi's army is the fourth largest in the world and Vietnam has emerged as a Soviet satellite and imperialist aggressor in its own right, subverting the inde-pendence of Laos, invading and colonizing Cambodia.

These facts confronted me with a supreme irony: the nation I had believed to be governed by corporate interests, a fountainhead of world reaction, was halted in mid-course by its conscience-stricken and morally aroused popu-lace; the forces I had identified with progress, once freed from the grip of U.S. "imperialism," revealed themselves to be oppressive, unspeak-ably ruthless and predatory. Nor were they able to bring their own or any of their captive peoples the economic benefits they had prom-ised. I was left with this question: what true friend of the South Vietnamese, or the Cambo-dians, or the Afghanis, or Ethiopians, would not wish that *Pax Americana* were still in force?

There was yet another Vietnam lesson for me when I pondered the question put by Jeane Kirkpatrick to the still active veterans of the new left: "How can it be that persons so deeply committed to the liberation of South Vietnam and Cambodia from Generals Thieu and Lon Nol were so little affected by the enslavement that followed their liberation? Why was there so little anguish among the American accomplices who helped Pol Pot to power?" Indeed, why have the passionate advocates of Third World liberation not raised their voices in protest over the rape of Afghanistan or the Cuban abetted catastrophe to Ethiopia?

Not only has the left failed to make a cause of these Marxist atrocities, it has failed to consider the implications of what we now know about Hanoi's role in South Vietnam's "civil war." For North Vietnam's victors have boldly acknowledged that they had infiltrated even more troops into the South than was claimed by the Presidential White Paper which was used to justify America's original commitment of mili-tary forces—a White Paper which we leftists scorned at the time as a fiction based on anti-Communist paranoia and deception. But to-day's left is too busy denigrating Ronald Rea-gan's White Papers on Soviet and Cuban intervention in Central America to consider the implications of this past history to the present.

My experience has convinced me that histor-ical ignorance and moral blindness are endemic to the American left, necessary conditions of its existence. It does not value the bounty it actu-ally has in this country, and in the effort to achieve a historically bankrupt fantasy—call it socialism, call it "liberation"—undermines the very privileges and rights it is the first to claim. Its most visible and lasting effect is to strengthen and promote a rapacious Communist world empire.

The lesson I learned from the Vietnam War was not a lesson in theory but in practice. Observing America go through its worst histor-ical hour, from a vantage point on the other side of the barricade, I came to understand that democratic values are easily lost and histori-cally only rarely achieved, that—however flawed—America is a precious gift, a unique presence in the world of nations, an unparal-leled plurality of ethnic, economic and political communities. Morever, because it is the stron-gest of the handful of democratic societies that mankind has managed to create, it is also a fortress that stands between the free nations of the world and the dark, totalitarian forces which threaten to engulf them.

My values have not changed, but my sense of what supports and makes them possible has. I no longer can join "anti-war" movements that seek to disarm the western democracies in the face of the danger that confronts them. I support the current efforts of America's leadership to rebuild our dangerously weakened military defenses, and I endorse the conservative argument that America needs to be vigilant, strong and clear of purpose in its life and death struggle with its global totalitarian adversaries. As an ex-radical, I would only add that in this struggle Americans need to respect and encourage their own generosity—their tolerance for internal dissent and their willingness to come to the aid of people who are fighting for their freedom.

QUESTIONS FOR DISCUSSION

1 Was the U.S. intervention in Vietnam motivated primarily by antipathy toward the Soviet Union?
2 Were the Vietcong and North Vietnamese puppets of either the Soviet Union or China?
3 Could the United States have won in Vietnam? If so, how?
4 Was domestic opposition to the Vietnamese war the principal reason for the U.S. failure?
5 What have been the consequences for U.S. foreign policy makers of the failure in Vietnam?

SUGGESTED READINGS

Fromkin, David, and James Chace. "What *Are* the-Lessons of Vietnam?" *Foreign Affairs,* **63** (Spring 1985), pp. 722–746.

Herring, George C. *America's Longest War: The United States and Vietnam.* New York: Wiley, 1979.

Hofmann, Margret, ed. *Vietnam Viewpoints: A Handbook for Concerned Citizens.* Austin, Tex.: Margret Hofmann, 1968.

Kahin, George McT. *Intervention: How America Became Involved in the War.* New York: Knopf, 1986.

Karnow, Stanley. *Vietnam: A History.* New York: Viking, 1983.

Kissinger, Henry. *White House Years.* Boston: Little, Brown, 1979.

———. *Years of Upheaval.* Boston: Little, Brown, 1982.

Kolko, Gabriel. *Anatomy of War: Vietnam, the United States, and the Modern Historical Experience.* New York: Pantheon, 1986.

Lewy, Guenter. *America in Vietnam.* New York: Oxford Univ. Press, 1978.

Nixon, Richard M. *RN, The Memoirs of Richard Nixon.* New York: Grosset and Dunlap, 1978.

Podhoretz, Norman. "Vietnam: The Revised Standard Version," *Commentary,* **77** (Apr. 1984), pp. 35–41.

Shultz, George. "The Meaning of Vietnam," *Department of State Bulletin,* **85** (June 1985), pp. 13–16.

Smith, R. B. *An International History of the Vietnam War: The Kennedy Challenge.* New York: St. Martin's Press, 1986.

Toai, Doan Van. "Vietnam: How We Deceived Ourselves," *Commentary,* **81** (Mar. 1986), pp. 40–43.

Zimmerman, William, and Robert Axelrod. " 'The Lessons' of Vietnam and Soviet Foreign Policy," *World Politics,* **34** (Oct. 1981), pp. 1–24.

4 Was U.S. acceptance of the Helsinki Accords a mistake?

YES

Eric Breindel

The Price of Helsinki

NO

Leonard R. Sussman

In Support of the Helsinki Process

The Price of Helsinki

Eric Breindel

No one contends, on the tenth anniversary of the Helsinki Accords, that they have led to improvements in the state of human rights behind the Iron Curtain. In fact, virtually all groups in the West that monitor international human rights agree that abuses have gotten considerably worse in the Soviet Union and in the East bloc over the last decade.

The notion that the accords have actually had a harmful effect seems farfetched. Yet, ironically, they did create a new, discrete class for Soviet authorities to persecute members of the Helsinki Watch groups. Of the original Soviet group of would-be monitors, more than half are today incarcerated—in prisons, psychiatric hospitals, and the camps of the Gulag. A number of other monitors have died due to maltreatment in prison, or under mysterious circumstances. Of the rest, some are at large in the Soviet Union, having been freed from incarceration. Others are in the West—in forced exile. The work of the Soviet Helsinki Watch, the entire internal effort to monitor compliance with the human rights provisions of the accords, has ceased altogether.

Helsinki represents the clearest possible case of an agreement with which one side complied while the other did not; a pact from which one side got what it wanted while the other did not. (Helsinki, it should be noted, is not, technically, a treaty. If it were, it would arguably have lapsed automatically by now, due to noncompliance.) The Soviet Union was extremely anxious for the security provisions of Helsinki—Basket I of the Final Act—understanding them, as does the entire world, as representing formal acknowledgment of Soviet hegemony in Eastern Europe and the Baltic. Whether or not this formal recognition of the status quo is of any

Eric Breindel,"The Price of Helsinki," *The New Republic,* **193** (Sept. 2, 1985), pp. 6–7.

particular consequence is not the point. Moscow came to the negotiating table wanting this official recognition of the post–Second World War frontiers in Europe very badly—and got it.

The United States and its allies, in turn, pressed for Basket III—a commitment on the part of the Soviet Union and its allies to respect basic human rights and freedoms: among them, freedom of "thought, conscience, religion or belief"; freedom of access to information; the right to emigrate, particularly to achieve family reunification; and a host of other familiar "humanitarian" principles.

Given the virtually unanimous agreement that Moscow has failed to comply even minimally with its Helsinki obligations, why do so few people argue that the United States should repudiate the accords? The principal argument against nullification is that Helsinki affords the West the right, for the first time, to call the Soviets to account for human rights abuses, a preserve hitherto protected by the claim that such issues represent "internal matters." No longer, it is suggested, can Moscow rebuff Western human rights inquiries out of hand. And the accords provide for a regular forum—the review conferences in Belgrade, Madrid, Ottawa—in which to raise these concerns. These are forums that the Soviets and their satellites, it is said, dare not boycott.

Thus the purported virtue, for the West, of Helsinki: public diplomacy—a guaranteed opportunity to propagandize. This conception is both flawed in its premises and deeply disturbing. The truth is that the U.S. and the Soviet Union are already bound by the Universal Declaration of Human Rights to uphold essentially the same principles identified in Basket III of Helsinki. And there is already an international forum, the U.N. Human Rights Commission, which meets annually to review compliance. There, in Geneva—as in Belgrade,

Madrid, and Ottawa—charges and counter-charges are traded. In addition, just two years before Helsinki the Soviet Union ratified the U.N. Human Rights Treaty.

The Helsinki Accords created something that was, in essence, already in existence. The advantages of this new forum, without the U.N.'s Soviet bloc-"non-aligned" automatic majority, are not to be discounted. Nor are the benefits of yet another arena in which to rail at the Soviets with the rest of the world, including the peoples of the East bloc and the U.S.S.R. looking on (thanks to Radio Free Europe, the BBC, and the Voice of America). But it remains a fact that these sessions have no effect whatever on Soviet domestic policy in the human rights theater. The last ten years are ample proof of that.

If there were no price to pay for these propaganda forums, it would make sense to wish for as many as possible. But in the case of Helsinki, the price is enormously steep. The United States—and its allies—entered into a solemn international agreement knowing that its adversary and cosignatory would not, *could* not, honor its terms. The Soviet Union would not be the Soviet Union if it permitted freedom of expression. The issue here is moral corruption. Should Washington, under any circumstance, be party to a sham agreement? What does this say about the United States's attitude toward international pacts in general? Are there some that are meant to be taken seriously, letter and spirit, and others simply not?

And what about America's commitment to the rights and freedoms enshrined in Basket III of Helsinki? Do we take freedom of religion seriously—or is it, as the Marxists contend, a "bourgeois freedom" and, as such, relative? The process of entry into a phony agreement is altogether treacherous. The United States is drawn into an Orwellian newspeak universe where things are not as they seem and people do not mean what they say. America adopts the Soviet view of international agreements and comes to acquiesce in a fraud.

The way out of this quagmire is clear. Those who are perhaps in the best position to determine the merits of Helsinki, the former Helsinki monitors now in the West, have made their view plain: repudiate the accords.

In Support of the Helsinki Process

Leonard R. Sussman

The Helsinki Accords were signed August 1, 1975. Several weeks later, Freedom House in an editorial urged the creation of a "Helsinki Watch"—the regular monitoring of compliance with the far-reaching commitments made at Helsinki. Now, ten years later, there is some disillusionment with that Helsinki Process. A reassessment is, therefore, in order. Let me state at the outset my position on the Helsinki Process (the continuing review of compliance

Leonard R. Sussman, "In Support of the Helsinki Process," *Freedom at Issue,* no. 86 (Sept.–Oct. 1985), pp. 14–17.

with the 1975 Final Act of the Conference on Security and Cooperation in Europe, the CSCE):

In the entire East bloc—with only variations in degree—human rights are observed mainly in the breach. Opportunities for normal contact between East and West are strictly limited. Cross-border communications are severely restricted, as are opportunities for dissent and diversity within each East-bloc country. Yet the instinctive, universal yearning for human rights—especially when they are institutionally violated—affects even the most pervasive violators of human rights. They must find some rationale for their anti-humane activities. That places some limit even on *their* tyrannies.

By violating the human rights of their own citizens, some consequences follow that would not occur if the Helsinki Accords did not exist. I shall return to that crucial factor after discussing the conditions which inspired initiation of the Helsinki Process.

THE PROCESS AS COMMUNICATION

In all East-bloc countries, ideological commitment to Marxism-Leninism results in authoritarian or totalitarian controls. This statism is diametrically opposed to individualism, which promises each person the right to exert a meaningful choice of governmental leaders and policies, and without penalty for making or publicly discussing such choices. For such freedoms pledge the right to public assembly and free association whether for religious, social, trade union, economic, or political purposes.

Intimately associated with each of these freedoms is the independence of the media of mass communication. Throughout the East bloc, governmental ownership of the means of communication—even the licensing of typewriters in some places—is the absolute law. The regime dominates the content of the print and broadcast media. Journalists, so-called, are really government spokesmen. They know they will be banished, at the least, if they express personal views of dissent. The Soviet broadcaster who diverged from the official line about the Afghanistan invasion was sent to a psychiatric institution.

Proof of the ironclad control over communication are the courageous dissenters who write and circulate *samizdat* in the Soviet Union, the Charter 77 people in Czechoslovakia, the prolific Solidarity movement in Poland, and others. These inspired exceptions prove the rule.

How, then, can free men and women outside the Great Gulag that is the East bloc make contact people-to-people? Authorized contacts—cultural, scientific, and journalist exchanges—are carefully controlled. East-bloc travelers are highly indoctrinated, mainly trustworthy carriers of governmental ideology. Occasionally a defector appears, but the rarity underscores the effectiveness of the authoritarian and totalitarian indoctrination in the homelands.

That is not said to denigrate cultural and other exchanges. They should continue, and be expanded. One may assume that Westerners, for their part, can make a certain positive impact on the East-bloc citizens they meet inside Soviet-dominated countries. The fact that cultural and other exchanges have limited effect suggests, however, that additional channels such as the Helsinki Process are necessary. That process must not be examined in isolation as simply a discussion of thirty-five delegates behind closed doors, or even as a conference producing a single, concluding statement that is bound to be consensual and mainly innocuous. The Helsinki Process should be seen as ideological ammunition to be fed continuously into established Western communication channels that reach regularly into East-bloc homelands. We do ourselves a disservice if we regard the Helsinki Process from *our* viewpoint rather than from the *Soviets'* perspective. There must be some reason why they dread facing in public human-rights reviews in the Helsinki Process. They fought long and hard before the Belgrade, Madrid, and Ottawa conferences to restrict press and NGO observation of the compliance discussions.

The reason is obvious: the Soviets don't want the world outside, particularly the 110 developing countries, to see the U.S.S.R. repeatedly stigmatized as a modern tyranny, and not the Marxist utopia that was promised. Beyond the observation of other countries, however, the Soviets mainly dread the magnification of the Helsinki Process through the Freedom Radios. They broadcast the facts of human-rights violations directly to the citizens of the Soviet bloc. One cannot fully estimate the impact of the Helsinki Process without factoring in the continuous use of the discussions by Radio Free Europe/Radio Liberty, the Voice of America, the BBC, Deutsche Welle, and other Western radios. The stepped-up jamming of American broadcasts by the Soviet Union is further proof that our radios are effective. How else can free people speak over the heads of totalitarians—as speak they must—to reach the peoples of the Soviet bloc?

THE TERRITORIAL BORDER QUESTION

For more than six decades, Western efforts to help liberalize the Soviet Union from the outside have largely failed. We have tried approaches called Cold War, detente, or a blend of the two—with little short-term success. These were largely approaches devised by, or in response to, the Marxist-Leninist system itself. The Helsinki Process is different. It is a Western concept. It was, to be sure, almost an afterthought when Western Europeans finally agreed to hold a postwar conference which the Soviet Union had long demanded. The West Europeans, and reluctantly the United States, agreed, provided human rights were as thoroughly examined as security and economic matters. It was to be understood that every word in the entire Final Act would be approved by all thirty-five signatories, and every word—human rights included—would carry equal weight. The Soviets thus committed themselves to standards of human rights which were not theirs in practice or in promise; standards that would, if complied with, transform their country and all East-bloc countries into far freer societies.

The Soviets were apparently willing to take that risk in order to achieve Europe-wide approval of existing borders. Did they achieve their primary objective? The answer is no, unless the West out of a perpetual sense of inferiority assumes the Soviets must have won what they sought. For, after all, the Soviets yielded a good deal by agreeing to Basket Three, the human-rights standards. And those issues dominate the Helsinki Process.

Examine the borders question. Critics of the Helsinki Accords, particularly Americans, do the free world a great disservice. They repeat the Soviet interpretation that at Helsinki the World War II borders of Europe were formally accepted for the first time. Helsinki, it is said, was the peace treaty the communists long sought in order to secure universal approval for their wartime and postwar accessions in Europe. That is *not* what happened at Helsinki in 1975. The accords did not affirm as inviolable the existing territorial boundaries. On the contrary, the declaration speaks clearly on this point: "Frontiers can be changed," it states, "in accordance with international law, by peaceful means and by agreement." That is given in the first principle. The third principle governing the document says that states "will refrain now and in the future from assaulting" one another's frontiers. When read with the first principle, the document opposes changes in borders by force but upholds changes resulting from peaceful agreement. Moreover, President Ford stipulated clearly as he signed the accords: "The United States has never recognized the Soviet incorporation of Lithuania, Latvia, and Estonia and is not doing so now." Indeed, a crucial territorial division, the Oder-Neisse line between the G.D.R. and Poland, was settled in 1970, five years before the Helsinki Final Act.

The principal American negotiator (Harold S. Russell) writes that he and "all the Western negotiators" believe the "U.S.S.R. failed in large part to achieve the kind of language it originally sought." The document, he says, "does not depart materially from previous international agreements on frontiers and does nothing to recognize existing frontiers in Europe." The two sentences in the accords "comprising the inviolability principle occupied four months'' of negotiation, and eliminated ''virtually all'' of the essential elements of the Soviets' initial draft.

However, what the Soviets failed to achieve in the CSCE negotiations they ''almost totally recouped at Helsinki through the American press''—that, too, from the American negotiator. And, I will add, our press continues to serve up the Soviet line that Helsinki gave the East bloc its present borders. It did not.

West German Foreign Minister Hans-Dietrich Genscher put it properly in the Bundestag: ''The Conference has not finalized the *status quo* in Europe,'' he said. ''And what the Conference did not do by text we should not do by words.'' President Ford stated explicitly as he signed the Helsinki Accords that he did not accept the interpretation that the CSCE ''will put a seal of approval on the political division of Europe.'' If he believed that it would, he said, he would not go to Helsinki.

Americans can be too prone to cast a skeptical eye on international negotiations. We are also quick to assume guilt for *our* policies, and believe the Soviets are ten feet tall. Helsinki was a different case. The Soviets did not get the territorial approval they sought. Instead, they got Basket Three—the human-rights commitments. By the time it was clear they could not get the territorial commitment, they were too deeply enmeshed in the three-sided process to pull out of one, and thus kill any territorial reference. Had they done so, it would have been impossible even to convert a bland territorial statement into a propagandized commitment they wanted but didn't get. Sadly, Americans are helping make that conversion after the fact. Instead of wringing our hands over a bad bargain, we should repeatedly proclaim the truth: Helsinki, far from providing territorial commitments, created a vast set of human-rights standards and commitments. These should be hailed, not rued.

HELSINKI'S PUBLIC NATURE

I turn next to what the Helsinki Process is, and is not. The latter first: it is not a legally binding commitment, as today's critics point out. Why so? Because for two years of negotiations before 1975, the *Americans* insisted that the Final Act would not be legally binding. And probably for good reason. Without resort to the military, it would be difficult to enforce commitments to internal relations. Realities would probably be no different in the Gulags today if the act had been legally binding, but the fragile rule of law would have been further weakened.

Critics also suggest that the Helsinki Process is an elaborate pretense, that we and the Soviets are seemingly in accord about the values and the violations of free expression, free trade unions, freedom to travel, and other matters. That criticism entirely misses the value of the process. The framing of the standards, important though they are, is only the beginning of the process. The key is holding the Soviet bloc to *our* interpretations of those standards. We have devised the most effective mechanism so far to bring Soviet spokesmen to the dock at Helsinki and charge them—citing names, cases, and institutional procedures—with violations of the approved code of human practice. Of course the Soviets counterattack, and of course they charge interference in their internal affairs. But that, on their part, is purely damage control.

The Helsinki Process is aired regularly, world-wide, over the Freedom Radios. These are heard, even through jamming, inside the Soviet bloc. The bloc bureaucrats, and probably their families, friends, and associates, must hear in detail of the charges made against them in the Helsinki Process. They must devise answers often of a relatively specific nature—answers which are transparently specious even to them. Such charges must seep through the internal communications channels. Certainly such attacks make many Soviet satellite bureaucrats uneasy and perhaps eventually help to Polandize their countries. At the very least, such attacks place a strain on Soviet relations with their satellites.

The most important aspect of the Helsinki Process is its public nature. If the review conferences at Belgrade and Madrid, and the human-rights experts' meeting at Ottawa, were held in the absence of publicity, I would agree the main value would be eliminated. That is why the Soviets insisted before the Ottawa conference that it be closed to the press and the NGOs. The U.S. delegation fought to keep it as open as possible. Clearly, the watching world sees that it is the Soviets who have something to hide. Each day, then, an American spokesman emerged from the session to report to the press what had transpired that day. And press materials spell out in detail the names, events, and institutional procedures that have resulted in serious Soviet violations of human rights. It is then the business of the free press to carry these charges around the world. To the extent that the press does not convey this information, people everywhere—including the mass media themselves—suffer. For violators of humane standards are let off too easily. But that is not the fault of the Helsinki Process; rather it is a sign of misunderstanding or indifference.

The press, which largely misinterpreted the territorial intent of the CSCE, may further advance Soviet objectives by playing down the stringent naming of names, and other issues set forth at Ottawa mainly by the American and British delegations. Ambassador Max M. Kampelman, board-chairman-on-leave of Freedom House, pursued that policy at Madrid from 1980 to 1983. Ambassador Richard Schifter did the same at Ottawa.

We should also credit the Helsinki Process with the diverse activities of the American CSCE—the joint Executive-Legislative Commission. The commission carefully monitors lists of human-rights violations. A substantial number of the 1,800 family-reunion cases submitted to the Romanian government, for example, have been successfully resolved, and the last outstanding Hungarian-U.S. family reunification case was concluded. The commission has held hearings, widely reported in the press, on the plight of Jews in the Soviet Union, psychiatric abuse in the Soviet Union, forced labor in the U.S.S.R., and the status of Andrei Sakharov and the unofficial peace groups in Eastern Europe. All of these public manifestations were possible because the Helsinki Process created both framework and newsworthiness. Given the nature of Western journalism, in the absence of such organized activities in defense of human rights, it is highly unlikely the press would cover individual appeals. Isolated, *ad hoc* complaints generally go unreported.

Human rights is one of three general concerns of the CSCE. The Madrid review conference, for example, helped spotlight the Soviet invasion of Afghanistan, the repression of Poland, and the shooting down of the Korean airliner. The meeting had the unusual effect of unifying the Western nations, including the neutrals and nonaligned, in the face of East-bloc opposition. And a fact not often publicized is that the Madrid review also served as an open channel for East-West communication during the time when other contacts were shut down. The Madrid conference also mandated the Stockholm meeting on confidence-building measures in the security field. While no rapid results may be anticipated there, the effort to avoid destabilizing military surprises can be useful.

"The Madrid meeting," in the words of Ambassador Kampelman, was "the appropriate forum at which to insert political and moral pressure into the process." The message to the Soviet Union was clear: "Conform to the promises made in 1975 if you wish to be recognized as a responsible member of the international community."

THE ESSENTIAL ALTERNATIVE

In a militarized, adversarial world the application of moral and political pressure is the essential alternative, and free men and women should support it to the fullest. Yet some Soviet dissidents now call for the abrogation of the Helsinki Accords. They say that in the ten years since the Final Act was approved the human condition has worsened in the East bloc, Afghanistan has been invaded, and the very dissidents who supported the Helsinki Process—the monitors inside the East bloc—have been imprisoned, and some died. All of this is true.

But would these evils have happened in the absence of the Helsinki Accords? Undoubtedly. Did any realist believe the accords would significantly reverse the sixty-eight years of Marxism-Leninism, even in ten years? Hardly. What, then, is the value of the Helsinki Process? Simply this: it is the only means the Western nations of Europe, and the neutrals, and Canada and the United States have devised to provide a public judgment seat for violations by the Soviet bloc.

Would the world be better without such judgments? I think not. Is there an effective alternative public system for exposing the Soviet bloc? I know of no other regularized way. Is there another method of changing the internal Soviet system? Isolation? Surely that would only increase the internal suffering, to the delight of the Soviet masters. Now, public attention provides some brake—as the very dissidents who now attack the Helsinki Process were quick to tell us personally as each of them was freed. "Keep up the publicity," they would tell us—each of them—"it helps." It still does. Helsinki is institutionalized publicity on behalf of human freedom.

I know that after ten years there are frustrations among the émigrés. Properly so. Worse still must be the cruel disappointment and suffering of the supporters of the Helsinki Process now in Soviet prisons and labor camps. We must understand and honor their anguish. Yet to this day, when these dissidents or other human-rights activists appeal for assistance, they invariably seek to hold the guilty state to

its commitment to the same Helsinki Accords, as well as to the Universal Declaration of Human Rights. Yet we never hear cries to abrogate the Universal Declaration of Human Rights. On the contrary, the appeal is always to comply with the declaration. Ironically, the Universal Declaration has no mechanism such as the Helsinki Process for monitoring compliance and bringing the guilty to the dock of world opinion.

We should not be complacent about the Helsinki or any other approach, as long as the world is divided between free and not free. Yet we should use the Helsinki Process ceaselessly to call on the Soviet bloc to comply. We should exploit to the fullest the so-far-unequaled opportunity to attack the violators in the only way open, short of military force—the use of the word addressed to the mind and the heart of the free and, yes, the not-yet-free of this world.

QUESTIONS FOR DISCUSSION

1 Did the United States recognize at Helsinki in 1975 the postwar territorial settlement in Europe? If so, was it justified in so doing?
2 Did U.S. leaders in 1975 expect the Soviets to adhere to articles in the Helsinki Accords relating to human rights?
3 Do Soviet failures in the matter of human rights now justify a U.S. withdrawal from the Helsinki Accords?
4 Why did the Soviet Union welcome the Helsinki Accords?
5 Have the Helsinki Accords made war in Europe less likely?

SUGGESTED READINGS

Bowker, Mike, and Phil Williams. "Helsinki and West European Security," *International Affairs* (London), **61** (Autumn 1985), pp. 607–618.
Ceska, Franz. "The Significance of 'Basket III' of the CSCE—Impact and Prospects," *NATO Review,* **33** (Aug. 1985), pp. 19–25.
Daniloff, Nicholas, and James Wallace. "The Helsinki Accords: An Exercise in Futility?" *U.S.*

News and World Report, **99** (Aug. 5, 1985), pp. 36–37.

Drinan, Robert F. "The Tenth Anniversary of Helsinki," *America,* **153** (Aug. 10, 1985), pp. 43–44.

Edwards, Geoffrey. "Human Rights and Basket III Issues: Areas of Change and Continuity," *International Affairs* (London), **61** (Autumn 1985), pp. 631–642.

Elliott, Laurence. "At Helsinki: Shadows of Yalta," *Reader's Digest,* **127** (Aug. 1985), pp. 122–126.

Howard, Michael. "Helsinki Reconsidered: East-West Relations Two Years after the 'Final Act,' " *Round Table* (London), no. 267 (July 1977), pp. 241–248.

Maresca, John J. *To Helsinki: The Conference on Security and Cooperation in Europe 1973–75.* Durham, N.C.: Duke Univ. Press, 1985.

Mellbin, Skjold G. "The Helsinki Process: Issues of Security and of Confidence-Building," *NATO Review,* **33** (Aug. 1985), pp. 7–13.

Will, George F. "Iron Curtain, Rubber Words," *Newsweek,* **105** (Apr. 1, 1985), p. 90.

5 Was détente of mutual benefit to the United States and the Soviet Union?

YES

Henry A. Kissinger

[*Détente*]

NO

George Meany

[*The Case against Détente*]

[Détente]

Henry A. Kissinger

I. THE CHALLENGE

Since the dawn of the nuclear age the world's fears of holocaust and its hopes for peace have turned on the relationship between the United States and the Soviet Union.

Throughout history men have sought peace but suffered war; all too often deliberate decisions or miscalculations have brought violence and destruction to a world yearning for tranquility. Tragic as the consequences of violence may have been in the past, the issue of peace and war takes on unprecedented urgency when, for the first time in history, two nations have the capacity to destroy mankind. In the nuclear age, as President Eisenhower pointed out two decades ago, "there is no longer any alternative to peace."

The destructiveness of modern weapons defines the necessity of the task; deep differences in philosophy and interests between the United States and the Soviet Union point up its difficulty. These differences do not spring from misunderstanding, or personalities, or transitory factors:

They are rooted in history, and in the way the two countries have developed.

They are nourished by conflicting values and opposing ideologies.

They are expressed in diverging national interests that produce political and military competition.

They are influenced by allies and friends whose association we value and whose interests we will not sacrifice.

Paradox confuses our perception of the problem of peaceful coexistence: if peace is pursued

From U.S. Cong., Senate, *Détente*, Hearings before the Committee on Foreign Relations, 93d Cong., 2d Sess., 1974, pp. 247–60.

to the exclusion of any other goal, other values will be compromised and perhaps lost; but if unconstrained rivalry leads to nuclear conflict, these values, along with everything else, will be destroyed in the resulting holocaust. However competitive they may be at some level of their relationship, both major nuclear powers must base their policies on the premise that neither can expect to impose its will on the other without running an intolerable risk. The challenge of our time is to reconcile the reality of competition with the imperative of coexistence.

There can be no peaceful international order without a constructive relationship between the United States and the Soviet Union. There will be no international stability unless both the Soviet Union and the United States conduct themselves with restraint and unless they use their enormous power for the benefit of mankind.

Thus we must be clear at the outset on what the term "détente" entails. It is the search for a more constructive relationship with the Soviet Union reflecting the realities I have outlined. It is a continuing process, not a final condition that has been or can be realized at any one specific point in time. And it has been pursued by successive American leaders though the means have varied as have world conditions.

Some fundamental principles guide this policy:

The United States does not base its policy solely on Moscow's good intentions. But neither can we insist that all forward movement must await a convergence of American and Soviet purposes. We seek, regardless of Soviet intentions, to serve peace through a systematic resistance to pressure and conciliatory responses to moderate behavior.

We must oppose aggressive actions, but we must not seek confrontations lightly.

We must maintain a strong national defense while recognizing that in the nuclear age the relationship between military strength and politically usable power is the most complex in all history.

Where the age-old antagonism between freedom and tyranny is concerned we are not neutral. But other imperatives impose limits on our ability to produce internal changes in foreign countries. Consciousness of our limits is a recognition of the necessity of peace—not moral callousness. The preservation of human life and human society are moral values too.

We must be mature enough to recognize that to be stable a relationship must provide advantages to both sides and that the most constructive international relationships are those in which both parties perceive an element of gain. Moscow will benefit from certain measures just as we will from others. The balance cannot be struck on each issue every day, but only over the whole range of relations and over a period of time.

II. THE COURSE OF SOVIET-AMERICAN RELATIONS

In the first two decades of the postwar period U.S.-Soviet relations were characterized by many fits and starts. Some encouraging developments followed the Cuban missile crisis of 1962, for example. But at the end of the decade the invasion of Czechoslovakia brought progress to a halt and threw a deepening shadow over East-West relations.

During those difficult days some were tempted to conclude that antagonism was the central feature of the relationship and that U.S. policy—even while the Vietnam agony raised questions about the readiness of the American people to sustain a policy of confrontation—had to be geared to this grim reality. Others recommended a basic change of policy: there was a barrage of demands to hold an immediate summit to establish a better atmosphere, to launch the SALT talks, and to end the decades-old trade discrimination against the Soviet Union which was widely criticized as anachronistic, futile, and counterproductive.

These two approaches reflected the extremes of the debate that had dominated most of the postwar period; they also revealed deep-seated differences between the American and the Soviet reactions to the process of international relations.

For many Americans, tensions and enmity in international relations are anomalies, the cause of which is attributed either to deliberate malice or misunderstanding, Malice is to be combatted by force, or at least isolation; misunderstanding is to be removed by the strenuous exercise of good will. Communist states on the other hand, regard tensions as inevitable by-products of a struggle between opposing social systems.

Most Americans perceive relations between states as either friendly or hostile, both defined in nearly absolute terms. Soviet foreign policy, by comparison, is conducted in a grey area heavily influenced by the Soviet conception of the balance of forces. Thus, Soviet diplomacy is never free of tactical pressures or adjustments, and it is never determined in isolation from the prevailing military balance. For Moscow, East-West contacts and negotiations are in part designed to promote Soviet influence abroad, especially in Western Europe—and to gain formal acceptance of those elements of the status quo most agreeable to Moscow.

The issue, however, is not whether peace and stability serve Soviet purposes, but whether they serve our own. Indeed, to the extent that our attention focuses largely on Soviet intentions we create a latent vulnerability. If détente can be justified only by a basic change in Soviet motivation, the temptation becomes overwhelming to base U.S.-Soviet relations not on realistic appraisal but on tenuous hopes: a change in Soviet tone is taken as a sign of a basic change of philosophy. Atmosphere is confused with substance. Policy oscillates between poles of suspicion and euphoria.

Neither extreme is realistic, and both are dangerous. The hopeful view ignores that we and the Soviets are bound to compete for the foreseeable future. The pessimistic view ignores that we have some parallel interests and that we are compelled to coexist. Détente encourages an environment in which competitors can regulate and restrain their differences and ultimately move from competition to cooperation.

A. American goals

America's aspiration for the kind of political environment we now call détente is not new.

The effort to achieve a more constructive relationship with the Soviet Union is not made in the name of any one administration, or one party, or for any one period of time. It expresses the continuing desire of the vast majority of the American people for an easing of international tensions, and their expectation that any responsible government will strive for peace. No aspect of our policies, domestic or foreign, enjoys more consistent bipartisan support. No aspect is more in the interest of mankind.

In the postwar period repeated efforts were made to improve our relationship with Moscow. The spirits of Geneva, Camp David and Glassboro were evanescent moments in a quarter century otherwise marked by tensions and by sporadic confrontation. What is new in the current period of relaxation of tensions is its duration, the scope of the relationship which has evolved and the continuity and intensity of contact and consultation which it has produced.

A number of factors have produced this change in the international environment. By the end of the sixties and the beginning of the seventies the time was propitious—no matter what administration was in office in the United States—for a major attempt to improve U.S.-Soviet relations. Contradictory tendencies contested for preeminence in Soviet policy; events could have tipped the scales towards either increased aggressiveness or towards conciliation.

The fragmentation in the Communist world in the 1960s challenged the leading position of the U.S.S.R. and its claim to be the arbiter of orthodoxy. The U.S.S.R. could have reacted by adopting a more aggressive attitude toward the capitalist world in order to assert its militant vigilance; instead the changing situation and U.S. policy seem to have encouraged Soviet leaders to cooperate in at least a temporary lessening of tension with the West.

The prospect of achieving a military position of near parity with the U.S. in strategic forces could have tempted Moscow to use its expanding military capability to strive more determinedly for expansion; in fact it tempered the militancy of some of its actions and sought to stabilize at least some aspects of the military competition through negotiations.

The very real economic problems of the U.S.S.R. and Eastern Europe could have reinforced autarkic policies and the tendency to create a closed system; in actuality the Soviet Union and its allies have come closer to acknowledging the reality of an interdependent world economy.

Finally, when faced with the hopes of its own people for greater well-being, the Soviet government could have continued to stimulate the suspicions of the Cold War to further isolate Soviet society; in fact it chose—however inadequately and slowly—to seek to calm its public opinion by joining in a relaxation of tensions.

For the United States the choice was clear: to provide as many incentives as possible for those actions by the Soviet Union most conducive to peace and individual well-being and to overcome the swings between illusionary optimism and harsh antagonism that had characterized most of the postwar period. We could capitalize on the tentative beginnings made in the sixties by taking advantage of the compelling new conditions of the 1970s.

We have sought to explore every avenue towards an honorable and just accommodation while remaining determined not to settle for mere atmospherics. We relied on a balance of mutual interests rather than Soviet intentions. When challenged—such as in the Middle East, the Caribbean or Berlin—we always responded firmly. And when Soviet policy moved towards conciliation we sought to turn what may have started as a tactical maneuver into a durable pattern of conduct.

Our approach proceeds from the conviction that in moving forward across a wide spectrum of negotiations, progress in one area adds momentum to progress in other areas. If we succeed, then no agreement stands alone as an isolated accomplishment vulnerable to the next crisis. We did not invent the interrelationship; it was a reality because of the range of problems and areas in which the interests of the United States and the Soviet Union impinge on each other. We have looked for progress in a series of agreements settling specific political issues and we have sought to relate these to a new standard of international conduct appropriate to the dangers of the nuclear age. By acquiring a stake in this network of relationships with the West, the Soviet Union may become more conscious of what it would lose by a return to confrontation. Indeed it is our expectation that it will develop a self-interest in fostering the entire process of relaxation of tensions.

B. The global necessities

In the late 1940s this nation engaged in a great debate about the role it would play in the postwar world. We forged a bipartisan consensus on which our policies were built for more than two decades. By the end of the 1960s the international environment which molded that consensus had been transformed. What in the fifties had seemed a solid bloc of adversaries had fragmented into competing centers of power and doctrine; old allies had gained new strength and self-assurance; scores of new nations had emerged and formed blocs of their own; and all nations were being swept up in a technology that was

compressing the planet and deepening our mutual dependence.

Then, as now, it was clear that the international structure formed in the immediate postwar period was in fundamental flux, and that a new international system was emerging. America's historic opportunity was to help shape a new set of international relationships—more pluralistic, less dominated by military power, less susceptible to confrontation, more open to genuine cooperation among the free and diverse elements of the globe. This new, more positive international environment is possible only if all the major powers—and especially the world's strongest nuclear powers—anchor their policies in the principles of moderation and restraint. They no longer have the power to dominate; they do have the capacity to thwart. They cannot build the new international structure alone; they can make its realization impossible by their rivalry.

Détente is all the more important because of what the creation of a new set of international relations demands of us with respect to other countries and areas. President Ford has assigned the highest priority to maintaining the vitality of our partnerships in Europe, Asia and Latin America. Our security ties with our allies are essential, but we also believe that recognition of the interdependence of the contemporary world requires cooperation in many other fields. Cooperation becomes more difficult if the United States is perceived by allied public opinion as an obstacle to peace and if public debate is polarized on the issue of whether friendship with the United States is inconsistent with East-West reconciliation.

One important area for invigorated cooperative action is economic policy. The international economic system has been severely tested. The Middle East war demonstrated dramatically the integral relationship between economics and politics. Clearly whatever the state of our relations with the U.S.S.R. the international economic agenda must be addressed. But the task would be infinitely more complex if we proceeded in a Cold War environment.

International economic problems cut across political dividing lines. All nations, regardless of ideology, face the problems of energy and economic growth, feeding burgeoning populations, regulating the use of the oceans, and preserving the environment.

At a minimum, easing international tensions allows the West to devote more intellectual and material resources to these problems. As security concerns recede, humane concerns come again to the fore. International organizations take on greater significance and responsibility, less obstructed by Cold War antagonisms. The climate of lessened tensions even opens prospects for broader collaboration between East and West. It is significant that some of these global issues—such as energy, cooperation in science and health, and the protection of the environment—have already reached the U.S.-Soviet agenda.

In the present period mankind may be menaced as much by international economic and political chaos as by the danger of war. Avoiding either hazard demands a cooperative world structure for which improved East-West relations are essential.

III. THE EVOLUTION OF DÉTENTE—THE BALANCE OF RISKS AND INCENTIVES

The course of détente has not been smooth or even. As late as 1969, Soviet-American relations were ambiguous and uncertain. To be sure, negotiations on Berlin and SALT had begun. But the tendency towards confrontation appeared dominant.

We were challenged by Soviet conduct in the Middle East ceasefire of August 1970, during the Syrian invasion of Jordan in September 1970, on the question of a possible Soviet submarine base in Cuba, in actions around Berlin, and during the Indo-Pakistani war. Soviet policy seemed directed toward fashioning a

détente in bilateral relations with our Western European allies, while challenging the U.S.

We demonstrated then, and stand ready to do so again, that America will not yield to pressure or the threat of force. We made clear then—as we do today—that détente cannot be pursued selectively in one area or towards one group of countries only. For us détente is indivisible.

Finally, a breakthrough was made in 1971 on several fronts—in the Berlin settlement, in the SALT talks, in other arms control negotiations—that generated the process of détente. It consists of these elements: an elaboration of principles; political discussions to solve outstanding issues and to reach cooperative agreements; economic relations; and arms control negotiations, particularly those concerning strategic arms.

A. The elaboration of principles

Cooperative relations, in our view, must be more than a series of isolated agreements. They must reflect an acceptance of mutual obligations and of the need for accommodation and restraint.

To set forth principles of behavior in formal documents is hardly to guarantee their observance. But they are reference points against which to judge actions and set goals.

The first of the series of documents is the Statement of Principles signed in Moscow in 1972. It affirms: (1) the necessity of avoiding confrontation; (2) the imperative of mutual restraint; (3) the rejection of attempts to exploit tensions to gain unilateral advantages; (4) the renunciation of claims of special influence in the world; and (5) the willingness, on this new basis, to coexist peacefully and build a firm long-term relationship.

An agreement for the prevention of nuclear war based on these principles was signed in 1973. It affirms that the objective of the policies of the U.S. and U.S.S.R. is to remove the danger of nuclear conflict and the use of nuclear weapons. But it emphasizes that this objective presupposes the renunciation of any war or threat of war not only by the two nuclear superpowers against each other, but also against allies or third countries. In other words, the principle of restraint is not confined to relations between the U.S. and the U.S.S.R.; it is explicitly extended to include all countries.

These statements of principles are not an American concession; indeed we have been affirming them unilaterally for two decades. Nor are they a legal contract; rather they are an aspiration and a yardstick by which we assess Soviet behavior. We have never intended to "rely" on Soviet compliance with every principle; we do seek to elaborate standards of conduct which the Soviet Union would violate only to its cost. And if over the long term the more durable relationship takes hold, the basic principles will give it definition, structure and hope.

B. Political dialogue and cooperative agreements

One of the features of the current phase of U.S.-Soviet relations is the unprecedented consultation between leaders either face-to-face or through diplomatic channels.

Although consultation has reached a level of candor and frequency without precedent, we know that consultation does not guarantee that policies are compatible. It does provide a mechanism for the resolution of differences before they escalate to the point of public confrontation and commit the prestige of both sides.

The channel between the leaders of the two nations has proved its worth in many crises; it reduces the risk that either side might feel driven to act or to react on the basis of incomplete on confusing information. The channel of communication has continued without interruption under President Ford.

But crisis management is not an end in itself. The more fundamental goal is the elaboration of a political relationship which in time will make crises less likely to arise.

It was difficult in the past to speak of a U.S.-Soviet bilateral relationship in any normal sense of the phrase. Trade was negligible. Contacts between various institutions and between the peoples of the two countries were at best sporadic. There were no cooperative efforts in science and technology. Cultural exchange was modest. As a result there was no tangible inducement toward cooperation and penalty for aggressive behavior. Today, by joining our efforts even in such seemingly apolitical fields as medical research or environmental protection, we and the Soviets can benefit not only our two peoples but all mankind; in addition we generate incentives for restraint.

Since 1972 we have concluded agreements on a common effort against cancer, on research to protect the environment, on studying the use of the ocean's resources, on the use of atomic energy for peaceful purposes, on studying methods for conserving energy, on examining construction techniques for regions subject to earthquakes, and on devising new transportation methods. Other bilateral areas for cooperation include an agreement on preventing incidents at sea, an agreement to exchange information and research methods in agriculture, and the training of astronauts for the Soviet-U.S. rendezvous and docking mission planned for 1975.

Each project must be judged by the concrete benefits it brings. But in their sum—in their exchange of information and people as well as in their establishment of joint mechanisms— they also constitute a commitment in both countries to work together across a broad spectrum.

C. The economic component

During the period of the Cold War economic contact between ourselves and the U.S.S.R. was virtually non-existent. Even then many argued that improved economic relations might mitigate international tensions; in fact there were several Congressional resolutions to that effect. But recurrent crises prevented any sustained progress.

The period of confrontation should have left little doubt, however, that economic boycott would not transform the Soviet system or impose upon it a conciliatory foreign policy. Throughout this period the U.S.S.R. was quite prepared to maintain heavy military outlays and to concentrate on capital growth by using the resources of the Communist world alone. Moreover it proved impossible to mount an airtight boycott in practice, since over time, most if not all the other major industrial countries became involved in trade with the East.

The question then became how trade and economic contact—in which the Soviet Union is obviously interested—could serve the purposes of peace. On the one hand, economic relations cannot be separated from the political context. Clearly, we cannot be asked to reward hostile conduct with economic benefits even if in the process we deny ourselves some commercially profitable opportunities. On the other hand, when political relations begin to normalize it is difficult to explain why economic relations should not be normalized as well.

We have approached the question of economic relations with deliberation and circumspection and as an act of policy not primarily of commercial opportunity. As political relations have improved on a broad basis, economic issues have been dealt with on a comparably broad front. A series of interlocking economic agreements with the U.S.S.R. has been negotiated, side by side with the political progress already noted. The 25-year-old lend-lease debt was settled; the reciprocal extension of most favored nation treatment was negotiated, together with safeguards against the possible disruption of our markets and a series of practical arrangements to facilitate the conduct of business in the U.S.S.R. by American firms; our government credit facilities were made available for trade with the U.S.S.R.; and a maritime

agreement regulating the carriage of goods has been signed.

These were all primarily regulatory agreements conferring no immediate benefits on the Soviet Union but serving as blueprints for an expanded economic relationship if the political improvement continued.

This approach commanded widespread domestic approval. It was considered a natural outgrowth of political progress. At no time were issues regarding Soviet domestic political practices raised. Indeed, not until after the 1972 agreements was the Soviet domestic order invoked as a reason for arresting or reversing the progress so painstakingly achieved.

This sudden, ex post facto form of linkage raises serious questions:

For the Soviet Union, it casts doubt on our reliability as a negotiating partner;

The significance of trade, originally envisaged as only one ingredient of a complex and evolving relationship, is inflated out of all proportion;

The hoped-for results of policy become transformed into pre-conditions for any policy at all.

We recognize the depth and validity of the moral concerns expressed by those who oppose—or put conditions on—expanded trade with the U.S.S.R. But a sense of proportion must be maintained about the leverage our economic relations give us with the U.S.S.R.:

Denial of economic relations cannot by itself achieve what it failed to do when it was part of a determined policy of political and military confrontation.

The economic bargaining ability of Most Favored Nation status is marginal. MFN grants no special privilege to the U.S.S.R.; in fact it is a misnomer since we have such agreements with over 100 countries. To enact it would be to remove a discriminatory hold-over of the days of the Cold War. To continue to deny it is more a political than an economic act.

Trade benefits are not a one-way street; the laws of mutual advantage operate, or there will be no trade.

The technology that flows to the U.S.S.R. as a result of expanded U.S.-Soviet trade may have a few indirect uses for military production. But with our continuing restrictions on strategic exports, we can maintain adequate controls—and we intend to do so. Moreover, the same technology has been available to the U.S.S.R. and will be increasingly so from other non-Communist sources. Boycott denies us a means of influence and possible commercial gain; it does not deprive the U.S.S.R. of technology.

The actual and potential flow of credits from the U.S. represents a tiny fraction of the capital available to the U.S.S.R. domestically and elsewhere, including Western Europe and Japan. But it does allow us to exercise some influence through our ability to control the scope of trade relationships.

Over time, trade and investment may leaven the autarkic tendencies of the Soviet system, invite gradual association of the Soviet economy with the world economy, and foster a degree of interdependence that adds an element of stability to the political relationship.

D. The strategic relationship

We cannot expect to relax international tensions or achieve a more stable international system should the two stronger nuclear powers conduct an unrestrained strategic arms race. Thus, perhaps the single most important component of our policy toward the Soviet Union is the effort to limit strategic weapons competition.

The competition in which we now find ourselves is historically unique:

Each side has the capacity to destroy civilization as we know it.

Failure to maintain equivalence could jeopardize not only our freedom but our very survival.

The lead time for technological innovation is so long, yet the pace of change so relentless that the arms race and strategic policy itself are in danger of being driven by technological necessity.

When nuclear arsenals reach levels involving thousands of launchers and over ten thousand warheads, and when the characteristics of the weapons of the two sides are so incommensurable, it becomes difficult to determine what combination of numbers of strategic weapons and performance capabilities would give one side a military and political superiority. At a minimum clear changes in the strategic balance can be achieved only by efforts so enormous and by increments so large that the very attempt is highly destabilizing.

The prospect of a decisive military advantage, even if theoretically possible, is politically intolerable; neither side will passively permit a massive shift in the nuclear balance. Therefore, the probable outcome of each succeeding round of competition is the restoration of a strategic equilibrium, but at increasingly higher and more complex levels of forces.

The arms race is driven by political as well as military factors. While a decisive advantage is hard to calculate, the appearance of inferiority—whatever its actual significance—can have serious political consequences. With weapons that are unlikely to be used and for which there is no operational experience, the psychological impact can be crucial. Thus each side has a high incentive to achieve not only the reality but the appearance of equality. In a very real sense each side shapes the military establishment of the other.

If we are driven to it, the United States will sustain an arms race. Indeed, it is likely that the United States would emerge from such a competition with an edge over the Soviet Union in most significant categories of strategic arms. But the political or military benefit which would flow from such a situation would remain elusive. Indeed after such an evolution it might well be that both sides would be worse off than before the race began. The enormous destructiveness of weapons and the uncertainties regarding their effects combine to make the massive use of such weapons increasingly incredible.

The Soviet Union must realize that the overall relationship with the United States will be less stable if strategic balance is sought through unrestrained competitive programs. Sustaining the buildup requires exhortations by both sides that in time may prove incompatible with restrained international conduct. The very fact of a strategic arms race has a high potential for feeding attitudes of hostility and suspicion on both sides, transforming the fears of those who demand more weapons into self-fulfilling prophecies.

The American people can be asked to bear the cost and political instability of a race which is doomed to stalemate only if it is clear that every effort has been made to prevent it. That is why every President since Eisenhower has pursued negotiations for the limitation of strategic arms while maintaining the military programs essential to strategic balance.

There are more subtle strategic reasons for our interest in SALT. Our supreme strategic purpose is the prevention of nuclear conflict, through the maintenance of sufficient political and strategic power. Estimates of what constitutes "sufficiency" have been contentious. Our judgments have changed with our experience in deploying these weapons and as the Soviets expanded their own nuclear forces. When in the late 1960s it became apparent that the Soviet Union, for practical purposes, had achieved a kind of rough parity with the United States, we adopted the current strategic doctrine.

We determined that stability required strategic forces invulnerable to attack, thus removing the incentive on either side to strike first. Reality reinforced doctrine. As technology advanced, it became apparent that neither side *could* realistically expect to develop a credible disarming capability against the other except through efforts so gigantic as to represent a major threat to political stability.

One result of our doctrine was basing our strategic planning on the assumption that in the unlikely event of nuclear attack, the President should have a wide range of options available in deciding at what level and against what targets to respond. We designed our strategic forces with a substantial measure of flexibility, so that the United States response need not include an attack on the aggressor's cities—thus inviting the destruction of our own—but could instead hit other targets. Translating this capability into a coherent system of planning became a novel, and as yet uncompleted, task of great complexity; but progress has been made. In our view such flexibility enhances the certainty of retaliation and thereby makes an attack less likely. Above all, it preserves the capability for human decision even in the ultimate crisis.

Another, at first seemingly paradoxical, result was a growing commitment to negotiated agreements on strategic arms. SALT has become one means by which we and the Soviet Union could enhance stability by setting mutual constraints on our respective forces and by gradually reaching an understanding of the doctrinal considerations that underlie the deployment of nuclear weapons. Through SALT the two sides can reduce the suspicions and fears which fuel strategic competition. SALT, in the American conception, is a means to achieve strategic stability by methods other than the arms race.

Our specific objectives have been:

(1) to break the momentum of ever increasing levels of armaments;

(2) to control certain qualitative aspects—particularly MIRV's;

(3) to moderate the pace of new deployments; and

(4) ultimately, to achieve reductions in force levels.

The SALT agreements already signed represent a major contribution to strategic stability and a significant first step toward a longer term and possibly broader agreement.

When the first agreements in 1972 were signed, the future strategic picture was not bright:

The Soviet Union was engaged in a dynamic program that had closed the numerical gap in ballistic missiles; they were deploying three types of ICBMs at a rate of over 200 annually, and launching on the average eight submarines a year with 16 ballistic missiles each.

The United States had ended its numerical buildup in the late 1960s at a level of 1054 ICBMs and 656 SLBMs. We were emphasizing technological improvements, particularly in MIRV's for the Poseidon and Minuteman missiles. Our replacement systems were intended for the late 1970s and early 1980s;

By most reasonable measurements of strategic power, we held an important advantage, which still continues. But it was also clear that if existing trends were maintained, the Soviet Union would, first, exceed our numerical levels by a considerable margin, and then develop the same technologies we had already mastered.

The agreements signed in May 1972, which limited antiballistic missile defenses and froze the level of ballistic missile forces on both sides, represented the essential first step towards a less volatile strategic environment.

By limiting antiballistic missiles (ABMs) to very low levels of deployment, the United States and the Soviet Union removed a potential source of instability; for one side to build an extensive defense for its cities would inevitably be interpreted...[as a means by which] a potential aggressor would want to protect his population centers from incoming nuclear weapons.

Some have alleged that the interim agreement, which expires in October 1977, penalizes the United States by permitting the Soviet Union to deploy more strategic missile launchers than the United States. Such a view is misleading. When the agreement was signed in May 1972, the Soviet Union already possessed more land-based intercontinental ballistic missiles (ICBMs) than the United States and, given the pace of its submarine construction program, it could have built virtually twice as many nuclear ballistic missile submarines.

The interim agreement confined an existing Soviet ICBM program to the then existing level; it put a ceiling on the heaviest Soviet ICBMs, and it set an upper limit on the Soviet submarine-launched ballistic missile (SLBM) program. No American program was abandoned or curtailed. We remained free to deploy multiple warheads. No restraints were placed on bombers—a weapons system in which we have a large advantage. Indeed, the U.S. lead in missile warheads is likely to be somewhat greater at the end of this agreement than at the time of its signature.

The SALT I agreements were the first deliberate attempt by the nuclear superpowers to bring about strategic stability through negotiation. This very process is conducive to further restraint. For example, in the first round of SALT negotiations in 1970–1972 both sides bitterly contested the number of ABM sites permitted by the agreement; two years later both sides gave up the right to build more than one site. In sum, we believed when we signed these agreements—and we believe now—that they had reduced the danger of nuclear war, that both sides had acquired some greater interest in restraint, and that the basis had been created for the present effort to reach broader agreement.

The goal of the current negotiations is an agreement for a ten-year period. We had aimed at extending the Interim Agreement with adjustments in the numbers and new provisions aimed at dealing with the problem of MIRVs. We found, however, that our negotiation for a two- or three-year extension was constantly threatened with irrelevance by the on-going programs of both sides that were due to be deployed at the end of or just after the period. This distorted the negotiation, and indeed devalued its significance. We shifted to the ten-year approach because the period is long enough to cover all current and planned forces but not so long as to invite hedges that would defeat the purpose of an arms control agreement. In fact it invites a slowing down of planned deployments; further, a period of this length will allow us to set realistic ceilings that represent more than a temporary plateau from which to launch a new cycle in the arms race. Future reductions thus become a realistic objective.

With respect to ceilings on strategic forces, we have defined our goal as essential equivalence in strategic capabilities. What constitutes equivalence involves subjective judgment. Because U.S. and Soviet forces are different from each other—in number and size of weapons, in technological refinement, in performance characteristics—they are difficult to compare.

Yet in the negotiations we shall, for example, have to compare heavy bombers in which the United States is ahead with heavy missiles which the U.S.S.R. has emphasized. We shall have to decide whether to insist on equivalence in every category or whether to permit trade-offs in which an advantage in one category compensates for a disadvantage in another. The equation does not remain static. We shall have to relate present advantages to potential development, existing disparities to future trends. This is a difficult process, but we are confident that it can be solved.

Numerical balance is no longer enough. To achieve stability, it will be necessary to consider as well the impact of technological change in such areas as missile throw weight, multiple

reentry vehicles and missile accuracy. The difficulty is that we are dealing not only with disparate levels of forces but with disparate capabilities—MIRV technology being a conspicuous example. The rate of increase of warheads is surging far ahead of the increase in delivery vehicles. This is why the United States considers MIRV limitation an essential component of the next phase of the SALT negotiations. If we fail, the rate of technology will outstrip our capacity to design effective limitations; constantly proliferating warheads of increasing accuracy will overwhelm fixed launchers. An arms race will be virtually inevitable.

The third area for negotiations is the pace of deployments of new or more modern systems. Neither side will remain in its present position without change for another decade. The Soviets are already embarked on testing an initial deployment of a third generation of ICBMs and on a third modification of submarine-launched missiles—though the rate of deployment so far has been far short of the maximum pace of the late sixties.

For our part we are planning to introduce the Trident system, and to replace the B–52 force with the B–1; we also have the capability of improving our Minuteman ICBM system, adding to the number as well as capability of MIRV missiles, and, if we choose, of deploying mobile systems, land based or airborne. Thus, our task is to see whether the two sides can agree to slow the pace of deployment so that modernization is less likely to threaten the overall balance or trigger an excessive reaction.

Finally, a ten-year program gives us a chance to negotiate reductions. Reductions have occasionally been proposed as an alternative to ceilings; they are often seen as more desirable, or, at least, easier to negotiate. In fact, it is a far more complicated problem. Reductions in launchers, for example, if not accompanied by restrictions on the number of warheads, will only magnify vulnerability. The fewer the aim points, the simpler it would be to calculate an attack. At the same time, reductions will have to proceed from some base line and must therefore be preceded by agreed ceilings—if only of an interim nature. But a ten-year program should permit the negotiations of stable ceilings resulting from the start of a process of reductions.

Détente is admittedly far from a modern equivalent to the kind of stable peace that characterized most of the nineteenth century. But it is a long step away from the bitter and aggressive spirit that has characterized so much of the postwar period. When linked to such broad and unprecedented projects as SALT, détente takes on added meaning and opens prospects of a more stable peace. SALT agreements should be seen as steps in a process leading to progressively greater stability. It is in that light that SALT and related projects will be judged by history.

IV. AN ASSESSMENT OF DÉTENTE

Where has the process of détente taken us so far? What are the principles that must continue to guide our course?

Major progress has been made:

Berlin's potential as Europe's perennial flash point has been substantially reduced through the Quadripartite agreement of 1971. The U.S. considers strict adherence to the agreement a major test of détente.

We and our allies are launched on negotiations with the Warsaw Pact and other countries in the European Conference on Security and Cooperation—a conference designed to foster East-West dialogue and cooperation.

At the same time NATO and the Warsaw Pact are negotiating the reduction of their forces in Central Europe.

The honorable termination of America's direct military involvement in Indochina and the substantial lowering of regional conflict were made possible by many factors. But this achievement would have been much more dif-

ficult—if not impossible—in an era of Soviet and Chinese hostility toward the United States.

America's principal alliances have proved their durability in a new era. Many feared that détente would undermine them. Instead, détente has helped to place our alliance ties on a more enduring basis by removing the fear that friendship with the United States involved the risk of unnecessary confrontation with the U.S.S.R.

Many incipient crises with the Soviet Union have been contained or settled without ever reaching the point of public disagreement. The world has been freer of East-West tensions and conflict than in the fifties and sixties.

A series of bilateral cooperative relations have turned the U.S.-Soviet relationship in a far more positive direction.

We have achieved unprecedented agreements in arms limitation and measures to avoid accidental war.

New possibilities for positive U.S.-Soviet cooperation have emerged on issues in which the globe is interdependent—science and technology, environment, energy.

These accomplishments do not guarantee peace. But they have served to lessen the rigidities of the past and offer hope for a better era. Despite fluctuations, a trend has been established; the character of international politics has been markedly changed.

It is too early to judge conclusively whether this change should be ascribed to tactical considerations. But in a sense, that is immaterial. For whether the change is temporary and tactical, or lasting and basic, our task is essentially the same: to transform that change into a permanent condition devoted to the purpose of secure peace and mankind's aspiration for a better life. A tactical change sufficiently prolonged becomes a lasting transformation.

But the whole process can be jeopardized if it is taken for granted. As the Cold War recedes in memory, détente can come to seem so natural that it appears safe to levy progressively greater demands on it. The temptation to combine détente with increasing pressure on the Soviet Union will grow. Such an attitude would be disastrous. We would not accept it from Moscow; Moscow will not accept it from us. We will finally wind up again with the Cold War and fail to achieve either peace or any humane goal.

To be sure, the process of détente raises serious issues for many people. Let me deal with these in terms of the principles which underlie our policy.

First, if détente is to endure, both sides must benefit.

There is no question that the Soviet Union obtains benefits from détente. On what other grounds would the tough-minded members of the Politburo sustain it? But the essential point surely must be that détente serves American and world interests as well. If these coincide with some Soviet interests, this will only strengthen the durability of the process.

On the global scale, in terms of the conventional measures of power, influence and position, our interests have not suffered—they have generally prospered. In many areas of the world the influence and the respect we enjoy are greater than was the case for many years. It is also true that Soviet influence and presence are felt in many parts of the world. But this is a reality that would exist without détente. The record shows that détente does not deny us the opportunity to react to it and to offset it.

Our bilateral relations with the U.S.S.R. are beginning to proliferate across a broad range of activities in our societies. Many of the projects now underway are in their infancy; we have many safeguards against unequal benefits—in our laws, in the agreements themselves and in plain common sense. Of course, there are instances where the Soviet Union has obtained some particular advantage. But we seek in each agreement or project to provide for benefits that are mutual. We attempt to make sure that there

are trade-offs among the various programs that are implemented. Americans surely are the last who need fear hard bargaining or lack confidence in competition.

Second, building a new relationship with the Soviet Union does not entail any devaluation of traditional Alliance relations.

Our approach to relations with the U.S.S.R. has always been, and will continue to be, rooted in the belief that the cohesion of our alliances, and particularly the Atlantic Alliance, is a precondition to establishing a more constructive relationship with the U.S.S.R.

Crucial, indeed unique, as may be our concern with Soviet power, we do not delude ourselves that we should deal with it alone. When we speak of Europe and Japan as representing centers of power and influence, we describe not merely an observable fact but an indispensable element in the equilibrium needed to keep the world at peace. The cooperation and partnership between us transcend formal agreements: they reflect values and traditions not soon, if ever, to be shared with our adversaries.

Inevitably, a greater sense of drama accompanies our dealings with the Soviet Union because the central issues of war and peace cannot be other than dramatic. It was precisely a recognition of this fact and our concern that Alliance relations not be taken for granted that led to the American initiative in April of 1973 to put new emphasis on our traditional associations. We sought political acts of will which would transcend the technical issues at hand, symbolize our enduring goals and thus enhance our fundamental bonds. Much has been accomplished. The complications attendant to adapting U.S.-European relations should not be confused with their basic character. We were tested in difficult conditions that do not affect our central purposes. Today relations with Europe and Japan are strong and improving. We have made progress in developing common positions on security, détente and energy. The experience of the past year has demonstrated that there is no contradiction between vigorous, organic alliance relations and a more positive relationship with adversaries; indeed they are mutually reinforcing.

Third, the emergence of more normal relations with the Soviet Union must not undermine our resolve to maintain our national defense.

There is a tendency in democratic societies to relax as dangers seem to recede, there is an inclination to view the maintenance of strength as incompatible with relaxation of tensions, rather than its precondition. But this is primarily a question of leadership. We shall attempt to be vigilant to the dangers facing America. This Administration will not be misled—or mislead—on issues of national defense. At the same time we do not accept the proposition that we need crises to sustain our defense. A society that needs artificial crises to do what is needed for survival will soon find itself in mortal danger.

Fourth, we must know what can and cannot be achieved in changing human conditions in the East.

The question of dealing with Communist governments has troubled the American people and the Congress since 1917. There has always been a fear that by working with a government whose internal policies differ so sharply with our own, we are in some manner condoning these policies or encouraging their continuation. Some argue that until there is a genuine "liberalization"—or signs of serious progress in this direction—all elements of conciliation in Soviet policy must be regarded as temporary and tactical. In that view, demands for internal changes must be the precondition for the pursuit of a relaxation of tensions with the Soviet Union.

Our view is different. We shall insist on responsible international behavior by the Soviet Union and use it as the primary index of our relationship. Beyond this we will use our influence to the maximum to alleviate suffering and to respond to humane appeals. We know what we stand for, and we shall leave no doubt about it.

Both as a government and as a people we have made the attitude of the American people clear on countless occasions, in ways that have produced results. I believe that both the Executive and the Congress, each playing its proper role, have been effective. With respect to the specific issue of Jewish emigration:

The education exit tax of 1971 is no longer being collected. We have been assured that it will not be reapplied.

Hardship cases submitted to the Soviet Government have been given increased attention, and remedies have been forthcoming in many well-known instances.

The volume of Jewish emigration has increased from a trickle to tens of thousands.

And we are now moving toward an understanding that should significantly diminish the obstacles to emigration and ease the hardship of prospective emigrants.

We have accomplished much. But we cannot demand that the Soviet Union, in effect, suddenly reverse five decades of Soviet, and centuries of Russian, history.

Such an attempt would be futile and at the same time hazard all that has already been achieved. Changes in Soviet society have already occurred, and more will come. But they are most likely to develop through an evolution that can best go forward in an environment of decreasing international tensions. A renewal of the Cold War will hardly encourage the Soviet Union to change its emigration policies or adopt a more benevolent attitude towards dissent.

V. AGENDA FOR THE FUTURE

Détente is a process, not a permanent achievement. The agenda is full and continuing. Obviously, the main concern must be to reduce the sources of potential conflict. This requires efforts in several interrelated areas:

The military competition in all its aspects must be subject to increasingly firm restraints by both sides.

Political competition, especially in moments of crisis, must be guided by the principles of restraint set forth in the documents described earlier. Crises there will be, but the United States and the Soviet Union have a special obligation deriving from the unimaginable military power that they wield and represent. Exploitation of crisis situations for unilateral gain is not acceptable.

Restraint in crises must be augmented by cooperation in removing the causes of crises. There have been too many instances, notably in the Middle East, which demonstrate that policies of unilateral advantage sooner or later run out of control and lead to the brink of war, if not beyond.

The process of negotiations and consultation must be continuous and intense. But no agreement between the nuclear superpowers can be durable if made over the heads of other nations which have a stake in the outcome. We should not seek to impose peace; we can, however, see that our own actions and conduct are conducive to peace.

In the coming months we shall strive:

to complete the negotiations for comprehensive and equitable limitations on strategic arms until at least 1985;

to complete the multilateral negotiations on mutual force reductions in Central Europe, so that security will be enhanced for all the countries of Europe;

to conclude the Conference of European Security and Cooperation in a manner that promotes both security and human aspirations;

to continue the efforts to limit the spread of nuclear weapons to additional countries with-

out depriving those countries of the peaceful benefits of atomic energy;

to complete ratification of the recently negotiated treaty banning underground nuclear testing by the U.S. and U.S.S.R. above a certain threshold;

to begin negotiations on the recently agreed effort to overcome the possible dangers of environmental modification techniques for military purposes;

to resolve the long-standing attempts to cope with the dangers of chemical weaponry.

We must never forget that the process of détente depends ultimately on habits and modes of conduct that extend beyond the letters of agreements to the spirit of relations as a whole. This is why the whole process must be carefully nurtured.

In cataloging the desirable, we must take care not to jeopardize what is attainable. We must consider what alternative policies are available, and what their consequences would be. And, the implications of alternatives must be examined, not just in terms of a single issue, but for how they might affect the entire range of Soviet-American relations and the prospects for world peace.

We must assess not only individual challenges to détente, but also their cumulative impact:

If we justify each agreement with Moscow only when we can show unilateral gain;

If we strive for an elusive strategic "superiority";

If we systematically block benefits to the Soviet Union;

If we try to transform the Soviet system by pressure;

If, in short, we look for final results before we agree to any results, then we would be reviving the doctrines of liberation and massive retaliation of the 1950s. And we would do so at a time when Soviet physical power and influence on the world are greater than a quarter century ago when those policies were devised and failed. The futility of such a course is as certain as its danger.

Let there be no question, however, that Soviet actions could destroy détente, as well.

If the Soviet Union uses détente to strengthen its military capacity in all fields:

If in crises it acts to sharpen tension;

If it does not contribute to progress towards stability;

If it seeks to undermine our alliances;

If it is deaf to the urgent needs of the least developed and the emerging issues of interdependence, then it in turn tempts a return to the tensions and conflicts we have made such efforts to overcome. The policy of confrontation has worked for neither of the superpowers.

We have insisted toward the Soviet Union that we cannot have the atmosphere of détente without the substance. It is equally clear that the substance of détente will disappear in an atmosphere of suspicion and hostility.

We have profound differences with the Soviet Union—in our values, our methods, our vision of the future. But it is these very differences which compel any responsible administration to make a major effort to create a more constructive relationship.

We face an opportunity that was not possible 25 years ago, or even a decade ago. If that opportunity is lost, its moment will not quickly come again. Indeed, it may not come at all. As President Kennedy in 1963 pointed out: "For in the final analysis our most basic common link is that we all inhabit this small planet. We all breathe the same air. We all cherish our children's future, and we are all mortal."

[The Case against Détente]

George Meany

I am president of the AFL-CIO, and I am very happy to have this opportunity to present to this committee my views and the views of the AFL-CIO on the subject of détente.

I suspect, Mr. Chairman, that you are not altogether unfamiliar with my views on this subject. They have been reported in the press, sometimes quite colorfully. And sometimes quite accurately. Let me read to you from an editorial in a little newspaper called the Torrington, Connecticut *Register,* under date of May 24, 1973—and I quote:

"Once upon a time," according to this Connecticut paper, "organized labor in this country was in the vanguard of the liberal movement in foreign policy as well as domestic. But not any

From U.S. Cong., Senate, *Détente,* Hearings before the Committee on Foreign Relations, 93d Cong., 2d Sess., 1974, pp. 371–86.

longer. Today its liberalism stops abruptly at the water's edge. On issues involving normalization of relations with the Communist world, the AFL-CIO as represented by aging George Meany, often makes the U.S. Chamber of Commerce sound like a cabal of wild-eyed Bolsheviks."

Well, aging or not, I have no desire to undertake a defense of the Chamber of Commerce from the charge of wild-eyed Bolshevism. I might suggest, however, that what you see in their eyes isn't the Red flag. It's dollar signs.

WHAT HAS BECOME OF THE WORD "LIBERALISM"?

But more to the point. I cannot help but wonder what has become of the word "liberalism." I always thought that liberalism had to do with the defense of freedom—and that the defense of freedom did not stop at the water's edge.

Now, I don't know how many liberals would accept the clear implication of this editorial that liberalism is to be defined as a softer or friendlier attitude toward totalitarian powers, whereas conservatism means a harder or more hostile attitude toward totalitarian powers.

I've always felt that this was a slanderous and silly notion of "liberalism"—a notion to which, I must admit, some liberals have contributed to their own abundant confusion.

Nonetheless, I don't see any necessary connection between a liberal commitment to social and economic justice at home and a policy of appeasement of Communist aggression abroad.

WE LIVE IN STRANGE TIMES

We live in strange times. We live in a time when a man [Richard Nixon] whose whole political career was built on rabid anticommunism can become President and overnight be transformed into the chief advocate of unilateral concessions to the Soviet Union.

We live in a time when the President of Pepsi-Cola is transported into ecstasy by Leonid Brezhnev, about whom he says he was tremendously impressed.

"By the candor and sincerity of this man and by his clear commitment to pursue not only peace, but also...the enrichment of life in his country."

This is Don Kendall speaking. He's the man whose company fills our airwaves with jingles about "feeling free."

I am sure you have all heard the Pepsi jingle which winds up with these lines: "Join the Pepsi people, feeling free, feeling free. All across the Nation, it's the Pepsi generation. Here today. Here to stay. Feeling free."

What wonderful background music this would make to Soviet bulldozers breaking up art shows.

FIRST PRINCIPLES OF THE LABOR MOVEMENT

So, in this topsy-turvy world, Mr. Chairman, we think we need to regain our bearings. We in the labor movement are not guided or influenced by the label-peddlers or by the demagogs who see a "cold warrior" under every bed. We are guided, rather, by the first principles of the labor movement. They were put very well by Sam Gompers, who said:

> I do not value the labor movement only for its ability to give higher wages, better clothes and better homes. Its ultimate goal is to be found in the progressively evolving life possibilities for those who work and in its devotion to advancing the basic idea of freedom for all people everywhere.

That's where we stand, Mr. Chairman—for "the basic idea of freedom for all people everywhere." And everywhere means everywhere, as far as American labor is concerned—from Little Rock to Moscow.

So, in appearing before this committee, the AFL-CIO is not departing from the best traditions of the labor movement, but rather continuing a long tradition of involvement and concern—a tradition of caring about working people everywhere, about the cause of freedom everywhere.

WHAT IS DÉTENTE?

And this is the vantage point from which we look at this thing called détente.

What is it?

I think it makes a big difference how we define it. It's not an academic exercise. If we don't know what it is, then we can't really measure or evaluate it. If we don't know what it is, then we don't have a yardstick, no criteria, for determining whether we are making progress in our relations with the Soviet Union or whether we are moving backward. How do we know if détente is working, unless we know what détente is?

And so I began to hunt around for a good definition of détente. And I discovered something interesting. I discovered that this détente has suddenly become very ambiguous. Suddenly this great idea—this "conceptual breakthrough," to use one of Henry Kissinger's favorite phrases—is like gossamer. You can't grab hold of it.

I wondered how we could have gotten so excited about something that wasn't much of anything anyway.

The truth is, of course, a little different. What has happened is that, as public disillusionment with détente mounts, its proponents are retreating into a rhetoric of dampened expectations, of fuzzy ambiguity. You might call it a revolution of falling expectations.

At least two members of this committee have, in my judgement, contributed to this process of obfuscation through excessive refinement. Here, for example, is Senator Church's idea of détente—and I quote:

> In long-term perspective, a détente may carry promise, or at least the hope, of future friendship, but in present fact, it represents no more than the imposition of restraints on an otherwise costly and dangerous rivalry.

In other words, détente is the "imposition of restraints"—no more. Therefore, as Senator Church goes on to say:

> There is no use asking, for instance, whether the Soviet Union has acted as a partner for peace in the Middle East. Clearly she has not, but that was not to be expected, because we and the Russians are not friends; we are rivals. The right question from the standpoint of détente is whether the rivalry has been restrained by an awareness of the danger of confrontation.

The answer to that, the Senator says, is yes. Which goes to prove, I suppose, that if you phrase the question properly you get the answer you want. Détente is working because we didn't go to war with the Russians over the Middle East.

A similar view has been expressed by the chairman of this committee. He has said—and I quote:

> Détente in its essence is an agreement not to let these differences—that is, the differences between the two superpowers—explode into nuclear war.

And to the Secretary of State, Dr. Kissinger, détente means that—and I quote—"confrontations are kept within bounds that do not threaten civilized life."

Now a common thread runs through all these definitions of détente. They all boil down to the same thing: Détente is the avoidance of nuclear war. Détente is the imposition of restraints so that the two superpowers don't blow each other up.

If this is the meaning of détente, then I have a question. What is the difference between détente and cold war? Isn't cold war also an avoidance of hot war?

If we have decided that this is all détente means—just that both sides restrain themselves—then what's all the fuss about? Why the vitriolic attacks, by Senator Church among others, on the "old-time cold warriors?" Perhaps we owe the cold warriors an apology. Or perhaps, as the distinguished writer Theodore Draper has recently said:

> It is time to stop using cold war as a scare term and détente as a sedative term; in their relation to nuclear war, they are not all that different.

Perhaps, as someone has quipped, détente is the cold war pursued by other means—and sometimes by the same.

WHAT DÉTENTE MEANS TO THE U.S. PUBLIC

Be that as it may, this is not what the man on the street thinks is meant by détente. And I contend that what the man on the street thinks—in other words, what the American people think—is important. And I also contend that this is not how détente was sold to the American people by Mr. Nixon and Mr. Kissinger. They didn't sell it as the cold war pursued by other means.

That's not how détente was sold to the American people when the Soviet wheat deal was being pulled off.

No; the American people thought they were buying something more. To them détente meant not just something negative but something positive—not just restraint but cooperation. Cooperation not only to reduce armaments, but to further world peace. To prevent small wars.

To the American people, détente meant a give and take on both sides, a kind of good-faith bargaining between adversaries.

Where did the people get this idea? Did they suck it out of their thumbs? Was it just "blowin' in the wind?" No. They got it from Mr. Nixon and Mr. Brezhnev, from their summit meeting of May 1972. The two leaders declared that—and I quote:

> The U.S.A. and the U.S.S.R. have a special responsibility...to do everything in their power so that conflicts or situations will not arise which would increase international tensions.

This was no negative prescription for détente. It was positive. Cooperation between the superpowers is implicit. How else, but through cooperation, can they do "everything in their power"—not just to avoid confrontation, but to prevent situations from even arising in the first place that could increase tension?

DÉTENTE'S TWELVE BASIC PRINCIPLES AND MIDDLE EAST SITUATION

There's nothing vague or amorphous about this. It's written out in twelve "Basic Principles of Relations Between the United States and the Union of Soviet Socialist Republics." The text is available from the Department of State. It's a specific code of conduct.

This is détente. Not what Secretary Kissinger says it is. Not what Chairman Fulbright says it is. Not what Senator Church says it is.

And it's not just what Mr. Brezhnev says it means on this or that day of the week.

Détente involves a specific code of conduct agreed to by Mr. Brezhnev and Mr. Nixon on behalf of their two countries.

According to this code, the two powers will "do their utmost to avoid military confrontations"—yes. But it goes further. The two powers will "prevent the development of situations capable of causing a dangerous exacerbation of their relations."

Was not the Yom Kippur war such a situation?

The two powers will "recognize that efforts to obtain unilateral advantage at the expense of the other, directly or indirectly, are inconsistent with these objectives." Did not the Arabs launch precisely such an effort?

The Basic Principles go further still. The two powers would "make no claim for themselves and would not recognize the claims of anyone else to any special rights or advantages in world affairs. They recognize the sovereign equality of all states." Did the Soviet Union really recognize the sovereign equality of Israel?

There is more, but this should be enough to make the point. The point is that Senator Church is exactly wrong about what we were led to expect from détente—and especially in the Middle East.

The point is not whether we and the Russians are friends or rivals. Nor is the point whether the Soviet Union acted as "a partner for peace." That's mere phrase-mongering.

The question is whether the Soviet Union cooperated with us to "prevent the development" of a situation "capable of causing a dangerous exacerbation of our relations."

The question is whether the Soviet Union recognized its "special responsibility...to do everything in their power so that conflicts or situations will not arise which would serve to increase international tensions.''

The question is whether in its Middle East policy the Soviet Union recognized "the sovereign equality of all states.''

DÉTENTE'S BASIC PRINCIPLES AND MIDDLE EAST SITUATION

This is the language, the specific language, agreed to by Mr. Brezhnev in May 1972. This is not a matter of interpretation. These "Basic Principles'' were not just thrown together. The idea for them was proposed by the Soviet Union in the first place. Several months were spent working it out to everybody's satisfaction. They were binding on both parties. The question is: did the Soviet Union live up to these twelve "Basic Principles'' in the Middle East situation?

The answer, obviously, is no. There is no way that question can be answered ambiguously.

The Russians knew about the impending Arab attack on Israel at least 4 days before it happened. They had an obligation, spelled out in the Basic Principles, to warn us in advance. They did not.

Not only did they fail to warn us, not only did they fail to try to limit the scope of the October War, but they actually attempted to widen it.

For one thing, the Soviets transported Moroccan troops into the conflict. As if that were not enough, the Soviet leaders, according to the *Washington Post* of May 2, "immediately issued a decision for a partial alert of the Soviet forces. Seven Soviet military divisions were mobilized and put on the ready to be taken to fight on the Egyptian front. In fact, an advance group actually arrived in Cairo.''

And then, Mr. Chairman, the same Leonid Brezhnev who smiled on Richard Nixon and promised to do everything in his power to prevent conflicts from arising "which

would increase international tensions,'' delivered this message to Boumedienne of Algeria—some 72 hours after the Arab attack on Israel:

> "Today, more than ever, the Arab brotherly solidarity must play its decisive role. Syria and Egypt must not remain alone in their fight against a perfidious enemy.''

This message was dated October 9—3 days after the outbreak of the Yom Kippur war. The very next day—October 10—a similar message went out to all the other Arab countries.

But that's not all, Mr. Chairman. Believe it or not, 24 hours before he wrote his message to Boumedienne—on October 8, to be precise— Mr. Brezhnev gave a speech in Moscow in which he said that he hoped the war would not interfere with the Soviet–United States détente. He went on to call for—and I quote—"a just and stable peace'' and "guaranteed security for all countries and peoples of the area.''

Mr. Chairman, this is the high act of diplomatic hypocrisy as practiced by one of the alltime experts.

Thus did Mr. Brezhnev—this man of "candor and sincerity,'' this man "committed to peace''—seek to push Algeria, Iraq, Jordan, and other Arab countries into a war with Israel which should never have been allowed to develop in the first place according to the "Basic Principles,'' agreed to by Mr. Brezhnev and Mr. Nixon.

The only impact of these "Basic Principles'' on the Middle East situation appears to have been to confuse our own intelligence people.

They were so certain the Russians and their Arab clients would abide by the détente that they concluded it must have been the Israelis who started the war.

That kind of détente we don't need. Even now the Russians are arming the Syrians to the teeth. This is how they discharged their so-called "special responsibility.''

DÉTENTE FROM RUSSIAN PERSPECTIVE

Clearly, something is wrong here. I think most Americans have a pretty good understanding of what our side means by détente, what we want out of it. But do we understand what the Russians want?

I think we need to look at détente from their perspective. They mean something very different—and that is the source of our problem.

In a sense, détente is not really new. Lenin, in the days of N.E.P.—the so-called New Economic Policy—sought a kind of détente with the West as a way of attracting desperately needed capital investment into his war-torn country. In 1921 he wrote these words, which echo down the decades, with an eerie prophetic quality:

> As a result of my own personal observations during the years of my emigration, I must say that the so-called cultural strata of Western Europe and America are not capable of understanding the contemporary state of affairs nor the actual alignment of forces; we must regard these strata as deaf mutes and act with respect to them accordingly.... The capitalists of the entire world, and their governments, in the rush of conquering Soviet markets, will close their eyes to the realities, and will thus become blind deaf mutes. They will open credits which will serve as a support for the Communist Party in their countries and will provide us with essential materials and technology thus restoring our military industries, essential for our future victorious attacks on our suppliers. Speaking otherwise, they will be working to prepare their own suicides.

This quote from Lenin hardly needs comment.

If the objective of détente, from our point of view, is a relaxation of international tension, a reduction of conflict, we have a right to ask: Do the Russians share that view or are they interested in something else?

In this connection, Mr. Chairman, I was very interested to read—as I am sure you were too— the editorial in last Thursday's *New York Times,* September 26 [1974]. The *Times,* which has been closer to your views than to mine on the subject of détente, says—and I quote:

> The chief reservation about the policy of détente as conceived by Mr. Kissinger under two Presidents now, is that this country may find itself settling for minimal tangible benefit for itself in pursuit of a desirable abstraction, while the Soviet leadership successfully extracts real concessions in return for empty lip service.

That's putting it mildly. I would use different language. For the point is, Mr. Chairman, that it is significant when a publication like *The New York Times* begins to have the kind of reservations about this détente that we in the AFL-CIO have been expressing for some time.

All you have to do, Mr. Chairman, is read what the Russian leaders say.

Mr. Nixon did not end the cold war. Before Mr. Nixon became President, the Soviet Union had decided it was to its advantage to relax the cold war. Here's what Mr. Brezhnev told a conference of select Communist representatives at Karlovy Vary on April 24, 1967—before Mr. Nixon became President, and before Henry Kissinger became a household name, and I am quoting now from Mr. Brezhnev:

> Experience teaches, in particular, that the "cold war" and the confrontation of military blocs, the atmosphere of military threats, seriously hampers the activity of revolutionary democratic forces. In conditions of international tension in bourgeois countries the reactionary elements become active, the military raise their heads, antidemocratic tendencies and anticommunism are strengthened.
>
> And, conversely, the past few years have shown quite clearly that, in conditions of slackened international tension, the pointer of the political barometer moves left. Certain changes in relations between Communists and social democrats in certain countries, a noticeable falling off in anti-Communist hysteria, and the increase in the influence of West European Communist parties is most directly correlated with the reduction in tension which has taken place in Europe.

What does all this mean? What Comrade Brezhnev is saying is that détente should not be construed as signifying a change in Soviet international objectives. In fact, détente is simply a new tactic, a new means toward the old end—the worldwide advance and ultimate victory of Communism.

What he is saying is that the cold war should be ended, not in the interest of peace, but because it hampers the "activity of the revolutionary democratic forces"—that's the way they describe themselves even though they are neither revolutionary or democratic, but static and totalitarian. And it activates the "reactionary elements" in the "bourgeois countries"—that's us. We're No. 1 bourgeois country.

SOVIET VIEW OF DÉTENTE

In other words, the fundamental conflict between our two social systems will not be abated. In fact, in some ways it will be intensified. The influence of the Communist parties in Europe will grow, and they will make new overtures to the social-democratic forces in certain countries.

Certainly, in respect to the European situation, there is considerable evidence that the Communist détente strategy has enjoyed some success.

But Brezhnev's 1967 speech is not the only indication we get of the Soviet's view of détente. Three years later, and 2 years after Mr. Nixon entered the White House, Mr. Brezhnev boasted—and I quote:

> The Soviet Union is on the offensive and the West on the defensive; the impact of our ideology is tremendous; it is mounting with every day, undermining the mainstay of the non-Soviet system from within.

How do you like that? "Undermining the non-Soviet system from within." And I thought the Russians were against any interference in the "internal affairs of other countries." I guess

that's only when it comes to the right of emigration for Soviet Jews.

But there's more. Two years later, in June 1972, at a dinner honoring Fidel Castro, Brezhnev had these words of inspiration—and I quote:

> We are aware that success in this important matter—referring to the struggle for peaceful coexistence—in no way implies the possibility of relaxing the ideological struggle. On the contrary, we must be prepared for this struggle to be intensified and becoming an ever sharper form of the confrontation between the systems.

So, Mr. Chairman, for the Communists, détente means an intensification of the ideological conflict—a sharper confrontation between the systems.

WHAT SOVIET VIEW OF DÉTENTE MEANS IN PRACTICE

What does this mean in practice? In practice it means that the Soviet Union can maintain and accelerate its campaign of propaganda against the United States—but we cannot criticize the Russians.

Mr. Nixon and Mr. Kissinger could not even bring themselves to a manly defense of Alexandr Solzhenitsyn because that would be "interfering in the internal affairs of another country" and that's a no-no. That would make the Russians very much displeased.

It is quite all right, however, for the Russians to go full steam ahead with their continuing propaganda onslaughts against the United States.

Compare this self-confident Russian propaganda drive with the remarks of our Secretary of State in response to the appeal of Andre Sakharov. The best Mr. Kissinger could muster was—and I quote:

> Painful as I find the Sakharov document, emotionally connected though I find myself to him, I feel nevertheless that we must proceed on the

course on which we are. And I continue to recommend most-favored-nation status for the Soviet Union.

Mr. Chairman, if you will forgive me, I find that a less than vigorous and forceful defense of human rights.

And if ever we needed a forceful reminder of the state of human rights in the Soviet Union, it was sadly provided by those Russian secret policemen who disguised themselves as workers and dispersed an open-air art show in the suburbs of Moscow.

What kind of society is it that has to turn bulldozers loose on paintings?

But instead of a national leadership that expresses the outrage of a free people at such incidents, we seem saddled with a leadership eager to see signs of convergence and parallelism between our basically democratic society and Soviet totalitarianism.

How else can one explain Dr. Kissinger's craven comparison of our so-called military-industrial complex and the Soviet war machine?

HOW SOVIET UNION SEES DÉTENTE

To return to the Soviet view of détente, I was interested to read the following analysis by Arnaud de Borchgrave, the distinguished senior editor of *Newsweek,* in the July 2, 1973, issue of that magazine. He writes—and I quote:

> Only a few experts know or care that Soviet Party Chief Leonid Brezhnev won his arguments for a "new look" foreign policy by convincing his colleagues that it would be the most effective way to break up NATO and neutralize Western Europe. While Moscow has made an important shift in tactics, policy planners say the goals the Kremlin has pursued since the early 1950s are unchanged. For practical purposes, Moscow has achieved two of its four main geopolitical objectives: conventional military superiority in Europe over the U.S. and its allies, and recognition of Moscow's hold on Eastern Europe. Next on the Kremlin's hit parade is the withdrawal of U.S.

> forces from Europe and the collapse of NATO. This, in the Kremlin scenario, is to come about as a result of internal pressures in the United States and growing European doubts about American reliability.

In other words, Mr. Chairman, while détente has produced a silly euphoria in the West, it is viewed with cold calculation in the Soviet Union. While détente has made anti-communism unfashionable in the West—and you know, of course, that anti-communism is out of style with the best people—in the East, détente means an intensification of ideological struggle.

Here's how the Soviet Union sees détente:

Détente is based on U.S. weakness.
Détente means intensification of ideological warfare.
Détente means an undermining of NATO.
Détente means ultimate Soviet military superiority over the West.
Détente means recognition by the West of the Soviet Union's ownership of Eastern Europe.
Détente means withdrawal of American forces from Europe.

That's what détente really means to the Soviet Union.

DÉTENTE AND U.S. BIG BUSINESS

What does it mean to us?

Well, to American big business, it means beautiful visions of new profits and expanded markets—the old quest for the almighty dollar now transplanted to the land of the commissars.

Let me quote again from the *Times* editorial of last Thursday [September 26, 1984]:

> While the Soviets envisage their many transactions in the broad context of political and economic needs, the American side has too often been content to let private entrepreneurs make their own deals on a purely commercial basis. If

the Government finally moves in to consider these transactions from a national interest viewpoint, it may be too late to matter.

Now, I have nothing against a man making an honest buck. But what's happening here is that some American businessmen are developing a vested interest in downplaying the repressive and inhuman character of the Soviet regime—or in selling the idea that this has nothing to do with us.

Is it possible that Adolf Hitler was born 50 years too soon?

They make sickening speeches about how wrong it would be for us to use our economic superiority as a weapon to force the regime to grant concessions to their own people. After all, they say, we wouldn't want the Russians to interfere in our internal affairs.

Mr. Chairman, I think there is something fundamentally wrong with businessmen who have gotten rich off this country—and its workers—comparing our pressures for greater freedom in the Soviet Union with Soviet intervention against human rights in other countries.

Not only would some of our businessmen like to desensitize American public opinion to Soviet abrogations of human rights, but they also feel compelled to foster the myth that trade is the road to peace.

Mr. Chairman, the idea sounds nice, very nice. It's very good for public relations—you know, "Businessmen for Peace. Businessmen for Trade." What's good for Pepsi-Cola, Chase Manhattan, or General Motors is not only good for America, it's good for the Soviet Union. And it's also good for the whole world.

There's one trouble with this idea. It's not true. There's not one shred of historical evidence to support it, and a considerable amount to support the opposite conclusion. Indeed, the argument could be made that trade and investment generate friction and conflict—even among friends.

After all, Germany was Russia's biggest trading partner just before the break in their relations.

Secretary Kissinger, on March 7 of this year [1974], admitted in testimony before the Senate Finance Committee, and I quote:

> ...if you remember, prior to World War I, there was essentially free trade in Europe, but nevertheless, this did not prevent the outbreak of a cataclysmic war.

Friction and conflict have arisen between trading partners with the same economic and social systems. Why do we assume this will not happen between countries with diametrically opposed economic and social systems?

Have our businessmen given any serious thought to the problems of trade and investment in a country whose economy is run by the state, which can—and will—make economic decisions on a political basis, not just on a basis of profits?

How do our businessmen, who sing the praises of free enterprise at home, conduct themselves in relation to a society from which economic competition has been officially eliminated?

How do our business friends intend to conduct themselves in relation to a work force that is not represented by unions, that does not enjoy the blessings of collective bargaining, that does not have the right to strike—that is, in fact, enslaved?

I don't know whether our business friends have thought about these questions. I don't know whether these "wild-eyed Bolsheviks" at the U.S. Chamber of Commerce have thought much about these questions. Perhaps they are the blind deaf mutes Lenin took them for.

MFN AND SOVIET EMIGRATION POLICIES

But we have thought about it, Mr. Chairman. The labor movement has thought about it. And we don't want any part of it. We're not interested in seeing cheap goods made by Soviet slave labor pour into this country. We're not interested in seeing American workers displaced by slave labor.

And that's why we're against granting the Soviet Union most-favored-nation treatment. It is obviously not one of our most-favored nations.

Yet, it is being proposed today that we grant the Soviet Union MFN status in exchange for their agreeing to liberalize their emigration policies. In other words, we will bribe the Soviet Union to do what it is already obligated to do under international law.

You see, there's something called the International Covenant on Civil and Political Rights. Moscow signed the covenant in March of 1968. Article 12 of that covenant says—and I quote—"Everyone should be free to leave any country, including his own."

"Everyone"—"any country." Everyone. Any country. That's pretty clear language, Mr. Chairman. Nothing ambiguous about it.

But the Russians decided to violate it. And what's the consequence? We give them MFN. Rewarding deception—and I can say there, Mr. Chairman, that's a hell of a way to run a foreign policy.

SYMBOLIC AND POLITICAL IMPORTANCE OF MFN

It has been said—in fact, by the Secretary of State, in this room—that MFN isn't that important anyway. Soviet imports into the United States don't, and won't, amount to very much anyway. The MFN is only a symbolic issue.

Well, there's some truth in that—in the sense that the Russians' main interest is not in exporting their goods to the United States, but rather in receiving our credits and technology. I will have more to say about that in a moment. I do think, however, that it would be wrong for us to completely dismiss the symbolic and political importance of most-favored-nation for the Russians.

ECONOMIC AND POLITICAL BENEFITS OF MFN

I think we will be under growing pressure to take whatever imports the Russians decide to send us in order to give them the means for paying for the credits we give them to buy our exports.

You may be interested to know that the latest United States–Soviet trade figures show that in the first half of this year, U.S. exports were down over 54 percent from the first half of last year, while imports from the Soviet Union rose by 125 percent.

There is no economic benefit for the United States in this deal. All the economic benefits flow to the Soviet Union. The most we can hope for are political benefits—but these are very, very doubtful. Let me quote to you from a Library of Congress study on United States–Soviet commercial relations: The Interplay of Economics, Technology Transfer and Diplomacy:

> The political benefits to the United States must by their nature be uncertain of fulfillment, especially in the short run. On the other hand, the economic benefits to the Soviet Union from improved commercial relations may be certain and significant. Thus, the risk of unfulfilled expectations appears greater for the United States than for the Soviet Union. More specifically, increased technology transfers to the Soviet Union may show only long-term benefits to the United States in the diplomatic and political area.

Mr. Chairman, these diplomatic and political benefits to us must be very long-term indeed—because at this time, I don't see any sign of them whatever.

PROVIDING SOVIET UNION WITH WESTERN TECHNOLOGY QUESTIONED

What I see is a one-way street in which the Soviet Union maintains all of its basic political objectives which are fundamentally antagonistic to the West, while it acquires from the West the technology it needs to help overcome the disastrous economic consequences of totalitarian planning.

And, make no mistake about it, this is the name of the game. Let me quote again from *The New York Times* editorial:

> Easing of nuclear tensions, formal recognition of the European status quo—these are desired goals of Soviet foreign policy; but the desperate driving impulse of detente is access to Western advanced technology.

Any student of Soviet society will tell you how desperately the Soviets need our technological know-how. As late as 1971—3 years ago—the productivity of Soviet labor was only about 40 percent of the American level.

The Soviet Union has 50 million more people than we do—yet its consumers can get only about one-third the goods and services available to the American people.

The distortions and imbalances in the Soviet economy are not due simply to backwardness, to the legacies of czarism. They are the direct product of Soviet concentration on military hardware, which is the inevitable companion to an expansionist imperialist foreign policy.

This Soviet concentration on military and space hardware, to the neglect of the Russian people's need for food and consumer goods, is possible only because of the totalitarian political structures that snuff out the will of the people.

There is thus a direct connection between the brutal suppression of democracy in the Soviet Union, the Soviet crisis in agricultural and consumer production, and the foreign policies of the Soviet Union. There is no way you can separate all of these things and say, "Their internal affairs are none of our business."

The decision to provide the Soviet Union with Western technology is a decision to bail out the Russian leaders. It is a decision to save them the hard choice between production for war and production for people.

It is, indeed—if I may say so, Mr. Chairman—a decision to give them what we were told a couple of years ago we could not have—guns and butter.

In this sense, the issue here cannot be narrowed down to whether this or that piece of technology has a military potential. Most modern technology has a military potential. And to the extent that this transfer of Western technology enables the Soviet regime to escape the consequences of its dictatorially imposed decisions upon its own people, we help to rescue a regime which has shown in situation after situation that it is not healthy for children and other living things.

The volume of this one-way flow of American goodies is already alarming. Let's leave aside for the moment our huge food shipments to the Soviet Union since May of 1972—shipments which have cost the American housewife and taxpayer mightily.

EXPORT-IMPORT BANK OPERATIONS

Let's look at the operations of the Export-Import Bank. Here's an institution that is backed by taxpayer money—not private enterprise. It was originally set up to encourage American exports by making loans available to foreign buyers. In this way, it was supposed to promote American sales and jobs.

But now it is playing the game of the multinational corporations. It is subsidizing overseas production that will hurt American exports and employers. And one of the beneficiaries of this largesse is the Soviet Union.

In the past year and a half, the Eximbank lent the Russians almost $469 million—most of it at 6 percent and a small portion at 7 percent.

What American worker can get a loan at 6 or 7 percent? You can't get a mortgage for under 10 unless you're lucky.

This isn't trade. This is an economic aid program. This is a welfare program for the benefit of the Soviet leaders.

It's not just the amounts that concern me—although I don't know why these sums are leaving our country when we have such tight money problems here. What really concerns me is how the money is being used.

The Eximbank put up $180 million of American money at a low interest rate to develop nitrogen fertilizer production in the Soviet Union. What will the Russians do with this fertilizer? Export it back to the United States? Or will they sell it—at a profit—to some of the overdeveloped distressed nations of Europe? Of course, they can always withhold it, as the Arabs did their oil.

But why don't we invest in our own fertilizer production here? Because we have to give the Russians a way to pay back credits. Why do we give them credits in the first place? So they can acquire our technological know-how. Why do we want them to acquire our technological know-how? So we can have détente—a more peaceful world. Then why did the Russians encourage Arab aggression in the Middle East—not to mention Arab oil blackmail? Because they are not yet our "partners in peace." We evidently have to give much more.

This is a circular argument, Mr. Chairman, and it leads nowhere—except to growing Soviet advantages.

Look at another Eximbank loan—$153,950,000 for the Kama River Truck project—again most of it at 6 percent. This is the largest truck production facility in the world. And this was a project approved by our Government despite the fact that it had a military potential acknowledged by our own Department of Commerce.

This fact, Mr. Chairman, is documented in an important new book which I commend to your attention. It is entitled "Western Technology and Soviet Economic Development, 1945 to 1965," by Anthony C. Sutton of Stanford University. This book also documents the thesis that Western technology is "the most important factor in Soviet economic development."

PAST U.S. ASSISTANCE TO AND INVESTMENT IN SOVIET UNION

You may recall that it was an American firm, the McKee Corp., that built the world's biggest iron and steel plant at Magmitogorsk. It was Ford that built the first Soviet automotive plant. It was General Electric that built the famous Dnieper hydroelectric dam.

In fact, some years ago, Stalin himself told the American industrialist Eric Johnson that—and I quote—"about two-thirds of all the large industrial enterprises in the U.S.S.R. have been built with U.S. materials or technical assistance."

So, Mr. Chairman, American economic aid to the Soviet Union goes way back. American capital investment in the Soviet Union goes way back. And so does technological assistance....

Out of this history, the question inevitably arises: What good did it do? Did it bring us closer to peace? What it brought us was something we called "the cold war." Or was it really détente pursued by other means?

But it appears our big corporate executives don't read history. They're cutting their own private deals with the Soviets—giving them computer technology, integrated circuits, telecommunications, photo-optical equipment, sophisticated machine tools, oscilloscopes, aircraft parts, ship and submarine quieting techniques—all that sort of thing and at bargain rate credits that are subsidized by the American taxpayers. That's the same taxpayer, incidentally, who subsidized the research and development costs of this technology in the first place.

LIMIT TO AVERAGE U.S. CITIZEN'S PATIENCE SUGGESTED

Mr. Chairman, let me suggest that there is a limit to the patience of the average American citizen. He's no dope. He knows he's being ripped off from every angle. This is certainly true of the average worker.

He has seen his standard of living decline in the last couple of years.

He has seen prices go through the roof, while his wages increase only modestly.

He sees that a big part of the inflation is due to spiraling food costs—and he knows the Soviet wheat deal had a lot to do with that.

He sees his fuel bills rising geometrically—and he knows that Soviet-Arab oil blackmail had a lot to do with that.

He sees corporate profits going up astronomically, especially oil profits—while he is less and less able to make ends meet.

He sees American capital flowing out of this country into the Soviet Union at 6 and 7 percent—while his bank refuses to give him a mortgage.

He listens to Mr. Kendall sing the praises of the Soviet dictator, and he sees Mr. Kissinger and Mr. Brezhnev blowing kisses at each other—and he thinks of the dead in Vietnam and the sacrifices of the brave Israelis.

Mr. Chairman, how much longer do you think this American is going to tolerate this phony détente?

How much longer do you think he's going to put up with the politicians who put this con game over on us? How much longer before this thing blows up in the faces of its authors—those who gave us Watergate, inflation, recession, and countless other calamaties?

Not much longer, in my opinion.

But that does not mean we are for nuclear war. It does not mean we are for confrontation. It does not mean that we are against negotiation. It does not mean that we are against détente.

A GENUINE DÉTENTE SUPPORTED

We are for a real détente. We're for a genuine détente.

We are for a détente in which the Soviet Union stops its ideological warfare against the West. Only then can we realistically anticipate a relaxation of international tensions.

We are for a détente in which the Soviet Union shows an honest willingness to reverse the arms buildup and to abandon its goal of military superiority in the SALT II negotiations.

We are for a détente in which the flow of Western aid to East is matched by a free flow of people and ideas in Eastern Europe and the Soviet Union.

We are for a détente in which the Soviet Union will stop sabotaging the efforts to build peace in the Middle East.

We are for a détente in which the Soviet Union will stop arming and encouraging guerrilla movements and other efforts of subversion.

Such a détente—a real détente—would be welcomed by the American labor movement, by the American people as a whole, and by all the peoples of the world.

But that is not what we have today. We are not building lasting structures of peace. We are building castles of sand on the watery foundations of petty greed, wishful thinking, irresponsibility, self-indulgence, and plain old ignorance.

The inability to face the world as it is, and to understand clearly the nature of freedom's enemies everywhere, is really the greatest threat to peace today. That threat is nowhere more clearly posed than in the delusion we call détente.

QUESTIONS FOR DISCUSSION

1 Did the Soviets and the Americans mean the same thing in the 1970s when they referred to détente?
2 Did détente make war between the superpowers less likely?
3 Why did détente collapse?
4 Should détente be revived?
5 What assumptions about the causes of war are made in Kissinger's description of détente?

SUGGESTED READINGS

Booth, Ken, and Phil Williams. "Fact and Fiction in U.S. Foreign Policy: Reagan's Myths about Détente," *World Policy Journal,* **2** (Summer 1985), pp. 501–532.

Cox, Michael. "From Détente to the 'New Cold War': The Crisis of the Cold War System," *Millennium: Journal of International Studies* (London), **13** (Winter 1984), pp. 265–291.

Gaddis, John Lewis. "The Rise, Fall and Future of Détente," *Foreign Affairs,* **62** (Winter 1983–84), pp. 354–377.

Garthoff, Raymond L. *Détente and Confrontation: American-Soviet Relations from Nixon to Reagan.* Washington, D.C.: Brookings Institution, 1985.

Gelman, Harry. "Rise and Fall of Détente," *Problems of Communism,* **34** (Mar.–Apr. 1985), pp. 51–72.

Hulett, Louisa Sue. *Decade of Détente: Shifting Definitions and Denouement.* Washington, D.C.: University Press of America, 1982.

Kissinger, Henry. *White House Years.* Boston: Little, Brown, 1979.

———. *Years of Upheaval.* Boston: Little, Brown, 1982.

Litwak, Robert S. *Détente and the Nixon Doctrine: American Foreign Policy and the Pursuit of Stability, 1969–76.* New York: Cambridge Univ. Press, 1984.

Stevenson, Richard W. *The Rise and Fall of Détente.* Urbana, Ill.: Univ. of Illinois Press, 1985.

U.S. Cong., House of Representatives. *Détente,* Hearings before the Subcommittee on Europe of the Committee on Foreign Affairs, 93d Cong., 2d Sess., 1974.

U.S. Cong., Senate. *Détente,* Hearings before the Committee on Foreign Relations, 93d Cong., 2d Sess., 1974.

Wallensteen, Peter. "American-Soviet Détente: What Went Wrong?" *Journal of Peace Research,* **22,** no. 1 (1985), pp. 1–8.

Weeks, Albert L. *The Troubled Détente.* New York: New York Univ. Press, 1976.

Williams, Phil. "Détente and U.S. Domestic Politics," *International Affairs* (London), **61** (Summer 1985), pp. 431–447.

6 Was the United States primarily responsible for the Cold War?

YES

D. F. Fleming

[*The Cold War: Origins and Developments*]

NO

Robert J. Maddox

The Rise and Fall of Cold War Revisionism

[The Cold War: Origins and Developments]

D. F. Fleming

Our cold war with the Soviet Union... has been due to two factors, both closely related. Our leaders after World War II were unwilling to accept a Communist state as a great world power and unable to recognize Russia's overwhelming need for firm security in Eastern Europe.

The anti-Communist aversion is basic. The Communist abolition of private profits is the supreme heresy, the unforgivable sin. Its proclamation in Russia in November 1918 led to a desperate civil war, during which all the governing, well-to-do classes were driven into exile, into labor battalions, or killed.

THE WESTERN INTERVENTIONS

The West European democracies did all that their war-weary peoples would permit to help the Russian Whites to defeat the Reds. From 1918 to 1920, they first did their utmost for the government of Admiral Kolchak in Siberia. The British gave him 79 shiploads of supplies and arms for 100,000 men, but his defeat led to one of the most ghastly mass retreats of all time.

In South Russia, about 500,000 Allied troops tried to aid the attempt of General Denikin to take Moscow. Equipment for 250,000 men was sent, along with all kinds of advisers and instructions, but the result was another terrible retreat in which a quarter of a million people died of typhus and exposure.

Then Poland made a major effort to carve out a great empire in Russia, but was defeated and saved only by military aid from the West.

These failures did not prevent the Allies from giving White General Yudenitch's forces equip-ment, including American gasoline, supplied by Herbert Hoover, for a drive up the Baltic coast to Leningrad.

The result was another tragic retreat. Simultaneously, too, the Allies were intervening in north Russia, at first to protect large dumps of supplies which we had laid down there from being captured by the Germans, then later to fight the Reds.

The first motive had also been a factor at Vladivostok in the east, where we had 7,000 troops, along with British, French, and Japanese forces. The Japanese had 70,000.

Though our men only guarded property, the other invading forces were anti-Red, a part of the effort to scotch bolshevism at its birth by invasions from all four sides of the Russian realm.

When it was all over, Russia was devastated throughout her vast expanses. ''Millions of poor civilians had died of abuse, exposure, and famine, which was soon to claim millions more.''

Everything was in a far worse state than at the end of Russia's immense effort in World War I, bad as that was. Hatred and degradation filled the land, and the upper classes were finished.[1]

Worse still, from our standpoint, the great foreign interventions had enabled the Reds to create a big military machine and to forge the first totalitarian regime. Without the compulsions of the Western interventions, the Soviet regime would probably have evolved more mildly.

Furthermore, neither the Soviet leaders or peoples can easily forget the frightful experiences of the time. To them it was a long ordeal of fire and blood, famine and death. To us it was a distant incident, vaguely understood and soon forgotten.

From U.S. Cong., House of Representatives, *The Cold War: Origins and Developments,* Hearings before the Subcommittee on Europe of the Committee on Foreign Affairs, 92d Cong., 1st Sess., 1971, pp. 11–16.

[1]D. F. Fleming, *The Cold War and Its Origins, 1917–1960,* pp. 16–35, especially pp. 30–35.

RUSSIA'S ORDEAL IN WORLD WAR I

Just before the Western interventions, the Russians had suffered the agonies of World War I, as we never did. The Tsarist bureaucracy had mobilized 15 million men, mainly illiterate peasants, for whom there was neither adequate transportation, barracks, or arms, or anything else. Yet, these hordes of men pouring into east Prussia had helped the Western Allies to succeed in the First Battle of the Marne in France in 1914, and by overwhelming the Austrians repeatedly with mass animal power, really, they had contributed to the final Allied victory.

However, by the summer of 1917, this largest of armies had become "an enormous, exhausted, badly clothed, badly fed, embittered mob of people, united by thirst for peace and general disillusionment."[2]

These memories, too, are deep in the Russian soul.

Yet, after seeing communism develop out of World War I, the U.S. Senate defeated the heroic efforts of Woodrow Wilson to create a strong League of Nations to keep the peace, and we retired into political isolation and unrestrained moneymaking, until World War II engulfed us again and brought communism to China.[3]

RUSSIA IN WORLD WAR II

Once more we suffered, but not as the Russians did. Again, they mobilized 10 million men, but this time well equipped for battle. They held the Nazi armies, the mightiest ever assembled, deep in Russia; and after nearly 3 years, drove them back behind Berlin and Vienna, both of which the Russians occupied.

It was a tremendous victory, but gained at abysmal costs: 15 cities, 1,700 towns, and 70,000 villages largely destroyed; 88 million people subjected to invasion, and 25 million deprived of shelter; 6 million buildings destroyed; 70 million head of livestock carried away; 40,000 hospitals, 84,000 schools, 44,000 theaters, and 43,000 libraries looted and destroyed—along with industrial enterprises, highways, bridges, postal, and telegraph stations.

Can we imagine what our country would have been like if all that had happened here?

Also, while all this was happening, the Anglo-Americans, due to British insistence, delayed until June 1944 the opening of a second front in Europe that would ease the pressure on Russia.

To the Russians, this was an eternity of more than 2 years; to us it was justified time to prepare efficiently. In the same period, too, we urgently desired Russia's entry into the war against Japan. She was bearing the main brunt of the war in Europe so well that we thought she could be a big help in Asia, also.

Generals MacArthur and Wedemeyer were strongly for Russia helping us in the Far East, as were the American people; and it was our main objective at the Yalta Conference, in early 1945, where Stalin agreed to be ready to fight Japan in Manchuria 3 months after Victory in Europe Day.

Events in Europe soon fixed this date as August 8, 1945. At that time the Russians were ready in the Far East, but on August 6 we hastily dropped the first A-bomb on Hiroshima, to save lives it was alleged, as 80,000 people died and an equal number were maimed horribly for life.

On August 9, our other A-bomb was used on Nagasaki, with comparable results, and Japan sued for peace the next day, leaving Russian faces red as we announced that the war was over,[4] just as they were ready to come in, according to their promise.

---

[2]*Ibid.*, vol. I, p. 11.

[3]My books about this period are: *The United States and the League of Nations, 1918–1920,* and *The United States and World Organizations, 1920–1933.*

[4]Fleming, *The Cold War and Its Origins, 1917–1960,* pp. 171, 193–98. Truman greeted the news from Hiroshima as "the greatest thing in history." He had "no qualms" about his use of the A-bomb. (p. 304.)

These two wartime threads of military-diplomatic history help to explain Russia's determination to hold East Europe and to do everything possible to delay a German revival.

THE RUSSIANS IN EAST EUROPE

Can any American begin to imagine the human suffering involved in Russia's tremendous World War II ordeal? Yet, this was the third long trauma from foreign invasion in the lifetime of most Russians.

Is it any wonder that Stalin made it clear to Eden in December 1941 that because of these three immense invasions through Eastern Europe "in 35 years," he did not intend to let that region fall into hostile hands again?[5]

Would any Soviet leader in his senses have resolved differently? Nevertheless, when East Europe was occupied by the Russians in 1945, in pursuit of the Germans, most Westerners thought that they should go back home and let the East Europeans have their usual anti-Soviet governments, especially in Poland.

Only a minority understood that the Soviets could trust only Communist governments to secure the region, with Moscow's aid and under its control.

Even Roosevelt may have thought that he could eventually persuade Stalin to let the Poles manage their own affairs, but both FDR and Secretary of State Hull did have a clear understanding of the immense losses and achievements of the Russians in World War II, and of the urgency of remaining friends with them and organizing the world for peace with their cooperation.

At the Moscow Conference in October 1943, Hull found that both Stalin and Molotov assented warmly to his statement that the closest relations and agreement between their two countries were of vast importance.[6]

FRANKLIN D. ROOSEVELT'S PREMONITIONS

After the Teheran Conference, a month later, still in 1943, Roosevelt also felt that its biggest achievement had been to make clear to Stalin that the United States and Britain were not teamed up against Russia. That would be the one thing, he said, that would "upset the applecart" after the war; and on his last Christmas Day, in 1944, he talked reflectively of British ability to get other countries to combine in some sort of bloc against the Soviet Union and said soberly: "It's what we've got to expect."

Again on March 3, 1945, he said that at Yalta many points had been disputed between Stalin and Churchill, but Stalin, said Roosevelt, "agreed to every single suggestion I made," and he added emphatically: "I am convinced that we are going to get along."

On April 12, 1945, just before his death, FDR sent a cable to Churchill about recent disputes with Russia concerning the problems of ending the war, saying that, "We must be firm, however, and our course thus far is correct."[7]

SUDDEN REVERSAL

A year later, on March 5, 1946, President Harry S. Truman sat on a college platform at Fulton, Mo., to applaud a speech by Winston Churchill, which he had already approved.

It portrayed in the most portentous terms the terrible Russian danger which had arisen, the "police governments" of Eastern Europe.

To cope with Russia and communism, Churchill pleaded for an alliance of the English-speaking peoples, with joint use of their naval and air bases all over the world. "At this sad and breathless moment" he saw "an iron curtain" from Stettin to Trieste. Nobody knew, he said, what Soviet Russia and its international Communist organization intended to do in the future, "or what are the limits of any of their expansion and proselytizing tendencies." Be-

[5]*Ibid.*, p. 147.
[6]*The Cold War and Its Origins, 1917–1960*, p. 160.

[7]*Ibid.*, pp. 162, 213, 215.

ware, he warned. Time might be short. "The Dark Ages may return, the Stone Age."[8]

All that Roosevelt had so clearly foreseen and feared had come to pass. Eleven days after his death, Truman had given Molotov a tongue-lashing in the White House, about Poland, using Missouri mule-driver's language, against the advice of his three leading advisers: Stimson, Marshall, and Leahy.[9]

25 YEARS OF COLD WAR

Given our aversion to Soviet and Communist control of East Europe, it was natural that NATO should be organized to protect West Europe, to be followed by the Warsaw Pact Alliance. It was natural that we should create the Marshall Plan, a wonderful achievement. The division of Germany and Berlin's anomalous status was also inherent in the situation.

It was soon assumed that both the terribly wounded Russians and communism were out to take over the world, but it was not inevitable that President Truman should deliver his famous doctrine, on March 12, 1947,...in which he practically forbade all future revolutions, lest they turn Communist, and allied himself and us with all reactionary regimes around the globe.

This was blindness on a gigantic scale. For us "to declare that revolution was finished was to kill the American dream. It was to shut us out of the future at a time when a billion and a half people, nurtured in our revolutionary tradition, were determined to move upward into a better life."[10]

Yet, upon this doctrinal base we erected alliance structures encircling the globe and

[8]*Ibid.*, pp. 348–49.
[9]*Ibid.*, p. 268. Some 3 months earlier, on January 10, 1945, Republican Senator Arthur H. Vandenberg had made a name for himself in a long Senate speech demanding "justice" for Poland, in which he had proposed a treaty with Russia promising to protect her from future invasions if she would let Poland alone. (p. 275.)
[10]Fleming, p. 447.

built an immense military machine to see to it, after China became Communist in 1949, that no other spot on earth did.

South Korea was saved in 1950, at a cost of 2 million dead, but saving South Vietnam has proved to be beyond our power.

There we have struggled for some 15 years, using finally our full air power—save only atomic bombs—to blast and burn and poison everything that may be underneath our bombers and planes. Several hundreds of thousands of helpless people have been killed and some 3 million others driven from their homes into penury in the cities.

We have used every kind of weapon on the ground and some 50,000 of our troops have died, yet the little yellow men in the jungles have defeated our mammoth military machine, and our own people have become outraged by the huge squandering of our resources until they are forcing the end of the sad struggle that has won us condemnation all over the planet and entailed the neglect of our own dangerous social problems until internal disintegration threatens.

This is the penalty for wasting some $200 billions in Vietnam and for spending a total that approaches a trillion dollars on the cold war, plus all the time, attention, and effort involved.

Could anyone possibly conjure up a more tragic and absurd end to the cold war than our adventure in Southeast Asia?

PROGRESS IN RUSSIA AND CHINA

While we have run the cold war deeply into the ground in Vietnamese jungles, Red China, which we thought we were containing over there, has emerged as a vast nation, the world's largest, all of whose people are fed, decently clothed, and housed.

In the same decades, too, the Soviet Union has developed military power virtually equal to our own, and it has given its great union of peoples good education, excellent health care, and full employment, these things for every-body.

CAN WE RECOVER?

The successes of the two mammoth Communist states, which we have been endeavoring to "con-tain," now compel us to engage in long and devoted efforts to save our own failing society; to cope with the immense misery in our huge urban ghettos; to stop the hopeless piling up of our people into the heavens in a few places; to reform our overloaded courts and shocking penal sys-tems; to build hospitals and health care for all; to renovate our sadly neglected schools, including many colleges; to provide better care for our old people; to build really adequate modern mass transportation systems, partly to save us from asphyxiation by the omnipresent automobile; and to save our natural environment from other kinds of pollution.

It may be too late for us to cope with all of these accumulated deficits, and others, but if we are to compete with the two Communist giants we must prove to the world and to ourselves that we too can abolish poverty and provide acceptable lives for all.

To do less is to condemn our way of life to a troubled end. It has wonderful advantages—as I have experienced all my life long—but it must also distribute the essentials for living to every-one.

Fortunately, our Government is now disposed to welcome China into the family of nations and to negotiate a more bearable level of nuclear stalemate with the Soviet Union.

These negotiations, said the Sunday *Times* of London, will be "the most momentous in dip-lomatic history."

So they will be. A reconciliation with China and the Soviet Union, or even a modus vivendi, should give us time to put our own house in order and to demonstrate to the other peoples that our Nation does have a future, that it can survive the cold war.

In this great endeavor we can succeed, if we have learned that power is a thing of the spirit, that it resides in the minds and hearts of men, not in the means of destruction.

The Rise and Fall of Cold War Revisionism

Robert J. Maddox

American historiography of the Cold War tells us very little of the Cold War, much of the American intellectual history in the 1960s and 1970s.

D.C. Watt
London School of Economics

A decade ago one of the most significant devel-opments in the writing of American history appeared to be the emergence of what was called, however imprecisely, "New Left" revi-sionism. Any historical study is revisionist in-

Robert J. Maddox, "The Rise and Fall of Cold War Revisionism," *The Historian,* **46** (May 1984), pp. 416–428.

sofar as it alters our understanding of the past, but the collective import of New Left works had revolutionary implications. The interpreta-tions they put forward, if valid, rendered obso-lete almost everything previously written about recent American foreign policy. Even more important; to the extent one accepted those interpretations, to that extent one had to view the present and future condition of the American society itself in a light radically different from the conventional wisdom. This new dispensation had attracted so much support in academic circles as to permit one scholar to predict that it would "construct a picture of American history that will move so far away from...[liberal interpretations] that the present revisionists will be revised."[1] Nothing of the sort happened. Instead, the thrust of recent scholarship has so thoroughly undermined revisionism that it can better be characterized as an aberration than as the wave of the future. The story of the rise and fall of revisionism contains a number of important lessons.

Although revisionists wrote about a variety of topics, they concentrated most heavily on the origins of the Cold War. The prevailing interpretation of that conflict had been, as Arthur Schlesinger once wrote, that it was "the brave and essential response of free men to communist aggression." "Orthodox" or "Traditionalist" scholars, as they came to be known, had disagreed widely among themselves over the causes of Soviet behavior and over the wisdom of the American response. They agreed, however, that Soviet initiatives bore the primary responsibility. This consensus the revisionists challenged in all its particulars.

The seminal revisionist work was William Appleman Williams's *Tragedy of American Diplomacy,* first published in 1959, revised and expanded in 1962. An admiring scholar referred to it as "perhaps the finest interpretive essay on American foreign policy ever written."[2] *Tragedy* was a comprehensive interpretation of American foreign policy, but its passages on the Cold War attracted the most attention. Most of the themes that later revisionists of the Cold

War elaborated upon can be found in Williams's book.

To Williams the "tragedy" of American diplomacy was the evolution of the Open Door policy "from an intellectual outlook for changing the world into one concerned with preserving it in the traditional mold." Formulated within the context of depression and the closing of the frontier in the 1890s, this policy represented an effort to resolve capitalism's internal contradictions—chronic overproduction, recurrent depressions—without fundamentally altering the system itself. First applied to secure equal access in China for American goods and investments but quickly extended to the entire world, this policy came to be based on the "dogmatic belief" that American *domestic* well-being depended on and derived from continuous overseas economic expansion. As Williams put it so starkly, "the history of the Open Door Notes became the history of American foreign relations" since 1900.

Assuming that unfettered economic expansion was crucial, American leaders perforce came to see efforts by other powers to obstruct this goal as a threat to the very existence of the American system. Only Franklin D. Roosevelt, of all the twentieth-century presidents, perceived the dangers such an approach entailed, and at times he appeared to be moving tentatively towards a restructuring of the American political economy. In the final analysis, however, FDR backed off and resumed "the traditional strategy of the Open Door Policy" in foreign affairs. Harry S. Truman, who lacked his predecessor's insight, seemed "to react, think, and act as an almost classic personification of the Open Door Policy." This world view caused him to pursue ends which made the Cold War inevitable.

Stalin, according to Williams, entertained no such global pretensions. His goals were limited to three major objectives: friendly governments on Russia's western borders, guarantees against a resurgent Germany, and securing the

[1]James V. Compton, ed., *America and the Origins of the Cold War* (Boston, 1972), 185.

[2]David Horowitz, *The Free World Colossus,* rev. ed. (New York, 1971), 4.

wherewithal to help reconstruct Russia's war-ravaged economy. On other matters he was flexible and inclined to cooperate with his western allies. Had the United States been sympathetic towards Russia's minimum needs the Cold War could have been avoided. Instead the American determination to achieve an Open Door in Eastern Europe (which to Williams meant pro-Western governments there) constituted a direct threat to one of Stalin's modest goals, and strategies subsequently pursued jeopardized the other two. These strategies, economic coercion and "Atomic Diplomacy" to name just two, became standard themes in most of the revisionist works which followed.[3]

Two years after *Tragedy* first appeared, D. F. Fleming published *The Cold War and Its Origins,* a lengthy, two-volume account.[4] Fleming corroborated most of Williams's themes in copious detail. For example, he contended that Truman had employed economic coercion by curtailing Lend-Lease aid to Russia at the close of the war in Europe, and he emphatically supported the idea that a crude atomic diplomacy had been employed. Fleming was particularly strident in his treatment of Harry Truman, whom he accused of being ready to launch the Cold War "before he had been in office two weeks." Truman's "sudden reversal" of Roosevelt's policies, according to Fleming, "cancelled out" the latter's years of labor thereby precipitating a needless conflict.

Fleming and Williams differed in one important respect. Truman's temperament and personal animosity towards the Soviet Union, according to Fleming, led him to adopt the course advocated by the hard-liners around him. The significance of this interpretation is limited, for it suggests that Roosevelt (had he lived) or a more moderate successor could have kept the wartime coalition alive. Some later revisionists also emphasized Truman's personal responsibility. Williams and those who shared his views sought to fry much larger fish. Individuals were relatively unimportant, they contended, because *all* American policymakers agreed on the necessity of constructing a world order which would permit the unhindered expansion of the economic system. Stalin's refusal to accept U.S. world hegemony made something very much like the Cold War inevitable, personal styles notwithstanding. Such a thesis has enormous implications: without a radical restructuring (some form of socialism) of the existing system, the United States was and is compelled to inflict upon a hapless world endless conflict and misery in its quest to satisfy the needs of its own economic juggernaut. The Vietnam war, from this viewpoint, was merely the "culmination of American expansion and the requirements which the domestic system imposed upon that expansion."[5]

In 1965 two more revisionist works appeared. David Horowitz's *Free World Colossus: A Critique of American Foreign Policy in the Cold War* resembled nothing so much as a condensed version of Fleming's account with even harsher verdicts rendered against Truman and those around him.[6] The book received less attention at the time than did a revised edition (1971) which was published when revisionism was in full flower. This fact the author attributed to a repressive conspiracy within the "academic establishment." Later, however, when opposition to the Vietnam war began to crest, "so the guardians of the academic establishment began to lose their control of the ivory tower." Having for two decades "promulgated

---

[3]All the above quotations from William Appleman Williams, *The Tragedy of American Diplomacy,* rev. ed. (New York, 1962), 11, 45, 205, 239.

[4]D. F. Fleming, *The Cold War and Its Origins,* 2 vols. (New York, 1961); quotes from 1:268-69.

[5]Walter LaFeber, in Compton, *America,* 179.

[6]In the revised edition, Horowitz denied that his book, as some reviewers had pointed out, was a shortened version of Fleming's work. The latter was "indispensable," however, "because it stood alone as a reliable source against a sea of academic variations on themes originating in the U.S. Department of State." *Colossus,* 8.

and inculcated a propagandistic view of the history of the post war years," the establishment's days were "clearly numbered." Presumably the number of days left would be reduced by republication of *Colossus* since, as Horowitz modestly proclaimed, "Neither its analyses not its account of events has been seriously challenged."[7]

Gar Alperovitz's *Atomic Diplomacy: Hiroshima and Potsdam, The Use of the Atomic Bomb and the American Confrontation with Soviet Power,* published a month before *Colossus,* had a far greater impact.[8] *Atomic Diplomacy,* according to Christopher Lasch, "made it difficult for conscientious scholars any longer to avoid the challenge of revisionist historians." Alperovitz agreed with Fleming's thesis that Harry Truman had precipitated the Cold War by his "sudden reversal" of Roosevelt's policy of cooperation with the Soviet Union. When economic coercion failed, according to Alperovitz, Truman bided his time until the United States acquired the atomic bomb, with which he meant to bully the Russians into submission. The evidence "strongly suggests," he wrote, that the primary aim in using the weapon was not to defeat Japan—she was done for anyway—but to impress upon the Soviet Union the enormity of American power. Stalin's conduct? He was merely trying to satisfy Russia's legitimate security needs in the face of growing American militance.

Alperovitz's book was distinctive. Here was an entire volume devoted almost exclusively to the five-month period between the Yalta and Potsdam conferences in 1945. Its analysis of events during this time were far more intensive

than anything Williams and Fleming had done, and it was heavily documented with references to fresh primary sources, most notably the diaries of Secretary of War Henry L. Stimson. Even orthodox scholars treated *Atomic Diplomacy* as a scholarly book to be reckoned with, and portions of it began appearing in most anthologies devoted to the origins of the Cold War. It was, as David Horowitz put it, "the first public breakthrough for the revisionist thesis."[9]

By the late 1960s revisionism had become a growth industry. Developments within the nation and abroad greatly contributed to this phenomenon. The "conservative consensus," as the revisionist Barton J. Bernstein called it, had begun breaking down even earlier. "For many," he wrote, "the rediscovery of poverty and racism, the commitment to civil rights for Negroes, the criticism of intervention in Cuba and Vietnam, shattered many of the assumptions of the fifties and compelled intellectuals to re-examine the American past."[10] This mood deepened as the war in Vietnam ground on year after year with no resolution. And, as Walter LaFeber put it, "revisionist history, rather than liberal history, better explains—and even forecasts—such a tragedy."[11]

The growing receptivity to revisionism was made evident with the appearance in 1968 of Gabriel Kolko's *Politics of War: The World and United States Foreign Policy, 1943–1945.*[12] Phrases such as "immense achievement" and "a turning point in the historiography of the war and postwar period" could be found in reviews by revisionists and traditionalists alike.[13] As indicated by the subtitle, Kolko's book was

[7]All quotes in this paragraph from Horowitz, *Colossus,* 4-8.

[8]Gar Alperovitz, *Atomic Diplomacy: Hiroshima and Potsdam, The Use of the Atomic Bomb and the American Confrontation with Soviet Power* (New York, 1965). The Lasch quotation is from his introduction to Alperovitz, *Cold War Essays* (New York, 1970), 12.

[9]Horowitz, *Colossus,* 5.

[10]Barton J. Bernstein, ed., *Towards a New Past: Dissenting Essays in American History* (New York, 1969), ix.

[11]LaFeber, in Compton, *America,* 185.

[12]Gabriel Kolko, *The Politics of War: The World and United States Foreign Policy, 1943–1945* (New York, 1968).

[13]Above phrases can be found in Ronald Radosh, *Nation,* 6 October 1969, 350-51, and Hans J. Morgenthau, *New York Review of Books,* 10 July 1969, 10-17.

ambitious in scope and also rested on documentation from an impressive number of primary and secondary sources.

Like Williams, Kolko placed less emphasis upon individuals than upon the perceived needs of the American economic system. American policymakers, whatever their differences over specific situations, agreed that the creation of a new world order—"an integrated world capitalism," to use his phrase—was an absolute necessity. This goal by definition required the establishment of governments, wherever possible, which would be amenable to the American vision. Washington officials pursued these ends with a single-minded ardor, never hesitating to break agreements, betray allies, or sell out the freedoms of smaller nations. Since fulfillment of this program would have denied the Soviet Union its basic security requirements, the United States made the Cold War inevitable.[14]

Two more important revisionist books were published at the end of the decade: Diane Shaver Clemens's *Yalta* and Lloyd C. Gardner's *Architects of Illusions; Men and Ideas in American Foreign Policy, 1941-1949*.[15] Clemens followed Fleming and Alperovitz in stressing individual personalities rather than systemic needs. She rejected the "sudden reversal" thesis, however, arguing instead that Roosevelt himself "demonstrated many of the views and attitudes that found a logical conclusion in the Truman administration." Gardner, formerly a student of Williams, put forward a less crude version of the latter's thesis. Whereas Williams had rested his case on the importance of markets in Eastern Europe, an insupportable contention by any measure, Gardner admitted they were not "essential."

Rather, he argued, the region became the "locus of a broader conflict" involving spheres of influence in the rest of Europe and in Asia. American leaders held the "illusion" that they could construct a liberal world order based on Open Door principles even though such a goal was in direct conflict with Russia's definition of her security needs. "Responsibility for the *way* in which the Cold War developed, at least," Gardner wrote, "belongs to the United States."

In addition to the basic works of revisionism discussed here, there appeared during the latter part of the 1960s and the early 1970s numerous articles, anthologies, and popularizations which advanced revisionist themes.[16] Journals such as the *Nation,* the *New Republic,* and the *New York Review of Books* published essays by revisionists and almost invariably assigned reviewers who were favorably disposed towards their books. And it was in the *New York Times Book Review* that Gabriel Kolko's *Politics of War* was described as "the most important and stimulating discussion of American policy during World War II to appear in more than a decade."[17]

One might have expected that such a challenge to the conventional wisdom would have touched off an intense debate within scholarly circles. Such was not the case. A few individuals, such as Arthur Schlesinger and Henry Pachter, published essays critical of revisionism in the late 1960s, and between 1970 and 1972 several more nonrevisionists added their voices.[18] Still, within a profession which nor-

---

[14]Kolko was one of the few revisionists who explicitly denied that the United States tried to practice "atomic diplomacy."

[15]Diane Shaver Clemens, *Yalta* (New York, 1970), and Lloyd C. Gardner, *Architects of Illusion: Men and Ideas in American Foreign Policy, 1941-1949* (Chicago, 1970). Quote from Clemens, page 279; quotes from Gardner, 317, 319.

[16]Though not comprehensive, a good sampling can be found in the bibliography of Compton, *America.*

[17]Gaddis Smith, *New York Times Book Review,* 13 April 1969, 6.

[18]See Arthur M. Schlesinger, Jr., "Origins of the Cold War," *Foreign Affairs,* October 1967, and Henry M. Pachter, "Revisionist Historians and the Cold War, *Dissent,* November 1968. The best critiques in the following years were Robert W. Tucker, *The Radical Left and American Foreign* Policy (Baltimore, 1971); Charles S. Maier, "Revisionism and the Interpretation of Cold War Origins," *Perspectives in American History,* 1970; and J. L. Richardson, "Cold War Revisionism: A Critique," *World Politics,* July 1972.

mally thrives on controversy, the response was mild to say the least.

Why did those whose views the revisionists were assaulting respond so meekly? Perhaps the Australian political scientist J. L. Richardson put it best in 1972: "In the case of the new generation coming to political awareness, analogies drawn or suggested between Vietnam and the period of the origins of the Cold War carry immediate conviction: *many others have had their image of contemporary history challenged or even shattered, and those not persuaded by the revisionist case would acknowledge that important questions have been raised.*"[19] (Italics added.) There is little question that a sense of guilt and frustration over Vietnam had come to pervade the liberal community from the mid-1960s onward. What had gone wrong? Who was at fault? Revisionists, of course, supplied an answer. It seems reasonable to suggest that liberal scholars, who themselves were calling into question previously held assumptions, were emotionally unprepared to subject revisionism to hard analysis. And besides, for those liberals who had come to oppose the Vietnam war, attacking revisionism would have placed them in the position of seeming to defend the hawks.

If the revisionists' early opposition to the war placed them in a morally superior position with regard to liberals (many of whom earlier had supported American policies in Southeast Asia), so too did their interpretations appear intellectually superior. Many liberal scholars had criticized various aspects of American diplomacy, including those pursued during the course of the Cold War. The difference was that revisionist history, if valid, rendered much of what the liberals had written superfluous. Revisionists of the more radical persuasion had argued that the path to Vietnam could be traced back through the Truman Doctrine and the Atlantic Charter and to Woodrow Wilson's

Fourteen Points. If they were correct, the scholarship which failed to detect this evolution was by definition inadequate. It might also be suggested, therefore, that increasing doubts about the relevance of their own work influenced liberal attitudes toward revisionism.

In 1973 a new ingredient was added to what had been a relatively decorous exchange. Until that time those who had criticized the revisionists had done so almost exclusively in terms of the latter's assumptions about the motives of American leaders, the alleged needs of the capitalist system, and the selection of evidence used. The present writer's *New Left and the Origins of the Cold War* employed a different approach. Comparing examples of evidence used by the revisionists to support their interpretations with the sources, *The New Left* attempted to show that the most prominent revisionist works were shot through with errors of the most rudimentary sort, which invariably lent support to their themes. These errors were caused by practices such as splicing together diverse statements to produce fictitious speeches and conversations, altering the meaning of sentences through the use of ellipses, and wrenching phrases out of time sequences and contexts, among other things. "Although the frequency varies from volume to volume," I wrote, "even the best fails to attain the most flexible definition of scholarship." The allegation of such practices subsequently was confirmed by, among others, Robert H. Ferrell, Thomas T. Hammond, Robert J. Loewenberg, and Edward S. Shapiro.[20]

---

[19]Richardson, "Cold War Revisionism," 579.

[20]Robert J. Maddox, *The New Left and the Origins of the Cold War* (Princeton, 1973), 10. For additional examples of how Alperovitz in particular "created" his evidence, see Robert H. Ferrell, "Truman's Foreign Policy: A Traditionalist View," in *The Truman Period as a Research Field: A Reappraisal*, ed. Richard S. Kirkendall, rev. ed. (Columbia, Mo., 1974): 17-20; Edward S. Shapiro, "Responsibility for the Cold War: A Bibliographical Review," *Intercollegiate Review*, Winter 1976-77, 113-20, and a more detailed examination available from Shapiro at Department of History, Seton Hall University; Thomas T. Hammond,

The reception accorded *The New Left* was revealing. "It marks a milestone in American historical writing since the Second World War," a reviewer wrote, while a less enthusiastic one called it "an act of verbal mugging." What appeared to one scholar as "a salutary operation...performed with grace and skill" caused another to write that "by literary or forensic standards this is a poorly written book." On the one hand, "Maddox meticulously lays out the evidence, lacing his prose with a mordant wit"; on the other, "Mr. Maddox's book is either irresponsible or fraudulent." And so it went. Reviews are often mixed but these contrasted so wildly as to make a reader wonder whether they applied to the same book.[21]

Why, it must be asked, should a volume devoted almost exclusively to factual matters strike various reviewers (to whom most of the sources were readily available) so differently?[22] The answer has depressing implications for the state of historical scholarship then and now. In a review essay, Edward S. Shapiro found that "the various evaluations of Maddox's book roughly corresponded to the reviewers' attitudes regarding the broader debate as to the responsibility for the Cold War."[23] In short, the Cold War had claimed yet another casualty: the critical detachment that professional scholars once strived for.

What impact the various criticisms of the revisionists have had within the historical community is impossible to ascertain. What is clear is that Walter LaFeber's prophecy that the trend would continue to such an extent that "present revisionists will be revised" has proven baseless. Indeed, the more extreme claims made by writers such as Williams, Alperovitz, and Kolko have been ignored or severely modified even by those generally favorable to the revisionist position.[24] Probably a number of factors accounted for this, not least of which has been the diminution of the high fervors so characteristic of the late 1960s and the early 70s. And, as J. L. Richardson has pointed out, historical controversies have tended to follow a pattern. Those who first challenge a prevailing interpretation often do so with reckless enthusiasm. Then, however, "the polemical generation gives way to more discriminating successors who discard the excesses but retain what is of value in the revisionist critique."[25]

Most damaging of all to the tenets of revisionism has been the ever greater availability of primary sources. Given the relative scarcity of such documentation earlier, it was plausible to construct on the basis of circumstantial evidence the "real" American policies as opposed to official versions. But an enormous body of materials has since become available, materials consisting of what American policymakers were saying and writing to one another at the time. Scholars using

---

"Atomic Diplomacy Revisited," *Orbis*, Winter 1976, 1403-28. For a critique of Kolko, see Robert J. Loewenberg, in " 'Value-Free' versus 'Value-Laden' History: A Distinction without a Difference," *Historian* (May 1976), 439-54. It is interesting to note that J. L. Richardson, whose 1972 critique complimented Alperovitz and Kolko on their "impressive scholarship," despite disagreeing with their conclusions, subsequently retracted that judgment. "It is quasi-scholarship," he wrote, "quasi-supported by a plethora of footnotes." Richardson to the editors of the *New York Review of Books*, 13 June 1973, copy in author's possession.

[21]For a convenient sampling of such reviews, see Shapiro, "Responsibility for the Cold War."

[22]For a published attempt to systematically rebut *The New Left*, see Warren F. Kimball, "The Cold War Warmed Over," *American Historical Review*, October 1974, 1124-35. In doing this, Kimball used many of the procedures that the revisionists had used. In one place, he spliced together a phrase from the book's introduction and one from the conclusion to create a statement never written. "Maddox's approach," he wrote in another passage, "is to look narrowly at the exact quotation...," as opposed, one imagines, to looking broadly at the inexact quotation. For an effective rebuttal, see Loewenberg, " 'Value-Free' versus 'Value-Laden' History."

[23]Shapiro, "Responsibility for the Cold War," 115.

[24]See, for instance, Thomas G. Paterson, *On Every Front: The Making of the Cold War* (New York, 1979).

[25]Richardson, "Cold War Revisionism," 581.

these documents have demolished the most prominent themes in revisionist literature. Thus Wilson D. Miscamble has shown that Truman's famous confrontation with Molotov on April 23, 1945, represented neither a "sudden reversal" (Fleming) nor a strategy of "immediate show-down" (Alperovitz) but resulted from a hasty decision made by Truman because British Foreign Minister Anthony Eden had convinced him that blunt talk provided the best hope for breaking down the impasse over Poland.[26] George C. Herring, Jr., has effectively rebutted the notion, a staple in revisionist literature, that the Lend-Lease curtailment of May 1945 constituted a deliberate effort on Truman's part to coerce the Soviet Union.[27]

The list can be extended almost indefinitely, and on more significant issues. Lynn Etheridge Davis and Geir Lundestad have eviscerated the revisionist contention that the United States followed a coherent, aggressive policy in Eastern Europe. Time after time, Davis shows, the State Department overruled or ignored recommendations by officials on the scene who actually wanted to *do* something. Instead the Department contented itself with issuing periodic statements of high ideals. Lundestad agrees with Davis that the United States did almost nothing to prevent Soviet economic domination of the East European states. The title of his book is apt: *The American Non-Policy towards Eastern Europe, 1943-1947.*[28] Atomic diplomacy? Not a shred of direct evidence has ever been adduced to support the idea that the

United States actively pursued such a course, and Alperovitz's book on the subject has been discredited by a number of scholars.[29]

What, then, can one say about the contribution of revisionism to our understanding of the origins of the Cold War? Perhaps the most generous assessment possible by one not imbued with the revisionist faith has been written by John Lewis Gaddis. Surveying the most recent literature on the subject, Gaddis finds no substantiation for two of the most important revisionist contentions:

(1) That postwar American foreign policy approximated the classical Leninist model of imperialism—that is, that an unwillingness or inability to redistribute wealth at home produced an aggressive search for markets and investment opportunities overseas, without which, it was thought, the capitalist system in the United States could not survive.

(2) That this internally motivated drive for empire left little room for accommodating the legitimate security interests of the Soviet Union, thereby ensuring the breakdown of wartime cooperation.[30]

With regard to the latter point, Gaddis emphasizes the importance of Vojtech Mastny's *Russia's Road to the Cold War* which convincingly shows that Stalin, far from being committed to

[26]Wilson D. Miscamble, "Anthony Eden and the Truman-Molotov Conversations, April 1945," *Diplomatic History*, Spring 1978, 167-80.

[27]George C. Herring, "Lend Lease to Russia and the Origins of the Cold War, 1944-1945," *Journal of American History*, June 1969, 93-114.

[28]Lynn Etheridge Davis, *The Cold War Begins: Soviet-American Conflict over Eastern Europe* (Princeton, 1974). Geir Lundestad, *The American Non-Policy towards Eastern Europe, 1943-1947: Universalism in an Area Not of Essential Interest to the United States* (New York, 1975).

[29]See footnote 20. Some scholars have continued to use the phrase "atomic diplomacy," but they employ it in such a watered-down version as to render it all but meaningless. Martin J. Sherwin, for instance, has defined it as "either the overt diplomatic or military brandishing of atomic weapons ...[or] a covert diplomatic strategy based upon considerations related to atomic weapons." Sherwin, *A World Destroyed: The Atomic Bomb and the Grand Alliance* (New York, 1975), 191-92. No recent scholars have used the phrase in the sense of "brandishing" atomic weapons, as did Williams, Fleming, et al.

[30]John Lewis Gaddis, "The Emerging Post-Revisionist Synthesis on the Origins of the Cold War," *Diplomatic History* (Summer 1983), 171-90. In a rather lame rejoinder, revisionist Lloyd C. Gardner said he agreed with Gaddis that the "whole" of American imperialism could not be contained within the Leninist model. Gardner left unanswered the matter as to whether American policy "approximated" the Leninist model, which was Gaddis's point.

a policy of cooperation, pursued his ends uni-laterally without regard to Western sensibilities. Even more important, it is still not clear what the scope of Stalin's ambitions really was or whether he had any clear-cut notions of what was "sufficient" for Russian security. It is easy enough in hindsight to say what Stalin "only" wanted, but American policymakers at the time had no way of knowing.[31]

Of all the aspects of revisionism pertaining to the *origins* of the Cold War, Gaddis finds only two which at least in part have been borne out by more recent scholarship: First, that ortho-dox historians had minimized or ignored the degree to which American policymakers tried to employ economic pressures against the Soviet Union. Gaddis points out, however, that "economic instruments were used to serve po-litical ends, not the other way around" as some of the revisionists would have it. Second, that traditionalist accounts tended to accept without evidence the notion that Stalin's actions repre-sented the carrying out of some master plan for world domination, a view which the revisionists rightly called into question. Gaddis might have added, but did not, that some of the revisionists went so far in the other direction as to portray the Soviet leader as a cooperative partner who was pushed into opposition by American and British intransigence. The latest scholarship rejects both extremes, instead depicting Stalin as a "cagy but insecure opportunist."[32] In short, with the exception of the two points noted above, what once appeared well on its way to becoming the new dispensation has disappeared almost without a trace in the writings of younger scholars who by no stretch of the imagination can be referred to as Cold Warriors.

The broad effects of revisionist interpretations at the time they were presented can only be guessed. Certainly they received wide dissemina-tion on campuses, as they did through journals of opinion. A survey taken of American historians during that period revealed that Williams's *Trag-edy of American Diplomacy* was considered by many to be the most influential recent book in the field, and another poll showed that revisionist-oriented textbooks in diplomatic history were extremely popular. The number of "conflicting interpretation" readers published during that era was impressive, and almost all contained a gen-erous sampling of revisionist writing. What can be said with assurance is that revisionism helped nourish a developing mood on campuses across the country.

The rise and decline of revisionism—recent writers seem to prefer being described as "post-revisionists" or as "having gone beyond revi-sionism"—illustrates several problems con-fronting the intellectual community. "It is past time, the revisionists believe," Walter LaFeber wrote, "for the admission that for American historians history begins and ends with ideology."[33] Whether there was anything left in the middle he did not say, but revisionist liter-ature provides countless examples of the ex-cesses to which "commitment" can lead. Com-plete objectivity is unobtainable, of course, but to abandon this quest in order to find a past "usable" to promote one's present views can easily lead to acts of vandalism supposedly in behalf of some higher good. If some of the more ardent orthodox historians acted as defense attorneys for American foreign policy, revision-ists assumed the role of prosecutors. This failed to provide a more balanced view; rather, it created a series of fictions which later scholars had to clear away.

---

[31]Vojtech Mastny, *Russia's Road to the Cold War: Diplomacy, Warfare, and the Politics of Communism, 1941-1945* (New York, 1979).

[32]Gaddis, "The Emerging Post-Revisionist Synthesis," 175, 181. Gaddis credits the revisionists with making two other valuable points: that American leaders from time to time exaggerated external threats to achieve internal goals, and that an American "empire" was created during the course of the Cold War. Whatever their merits, these themes pertain to the period *after* the Cold War began.

[33]LaFeber, in Compton, *America,* 185.

The largely uncritical response to revisionism, when it first began to appear, raises another issue. In some disciplines, whenever important new hypotheses are offered, it is commonplace for others in the field to examine the evidence and the procedures used to support those hypotheses. This historians seem unwilling to do. Indeed, in his essay on the revisionists Gaddis made the remarkable statement that such a practice was "shocking." Shocking it may be, but if scholars in the field had performed this service at the time, it would not have taken almost a decade to expose revisionism's grave deficiencies.

QUESTIONS FOR DISCUSSION

1 If Western nations had not intervened in the aftermath of the Bolshevik Revolution, would the Soviet regime have "evolved more mildly"?
2 Was overseas economic expansion by the United States a cause of the Cold War?
3 How important was historical revisionism about the early Cold War in shaping the evolution of the U.S. national mood in the 1970s?
4 How far did Stalin's reputation benefit from U.S. historical revisionism on the Cold War?

SUGGESTED READINGS

Gaddis, John Lewis. "The Emerging Post-Revisionist Synthesis on the Origins of the Cold War," *Diplomatic History*, **7** (Summer 1983), pp. 171–190.
———. *Strategies of Containment: A Critical Appraisal of Postwar American National Security Policy*. New York: Oxford Univ. Press, 1981.
Gardner, Lloyd C., Arthur Schlesinger, Jr., and Hans J. Morgenthau. *The Origins of the Cold War*. Waltham, Mass.: Ginn-Blaisdell, 1970.
Hammond, Thomas T. (ed.). *Witnesses to the Origins of the Cold War*. Seattle, Wash.: Univ. of Washington Press, 1982.
LaFeber, Walter. *America, Russia, and the Cold War, 1945–1984*. 5th ed. New York: Knopf, 1985.
Leigh, Michael. "Is There a Revisionist Thesis on the Origins of the Cold War?" *Political Science Quarterly*, **89** (Mar. 1974), pp. 101–116.
Maddox, Robert James. *The New Left and the Origins of the Cold War*. Princeton, N.J.: Princeton Univ. Press, 1973.
Mastny, Vojtech. *Russia's Road to the Cold War*. New York: Columbia Univ. Press, 1979.
Paterson, Thomas G. (ed.). *Cold War Critics: Alternatives to American Foreign Policy in the Truman Years*. Chicago, Ill.: Quadrangle Books, 1971.
———. *On Every Front: The Making of the Cold War*. New York: Norton, 1979.
Pollard, Robert A. *Economic Security and the Origins of the Cold War, 1945–1950*. New York: Columbia Univ. Press, 1985.
Schaller, Michael. *The American Occupation of Japan: The Origins of the Cold War in Asia*. New York: Oxford Univ. Press, 1985.
Sivachev, Nikolai V., and Nikolai N. Yakoviev. *Russia and the United States*. Olga Adler Titelbaum, trans. Chicago, Ill.: Univ. of Chicago Press, 1979.
Taubman, William. *Stalin's American Policy*. New York: W. W. Norton, 1982.
Thompson, Kenneth W. *Cold War Theories*. Vol. 1: *World Polarization, 1943–1953*. Baton Rouge, La.: Louisiana State Univ. Press, 1981.

CHAPTER 2

INTERNATIONAL SYSTEM

The patterns of relations among the principal actors of world politics—or what has been called the international system—have varied considerably over time. Actors include states, private groups, and international organizations. Since the Treaty of Westphalia of 1648, however, states have been the primary actors in world politics.

In the period between 1648 and 1945, the international system was characterized by a dispersion of power. No single state was so powerful as to be able to dominate the others. This international system could thus be described as "multipolar." On some occasions, one country sought to expand its power so as to threaten the security of many other nations. Such, for example, was the case of Louis XIV or Napoleon in France and Adolf Hitler in Germany. But such efforts were thwarted by grand alliances.

In the aftermath of World War II, however, the structure of the international system gradually came to be seen as "bipolar," that is, a system in which there are two principal power centers. With the defeat of the Axis powers, the United States and the Soviet Union had in fact become the two dominant powers in the world. Most of Europe had been devastated by the war. Japan was occupied by the United States. And most of Africa and Asia were still under somewhat shaky Western European imperial rule.

Only Great Britain was briefly considered to be a possible contender against U.S.-Soviet domination. But its economic base had been destroyed by World War II, and it was also faced with irresistible pressures to terminate its empire, a process begun in 1947 with the granting of independence to India. And such pretensions as Great Britain had to being in any way in the same league as the United States and the Soviet Union were decisively and vividly punctured in

1956 when it was unsuccessful in its efforts to compel Egypt to abandon its seizure of the Suez Canal. Thereafter the existence of only two superpowers was almost universally recognized.

The United States had, of course, escaped the devastation of the war. It was the first country to possess atomic weapons, and it retained its monopoly of those weapons until 1949. Its economy was strong, and it helped to restore the economic strength of other countries, particularly in Western Europe. As for the Soviet Union, although it experienced the greatest number of casualties in the war, it possessed the strongest military establishment in Europe.

As noted in the last chapter, the two superpowers soon confronted each other at various points around the world. Such confrontation did not lead to war between them, but it produced political, economic, and ideological conflicts that were perceived by many observers to be so dangerous as to arouse genuine fears that war could result. The bipolar arrangement solidified into blocs with the establishment of the North Atlantic Treaty Organization in 1949, in which the United States joined with most Western European states to form a military pact, and the Warsaw Pact in 1955, in which the Soviet Union allied with Eastern European countries under its control.

The fact that both the United States and the Soviet Union came to be seen as superpowers gave them for a time substantial, if not total, control over their allies. Gradually, however, the bipolar character of world politics has been modified, and the power of both the United States and the Soviet Union has diminished. In accounting for this evolution, we need to consider military, political, economic, and ideological factors.

Militarily, the U.S. monopoly of atomic weapons ended in 1949. Today a situation of approximate nuclear parity is widely thought to characterize the nuclear arsenals of both superpowers. But other nations have nuclear weapons, too. The list now includes China, France, and Great Britain. India detonated what it called a peaceful nuclear explosion in 1974. Israel is believed to have nuclear weapons, although it does not admit to having them. Pakistan is believed to be quite close to producing nuclear weapons. Other countries are capable of manufacturing those weapons. Compared to other nuclear weapon states, the United States and the Soviet Union are at present in a different league in terms of numbers of bombs and means of delivery. But they cannot leave the others out of account—not least if major nuclear arms reductions are to take place.

Conventional weapons are now produced by many countries, not only the superpowers. Great Britain, France, Czechoslovakia, Brazil, and Israel are some of the many nations that engage in a vigorous arms trade. Even the overwhelming military strength of the United States, moreover, could not prevent communist governments from gaining control of Cuba, ninety miles from U.S. territory, or of South Vietnam and neighboring states. Nor could superior military strength assure the Soviets of an easy victory over rebels in Afghanistan seeking to topple a pro-Soviet Afghan government.

The rise of independent nations in Asia and Africa has brought new actors into the global arena. Although the superpowers have sought to retain their interests in the Third World, they have been cautious about military intervention. Where they have intervened militarily, as in the case of the United States in Vietnam and the Soviet Union in Afghanistan, they have been sharply criticized by many nonaligned nations.

Politically, too, divisions within the Western and communist worlds have emerged. France has withdrawn from military cooperation with the NATO alliance and has built an independent nuclear force. Divisions in the West have surfaced on such issues as nuclear strategy, arms control, trade embargoes against the Soviet Union, Central America, and overall economic policy. The Soviet preeminence in the communist world has also been challenged, most notably by Yugoslavia in 1948 and, subsequently, by China and Albania (successfully), and by Hungary and Czechoslovakia (unsuccessfully). The failure of the Soviet Union to completely quell the Solidarity labor movement in Poland is often perceived as another example of the Soviets' inability to discipline their allies. The emergence of the Eurocommunism movement, in which some communist parties of Western European nations have asserted their commitment to political democracy and independence from the Soviet Union, has further weakened Soviet domination of communist parties abroad.

Economically, U.S. preeminence has declined. The rise of the economies of Western Europe and the Pacific Basin countries in particular has resulted in a diminished economic role for the United States, and trade and tariff conflicts as well. On the other hand, far-flung Soviet foreign commitments have put a strain on the Soviet economy.

The ideological orientation of the superpowers has also seen change. Communism as an ideology still had a worldwide appeal in the immediate aftermath of World War II, although many adherents had become disenchanted with the ideology and the Soviet Union in large part because of Stalin's domestic and foreign policy actions. Still, the Soviet Union dominated communist parties throughout the world, and communist ideology had its core of supporters in noncommunist countries. Some Western intellectuals, viewing their own societies as corrupt and exploitive, saw the Soviet Union as a model to follow. Leaders of the anticolonial movement in the Third World often found communist ideology useful in explaining their countries' poverty as caused by Western colonialism and exploitation.

Over time, however, the ideological appeal of communism diminished. Mao Zedong in China denounced the Soviet Union for lack of revolutionary fervor and thus interpreted Marxism-Leninism in a manner different from Soviet Communist party officials. Advocates of Eurocommunism, moreover, challenged much Soviet communist theory.

In the United States especially, but in other Western countries as well, an anticommunist ideology became prominent soon after World War II. Proponents of this ideology saw the United States in particular, and the West in general, as the embodiment of the "Free World," and the Soviet Union and other communist countries as the embodiment of the "Slave World." Even after the death of Stalin, Dulles, who was secretary of state in the Eisenhower administration, viewed nonalignment as immoral since he perceived communism to be an evil.

This anticommunist ideology has since lost its vigor. The movement away from Soviet control, the conflict between the Soviet Union and the People's Republic of China, the increasing trade between the communist and Western worlds, Nixon's trip to China, and the stronger Sino-U.S. ties since the Nixon administration have all eroded the bitter anticommunist feeling. The enormous increase in the power of nuclear weapons, moreover, has generated a movement toward negotiation with the Soviet Union. To be sure, there is an anticommunist sentiment in the United States and other Western nations, but it does not have the vehemence or acceptance that it had in the postwar Stalin years.

These military, political, economic, and ideological factors, then, have played a role in changing the international system. Two debates that are considered below deal with assessing the power of the Soviet Union and the United States and raise issues about the current state of the international system.

CENTRAL AMERICA

Since 1945, Soviet power and influence have expanded to areas of the world beyond Soviet borders. The Soviet Union has bases in Vietnam and in Ethiopia, for example. It has been closely tied to such countries as Syria and, in the early 1970s, to Egypt.

Although the Soviet Union supported communists throughout the world, it was not until Fidel Castro turned Cuba into a communist state by the early 1960s that U.S. security became immediately threatened in the Western hemisphere. The Cuban-Soviet tie has been a strong one, and it led to a major confrontation between the superpowers in 1962 when the Soviets planned to install nuclear missiles in Cuba. The Soviets have invested vast sums in Cuban economic development. Cuban military forces have also fought in Angola and Mozambique. These forces have been described by anti-Castro organizations as surrogates for the Soviet Union. Pro-Castro partisans regard these forces as prorevolution and liberation.

The United States has been particularly concerned with the threat of Soviet expansion in the Western hemisphere. With the collapse of the Anastazio Somoza government in Nicaragua in the late 1970s, the United States watched as the Marxist Sandinistas, under the leadership of Daniel Ortega, took over that country. In 1983, the United States sent troops to Grenada and succeeded in toppling a Marxist regime.

Does the coming to power of Marxist regimes in Central America inevitably mean a strengthening of the Soviet Union? Carl Gershman, who served as a member of the U.S. delegation to the United Nations and is now president of the National Endowment for Democracy, argues that it does. He assesses the activities of the Soviet Union primarily in Cuba, Nicaragua, and El Salvador and concludes that the rise of Soviet and Cuban power in the hemisphere is a threat to U.S. security. He points to the implications the strengthening of Marxist forces has for U.S. strategy and credibility as a world power.

A contrary view is taken by Sol M. Linowitz, who served as the U.S. ambassador to the Organization of American States in the Kennedy administration. He sees the major problems of Latin America as economic, social, and political—and not military. Finally, he describes the sources of insecurity as mainly internal to each nation, and external influences as secondary.

U.S. HEGEMONY

Power has been defined as the ability to make people do what they may not want to do. Both in domestic politics and world politics, however, it is difficult to define the components of power, let alone evaluate the relative power of different countries. Policy makers do not always know power when they see it—although they know it when they feel it.

Those who assess power weigh a variety of factors, including military capability, economic resources, domestic constraints, political resolve, capable leadership, and diplomatic skill. Leaders are forced to make guesses about power relationships, and they are often wrong in their assessments.

But what of U.S. power in the world? For reasons discussed above, it was not uncommon in the aftermath of World War II to hear the United States described as hegemonic. The character of U.S. power has surely changed in more than four decades. But has U.S. hegemony declined over recent years?

Kenneth A. Oye offers a rather traditional view arguing the affirmative position. He cites the economic climb of Western Europe, Japan, and some developing nations. He notes the expansion of Soviet military capabilities. Writing in the early 1980s, he says that there is nothing the Reagan administration can do to restore American economic and military preeminence.

A contrary position about the current status of U.S. hegemony is taken by Bruce Russett. He agrees that the power base of the United States has declined, but he contends that there is no consensus on the extent of that decline. More important than the decline of the U.S. power base, he says, is the significance of that decline in affecting outcomes. By analyzing military, economic, and cultural developments, he contends that the demise of U.S. hegemony has been greatly exaggerated.

7 Does the coming to power of Marxist regimes in Central America inevitably mean a strengthening of the Soviet Union?

YES

Carl Gershman

Soviet Power in Central America and the Caribbean: The Growing Threat to American Security

NO

Sol M. Linowitz

[*The United States and Central America*]

Soviet Power in Central America and the Caribbean: The Growing Threat to American Security

Carl Gershman

The significance to the United States of developments in Central America and the Caribbean Basin cannot be appreciated apart from a consideration of the Soviet Union's role in the region and its implications for American national security. Over the last quarter of a century, with the imposition in Cuba of a Communist regime allied with Moscow, the Soviet Union has steadily, if at times imperceptibly, expanded its power and presence in the region. This steady advance, which is reflected in Soviet doctrinal shifts registering Moscow's heightened capabilities and ambitions in the region, has been marked by an immense increase in Cuba's military capability and greatly stepped up aid to regional insurgent forces. With the coming to power in 1979 of pro-Cuban groups in Nicaragua and Grenada, the ability of the Soviet Union and Cuba to promote armed struggle and to project military power throughout the region was vastly enhanced.

These developments, especially if viewed in the context of the Soviet Union's growing global power and its unprecedented peacetime military build-up, pose a grave and growing threat to what Hans J. Morgenthau once called "the permanent national interest of the United States in the Western Hemisphere." They also threaten the well-being of the region's peoples who have suffered from escalating levels of violence, economic destruction, and social dislocation. Not least, the deteriorating regional conditions threaten the NATO Alliance owing to the special importance of the Caribbean Basin as a geopolitical zone—the "strategic

From *Report of the National Bipartisan Commission on Central America, Appendix* (Washington, D.C.: Government Printing Office, 1984), pp. 328–359.

rear," as the Soviets call it, of United States global power.

The critical importance of the Caribbean Basin to American security and the growing threat to U.S. interests there is still not adequately appreciated in this country. As Americans, we have been so accustomed throughout most of our history to security in our own Hemisphere that we have come to think, as Walter Lippmann wrote four decades ago, "that our privileged position was a natural right." In fact, it was the divisions in Europe and the supremacy of British seapower that allowed us to uphold the Monroe Doctrine with minimal effort during the last century. The only significant breach of the Doctrine came during the American Civil War when Napoleon III, taking advantage of our debilitating internal conflict, installed an Austrian archduke in Mexico City and Spain briefly reannexed Santo Domingo. The Monroe Doctrine remained essentially intact for a full century thereafter, until the intrusion of Communism into Cuba.

That event, which prompted Khrushchev to declare that the Monroe Doctrine had "outlived its times" and had died "a natural death," might have been expected to challenge the complacency with which Americans have tended to regard their security in the Hemisphere. But the 1962 understanding with the Soviet Union, according to which the Soviets would not introduce offensive weapons into Cuba and would curtail Cuban aggression in the Hemisphere in exchange for our assurances against invading Cuba, allowed the belief that "the Cuban problem" had been effectively contained. Subsequent history has shown, however, that this belief was both premature and mistaken.

In the aftermath of the 1962 agreement, the Soviet Union and Cuba followed different policies toward the Hemisphere. Cuba, hoping to replicate its own revolution in other countries, followed the *foco* theory of Castro and Che Guevara which was based upon the belief that protracted guerrilla warfare in the countryside could create the political as well as military conditions for the overthrow of established governments. The Soviets, showing a Leninist distrust of "infantile leftism," preferred to prepare the ground slowly and systematically for a future challenge to the U.S. While not opposing Cuban support for armed struggle in Venezuela, Colombia, Guatemala and several other countries, the Soviets concentrated on expanding their diplomatic, economic, and cultural ties in the region and on strengthening the influence of local Communist parties in broad electoral fronts and the trade unions.

By the late 1960s and early 1970s, this strategy appeared to be paying off. While Cuban-supported guerrillas suffered repeated setbacks, the Soviets were encouraged by the victory of Allende in Chile, the success of the Broad Front in Uruguay, and the return of Peron to Argentina, as well as by "progressive" military coups in Peru, Ecuador, Bolivia, and Panama. In 1971, Boris N. Ponomarev, the chairman of the international department of the Central Committee of the Soviet Communist Party, welcomed "the upsurge of the revolutionary movement on the Latin American continent" which had "tremendous importance to the world revolutionary process." Emphasizing the strategic significance of this development, Ponomarev wrote,

> Seemingly quite reliable rear lines of American imperialism are becoming a tremendous hotbed of anti-imperialist revolution. A tremendously powerful revolutionary movement is developing by the side of the main citadel of imperialism, the U.S. These changes are having and, unquestionably will continue to have, a strong impact on the further changes in the correlation of world forces

in favor of the international working class and socialism. A number of developments came together in the 1970s causing the Soviet Union to abandon the relatively cautious approach it followed in the decade after 1962 and to adopt a policy of revolutionary armed struggle, thus setting the stage for the current crisis in Central America.

The first of these developments was the overthrow of Allende in Chile and the subsequent right-wing takeovers in Uruguay, Argentina, and Bolivia. The effect of these events was to discredit the Soviet line concerning the "peaceful path" to Communism in Latin America. While the Soviets continued officially to uphold this line—they did not abandon it completely until the Sandinista victory in 1979—they also embraced the armed struggle, as indicated by the Havana Declaration of Latin American and Caribbean Communist parties in 1979:

> The utilization of all legal possibilities is an indispensable obligation of the anti-imperialist forces ....Revolutionaries are not the first to resort to violence. But it is the right and duty of all revolutionary forces to be ready to answer counter-revolutionary violence with revolutionary violence.

Second, with the triumph of Soviet-backed forces in Indochina, Angola, Mozambique, Ethiopia, and South Yemen, the Soviets adopted a much more aggressive policy toward the Third World, reflecting their view that the "correlation of forces" had shifted dramatically against the West. In the Soviet view, changes in the balance of strategic and conventional forces had created the conditions for further Soviet gains in Third World struggles, which the Chief of the Soviet General Staff Academy, I. Shavrov, called "epicenters" in the global East-West struggle. Under these favorable conditions, wrote Soviet Central Committee member and Third World specialist Karen Brutents, the decisive issue was no longer the defense of the

Soviet Union but "carrying on the offensive against imperialism and world capitalism as a whole in order to do away with them."

Third, the Soviets dramatically strengthened their military capability in the Caribbean, in line with their global build-up. This development was marked by the "Sovietization" of Cuba, which fell into line behind Soviet policy after 1968, and by a dramatic increase in Cuban military forces. Cuba's total armed forces, which numbered less than 50,000 in 1960, more than doubled by 1970 to 109,500. With the beginning of Cuba's Africa operations in the mid-1970s, these forces expanded once again, from 117,000 in 1975 to 175,000 in 1976. In addition to acquiring valuable combat experience in Africa, these forces received upgraded training and sophisticated weaponry, including an impressive array of tanks, armored cars and personnel carriers, heavy artillery, surface-to-surface missiles, anti-tank guided missiles, self-propelled anti-aircraft weapons, and surface-to-air missiles. This build-up included an expansion of the Cuban Navy, which acquired Osa patrol boats equipped with Styx surface-to-surface missiles, as well as the expansion and modernization of the Cuban Air Force, which received advance models of the MiG-21MF in 1975 and MiG-23/27 fighter bombers in 1978.

The Soviet military presence in the Caribbean also increased dramatically during this period. A seven-ship Soviet task force entered the Caribbean in July 1969, beginning a series of regular visits that gave the Soviets a routine naval presence in the region. Though the Soviets were forced to halt their construction of a nuclear submarine base at Cienfuegos in the fall of 1970, Soviet nuclear submarines and diesel-powered ballistic missile submarines made repeated visits to Cuban ports thereafter, and new naval basing and repair facilities were under construction at Cienfuegos by the end of the decade. In addition, Soviet TU-95 Bear reconnaissance aircraft began to be deployed in Cuba in 1975, and several new airfields were constructed capable of accommodating the Backfire strategic bomber. Increased numbers of Soviet military advisers, technicians, and instructors arrived to supervise and service the build-up of Soviet and Cuban forces.

As an indication of the increasingly close collaboration between these forces, significant numbers of Soviet pilots were sent to Cuba in 1976 and 1978 to replace the Cuban pilots who were sent to Africa to defend the pro-Soviet regimes in Angola and Ethiopia. The 3,000-man Soviet brigade in Cuba also indirectly aided Cuban military activities: as a guarantee of the Soviet commitment to the survival of the Castro regime, it allowed Cuba to pursue a more aggressive policy in the region without fear of a retaliatory U.S. strike.

Fourth, just as the increase in Soviet global power was accompanied by a major build-up in the region, the retreat of U.S. global power during the same period was matched by a corresponding regional decline. Between 1968 and 1981, U.S. military personnel in the Basin decreased from over 25,000 to under 16,000, and U.S. military installations in Panama, Puerto Rico, and Guantanamo were downgraded or closed down entirely. At the same time, the rise of the "Vietnam syndrome" in the United States created a climate of indifference to U.S. security concerns in the Basin and stimulated calls for ending what some disparagingly called the American "hegemonic presumption." The resulting power vacuum altered the geopolitical dynamics of the region, inviting new foreign intervention—from the Socialist International as well as the Soviet bloc—and contributing to increased Balkanization and political instability. These trends were accelerated by the enunciation of a new human rights doctrine during the Carter Administration which signaled the withdrawal of support for Central American governments previously backed by the United States.

Fifth, rapid social and economic changes in Central America during the previous quarter of a century forced new pressures to the surface in the mid-1970s that made the region an inviting target for insurgency. The sustained economic growth of the 1960s produced a new middle class and an urban working class whose political aspirations were blocked by the traditional oligarchs, and whose rising economic expectations were frustrated during the recession that followed the first OPEC oil price rise of 1973–74. The shattering impact of the second oil price rise of 1979–80 brought to a head seething social conflicts which, as they turned more violent, worsened the economic collapse.

Sixth, by the mid-1970s and increasingly thereafter, Cuba had developed a much greater institutional capacity to promote guerrilla warfare than it possessed during the previous decade, and its revolutionary strategy was much more sophisticated than the failed *foco* strategy of Che Guevara. The principal institutional instrument for promoting insurgencies was the Americas Department, which was established in 1974 to centralize Cuba's operational control over covert revolutionary activities throughout the Hemisphere and particularly in Central America. The Americas Department brought together the expertise of the Cuban military and the General Directorate of Intelligence (DGI) in a coordinated operation that included covert operations in the field, networks for the movement of intelligence and other personnel and material between Cuba and abroad, and extensive cultural and propaganda activities tailored to discredit targeted governments and to build support for armed opposition groups. The Department's activities also included supervision of a network of guerrilla training camps and indoctrination schools on the island where trainees from throughout Latin America received 3 to 6 months of instruction in guerrilla warfare tactics, weapons use, and propaganda and agitation.

The revolutionary strategy pursued by Cuba in target countries involved the creation of separate military and political fronts, as well as the establishment by such fronts of relations with a broad array of non-Communist allies, both domestic and foreign. This strategy, as it developed in the course of the Nicaraguan revolution, required in the first instance the unification of traditionally splintered insurgent groups as a condition for increased Cuban military advice and assistance. Just as the creation of such unified military fronts allowed Cuba to exercise control over the armed struggle, so too did the creation of broad political fronts with non-Communist oppositionists allow the guerrillas to coopt such forces and neutralize them as rival alternatives to the existing government. This objective was also served by the armed struggle itself, which undermined the political center by sharpening the increasingly violent confrontation between left and right.

The popular-front tactic had the added advantage of allowing the guerrillas to disarm critics by posing as non-Communist democrats, a posture given further credibility by the alliances formed with non-Communist Latin governments, European Socialists, political forces in the United States, and church and human rights groups. These alliances strengthened the international legitimacy of the guerrillas and helped delegitimize the target government, and they neutralized U.S. opposition even as they legitimized support from Cuba as just one of many foreign backers of the insurgents.

This highly sophisticated and subtle strategy was successfully applied in Nicaragua, with far-reaching consequences for the future of Central America. In March 1979, after more than a year of effort, Castro announced the unification of the three guerrilla factions of the Sandinista National Liberation Front (FSLN). During the next three months, Cuba escalated—but also cleverly masked—its military involvement, transshipping through Panama to Costa Rica 450 tons of weapons for use in the "final offensive." It also provided the FSLN with some 200 military advisers, who manned the heavy artillery and other sophisticated weapons, and with an "internationalist brigade" drawn from Central and South American terrorist groups. In addition, an intelligence center was set up at the Cuban Embassy in San Jose under the control of Julian Lopez, the DGI officer sent to Costa Rica the previous year to coordinate Cuba's assistance to the FSLN.

In the meantime, a Broad Opposition Front (FAO) had been established in 1978 consisting of political representatives of the FSLN (the so-called "Group of 12") and leaders of political parties, trade unions, and business and professional groups. Though the FAO was disbanded after the militarization of the conflict had given the FSLN preeminence in the opposition, the Front had, in the words of an FSLN document, "allowed the channeling of external help from many sources and without restrictions, while limiting the maneuvering of the most reactionary forces within the U.S."

Among the principal sources of such external help were the governments of Venezuela, Panama, and Costa Rica, which provided important material, logistic, and political assistance. Other sources included Western European Socialist Governments and the Socialist International, and human rights, church, and political groups in the United States. Instead of moderating the revolution, as many of these external actors had surely hoped to do, they supported the democrats and the "extreme left" without distinction, thus conferring democratic legitimacy on the latter and limiting the options available to the U.S. Their involvement also helped Cuba conceal its decisive role.

The success of the armed struggle in Nicaragua brought about a basic revision of Soviet doctrine regarding revolution in Central and Latin America. The editor of *Latinskaya Amerika,* Sergo Mikoyan, called the Nicaragua revolution an event of "colossal international importance" demanding a "reexamination of established conceptions" in light of the fact that "only the armed road has led to victory in Latin America." Another contributor to the Soviet

publication stated that "The Nicaraguan experience demolished the previous simplistic interpretation of guerrilla actions, confirmed the justice of many of Che Guevara's strategic principles and crystallized his idea of creating a powerful popular guerrilla movement." The President of the Soviet Association of Friendship with Latin American Countries, Viktor Volski, called the armed victory in Nicaragua a "model" to be followed in other countries, while Boris Ponomarev included for the first time the countries of Central America among Third World states undergoing revolutionary changes of "a socialist orientation."

The new line was unanimously endorsed by the leaders of the Central American Communist parties. For example, the Communist Party of El Salvador (PCES), which had previously described the country's insurgent groups as "adventurist" and "bound to fail"—and was accused, in turn, of "decadence" and "revisionism"—made a complete about face and established itself as the revolutionary arm of its front group, the National Democratic Union (UDN). The party secretary Shafik Jorge Handel wrote in *Kommunist,* the theoretical organ of the Soviet Communist Party, that the Salvadoran revolution "will be victorious by the armed road...there is no other way."

The change of line was also embraced by Communist party leaders from elsewhere in Latin America. Luis Corvalan, the leader of the Chilean Communist party who had earlier derided the Castroites as "petty-bourgeois revolutionaries," now called for armed struggle, as did Rodney Arismendi, the first secretary of the Uruguayan Communist party.

The change in doctrine was accompanied by a new build-up of Cuban and now also Nicaraguan military forces, and by an effort to export the Nicaraguan revolution. By the early 1980s, Cuba had become by far the most formidable military power south of the United States, "a kind of vast floating military base," as Robert S. Leiken has aptly put it, "united by a Soviet-built central strategic highway and railway system...." Including army ready reserves, Cuban armed forces in 1981 totalled 227,000. This represented over 2.3 percent of the population, fully 10 times the average proportion of military personnel to population in ten other leading countries of the Basin (including Mexico, Venezuela, Colombia, and the Central American states). Moreover, this figure does not include a paramilitary force of 780,000 consisting of a Youth Labor Army (100,000), a Civil Defense Force (100,000), a Territorial Troop Militia (over 500,000), Border Guard Troops (3,000), the National Revolutionary Police (10,000 plus 52,000 auxiliaries), and the Department of State Security (10,000–15,000).

Whereas the Soviet Union annually delivered an average of 15,000 tons of military equipment to Cuba during the 1970s build-up, 66,000 tons arrived in 1981 and about the same amount the following year. The new equipment enhanced the mobility and firepower of Cuba's ground forces, which have an overwhelming numerical superiority in weapons over Cuba's Latin neighbors, as well as a qualitative advantage. The Cuban Air Force now possesses more than 200 combat jet aircraft, including three squadrons of MiG-23s whose combat radius, if they could refuel in Nicaragua and Grenada, would encompass all of Central America and the eastern Caribbean, southern Mexico, and northern South America. The Air Force is also equipped with Mi-8 helicopter gunships and Mi-24 assault helicopters, as well as AN-26 and other transport aircraft which give Cuba a logistic capability much greater than it had at the time of the airlift to Luanda in 1975. This capability could be used to deploy quickly to crisis points within the region the Special Troops Battalion, a [3,000]–4,000 man all-purpose elite force under Castro's personal command. The expansion of the Cuban Navy that began in the mid-1970s has continued with the acquisition of three Foxtrot- and Whiskey-class submarines, a Koni-class frigate, 24 fast-

attack missile craft, 24 fast-attack torpedo craft, and 22 fast-attack patrol craft, as well as coastal patrol craft, minesweepers, and landing craft.

A corresponding military build-up has taken place in Nicaragua. According to Nicaraguan army commander Joachin Cuadra, by the end of 1982 the Nicaraguan forces had grown to be "four times as big and eight times as strong" as Somoza's Guardia Nacional. With a population of just 2.7 million, Nicaragua has 25,000 regulars and 80,000 reserves and militias, a force that already vastly overshadows that of Honduras, with only a 15,000 man force, and Costa Rica, which has no armed forces at all. Moreover, the Nicaraguan force is rapidly being built up through broad-based conscription and Soviet bloc logistic support.

Nicaragua has added nearly 40 new military bases, as well as a powerful array of Soviet Bloc weaponry, including some 50–60 T-54/55 tanks—the heaviest by far in Central America—1,000 East German trucks and armored personnel carriers, heavy artillery, assualt helicopters, antiaircraft weapons, mobile multiple rocket launchers, patrol boats, and amphibious ferries. The first delivery of sophisticated Soviet electronic gear of a type seen previously in Cuba took place in December 1982, giving Nicaragua the ability to intercept signals from throughout Central America that would be especially useful in locating Honduran military communication sites.

The acquisition of these and other weapons accelerated during 1983, with 14 deliveries arriving from the Soviet Union between January and August, compared to 11 such deliveries in all of 1982. Libya has also succeeded in delivering military equipment to Nicaragua after its failed attempt earlier [in 1983] to transship through Brazil arms labelled as medical equipment.

The foreign military presence in Nicaragua includes Soviet, East European, Libyan, and PLO advisers, along with a 2,000 man Cuban force that is reportedly headed now by the former commander of the Cuban forces in Angola and Ethiopia. East German advisers have reorganized Nicaragua's internal security apparatus and intelligence system and set up a military communications network linking Managua with Havana and Moscow, while the Soviets are supervising the reorganization and "Sovietization" of the Nicaraguan economy. The Cubans have constructed a major strategic road between Puerto Cabezas and the interior, facilitating the movement of troops and supplies to suppress and remove indigenous Indian residents of the region. They have also supervised the extension of the airfields at Puerto Cabezas and Bluefields on the Atlantic Coast and Montlimar on the Pacific Coast to accommodate advanced jet aircraft. About 70 Nicaraguan pilots who were trained in Bulgaria are now in Cuba, where it is reported that about an equal number of advanced MiG warplanes designated for Nicaragua have recently arrived.

The Nicaraguan leaders have made no secret of their intention to use this new military capability to promote revolution through armed struggle in Central America. The *Economist* (May 16, [1983]) quoted Defense Minister Humberto Ortega as follows: "Of course we are not ashamed to be helping El Salvador. We would like to help all revolutions." Similarly, Interior Minister Tomas Borge told columnists Evans and Novak earlier [in 1983] that the Sandinista revolution was the vanguard for similar revolutions throughout the region and that "the energies released here will be universal in all Central America."

The effort to export the Nicaraguan revolution to El Salvador began almost as soon as the Sandinistas had seized power in Managua. As had earlier been the case in Nicaragua, the first priority was to unite the various Salvadoran guerrilla factions. A meeting in Havana in December 1979 resulted in an initial unity agreement, after which a combined military command was formed called the Unified Revolutionary Directorate (DRU). A joint com

mand and control apparatus was established in the Managua area, and logistic and training support for the guerrillas was organized on Nicaraguan soil with Cuban and other Soviet Bloc assistance.

The training of the Salvadoran guerrillas in military tactics, sabotage, explosives, and special commando operations has taken place in Cuba as well as in Nicaragua. One Salvadoran guerrilla who defected to Honduras in September 1981, for example, reported that he and 12 others were sent for training from Nicaragua to Cuba, where over 900 other Salvadorans were also being trained.

Cuba is also intimately involved in the arms supply to Salvadoran guerrillas, both by shipping arms destined for El Salvador directly to Nicaragua and by coordinating the acquisition and delivery of arms from Vietnam, Ethiopia, and Eastern Europe. In December 1981, after meetings in Havana with Salvadoran guerrilla leaders, Castro directed that external supplies of arms to FMLN [Farabundo Marti National Liberation Front] units be stepped up with a view toward mounting an offensive that would disrupt the elections planned for March 1982. In addition to ammunition, these supply operations have included greater quantities of sophisticated heavy weapons, including M-60 machine guns, M-79 grenade launchers, and M-72 antitank weapons. Confirmation that Nicaragua remains the primary source of these weapons was given by Alejandro Montenegro, a high-level Salvadoran FMLN leader captured during a raid on a guerrilla safehouse in Honduras in August 1982. One of the guerrillas captured with Montenegro had already made five trips to Managua that year to pick up arms for the insurgents, using a truck modified by the Sandinistas to carry concealed weapons.

Montenegro also provided evidence of the role played by Cuba and Nicaragua in the Salvadoran armed struggle. He said that he personally had attended two high-level meetings with Cuban officials in 1981, one in Havana and the other in Managua, to review the situation in El Salvador and to receive strategic advice. Another captured Salvadoran guerrilla leader, Lopez Arriola, admitted to attending a platoon leaders course in Cuba in July 1979. He also confirmed that the Sandinistas control weapons delivered to Nicaragua for the Salvadoran insurgents, and that the guerrillas have to seek permission from the Sandinista authorities to draw on the supplies. He added that the Sandinistas give the insurgents an extensive base of operations in and around Managua, and even provide a school for their children.

After years of combat, the Salvadoran guerrilla headquarters in Nicaragua has evolved into an extremely sophisticated command and control center. Guerrilla planning and operations are guided from this headquarters, and Cuban and Nicaraguan officers are involved in command and control, coordinating logistical support for the insurgents which includes food, medicines, clothing, and money as well as weapons and ammunition.

The Salvadoran insurgents have not denied their relationship with Cuba and Nicaragua. In a broadcast last year, the Salvadoran guerrilla Radio Venceremos declared, "We are and will continue to be friends of the peoples and Governments of Cuba and Nicaragua, and we are not ashamed of this." It added: "We have conducted important logistics operations clandestinely, which have served to provide our forces with arms and ammunition for long periods of time. We have conducted these operations using all the means available, and, therefore, have used the entire Central American region and other countries." The purpose of these operations, the broadcast pointed out, was the destruction of the Salvadoran economy.

This past spring, for example, the guerrillas announced a heightened campaign to disrupt the planting of cotton and the processing of coffee, products that account for 60 percent of El Salvador's export earnings. In an effort to stop trade and communication between El Salvador and Honduras, they increased the destruction of bridges. Following the destruction of the bridge at El Amantillo in April, the guerrillas announced that they would kill anyone who tried to repair it. They have attacked the rail system, hoping that the paralysis of traffic between the capital and the East Coast would discourage growers and investors. They have also ordered continued operations against energy and transportation facilities and have destroyed hydro-electric plants.

As a result of these massive attacks, unemployment has increased from 7 percent to 40 percent since 1979, per capita income is down by over 30 percent, the eastern part of the country has been blacked out for most of the year, half of the country's buses have been destroyed, schools have been closed, and hundreds of thousands have fled, including many of the best educated and trained citizens.

El Salvador has not been the only target of the armed struggle in Central America. Guatemala exemplifies Cuban and Nicaraguan efforts to create a unified guerrilla command as a first step in mounting a sustained insurgency. In the fall of 1980 the four major Guatemalan guerrilla groups met in Managua to negotiate a unity agreement. It was signed in November—in Managua—in the presence of Manuel Pineiro Losada, the Chief of Cuba's Americas Department. Following the unity agreement, which set the goal of establishing a Marxist-Leninist state, Cuba agreed to increase military training and assistance for the Guatemalan guerrillas, including instruction in the use of heavy weapons. Arms smuggled from Nicaragua overland through Honduras have included 50mm mortars, submachine guns, rocket launchers, and M-16 rifles that have been traced to U.S. forces in Vietnam.

Reflecting the Nicaraguan experience, the Guatemalan guerrillas have adopted a comprehensive political-military strategy which combines a commitment to prolonged armed struggle with an awareness of the need to establish popular front organizations and links with the media, churches of all denominations, human rights organizations, trade unions, political parties, and sympathetic governments. A General Revolutionary Command (CGR) has been established by the leaders of the four insurgent groups to plan military strategies and strengthen ties to front organizations and international solidarity networks in Mexico, Central America, the United States, and Europe.

Honduras has also become a target of Cuban and Nicaraguan assisted armed struggle. Until 1981, Havana and Managua maintained links with Honduran terrorist groups primarily for the purpose of transporting arms to insurgents in El Salvador and Guatemala. At the same time, the ground was laid for armed struggle with the formation of the Morazanist Front for the Liberation of Honduras (FMLH). In *El Nuevo Diario,* the pro-government Nicaraguan newspaper, a founder of the FMLH described it as a political-military organization formed as part of the "increasing regionalization of the Central American conflict." Evidence of Nicaraguan and Cuban involvement came when Honduran authorities raided several guerrilla safehouses in late November 1981, detaining a number of guerrillas, including several Nicarguans. Captured documents and statements by detained guerrillas revealed that the group was formed in Nicaragua at the instigation of high-level Sandinista leaders, that its chief of operations resided in Nicaragua, and that members of the group had received military training in Nicaragua and Cuba.

The strategy pursued in Honduras until March 1983 involved a series of urban terrorist incidents, most of which saw Salvadoran guerrilla groups working together with Hondurans. Captured Salvadoran and Honduran terrorists have admitted that explosives used in bombing attacks in the Honduran capital were obtained in Nicaragua. Other information indicates that the Cubans had a hand in planning the seizure of 108 hostages in San Pedro Sula in September 1983.

In March 1983 the Communist effort to destabilize Honduras took a new turn with the announcement that four extreme left groups had formed a Unified Revolutionary Coordinating Board. The April 21 issue of *Barricada*, the Sandinista organ, published the new group's declaration of "Popular Revolutionary War" which called on the Honduran people to rise up against the government and armed forces and against "U.S. imperialism."

Subsequently, on July 19, 96 Honduran guerrillas launched an unsuccessful raid from Nicaragua into Olancho Department. The 24 guerrillas who deserted or were captured told a fairly consistent story of their recruitment and training. In almost all cases they were recruited by deception, having been told that they would receive some type of training in mechanics or agriculture. They were not told that they would be sent to Cuba. The training took up to two years and included 4 to 6 months in Cuba at the guerrilla training school in Pinar del Rio. There they received instructions in ideology, weapons, intelligence, and military tactics. At the same camp were guerrilla trainees from other countries, including El Salvador and Guatemala. For some, the stay in Cuba included "volunteer labor" as farm workers or servants at state guest houses. Following their stay in Cuba, they were sent to Nicaragua for additional training before their entry into Honduras on July 19. Statements by Havana and Managua indicate that despite the failure of this raid they will persist in efforts at rural insurgency and destabilization in Honduras.

Costa Rica remains the most politically stable nation in Central America but it, too, has not been able to isolate itself from the turmoil in the region. For the past two years, Cuba and Nicaragua have used terrorism and diplomacy to intimidate Costa Rica into neutralism. The July 1982 bombing of the Honduran Airline office in San Jose, for example, took place at Nicaragua's direction. The captured terrorist who placed the bomb said that Nicaraguan diplomats in Costa Rica had recruited and trained him for the operation. Though Nicaragua denied complicity, the accused diplomats were caught *in flagrante,* declared *persona non grata,* and expelled from the country. The captured terrorist also stated that the bombing had been part of a broader Nicaraguan plan which included sabotage, kidnapping, bank robberies, and other acts designed to discredit Costa Rica internationally. Since the beginning of 1982, several guerrilla arms caches and safehouses have been uncovered in Costa Rica.

Terrorist attacks have continued to occur in San Jose, along with a joint Cuban, Soviet, and Nicaraguan campaign attacking Costa Rican democracy. There have also been incidents involving Sandinista forces along the border, including the recent Nicaraguan attack on the Costa Rican border installation at Penas Blancas which Costa Rica denounced at a specially called meeting of the OAS Permanent Council.

The cumulative effect of the armed assault on Central America and of the overall growth of Soviet and Cuban military power in the Caribbean Basin has been to pose a major threat to the "strategic rear" of the United States. The view that U.S. security is only threatened by the establishment of Soviet military bases in the region or by the deployment of SS-20 missiles there—a step repeatedly threatened by the Soviets, most recently by the chief of the Warsaw Pact forces in connection with the planned deployment of U.S. intermediate range missiles in Europe—overlooks the vital strategic importance to the United States of a secure Basin.

Until now, the United States has been able to act on the assumption that its "strategic rear" was secure and did not require a large diversion of military resources for its protection. The Western Alliance has benefited from this "economy of force" posture since, as Congressman Dante B. Fascell has pointed out, "in a real sense it is the nonthreatening environment close to home that permits the United States to concentrate so much manpower, equipment, and attention on Europe."

This situation has already begun to change as the United States has had to expend increased military resources and growing attention on the crisis in Central America. In the event of a collapse there, the reversal of our posture would be swift and drastic, requiring the diversion of significant resources to protect our southern border and the Caribbean Basin. Were the United States ever to be tied down within this region in such a manner, our ability to fulfill commitments in Europe and elsewhere in the world, not to speak of our own security and well-being, would inevitably suffer.

The Basin is also important strategically, since as much as 70 percent of U.S. seaborne reinforcements to NATO would transit the sealanes leading from the Gulf Coast and the Panama Canal in the event of a Soviet armed attack in Europe. The goal of interdicting such reinforcements is an important element in Soviet strategic thinking, as set forth in 1979 by Soviet Navy Fleet Admiral Sergei Gorshkov in his book, *Naval Power in Soviet Policy*:

> To achieve superiority of forces over the enemy in the main sector and pin him down in secondary sectors...means to achieve sea control in a theater or a sector of a theater...the enemy will be paralyzed or constrained in his operations...and thereby hampered from interfering with our operations.

The Soviets have already achieved a far greater interdiction capability than the Nazis had during World War Two, when 50 percent of U.S. supplies to Europe and Africa were shipped from Gulf ports. At that time, German U-boats were able to sink 260 merchant ships in just six months, despite the fact that the Allied forces enjoyed many advantages, including a two-to-one edge in submarines and the use of Cuba for resupply and basing operations. The Germans, meanwhile, had to operate from the Bay of Biscay, 4,000 miles across the Atlantic and without the benefit of aircover. Today these advantages have been reversed. It is the Soviet Union that now has the two-to-one edge in submarines and can operate and receive aircover from Cuba, a point from which all 13 Caribbean sealanes passing through four choke-points are vulnerable to interdiction.

The Soviet ability to carry out a strategy of "strategic denial" is further enhanced by the presence near Havana of the largest Soviet-managed electronic monitoring complex outside the Soviet Union, as well as by the deployment of TU-95 Bear reconnaissance aircraft.

The strategic position of the Soviet Union in the Caribbean would be considerably strengthened if Grenada were used for refueling and stationing tactical and transport aircraft or as a site for naval refueling, both real possibilities with the construction of a new airport at Port Salines and the reports of Soviet plans to build naval facilities on the island. The establishment of new Soviet military positions in Grenada would give Moscow a routine military presence in the Eastern Caribbean, while the acquisition of new positions in Nicaragua—especially the construction of a naval base on the Pacific Coast, where a fishing port is being built— would extend the Soviet reach to the Pacific Basin. Either development would constitute a major gain for Soviet strategy.*

The sea routes of the Caribbean are also important economically to the United States, since they now carry nearly half of all the crude oil and other foreign cargo shipped to this country. Moreover, the Basin itself is a growing source of critical raw materials. Mexico supplies 33 percent of the crude oil currently imported by the U.S. and has reserves estimated at 45 billion barrels, roughly equal to the reserves of such major producers as Iraq and Abu Dhabi. Venezuela and Trinidad and Tobago supply another 8 percent of U.S. crude oil

imports, while 56 percent of the refined petroleum products imported to the U.S. come from Basin refineries. In addition, Jamaica and several other Basin countries supply 85 percent of the bauxite imported to the U.S. and nearly 40 percent of the alumina.

Beyond the issue of U.S. strategic interests in the Basin, the overriding fact is that our credibility worldwide is inevitably engaged in an area so close to the United States. The triumph of hostile forces in our "strategic rear" would be read as a sign of U.S. impotence—the inability successfully to define our objectives, manage our policy, and defend our interests.

A consensus on policy would need to be based upon a common understanding of the nature of the problem facing the United States in Central America. The view heard frequently that the problem is essentially internal, deriving from poverty and repression, does not take adequate account of the scope of the external threat facing the region and the extent to which the Soviet Union and Cuba are exploiting the serious problems of very vulnerable Central American societies. Since their strategy of armed struggle wreaks havoc with any effort to promote economic opportunity, a democratic political center and free institutions, and a more professional military—the pillars of any meaningful policy of reform in Central America—it is hard to see how it is possible to deal effectively with internal problems without resisting the external threat. As President Kennedy's Latin American task force declared in its report that led to the creation of the Alliance for Progress, "good wishes and economic plans do not stop bullets or hand grenades or armed bands."

Today the threat is greater—far greater— than it was in 1961 when the task force declared that it "resembles, but is more dangerous than, the Nazi-Fascist threat of the Franklin Roosevelt period and demands an even bolder and

* *Editors' note:* In October 1983 a U.S. military intervention in Grenada toppled the Marxist government there.

more imaginative response." Moreover, today we have fewer resources at our disposal—economically, militarily, strategically, politically. We are still, ten years after the withdrawal from Vietnam, divided over our foreign policy and national purpose, over our understanding of the threat we face and our sense of our proper role in the world.

The deterioration in the region to our immediate south has been such, however, that we cannot afford paralysis in defending our national interests and in achieving our national purposes. The fact that such paralysis could be attributed to the continuing absence of a national consensus on foreign policy in the United States would not mitigate the consequences of failure. As George Kennan once wrote, "History does not forgive us our national mistakes because they are explicable in terms of our domestic politics."

[The United States and Central America]

Sol M. Linowitz

I am very pleased to have been invited to meet with your Commission in order to talk about some of the critical problems we face in Central America. Let me say at the outset that I believe the only way to understand the problems of Central America and what lies behind them is to view them against the backdrop of United States–Latin American relations over the years. For I submit to you that it will not be possible to deal effectively and thoughtfully with the challenges we confront in Central America today unless we have some sense of what has gone before in our Hemispheric relationships:

Unhappily, Latin America is an area of the world which has been largely overlooked, ignored or disregarded in the United States. James Reston once said that Americans will do anything for Latin America except read about it, and I am afraid that he is all too accurate. No responsible American leader since the days of President Monroe has dared to tell the American people that we can neglect or ignore Latin America, yet we have consistently relegated Latin America to the backwash of history—

From *Report of the National Bipartisan Commission* on *Central America, Appendix* (Washington, D.C.: Government Printing Office, 1984), pp. 666–679.

focusing on it only in moments of crisis. Over the years we have tended to take Latin America for granted or to use the region to score points and teach lessons rather than to build constructive relationships.

Ask most Americans about Latin America and you get a glazed look. Few can name as many as ten Latin American countries. Few know the immense differences—cultural, physical, political, sociological—that separate the countries and permit you to change five centuries by crossing a border. Relatively few recognize that Latin America consists of individual nations at critical points in their history determined to fulfill their destiny in their own way.

Now we have suddenly rediscovered Latin America and its significance to the United States. The strife in Central America; the aftermath of the war in the South Atlantic; the financial upheavals in Mexico, Brazil, Venezuela, Argentina and elsewhere; the dramatic flow of migrants from Mexico, Haiti, Cuba and other countries—reveal all too clearly that what happens in Latin America deeply affects the security, welfare, culture and politics of the United States. And by the same token, what happens in the United States has a great impact on Latin America.

Because of my own concern about these problems and my own involvement in Latin American relations over the years, some months ago I talked to a number of men and women both in the United States and in Latin America—people of different parties from different professional perspectives and different generations—about the need to come together in order to exchange ideas on how we might approach the problems in inter-American relations today.

I was struck by how much had changed in Hemispheric relationships since the 1970's when I had served as Chairman of the Commission on United States–Latin American relations.

In the mid-1970's we thought that revising the Panama Canal Treaty was the most urgent issue in United States–Latin American relations. Today that problem is largely behind us.

In the mid-1970's because of Latin America's dynamic growth and prospects, we viewed Latin America's economic future with great optimism. Today we know all too well that Latin America faces a severe economic downturn and an acute crisis of overwhelming debts and high unemployment.

In the mid-1970's, territorial conflicts were not regarded as particularly significant. Today these questions are hard to avoid, and they in turn raise other issues such as the arms races, peace-keeping capabilities and the like.

In the mid-1970's, we were disturbed by what we called a "plague of repression" sweeping the Americas. Today we are aware of deep stirrings for a return to democracy in many countries, and the struggle in many nations to achieve progress toward a fuller respect for human rights.

In the 1970's, we paid little attention to Central America which we regarded as a relatively tranquil corner of the Hemisphere. Today we know all too well that we did not have enough understanding to anticipate the fierce struggles now being waged in that region.

And in the 1970's, while we were aware that the so-called "special relationship" in the Hemisphere was declining, we could not have imagined that the United States and major Latin American countries would actually line up on opposite sides of a war.

All these developments made unmistakably clear that there had been drastic changes in inter-American relations in a relatively few years, and what was needed was a new look, free of preconceptions and prejudices.

Dr. Galo Plaza, former President of Ecuador and former Secretary General of the Organization of American States, joined me in convening a group of distinguished opinion leaders from all over the Hemisphere in order to examine the issues in an Inter-American Dialogue. Twenty-four leaders from 15 countries of Latin America, one Canadian and 23 from the United States responded to our invitation. Our group included two former Latin American Presidents, four former Foreign Ministers, six former Finance Ministers, and such distinguished North Americans—Republicans and Democrats alike—as David Rockefeller; General David Jones; Father Theodore Hesburgh; Cyrus Vance; Edmund Muskie; Elliot Richardson; Robert McNamara; Ralph Davidson, Chairman of Time, Inc.; Frank Shakespeare, Chairman of the Heritage Foundation; and Mayor Henry Cisneros, a member of this Commission.

Our studies and deliberations went on for a period of six months, and during that time we consulted extensively with high officials in a number of countries. In the United States, for example, we met with Secretary of State Shultz, Vice President Bush, Assistant Secretary of State Enders and others. Working together in the Dialogue, we had a chance to look beyond today's headlines and to think hard and carefully about the kind of tomorrow we wanted in the Americas, and how to help achieve it.

The opening words of our Report were these: "The Western Hemisphere today faces challenges more serious than any since World War II, or perhaps even the Great Depression.'' And we undertook to examine some of the most important economic, political, social and security problems confronting the Americas.

We started with the grave economic and financial crisis in Latin America today—a crisis which, in my judgment, is no less serious and threatening to the security and stability of the Americas than the wars being fought in Central America.

To put it briefly, the debt crisis in Latin America which has plunged Mexico, Brazil, Argentina, Venezuela, Chile and Costa Rica, among others, into deep trouble is also a serious problem for the United States; and our entire closely interlinked financial system is under challenge. To address these problems, we suggested measures to deal with the immediate liquidity crisis and also offered recommendations for resuming the sustained economic growth and development which will be required for a longer term solution. Let me just mention some of the specific recommendations on which we focused attention in our Report.

The strengthening of the International Monetary Fund; the expansion of the role of the multi-lateral development banks; extension of the maturities of existing debt in various Latin American countries; an increase in flows of private, direct investment; resistance to protectionist sentiment both in the Hemisphere and worldwide; the stabilization of commodity export earnings; and the speedy approval of the Administration's Caribbean Basin Initiative.

I suggest that all of these are relevant to your own charge as a Commission to review the economic problems affecting Central America and to develop recommendations for long-term economic policies. Money used for debt servicing is not available for development. And economic austerity programs imposed insensitively can have drastic social and political effects.

In recent weeks we have heard much about a possible Marshall Plan for Central America.

The term is appealing, but I submit that it is very important to be clear as to exactly what it means and what it does not mean.

The simple fact is that the problems of Central America and of Latin America are not like those of Europe a generation ago when we evolved the Marshall Plan for the reconstruction of Europe. There is too little to reconstruct, recover or rebuild in Central America. What can be borrowed from the Marshall Plan is the overriding objective—*a multilateral undertaking not directed against any country or ideology, but against poverty, chaos and distress*. This is essentially the goal set forth in the OAS Charter which enunciates our joint objectives in the Americas in these words: ''A united effort to insure social justice in the Hemisphere and dynamic and balanced economic development for their peoples, as conditions essential for peace and security.''

In that connection, we must recognize that Latin America is today at a political crossroads. During the last several years, much of Latin America has moved toward more open and representative policies, and the bases are being laid for a renewal of democracy in much of the Western Hemisphere.

If these democratic openings are to take hold, governments and political movements must enlist the participation of the great majority of Latin Americans by responding to their desire for improved conditions of life. Latin American countries have made substantial gains in recent years in such areas as health and education. But World Bank estimates still show that one-half of Latin America's rural population and one-quarter its city dwellers remain in ''absolute poverty.'' At least another one-third of the region's population is poor by contemporary standards.

The persistent poverty of two-thirds of the people of Latin America is the major cause of the Hemisphere's social unrest. Poverty, inequality and injustice lead to political protest and polarization. Polarization, in turn, frequently leads to repression, followed by cycles of violent opposition, widespread violations of human rights, and greater social injustice. To break this cycle, to increase the opportunities for human fulfillment, and to build more stable societies, sustained commitments to alleviate poverty will have to be made throughout the Americas.

The renewal and expansion of democratic procedures offer the best hope of progress toward greater social justice. But democratization is by its nature a national process for which individuals and institutions within each country must be responsible. Democracy is not a set of formal mechanisms and procedures that can be sent abroad. It is a process, a set of commitments rooted in the history and culture of a nation, a process that can be nurtured and encouraged but not transplanted or imposed. While outside countries can and should encourage the growth of democratic institutions, it is doubtful that any government—perhaps least of all that of the most powerful country in the Hemisphere—can in a direct way undertake to build democratic political institutions in other countries.

Accordingly, the recommendations in our Report for advancing democracy in the Hemisphere were quite modest.

First, we oppose any activities—covert or overt—by government and other institutions which undermine the political autonomy or integrity of any country. We believe that the principle of non-intervention is vital for safeguarding democratization.

Second, we believe that foreign governments, international organizations and private institutions can contribute importantly but indirectly to democratization through support of equitable economic and social development.

Third, we believe that governments can help create a climate favorable to democracy through the tone and quality of their diplomatic relations. We hope that democratic countries in the Americas will maintain warmer and more supportive relations with other democracies.

But we would counsel against breaking diplomatic relations with authoritarian governments, since this tends to rally nationalist support for a regime and to reinforce rigidity.

On the issue of human rights, clearly the protection and advancement of human rights is primarily the domestic responsibility of the national government. But it is also a legitimate international concern. And this should be reflected in the foreign policies of the governments and in the programs of international organizations. For carefully considered multilateral action to protect fundamental human rights is not intervention, but an international obligation. Direct unilateral intervention of any government in the domestic affairs of others, even on behalf of human rights, can have unfortunate consequences. But silence and inaction in the face of clear abuses are inexcusable. For these can threaten both the security and the stability of the Hemisphere.

In focusing on the issue of security, we agreed on two important points: First, that the basic roots of insecurity—and the basic problems of security—in the Hemisphere are primarily economic, social and political, not military. Second, that sources of insecurity are mainly internal to each nation, and external influences are secondary.

It was also our firm conviction that even when there is a military dimension to conflict as in Central America, the solutions ultimately lie in economic and social development and political dialogue and not in weapons or military advisors. Even when external support for insurrection clearly is present, as in El Salvador, the underlying problems remain domestic.

There are significant differences in the way security is conceived and defined in the United States as against the way it is understood in Latin America. When Latin Americans think of security, most of them tend to think of the internal challenges of national unity, of border issues with neighboring states, and, in some cases, of the possibility of intervention by the United States.

In the United States, the focus on security is external, global and strategic. Because of its worldwide interest and role, the United States generally seeks to assure political stability by supporting the status quo under sharp internal or regional challenge. Many Latin Americans, on the other hand, feel that profound change in the region is inevitable and that an emphasis on immediate stability is, therefore, misguided.

These differences are reconcilable. For both North Americans and Latin Americans stress self-determination and non-intervention as norms. Both favor keeping Latin America and the Caribbean out of the East-West conflict to the greatest extent possible. Both understand that social and economic progress is vital for achieving political stability and protecting national and international security.

Our approach toward the Central American conflict was based on two major premises. First, that most citizens and governments throughout the Hemisphere oppose an expansion of Soviet and Cuban military presence in the Americas. Second, that the United States could do much to foster a climate of security in the region by making unequivocally clear its commitment to respect national sovereignty.

Accordingly, we strongly endorsed the initiative taken by Colombia, Mexico, Panama and Venezuela in the Contadora Declaration, offering their good offices in seeking peaceful solutions to Central America's problems. We urged the United States to declare its full support for the Contadora group's efforts and its readiness to participate in the discussions as might be deemed appropriate.

Such an American commitment must make unmistakably clear by word and deed that this regional approach is *central* to our planning for the resolution of the conflicts—and not just peripheral to it; and that we stand resolutely with the Contadora countries as partners in this common effort. I am afraid that such a commitment is still lacking.

We also made a further recommendation, suggesting that it might be worth exploring the possibility that the United States–Soviet understandings of 1962, 1970 and 1979 with respect to Cuba might provide a basis for a wider accord that could enhance the collective security of the entire region. We proposed that this could be explored informally and quietly with both the Soviet Union and Cuba in order to determine the possibility of arriving at understandings.

Recent statements by Fidel Castro appear to encourage such an approach and suggest that we should indeed, in the President's words, give Castro "the benefit of the doubt" and ask our Contadora friends to explore the seriousness of his own proposal along this line.

Of course, we cannot be sure that such discussions would succeed. But we are sure that the perils and costs of allowing the Central American conflicts to grow are grave and raise the specter of wider conflicts. And the dangers are growing—for time is not on the side of peace. Accordingly, we firmly believe—all of us from North and South America and covering a wide spectrum of views and experience—that negotiations should and must be tried—on all levels.

In both El Salvador and Nicaragua, negotiations should be pursued with the help of the Contadora countries to arrange for free internationally supervised elections on the basis of security guarantees for all parties and participants. And in the region as a whole, a major effort should be undertaken in conjunction with our Latin American friends to find a way to settle the conflicts.

All of this suggests a few basic principles which I believe should guide us in dealing with the Central American situation today.

First, we must recognize that the problems of Central America are primarily regional ones, affecting all of the countries in the area and not just the United States. Accordingly, we cannot and must not undertake unilaterally to deal with the issue as if it were ours alone to solve.

Second, as a regional issue it is a problem which must and can be dealt with only on a regional and cooperative basis. The Contadora countries have taken leadership in exploring avenues for peaceful negotiation of the conflicts and we should make unequivocally clear our full commitment to their efforts.

Third, we must understand that the basic problem of Central America today is essentially a political problem with a military dimension rather than—as our present policy seems to suggest—a military problem with a political dimension. Accordingly, we must recognize that a military response in Central America will not by itself achieve a solution.

Fourth, we must be clear about what we seek to achieve in Central America and consistent in our words and actions moving toward that objective. We cannot, for example, assert that we are committed to regional cooperation and, at the same time, pursue our own course without regard to the views of our friends and allies. We cannot maintain that we are committed to self-determination and freedom of choice for the people of Central America, yet assume we can undertake to prescribe what that choice must be.

In short, the United States of America must stand for the peaceful resolution of the conflicts through negotiation, making unmistakably clear our commitment to non-intervention and self-determination as fundamental principles.

I believe that Central America is less a test of our resolve to stand up to the Soviet Union than of our capacity for farsighted leadership and cooperation within our hemisphere—whether we can conduct ourselves with requisite vision, restraint, flexibility and self-confidence, not just as a great power—but as a great democracy.

It may be significant that all who participated in our Report agreed that the security of the Americas had probably been *advanced* more in recent years by the Panama Canal Treaties than by any other single development.

For the Treaties did much to enhance the spirit of cooperation between the two halves of America; and they reinforced the stakes held in common by allowing Latin Americans to take responsibility commensurate with their stakes.

That was the essence of the approach in our Report—not to deny differences in interest and perspective between the United States and Latin America, but to emphasize the important interests we share, and the importance of mutual respect for vital concerns. For as the Mexican patriot Benito Juarez once said: "Respect for the rights of others is peace."

Today we are at a moment of crisis in Central America and in the Hemisphere at large. When conditions of crisis are faced imaginatively, opportunities for progress exist. Such opportunities do exist—especially for the United States. The question is how we will respond to them.

Many years ago, President Theodore Roosevelt described those opportunities in some words singularly applicable to our role in Latin America today—and to your role as members of this Commission: "The United States does not have the option as to whether it will or will not play a great part. It must play a great part. The only question is whether it will play that part well or badly."

QUESTIONS FOR DISCUSSION

1 What are the security threats faced by the United States in the establishment of Marxist governments in the Western hemisphere?

2 What assumptions does Linowitz make about the causes of instability in Central America? On the basis of what you know from history, evaluate the soundness of his assumptions.

3 Does the experience of the political behavior of communist regimes which have differed and sometimes been hostile to the Soviet Union (China, Yugoslavia, and Albania, for example) have any bearing on this debate?

4 Are there any conditions under which the United States should use military force to oust the Sandinista government?

5 What would be the consequences for the United States if it abandoned its support of the Contras in Nicaragua?

SUGGESTED READINGS

Abrams, Elliott. "Intervention in Latin America: Cuba Si, Yanqui No?" *National Interest,* no. 4 (Summer 1986), pp. 74–78.

Barrett, Jeffrey W. *Impulse to Revolution in Latin America.* New York: Praeger, 1985.

"The Case for the Contras," *New Republic,* **194** (Mar. 24, 1986), pp. 7–9.

Coll, Alberto O. "Soviet Arms and Central American Turmoil," *World Affairs,* **148** (Summer 1985), pp. 7–17.

Duncan, W. Raymond. *The Soviet Union and Cuba: Interests and Influence.* New York: Praeger, 1985.

Falcoff, Mark. "How to Understand Central America," *Commentary,* **78** (Sept. 1984), pp. 30–38.

Gonzalez, Edward. "The Cuban and Soviet Challenge in the Caribbean Basin," *Orbis,* **29** (Spring 1985), pp. 73–94.

LaFeber, Walter. "The Reagan Administration and Revolutions in Central America," *Political Science Quarterly,* **99** (Spring 1984), pp. 1–25.

LeoGrande, William M. "Through the Looking Glass: The Report of the National Bipartisan Commission on Central America," *World Policy Journal,* **1** (Winter 1984), pp. 251–284.

Persky, Stan. *America, The Last Domino: U.S. Foreign Policy in Central America under Reagan.* Vancouver, Canada: New Star Books, 1984.

Report of the National Bipartisan Commission on Central America. Washington, D.C.: Government Printing Office, 1984.

Treverton, Gregory F. "U.S. Strategy in Central America," *Survival* (London), **28** (Mar.–Apr. 1986), pp. 128–139.

8 Has U.S. hegemony declined drastically over recent years?

YES

Kenneth A. Oye

International Systems Structure and American Foreign Policy

NO

Bruce Russett

The Mysterious Case of Vanishing Hegemony; or, Is Mark Twain Really Dead?

International Systems Structure and American Foreign Policy

Kenneth A. Oye

HEGEMONIC DECLINE AND STRATEGIES OF RESTORATION

In the thirty-five years since the end of the Second World War, American military and economic preeminence has clearly faded. Western Europe, Japan, and the upper tier of the developing world grew more rapidly than the United States, and American comparative weight in the international economic system declined. The Soviet Union's military capabilities grew more rapidly than American military capabilities, and the United States' comparative weight in the international security system declined. The erosion of American hegemony reflects the dispersion of power as other nations' capabilities have increased relative to those of the United States. Power, defined in terms of ability to influence or control events, cannot be directly measured. Imperfect surrogates can provide a crude sense of the changing American position in the international system. Before turning to the problem of explaining power redistribution, it is useful to assess the magnitude and timing of shifts.

Gross Domestic Product provides a basic measure of the resources a nation can choose to apply to military programs, consumption, and capital investment. Table 1-1...presents estimates of percentage shares of gross world product for 1950, 1960, 1970, and 1980. Discrepancies between the two overlapping series reflect the intrinsic imprecision of the exercise, and give warning of the many opportunities for chicanery in comparing disparate national in-

From Kenneth A. Oye, "International Systems Structure and American Foreign Policy," in Kenneth A. Oye, Robert J. Lieber, and Donald Rothchild, eds., *Eagle Defiant: United States Foreign Policy in the 1980s* (Boston, Mass.: Little, Brown, 1983), pp. 7–16. Copyright © 1983 by Kenneth A. Oye. Reprinted by permission of Little, Brown and Company and Kenneth A. Oye.

comes. Nevertheless, the trends are clear. The American share of world product declined sharply during the 1950s, and more slowly during the 1960s and 1970s. How do the shares of the two competing security blocs compare? The product of the Western advanced industrial states dwarfs that of the Soviet bloc, and the ratio of Western to Eastern production has remained fairly constant over thirty years. The declining weight of the United States in international economic affairs is revealed clearly by comparing the American share with those of Japan, the European Community, and the developing countries. It is important to keep in mind both trends and final position. Even after decades of relatively rapid growth, the nations of the Third World account for less than 15 percent of world product, while the developed Western nations account for over 60 percent of world product.

Military spending and personnel provide a crude measure of military capabilities. Barry Posen and Stephen Van Evera provide an extended assessment of the *adequacy* of American and allied military forces for varied contingencies in Chapter 3 [of *Eagle Defiant*], "Defense Policy: Departure from Containment." As they note, Western military capabilities have not declined relative to the capabilities of the Soviet bloc. However, the simple figures in Table 1-2 confirm perceptions of a decline in the American share of world military spending between 1960 and 1980. Increases in Soviet military spending, the rapid expansion of military spending and forces in the Third World, and increases in Western European military spending are reflected in the figures for world spending and personnel. The sharp decline in the American share of world spending and personnel between 1970 and 1980 reflects both the reallocation of American resources

TABLE 1-1.   SHARES OF GROSS WORLD PRODUCT (PERCENTAGES)

	Council on International Economic Policy Series			Central Intelligence Agency Series		
	1950	**1960**	**1970**	**1960**	**1970**	**1980**
Developed Countries	67.4%	65.2	64.5	66.5	65.7	62.7
United States	39.3	33.9	30.2	25.9	23.0	21.5
European Community	16.1	17.5	18.4	26.0	24.7	22.5
Japan	1.5	2.9	6.2	4.5	7.7	9.0
Other	10.5	10.9	9.7	10.1	10.3	9.7
Less Developed Countries	9.1	9.5	10.0	11.1	12.3	14.8
Communist Countries	23.5	25.3	25.5	22.4	22.0	22.0
Soviet Union	13.5	15.5	16.5	12.5	12.4	11.4
China	4.0	4.5	4.0	3.1	3.4	4.5
Other	6.0	5.3	5.0	6.8	6.2	6.1
Gross World Product in Trillions of 1980 Dollars	$2.4	3.9	6.3	5.0	8.4	12.2

Sources: U.S. Council on International Economic Policy, *The United States in the Changing World Economy* (Washington: GPO, 1971) Volume II, Chart 1. U.S. Central Intelligence Agency, National Foreign Assessment Center, *Handbook of Economic Statistics 1981* (Washington: GPO, 1981), percentages calculated from Table 9. Gross World Product for C.I.E.P. Series derived by dividing U.S. GNP in 1980 dollars (*Economic Report of the President 1982,* Tables B-1 and B-3) by the C.I.E.P. estimate of the U.S. share of Gross World Product. European Community adjusted to include the United Kingdom for all years in both series. Some of the major disparities between the C.I.E.P. and C.I.A. figures for the overlapping years of 1960 and 1970 appear to rest on the following factors: (1) European Community and Japan—Exchange rates used to value national product in dollars; (2) Less Developed Countries and China—Quantity and value of subsistence sector plus exchange rates; and (3) Communist Countries—Quantity and value of production in command economy plus exchange rates.

during the 1970s and the unusually high military effort in 1970 related to the Vietnam War.

What factors account for the clear relative American decline? The pattern of economic and military changes summarized in Tables 1-1 and 1-2 are partially the product of national choices that were, in turn, conditioned by the international distribution of power. Finite economic resource bases create a tradeoff among military spending, investment, and consumption. The priority that nations assign to guns, growth, and butter is the best single predictor of changes in economic and military strength. Table 1-3 summarizes the choices and growth rates of the United States, United Kingdom, West Germany, Japan, and the Soviet Union in the period 1960 through 1979. The Soviet Union financed very high investment and very high levels of military spending by repressing consumption and thereby attained military parity with the United States while sustaining a moderately high, but declining,

growth rate. Japan opted for very high levels of investment and moderate levels of consumption while spending little on defense, and it achieved an astonishing growth rate of 8.5 percent per year. Germany balanced moderate investment, military spending, and consumption, and grew at 4.7 percent in the 1960s and 2.9 percent in the 1970s. Britain's high consumption, high military spending, and low investment strategy yielded an average 2.5 percent growth rate. The United States' high consumption, low investment, and moderately high military spending approach yielded a growth rate of 3.6 percent. In summary, the United States did not match German and Japanese economic and Soviet military investments simultaneously.

These figures summarizing national allocation of resources to investment, defense, and consumption are clear and consequential, but they raise a difficult basic question. How can we explain these national choices? Robert Gil-

TABLE 1-2.   UNITED STATES SHARE OF WORLD MILITARY SPENDING AND PERSONNEL

	1960	1970	1980
U.S. Military Spending as a Share of World Spending	51%	42%	28%
World Military Spending in billions 1978 $	$341	$469	$570
U.S. Armed Forces Personnel as a Share of World Personnel	13%	14%	8.3%
World Armed Forces Personnel in thousands	18,550	21,484	24,435

Sources: Computed from *Department of Defense Annual Report for Fiscal Year 1983*, pages I-5 and C-3; Ruth Sivard, *World Military and Social Expenditures*, p. 24; and *Economic Report of the President*, Table B-3.

pin's important recent book, *War and Change in World Politics,* examines the decline of the Athenian, Roman, Dutch, British, and American empires, and develops a set of propositions to account for regularities in cycles of hegemonic decline. In each case, *external burdens of leadership, internal secular tendencies toward rising consumption,* and *the international diffusion of technology* appear to explain hegemonic recession. How well do these factors account for the American decline? Which factors bear on Soviet prospects?

Every strategy of dominance undercuts the economic bases of dominance. The United States' strategy of containment centers on the protection of Western Europe and Japan. Table 1-3 indicates clearly that the United States bears a disproportionate share of the burden of defense. In "An Economic Theory of Alliances," Mancur Olson and Richard Zeckhauser note that because the dominant state in an alliance has an absolute interest in offering protection, smaller allies have little incentive to contribute proportionately to their own defense.[1] Because the loss of the technologically advanced Western nations would have catastrophic effects on American interests, the United States cannot credibly threaten to retract American protection and therefore lacks leverage to coerce increases in allied defense spending. Lesser threats and jawboning by the Nixon, Ford, and Carter administrations did succeed in doubling the Europeans' share of the NATO burden, but the persistent tendency of the United States to devote a disproportionate share of national product to defense remains. American, Western European, and Japanese "choices" of guns, growth, and butter are conditioned by this elemental aspect of alliance relationships. Even with overt and covert coercive means, the Soviet Union bears an even more highly

[1]Mancur Olson and Richard Zeckhauser, "An Economic Theory of Alliances," *The Review of Economics and Statistics* 48 (1966), pp. 266–279.

TABLE 1-3.   ALLOCATION OF GROSS DOMESTIC PRODUCT—AVERAGE PERCENTAGES 1960-1979

	Annual Growth Rate	Fixed Capital Formation	Military Spending	Consumption Gov't+Private=Total		
United States	3.6%	17.6	7.4	10.9	63.0	73.9
United Kingdom	2.5	18.4	5.4	13.0	62.8	75.8
West Germany	3.9	24.1	3.9	13.2	55.6	68.8
Japan	8.5	32.7	.9	7.7	55.4	63.1
*Soviet Union**	4.1	28.7	14.0	-	-	54.1

Sources: For Western nations, see Robert DeGrasse, *The Costs and Consequences of Reagan's Military Buildup* (New York: Council on Economic Priorities, 1982). For the Soviet Union, see C.I.A., *Handbook of Economic Statistics 1981,* Table 37 on Fixed Capital Formation and Consumption, and Department of Defense, *Annual Report to Congress Fiscal Year 1983* for estimated military spending.
   * The Soviet figures do not add to 100 because different sources were used for estimates of investment and consumption and of military spending. The C.I.A. estimate for "R&D, inventory change, net exports, outlays and defense" over this period comes to 17.25 percent of Soviet product.

disproportionate share of military spending within the Warsaw Pact.

A second burden of leadership is at least partially self-imposed. During the 1950s and 1960s, the United States guaranteed the security of anticommunist governments in peripheral regions against internal and external threats. The globalization of containment rested on American willingness to intervene to forestall revolution under disadvantageous circumstances. The apotheosis of global containment—the American intervention in Indochina—entailed enormous costs in blood and treasure and triggered the Nixon's administration's search for less costly means of counterrevolution and the Carter administration's more tolerant attitude toward revolutionary nationalism. The diversion of resources into military consumption undercuts both military and economic investment. Prior to its invasion of Afghanistan, the Soviet Union avoided direct military interventions outside Eastern Europe. However, the recurrent costs of controlling Eastern Europe through invasion and occupation and the uncertain costs of the ongoing Afghan invasion must both be reckoned as substantial costs of dominance.

The costs of bidding for allegiances and bolstering the strength of allies are a third burden of leadership. American postwar promotion of European and Japanese recovery through direct financial assistance and tolerance of trade asymmetries, and security supporting assistance to many Third World states are not reflected in any of the figures in Table 1-3, but they clearly entail economic costs. The Soviet Union's strategy of alternating exploitation and subsidization of Eastern Europe and of providing more modest support for Third World clients lessens this cost of dominance. However, the continuing instability of Eastern Europe and defection of China follow, at least in part, from Soviet efforts to concentrate resources on Soviet economic and military growth.

The second major factor, a secular tendency toward increasing consumption, is directly reflected in Table 1-3. A former hegemonic power, Great Britain, and a declining hegemonic power, the United States, top the list in terms of proportion of national product devoted to consumption. Democratic governments may be incapable of cutting domestic consumption to maintain international position, and authoritarian governments may cut consumption only at the risk of increasing domestic political instability. Are the Soviets immune from this tendency toward rising consumption? Grumblings over the quality of life in the Soviet Union and Eastern Europe are endemic, and the recent rise of Solidarity in Poland was based on both economic and political discontent. Even if a totalitarian state can sustain extremely high levels of investment and military spending by suppressing consumption, the ends of economic growth and perhaps even greater military capabilities may be undercut by economic discontent and inefficiency. In the period 1960-1979, the Soviet Union devoted almost as great a share of national product to investment as did Japan, but it grew at less than half the rate. In the late 1970s and early 1980s, Soviet growth has been stagnant or negative.

The third major factor accounting for hegemonic decline—a tendency towards the international diffusion of technology—operates by eroding margins of technological superiority on which economic and military advantage may be based. Knowledge is intrinsically difficult to control, and the argument that technological superiority inevitably fades is substantiated by the narrowing or nonexistent margin of American technological superiority over Japan and Western Europe. If differences in rates of growth in Table 1-3 are explained by both levels of investment *and* technological borrowing, then more equal growth is likely to follow from technological equality. The Soviet Union can limit technological diffusion through controls over emigration and publication. However, this clear advantage is of less consequence to a nation whose power does not rest on broad-based technological superiority.

The programs and policies of the Reagan administration fail to address the first and third causes of hegemonic decline. The first factor, the burden of leadership, is likely to grow heavier under the Reagan administration. The Reagan administration's security strategy expands American commitments, and the acceleration of defense spending may well assuage Japanese and Western European fears and trigger reductions in their defense spending. The third factor, technological diffusion, cannot be addressed without eliminating freedoms of communication that appear necessary for technological advance. In any event, the narrow or nonexistent gap between the United States and other advanced industrial states may have mooted the significance of this factor. The Reagan administration's program for reversing movement toward the international diffusion of power rests ultimately on managing the tradeoff among investment, military spending, and consumption.

The initial domestic economic program of the Reagan administration offered a remedy for headaches caused by the need to choose among guns, butter, and growth. The administration expected its package of tax and domestic spending cuts, investment incentives, regulatory reform, and monetary restraint to evoke a vigorous "supply-side" response and expand the capacity of the American economy. Reaganomics with the Laffer curve promised tax reductions without revenue reductions and rapid growth with declining inflation. A larger economic base would permit the administration to increase defense spending and investment without reducing consumption. By the autumn of 1982, continuing economic stagnation had demolished expectations of a quick and painless expansion of economic capacity.

Reaganomics without the Laffer curve is a program to reduce consumption to finance investment and military spending. The domestic spending cuts and regressive tax policies of the administration redistribute income away from the poor, with their tendency to devote resources to food and shelter, toward high-income groups with higher savings rates.[2] A tight monetary policy would further stimulate savings by sustaining high real interest rates. Taken together, these policies can repress consumption and spur savings, but they do not address the problem of managing the tradeoff between military spending and economic growth.

The Reagan Administration's Five Year Defense Plan projects a 7.4 percent annual real growth rate in defense spending over the period 1983-1987. The defense plan aims at building what Secretary Weinberger calls "the capital stock of the nation's defense establishment" by emphasizing procurement of defense durable goods.[3] James R. Capra, of the Federal Reserve Bank of New York, observes, "In procurement, the projected increase is larger, more rapid, and of longer duration than the Vietnam buildup."[4] The $1.7 trillion five year defense plan and the Reagan domestic package are the central elements of the administration's program to reverse trends towards the recession of American power. How are these two programs related?

In his FY 1983 Report to Congress, Secretary Weinberger declared:

Fears that the defense budget of this Administration will strain the American economy are unfounded. In the 1950s and 1960s, when defense spending as a percentage of GNP was much larger than today, annual inflation rates ranged from about one to seven percent. Economic studies have found little difference in the effect of defense spending on inflation. Defense spending, like

[2]For Urban Institute estimates of the effects of tax and spending changes on groups of families stratified by income, see *The Economist,* September 25, 1982.

[3]U.S. Department of Defense, *Annual Report to Congress Fiscal Year 1983* (Washington: U.S. Government Printing Office, 1982), p. I-6.

[4]James R. Capra, "The National Defense Budget and Its Economic Effects," *Federal Reserve Bank of New York Quarterly Review* (Summer 1981), p. 21.

other Federal spending, produces something which contributes to the people's welfare.[5]

The relationship between military spending and economic performance is more complex than Secretary Weinberger suggests.

The nature of the tradeoff hinges on the extent of underutilization of the economy as a whole and defense sectors in particular, inflation rates, and monetary and fiscal policy. Consider two macroeconomic scenarios. If the Reagan domestic economic program succeeds in triggering growth in domestic fixed capital formation and production, then the Defense Plan would encounter serious bottlenecks and capacity limits. The defense sector and private sectors would be forced to bid against each other for scarce plant and engineering talent. The quality of volunteer enlistments would decline and the price of attracting and retaining skilled personnel would increase. With a domestic economy operating at or near capacity, the price of defense would increase, and price increases in the defense sector would spill over into the private sector. In the period 1975 through 1980, price increases in the defense sector averaged 2 percent more than general inflation as measured by the GNP deflator.[6] In a tight economy, the sharp Reagan defense spending increases would increase the spread even more. To date, the Reagan economic program has not stimulated capital formation or growth, and the American economy operates at far less than capacity. Industrial slack seems ample for defense production and the all-volunteer force is functioning as an employer of last resort. In Emma Rothschild's words, "Mr. Reagan, the first military Keynesian, may be spending his way out of the recession of 1982."[7] But all is not well.

With stagnation, financial/interest rate problems replace the capacity/inflation problems of the first macroeconomic scenario. Federal revenues have run well below initial administration projections, and federal budgetary deficits are large. Although both domestic and defense spending contribute to deficits, in practical terms it is fair to speak of defense deficits. Under the Five Year Defense Plan, the military share of all federal spending is to increase from 25 to 38 percent, and the military share of the "disposable" federal budget—outlays excluding trust funds and interest on national debt—will increase from 50 to 75 percent.[8] With a substantial proportion of all lending projected to go to deficit financing, the Reagan administration effectively discourages private sector capital formation and thereby compromises its own long-term plans for stimulating productivity and growth. Furthermore, the shift from domestic spending to defense procurement may reduce employment for any given size budget. Defense durable goods are highly knowledge- and capital-intensive, and defense investment appears to compare unfavorably with other federal spending in terms of reducing unemployment.[9]

In short, if the Reagan domestic economic program begins to achieve its growth and investment targets, the ambitious defense procurement program is likely to produce capital goods bottlenecks and contribute to inflation. If the Reagan tax cuts fail to produce a strong supply-side response and growth, and the Federal Reserve Board restrains monetary growth, the defense increases will contribute to large budgetary deficits and high interest rates. Either a capacity/inflation or finance/interest rate problem is very likely to compel reductions in the growth of military spending. By developing defense and economic programs based on the assumption that no tradeoff exists, the administration may have

[5]U.S. Department of Defense, *Annual Report to Congress Fiscal Year 1983*, p. I-9.

[6]Capra, p. 25.

[7]Emma Rothschild, "The Philosophy of Reaganism," *The New York Review of Books,* April 15, 1982.

[8]Council on Economic Priorities, *Machinists and Aerospace Workers Report,* 1982.

[9]*Ibid.,* p. 27.

inadvertently worsened the terms of the tradeoff. Secretary Weinberger notes that achieving defense savings in midstream has disproportionate effects on capabilities:

> Because of Defense spendout patterns, outlay reductions require program reductions about four times as large. This causes serious program disruptions and impacts heavily on faster spending readiness functions.[10]

The first installment of the defense program commits the government to multiple-year contracts with weapons producers and researchers. Because these future commitments can be abrogated only at substantial cost, reductions in the growth of the defense budget are likely to come at the expense of bread-and-butter operations and maintenance. Projecting massive increases in defense spending and then retrenching to a lower rate of growth produces *less* effective defense capability than planning and carrying out a far more modest defense program.

These short-term economic effects of the Reagan Defense Plan are of secondary importance. The administration's goals are long-term, and the administration's programs must be evaluated with respect to the long-term compatibility of defense and economic goals. Bruce Carter Jackson of Brown Brothers, Harriman & Company found that high levels of defense spending correlate with low economic growth for the seven advanced industrial states. He argues that military spending diverts resources and distorts their allocation, thereby hindering growth and contributing to inflation.[11] A recent study by the Council on Economic Priorities found that among advanced industrial states in the 1970s, economic growth, growth in productivity, and

gross domestic fixed capital formation were strongly and negatively associated with military spending. The United States' position in international trade may be expected to erode as resources are drawn from commercial to military applications. Even without the Five Year Plan, the United States devotes a far higher share of national resources to defense than do other advanced industrial states. In the period 1960-1976, the United States devoted well over half of each research and development dollar to defense. Over the same period, 90 percent of German and 95 percent of Japanese research and development was devoted to nondefense purposes.[12] Any economy has finite resources, and spending on defense must come at the expense of consumption or investment. In practice, high rates of growth and capital formation are difficult to sustain in the face of high levels of military spending.

The Reagan administration can increase American near-term military capabilities at the expense of domestic economic welfare and international economic position. Ultimately, the tradeoff among military position, international economic position, and domestic economic welfare cannot be fudged; to argue otherwise is disingenuous. Even if the administration succeeds in repressing consumption to finance investment and military spending, it will not address other causes of the international diffusion of power. The international diffusion of technology appears irreversible, and economic burdens of leadership are increased by the administration's core security policy. American policy, alone, cannot arrest or reverse structural tendencies toward cyclical hegemonic decline. The goal of restoring American economic and military preeminence to what it was a generation ago is alluring and unattainable.

---

[10]U.S. Department of Defense, *Annual Report to Congress Fiscal Year 1983*, p. I-44.

[11]Bruce Carter Jackson, *Military Expenditures, Growth, and Inflation in Seven Leading Industrial Countries* (New York: Brown Brothers, Harriman & Co., 1981).

[12]Council on Economic Priorities, p. 23.

The Mysterious Case of Vanishing Hegemony; or, Is Mark Twain Really Dead?

Bruce Russett

Has American hegemony greatly declined over recent years? Much of the recent literature on "hegemonic stability" has been devoted to explaining the effects of a decline in American hegemony on the international system since the high point immediately after 1945. In a variant of the theme scholars have searched for ways in which to maintain an international regime established during that lost hegemony. Others have perceived an ethnocentric bias in some of this angst.[1]

The very premise of a major decline in American hegemony has, however, gone largely unexamined, and it is to such an examination that this article is devoted. I shall first make the familiar but crucial distinction between power base and power as control over outcomes. I am much readier to concede decline in America's position in the former—though it too can be exaggerated by choice of baseline for evaluation—than in the latter. Simple versions of hegemonic stability theory predict that control over outcomes will decline as power base deteriorates. Collective goods theory, moreover, a key component of the hegemonic stability literature, seems to predict both that the achievement of these goods will

decline and that the goods will be achieved only to a suboptimal degree. I question those predictions.

Turning to control over outcomes—the achievement of various "goods" in the global system and the regimes by which those goods are achieved—I distinguish between security goods and economic goods. A sensitivity to demands and achievements in the domain of international security helps to temper assessments, based primarily on political economy, that the decline of American power has been great. I evaluate the degree to which achievement of those various goods has in fact declined in the past three or four decades. The decline has been substantially less than would be expected had they been collective goods, and less than many variants of hegemonic stability theory would predict.

This substantial continuity of outcomes must be explained. Some variants of hegemonic stability theory emphasize institutionalization as a partial explanation. But, as I shall argue, many of the gains from hegemony have been less collective goods than private ones, accruing primarily to the hegemon and thus helping maintain its hegemony; this applies to short-term as well as to long-term gains; the hegemon has not really borne the costs of achieving these goods (both collective and private) as unequally as might have been the case had they been relatively pure collective goods; and one very important kind of gain, cultural hegemony, has proved a major resource to the hegemon in maintaining its more general hegemony.

These gains have helped the United States both to maintain its power base in ways not readily measured by standard indicators and to continue to control outcomes. Specifically, the international system has been structurally

Bruce Russett, "The Mysterious Case of Vanishing Hegemony; or, Is Mark Twain Really Dead?" *International Organization*, 39 (Spring 1985). pp. 207–231. Reprinted by permission of Bruce Russett.

I wrote this article while a Fellow at the Netherlands Institute for Advanced Study and am very grateful to the staff and other Fellows for making the institute such a pleasant and productive environment. I am also grateful to the General Service Foundation and to the Yale Center for International and Area Studies for financial support and to several colleagues—especially Robert Keohane, Stephen Krasner, Jim Lindsay, Susan Strange, William R. Thompson, and H. Bradford Westerfield—for insightful comments on an earlier draft.

[1] For example, Susan Strange, "Cave! Hic Dragones: A Critique of Regime Analysis," *International Organization* 36 (Spring 1982), pp. 299–324.

transformed, largely by the United States. This transformation of preferences and expectations continues to produce the goods (e.g., free trade) that the United States and the dominant elements of the rest of the world (especially in the other industrialized, noncommunist states) need to maintain a compatible international system. Since the transformation took place the United States has not had to exert such overt control over others in order to maintain control over outcomes.

POWER BASE AND CONTROL

The perception of a significant decline in American power over the last two decades is widespread, indeed virtually universal. Many observers, writing from diverse perspectives, characterize the decline in strong terms. Richard Rosecrance, for example, says the American "role as maintainer of the system is at an end," Kenneth Oye speaks of "the end of American hegemony," and George Liska repeatedly applies the word "dissolution" to the state of the "American empire."[2] The perception is particularly common, however, in the literature on international regimes and most straightforward in that part of the literature identified with "hegemonic stability" theory. Strong characterizations of decline are frequently associated with the work of Robert Gilpin, Stephen Krasner, Charles Kindleberger, and even Robert Keohane.[3]

To be sure, most of these characterizations are nuanced, and they change in a literature and a world that are rapidly evolving. Nearly everyone recognizes that the United States retains great power and, in the economic sphere at least, greater power than any other state. These same writers typically remind us of a continuing degree of American preeminence. The decline, then, is relative—relative to past American power or perhaps relative to what a hegemon needs to maintain essential elements of the world economic order. My purpose is to point out the assumptions and consequences of this emphasis on decline rather than continuity, for there is a great deal still to be said for the latter perspective.

The standards against which to measure the American decline are seldom made clear. Part of the difficulty stems from a lack of agreement about how much power is necessary to produce "hegemony." Unless there is some rather sharp step-level jump at which hegemony comes into existence or is lost (a level that has never been specified), relative power is necessarily distributed continuously. The theoretical problem is basic: there is always room for argument about whether a given degree of superiority is enough to produce particular (and also rarely well-specified) results.

[2] See Richard Rosecrance's "Introduction" to his edited volume, *America as an Ordinary Country* (Ithaca: Cornell University Press, 1976), p. 1; Kenneth A. Oye, "The Domain of Choice," in Oye, Donald Rothchild, and Robert J. Lieber, eds., *Eagle Entangled: U.S. Foreign Policy in a Complex World* (New York: Longman, 1979), pp. 4–5; and George Liska, *Career of Empire* (Baltimore: Johns Hopkins University Press, 1978), chap. 10.

[3] See Robert Gilpin, *U.S. Power and the Multinational Corporation: The Political Economy of Direct Foreign Investment* (New York: Basic Books, 1975), and Gilpin, *War and Change in the International System* (Cambridge: Cambridge University Press, 1981), esp. p. 231: "By the 1980s the Pax Americana was in a state of disarray"; Stephen Krasner, "Transforming International Regimes: What the Third World Wants and Why," *International Studies Quarterly* 25 (March

1981), pp. 119–48; Charles Kindleberger, "Systems of International Economic Organization," in David Calleo, ed., *Money and the Coming World Order* (New York: New York University Press, 1976); and also many of the contributors to the special issue of *International Organization* 36 (Spring 1982). Robert O. Keohane's *After Hegemony: Cooperation and Discord in the World Political System* (Princeton: Princeton University Press, 1984), represents a special case. His is the most sophisticated version of hegemonic stability theory, and he explicitly argues against equating a decline in power base with an equivalent decline in the characteristics of a regime. Nevertheless he repeatedly uses such phrases as "a post-hegemony world" (p. 216) and "the legacy of American hegemony" and "hegemony will not be restored in our lifetime" (p. 244), justifying the book's title. The only strong emphasis on the continuity of American power that I have been able to find is Susan Strange, "Still an Extraordinary Power: America's Role in a Global Monetary System," in Raymond E. Lombra and William E. Witte, eds., *Political Economy of International and Domestic Monetary Relations* (Ames: Iowa State University Press, 1982).

A second and related difficulty stems from a lack of agreement on the relevant dimensions and indicators of power. In some amorphous manner, of course, our senses do not deceive us. American power, as measured by various power base indicators, surely has declined. The litany is too familiar to require full recitation, and some examples will suffice: loss of strategic nuclear predominance; decline in conventional military capabilities relative to the U.S.S.R., especially for intervention; diminished economic size in relative gross national product, productivity, and terms of trade with some commodity producers (principally of oil); loss of a reliable majority in the United Nations; and loss of assured scientific preeminence in the "knowledge industries" at the "cutting edge" and even in the numerical and financial base that enabled U.S. scholars to dominate global social science.

Even with these power base indicators, however, it is not quite a case where "all the instruments agree" it is a dark, cold day. President Reagan's rhetoric about "a definite margin of superiority for the Soviet Union" had to be corrected the next day by his own director of the Bureau of Politico-Military Affairs of the State Department, his talk of a "window of vulnerability" by his own Scowcroft Commission. Reasonable (if, on both sides, rather ideological) people can debate the relative importance of warheads vs. throw-weights vs. "kill ratios," the proper exchange rates for comparing Soviet with American military expenditures, and the true balance of conventional forces between NATO and the Warsaw Pact. U.S. economic industrial predominance in the world looks slightly less impressive if one takes its share of world GNP rather than its share of world energy consumption. While virtually all power base measures show a clear decline in American predominance over the past forty years, they do not agree on the rate or the depth of that decline. Some few show the United States slipping to second place in the world, but many more show merely a shrunken lead for the front-runner.[4]

When in time one begins measuring the power base indicators also makes a great difference. If one begins with 1945, all indicators show a significant, though never precipitous, decline in American power base over the subsequent four decades.[5] But 1945 represents the absolute peak of American strength. The old powers of Europe and Japan were physically and economically devastated, the United States unscathed. That situation could not continue, the United States hastened its passing, and by 1955 the former powers had significantly recovered. The first decade, with the sharpest slope of decline in American predominance, represented a substantial "return to normality." The immediate postwar years look even more peculiar if one starts with 1938 or earlier. America's military preeminence dates, without question, only from World War II. Its predominance in 1945 over the existing military capability of any other state (even, at that point, the Soviet Union) could be matched by no state since at least the time of Napoleon. Since 1945 the Soviet Union has achieved parity, but the dominance of the two states over all other powers, including those of the Western alliance, remains. The name of the Soviet-American military game is duopoly.

A long time-perspective on economic power makes clear the unusual degree of American superiority in 1945 in that power base as well. Table 1 provides a historical perspective on hegemons' ability to dominate three of the most commonly used dimensions of national power

[4] Keohane, *After Hegemony,* identifies four criteria by which to judge a hegemon of world political economy: a preponderance of material resources in raw materials, capital, markets, and production of highly valued goods. A broader view of hegemony, however, requires inclusion of military, scientific, and other resources.

[5] For example, Mark E. Rupert and David P. Rapkin, "The Erosion of U.S. Leadership Capabilities," in Paul Johnson and William R. Thompson, eds., *Rhythms in International Politics and Economics* (New York: Praeger, 1985).

TABLE 1   FOUR LEADING POWERS INDEXED TO "HEGEMON," 1830–1983[a]

Year	Country and percentage of "hegemon's" value							
	Largest		2d largest		3d largest		4th largest	
Gross National Product								
1983	U.S.A.	100	U.S.S.R.	41	Japan	35	W. Germany	20
1950	U.S.A.	100	U.S.S.R.	29	U.K.	19	France	13
1938	U.S.A.	100	Germany	37	U.S.S.R.	37	U.K.	27
1913	U.S.A.	306	Russia	123	Germany	113	U.K.	100
1870	U.S.A.	117	Russia	117	U.K.	100	France	86
1830	Russia	132	France	105	U.K.	100	A.-H.	87
Military Expenditures								
1983	U.S.A.	100	U.S.S.R.	100	China	19	U.K.	16
1950	U.S.S.R.	106	U.S.A.	100	China	18	U.K.	16
1938[b]	Germany	657	U.S.S.R.	481	U.K.	161	Japan	154
1913	Germany	129	Russia	125	U.K.	100	France	99
1872[c]	Russia	127	France	119	U.K.	100	Germany	68
1830	France	148	U.K.	100	Russia	92	A.-H.	54
Manufacturing Production								
1980	U.S.A.	100	U.S.S.R.	47	Japan	29	W. Germany	17
1953	U.S.A.	100	U.S.S.R.	24	U.K.	19	W. Germany	13
1938	U.S.A.	100	Germany	40	U.K.	34	U.S.S.R.	29
1913	U.S.A.	235	Germany	109	U.K.	100	Russia	26
1870	U.K.	100	China	75	U.S.A	51	France	37
1830	China	319	India	185	U.K.	100	Russia	59

[a] "Hegemon" at the time is underlined; there was no hegemon in 1938, but I have arbitrarily used the U.S. values as the base.

[b] U.S.A. ranked fifth.

[c] 1872 data used, as figures for French and German (Prussian) military spending were inflated in 1870 and 1871 by the Franco-Prussian War.
  Sources. GNP data 1983 from OECD, *Main Economic Indicators* (Paris, May 1984), p. 182; U.S.S.R. total is estimated. Other GNP data from Paul Bairoch, "Europe's Gross National Product, 1800–1975," *Journal of European Economic History* 5, 2 (1976), pp. 273–340, and U.S. Bureau of the Census, *Historical Statistics of the United States: Colonial Times to 1970* (Washington, D.C., 1975). Military expenditures 1983 from *World Armaments and Disarmament: SIPRI Yearbook, 1984* (London: Taylor & Francis, 1984), pp. 117–18. SIPRI lists U.S.S.R. military expenses as 74% of the U.S. figure, but U.S. government sources (C.I.A. and D.I.A.) give U.S.S.R. expenditures as exceeding those of U.S.A. I have set the two countries as equal. The estimate for China, given by SIPRI and used here, may be somewhat low. Military expenditure data for previous years are from the Correlates of War national capabilities data provided by Professor J. David Singer. Manufacturing production data from Paul Bairoch, "International Industrialization Levels from 1750 to 1980," *Journal of European Economic History* 11, 2 (1982), pp. 269–333. Data for 1870 are interpolated between Bairoch's figures for 1860 and 1880.

base. Gross national product is the most fungible of resources, usable to exert many kinds of influence; it also represents market size, the attraction of which can give important advantages in international trade negotiations. It represents the basis of structural power, that is, the ability to define the context within which others must make decisions. Military expenditures give a good if hardly perfect indication of relative military strength. Manufacturing production is a basic source of both economic and military strength.

These data make several facts apparent. First, the United Kingdom was *never,* even at its peak in the 19th century, the dominant power as measured by either GNP or military expenditures. The wealth provided by its industrial strength was always overwhelmed in terms of GNP by the demographic base of its sometimes less wealthy but more populous chief competitors; its military expenditures were always markedly below one or more of its continental rivals. Only in manufacturing production, and then only rather briefly, did it lead the world. (For purposes of this analysis, however, we should probably discount the surprising manufacturing capacity of China and India, as they were hardly great powers in the world system.) These data should encourage a cautious interpretation of Britain's "hegemonic" power. Britain's commercial power, reflected in trade or financial indicators, is not evident in other very important indicators of power base. Second, despite slippage since filling the void immediately after World War II, the United States retains on all these indicators a degree of dominance reached by the United Kingdom at no point, and one that compares well with the U.S. position in 1938. (U.S. military expenditures for 1950 do not reflect the Korean War and are artificially low for the Cold War period.) The basis of American hegemony may have declined, but it has hardly vanished.

Other indicators are imaginable, but many data are not available for a long time span, and length of historical perspective is essential to the argument. Moreover, the meaning of some potential indicators is not entirely clear: for example, does a large volume of foreign trade indicate market dominance or vulnerability?[6] Nevertheless, any truly scientific assessment will require more and more rigorous, measurement than Table 1 provides, as well as some agreement on appropriate baselines for temporal comparison. With conceptual and theoreti-cal clarity, one could establish appropriate rules for measuring certain kinds of power base decline. Until that time it would be well to remember Galileo's experiment with falling bodies: if one would explain the velocity of those bodies, one must first determine what the velocity is! The hegemonic stability literature, to be persuasive, demands better measurement than it has enjoyed so far.

The more important question, however, is "so what?" In what ways has decline produced (or, perhaps, been reflected in) a decline in American power as control over outcomes—that is, "ability to prevail in conflict and overcome obstacles"?[7] Surely it is this control over outcomes that really interests us. If we are to have a matter worth investigating, we must identify hegemony at least with success in determining and maintaining essential rules, not merely with power base or resource share. Hegemony is a condition, as Keohane and Nye recognize, in which "one state is powerful enough to maintain the essential rules governing interstate relations, and willing to do so." We must avoid making a tautology out of Krasner's statement that, "The theory of hege-monic leadership suggests that under conditions of declining hegemony there will be a weakening of regimes."[8] Rather, we should ask whether, when predominance in the power base declines, the basic regime (the network of rules, norms, etc.) weakens or the ability of the preponderant state to determine rules lessens. The former, a weakening of the network, is difficult to investi-gate empirically though good efforts have been made, especially with aspects of the trade regime. Here, however, I address the latter, the influence of the preponderant state. I emphasize the distri-bution of *desired outcomes* as a result of the

---

[6] See, for instance, Kenneth Waltz, *Theory of International Politics* (Reading, Mass: Addison-Wesley, 1979), esp. chap. 7, who regards the United States as more autonomous, and hence stronger, than more internationally involved states.

[7] Karl W. Deutsch, *The Analysis of International Relations,* 2d ed. (Englewood Cliffs, N.J.: Prentice-Hall, 1978).

[8] Robert O. Keohane and Joseph Nye, *Power and Interdependence* (Boston: Little, Brown, 1977), p. 44, and Stephen Krasner, "Structural Causes and Regime Consequences: Regimes as Intervening Variables," *International Organization* 36 (Spring 1982), p. 199.

rules, in conformity with Krasner's formulation of a causal chain from "basic causal factors" to regimes to outcomes and behaviors.

It is widely acknowledged that the United States did occupy a position of hegemony in the international system immediately after World War II. Its enemies were defeated and its allies exhausted. The productive base of the American economy alone escaped wartime devastation; indeed, it was enormously expanded by the war effort. The United States was the world's foremost military power, and only it had the nuclear "winning weapon." While U.S. preponderance was not so overwhelming as to enable it to set all the rules for the entire world system, it did permit it to establish the basic principles for the new economic order in the over 80 percent of the world economy controlled by capitalist states and to organize a system of collective security to maintain political and economic control over that 80 percent. While U.S. power was not complete, virtually all analysts of the regimes school agree that the United States in about 1946 came closer to meeting the criteria of global hegemony than has any other state in world history. Indeed, as Timothy McKeown and Keohane have argued, one should have important reservations about the "supposed hegemonic leadership" of 19th-century Britain and must wonder whether Britain was hegemonic in any meaningful sense.[9]

One can also have reservations about the scientific status of a theory derived in large part from a single case and attempting to explain behavior in that same case. Proponents of hegemonic stability theory frequently acknowledge this problem, which does not greatly concern me here. One can appropriately seek to extend insights and test propositions by looking at various "issue-area" regimes within the overall set of rules and by looking at the behavior and outcomes of actors in various kinds of arenas (as in small groups of individuals or in coalitions within organizations) where degrees of hegemony may be examined, compared, and even manipulated. Empirical tests of the theory of collective goods have been made in just such arenas; with care their findings can, and because the questions are important should, be extended to the global situation. Nevertheless, in these arenas global conditions are but crudely approximated, and we should look very closely at some key assumptions about the goods provided by a regime (do they truly meet the definition of collective goods?),[10] about behavior by unitary actors,[11] and about "fairness" in the distribution of costs and benefits.[12] I shall return to these matters below.

ACHIEVEMENTS, GOODS, AND REGIMES

In the years immediately following World War II the United States emerged as a hegemonic power, perhaps following in the path George Modelski characterizes as occurring at roughly hundred-year intervals.[13] The United States provided the world with a variety of "goods," some of them collective goods, of security, international organization, and a framework for international economic relations. The idea that a hegemon provides collective goods to permit peace and prosperity within a wider area is an

[9] Timothy J. McKeown, "Tariffs and Hegemonic Stability Theory," *International Organization* 37 (Winter 1983), pp. 73–93, and Keohane, *After Hegemony,* p. 37.

[10] Duncan Snidal, "Public Goods, Property Rights, and Political Organization," *International Studies Quarterly* 23 (December 1979), pp. 532–66.

[11] Stephen Krasner, "State Power and the Structure of International Trade," *World Politics* 27 (April 1975), pp. 314–47, and John Ruggie's review of Krasner's book in *American Political Science Review* 74 (March 1980), pp. 296–99.

[12] Joe Oppenheimer, "Collective Goods and Alliances: A Reassessment," *Journal of Conflict Resolution* 23 (September 1979), pp. 387–407.

[13] George Modelski, "The Long Cycle of Global Politics and the Nation-State," *Comparative Studies in Society and History* 20 (April 1978), pp. 214–35.

old one; Karl Deutsch's work on integration anticipated much of what emerged in the regimes literature of the 1970s.[14]

But there is more than one way of looking at the provision of goods in the postwar international system. A radical perspective exists. Recognizing the existence of a Pax Americana, it identifies achievements that are not necessarily collective goods:

> The pacification of capitalist interstate relations and the imperial guarantee against nationalization created a reliable world legal framework which reduced the risks of transnational expansion; decolonization opened up the entire periphery to primary transnational expansion based on comparative advantage rather than on the monopolistic privileges and restrictions with which rival metropolitan states had increasingly enmeshed their colonial possessions; the gold-dollar standard restored the possibility of capitalist accounting on a world scale, thus enhancing secondary transnational expansion, which depends decisively upon reliable calculations of the cost advantages of alternative locations of production.[15]

Giovanni Arrighi recognizes two kinds of achievements or goods: security (peace) and economy (prosperity). Each can be broken down further, and we can ask what conditions or regime made possible those achievements.[16]

Arrighi speaks of the "pacification" of relations among capitalist states, and indeed there have been no wars between capitalist states, at least between developed (capitalist) industrial states, since 1945. Whether this absence of war is attributable more to the spread of advanced industrial capitalism or to the spread of representative democracy in the world is hard to say, because the two potential explanatory variables are so closely correlated. Various arguments do not necessarily agree on the direction of causality, and indeed, all the correlations may be spurious.[17] Nevertheless, the absence of interstate war is indisputable, and by fairly early in the postwar era even preparation for, and expectation of, war among capitalist states had diminished nearly to the vanishing point. By the end of the 1950s one could say with reasonable confidence that a "security community" or "stable peace" had been established nearly everywhere in the OECD area, even between traditional enemies.[18] Nor have there been any civil wars (involving 1,000 or more deaths) within any of the advanced capitalist countries, nor hardly any serious expectation of such. (Violence in Northern Ireland and the Spanish Basque country could possibly escalate above this threshold.) One could argue that the absence of war between democracies has been a fact of life since the end of the Napoleonic

[14] Karl W. Deutsch et al., *Political Community and the North Atlantic Area* (Princeton: Princeton University Press, 1957).

[15] Giovanni Arrighi, "A Crisis of Hegemony," in Samir Amin et al., *Dynamics of Global Crisis* (New York: Monthly Review Press, 1982), p. 77.

[16] I am aware that much of the hegemonic stability literature (for example, a "founding father," Charles Kindleberger, *The World in Depression, 1929–1939* [Berkeley: University of California Press, 1973]) is concerned with very specific issue-areas and goods rather than with such broader achievements or "goods" as "peace and prosperity." Focus on narrow issue-areas makes the thesis of a decline in American hegemony more plausible—at least for those selected issue-areas. Nevertheless, issue-areas are usually selected because they are assumed, implicitly or explicitly, to be symptomatic of a broad decline in U.S. ability to maintain the conditions of global prosperity.

"Peace" among industrial capitalist powers (and containment of the Soviet Union) is one of those conditions. Thus, while some hegemonic stability writing can escape the strictures of my critique, a general evaluation of the state of American "hegemony" and its consequences—an evaluation that is both common and necessary—must carry the discussion beyond selected, rather narrow issue-areas. Gilpin, *War and Change,* and many of the contributors to the Spring 1982 special issue of *International Organization* would surely agree.

[17] See Bruce Russett and Harvey Starr, *World Politics: The Menu for Choice,* 2d ed. (New York: W. H. Freeman, 1985), chap. 15, and Michael Doyle, "Kant, Liberal Legacies, and Foreign Affairs," *Philosophy and Public Affairs* 12 (Summer 1983), pp. 205–35.

[18] The terms are, respectively, from Deutsch et al., *Political Community,* and Kenneth E. Boulding, *Stable Peace* (Austin: University of Texas Press, 1978).

era,[19] but the recent extension of stable democracy and also (therefore?) a "zone of peace" to
various industrialized countries where it was
previously fragile—Germany, Italy, Japan—is
surely a major achievement. It is, moreover, an
achievement that can be credited in some degree to the United States, either as a result of
enforced suppression of hostilities[20] or, in Arrighi's terms, by provision of a "cohesive political and ideological framework."

Stable peace has not been achieved to anything like the same degree in the Third World
and between its capitalist states. Virtually all
post-1945 wars have been fought on the territories of Third World states, between or within
Third World states or between Third World
states and intervening First or Second World
states. Open insurgency has often been avoided
only because of the threat of direct foreign
intervention or because of the establishment of
powerful coercive states within Third World
countries, usually with strong external support.
It is all too often a "peace" based on threats,
either the mutual threats of deterrence or the
one-sided threats of dominance.

From the point of view of Third World
peoples, this sort of peace may well be no great
achievement. From the point of view of the
United States, however, the judgment will be
less certain. Wars have been fought in Third
World countries, civilian casualties have been
incurred there, and it is Third World peoples
who have borne most of the costs of maintaining coercive states. The result has been sufficient "pacification" to provide a "reliable legal
framework" for transnational corporate expansion and to discourage most large-scale nation-
alizations without "fair" compensation. Some

parts of the Third World (some countries, some
classes) have shared in the resulting prosperity,
others have not. But by historic standards, even
compared with the colonial era of direct control, the overall results show not a bad ratio of
costs and benefits for the United States.

If stable peace has been achieved among and
within many capitalist countries, it has surely
not been achieved between capitalist and communist countries. Instead, we can speak only of
containment or deterrence and the ability of
American hegemony to maintain stable boundaries between the capitalist and communist
worlds. The United States was able to erect
around the Soviet Union, in the first decade
after the war, a *cordon sanitaire* that held from
the "loss" of China to the accession of Castro.
It is a "peace" maintained by deterrence. Initially somewhat one-sided (Soviet conventional
superiority in Europe gave some compensation
for American nuclear monopoly), it has become
increasingly based on a system of mutual
threat. While there are many flaws and dangers
in this system, the substantial success for "containment" and the avoidance of superpower
war should not be dismissed.

Is it appropriate to refer to these achievements as "regimes"? If we use Krasner's definition ("principles, norms, and decision-
making procedures around which actor
expectations converge"),[21] it seems reasonable to do so, at least for "stable peace." Stable
peace is built on a set of norms and rules for
regulating, limiting, and resolving conflict.
While not necessarily embodied in organized
institutions, they do involve a set of stable
expectations about others' behavior and principles to guide one's own—what acts and demands are appropriate, permissible, or unacceptable. Students of international political
economy miss insights into the regimes directly
of interest to them when they ignore the regime
of stable peace.

---

[19] See J. David Singer and Melvin Small, "The War-
Proneness of Democratic Regimes, 1815–1965," *Jerusalem
Journal of International Relations* 1, 1 (1976), pp. 50–69.

[20] Not to me the most persuasive explanation, though
see Erich Weede, "Extended Deterrence by Superpower
Alliance," *Journal of Conflict Resolution* 27 (June 1983),
pp. 231–53.

[21] Krasner, "Structural Causes," p. 185.

Whether one can use "regime" to characterize superpower deterrence is less certain. Robert Jervis is not inclined to, yet admits that "the subject is so complex that I lack confidence in this judgment."[22] Certainly the element of pure threat, as contrasted with established norms for resolving conflict and pursuing mutual reward, is much greater. As Jervis notes, the restraints have been, in large part, shifting, narrow, and short-term. Still, norms and rules for behavior were built up, embodied both in formal arms control treaties and in various implicit understandings about what kinds of acts (e.g., military alerts, weapons procurements, troop deployments beyond one's borders) may be legitimate to achieve certain ends or to signal intentions, what kinds may be too provocative and threatening. The element of building rules and norms was especially important during the era of détente; and then, it seems to me, the term fits as well as it does in its wide application in political economy.

The second gain that Arrighi identifies from establishment of the Pax Americana is decolonization and the consequent entry of the United States into previously closed markets and sources of supply for raw materials. The price of American assistance for postwar reconstruction was the demand that former colonial powers accede to demands from their colonial peoples for independence. Clear-cut examples include the experience in 1949 when the threat to cut off American economic aid halted the Dutch military operation to restore control over the Dutch East Indies, American pressure in 1962 that helped impel the Dutch effectively to cede West New Guinea (Irian Jaya) to Indonesia, and the American refusal to approve an urgent IMF loan that forced the British and French to retreat from their effort to reoccupy the Suez Canal in 1956.[23]

The American goal was more than mere nominal independence for colonies; to follow was the dismantling of the formal and informal barriers that had largely restricted colonies' trade to their metropoles. Britain, for instance, was strongly pressured to give up Commonwealth Preference and the Sterling Area, which had provided it with a relatively closed, secure market. Britain was also forced, most notably as part of the settlement of the Anglo-Iranian Oil nationalization in 1953, to give American-based multinationals a dominant share of Middle Eastern oil supplies. Decolonization as an ideology was attractive to Americans; it cost them almost nothing (the only American colony was the Philippines) while creating enormous economic opportunities. With its dominant technology and industrial organization, the United States was ready and able to move into hitherto closed markets. Decolonization meant acceleration of the introduction of advanced capitalism into the Third World, and the United States was the most efficient capitalist. The postwar regimes in international trade and finance brought worldwide prosperity, not least to the United States.

CONTINUITY AND DISTRIBUTION OF GAINS

These achievements, often embodied in regimes, are very important products of American hegemony. Moreover, they represent a continued achievement of outcomes desired by the United States, even at a time of discernible decline in standard indicators of the American power base. If one looks not at narrow issue-area regimes but at broader aspects of the international environment after World War II, one has to be impressed by the degree to which perceived American interests, not just the interests of all states, were served. Strong elements of continuity, of sustained reward, characterize these achievements. These two

---

[22] Robert Jervis, "Security Regimes," *International Organization* 36 (Spring 1982), p. 371.

[23] See Arend Lijphart, *The Trauma of Decolonization: The Dutch and West New Guinea* (New Haven: Yale University Press, 1966), chap. 11; and Townsend Hoopes,

The Devil and John Foster Dulles (Boston: Little, Brown, 1973), p. 384.

elements—important gains to the United States and the continuity of gains—are interlinked.

Over the past decade we have seen a breakdown in détente, a breakdown in the rules and norms governing Soviet-American behavior. "Prompt hard-target kill" weapons have been acquired, in numbers and capabilities formerly avoided; troops have crossed some of the implicit boundaries between East and West; and continued adherence to formal agreements, among them SALT and the ABM treaty, is in doubt. Yet the rules and norms built up over the decades have not been entirely abandoned. Some vestige of a regime in East-West relations survives. More dubious is the continuity of containment, but even there the argument of drastic decline is readily exaggerated. American strategic nuclear predominance is gone (forever, in my opinion, though members of the Reagan administration may disagree). Most of us now feel less secure about maintenance of the balance of terror than we did formerly, especially about the risks of low-level political or military conflict spiraling into Armageddon. But the risks of deliberate Soviet nuclear attack still seem remote and are likely to remain so indefinitely, barring either gross American provocation or gross American negligence in providing a secure nuclear deterrent.

Despite some breaches, the *cordon sanitaire* around the Soviet Union still looks quite effective. Counterbalancing Soviet gains in Afghanistan, Vietnam, and parts of Africa has been the Soviet loss of China, once its foremost ally. By any standards of resources or population, the reentry of China to the world economy and the reorientation of Chinese foreign policy more than compensate for losses to the "free world" elsewhere. American losses in the Middle East (e.g., Iran) have by no means translated into Soviet gains.[24] The biggest real switch in that part of the world was Egypt, from "them" to "us." Soviet penetration into Latin America since Cuba still remains more of a threat than a reality (and the Soviets "acquired" Cuba despite the American nuclear predominance of the time).

Continuity also applies in America's relations with the industrialized countries. The hegemonic stability literature does not give precise predictions about whether, and particularly how much, the achievement of goals will decline as the relative power base of the hegemon declines. Except in its vulgar form as what Keohane calls "crude theory," it emphasizes the mediating and conditioning roles of, for example, international institutions and the characteristics of domestic political systems.[25] Nevertheless, some decline, particularly in light of the sharp decline in American military power, might be expected. It has not happened. By no reasonable criterion has stable peace declined among the advanced capitalist countries. They are hardly able to solve all their common problems, but—and it is no small achievement—war among them is now less thinkable than ever. War among them, moreover, became no more thinkable during the 1970s, when the apparent common threat, the Soviet Union, became less threatening. And while wars in the Third World remain common, they do not tend to happen more frequently than they did in the past.[26]

If American predominance (hegemony) vis-à-vis the Soviet Union is gone, American nuclear predominance (hegemony) over all other states remains, perhaps stronger than ever, and there is little sign that it will erode in the future. Western Europe seems unable to put together a substantial deterrent of its own, and any Soviet-American success in constructing space-based antimissile systems will only reinforce their nuclear duopoly by drastically reducing the effectiveness of smaller and less sophisticated

---

[24] See Zalmay Khalilzad, "Islamic Iran: Soviet Dilemma," *Problems of Communism* 33 (January–February 1984), pp. 1–20.

[25] Keohane, *After Hegemony*, p. 34.
[26] Melvin Small and J. David Singer, *Resort to Arms* (Beverly Hills: Sage, 1982), p. 134.

forces. In a nuclear world American military hegemony over its allies may never end. That kind of hegemony gives the United States some fungible resources with which to maintain a degree of hegemony in other areas. ("Open up your domestic market more, or Congress may tire of keeping our military commitment.")

In economic matters the structure of a relatively open world economy (the GATT, various rounds of trade liberalization, etc.) remains substantially intact. Despite the spread of such measures as "voluntary" export restraints and many observers' anticipation of a major relapse into protectionism, the sky has not fallen. It is significant that world trade fell only in 1982, and by only 1 percent, after a decade of increased protectionist efforts. The inflation-adjusted increase in world trade between 1973 and 1983 was between 6 and 7 percent, as contrasted with a 28 percent drop from 1926 to 1935. Progress in opening up the best-protected capitalist economy outside the United States, that of Japan, continues to creep forward.[27] Currencies remain

convertible. The United States can use the attractiveness of its financial markets, with high interest rates, to finance its military buildup with other people's money.

It would be perverse to deny that there has been some demonstrable (if less easily measurable) decline in recent decades in America's ability to get others to do as it wished. That decline has been well documented in the regimes literature, though it is often exaggerated. Arrighi, whom I quoted earlier on the gains achieved by the United States by its world predominance, also considers both the persistence and the decay of those gains:

> In general, the U.S. government has simply exploited, in the pursuance of national interests, the core position that the U.S. national economy still retains in the "world-economy." Its internal reserves of energy and other natural resources, the sheer size of its internal market, and the density and complexity of its linkages with the rest of the capitalist world imply a basic asymmetry in the relation of the U.S. economy to other national economies: conditions within the U.S. state's boundaries influence, much more than they are influenced by, conditions within the boundaries of any other national economy. This asymmetrical relation, though independently eroded by other factors, has not yet been significantly affected by the undoing of the U.S. imperial order. What has been affected is the *use* made by the U.S. state of its world economic power: while in the 1950s and 1960s the national interest was often subordinated to the establishment and reproduction of a world capitalist order, in the middle and late 1970s the reproduction of such an order has been subordinated to the pursuit of the national interest as expressed in efforts to increase domestic economic growth.

In such a sense, this redeployment of U.S. world political-economic power in the pursuit of national interests has been a major symptom of, and factor explaining, the state of anarchy that

[27] For the comparative data on trade I am indebted to Susan Strange, "Protectionism and World Politics," *International Organization* 39 (Spring 1985). Helen Hughes and Jean Waelbroeck, "Foreign Trade and Structural Adjustment—Is There a New Protectionism?" in Hans-Gert Braun et al., eds., *The European Economy in the 1980s* (Aldershot: Gower, 1983), reply that the increase in protectionism during the 1970s was very small. There is some evidence that protectionism rises during periods of cyclical economic downturn, but those increases must not be mistaken for long-term trends. On the collapse of the Bretton Woods fixed-exchange-rate system see Hugh Patrick and Henry Rosovsky, "The End of Eras? Japan and the Western World in the 1970–1980s" (paper presented at the Japan Political Economy Research Conference, Honolulu, July 1983), p. 38: "In our view, despite excessively wide swings in real rates among currencies, the flexible exchange rate system was a way of maintaining the liberal international economic order rather than being a cause of its demise." Also see Keohane, *After Hegemony,* p. 213: "Substantial erosion of the trade regime...has occurred, but...what is equally striking is the persistence of cooperation even if not always addressed to liberal ends. Trade wars have not taken place, despite economic distress. On the contrary, what we see are intensive efforts at cooperation, in response to discord in textiles, steel, electronics, and other

areas." On liberalization of the Japanese economy see Raymond Vernon, *Two Hungry Giants: The United States and Japan in the Quest for Oil and Ores* (Cambridge: Harvard University Press, 1983).

has characterized international economic relations since 1973. It is important to realize, however, that at least insofar as the advanced capitalist countries are concerned, this state of anarchy in interstate relations has been strictly limited to monetary and budgetary policies and that it has yet to undermine the two main "products" of formal U.S. hegemony: the unity of the world market and the transnational expansion of capital. These substantive aspects of U.S. hegemony have survived the downfall of the U.S. imperial order; and their operating reach throughout the world capitalist economy has, if anything, been continually extended.[28]

As will shortly become apparent, I disagree with several counts of Arrighi's assessment. I contend that the U.S. national interest *was* served, even in the short run, by the policies of the 1950s. I also regard his characterization of a "state of anarchy"—even applied only to monetary and budgetary policies—as much too strong. A literal "absence of government" is not necessarily synonymous with chaos, as Hedley Bull and others have urged.[29] (It is worth emphasizing that, with the world capitalist order once established, the tasks of maintaining and reproducing it are far easier.) Nevertheless, Arrighi's emphasis on asymmetries rather than simplistic uses of "interdependence," and hence the remaining power of the United States to influence others, is of major importance.

If significant continuity in the ability of the United States to get what it wants is accepted, then it must be explained. The explanation starts with our noting that the institutions for political and economic cooperation have themselves been maintained. Keohane rightly stresses the role of institutions as "arrange-

ments permitting communication and therefore facilitating the exchange of information."[30] By providing reliable information and reducing the costs of transactions, institutions can permit cooperation to continue even after a hegemon's influence has eroded. Institutions provide opportunities for commitment and for observing whether others keep their commitments. Such opportunities are virtually essential to cooperation in non-zero-sum situations, as gaming experiments demonstrate.[31] Declining hegemony and stagnant (but not decaying) institutions may therefore be consistent with a stable provision of desired outcomes, although the ability to promote new levels of cooperation to deal with new problems (e.g., energy supplies, environmental protection) is more problematic. Institutions nevertheless provide a part of the necessary explanation.

COLLECTIVE OR PRIVATE GOODS?

The nature of the institutions themselves must, however, be examined. They were shaped in the years immediately after World War II by the United States and they, and the regimes of which they are a part, have significantly endured. The American willingness to establish those regimes and their institutions is sometimes explained in terms of the theory of collective goods. It is a commonplace in the regimes literature that the United States, in so doing, was providing not only private goods for its own benefit but also (and perhaps especially) collective goods desired by, and for the benefit of, other capitalist states. (Particular care is needed here about equating state interest with "national" interest.) Not only was the United States protecting its own territory and commer-

[28] Arrighi, "A Crisis of Hegemony," p. 65. One could quarrel with the use of "national interest," and qualify it by reference to the interests of the ruling classes, but on the whole I am not inclined to do so—major qualification would require some near-heroic assumptions about false consciousness.

[29] Hedley Bull, *The Anarchical Society* (New York: Columbia University Press, 1977).

[30] Robert O. Keohane, "The Demand for International Regimes," *International Organization* 36 (Spring 1982), p. 348. Keohane's discussion is reminiscent of Karl W. Deutsch, *The Nerves of Government* (New York: Free Press, 1963).

[31] Robert Axelrod, *The Evolution of Cooperation* (New York: Basic Books, 1984).

cial enterprises, it was providing military protection for some fifty allies and almost as many neutrals. Not only was it ensuring a liberal, open, near-global economy for its own prosperity, it was providing the basis for the prosperity of all capitalist states and even for some states organized on noncapitalist principles (those willing to abide by the basic rules established to govern international trade and finance). While such behavior was not exactly selfless or altruistic, certainly the benefits—however distributed by class, state, or region—did accrue to many others, not just to Americans. Coupled with this commonplace argument is the implication that the United States paid substantial costs in the immediate postwar period to set in place the basis for it and others to accrue long-term benefits.[32]

If this were a case of providing a collective good, several conclusions would follow. First is the prediction of collective goods theory that, in the absence of a strong central authority able to coerce members to pay appropriate contributions, a collective good will be supplied to only a suboptimal degree. Second, the costs of providing the good will be borne unequally, and disproportionately by the hegemon. Usually implicit in the assessment of inequality in burden sharing is an assumption of inequity or unfairness, implying that while the hegemon bears disproportionate costs, the nonhegemonic powers desire the good as much as, or almost as much as, the hegemon does. (This proposition should alert us to the normative implications of the prior assumption that the principal goods provided are truly collective. If the goods largely benefit the hegemon, it is hardly fair to berate smaller states for an unwillingness to pay an equal share of the costs.)

Finally there is an implication not so common in collective goods theory per se as in many of its applications to problems of hegemonic stability: costs must typically be incurred in the short run whereas benefits are primarily gained in the long term. Most collective goods, after all, involve a significant investment that, once in place, will pay returns for a long time. Deterrence, stable peace, a liberal trading order that undergirds prosperity, all fit this characterization.

Serious doubt about the willingness and even the ability of the hegemon to continue to pay the costs is a corollary to this last conclusion. The short-term costs were so heavy, the argument holds, and the benefits distributed so widely to those who never paid the costs, that a weakening of the United States and a loss of its hegemony were inevitable. Equally inevitable, except as retarded by such factors as institutionalization, mentioned earlier, was a weakening of the regimes that the United States had established and sustained.

Collective goods theory, so applied, predicts the very weakening whose existence I have contested. Yet the absence of that weakening can itself be understood by a different application of collective goods theory. This interpretation requires a careful examination of the goods provided and an awareness of the degree to which they were not collective, but private. To the degree that they were private goods—benefits to the United States itself—they have brought important if sometimes obscured resources to the United States, resources that help it to maintain regimes and to obtain further private goods for itself.

---

[32] Keohane, *After Hegemony*, p. 270: "So the United States farsightedly made short-term sacrifices—in growing financial aid, and in permitting discrimination against American exports—in order to accomplish the longer-term objective of creating a stable and prosperous international economic order in which liberal capitalism would prevail and American influence would be predominant." The proposition that the burdens of empire almost inevitably outweigh its benefits is of course a common one. Note Mark Elvin, *The Pattern of the Chinese Past* (London: Methuen, 1973): "The burdens of size consist mainly in the need to maintain a more extended bureaucracy with more intermediate layers, the growing difficulties of effective co-ordination as territorial area increases, and the heavier costs of maintaining troops on longer front lines further removed from the main sources of trustworthy manpower and supplies" (p. 19).

A "collective good" must meet the two standard criteria of nonrivalness and nonexclusiveness. By the first is meant that one's enjoyment or consumption of a good does not diminish the amount of the good available to anyone else; by the second, that it is not possible to exclude any party from enjoyment of the good, as a result of which many actors may be "free riders" unwilling to pay any of the costs for providing the good. Few goods ever fit these criteria perfectly; one can usually find some possibilities of rivalness and exclusion, but judgments of less and more are perfectly feasible.[33]

None of the major goods identified earlier primarily meet the criteria for collective goods, I shall argue. In many ways they represent private goods accruing as much to the United States as to others. The conclusion that the exercise of hegemony necessarily weakened the United States does not follow. If the United States has not been severely weakened, moreover, we need not be surprised at its continued willingness and ability to secure these goods.

The first of the goods at issue is stable peace, particularly among the industrialized states. It probably satisfies the criterion of nonrivalness, though some radical critics contend that peace within and among the industrialized states is achieved only at the price of exploiting (through dominance, military threats, and military intervention) the Third World. Whatever one thinks of that assessment, peace clearly does not meet the criterion of nonexclusiveness. It certainly is feasible to exclude various countries or areas from stable peace, if one so wishes, by attacking or invading. Even for "peace" by dominance one can choose boundaries to the area one pacifies.

Many Western observers would probably judge containment to be largely a collective good. It was desired by *most* of the citizens of all the countries protected, not just by the United States. The unanimity of this desire has weakened recently, however, as many of its

beneficiaries, notably in Western Europe, have come to doubt the reality of a Soviet military threat to their security or way of life. Containment is achieved both by deterrence and by a willingness to defend. It is neither entirely nonrival nor entirely nonexclusive. As the distinction in the alliance literature makes clear, deterrence satisfies the criterion of nonrivalness well and that of nonexclusiveness reasonably well, but defense is another matter.[34] Fortifying one area may require the adversary to concentrate troops there, actually enhancing the defense of other areas; or, by drawing the hegemon's resources away from other areas, it may indeed prove to be "rival" by leaving weak spots elsewhere in the perimeter. (In the Korean War many American analysts feared that too great an involvement would divert needed forces from the European theater.) One may attempt to exclude "unimportant" countries or uncooperative governments from one's defensive or deterrent umbrella, though as South Korea in 1950 suggests, it is not always possible to stick to the resolve to exclude them. Since defense is significantly a private good, small and large states have strong incentives to provide substantial military capabilities of their own. Other important goods can also be derived from military forces, among them technological knowledge, prestige, and internal security.[35]

Prosperity, as provided by an open world economy, is also to be found somewhere on the continuum between private and collective

---

[33] See Russett and Starr, *World Politics,* chap. 18.

[34] Bruce Russett, *What Price Vigilance? The Burdens of National Defense* (New Haven: Yale University Press, 1970), chap. 4.

[35] Karen Rasler and William R. Thompson, "Global Wars, Public Debts, and the Long Cycle," *World Politics* 36 (October 1983), pp. 489–516, carefully recognize the particular private benefits, to the commercially extended hegemon, of providing defense and deterrence for others. This should be set against the more familiar argument that military expenditures become a private "bad" by inhibiting capital formation and growth in the hegemon. For evidence see Rasler and Thompson, "Longitudinal Change in Defense Burdens, Capital Formation, and Economic Growth," *Journal of Conflict Resolution,* forthcoming.

goods. It is partly nonrival and partly rival. General gains accrue from prosperous and expanding markets, yet a capitalist economy lives by competition, and one sells at the expense of a competitor. (The mixed-motive game characterization is appropriate.) States can be formally excluded from the most-favored-nation system—the system that provides much of the basis of international prosperity—as the Soviet Union has been.[36] Within the system, the rules of the international trade and finance game prohibit many kinds of discrimination (exclusion from benefits), but many loopholes can be found, as in various preferences, restrictions, and common market arrangements.

I have already argued that the United States was in the immediate postwar years well positioned to reap *at least* a proportionate share of the collective and private gains to be obtained from the prosperity induced by decolonization and a more open world market. In some sense there were costs, as the United States, in accordance with the liberal free-trade regime it was sponsoring, had to open its own previously protected markets. But these costs were, during the first decades after World War II, recouped many times over from the prosperity stimulated generally by a relatively open world market and specifically by American access to others' previously closed markets. These markets, of course, included those of the metropolitan countries of Europe as well as the Third World. The United States mitigated EEC discrimination against American trade by insisting that EEC trade and investment barriers be low and, save for agricultural products, it succeeded in gaining access on terms not much worse than those accorded to intra-EEC enterprises.

The gains from an open global economy surely exceeded the costs to the United States. Despite what ultimately proved to be heavy burdens that the United States shouldered to maintain the open economy, the balance sheet for Americans looks favorable when compared with the costs that other powers accepted in decolonization. (The costs associated with maintaining the dollar at a fixed price in gold, for example, eventually became too great, but for a long time they were substantially balanced by the gains from seigniorage and autonomy.) Indeed, gains from decolonization helped shield the United States from what might otherwise have been a *rapid* deterioration of its relative economic position resulting from the disproportionate economic burden (the Marshall Plan as well as high military expenditures) it carried in the interests of containment. The two defeated powers, Germany and Japan, did quickly close much of the per capita economic gap with the United States—as a consequence of deliberate American policy to build strong pillars of containment at either end of the Soviet Union. But the major power whose decolonization occurred after rather than during the war, Great Britain, was in no way able to close the gap.

A careful understanding of the kind of goods provided to various actors tells us that the picture of hegemonic America largely supplying others with collective goods is simply misleading. Earlier I also argued that the image of a gross long-term deterioration in benefits enjoyed by the United States was a serious distortion of reality, ignoring much continuity of gain. To recognize that distortion, however, is not to argue that the benefits to the United States were necessarily weighted in the direction of the long term. In fact, gains began to accrue rather quickly while many of the costs emerged only in the longer term, in the 1970s.

[36] Arthur A. Stein, "The Hegemon's Dilemma: Great Britain, the United States, and the International Economic Order," *International Organization* 38 (Spring 1984), pp. 355–86. For the argument that free trade is not necessarily a collective good see John Conybeare, "Public Goods, Prisoners' Dilemma, and the International Political Economy," *International Studies Quarterly* 28 (March 1984), pp. 5–22.

The Western alliance system to contain the Soviet Union was created quickly and was especially effective in the first decades. Stable peace was established among and within the OECD countries quite early, and it too was a quick as well as an enduring benefit.

The prosperity that both supported and was maintained by peace likewise began early, with the immediate rebuilding of war-torn economies, and it extended unbroken until the oil shocks of the 1970s. True, the postwar reconstruction entailed immediate large-scale costs to the United States, in the Marshall Plan and in trade concessions to Japan that in large part substituted for heavy grant assistance, but the United States had large amounts of surplus productive capacity after World War II, making the costs of overseas economic assistance not really very onerous. Furthermore, that excess capacity made postwar American prosperity dependent on foreign economic expansion in worldwide prosperity. Had the European or former colonial economies been allowed to stagnate, almost surely the American economy would have done likewise. Most major currencies had become convertible by the mid-1950s and at stable exchange rates, reducing, in Arrighi's words, "the risks to capital of, and so favoring, the expansion of international trade and investment."[37] Again, the United States was superbly positioned to capture its full share of those gains. It is also worth remembering that this open world economy did not, especially in the first decades, include the communist countries. When those states began to seek partial global economic integration, however, Eastern Europe in the 1960s and the Soviet Union and China somewhat later, the terms were largely the initial American specifications.

It is no more correct to describe the costs of obtaining noneconomic goods as disproportionately borne by the United States. Even in the instance most often cited, the cost of contain-

ment, the argument fails. It is true that in purely economic terms (i.e., share of GNP, a cost that the wealthy United States could most easily bear) the burden fell more heavily on Americans. But non-Americans have consistently provided the real estate and the manpower. For example, America's formal allies alone, in Europe and Asia, have maintained twice as many soldiers under arms as has the United States. They did so immediately after the war as well as in recent years, many of them with compulsory national service.

The balance sheet of costs and benefits to all parties, coupled with a rigorous application of the criteria for collective goods, casts a good deal of doubt on the proposition that the United States provided disproportionate benefits to others. The major goods provided by American postwar hegemony—"stable peace" within much of the industrialized world, a *cordon sanitaire* around the major perceived security threat, a relatively open, expanding, and largely predictable world economy—were obtained in degrees that were not markedly suboptimal from the American point of view. The burdens were not grossly unfair to the United States relative either to the gains to the United States or to the burdens borne by many other noncommunist countries. Nor did the United States incur especially large short-term costs for its own or others' long-term benefit. True, there were short-term costs, especially economic costs that the world's largest, richest economy could readily bear, but the benefits came pouring in quickly too.

This assessment fits with what is, after all, conventional wisdom about governmental decision makers, perhaps especially those in an elected system. Decision makers experience incentives to incur long-term costs (payable after election) to show short-term gains, or at least to avoid short-term losses.[38] It is possible

---

[37] Arrighi, "A Crisis of Hegemony," p. 57.

[38] Edward R. Tufte, *Political Control of the Economy* (Princeton: Princeton University Press, 1980); Daniel Ells-

that after great disruptive wars politicians are more likely to become statesmen, concerning themselves with a long-term institutionalization of a "structure of peace." Certainly there was a great deal of action after 1945 based on long-term vision, but at the same time the short-term gains were very far from trivial. Indeed, from many radical and even liberal perspectives American aid and rearmament expenditures—both in themselves and as stimulants in a wider and open world economy—prevented a postwar repetition of the Great Depression. For Americans it was the ideal outcome: one could do well by doing good.

CULTURAL HEGEMONY

How do we explain the U.S. ability to achieve and to maintain a rather favorable balance of costs and benefits? One answer, found in a few versions of the hegemonic stability literature, asserts that in the early years, at least, the United States was such a powerful hegemon that it could skew the division of private goods in its favor and *enforce* "adequate" burden sharing for collective goods by other noncommunist states. The United States, according to this interpretation, in effect provided something functionally equivalent to the coercive mechanism of central government that insures the provision of collective goods within nation-states.[39] In this sense American hegemony was essentially imposed and maintained by political-economic coercion, though not largely by the threat or fact of physical violence. Certainly

other countries were in a weak position to resist American demands in the immediate postwar era, and relatively strong international institutions—at least by comparison to those of the period before World War II—were created, dominated by the United States. But the qualification of "strong" as relative to what went before is an important one. I find it hard to believe that the institutions provided the basis for coercive, tax-collecting power necessary to enforce what was from an American point of view a near-optimal provision of collective goods at a distribution of costs that was not unfair to the United States. Coercive hegemony provides at best a challengeable answer.[40]

A final major gain to the United States from the Pax Americana has perhaps been less widely appreciated. It nevertheless proved of great significance in the short as well as in the long term: the pervasive cultural influence of the United States. This dimension of power base is often neglected. After World War II the authoritarian political cultures of Europe and Japan were utterly discredited, and the liberal democratic elements of those cultures revivified. The revival was most extensive and deliberate in the occupied powers of the Axis, where it was nurtured by drafting democratic constitutions, building democratic institutions, curbing the power of industrial trusts by decartelization and the rebuilding of trade unions, and imprisoning or discrediting much of the wartime leadership. American liberal ideas largely filled the cultural void. The effect was not so dramatic in the "victor" states whose regimes were reaffirmed (Britain, the Low and Scandinavian countries), but even there the United States and its culture was widely admired. The upper classes may often have thought it too "commercial," but in many respects American mass consumption culture was the most pervasive part of America's impact. American styles, tastes, and middle-class consumption patterns

berg, *Papers on the War* (New York: Simon & Schuster, 1972); and Leslie Gelb and Richard Betts, *The System Worked: The Irony of Vietnam* (Washington, D.C.: Brookings, 1979).

[39] In his brilliant paper Duncan Snidal, "Hegemonic Stability Theory Revisited," *International Organization*, forthcoming, notes that both Krasner, "State Power," and Gilpin, *War and Change*, fully recognize the degree to which the postwar regimes benefited the United States in particular, and that Gilpin particularly argues that the United States was significantly able to extract contributions as a quasi-government.

[40] See Keohane, *After Hegemony*.

were widely imitated, in a process that has come to bear the label "coca-colonization."

Altogether, the near-global acceptance of so many aspects of American culture—consumption, democracy, language—very quickly laid the basis for what Gramscians would call cultural hegemony. It paid immediate benefits, in markets and in a willingness of many people to bear significant burdens in order to establish and maintain the *cordon sanitaire*. In the longer term it shaped people's desires and perceptions of alternatives, so that their preferences in international politics and economics were concordant with those of Americans. (The rationalization of hegemony is itself part of this process.) Pervasive American cultural influence was part of a structural transformation of the international system. It meant that in many cases Americans would be able to retain substantial control over essential outcomes without having to exert power over others overtly.[41] Rather, others' values were already conditioned to be compatible with American wishes in ways that would benefit Americans as well as themselves (antiauthoritarianism and, within limits, acceptance of free-market economics).[42]

Gramscian ideas of influence are notoriously difficult to operationalize because by definition they leave no traces in events; overt persuasion is usually unnecessary, much less coercion. But they should not be dismissed.[43] Evidence of the mushroom expansion of American television, film, and printed matter in the world, often in spite of other governments' efforts to reinforce cultural boundaries, supports a Gramscian interpretation. It is truly a worldwide phenomenon, not limited to the industrial states of Europe and Japan. The internalization of Western (but especially American) norms by the rulers and middle classes of the Third World forms a constant theme in *dependencia* writing. Nor has it noticeably diminished over the years. De Gaulle and Mitterrand offer but ineffectual resistance in an industrial country, and only the draconian measures of Khomeini bring much success in an underdeveloped one.

The international institutionalization associated with regime building, noted earlier, helps spread common cultural and political norms, especially among governing elites, helping to achieve consensus on what problems must be solved and how. Norm-creating institutions broaden individuals' self-images; institutions may change the "decision criteria—members may become *joint* maximizers rather than just self-maximizers."[44]

The spread of American culture (democratic, capitalist, mass-consumption, anticommunist)

---

[41] That is, persuading someone to do something he or she would not otherwise do; see Robert A. Dahl, *Modern Political Analysis*, 4th ed. (Englewood Cliffs, N.J.: Prentice-Hall, 1984).

[42] Robert W. Cox and Harold K. Jacobson, "The United States and World Order: On Structures of World Power and Structural Transformation" (paper presented at the Twelfth World Congress of the International Political Science Association, Rio de Janeiro, August 1982), p. 7: "World hegemony is founded through a process of cultural and ideological development. This process is rooted mainly in the civil society of the founding country, though it has the support of the state in that country, and it extends to include groups from other countries." Also see Norbert Elias, *The Civilizing Process*, vol. 2: *State Formation and Civilization* (Oxford: Blackwell, 1982): "Just as it was not possible in the West itself, from a certain stage of interdependence onwards, to rule people solely by force and physical threats, so it also became necessary, in maintaining an empire that went beyond mere plantation-land and plantation-labour, to rule people in part through themselves, through the moulding of their superegos.... The outsiders absorb the code of the established groups and thus

undergo a process of assimilation. Their own affect-control, their own conduct, obeys the rules of the established groups. Partially they identify themselves with them, and even though the identification may show strong ambivalencies, still their own conscience, their whole superego apparatus, follows more or less the pattern of the established groups." Neither of these statements is meant to deny some reciprocal role of elites in the periphery in helping to shape the dominant world culture.

[43] They form, for instance, a key element in Alker's conception of power. Hayward R. Alker, "Power in a Schedule Sense," in Alker et al., eds., *Mathematical Approaches to Politics* (San Francisco: Jossey-Bass, 1972).

[44] Arthur A. Stein, "Coordination and Collaboration: Regimes in an Anarchic World," *International Organization* 36 (Spring 1982), p. 324.

has laid the basis for innumerable American economic and political gains. The spread of American culture has been a collective good in the sense of being nonrival. (We can state this observation more strongly: to the degree one state in the global system becomes more Americanized, others are influenced to become more, not less, so.) It also is not readily capable of being excluded. If one regards it normatively as a ''good,'' then all parties are beneficiaries, but even then the private benefits to the United States itself can hardly be ignored. Many peoples who would have liked to exclude American culture were unable to do so, and certainly to them it was hardly an unalloyed ''good.''

It was appropriate that Americans, who have reaped so many gains from cultural dominance, should pay whatever extremely modest costs it may have entailed. Cultural hegemony provides long-term influence that persists, and persists deeply, to this day. It is among the primary reasons why a decline in dominance over material power has not been reflected in an equivalent loss of control over outcomes.

CONCLUSION

These observations begin to untangle a central puzzle of the hegemonic stability literature. Two empirical assumptions at the ''hard core'' of the hegemonic stability research program depart so far from reality as to have seriously misleading effects. First, the characterization of hegemonic America as predominantly supplying itself and others with collective goods is inaccurate. Even for those goods which can correctly be called collective the United States had not paid at all disproportionate costs. Second, the description of American hegemony itself as having declined is a gross overstatement, particularly when one looks at the military and cultural as well as at the economic elements of hegemony.

The puzzle stems from trying to explain a phenomenon that has not really occurred. Mark Twain did die eventually, and so will American hegemony. But in both cases early reports of their demise have been greatly exaggerated.

QUESTIONS FOR DISCUSSION

1 What criteria should be used in evaluating whether U.S. hegemony has declined?
2 Has decolonization strengthened U.S. hegemony?
3 Does the pervasive cultural influence of the United States have any bearing on the issue of U.S. hegemony?
4 What will be the status of U.S. hegemony in the next 10 years? Why?
5 What kinds of developments in world politics could the United States influence in 1946 that it cannot influence today?
6 How can you relate your answer to Question 5 to the issue debated in the Oye and Russett articles?

SUGGESTED READINGS

Chomsky, Noam. ''Intervention in Vietnam and Central America: Parallels and Differences,'' *Radical America,* **19**, no. 1 (1985), pp. 49–66.

Galbraith, John Kenneth. ''The Second Imperial Requiem,'' *International Security,* **7** (Winter 1982–83), pp. 84–93.

''How Has the United States Met Its Major Challenges since 1945?: A Symposium,'' *Commentary,* **80** (Nov. 1985), pp. 25–107.

Hunter, Robert E. ''The Relevance of American Power,'' *SAIS Review,* **5** (Winter–Spring 1985), pp. 11–24.

Johnson, Robert H. ''Exaggerating America's Stakes in Third World Conflicts,'' *International Security,* **10** (Winter 1985–86), pp. 32–68.

Keohane, Robert O. *After Hegemony: Cooperation and Discord in the World Political System.* Princeton, N.J.: Princeton Univ. Press, 1984.

Maynes, Charles William. ''Logic, Bribes, and Threats,'' *Foreign Policy,* no. 60 (Fall 1985), pp. 111–129.

Mee, Charles L., Jr. *The Marshall Plan: The Launching of the Pax Americana.* New York: Simon and Schuster, 1984.

Nuechterlein, Donald E. *America Overcommitted: United States National Interests in the 1980s.* Lexington, Ky.: Univ. Press of Kentucky, 1985.

Rosecrance, Richard (ed.). *America as an Ordinary Country*. Ithaca, N.Y.: Cornell Univ. Press, 1976.

Rupert, Mark E., and David P. Rapkin. "The Erosion of U.S. Leadership Capabilities," in Paul Johnson and William R. Thompson (eds.), *Rhythms in International Politics and Economics*. New York: Praeger, 1985, pp. 155–180.

Strange, Susan. "Still an Extraordinary Power: America's Role in a Global Monetary System," in Raymond E. Lombra and William E. Witte (eds.), *Political Economy of International and Domestic Monetary Relations*. Ames, Ia.: Iowa State Univ. Press, 1982, pp. 73–93. (See also discussion by Robert Z. Aliber, Robert Solomon, Susan Strange, and others on pp. 94–103.)

CHAPTER 3

GOALS

All sovereign states can be said to have goals in international politics, but these are not necessarily coherent or held consistently over protracted periods of time. In fact, the foreign and security policies of states often result from the unpredictable interaction of the numerous actors within them—political leaders, bureaucrats, business leaders, opinion formers, media personnel, and even general publics. States, it is often claimed, pursue only their selfish interests. But, even if true, that may explain everything and yet really explain nothing, for rarely can two actors in a given state agree on precisely what those interests are. In 1986, for example, President Reagan's various advisers clearly did not agree on whether it was in the U.S. interest to seek better relations with Iran by offering arms shipments. Moreover actors are constantly moving on and off any particular stage. For example, most U.S. presidents in this century have served less than two full terms, and the number of postwar secretaries of state and of defense has also been disturbingly high for those who look for continuity and consistency.

A further important point is that actors tend to have both macrogoals and microgoals. At any particular moment of decision, it is never entirely predictable which will have priority if a clash between the two levels should occur. Thus, an actor may wish to see the advancement of a certain global ideology but nevertheless may be tempted, on a particular occasion, to accord that objective less importance than the pursuit of some short-term perceived gain. Or he or she may make the opposite choice. It is a matter for debate whether pluralistic democracies are more prone than dictatorships to put short-term goals first.

Analysis of goals has never been more widely attempted than in the case of the two superpowers that have emerged since the end of World War II, and it is not surprising that major differences of opinion have arisen among the multitude of analysts. This has been true for both military-security and political-ideological goals. And no effort to establish a hierarchy of alleged goals or to draw clear-cut lines between short-term and long-term goals has commanded any degree of consensus.

IDEOLOGY

Both the Soviet Union and the United States can be said to pay at least lip service to certain ideological objectives. But whether either or both take these ideologies seriously as guides for day-to-day action is a matter of great controversy, as our first debate between Herbert J. Ellison and Brian Thomas illustrates.

For some experts the Soviet Union is obsessively concerned with promoting world communism and does not hesitate to use armed force for this purpose whenever it safely can. A number of such experts would go on to say that the United States is no less committed to the ruthless promotion of *its* ideology, which can be seen as either ''freedom'' (and especially pluralistic democracy) or ''capitalism,'' or possibly both. An important divergence arises at this point, however, between those who thus think both superpowers are more-or-less equally ideological in their conduct and those who see the United States as much more pragmatic than the Soviet Union. Those who hold the second position tend to stress the importance of the body of literature known as Marxism-Leninism, which is taught like a religious catechism to all Soviet children and may possibly serve as the underlying rationale for all major Soviet actions in world affairs. The United States, by contrast, according to this interpretation, has no similar creed and hence evolves more or less in line with the fluctuations of majority opinion at any particular time—meaning that any consistent long-term ideological base to its foreign and security policies is largely absent. Others, including most Marxists, would think this supposed distinction between the superpowers a profound illusion.

There is a major school of thought, however, which holds that ideological beliefs are mere window dressing for the largely pragmatic conduct of both superpowers. According to this view, represented in our debate by Thomas, the Soviets are not really guided to any serious extent by the writings of V. I. Lenin (who has now been dead for more than 60 years) any more than U.S. presidents spend their time poring over the works of their nation's founding fathers. In short, world conditions in the 1980s are so fundamentally different from those applying in the distant past, and so complex, that no serious statesman could possibly operate successfully by trusting to any kind of ''automatic pilot.''

The argument then arises as to the meaning of various acts of external intervention (called ''aggression'' if one disapproves). The Soviet Union and the United States have both engaged in overt moves of this kind in the period since World War II: the former, for example, in East Central Europe and in

Afghanistan; the latter, for example, in the Dominican Republic and in Grenada. Moreover, both superpowers have also interfered in the internal affairs of many countries by methods that fall short of direct military invasion, especially in the Third World, where many so-called proxy actions have occurred. If these actions are not ideologically motivated, how are they to be explained? There are many who think that in the case of one or the other or both superpowers we should be looking for explanations mainly in terms of traditional power-political motives in the spheres-of-influence tradition, or perhaps as mere reactions to the perceived expansionist goals of the principal supposed adversary. After all, one does not usually explain, say, Anglo-German rivalry before World War I in terms of ideology—that is, no body of writing comparable to that of Lenin is held to be responsible, say, for the famous naval race or for the fact that the British and German soldiers slaughtered one another in such large numbers at the battle of the Somme. Others would point out, however, that neither Great Britain nor Imperial Germany before 1914 had elevated any single individual to the role of supposedly infallible prophet—which is the impression Western visitors to the Soviet Union sometimes get about the status of Lenin, who is practically deified in his mausoleum in Red Square and whose busts, portraits, and slogans are to be seen at every turn. In our debate Herbert J. Ellison represents the viewpoint that the Soviet Union is indeed uniquely motivated by Leninist ideology.

AFGHANISTAN

In recent years no Soviet action has had a more profound effect on U.S. opinion than the invasion of Afghanistan in 1979. President Carter, for example, decisively revised his earlier, relatively favorable opinion of the Soviet Union, and he did not recommend to the Senate the ratification of the SALT II Accords. In 1977 he had said, "Being confident of our own future we are now free of that inordinate fear of Communism which once led us to embrace any dictator who joined us in that fear."[1] But in the last year of his presidency he showed that this fear had to some extent returned, and he saw fit to promote American rearmament and to prepare for possible military moves against any further Soviet acts of aggression.

Few Western citizens approved of the Soviet invasion of Afghanistan, but there were nevertheless major differences of opinion about the motives that underlay it. These differences are reflected in our next debate between William E. Griffith and Geoffrey Stern. For those who took a gloomy view of Soviet aims, whether based primarily on ideological fanaticism or great-power imperialism, the invasion was nothing less than a central geopolitical challenge to the West. Afghanistan was seen as a possible future jumping-off point for a major Soviet thrust toward control of the Gulf Area and maybe also toward Soviet access to the Indian Ocean. In short, Pakistan, Iran, and the Arab Gulf

---

[1] President Jimmy Carter, Commencement Address at Notre Dame University, May 22, 1977.

States were all seen as menaced with destabilization and perhaps conquest. Western interests, not perhaps directly involved in Afghanistan per se, were thus seen as seriously threatened, since Soviet expansion into South Asia and the Gulf Area could have profound strategic implications and, for Western Europeans and Japan, possibly ruinous consequences in the light of their dependence for oil on the various Gulf States.

Other experts, including Stern, were less alarmed by the Soviet move, seeing it as more defensive than offensive in motivation. In 1979 the communist Afghan regime, established by a domestic coup, was on the point of collapse and had to be propped up if an anticommunist regime was to be kept out of power in Kabul. There are two broad reasons why the Soviets may have dreaded the latter outcome. One possibility is that they simply did not want a hostile regime on their doorstep and may have further feared the spread of fanatical Islamic beliefs into contiguous Islamic regions of the Soviet Union. Another broad possibility is that the Soviets acted from the essentially defensive ideological concern that no state having adopted a Marxist-Leninist regime can be permitted to backslide lest it undermine the oft-proclaimed communist belief in the inevitable march of history.

It is right to repeat that all assessments of Soviet motives can only, in the final analysis, be speculative, for authentic information about discussions that take place among the Soviet leaders simply cannot be had. Soviet society is closed; there are no "leakers" ready to rush to the media, and no tapes are ever released. In fact, the relevant Soviet archives for the entire postwar period remain closed. The contrast with general knowledge of U.S. policy making is thus rather striking.

In such circumstances, then, nothing very authoritative can be said about the invasion of Afghanistan. One thing indisputably is true, however. Fears that the seizure of Afghanistan would rapidly lead to Soviet attacks on neighboring countries did not materialize. At the time of writing, nearly a decade later, Iran, Pakistan, and the rest retain their independence. But we have no means of knowing whether the Soviets have been deterred or are just biding their time. Or perhaps they had no intention of extending their military operation beyond Afghanistan in the first place, though it should not be forgotten that the appetite can grow with the eating. In short, goals can and do change.

HUMAN RIGHTS

Many of those who believe ideological concerns are of great importance in determining the conduct of the superpowers write or speak as if this invariably is a matter for regret. Thus, the Soviets, held to be inspired by Lenin, seek with fanatical zeal to impose their system on unwilling victims. And the U.S. government, whose strings are supposedly pulled by greedy capitalistic exploiters, invade small neighboring states in Latin America to protect the dividends of stockholders on Wall Street. But in the case of the United States at least some supposedly ideologically motivated conduct is also warmly welcomed by an influential U.S. liberal constituency. Reference is to the promotion of human rights, which was a particular concern of the Carter administration. The form that promotion took became the subject of great controversy at the end of the 1970s, as our next debate illustrates. Jeane Kirkpatrick, herself at that time a Democrat, held in a celebrated article in *Commentary* (which we reprint) that the sentimental and inconsistent pursuit by the Carter administration of supposed human betterment had been profoundly damaging to American interests. She particularly deplored Carter's decision not to sustain Somoza in Nicaragua and the Shah in Iran on account of their poor human rights records. As a consequence new regimes emerged in these countries that Kirkpatrick considers in practice to have been as bad as or worse than their predecessors in the area of human rights, and which were undeniably anti-American.

In 1986, however, another test arose when the pro-American Ferdinand Marcos of the Philippines came under threat from domestic opponents. With vital U.S. defense interests at stake, one might have expected stout support for the Marcos regime from Carter's successor. Indeed, Reagan had appointed Kirkpatrick to his administration largely on the strength of her article in *Commentary*. In practice, however, both Reagan and Kirkpatrick, after wavering, endorsed the removal of Marcos and his replacement by Corazon Aquino, a left-leaning critic of Marcos. Sidney Blumenthal, in an article in the *Washington Post* (which we reprint), saw in this endorsement a practical refutation of the line taken by Kirkpatrick in her *Commentary* article and a belated vindication of Carter. Two debates between Kirkpatrick and Blumenthal about the role of human rights in foreign policy and the relevance of the downfall of Marcos are presented here.

THE REAGAN DOCTRINE

The so-called Reagan Doctrine establishes the ambitious goals to which the administration ostensibly became committed for the course of Reagan's second term. It amounts to supporting anticommunist insurgency movements as well as reviving more traditional policies of resisting all kinds of Soviet expansionism throughout the world. If put into practice, the Reagan Doctrine would mean a reversal of much in the very recent U.S. record in world affairs. For from the time things began to go seriously wrong in Vietnam, the United States has tended to reduce its commitments and to leave matters to take their course in many parts of the world.

The U.S. withdrawal from an active world role was first given authoritative articulation in July 1969 with the Guam speech of President Nixon. Eventually it came to be known as the Nixon Doctrine, and Nixon summarized it thus in his memoirs:

> I stated that the United States is a Pacific power and should remain so. But I felt that once the Vietnam War was settled, we would need a new Asian policy to ensure that there were no more Vietnams in the future. I began with the

proposition that we would keep all our existing treaty commitments, but that we would not make any more commitments unless they were required by our own vital interests.

In the past our policy had been to furnish the arms, men and matériel to help other nations defend themselves against aggression. That was what we had done in Korea, and that was how we started out in Vietnam. But from now on, I said, we would furnish only the matériel and the military and economic assistance to those nations willing to accept the responsibility of supplying the manpower to defend themselves. I made only one exception: in case a major nuclear power engaged in an aggression against one of our allies or friends, I said that we would respond with nuclear weapons.[2]

The Nixon Doctrine amounted to a watering down of the U.S. approach of the previous 2 decades—an approach best encapsulated in President Kennedy's declaration in his Inaugural Address in 1961 that he was willing "to pay any price, bear any burden, meet any hardship, support any friend, oppose any foe to assure the survival and success of liberty."[3]

The consequence of the new approach signaled by Nixon was soon seen in Vietnam. There ensued the "Vietnamization" of the war and the withdrawal of U.S. forces. The South Vietnamese government proved incapable of survival, with the result that the Communists finally seized power in 1975. Then in the Carter period, as we have seen, nothing much was done to prevent anti-American forces from seizing power in Nicaragua and in Iran, while the Soviet invasion of Afghanistan was deplored but not effectively resisted.

In spite of the rhetoric of the Republican administration enshrined in the Reagan Doctrine, there has been much skepticism about whether the United States could in the 1980s really become markedly more robust. Such efforts as were made to demonstrate increased U.S. assertiveness were of a relatively modest kind. For example, the U.S. invasion of Grenada in 1983 was a rapid affair, and it encountered negligible resistance. And even the bombing of Tripoli, Libya, in 1986 had something of a hit-and-run character. More instructive perhaps was the U.S. decision to withdraw its forces from Lebanon in 1983, when it became clear that losses were mounting and that no rapid achievement of U.S. purposes was in sight. So it is a matter for debate whether the Reagan Doctrine really amounts to any significant change in the direction of U.S. foreign policy.

The debate we have chosen here, however, is based on the premise, accepted by both participants, that the Reagan Doctrine ought to be taken seriously in the sense that it could in the future move from the realm of rhetoric to reality. Both our debators—Jack Wheeler and Christopher Layne—are in the tradition of American Republicanism. Wheeler is a supporter of the Reagan Doctrine, although he believes it needs to be pursued with greater vigor than

---

[2] Richard Nixon, *RN, The Memoirs of Richard Nixon* (New York: Grosset and Dunlap, 1978), pp. 394–395.
[3] President John F. Kennedy, Inaugural Address, Jan. 20, 1961.

has hitherto been the case. With robust U.S. policies, however, he foresees the possibility that what the Soviets call the "correlation of forces" may turn dramatically against them.

Layne is an opponent of what he considers to be the neoconservative approach of many Republicans. He sees himself as a real conservative and argues against global interventionist policies. He believes that in the postwar era the Republican who most clearly understood the nature of U.S. interests was Sen. Robert Taft, who was of course no communist sympathizer but held that the United States should avoid getting overextended with expensive and possibly unsustainable global commitments. Hence, Taft argued against the massive deployment of U.S. forces in Western Europe in the so-called Great Debate in the Senate in 1951. Layne believes that Taft's ideas were those whose time has now visibly come. The U.S. base in terms of economic and military strength is so limited, in his view, as to make desirable a highly selective approach to security guarantees. Layne bluntly concludes that only Central America seems at present to constitute a sufficiently vital interest to warrant possible U.S. military intervention. If Layne's view comes to be accepted by a future U.S. administration, we shall clearly see a transformation in the U.S.-Soviet relationship. But whether Americans would regret that transformation must remain a matter for speculation.

9 Is U.S.-Soviet Competition Influenced Primarily by Ideological Factors?

YES

Herbert J. Ellison

Soviet-American Intervention

NO

Brian Thomas

Ideology and the Cold War

Soviet-American Intervention

Herbert J. Ellison

It is an odd fact of U.S.-Soviet competition in the third world that the policies and motivations of the two sides are rarely discussed in the same context, but rather separately. Yet, the behavior of each side is affected by its perception of the actions and motives of its competitor. Therefore, in assessing the causes of past and present conflict and speculating about possibilities for the future, it is essential to review the performance of both sides.

The end of World War II marked one of the most dramatic and significant transformations of the global power structure in modern history. Sir Lewis Namier described it as the point at which world power passed from the major European states to "two essentially extra-European powers, the United States and the Soviet Union." Once the empires of Germany in Europe and Japan in East Asia had collapsed, the resultant power vacuum was bound to be filled either by the United States or by the Soviet Union. How the process of readjustment would proceed was heavily dependent upon the compatibility of the purposes of the two powers, and those purposes were fundamentally opposed, a fact which was initially less apparent to the Western leaders than to the Soviets.

Both the United States and the Soviet Union agreed on one issue: the colonial empires, much of which is today described as the third world, should be dismantled. The American plan—articulated in the Wilsonian tradition by President Roosevelt—called for a transformation of colonial dependencies into democratically governed independent states. Their independence would be guaranteed by the new United Nations organization and its Security Council.

Though difficult for the American political mind to conceive—and equally difficult to accept—the Soviet view and goal were radically different. In the Soviet view, the American program would merely replace overt colonial political control with a new scheme of economic controls based on American global economic preponderance. Soviet ideologists dutifully named the proposed system *neocolonialism*. The proper political objective was the replacement of colonial regimes with regimes in which communist parties would hold significant or dominant political power.

Soviet interest in the political development of the colonial world dates from the earliest months of the revolution. Even as the Bolsheviks fought a civil war for their survival, they formed in 1919 the Communist International (Comintern), and proceeded to organize communist parties abroad on the Bolshevik model. In the 1920's, they also set up the international organizations for labor (Profintern), peasants (Krestintern), and other groups which, working with the Comintern, aimed to broaden the base of communist power and thus help prepare for communist revolutions. To the same end, they trained communist party operatives in the Soviet Union and established special training schools for recruits from Asia, such as the Sun Yat-sen University and the Communist University for Workers of the East. They also developed, at an early date, the use of Soviet foreign policy and Soviet foreign representatives to aid local communist parties directly and indirectly. Such efforts were often frustrated in the huge portion of Asia controlled by the European colonial states. In China, however, the opportunity was available in the 1920's. Soviet cooperation with the Chinese Nationalists laid the basis for the communist-nationalist united front

Herbert J. Ellison, "Soviet-American Intervention," *Harvard International Review*, **8** (Jan.–Feb. 1986), pp. 3–6.

that proved instrumental in broadening the influence and support of the Chinese communists, helping them toward their eventual victory.

These were the ways in which the Soviets got started on the effort to remold the colonial world in their own image more than a generation before the United States. World War II and its aftermath brought important new openings for the Soviets and for the communist parties in Asia which they had helped to found. Parties in the Japanese-occupied territories were directed to form alliances with other willing political parties in a united front against the Japanese occupation (the same policy as in occupied Eastern Europe). As the Japanese empire collapsed the communists emerged as a powerful or dominant force in the political and military organizations of several of the major countries of East and Southeast Asia (Burma, Indonesia, Malaya, Vietnam, and the Philippines). In China, they had already won a territorial enclave in the north during the Communist-Nationalist struggles of the thirties. The wartime period enabled the Chinese communists, like communists elsewhere, to gain greater political credibility and a broader base of support by taking leadership of the national resistance against an alien occupation.

The communist policy of forming a broad united front, a coalition of ideologically dissimilar political groups united by a single purpose, was, and remains today, the major stratagem in the communist pursuit of political power. In the wartime period the common enemy in much of East and Southeast Asia was the Japanese occupying force. In the postwar period, it was often returning European colonial authority. When European colonialism was either defeated or voluntarily dismantled, the enemy became the successor government headed by native leaders. They were accused of being lackeys of the former colonial powers or of the new imperialist villain of postwar communist analysis, the United States.

Wherever broad political resistance coalitions were formed, the communists sought to build both a political and a military organization, and to assure themselves of internal leadership and control of both. This was then, as it is today, the basis of the confusion of opponents of communist power, who often supported a coalition resistance effort against an occupying power or an objectionable native government. Only when it was too late would they discover that the real power within the coalition was in communist hands and that they had served the communist cause unknowingly.

The organization and assistance of local communist parties is thus a central feature of Soviet third world policy and one that has made a policy response by the U.S. and other democratic states uniquely difficult. It was one thing to apply the major American postwar policy response to the spread of communism—containment—to a situation such as South Korea where there was clearly an invasion of one state by another with conventional warfare. It was an altogether different and more complicated matter when the communists emerged as the dominant organizers and leaders of the political/military apparatus of, say, postwar Vietnam, or post-Somoza Nicaragua. What the U.S. faced in its competition with the Soviets for leadership of the third world was often a strong local communist party which, through the united front stratagem, and with extensive political, economic, and military support from the Soviet Union and other communist states, was able to achieve an internal coup against an unpopular government. After dispensing with the coalition partners who had made the victory possible, a communist dictatorship could be organized. There is no political group more skillful at using the slogans of nationalism and of democracy; and there is no group more determined, on ideological principle, to obtain a monopoly of political power to pursue its program.

It is often asserted, especially since the emergence of the Soviet Union as a superpower, that the motivation of Soviet revolutionary ideology has been replaced by a more conventional great power imperialism. The proper response to the assertion is that the ruling communist party in the Soviet Union sees the resources of the Soviet states as the major force for advancing a global revolutionary process, the key element in what its leaders describe as the changing "correlation of forces" in the global arena. The other elements (and not only in the third world, of course) include the other communist parties, governing and non-governing, and all other political and social movements controlled by or friendly to the communist states and parties—in brief, all of the resources globally which can be counted as useful for the general cause.

Those who argue against the primacy of ideological motivation in Soviet third world policy point to the heavy emphasis on the use of military and police power in the enterprise and the enormous buildup of the military power of the Soviet Union. The fact is that Leninist communism has from the beginning seen military power as a major policy instrument. Soviet history texts speak openly of the role of the Red Army in carrying the revolution to Eastern Europe and East Asia after World War II, not to mention its role in spreading the revolution to the non-Russian borderlands of the former Russian empire following the Bolshevik Revolution. In recent years the advent of Soviet global power—specifically the air and naval forces which make possible global application of Soviet power—has brought the use of that power to further revolutionary activities in previously inaccessible regions of the world, such as Africa and Latin America.

Another feature of the activity is the close collaboration with fellow communist states. The role of Cuban military forces (transported by Soviet aircraft) in several parts of Africa (no fewer than 30,000 in Angola alone today) and the close collaboration of communist states in the supply of the military and other assistance to governments in such countries as Grenada and Nicaragua are further evidence of the uses

of military power for political purposes. It is worth remembering that shortly after the Russian Revolution the Soviet leaders created the largest army in Europe, and that Cuba, Vietnam, and Nicaragua have created the dominant military forces in their own regions. Like their Soviet mentors, other communist states have emphasized military power for making revolution internally, while defending and extending it externally.

One should emphasize, as the Soviets themselves have repeatedly done, the two special roles of military power in Soviet third world policy which go beyond forcible acquisition of power. The first is to suppress "counter-revolution"—a term which applies to any effort, internally or externally organized, to overturn a communist government in power. Recent examples are the Soviet military aid to the Angolan government in its effort to suppress Jonas Savimbi and UNITA and the most costly and difficult recent case—Afghanistan. The second role is to discourage intervention against communist-led or -supported revolutions. These uses are more difficult to identify, since they involve some speculation about the impact of the estimation of Soviet military capacities and intentions on the policies of competing powers. Certainly the perception of growing Soviet missile strength influenced U.S. policy toward Cuba in the early 1960's.

With the growth of Soviet military power and the achievement of a rough parity in strategic nuclear weaponry with the U.S., the Soviets feel less inhibited about taking military initiatives in support of revolution. The U.S., meanwhile, has tended to feel more inhibition about intervention against such efforts. Nikita Khrushchev remarked in his memoirs that the increase of Soviet military power in his time assured that the U.S. could not again deliver a credible demand for Soviet withdrawal, as it had done over Iran in 1946. Doubtless there is a clue here to the Soviet perception of the political uses of military power in the third world:

namely, the importance of being sufficiently powerful that one's initiatives cannot be diverted or blocked by the threat of superior American military force.

Thus the military element of Soviet third world policy is subordinated to ideologically-based political objectives. Military power is not an end in itself but an instrument, and in the defense and advancement of third world revolution it is an instrument of growing importance. It appeared as a factor outside the periphery of the Soviet Union for the first time with arms aid to Egypt in 1955 (Czech arms, but clearly Soviet authorized and negotiated). It has multiplied rapidly, and the Soviets today occupy one of the leading places in arms exports to the third world.

The exports are not, of course, solely to organizations engaged in armed insurrection, either guerrilla groups or communist states (such as North Vietnam during the Vietnamese War). They are also to non-aligned third world countries such as India where the arms exports are intended to complement other efforts to build friendship and diplomatic cooperation with the Soviet Union. This category of arms export has become an important part of Soviet exports. Where the arms are purchased with much-needed hard currency, as with the huge purchases of Libya, the benefits to the Soviets are substantial. Indeed arms appear to be one area of exports in which the Soviets are competitive on the global market.

When the assertion is made that the Soviets are mainly seeking strategic positions in their third world policy, the issue needs clarification. Clearly, Soviet third world policy has brought with it some highly important strategic gains. One thinks of the base at Camranh Bay, the strategic importance of Aden (and the communist regime in South Yemen), of Ethiopia, and of the new positions in Southern Africa gained from the collapse of the Portuguese Empire. In the Caribbean and Central America, the Soviets have also made impressive strategic gains, and there is no doubt that those gains have added greatly to the Soviet military-strategic advantages.

Is one, therefore, justified in imputing to the Soviets a motivation for such action based on military-strategic objectives? The answer is yes, but not chiefly. Clearly the military and strategic purposes—and advantages—are there and are pursued. But opportunities for acquiring such positions come, as often as not, as a sort of "fringe benefit" in a broader revolutionary enterprise. For example, Camranh Bay, a gain from North Vietnam's conquest of the South, was not even a base, nor was the Soviet-American rivalry a significant factor in international politics when Comintern strategists first supported the development of a communist party organization in Indochina in the 1920's. The growth of Soviet global military power, and the perception of the increased importance of that power in "the revolutionary process," have given greater prominence to the acquisition of the military-strategic position, as both the arena of revolutionary action and the arena of American-Soviet strategic competition have expanded. The rapid increase in the number of such positions acquired by the Soviets in recent years provides evidence for the point. And it is likely that the process will continue and expand in the future. The evidence of Soviet interest and activity in the island states of the Southwest Pacific is a recent development which suggests a search for strategic positions in that vital region to complement the expanding regional Soviet naval power and the effort to build a political influence and presence.

In sum, the Soviet approach to the third world is part of a complex policy which has its foundation in the ideological concepts of the global "revolutionary process," and which regards all elements of Soviet power—including military—as instruments for advancing that process. As Soviet military power has expanded—both in scope and in geographical outreach—so too has its role as an instrument of revolutionary ideology. The same is true of the role of the Soviet economy. The Soviet economy is, of course, a very large one—third behind the United States and Japan—yet its external impact beyond the company of communist states and a few special trading partners outside it, is relatively small. This fact has much to do with the general failure of the Soviet economy to produce exportable goods other than energy and raw materials. Soviet manufacturers and technology simply cannot compete effectively on world markets. Even third world countries such as India have tended to "outgrow" the Soviet suppliers and look to Western markets for their needs.

Soviet exports to third world countries have grown steadily during the past three decades, a function of the growth of the Soviet economy itself and of the growth of the trading activity of the third world economies. The only really impressive export growth has been in arms, and the general level of trade has remained much below what Soviet leaders wanted. Moreover, there appears to be little connection between Soviet economic interests as such and Soviet political intervention in the third world. Reviewing the areas where Soviet activity has been greatest in recent years—Asia, Africa, and Latin America—it is difficult to find one in which there was a prior economic interest. In view of declining Soviet oil production, however, the argument can be made for the attraction of the oil resources of the Middle East and Southwest Asia, and for the influence of this factor on current Soviet policy. Once again, however, this factor is added to a long-standing interest and activity in the region based on ideological objectives.

The American reaction to Soviet policies of third world revolution has been complex and changing and also requires a brief historical background. The guiding voices were those of Wilson and Roosevelt rather than Lenin and Stalin, seeking replacement of colonialism with democratic self-government and the integration of the newly independent countries into the global economy. The postwar political evolution of the former colonial states has brought both successes and failures. For the U.S., as for the Soviet Union, democratic post-colonial constitutions frequently gave way to civilian or military dictatorship, and market economic relationships to unsuccessful socialist experimentation. Moreover, the postwar era opened with communist revolution in China and North Korea, and communist insurrections in Indochina, Malaya, Burma, and the Philippines, a process which reached a climax with the North Korean invasion of the South in 1950.

In the years following the Korean War, American policymakers became increasingly involved in the third world in the task of "containment"—of limiting the outward threat of the power and influence of the communist states—especially the Soviet Union and China. The liberal idealists who saw European colonialism as the enemy and felt that its demise would bring independent democratic states were soon disillusioned. In American policymaking the third world was increasingly seen as an area of widespread political instability which could in many countries be exploited by local communists, in cooperation with Moscow or Peking, to achieve new communist victories. Fear of the strategic menace of the expanding power of the U.S.S.R. and China was added to an antipathy to communist rule. The result was an immensely ambitious third world policy which combined economic and military aid to strengthen client states with a commitment to their defense against both external and internal armed opposition.

Both American and Soviet third world policies have ideological foundations which bring them sharply into conflict, the inevitable conflict of the aims and values of communism and liberal democracy. But the translation of ideology into policy is vastly different in the two cases. For the Soviets, ideology is the foundation of organization and action. Military and economic policy are the handmaidens, not the equals, of ideology. The essence of the ideology is a dynamic concept of political change, with the world, including the third world, moving steadily forward to communism. Soviet energies are concentrated on supporting communist revolution in the third world. Each new victory, whether in Vietnam, Nicaragua, Angola, or elsewhere, is viewed as a base for launching new offensives. And each of these new initiatives creates new anxieties, and often countermoves, from the American rival.

The American interaction with the third world is vastly more complex than its Soviet counterpart, and its ideological element less dominant. Government-controlled economic relations are only a fraction of the American economic ties. Private economic relations are vastly larger than governmental and in most cases dwarf the Soviet economic participation and capacity. Being mainly private trade and investment, those relations are motivated by private profit and have little to do with ideological considerations. Indeed, many American—and Western—companies have often shown a preference for stable dictatorships of the right or left over unstable democratic regimes. The result of this fact is that independent motivation can outweigh or counter the ideological element in U.S. government policy in an individual case. Because of the pluralism of structure and power in American society, governmental representatives are but one of the actors in the American–third world relationship. It is more accurate in the American case to refer to a "relationship" than simply to a governmental policy.

While the American government controls and directs only a small part of the nation's total relationship with the third world, it still controls enormous economic and military power which it has applied in many ways, including political and military intervention. During and since World War II there has been considerable uniformity to the pattern of intervention. It has been directed against what has been perceived as communist political power, both that of the Soviet Union and other communist states, and that of armed communist insurgents within individual states. Moreover, American intervention has been motivated by the view that the communist power was aiming not just at forcible imposition of its will in a single country, but was also expansionist. Such was the ideological rationale that underlay the Truman Doctrine of 1947. Originally applied to Greece and Turkey, it was extended and integrated into a broader "containment" policy in the succeeding years. The policy acquired mature form in the postwar context of revolutionary transformation in Europe and Asia when the East-West conflict emerged as the centerpiece of global politics. It was simultaneously democratic—supporting democratic self-government, and anti-communist—viewing totalitarian communism as the antithesis of democracy. Its democratic commitment was evident in pressure on European allies to emancipate their colonies, and upon native successor governments to rule democratically.

The scope and complexity of American intervention, as well as its roots, grew impressively in the 1950's and 1960's. Military intervention was obviously the action of last resort. American policy developed an elaborate array of programs and agencies—political and economic—whose central task was to assist the development of democratic self-rule in third world states. But military intervention, too, was part of the policy, and its most prominent applications were Korea and Vietnam.

The enormously costly and painful failure in Vietnam left paralysis and bewilderment in American policy. This was precisely the time when the Soviets and their allies, especially Cuba, had acquired new capacities and new confidence, and when a wave of revolutionary change was sweeping parts of Africa and Latin America.

The revival of a policy of American intervention against communist revolution seemed wholly unlikely in the mid-1970's, when the exhaustion of the Vietnamese War produced a strong public and congressional sentiment against future involvements in third world political conflicts. But a series of Soviet and Cuban initiatives—in the Middle East, Africa, and Central America—climaxed by the Soviet invasion of Afghanistan and the 1980-81 crisis in Poland—brought a rapid change of view. Beginning in the last stage of the Carter Presidency and proceeding rapidly under President Reagan in the early 1980's, the change of mood has made possible limited American support for Salvadoran President Duarte and for a variety of anti-communist insurgencies, as well as a small direct military intervention in Grenada. Anti-interventionist public opinion, widely expressed in Congress and strengthened by a massive international propaganda campaign receiving extensive Soviet and Cuban support, makes repetition of a large-scale American intervention highly unlikely.

Nonetheless, American democratic ideology and security concerns are persistent factors which could again, separately or in combination, motivate American military intervention against third world communist revolution. The commitment of the Soviet Union and other communist states to that cause remains strong, and there continue to be a number of politically unstable areas of Latin America, the Middle East, Africa, and Southeast Asia which provide opportunities. The pressures for American intervention are therefore likely to reappear, but in a context greatly different from the pre-Vietnam era. The superpowers are more evenly balanced in military power. Also, while the expansionist communist states and parties may still find revolutionary opportunities, they will also find that they carry heavy risks and costs, both in relation to non-communist states and in support for infant communist regimes facing strong opposition, often military opposition. Moreover, the economic and political dynamism of the global system—created by the great industrial democracies of North America, Europe, and East Asia—has drawn to its circle a growing company of newly industrialized states of successful developing countries for whom communism has little appeal or social foundation. Such developments would appear simultaneously to reduce the appeal and increase the risks of intervention for the future.

Yet the evidence of many decades suggests a remarkable continuity of fundamental view and purpose in Soviet third world policy. The persistent economic and social problems and attendant political instability of much of the third world will continue to attract the Soviets and their allies, just as their initiatives will continue to activate familiar ideological responses and security concerns on the American side. Whether those responses and concerns will again motivate American intervention to go beyond support of communist opponents remains to be seen. It seems most likely where really significant American security interests are at issue. Unfortunately, it is precisely in several such areas that the Soviets are most active today.

Ideology and the Cold War

Brian Thomas

That U.S.-Soviet relations have ideological over-
tones is undeniable. Many on both sides of what
Isaac Deutscher called "The Great Contest" believe the relationship to be more than just the
simple rivalry of two continental powers. To
Winston Churchill it was essentially a "schism
between communism, on the one hand, and
Christian ethics on the other"; for both Harry S.
Truman and Clement Attlee the Iron Curtain was
a curtain between minds;[1] while Ronald Reagan's
reference to the Soviet Union as an empire of evil
recalled Thomas Jefferson's view of the United
States as an empire of liberty. The language of
ideology is thus continually used, and much time
has been spent by each side in probing the beliefs
of the other.

The argument of this paper is that translating
U.S.-Soviet rivalry into the language of ideology is largely wasted effort. Seventy years ago,
on the other hand, it might well have been
worth doing. For both the United States and the
Soviet Union were, and are, more than simply
nation-states. Each was committed from birth
to a particular view of the world and of its own
place in it. Both are products of war, dissent,
and revolution. The American Revolution and
the founding of the United States were seen, by
both supporters and opponents, as a reaction
against the whole European "system" of monarchies, police states, and colonial empires.
Likewise, the Russian Revolution and the
founding of the U.S.S.R. were regarded as a
blow against the European "system" of V.I.

Lenin's time. That is why one of Lenin's fir-st
acts was to withdraw from a European war and
to choose a name for his new state that would
resemble European ones as little as possible.

In this Lenin followed Tom Paine. Like
"U.S.S.R.," "U.S.A." as the name of a state
was somewhat imprecise, chosen so that like-
minded recruits could join with as little discom-
fort as possible. Potential members had only to
be in, or near, the American continent, republican in form, democratic in intent, and willing
to subscribe to the values enshrined in the U.S.
Constitution. The name "U.S.S.R." had, admittedly, no continental connotation, but its
constituent member states were obliged to be
both republican and "socialist" in form, organized in "soviets," and willing to profess the
beliefs set out in the Soviet Constitution.

It is true, also, that the early champions of
both states were convinced that their respective
belief systems were not just locally valid but
worthy of universal application. To an American, republicanism, democracy and national
independence were not merely different from
monarchy, autocracy and colonialism; they
were wholly superior. To this extent, therefore,
the expansion of the United States was both
conditioned and made palatable by ideology.
This is why the Monroe Doctrine of 1823 made
plain the United States's opposition not only to
European colonialism but to Europe's "essentially different" "political systems," and why
President Lyndon B. Johnson in 1965 felt able
to pronounce a ban on future communist governments in the Western hemisphere without
having to mention the Soviet Union.

One can concede, finally, the relevance of
ideology to at least two aspects of Soviet foreign
policy, one present, one past. As all who conduct
that policy are members of the ruling Communist
party, it is reasonable to assume that they will

Brian Thomas, "Ideology and the Cold War" was
written especially for *The Cold War Debated*.
[1] Isaac Deutscher, *The Great Contest: Russia and the
West* (London: Oxford University Press, 1960); W. S.
Churchill in *The Daily Telegraph* (London), Dec. 31, 1946;
H. S. Truman in *New York Times*, Mar. 13, 1947; C. R.
Attlee in House of Commons *Parliamentary Debates*, vol.
423, col. 2038, June 5, 1946.

bear at least some traces of whatever ideological training party members receive.

Of equal importance, perhaps, was the role played by ideology at the time Soviet foreign policy was first conceived, irrespective of its possible relevance today. It is this first ("Leninist") phase of Soviet history that has supplied the stereotype for those determined to find consistency and continuity in Soviet foreign policy over the past seventy years. Continuity of one kind there was, but it is the argument of this paper that the policy of Joseph Stalin and his successors since 1924 has more in common with that of the tsars than it ever had with Lenin and the early Bolsheviks.

Lenin believed that the U.S.S.R. arose from the triumph of the Russian proletariat in alliance with the peasants. It was a victory achieved by class struggle. His conclusion was that other "proletarian" states would soon arise from similar class struggles conducted elsewhere and that without these new allies the ultimate goal of communism would not be attained. The logic, at least, was faultless; for if communism meant the abolition of the state,[2] then communism in one country must always remain a contradiction in terms. Lenin expected, further, that these new class struggles would take more than one form. There would be a rebellion inside each state conducted by the proletariat against its "bourgeois" (or colonial) masters. There would also be, perhaps simultaneously, an attack by these same "bourgeois" states on whatever "proletarian" regimes managed to emerge from revolution, including of course the Soviet Union. So however insignificant they may appear in other respects, it was the wars of intervention of 1918–1920 that gave color to Lenin's belief and produced the most celebrated of his contemporary comments:

We are living not merely in a state, but in a system of states, and the existence of the Soviet Republic side by side with imperialist states for a long time is unthinkable. One or other must triumph in the end. And before that end comes, a series of frightful collisions between the Soviet Republic and bourgeois states will be inevitable.[3]

Although it is reasonably clear from the context (a debate on defense expenditure in the middle of the civil war) that Lenin was referring to future attacks on the Soviet Union rather than to Red Army attacks on others, this statement is still sometimes used to persuade the West that Lenin was predicting a Soviet onslaught on the entire "bourgeois" world.

While Lenin's words portray a "worst-case" situation, he believed that a fair number of proletarian revolts would in fact occur. So for that matter did David Lloyd George. But the most optimistic was G. E. Zinoviev, who predicted the triumph of communism all over Europe within a matter of months.

Once it became clear, however, that nothing of the sort was going to happen, Stalin and his supporters drew the appropriate conclusion and reverted to the first phase of Lenin's policy: that of consolidating the revolution in one country. It was a move that had immediate (and lasting) consequences for Soviet foreign policy. Once the Soviet government realized that it was now charged with the defense of nearly all the territory of what was once tsarist Russia, and that this defense must be conducted without allies, the Soviet outlook altered. Outside the U.S.S.R. capitalism recovered rather than foundered, and what revolutions there were after 1920 seemed to be nationalist or "fascist" instead of "proletarian" and Marxist. In consequence the new revolutionary state was transformed into a revived Eurasian one, and the continental rivalry with the

---

[2] "So long as the state exists there is no freedom. When there is freedom, there will be no state." V. I. Lenin, *The State and Revolution* (1917) (Moscow: Foreign Languages Publishing House, 1951), p. 152.

[3] March 18, 1919. V. I. Lenin, *Collected Works,* 3d Russian ed. (Moscow: Foreign Languages Publishing House, 1937), vol. 24, p. 122.

United States, suspended since the sale of Alaska, began to be resumed. However strenuously Lenin and Woodrow Wilson competed for possession of the European mind, their successors reverted to more traditional pursuits. "Ideology" gave way to economic development and political consolidation.

As a result, the preoccupation of presidents Warren G. Harding, Calvin Coolidge, and Herbert Hoover with the consumer boom of the 1920s, and of Franklin D. Roosevelt with the aftermath of the Wall Street debacle, was matched by Stalin's commitment to "socialism in one country" and by the metamorphosis of the Communist International of 1919 into a branch of the Soviet foreign office. Even the noun "revolutionary" had to be redefined by Stalin; it emerged as one concerned solely with the defense of the Soviet Union.

It was in this interwar period, and not, as is sometimes alleged, under Nikita Khrushchev, that the doctrine of "peaceful coexistence" was formulated as the international counterpart of "socialism in one country." It made a full-dress appearance at the Seventeenth and Eighteenth Communist Party Congresses in 1934 and 1939 and was meant to apply to Soviet relations with Germany, Italy, and Japan just as much as with Britain, France, and the United States. The emphasis on peace and, above all, on "business relations" with other states had much in common with contemporary American "isolationism," and Stalin's words concerning the need to share the planet with those whose "systems" were different echoed those of James Monroe a hundred years before. As a policy it found expression in the Nazi-Soviet Pact as much as in M. M. Litvinov's attempts to negotiate some kind of anti-German alliance. It explains the Soviet decision to join the League of Nations in 1934 and the United Nations in 1945.

Paradoxically, the U.S.S.R.'s decreasing concern with revolution after 1930 can quite easily be reconciled with the ideology that it still claimed to profess. In the first place, there is nothing in

either Karl Marx or Lenin about the long-term role of the proletarian state in isolation, which meant that the U.S.S.R.'s foreign policy could be formulated empirically, like that of every other state. This was the task, successively, of Stalin, Khrushchev, and Leonid Brezhnev, and it is a great mistake to treat the pronouncements of one or other of these leaders as if they constituted revisions of the old ideology. What they did was to fill the gap that ideology did not foresee, with the result that world communism became a dream of the far future.

And second, even on the assumption that revolution elsewhere would follow the pattern set by Russia, any form of intervention by the new Soviet state to accelerate the process was ruled out of court. An early remark of Lenin that suggested the opposite was quickly revised; and by 1918 he had come round to the view that "the idea that revolution in other countries can be secured by prodding is completely at variance with Marxism."[4] Here Lenin stood four square with Friedrich Engels: "One thing alone is certain. The victorious proletariat can force no blessings of any kind upon any foreign nation without undermining its own victory by so doing."[5]

The logic is clear enough. If revolution in Russia was spontaneous and natural, why should it be any different elsewhere? Moreover, Soviet assistance could be interpreted as foreign intervention, and provoke national resistance rather than proletarian enthusiasm. And again, the very fact of Soviet help could easily prompt the suspicion that perhaps the country concerned was not really ready for revolution after all. If apples are truly rotten, they should fall without the aid of a bulldozer. What Marxism suggests, therefore, is that Soviet intervention should take place, if at all, for reasons unconcerned with revolution.

[4]V. I. Lenin, Mar. 1, 1918, cited in Andrew Rothstein, *Peaceful Coexistence* (London: Penguin Books, 1955), p. 74.
[5]September 12, 1882, cited in Arkady Losev, *The Nations Can Live in Peace* (London: Soviet News, 1956), p.19.

With the slow death of the Communist International, a formula to explain the absence of "prodding" had to be devised. On their own, "business relations" and "peaceful coexistence" were insufficient, for neither mentioned revolution elsewhere. Stalin supplied the answer on March 1, 1936, and as it was repeated verbatim by G. M. Malenkov sixteen years later and elaborated by Khrushchev at three successive party congresses in 1956, 1959, and 1961, it is perhaps worth quoting in full:

> We Marxists believe that a revolution will also take place in other countries. But it will take place only when the revolutionaries in those countries think it possible or necessary. The export of revolution is nonsense. Every country will make its own revolution if it wants to, and if it does not want to there will be no revolution.[6]

Reactions to this statement have been fourfold. Because it was first heard by a U.S. newspaperman, Roy Howard, and published in *Pravda* only after some delay, it is sometimes regarded as having been made for foreign consumption only. But if this were so it would hardly have been given such prominence subsequently by two of Stalin's successors. Alternatively, it is occasionally accepted as definitive on the grounds that it does not rule out support for revolutions once they have taken root. In this respect it is in complete conformity with the Brezhnev Constitution of 1977. Third, the statement is sometimes used as evidence that "ideology" has been finally buried, which is hardly logical, since Stalin, like Lenin, is saying little more than did Engels fifty years before. Finally, it is often discounted because it appears to conflict with Soviet intervention in Eastern Europe or Afghanistan. But this assumes that the Soviets invaded these countries

to "export" revolution, a proposition that deserves critical examination.

Let us take, first, Eastern Europe. Although the U.S.S.R. would no doubt claim to repudiate spheres of influence on principle, much of its foreign policy since it was attacked by Germany has been directed at securing a zone of control in Eastern, and later Central, Europe. The extent of that control intensified with the onset of the Cold War, and as the prospect of a neutral Germany on "Austrian" lines receded.

The part played by ideology, so far as can be judged, is negligible. The determining factor is not ideology but geography. Soviet objectives were threefold: to rid Soviet soil of all the German invaders; to retain and secure her 1941 frontiers, as opposed to those she had prior to the Nazi-Soviet Pact; and to permit no hostile regimes inside Eastern or Central Europe. The U.S.S.R. was assisted by three factors, only one of which had anything to do with ideology. There was a general feeling expressed a number of times by Churchill and, most movingly, by John Kennedy in a notable speech at American University, Washington, D.C., which he delivered on July 10, 1963. It recognized that, in the matter of World War II, if (to paraphrase Stalin) it was the Americans who provided the material and the British the time, it was the Soviets who supplied the blood. Not only did their losses exceed 20 million, but some 74 percent of all German casualties were inflicted by the Red Army on the Eastern front. Eastern Europe, therefore, must remain for some time an area of special concern to the Soviet Union. Second, there was toward the end of the war an expression of "leftist," anticonservative, and (in consequence) pro-Soviet feeling throughout much of Europe. It was as evident in Czechoslovakia and Bulgaria as it was in France, Italy, and Britain. That Bulgaria, Rumania, and Hungary also happened to be "enemy" states with intensely conservative regimes made it that much easier for "the Left" to secure considerable support. Some it obtained from Stalin, but in each

---

[6] *Pravda*, March 5, 1936, cited also in G. M. Malenkov, *Report to the XIX Congress of the CPSU*, October 5, 1952 (Moscow: Foreign Languages Publishing House, 1953), pp. 43–44.

case his approval depended upon whether the new government was "loyal," not on whether it was communist. In time the two became the same, but they were not the same in 1945.

In his long reply to Churchill's speech at Fulton in March 1946, Stalin put the issue squarely in nonideological terms and with more than a hint of the language of Monroe:

> The following circumstances should not be forgotten. The Germans made their invasion of the U.S.S.R. through Finland, Poland, Rumania, Bulgaria, and Hungary. The Germans were able to make their invasion through these countries because, at the time, governments hostile to the Soviet Union existed in these countries. As a result of the German invasion the Soviet Union has lost irretrievably in the fighting against the Germans. . . . Possibly in some quarters an inclination is felt to forget about these colossal sacrifices . . . . But the Soviet Union cannot forget about them. And so what can there be surprising about the fact that the Soviet Union, anxious for its future safety, is trying to see to it that governments loyal in their attitude to the Soviet Union should exist in these countries?[7]

There is not a word about the triumph of "antifascism," much less that of the proletarian state. Stalin spoke as he acted, as the guardian of the territory of a sovereign state that had been pillaged. Certainly the language was less formal than that of the Brezhnev Doctrine twenty-two years later, but the essentials of that Doctrine were set out here, in 1946, with little trace of ambiguity. By contrast, the language of the more famous "election speech" of a few weeks earlier contained much more of the standard party rhetoric.[8]

There is little doubt that the attitude recorded here had its effect on contemporary Soviet policy in other fields, most notably in Soviet rejection of the U.S.-sponsored Baruch

Plan for the international control of atomic energy. That Stalin was not perhaps being unduly paranoid was a view taken at the time by one of the leading British physicists concerned:

> In the Hearings in 1954, [J. Robert] Oppenheimer states that at that time he did not expect the Soviet Union to accept the plan, because he thought that if they did so and opened their frontiers and freely admitted Western inspection, the Soviet system as it existed would collapse. Exactly the same view was expressed to me in New York in 1946 by the late Lord Inverchapel, then the British Ambassador in Washington. I am surprised now, as I was then, that it was considered realistic diplomacy to ask the Soviet Union voluntarily to accept a plan which, in the views of its author and the American and British Governments, would lead to the collapse of the system.[9]

Stalin's task was also made easier by the existence of a third factor: the apparent connivance of the West in 1944 and 1945, a phenomenon that, like that displayed at Munich in 1938, was distinctly "nonideological." However much certain politicians accused Stalin later on of aiming to dominate the world, they appeared to be under no such illusion at the time. The connivance bred from their familiarity with, and acceptance of, what Georg Schwarzenberger once described as "imperialism with good manners": the principle of spheres of influence.[10] As Anthony Eden's private secretary wrote in his diary on December 15, 1944: "There is much to be said for Russian claims to play leading part in East. . . as we claim in West. . . . We can't have our cake and eat it as HMG [His Majesty's Government] always expect."[11]

[7] *Pravda,* Mar. 13, 1946; *New York Times,* Mar. 14, 1946.

[8] *New York Times*, Feb. 10, 1946.

[9] P. M. S. Blackett, *Atomic Weapons and East-West Relations* (Cambridge, England: Cambridge Univ. Press, 1956), p. 90. See also *In the Matter of J. Robert Oppenheimer* (Washington, D.C.: U.S. Government Printing Office, 1954), p. 38.

[10] Georg Schwarzenberger, "Hegemonial Intervention," in *Yearbook of World Affairs* (London: Stevens & Son, 1959), p. 251.

[11] John Harvey (ed.), *War Diaries of Oliver Harvey* (London: Collins, 1978), p. 368.

That HMG sometimes heeded the advice of men like Sir Oliver Harvey is clear from the records of the famous Churchill-Stalin Percentages Agreement of October 9, 1944, which preempted Yalta by granting the Soviet Union a substantial degree of control in Rumania, Bulgaria, and (twenty-four hours later) Hungary "in exchange" for Greece. Stalin's advice to the Greek communists to cease fighting the British has been faithfully recorded by the Greek communists themselves, and on December 30, 1944, at the height of the civil war, Stalin even appointed an official ambassador to the very government the Greek communists were fighting to bring down. Although the Soviet government subsequently denied that Stalin did more than listen to Churchill's proposals, his actions in support of them speak even more eloquently than the graphic account supplied by Churchill himself.[12] Churchill's acknowledgement of Stalin's cooperation is also on record:

> ...in spite of the fact that all this was most disagreeable to him and to those around him ...Stalin...adhered strictly and faithfully to our agreement of October, and during all the long weeks of fighting the Communists in the streets of Athens not one word of reproach came from *Pravda* or *Izvestia*....If I pressed [Stalin] too much he might say, "I did not interfere with your action in Greece; why do you not give me the same latitude in Rumania?"...I was sure it would be a mistake to embark on such an argument.[13]

The myth that Yalta overrode the 1944 agreement by committing Stalin to hold free elections in Eastern Europe dies hard, but it is a myth nonetheless. The presence of the United States at Yalta made no serious difference to the arrangements already in force. Although Stalin was made to subscribe to the *principle* of free elections in liberated territories, his commitment did not extend to his holding (or supervising) them himself, or even persuading his satellites to do so. The role of a single great power as set out in the Declaration on Liberated Europe is extremely limited. Together the powers could do much more, but if one was perfectly happy with what was happening in, say, Rumania, it had only to say so, and that was the end of the matter.

Far from imposing any "ideology" of free elections on Eastern Europe, what Yalta did was to make democracy there a Soviet option rather than a Soviet commitment. This was clearly deliberate, for if free elections had been held in Poland or Rumania there is little doubt that they would have produced governments hostile to the U.S.S.R., or communism, or both; and, as U.S. Secretary of State James Byrnes declared on October 31, 1945, when comparing Soviet acts in Eastern Europe with those permitted the Americans in Latin America under the Monroe Doctrine: "We can appreciate the determination of the people of the Soviet Union that never again will they tolerate the pursuit of policies in these countries deliberately directed against the Soviet Union's security and way of life."[14]

Once again, it may be noted, there is not the slightest hint, much less accusation, that the U.S.S.R. was promoting the cause of world revolution. The inference was that the Soviet Union was permitted the same latitude in Central and Eastern Europe (Byrnes was careful to refer to both) as the United States in Latin America, while the remarkable inclusion of the last four words recalls Monroe's preoccupation with "essentially different" "political systems" as well as foreign aggression. Consequently, when U.S. activities in Cuba came to be discussed in the United Nations some seventeen years later, Adlai Stevenson's com-

---

[12] W. S. Churchill, *Triumph and Tragedy,* vol. 6: *The Second World War* (Boston: Houghton Mifflin, 1953), pp. 227–229.

[13] Ibid., pp. 293, 420, 421.

[14] *Department of State Bulletin*, vol. 13, no. 332 (November 4, 1945), pp. 709–711.

ments came remarkably close to the words as well as the sentiments of the *Pravda* article that formed the basis of the later Brezhnev Doctrine.[15]

Since then the Soviet position in Europe has been broadly maintained. Although pressed in some quarters to revive the Communist International in response to the Truman Doctrine of 1947, Stalin refused to do so,[16] with the result that the new Cominform played only a limited role, and did not long survive his death. Some disloyalty—in Albania, Rumania, and, marginally, in Hungary and Poland—is tolerated and occasionally ignored, but all major rebellions have been firmly crushed.

The allegation that it is the West rather than the East which imposes "ideology" from time to time is plausible, but rarely substantiated. Certainly the Truman Doctrine of March 12, 1947, contained elements of that "moralism" beloved by some U.S. presidents in the past, but far more of it was to be found in the Baylor University speech of the week before than in the address to Congress. More important, the remedies the Doctrine prescribed were reserved for those who had not succumbed to Soviet pressure, not for those who had. It was a doctrine of containment and not of liberation, and throughout his speech Truman was careful to identify "the enemy" with considerable precision. The "threat" to Turkey was Soviet rather than communist, so Turkey would be encouraged to resist "outside pressures." Conversely, the "threat" to Greece was communist rather than Soviet, so Greece would be helped to resist "armed minorities." The two targets, though linked, were never confused; and this, paradoxically, helped to make the later intervention in Vietnam easier to accept.

For their part, Stalin and his successors rarely supported those communists whom they could not immediately control, even when the prospects for revolution were excellent, as they were in Yugoslavia and China. Josip Broz Tito's expulsion from the Cominform in 1948 was the result of a long record of insubordination, in which "ideology" played no part whatever. In fact it was Tito's revolutionary zeal that irritated Stalin most. Time and time again during World War II Soviet help to the Yugoslav partisans was refused on the grounds that the latter were more interested in promoting "proletarian revolution" and "assuming a communist character" instead of fighting the Germans![17]

As for China, it is clear from remarks made by Stalin to the Yugoslavs and to the Chinese themselves that he did not envisage a communist China as part of the postwar world. On the very day, August 14, 1945, when Soviet armies crossed into Manchuria, Stalin signed a pact with Chiang Kai-shek, refusing to aid any other Chinese "faction" in return for Chiang's acknowledgment of Outer Mongolia's position as a Soviet satellite.[18] The contemptuous references to "margarine" communists followed Mao Zedong's repeated rejection of Stalin's advice to disband the Chinese Communist party until it could be formed by leaders of a less independent kind and no longer dominated by "peasants and mandarins." It is clear in retrospect that the Sino-Soviet split is one of long standing, in the course of which Mao's 1949 decision to "lean to one side" marked a temporary phase brought about by the worsening of U.S.-Soviet relations. Once the crisis had passed, China was ready to resume, at Bandung in 1955, her traditional role. It was a role from

---

[15] *New York Times,* October 9, 1962; compare S. Kovalev, in *Pravda,* September 26, 1968.

[16] Interview with Konni Zilliacus, M.P., on November 1, 1947, who reported Stalin's conversation of October 14, 1947. See also *The Times* (London), October 24, 1947.

[17] Mosha Pijade, in *Borba,* March 22 and 23, 1950.

[18] Stalin's remark that he made a mistake about the Chinese Communist party ("we admit we were wrong") is reported by Edvard Kardelj in Vladimir Dedijer, *Tito Speaks* (London: Weidenfeld & Nicolson, 1953), p. 331.

which the Soviet Union would henceforth be excluded.

The Soviet Union's reluctance to sponsor "left-wing" rebellions outside its sphere of influence has not, however, prevented it from offering support whenever one with pro-Soviet sympathies seems likely to fail, as in Afghanistan. Lenin's appeal to the peoples of the East to overthrow the imperialist "robbers and enslavers" has not been entirely forgotten.

The conclusion of this paper is that when great-power competition is misrepresented by both sides as some kind of moral crusade, many of the more powerful accusations simply fail to register. The word "imperialism" has been so overworked by Moscow that it is now susceptible of almost endless definitions. Similarly, the growth of the police state in areas well outside the communist camp has tended to make the West rather more cautious in its use of the term "totalitarian," which in the 1950s was little more than a synonym for "communist." Ideology certainly dictates the language of much of the Cold War and provides a lot of its invective, but it has had little effect on its character.

QUESTIONS FOR DISCUSSION

1 Does the Soviet Union have an ideology that shapes its day-to-day foreign policy? If so, has its ideology ever been modified?
2 Does the United States have an ideology? If so, in what way does it differ from that of the Soviet Union?
3 How important, if at all, is ideology in shaping the policies of the superpowers toward the Third World?

4 Must ideological competition culminate in military clashes between the superpowers?

SUGGESTED READINGS

Brennan, Edward J. "East-West Relations: The Role of Ideology," *Irish Studies in International Affairs* (Dublin), **2**, no. 1 (1985), pp. 51–101.

Caldwell, Dan (ed.). *Soviet International Behavior and U.S. Policy Options.* Lexington, Mass.: Lexington Books, 1985.

Cohen, Stephen F. *Rethinking the Soviet Experience: Politics and History since 1917.* New York: Oxford Univ. Press, 1985.

Hassner, Pierre. "Soviet Foreign Policy: Ideology and Realpolitik," *Problems of Communism,* **26** (Sept.–Oct. 1977), pp. 82–89.

Hough, Jerry F. *The Struggle for the Third World: Soviet Debates and American Options.* Washington, D.C.: Brookings Institution, 1986.

Luttwak, Edward N. *The Grand Strategy of the Soviet Union.* New York: St. Martin's Press, 1983.

Papp, Daniel S. *Soviet Perceptions of the Developing World in the 1980s.* Lexington, Mass.: Lexington Books, 1985.

Pipes, Richard. *Survival Is Not Enough: Soviet Realities and America's Future.* New York: Simon and Schuster, 1984.

Saivetz, Carol R., and Sylvia Woodby. *Soviet–Third World Relations.* Boulder, Colo.: Westview Press, 1985.

Ulam, Adam. *Expansion and Coexistence: Soviet Foreign Policy, 1917 to 1973,* 2d ed. New York: Praeger, 1974.

White, Stephen. "Propagating Communist Values in the U.S.S.R." *Problems of Communism,* **34** (Nov.–Dec. 1985), pp. 1–17.

Wiles, Peter. "Irreversibility: Theory and Practice," *Washington Quarterly,* **8** (Winter 1985), pp. 29–40.

10 Was the Soviet Invasion of Afghanistan a Major Geopolitical Challenge to the West?

YES

William E. Griffith

Super-Power Relations after Afghanistan

NO

Geoffrey Stern

The Soviet Union, Afghanistan and East-West Relations

Super-Power Relations after Afghanistan

William E. Griffith

The Soviet invasion of Afghanistan is important for two major reasons. First, it marked the first time since 1945 that Soviet troops have invaded a country which is not a member of the Warsaw Pact. Second and more important, because of Afghanistan's strategic location, the invasion improves the Soviet strategic position in the direction of the Indian Ocean and the oil of the Persian Gulf.[1]

In comparison, the question of whether or not the immediate, minimal Soviet purposes in invading Afghanistan were primarily defensive, to prevent the loss of what Moscow had gained there, is a secondary one. The indefinite presence of massive Soviet air and land forces in Afghanistan—which is what we must anticipate, since otherwise the regime in Kabul would fall—is bound to have major geopolitical results, regionally and globally favourable to the Soviet Union.

Whether, and how much, the response to the Soviet invasion, particularly by the United States and the Islamic countries, will outweigh these Soviet strategic gains is the most important question for the making of American foreign policy today.

REALPOLITIK AND IDEOLOGY

Soviet foreign policy, like that of any other major imperial power, has always been a mixture of *Realpolitik* and ideology. Because Russia has been a multinational empire for nearly five centuries, the domination of her Great Russian elite over other nations has been imperial (i.e., colonial) in nature *within* the Russian Empire. Thus Soviet imperialism abroad is basically an extension of her internal polity. As Tsar Alexander II remarked after he crushed the Polish rising of 1863, "I cannot give liberties to my subjects in Poland that I dare not give to my subjects in Russia." Thus the Russian Empire has no *natural* boundaries, only imperial ones.

Unlike Angola and Ethiopia, there is a continuous history of Russian interest in Afghanistan, which for more than a century has bordered on the Russian Empire.[2] In the 1820s, the Asian expansion of the Russian empire east and south-east towards the Indian Ocean began to aim at Afghanistan and thus, in London's view, to endanger British rule in India. From that time on until her departure from the subcontinent in 1947, Britain was therefore determined to prevent Soviet domination of Afghanistan.

With this aim Britain twice invaded Afghanistan in the nineteenth century, and twice, after bloody struggles, withdrew. Finally, Russia and Britain settled for her neutralization, the more

William E. Griffith, "Super-Power Relations after Afghanistan," *Survival* (London), **22** (July–Aug. 1980), pp. 146–151.

[1] Much of this essay is based on travels in the Middle East and Pakistan in July and August 1979, which were made possible by *The Reader's Digest,* of which I am a roving editor, and its editor-in-chief, Edward T. Thompson, to whom I am most grateful.

[2] Hannah Negaran (pseud.), "The Afghan Coup of April 1978: Revolution and International Security," *Orbis,* Spring 1979; Louis Dupree, "Afghanistan under the Khalq," *Problems of Communism,* July–Aug. 1979; Richard S. Newell, "Revolution and Revolt in Afghanistan," *The World Today,* Nov. 1979....[F]or regional background, see Zalmay Khalilzad, "The Superpowers and the Northern Tier," *International Security,* Winter 1979–80; for the implications for political development theories, Charyl Benard and Zalmay Khalilzad, "Secularization, Industrialization and Khomeini's Islamic Republic," *Political Science Quarterly,* Summer 1979; and for Islamic fundamentalism, William E. Griffith, "The Revival of Islamic Fundamentalism: The Case of Iran," *International Security,* Summer 1979.

so because, by the early twentieth century, they both feared rising imperial German power. (In 1907 this also caused their *de facto* partition of Iran, which was already influenced by oil, for the British fleet had begun to operate on oil from the Anglo-Iranian Company's wells in southern Iran.)

How different is Soviet from Imperial Russian foreign policy? Initially, it was less successful because the Soviet Union was weak and isolated, after her attempt to conquer Poland and revolutionize Germany failed at the end of World War I. However, Bolshevik ideology gave Russian expansionism an additional dynamic, "secular Calvinist" conviction of legitimacy, inevitable success and, paradoxically, the imperative to push history forward faster. The domestic legitimacy and the international Communist prestige of the ruling Soviet Communist party depend on its claim to lead the irresistible, irreversible course of history towards socialism. The encouragement of this course, that is to say, of "national liberation struggles," has therefore always been an integral part of Soviet ideology and foreign policy. It follows that Moscow has also always been determined to prevent the collapse of a once-established Communist regime.

While Lenin in theory supported "self-determination to the point of separation," that is to say, the right of the non-Russian nationalities of the Soviet Union to become independent states, in fact he and Stalin ruthlessly crushed all such attempts, including those in Muslim areas of the Soviet Union: in Soviet Azerbaijan, annexed from Persia by the Russian Empire in the early nineteenth century, and Kazakstan, Uzbekistan, and Tadjikistan, conquered in the mid-nineteenth century. Parts of these nations also live in Iran and Afghanistan.

The history of Soviet foreign policy since World War II has been one of constant, purposeful increase of military power and, under Stalin's successors, of more flexible, forward strategies to profit politically from it. After its defeat in the 1962 Cuban missile crisis, the Soviet leadership methodically developed its global nuclear, naval, and conventional capabilities.

Khrushchev also developed a policy of detente with the United States. One of its objectives was, and remains, to lower the risk of general or nuclear war by accident or miscalculation. The second was to cement the *status quo* in Europe, and especially the division of Germany—Moscow's most valuable gain in World War II. The third was to make Soviet third-world expansion less risky, by making a forceful U.S. response to it less likely. Successive American administrations have explicitly shared the first objective, implicitly shared the second and failed to understand the third.

"ARC OF CRISIS"

Unlike Stalin, Khrushchev and his successors tried to expand Soviet influence by allying with radical, anti-colonial, and anti-American third-world leaders (the "states of national democracy"), with mixed results. Russia historically followed the advice of Tsar Peter the Great (in his political testament) to expand southward towards Constantinople and the Indian Ocean and the Soviet thrust has also centred in those directions. Because of domestic radicalization, arising out of the strain of modernization and intensified by the Arabs' anti-Israeli (and therefore anti-American) impulses, the Soviet Union at first made great progress, notably in Egypt. She faced, however, three obstacles: her inability to gain decisive influence in Turkey and in Iran under the Shah, her unwillingness to fight with the Arabs against Israel, lest she run the risk of a military confrontation with the United States, the consequent Arab disillusionment with her; and, more recently, her evident inability to cope with the revival of Islam.

After the collapse of Soviet influence in Egypt in 1973, it seemed for a time that Soviet influence in the Middle East and South-west Asia had suffered a major and lasting blow. But during this same period U.S. foreign policy had been greatly weakened by the American defeat in Vietnam and the Watergate scandal. The Vietnam defeat had been caused in considerable part by massive Soviet arms aid to North Vietnam, which the United States, fearing the interruption of detente, had tried to interrupt only at the very end, after defeat was inevitable. Moreover, the United States had long embraced two illusions: that China was Vietnam's principal and most dangerous ally and that the Soviet Union could be persuaded to help bring the Vietnam war to an end without an American defeat. Behind these American errors were two others: U.S. slowness in understanding the extent of the Soviet military build-up and the significance of the 1959 Sino–Soviet split.

In contrast, the Soviet Union considered the United States her strongest and most dangerous short-range enemy, and China her most dangerous long-range one. The Soviet military build-up was therefore directed against both. The massive Soviet military deployment on the Chinese frontier continued, in addition to the rapid increase of Soviet forces in Europe and her overall military build-up against the U.S. Because the Soviet Union increasingly feared that she would be encircled by a Sino–American–Japanese–West-European alliance, she became determined to achieve parity with all of them and therefore, inevitably, superiority over any one, in particular the United States, who has refused to accept the consequent inferiority.

Moreover, Moscow became increasingly determined to break through this encirclement.[3] The Middle Eastern–South-west Asian "arc of crisis" was the natural place for Moscow to attempt this break-through for several reasons: Soviet fear of encirclement, the defeat in Egypt

and concern about the Islamic revival, the decisive Western dependence on Middle Eastern oil, the festering Palestinian issue and the trends towards radicalization in the area.

This is not to argue that Soviet expansion operates according to a "master plan." Rather, the Soviet dynamic view of history and its own duty to push history forward predispose Moscow to exploit low-risk opportunities offered to it. Recently these opportunities have primarily been in the Middle East and South-west Asia.

Like pre-1914 Imperial Germany, Soviet fears of encirclement have created it. Soviet attempts to break through it, like Imperial Germany's in the Balkans, have intensified it, raised international tension, and endangered détente.

After Sadat expelled the Soviet Union from Egypt in 1972 and Washington excluded her from the Middle East peace negotiations after 1973, she naturally began to try to improve her position on the periphery of the Middle East. The 1975 Soviet move into Angola was Moscow's first major third-world breakthrough. There Moscow demonstrated its long-range air- and sea-lift capability and its successful use of Cuban proxy troops. American inaction against this Soviet move was caused by post-Vietnam war-weariness and Dr. Kissinger's miscalculation, notably his counter-productive parallel policy with South Africa. More generally, the Carter Administration initially tried to de-emphasize Soviet–American tension and to give priority to arms control, north–south issues, human rights, nuclear non-proliferation, arms transfer cut-backs, and "Africa for the Africans." Although these policies increased American influence abroad, they also, like American inaction in Angola, encouraged Soviet third-world expansion.

The next Soviet move was in Ethiopia, where a radical nationalist revolution needed foreign support against the Somali invasion of the Ogaden and the Eritrean rebellion. Soviet arms and Cuban troops defeated the former but their unwillingness and Mengistu's inability to

[3] I owe this concept to William G. Hyland "The Sino-Soviet Conflict: A Search for New Security Strategies," in Richard H. Solomon, ed., *Asian Security in the 1980s: Problems and Policies for a Time of Transition*, RAND R-2492-ISA, Nov. 1979.

defeat the latter makes continued Soviet and Cuban presence in Ethiopia essential for his survival.

In Angola and Ethiopia, the U.S.S.R. supported the legitimate governments, that is, the ones recognized by the Organization of African States. In Angola the Soviet Union supported a movement, the MPLA, which was Marxist-Leninist in ideology and pro-Soviet in policy. In Ethiopia, Colonel Mengistu, like Castro, drifted towards Marxism-Leninism, and like Castro and Neto in Angola, ended up totally dependent on Soviet military and economic aid to prevent his own overthrow. In her operations in Ethiopia, the Soviet Union used the resupply base in Aden, where a ruling Marxist-Leninist regime had come into power—a hitherto unknown phenomenon in Arab politics. Thus the Soviet Union had victorious and dependent rulers in Luanda, Addis Ababa, and Aden, with the first and the last Marxist-Leninist and pro-Soviet, and Ethiopia moving in that direction.

The April 1978 coup in Kabul occurred at a time when, unnoticed by the American government, the Shah's position in Iran was in grave danger. His replacement in early 1979 by a fanatically Islamic regime has not so far brought the Soviet Union any direct influence in Iran. It has, however, meant the collapse of American influence there; an American preoccupation with Iran resulting from the imprisonment of the American hostages, which has detracted from American concern about other parts of the area; and the potential for a leftist, pro-Soviet takeover, if not, indeed, a Soviet invasion of Iranian Azerbaijan. All these developments have favoured Soviet interests.

SOVIET OBJECTIVES

After the British withdrawal from India in 1947, the Afghan government hoped to maintain its neutrality between East and West. However, strong American support to Pakistan, Afghan irredentist dreams of a "greater Pushtunistan"

and American disinterest, led Kabul after 1955 to move towards the Soviet Union, while remaining traditionalist and oligarchical at home. This meant not only large-scale Soviet military and economic aid but, most importantly, the training of most Afghan military officers in the Soviet Union. Moreover, even the slow modernization under the Afghan oligarchy had produced a significant number of educated young Afghans, some of whom, frustrated, became pro-Soviet Communists.

It serves little purpose here, because there is simply not enough evidence, to debate whether the Soviet Union was behind the April 1978 Communist coup in Kabul. It would be foolish to so underestimate the KGB as to believe that Moscow did not know of the plans for the coup and therefore could not have stopped it if it had wished. What is important was the result. It brought to power the Afghan Communist party, headed by a rather ineffective intellectual, Noor Mohammed Taraki, and his fiercely feuding associates. Their radical attempts at modernization inevitably sparked off tribal revolts, which made the Communists even more dependent on the Soviet Union and fed the revolts further. The overwhelming allegiance of Afghans to Islam made the Afghan Communists and their Soviet patrons feel it necessary to conceal from the public the fact that they were Communist. This was a new development: a "covert" Communist Soviet satellite.

It seems likely that, like the United States in Vietnam, the Soviet Union underestimated the difficulty of keeping a Communist government in power in Afghanistan. Moscow poured in military and economic advisers and arms, a process which only intensified the rebellion. The fierce factional struggles among the Afghan Communists must have exasperated the U.S.S.R. particularly when the Soviet-Taraki plan to dispose of Taraki's chief colleague, Amin, misfired. Instead, in September 1979 Amin had Taraki killed.

Amin was just as unsuccessful in crushing the

rebellion. He also showed some signs of resentment at total Soviet control. Moscow therefore probably concluded that he was untrustworthy as well as incompetent. Moreover, given her history, the Soviet Union could probably only have concluded that the rebellion was growing because of foreign (American and Chinese) help. That this appears to have been largely untrue is much less important than the probable Soviet perception of its validity. Since late 1979 the Iranian Islamic revolution was raging. In view of the indications of increasing Islamic activity in Soviet Azerbaijan and Soviet Central Asia, the U.S.S.R. can hardly have been unconcerned at the prospect of a Communist government in Kabul being replaced by a strongly anti-Soviet, pro-Islamic one. Moreover, the overthrow even of a "covert" Communist government would have cast doubt on the irreversibility of history's drive towards socialism.

The immediate, minimal Soviet aim in invading Afghanistan was indeed defensive. The Soviet Union was determined to preserve what she had gained there since 1955 and particularly since the April 1978 Communist coup. But no great power undertakes such a massive invasion without weighing maximal gains and losses as well. Since the 1820s all strong Russian rulers have aimed at Russian military domination of Afghanistan as a step towards a southward expansion. Moreover, the West is now far more dependent on the Middle East (for oil) than it was in the nineteenth century, and the U.S.S.R. will probably need Middle Eastern oil in the late 1980s. The revolution in Iran, even if Muslim and anti-Communist, must nevertheless have made Moscow hope that it would profit, at least because the West would lose, from the increasing instability in the Middle East and in South-west Asia.

Finally, the invasion put the Red Army on the borders of Pakistan. And that state, as Moscow well knows, is especially vulnerable. Her economy is nearly bankrupt and her economic development has been much slower than India's. The military government remains very

unpopular and her Punjabi oligarchy dominates and alienates the Pushtu, Sindhi and especially Baluch minorities. Moreover, the Pushtu overlap Afghanistan and Pakistan and the Baluch overlap Afghanistan, Pakistan, and Iran. Baluch separatism, one of the principal dangers to Pakistan's cohesion, is the obvious corridor through which Soviet influence may move to the Indian Ocean. Pro-Soviet Marxism is reportedly becoming more influential among separatist Baluchi intellectuals and students. They also resent the Punjabi majority profiting from Baluchi natural gas and minerals. Thus, in sum, the Soviet conquest of Afghanistan automatically destabilizes Pakistan and offers inviting separatist possibilities for Moscow to move closer to the oil of the Persian Gulf.

Why does the Soviet Union accept international near-isolation in order to maintain her grip on Afghanistan? The easiest answer is that the Soviet Union was also isolated after her invasion of Hungary in 1956 and Czechoslovakia in 1968, but she did not stay isolated very long. She sees the United States absorbed in, and frustrated by, Iran—a situation from which she also hopes to profit. (This hope must be greater after the U.S. failure of the April 1980 attempt to rescue the hostages in Tehran.) She has some reason, therefore, to expect her present near-isolation to be brief. The Soviet Union has lost her ideological, economic, and technological attractiveness abroad. Only her military power now gives her international influence. Moscow presumably calculates that the net result of its invasion of Afghanistan will be an intensified foreign perception of overwhelming successful Soviet military force, and that, isolation or not, the Soviet army and air force will be stationed much closer to the Indian Ocean and Persian Gulf—and that is what counts.

Finally, as the reactions in Paris and Bonn have shown, the Soviet Union justifiably believes that her continued advocacy of detente in Europe is reciprocated by France and the Federal Republic. Moscow thus expects to avoid economic and technological isolation. It hopes to encourage further strain between the United States and her West European allies. Indeed by Spring 1980 their relationship had deteriorated. Finally, it will probably try to exact some price from Western Europe for "allowing" it to remain an "island of détente" surrounded by a Soviet–American "new cold war"—and thereby to intensify U.S.–West European tensions.

AMERICAN RESPONSE

The most uncertain factor in all Soviet calculations must be American policy. Given the inaction of the Carter Administration with respect to Angola, Ethiopia, and South Yemen, is it any wonder that the Soviet Union felt that the United States would be essentially inactive about Afghanistan? But given American economic problems and social strains, will Moscow turn out to have miscalculated after all?

It is too early to answer this question definitively. The American measures taken in retaliation to the Soviet invasion of Afghanistan will hurt the Soviet Union economically (curtailment of grain exports and technology transfers), psychologically (withdrawal from the Moscow Olympic Games), politically (tilting more towards China) and militarily (U.S. arms build-up). America's allies seem so far not to be undercutting her retaliatory measures. And although France, West Germany, and Japan seem unlikely to match American economic and technological retaliation, they are unlikely to break with the U.S. on the issue. Moreover, the Soviet Union has lost greatly in the Islamic world, and in the Third World in general, on the Afghan issue and so has her ally Cuba.

The fundamental U.S. policy question, therefore, is whether the United States will stay the course. The Carter Administration did not distinguish itself, before the Iranian and Afghan crises, by decisiveness and persistence, but it has done so since. Will it continue to do so?

If American policy is to deter the U.S.S.R.

from further expansion, it must bring about a slow but sure change in the Soviet cost-benefit analysis of such moves. Washington can best do so by neither abandoning detente nor soon re-embracing it *in toto*. Now, and for some years to come, the U.S. should concentrate on making the Soviet Union realize the cost of her invasion of Afghanistan. But because only Moscow can destroy the United States and only the U.S. and/or the U.S.S.R. can destroy the world, the U.S. still shares with the Soviet Union a general interest in arms control and in limiting third-world competition. These are what detente is about and all that it *can* be about. The rest has all been American illusions and wishful thinking.

One of the principal lessons of Afghanistan is that detente is only one part of American foreign policy, as it is of Soviet foreign policy. Competition is, and will remain the larger part. The two cannot be separated: linkage is not only desirable but inevitable. If, and when, the Soviet Union reassesses her cost-benefit analysis of her expansionism, as she did to some extent after Stalin died, the United States should reciprocate. Until then, America should compete, more strongly, more firmly, and thereby more successfully. Insofar as she does not, there must be more retaliation against Soviet expansionism. Containment worked in the 1950s, and if there is no other alternative, it could, and should, be made to work again.

Nor should there be any pessimism about the future. Compared to the United States, Western Europe, Japan, and China, the Soviet Union is weak and encircled. Not that we should *want* to encircle it—we should want to preserve detente, including limited co-operation. But in the last analysis the Soviet Union will decide her own foreign policy. Let us hope she will turn from expansionism back to detente, and let us be ready to reciprocate. But if she does not, let us be equally ready to contain her expansionism until she once again realizes that detente, sooner or later, is her only choice.

The Soviet Union, Afghanistan and East-West Relations

Geoffrey Stern

There were at least four major military interventions in 1979, apart from the Soviet adventure in Afghanistan. The Vietnamese invaded Kampuchea, China bombarded Vietnam, Tanzania sent its troops into Uganda and French forces helped to unseat the Imperator and architect of the Central African Empire. Three of these four interventions resulted, as did the incursion into Afghanistan, in the removal of what was by common consent an extremely brutal and unpopular régime and the establishment of a new administration handpicked by the invaders. Most had received the tacit or explicit support of third parties. Yet the response to the Soviet action was somehow different. It was roundly condemned by an overwhelming majority in both the UN and the Islamic Conference Organization,[1] and although it is almost a year since some 85,000 Soviet troops established a presence in Afghanistan, the intervention has continued to engender widespread alarm and despondency.

That the offending party was in this instance the Soviet Union was bound to harden opinion among those who have long held:

1 that Russia is an imperialist power bent on world domination;

2 that Moscow's prime object in pursuit of her expansionist goal is to obtain direct access to the Indian Ocean and the Gulf so as to enjoy the benefits of both warm water ports and oil, and also to deny these to the West;

3 that Afghanistan is strategically placed to enable the Kremlin to move into position for an eventual onslaught on the Gulf area; and

4 that its unprecedented military power will have given Moscow the self-confidence to further her age-old expansionist ambitions, knowing that the crisis-ridden and divided West would be unwilling, or unable, to prevent the Soviet advance.[2]

Since, however, the Soviet strike into Afghanistan had occurred at a time when Western political and economic interests were perceived to be under threat in several different areas simultaneously, the neat simplicity of the traditional "cold warrior" explanation was to prove almost as beguiling to the political "soft centre" of the Jimmy Carter variety as to the "apoplectic Right" of the Reagan/Brzezinski school. It is, however, an explanation of Soviet conduct which, however seductive, is dangerously misleading. For though it contains kernels of truth, it is a partial account which in my judgment gives a distorted picture of the mood in the Kremlin and, moreover, raises more questions than it answers.

Geoffrey Stern, "The Soviet Union, Afghanistan and East-West Relations," *Millennium: Journal of International Studies,* 9 (Autumn 1980), pp. 135–146.

[1] In the General Assembly, January 14, 1980, 104 states called for the withdrawal of Soviet troops from Afghanistan and only 18, including the Soviet Union, Byelorussia and the Ukraine voted against. In the Islamic Foreign Ministers Conference in Islamabad, January 26, 1980, at least 36 members of the Islamic Conference Organisation condemned the Soviet Union for its "military aggression" against Afghanistan.

[2] Connoisseurs of the art of "Kremlin watching" will have been surprised neither by the speed with which many of the chilliest of the cold warriors went into print after the Soviet intervention in Afghanistan nor by the style and substance of the explanations preferred. For a representative sample see, for example, Robert Moss, "The Soviet Drive to the Sea," *The Daily Telegraph,* January 7, 1980; Brian Crozier's contribution to the Letters Page of *The Times,* January 10, 1980, and Geoffrey Stewart-Smith, "A Democracy's Response to Tyranny," *East-West Digest,* (Volume 16, No. 2, January 1980). For lengthier disquisitions along similar lines see Richard M. Nixon *The Real War* (London: Sidgwick & Jackson, 1980), and Harlan Cleveland, Andrew J. Goodpaster and Joseph J. Wolf *After Afghanistan: The Long Haul* (The Atlantic Council, 1980).

It is not contested here that Russia is an expansionist power. Indeed, given the historical record both before and after the Bolshevik Revolution it would be foolish to deny it; but does it follow from this that Moscow is bent on world conquest? After all, many other powers, including Britain and the U.S., have sought to expand their terrain and their economic and political influence, but we do not say of them that they are hell bent on world domination. Admittedly, Soviet propaganda speaks of a ''Communist world,'' but how real is Moscow's commitment to it, how much is it prepared to sacrifice to bring about that global transformation and where is it suggested that this 'earthly paradise' is to be brought about solely by force or by threat of Soviet arms? If the argument is that the growth of the Soviet military arm on land, sea, and in the air, is sufficient proof of the Soviet commitment to world conquest, it begs a number of questions—not least, why it is assumed that the purposes of a large Soviet military capability must necessarily be different from the purposes of a large American, Western European or even Chinese military capability. Indeed, given the country's frequent experience of armed attack,[3] its continued economic and technological inferiority *vis-à-vis* the West[4] and the perceived, if to some extent justifiable, hostility of so many of Russia's neighbours—to the East, West and South—could the Kremlin really justify the kinds of cuts in military expenditure its opponents demand of it?

As to warm water ports, while no doubt Russia's historical quest in this regard still has appeal, can it seriously be suggested that it retains the kind of salience that it had for the Tsars a century or two ago? Surely Russia's trading patterns have shifted decisively in recent years. While its economic links are indeed world wide, its main trading partners are in Eastern Europe—and it does not need warm water ports to secure these. Moreover, a not inconsiderable percentage of Russia's trade outside the Soviet bloc goes by air, a form of transportation which, again, requires no warm water ports. More importantly, Russia already has a number of warm water ports, for example, in Aden and Massawa, put at its disposal by friendly régimes, and it can share facilities with Western fleets in a number of other ports. It does, of course, lack overland access to such facilities, but if Moscow's designs on the Gulf were so insatiable, why did the Soviet leaders choose to launch their strike against a cul-de-sac like Afghanistan instead of going through Iran, the main highway, on whose borders the Russians have long had a military presence and which would hardly have been in a fit state to resist a Red Army advance? If, on the other hand, they are determined to win over Iran by bribery or stealth, why pursue an action in neighbouring Afghanistan that could only inflame the Islamic sensibilities of potential supports in Tehran?

If the contention is that it is not warm water ports that Russia needs so much as oil and the ability to deny it to the West, the question arises—why risk a world war for the sake of a commodity the Soviet Union has in abundance, of which she is the world's largest producer and of which she is a net exporter to the West?[5] No doubt Russia lacks the technology to exploit to the full her own vast oil reserves, but this is surely an argument for better relations with the technologically more advanced West, not for a

---

[3] A point elaborated in Chapter 11 of John Baylis, Ken Booth, John Garnett and Phil Williams *Contemporary Strategy* (London: Croom Helm, 1975), pp. 218-241.

[4] For a discussion of some of the structural weaknesses in the Soviet economy see, for example, Alec Nove *The Soviet Economy,* 3rd Edition (London: Allen & Unwin, 1969).

[5] See Marshall Goldman, ''Is there a Russian Energy Crisis?,'' *The Atlantic Monthly,* (September 1980) and Anthony Robinson, ''The Looming Soviet Factor in the World Oil Equation,'' *The Financial Times,* July 3, 1979.

global confrontation. In any case, the fact that Russia and her allies have been importing Middle Eastern oil for some years already does not seem, of itself, to have posed serious problems for East-West relations. And with the emphasis on conservation and the discovery and tapping of new energy sources, there is no logical reason to anticipate a major East-West conflict over oil.

As to the suggestion that the Russians are so confident that they feel strong enough to be able to challenge in a militarily significant way the deterrence strategy that the West has painfully built over the years, this is, to my mind, the most dangerous assumption of all. In the first place, any sensible analysis has to take into account constraints as well as capabilities, and no matter how formidable the Soviet Union's "overkill" capacity, the Russians know only too well that this makes them no more invincible than the thermonuclear powers which were humbled in Suez, Algeria, Vietnam, in the waters off Iceland or in the desert sands of Iran. Moreover, even if Moscow's enemies are far from united, they are quite capable, either singly or in concert, of inflicting unacceptable damage on the Soviet Union if provoked; and of course the Soviets have ample reason to know that even the successful use of military power may entail political costs which are intolerably high—as when China gravitated toward the Western powers in the aftermath of the Soviet invasion of Czechoslovakia.[6] Thus, the use of the Red Army is not something the Russians undertake lightly. Hitherto it has been called into operation only in countries in the Soviet Union's vicinity, which the Soviets regard as

being within their sphere of influence and where they see vital interests at stake. As will be argued subsequently, the intervention in Afghanistan represents in the Soviet perspective no departure from this practice, whereas a bid to take over the Gulf would.

If foolhardiness and reckless adventurism are not characteristics of Soviet foreign policy, neither is self-confidence. For, while as residual Marxist-Leninists the Soviet leaders feel that the long term future is assured, their schooling in dialectics combined with their understanding of Russia's historical experience both before and since the Revolution often leads them to a more pessimistic analysis of current trends than perhaps the facts warrant. For the dialectical principle with its attendant notions of contradiction, struggle and conflict merely tends to heighten the sense of insecurity in a country all too frequently invaded and embargoed and with a tally of 20 million dead following Germany's unprovoked and undeclared onslaught in 1941.

There is more than a hint of this lack of assurance in the response of the Soviet media to foreign criticisms of the Red Army's action in Afghanistan. For example, after Richard Nixon's anti-Soviet diatribes in *The Real War*, commentator Igor Dmitriyev, broadcasting on Moscow's World Service, chided American politicians for "flatly refusing for even a moment to look at world developments the way we see them here." He continued: "separated by two oceans, and having quiet borders with Canada and Mexico, the United States has been spared the political, military and economic turmoils and upheavals that most Europeans and all Russians have gone through. The sacrifices we have made since 1917 and the destruction we have gone through were so enormous they would have made a different nation out of the Americans. They have never had a feeling of being alone in an unfriendly world which is exactly what we felt before World War II. The trouble came from the West; and no

---

[6] That the Soviet invasion of Czechoslovakia might have had an important bearing on the Sino-American *entente* is hazarded by Allen S. Whiting in his contribution to Ian Wilson (ed.) *China and the World Community* [London:] (Angus and Robertson, 1973), pp. 70-89. My own discussions with Chinese and American officials lend credence to the critical importance of the Soviet invasion of Czechoslovakia in the calculations of Peking and Washington, respectively.

politician...should make such an impermissible error as ignoring history."[7]

The inference to be drawn from this, and from other similar comments in the officially controlled media, is that while many may depict the Soviet Union as a Great Bear bent on securing a stranglehold on the West's vital arteries, the men in the Kremlin tend to see themselves in part as a victim of historical circumstance. In their insecurity they fear not only attack, but also the subversion of their political and economic system and, worse, the disintegration of what is in effect a multinational empire masquerading as a single sovereign state.[8]

Moreover, while Western policy makers and their advisers will often portray the Soviet Union as a country whose military prowess is enabling it to go diplomatically from strength to strength, the Kremlin's perception is somewhat different, even if such military spokesmen as the Commander-in-Chief of the Soviet Navy, Admiral Gorshkov, appear to exude confidence. As will be indicated below, Moscow's political influence has not been commensurate with its rise in military strength, and if Western alarmists compare—as they tend to do—Western weaknesses with Soviet strengths, they produce a dangerous distortion of political reality. The fact is that Soviet fortunes have been far more mixed than the alarmists appreciate; and the Kremlin knows it.

II

Domestically, it is a period of great uncertainty as Russia's elderly and far from robust leaders (average age 70) fail to grapple with the problems of political succession[9] or of

economic growth rates in decline.[10] Abroad, too, Moscow faces serious difficulties. Yugoslavia and Albania have long since detached themselves from the Soviet orbit and Romania retains its semiautonomy. But these are problems Moscow has learnt to live with. What is of much more immediate concern is the fear of another serious threat to the Soviet alliance system along the lines of the East Berlin riots of 1953, the Revolution in Hungary in 1956 and the Reform Movement in Czechoslovakia of 1968. For with Eastern Europe increasingly affected by the economic recession which has caused so many difficulties for the West, the Kremlin fears that disillusioned workers may join with disaffected intellectuals in a united front against the Socialist system. In Poland, something of the kind has already happened. In the early 1970s it was the workers who took the law into their own hands, burning down the Communist Party Headquarters in Gdansk and Szczecin, staging strikes and sit-ins and refusing to load ships destined for Soviet ports because of their frustration with economic conditions. Further mass demonstrations occurred in 1975 and 1976, since when workers in trouble for dissident activities have had the advice and support of an organisation of intellectuals known as KOR—The Committee for Public Self-Defence. In August 1980, after their adroit use of the (illegal) strike weapon, a powerful combination of workers and intellectuals succeeded in obtaining major concessions regarding the establishment of "free" trade unions, with the right to strike and to publicize their case. Already, therefore, the

---

[7] *BBC Summary of World Broadcasts, Part I: The Soviet Union,* April 24, 1980.

[8] See Chapter 4 of Hugh Seton-Watson *The Imperialist Revolutionaries* (London: Hutchinson University Library, 1980), pp. 85-101.

[9] That the 76-year-old Prime Minister, Alexei Kosygin, was succeeded by a man only one year his junior and a

relative newcomer to the Politburo, is an indication of the reluctance of the present leadership to make long-term plans about the succession. Their reasons are examined in my article, "Brezhnev and the Future," *The Round Table,* (October 1978).

[10] The extent and implications of Moscow's current economic difficulties are analysed in S. Bialer, "The Politics of Stringency in the U.S.S.R.," *Problems of Communism,* (May-June 1980).

Poles have moved some considerable wayto-wards the political and economic pluralism espoused by the ''Euro-Communists,'' and the Soviets are not alone among Soviet blocleaders in fearing that what is happening in Poland might prove contagious.[11]

If the European Communist-ruled states pose problems for Soviet policy, the Kremlin perceives its Communist neighbour to the East as posing an even graver threat. At first sight, it is not easy to understand why the Chinese should cause Moscow any particular concern. For clearly in terms of military and industrial technology, political organisation and trained manpower the Soviet Union is vastly superior. In addition, Moscow has the means to destroy Peking's existing nuclear capability and its major cities. On the other hand, each year these advantages are diminished by China's own military and economic advance, and if the Americans can be whipped into a frenzy over the presence of some two to three thousand Soviet troops in Cuba, it is hardly surprising that the Russians get alarmed at the prospect of a thousand million potentially hostile Chinese beyond their Eastern frontier. Even now it is difficult for them to forget that of the many invasions against Russia, the most devastating have come from the East. After all, the Mongols destroyed and laid waste the original Russian state, and the Kremlin sees a bitter symbolism in the fact that the notorious leader of the Golden Horde, Genghis Khan, has recently been ''rehabilitated'' in China.

However, the main source of Moscow's current concern lies in the fact that China seems to be making common cause with Moscow's presumed enemies to the East and West, some of whom are only too eager to sell to Peking weapons they can no longer off-load onto Iran. As the Kremlin sees it, China is at the hub of a global anti-Soviet alignment which includes Japan, the U.S., much of Western Europe and even countries in Eastern Europe, such as Yugoslavia and, potentially, Romania. As such, this new diplomatic alignment represents in Moscow's eyes a new form of encirclement and symbolizes a significant tilt in the world's diplomatic balance to Russia's disadvantage.[12]

Regarding the Third World in general, while Western alarmists tend to see Soviet policy solely in terms of its opportunities for mischief-making and balance-tilting, the Russians are only too conscious of the difficulties of making long-term political capital out of areas where politics tend to be very volatile. For while Moscow has undoubtedly chalked up a considerable number of apparent successes, as it has done ever since Khrushchev chose the Third World as the major battleground on which the struggle against capitalism was to be fought,[13] many of these have turned out to be short-lived. In the 1970s alone, the governments of such countries as Egypt, the Sudan, Somalia, Bangladesh, Sri Lanka and Chile, amongst others, went from a pro-Soviet to an anti-Soviet orientation. Increasingly, Iraq and Mozambique, despite their reliance on Soviet arms, have been questioning their ties with the Kremlin, and Zimbabwe has not, as yet, turned out to be the Soviet ''satellite'' that some had predicted. Meanwhile, by the end of 1979, with Moscow's

---

[11] It is a sign of their unease that in November 1980 both East Germany and Czechoslovakia felt it necessary to impose restrictions on travel to and from Poland. Such anxieties amongst the Soviet bloc's ''old guard'' are explained and analysed by Teresa Rakowska-Harmstone in her contribution to M. Kaplan (ed.) *The Many Faces of Communism* (London: Collier Macmillan, 1978).

[12] Indications of Moscow's disquiet in this respect can be gleaned from many recent articles in the Soviet press. See, for example, N. Kapchenko, ''The Threat to Peace from Peking's Hegemonistic Policy,'' *International Affairs* (Moscow, February 1980). The Kremlin's anxieties about world diplomatic trends are encapsulated by Michael Binyon ''Is the Old Nightmare Coming True?,'' *The Times,* October 22, 1980.

[13] See R. C. Tucker's chapter on ''The Dialectics of Co-existence'' in his volume *The Soviet Political Mind* (New York: Praeger, 1963), pp. 201-222.

clients in Ethiopia, Angola and Afghanistan tied down in guerrilla conflicts they seemed incapable of suppressing Russia's image among the non-aligned, both as a purveyor of success and as an inveterate champion of national liberation movements, had begun to suffer. Furthermore, the credibility of Russia's commitments had been thrown in doubt when, in early 1979, Peking proceeded to "teach" Moscow's Vietnamese ally "a lesson" while the Russians in effect stood idly by.

Thus, at the very time when the Americans were agonising about the "drift" in American policy, the Russians had good reason to feel that the course of Soviet policy was hardly more assured. Yet if the Americans failed to perceive that their sense of frustration may have been shared by the Russians, they were also oblivious to another striking parallel—the feeling that their adversary was now cool towards détente was at least as strong in Moscow as in Washington. Washington's case against Moscow in this respect is well known: excessive military expenditure; the production and deployment of the SS-20; the Kremlin's backing of the Cuban presence in one African country after another; and, of course, the intervention in Afghanistan. But the Soviets have a case too. As the Kremlin sees it, Washington's commitment to détente was undermined the moment Jimmy Carter assumed the Presidency and championed the cause of "human rights." To Moscow, the Carter crusade was not directed at all authoritarian régimes, or, indeed, at all Communist régimes, since the President did not appear especially troubled by the "human rights" record of China, Pol Pot's Kampuchea or Yugoslavia. As the Kremlin perceived it, rightly or wrongly, it was a strategy designed to encourage dissidence in the Soviet Union and Eastern Europe and to destabilize the Soviet bloc. The Soviet leaders also saw in Carter's campaign an attempt to impose American values on the Soviet bloc, thereby interfering in Soviet politics and, hence, denying Russia that

parity of esteem and entitlement to equality of status which they believed had been secured in the SALT I agreement.[14]

They began to see, in such things as: the change in CIA accounting procedures which inflates the percentage increase in Soviet military budget;[15] Russia's exclusion from the President's attempts at Middle Eastern peace-making through the Camp David accords; the tilt towards China and the decision to allow Peking Most Favoured Nation treatment denied to Moscow; the furore over the presence in Cuba of a Soviet contingent that had apparently been there for seven or eight years; the non-ratification of SALT II; Western disinterest in the Soviet removal of some sophisticated weaponry and troops from East Germany; and the decision to deploy new American Medium Range Ballistic Missiles in West Germany and elsewhere in NATO's European theatre, proof of America's half-hearted approach to détente. And it only compounds all Russia's pent-up fears and suspicions when they see how easily liberal Democrats, who were "doves" on the Vietnam issue, can become "hawks" when it comes to co-operation with Moscow now.

III

It is possible that the Russians would have invaded Afghanistan whatever the state of East-West relations. Yet it is not inconceivable that the scale and urgency of the operation were determined in part by Moscow's disillusionment with the Americans. For whatever leverage the U.S. may have had over Soviet policy was virtually written off at the end of 1979 when

[14] See V. V. Aspaturian, "Soviet Global Power and the Correlation of Forces," *Problems of Communism*, (May-June 1980).

[15] See Ian Mather, "How CIA Measures Russia's War Threat" in *The Observer*, March 23, 1980, and also P. Holzman "Is There a Soviet-U.S. Military Spending Gulf?," *Challenge*, (Sept.-Oct. 1980).

SALT II was effectively shelved and NATO refused to defer its nuclear modernisation programme for Europe. Since Moscow's stock in America was already so low the Soviet leaders might well have concluded that there was no-longer much point in exercising restraint in Afghanistan.[16]

But then if the Russians were not in an over-confident mood and if an onslaught on the Gulf was not the primary consideration, what was? Once again, an American analogy would be helpful, for at the root of Moscow's interest in Afghanistan lie attitudes and anxieties not dissimilar from those which produced the Monroe Doctrine. If Washington can be alarmed by foreign intervention in Cuba, by a change of régime in Chile or turmoil in Nicaragua and El Salvador, Moscow can be equally disturbed by the prospect of anarchy in Afghanistan, of foreign intervention in neighbouring Iran, or a hardening of anti-Soviet opinion in Turkey. After all, these countries do represent the soft underbelly of Russia's southern flank and for well over one and a half centuries the Russians have repeatedly fought to try and prevent them from falling under foreign domination.[17] Not long after the Bolshevik Revolution, the Russians had followed American diplomatic practice by furnishing credits and military hardware to enable the governments beyond their southern frontiers to hold the British Raj at bay.[18] Although the aid policy had lapsed in

the early 1930s it was to be revived in respect of Afghanistan after Russia's other former southern clients, Turkey and Iran, had been absorbed into the Western Alliance system. Afghanistan was, indeed, the first country to benefit from the Soviet Union's renewed foreign assistance programme in 1954,[19] and since then Moscow had invested a great deal of economic, political and, of course, military capital to prevent it from going the way of Russia's other southern neighbours. By contrast, Western aid had been comparatively modest,[20] for lacking developed resources, modern agriculture, industry, education, health care or even effective government the country was hardly a glittering prize for Western economic interests. Effectively, Afghanistan was already in the Soviet orbit well before the coup which brought the country's first Marxist ruler to power in April 1978.

Though newspaper reporters at the time "detected" a Soviet hand in the Taraki coup, there is no reliable evidence that Moscow engineered or even sought it. But of course once Afghanistan had a Government that was not merely pro-Soviet but pro-Marxist as well, the Kremlin felt a special responsibility to assist it and preserve it from its many foes at home and abroad. Unfortunately, the Government to which Moscow gave its full blessing was both divided and acutely unpopular. It rapidly degenerated into warring Marxist factions,[21] while its Socialist and anti-Islamic platform so offended tribal values and tradi-

---

[16] A point elaborated in Dan Fisher, "Détente in Russian Deep Freeze," *The Guardian*, January 8, 1980 and in Lawrence Freedman, "Has Putting SALT on the Shelf Done Anyone Any Good?," *The Times*, January 15, 1980.

[17] See, for example, H. Seton-Watson *The Decline of Imperial Russia 1855-1914* (New York: Praeger, 1952); L. Adamec *Afghanistan's Foreign Affairs to the Mid-Twentieth Century* (Arizona: University of Arizona Press, 1974), and P. G. Fredericks *The Sepoy and the Cossack* (London: W. H. Allen, 1972).

[18] E. H. Carr *The Bolshevik Revolution 1917-1923, Volume III* (Harmondsworth: Penguin, 1966), pp. 239-251 and 290-298.

[19] Peter Calvocoressi *World Politics Since 1945*, Second Edition (London: Longmans, 1971), p. 272.

[20] See, for example, the statistical sections in *The Middle East and North Africa, 1973-4* (Europa Publications, 1973), p. 160, and *UN Statistical Year Book, 1978*, pp. 889-891.

[21] See, for example, Richard Wigg "In-fighting Among Afghanistan's Revolutionaries is Likely to Cause Growing Concern in Moscow," *The Times*, October 2, 1978; L. Dupree "Afghanistan Under the Khalq," *Problems of Communism*, (July-August 1979), and, also, Bruce Loudon "Deep Rift in Afghan Ruling Party," *The Daily Telegraph*, November 3, 1980.

tions that soon there were large-scale armed insurrections in the course of which no holds were barred on either side. Amid this bloody chaos the Government of Noor Mohammed Taraki demanded ever-increasing Soviet support, but as the protector of a hated régime the Soviet position became more and more untenable. Indicative of the surge of anti-Soviet feeling was the fact that in two uprisings—one in Herat near the Iranian border, the other in Jellalabad between Kabul and the Khyber Pass—up to a hundred Soviet advisers were reportedly publicly tortured, mutilated and killed by insurgents,[22] and the possibility of further attacks on Soviet personnel only increased as thousands of Soviet trained Afghan soldiers went over to the rebels, taking their weapons with them.[23]

The palace coup of September 1979 which brought Taraki's former Prime Minister, Hafizullah Amin to power only made things worse for the Soviets. For the evidence suggests that he was not a Moscow appointee,[24] and by his brutal excesses the situation inside Afghanistan was further inflamed. By December 1979 his hard-line Marxist Government was teetering on the edge of collapse, with all but a handful of the country's 28 provinces reported to be in rebel hands,[25] but with the Marxist government

in danger of defeat by Islamic rebels, enjoying the possibly active support of sympathisers abroad,[26] the Russians were faced with the kind of dilemma the Americans were confronted with in South Vietnam in the 1960s and 70s: either step up support of a friendly, if unpopular régime, or let the rebels take over. The fact that the Russians have a 20-year friendship treaty with Afghanistan dating from December 1978 gave Moscow a legal pretext for sending in the troops, but the political imperatives must have seemed even more compelling.

In the first place, the U.S.S.R. has a "domino theory" with, if anything, an even firmer historical base than that of the US. After all, the anti-Russian movements in the Caucasus had had a profound impact on the development of the Ukrainian, Polish and Tartar national movements in Tsarist times, and today the Kremlin fears that a successful "counter-revolution" in one of its client-states—say, in Hungary, Czechoslovakia, Poland or Afghanistan—might encourage "counter-revolution" elsewhere, especially when Moscow is preoccupied with so many domestic and international problems simultaneously. More importantly, if Afghanistan had gone the way of Iran, bringing a victory for Islamic fundamentalism, the impact inside the Soviet Union itself could have been incalculable. For amongst other elements within the country's 260 million population are between 40 and 50 million Muslims, most of them in Central Asia.[27] And if at present they do not appear to

---

[22] See, for example, Michael Binyon, "Why Moscow Ventured into the Afghan Quagmire," *The Sunday Times,* December 30, 1979, and Peter Wilshire (ed.), "Has Russia Won the Great Game?," *The Sunday Times,* January 6, 1980.

[23] See, for example, Andrew Wilson, "Kremlin Hawks Dictated Invasion," *The Observer,* January 13, 1980. It is worth noting that as early as June 23, 1979, *The Economist* was quoting Western sources to the effect that "More than two thousand Afghan officers and men" had deserted to the guerrillas and that "the rebels" were claiming "ten thousand defections, including an entire mechanised brigade of 2,500 troops."

[24] Moscow's dislike of Amin is attested in Michael Binyon, "Why Moscow Ventured into the Afghan Quagmire," *The Sunday Times,* December 30, 1979.

[25] It is difficult to be precise about the number of rebel-held provinces at the time of the Soviet intervention, but reports published in *The Sunday Times* suggest that on

the eve of the Soviet action "95%" of Afghanistan was "in uncontrolled revolt" and that the country was under a "beleaguered and tottering régime." Moreover, in an article in *The Observer,* February 17, 1980, it is suggested that even under Amin the Government had control "of only two or three provinces."

[26] F. Halliday in *The New Statesman,* (January 4, 1980), claimed that "the Islamic tribal forces in Afghanistan do benefit from substantial foreign assistance. Their base areas lie unmolested in Pakistan, and material aid has been provided by China, Iran, Kuwait and Saudi Arabia."

[27] Broadcasting in Turkish on Radio Moscow, April 5, 1979, Mufti Zia ud-Din Babakhanov gave the number of Soviet Muslims as numbering "over 40 million." A. Ben-

be highly imbued with that explosive combination of religion and nationalism which is playing such havoc elsewhere, what if their blood brothers in Afghanistan had succeeded in overthrowing a Marxist régime in the name of Islam? For some time there have been reports of the revival of illegal Moslem brotherhoods in various parts of Soviet Central Asia, and with the Islamic population rising much more rapidly than any other in the Soviet Union,[28] the Europeans who dominate the Kremlin are acutely sensitive to any trend which might encourage the politicisation of the religious and kinship ties of their Asian subjects. It may seem far-fetched to talk of the possible disintegration of Soviet rule in Central Asia but it is perhaps less so when one considers the depth of anti-colonial sentiment throughout the "crescent of crisis" on the U.S.S.R.'s periphery and the rapidity of the collapse of another well entrenched, authoritarian ruled multi-national state in the region—that of Iran under the Shah. All the more reason, then, for the Soviets to try to seal off the country's southern frontiers from the "contagion" of Islamic fundamentalism.

IV

However, motivations are one thing: implications another, and even if an assault on the Gulf was not a primary consideration, the Soviet strategic posture does appear to have been enhanced by its intervention in Afghanistan. If, for example, the Americans felt obliged to stage some form of intervention in the Gulf in the event of a threat to the Straits of Hormuz they

ningsen and C. Lemercier-Quelquejay in "Muslim Religious Conservatism and Dissent in the U.S.S.R.," *Religion in Communist Lands,* (Autumn 1978), suggest that the total is between 45 and 50 million, of which 75% live in Central Asia.

[28] In "Empire Building—Russian Style," *The Observer,* January 27, 1980, Mark Frankland draws attention to a Soviet demographic claim that "by the year 2,000...there may be a hundred million Muslims out of a total Soviet population of perhaps 320 million."

could hardly ignore Soviet interests as they had effectively done at Camp David. At the same time the Soviet Union has put itself in a position from which it might be able to secure, without risk, certain political or economic concessions, say, from Iran or Pakistan.

On the other hand, although a major projection of Soviet military power has occurred, we are no longer living in a world in which armed might necessarily brings political success, as America's failure to secure the "integrity" of South Vietnam or the quick release of the country's hostages from Iran demonstrates. In any case, while the disposition of Soviet forces may have been extended, the very visibility of the Soviet military arm could prove a disadvantage. Politically, it could alienate the prickly sensitivities of the non-aligned, who tend to despise the outward trappings of super-powerdom. Militarily, it could signify the over-extension of the country's commitments and, hence, vulnerability—as, for example, when each of the Soviet Union's four separate fleets passes through "choke points" which remain in pro-Western hands.

Moreover, these are for Moscow, no less than for Washington, uncertain times. In the long run the Red Army may be no more successful in securing Afghanistan than was the German Wehrmacht in securing Yugoslavia during the Second World War. Significantly, both countries are ideal terrain for guerrilla warfare, and counter-insurgency is not a military skill for which the Red Army is noted. In the meantime, what happens to Soviet morale as more and more coffins are returned to Russia for burial? Mounting casualties in incomprehensible overseas campaigns contributed to the sapping of American national morale during the Vietnam War and are helping to create disaffection today among the bereaved in Cuba. Then there are the political, military and economic costs of the Soviet intervention: the growing distrust of Moscow in the Islamic world, the facilities put at America's disposal by such-states as Israel, Egypt, Oman, Kenya and Somalia, the speed-up of the plan for a Rapid Deployment Force, the decision to deploy the Cruise Missile in Europe, the embargo on grain and advanced technology, to say nothing of the partial boycott of the Moscow Olympics (and all those unsold furry mascots called ''Misha'').

If I am right in suspecting that the uncertainty and insecurity in Washington is mirrored to some extent by uncertainty and insecurity in Moscow, this surely puts a new complexion on the kind of challenge which the Soviet intervention in Afghanistan poses, and on the appropriate response. To prepare for war may well be the best way to avoid it—but one does not have to be a ''wet Leftie'' to know that all ''stick'' and no ''carrot'' is hardly a sensible policy for the ther-monuclear age. Today each super-power is worried about the capabilities and intentions of the other; but each, too, faces threats which emanate not from its super-power rival but from the forces of anarchy and obscurantism that are disrupting the smooth functioning of the international system. The seizing of diplomatic hostages, the possible disintegration of established states, the sabotaging of oil installations in the Gulf and so forth can be seen as threatening the security of East and West alike.[29] Since both super-powers tend to be at their worst when they are at their most insecure, I would suggest that the need for some framework of discussions which is free from the public gaze and within which each could gauge the intentions, explore and if possible allay the anxieties of the other, is now more urgent than ever.[30]

Those who despair of rediscovering any such framework a year after the American shelving of SALT II and the Soviet intervention in Afghanistan might care to recall that since the 1950s periods of acute East-West tension have generally been followed by periods of international relaxation. President Reagan's formula for replacing SALT II with a new framework for East-West talks on Strategic Arms Limitation may not appear very promising, and the Russians could yet reject SALT III out of hand. But the Reagan proposal does at least serve as a signal that ''the cowboy wishes to parley,'' and the Russians might conceivably respond more favourably to an apparently strong President who wants a dialogue than an apparently weak one forced in his last full year of office to abandon serious discussions on curbing the arms race. None of this is to suggest that there is any easy answer to the predicament facing virtually all parties to the melée in Afghanistan. What it does indicate is that if there is eventually to be a reduction of the Soviet military presence in Afghanistan, it is more likely to follow the resumption of East-West dialogue than to precede it.

QUESTIONS FOR DISCUSSION

1 What is the most likely explanation for the Soviet invasion of Afghanistan?
2 Should the United States have come to the assistance of the Afghans? If so, how?
3 Is it likely that the Soviets intend to invade other countries in the Middle East or South Asia?
4 How far is Islam a threat to the stability of the Soviet Union?
5 On what terms, if any, would the Soviets be likely to withdraw from Afghanistan?

SUGGESTED READINGS

Brzezinski, Zbigniew. ''Afghanistan and Nicaragua,'' *National Interest,* no. 1 (Fall 1985), pp. 48–51.
Collins, Joseph J. *The Soviet Invasion of Afghanistan: A Study of the Use of Force in Soviet*

---

[29] In so far as the decrepit Soviet economy still needs Middle Eastern petroleum and feeds off the more vigorous Western economies, the continued flow of oil from the region may be as much a Soviet as a Western interest.

[30] The European Security Conference's review sessions clearly do not satisfy these requirements. They lack continuity, are the subject of too much publicity, and have tended to degenerate into propaganda forums.

Foreign Policy. Lexington, Mass.: Lexington Books, 1986.

Hauner, Milan. "Seizing the Third Parallel: Geopolitics and the Soviet Advance into Central Asia," *Orbis,* **29** (Spring 1985), pp. 5–31.

Karp, Craig M. "The War in Afghanistan," *Foreign Affairs,* **64** (Summer 1986), pp. 1026–1047.

Khalilzad, Zalmay. "Moscow's Afghan War," *Problems of Communism,* **35** (Jan.–Feb. 1986), pp. 1–20.

Rubinstein, Alvin Z. "The Soviet Union and Afghanistan," *Current History,* **82** (Oct. 1983), pp. 318–321, 337.

U.S. Cong., House of Representatives. *East-West Relations in the Aftermath of Soviet Invasion of Afghanistan,* Hearings before the Subcommittee on Europe and the Middle East of the Committee on Foreign Affairs, 96th Cong., 2d Sess., 1980.

U.S. Cong., Senate. *U.S. Security Interests and Policies in Southwest Asia,* Hearings before the Committee on Foreign Relations and the Subcommittee on Near Eastern and South Asian Affairs, 96th Cong., 2d Sess., 1980.

U.S. Cong., Senate. *Situation in Afghanistan,* Hearings before the Committee on Foreign Relations, 97th Cong., 2d Sess., 1982.

11A Does the application of an activist human rights policy by the United States against its allies hurt U.S. interests?

YES

Jeane Kirkpatrick

Dictatorships and Double Standards

NO

Sidney Blumenthal

An Ideology That Didn't Match Reality

Dictatorships and Double Standards

Jeane Kirkpatrick

The failure of the Carter administration's foreign policy is now clear to everyone except its architects, and even they must entertain private doubts, from time to time, about a policy whose crowning achievement has been to lay the groundwork for a transfer of the Panama Canal from the United States to a swaggering Latin dictator of Castroite bent. In the thirty-odd months since the inauguration of Jimmy Carter as President there has occurred a dramatic Soviet military build-up, matched by the stagnation of American armed forces, and a dramatic extension of Soviet influence in the Horn of Africa, Afghanistan, Southern Africa, and the Caribbean, matched by a declining American position in all these areas. The U.S. has never tried so hard and failed so utterly to make and keep friends in the Third World.

As if this were not bad enough, in the current year the United States has suffered two other major blows—in Iran and Nicaragua—of large and strategic significance. In each country, the Carter administration not only failed to prevent the undesired outcome, it actively collaborated in the replacement of moderate autocrats friendly to American interests with less friendly autocrats of extremist persuasion. It is too soon to be certain about what kind of regime will ultimately emerge in either Iran or Nicaragua, but accumulating evidence suggests that things are as likely to get worse as to get better in both countries. The Sandinistas in Nicaragua appear to be as skillful in consolidating power as the Ayatollah Khomeini is inept, and leaders of both revolutions display an intolerance and arrogance that do not bode well for the peaceful sharing of power or the establishment of constitutional governments, especially since those

leaders have made clear that they have no intention of seeking either.

It is at least possible that the SALT debate may stimulate new scrutiny of the nation's strategic position and defense policy, but there are no signs that anyone is giving serious attention to this nation's role in Iranian and Nicaraguan developments—despite clear warnings that the U.S. is confronted with similar situations and options in El Salvador, Guatemala, Morocco, Zaire, and elsewhere. Yet no problem of American foreign policy is more urgent than that of formulating a morally and strategically acceptable, and politically realistic, program for dealing with non-democratic governments who are threatened by Soviet-sponsored subversion. In the absence of such a policy, we can expect that the same reflexes that guided Washington in Iran and Nicaragua will be permitted to determine American actions from Korea to Mexico—with the same disastrous effects on the U.S. strategic position. (That the administration has not called its policies in Iran and Nicaragua a failure—and probably does not consider them such—complicates the problem without changing its nature.)

There were, of course, significant differences in the relations between the United States and each of these countries during the past two or three decades. Oil, size, and proximity to the Soviet Union gave Iran greater economic and strategic import than any Central American "republic," and closer relations were cultivated with the Shah, his counselors, and family than with President Somoza, his advisers, and family. Relations with the Shah were probably also enhanced by our approval of his manifest determination to modernize Iran regardless of the effects of modernization on traditional social and cultural patterns (including those which enhanced his own authority and legitimacy).

Jeane Kirkpatrick, "Dictatorships and Double Standards," *Commentary,* **68** (Nov. 1979), pp. 34–45.

Who lost Nicaragua?

And, of course, the Shah was much better looking and altogether more dashing than Somoza; his private life was much more romantic, more interesting to the media, popular and otherwise. Therefore, more Americans were more aware of the Shah than of the equally tenacious Somoza.

But even though Iran was rich, blessed with a product the U.S. and its allies needed badly, and led by a handsome king, while Nicaragua was poor and rocked along under a long-tenure president of less striking aspect, there were many similarities between the two countries and our relations with them. Both these small nations were led by men who had not been selected by free elections, who recognized no duty to submit themselves to searching tests of popular acceptability. Both did tolerate limited opposition, including opposition newspapers and political parties, but both were also confronted by radical, violent opponents bent on social and political revolution. Both rulers, therefore, sometimes invoked martial law to arrest, imprison, exile, and occasionally, it was alleged, torture their opponents. Both relied for public order on police forces whose personnel were said to be too harsh, too arbitrary, and too powerful. Each had what the American press termed "private armies," which is to say, armies pledging their allegiance to the ruler rather than the "constitution" or the "nation" or some other impersonal entity.

In short, both Somoza and the Shah were, in central ways, traditional rulers of semi-traditional societies. Although the Shah very badly wanted to create a technologically modern and powerful nation and Somoza tried hard to introduce modern agricultural methods, neither sought to reform his society in the light of any abstract idea of social justice or political virtue. Neither attempted to alter significantly the distribution of goods, status, or power (though the democratization of education and skills that accompanied modernization in Iran

did result in some redistribution of money and power there).

Both Somoza and the Shah enjoyed long tenure, large personal fortunes (much of which were no doubt appropriated from general revenues), and good relations with the United States. The Shah and Somoza were not only anti-Communist, they were positively friendly to the U.S., sending their sons and others to be educated in our universities, voting with us in the United Nations, and regularly supporting American interests and positions even when these entailed personal and political cost. The embassies of both governments were active in Washington social life, and were frequented by powerful Americans who occupied major roles in this nation's diplomatic, military, and political life. And the Shah and Somoza themselves were both welcome in Washington, and had many American friends.

Though each of the rulers was from time to time criticized by American officials for violating civil and human rights, the fact that the people of Iran and Nicaragua only intermittently enjoyed the rights accorded to citizens in the Western democracies did not prevent successive administrations from granting—with the necessary approval of successive Congresses—both military and economic aid. In the case of both Iran and Nicaragua, tangible and intangible tokens of U.S. support continued until the regime became the object of a major attack by forces explicitly hostile to the United States.

But once an attack was launched by opponents bent on destruction, everything changed. The rise of serious, violent opposition in Iran and Nicaragua set in motion a succession of events which bore a suggestive resemblance to one another and a suggestive similarity to our behavior in China before the fall of Chiang Kai-shek, in Cuba before the triumph of Castro, in certain crucial periods of the Vietnamese war, and, more recently, in Angola. In each of these countries, the American effort to impose liberalization and democratization on a government confronted with violent internal opposition not only failed, but actually <u>assisted</u> the coming to power of new regimes in which ordinary people enjoy fewer freedoms and less personal security than under the previous autocracy—regimes, moreover, hostile to American interests and policies.

The pattern is familiar enough: an established autocracy with a record of friendship with the U.S. is attacked by insurgents, some of whose leaders have long ties to the Communist movement, and most of whose arms are of Soviet, Chinese, or Czechoslovak origin. The "Marxist" presence is ignored and/or minimized by American officials and by the elite media on the ground that U.S. support for the dictator gives the rebels little choice but to seek aid "elsewhere." Violence spreads and American officials wonder aloud about the viability of a regime that "lacks the support of its own people." The absence of an opposition party is deplored and civil-rights violations are reviewed. Liberal columnists question the morality of continuing aid to a "rightist dictatorship" and provide assurances concerning the essential moderation of some insurgent leaders who "hope" for some sign that the U.S. will remember its own revolutionary origins. Requests for help from the beleaguered autocrat go unheeded, and the argument is increasingly voiced that ties should be established with rebel leaders "before it is too late." The President, delaying U.S. aid, appoints a special emissary who confirms the deterioration of the government position and its diminished capacity to control the situation and recommends various measures for "strengthening" and "liberalizing" the regime, all of which involve diluting its power.

The emissary's recommendations are presented in the context of a growing clamor for American disengagement on grounds that continued involvement confirms our status as an agent of imperialism, racism, and reaction; is inconsistent with support for human rights;

alienates us from the "forces of democracy"; and threatens to put the U.S. once more on the side of history's "losers." This chorus is supplemented daily by interviews with returning missionaries and "reasonable" rebels.

As the situation worsens, the President assures the world that the U.S. desires only that the "people choose their own form of government"; he blocks delivery of all arms to the government and undertakes negotiations to establish a "broadly based" coalition headed by a "moderate" critic of the regime who, once elevated, will move quickly to seek a "political" settlement to the conflict. Should the incumbent autocrat prove resistant to American demands that he step aside, he will be readily overwhelmed by the military strength of his opponents, whose patrons will have continued to provide sophisticated arms and advisers at the same time the U.S. cuts off military sales. Should the incumbent be so demoralized as to agree to yield power, he will be replaced by a "moderate" of American selection. Only after the insurgents have refused the proffered political solution and anarchy has spread throughout the nation will it be noticed that the new head of government has no significant following, no experience at governing, and no talent for leadership. By then, military commanders, no longer bound by loyalty to the chief of state, will depose the faltering "moderate" in favor of a fanatic of their own choosing.

In either case, the U.S. will have been led by its own misunderstanding of the situation to assist actively in deposing an erstwhile friend and ally and installing a government hostile to American interests and policies in the world. At best we will have lost access to friendly territory. At worst the Soviets will have gained a new base. And everywhere our friends will have noted that the U.S. cannot be counted on in times of difficulty and our enemies will have observed that American support provides no security against the forward march of history.

No particular crisis conforms exactly with the sequence of events described above; there are always variations on the theme. In Iran, for example, the Carter administration—and the President himself—offered the ruler support for a longer time, though by December 1978 the President was acknowledging that he did not know if the Shah would survive, adding that the U.S. would not get "directly involved." Neither did the U.S. ever call publicly for the Shah's resignation. However, the President's special emissary, George Ball, "reportedly concluded that the Shah cannot hope to maintain total power and must now bargain with a moderate segment of the opposition..." and was "known to have discussed various alternatives that would effectively ease the Shah out of total power" (Washington *Post,* December 15, 1978). There is, furthermore, not much doubt that the U.S. assisted the Shah's departure and helped arrange the succession of Bakhtiar. In Iran, the Carter administration's commitment to nonintervention proved stronger than strategic considerations or national pride. What the rest of the world regarded as a stinging American defeat, the U.S. government saw as a matter to be settled by Iranians. "We personally prefer that the Shah maintain a major role in the government," the President acknowledged, "but that is a decision for the Iranian people to make."

Events in Nicaragua also departed from the scenario presented above both because the Cuban and Soviet roles were clearer and because U.S. officials were more intensely and publicly working against Somoza. After the Somoza regime had defeated the first wave of Sandinista violence, the U.S. ceased aid, imposed sanctions, and took other steps which undermined the status and the credibility of the government in domestic and foreign affairs. Between the murder of ABC correspondent Bill Stewart by a National Guardsman in early June and the Sandinista victory in late July, the U.S. State Department assigned a new ambassador who refused to submit his credentials to Somoza even though Somoza was still chief of state, and called for replacing the government with a "broadly based provisional government that would include representatives of Sandinista guerillas." Americans were assured by Assistant Secretary of State Viron Vaky that "Nicaraguans and our democratic friends in Latin America have no intention of seeing Nicaragua turned into a second Cuba," even though the State Department knew that the top Sandinista leaders had close personal ties and were in continuing contact with Havana, and, more specifically, that a Cuban secret-police official, Julian Lopez, was frequently present in the Sandinista headquarters and that Cuban military advisers were present in Sandinista ranks.

In a manner uncharacteristic of the Carter administration, which generally seems willing to negotiate anything with anyone anywhere, the U.S. government adopted an oddly uncompromising posture in dealing with Somoza. "No end to the crisis is possible," said Vaky, "that does not start with the departure of Somoza from power and the end of his regime. No negotiation, mediation, or compromise can be achieved any longer with a Somoza government. The solution can only begin with a sharp break from the past." Trying hard, we not only banned all American arms sales to the government of Nicaragua but pressured Israel, Guatemala, and others to do likewise—all in the name of insuring a "democratic" outcome. Finally, as the Sandinista leaders consolidated control over weapons and communications, banned opposition, and took off for Cuba, President Carter warned us against attributing this "evolutionary change" to "Cuban machinations" and assured the world that the U.S. desired only to "let the people of Nicaragua choose their own form of government."

Yet despite all the variations, the Carter administration brought to the crises in Iran and Nicaragua several common assumptions each of which played a major role in hastening the victory of even more repressive dictatorships than had been in place before. These were, first, the belief that there existed at the moment of crisis a democratic alternative to the incumbent government; second, the belief that the continuation of the status quo was not possible; third, the belief that any change, including the establishment of a government headed by self-styled Marxist revolutionaries, was preferable to the present government. Each of these beliefs was (and is) widely shared in the liberal community generally. Not one of them can withstand close scrutiny.

Although most governments in the world are, as they always have been, autocracies of one kind or another, no idea holds greater sway in the mind of educated Americans than the belief that it is possible to democratize governments, anytime, anywhere, under any circumstances. This notion is belied by an enormous body of evidence based on the experience of dozens of countries which have attempted with more or less (usually less) success to move from autocratic to democratic government. Many of the wisest political scientists of this and previous centuries agree that democratic institutions are especially difficult to establish and maintain—because they make heavy demands on all portions of a population and because they depend on complex social, cultural, and economic conditions.

Two or three decades ago, when Marxism enjoyed its greatest prestige among American intellectuals, it was the economic prerequisites of democracy that were emphasized by social scientists. Democracy, they argued, could function only in relatively rich societies with an advanced economy, a substantial middle class, and a literate population, but it could be expected to emerge more or less automatically whenever these conditions prevailed. Today, this picture seems grossly oversimplified. While it surely helps to have an economy strong enough to provide decent levels of well-being for all, and "open" enough to provide mobility

and encourage achievement, a pluralistic society and the right kind of political culture—and time—are even more essential.

In his essay on *Representative Government,* John Stuart Mill identified three fundamental conditions which the Carter administration would do well to ponder. These are: "One, that the people should be willing to receive it [representative government]; two, that they should be willing and able to do what is necessary for its preservation; three, that they should be willing and able to fulfill the duties and discharge the functions which it imposes on them."

Fulfilling the duties and discharging the functions of representative government make heavy demands on leaders and citizens, demands for participation and restraint, for consensus and compromise. It is not necessary for all citizens to be avidly interested in politics or well-informed about public affairs—although far more widespread interest and mobilization are needed than in autocracies. What *is* necessary is that a substantial number of citizens think of themselves as participants in society's decision-making and not simply as subjects bound by its laws. Moreover, leaders of all major sectors of the society must agree to pursue power only by legal means, must eschew (at least in principle) violence, theft, and fraud, and must accept defeat when necessary. They must also be skilled at finding and creating common ground among diverse points of view and interests, and correlatively willing to compromise on all but the most basic values.

In addition to an appropriate political culture, democratic government requires institutions strong enough to channel and contain conflict. Voluntary, non-official institutions are needed to articulate and aggregate diverse interests and opinions present in the society. Otherwise, the formal governmental institutions will not be able to translate popular demands into public policy.

In the relatively few places where they exist, democratic governments have come into being slowly, after extended prior experience with more limited forms of participation during which leaders have reluctantly grown accustomed to tolerating dissent and opposition, opponents have accepted the notion that they may defeat but not destroy incumbents, and people have become aware of government's effects on their lives and of their own possible effects on government. Decades, if not centuries, are normally required for people to acquire the necessary disciplines and habits. In Britain, the road from the Magna Carta to the Act of Settlement, to the great Reform Bills of 1832, 1867, and 1885, took seven centuries to traverse. American history gives no better grounds for believing that democracy comes easily, quickly, or for the asking. A war of independence, an unsuccessful constitution, a civil war, a long process of gradual enfranchisement marked our progress toward constitutional democratic government. The French path was still more difficult. Terror, dictatorship, monarchy, instability, and incompetence followed on the revolution that was to usher in a millennium of brotherhood. Only in the 20th century did the democratic principle finally gain wide acceptance in France and not until after World War II were the principles of order and democracy, popular sovereignty and authority, finally reconciled in institutions strong enough to contain conflicting currents of public opinion.

Although there is no instance of a revolutionary "socialist" or Communist society being democratized, right-wing autocracies do sometimes evolve into democracies—given time, propitious economic, social, and political circumstances, talented leaders, and a strong indigenous demand for representative government. Something of the kind is in progress on the Iberian peninsula and the first steps have been taken in Brazil. Something similar could conceivably have also occurred in Iran and Nicaragua if contestation and participation had been more gradually expanded.

But it seems clear that the architects of contemporary American foreign policy have little idea of how to go about encouraging the liberalization of an autocracy. In neither Nicaragua nor Iran did they realize that the only likely result of an effort to replace an incumbent autocrat with one of his moderate critics or a "broad-based coalition" would be to sap the foundations of the existing regime without moving the nation any closer to democracy. Yet this outcome was entirely predictable. Authority in traditional autocracies is transmitted through personal relations: from the ruler to his close associates (relatives, household members, personal friends) and from them to people to whom the associates are related by personal ties resembling their own relation to the ruler. The fabric of authority unravels quickly when the power and status of the man at the top are undermined or eliminated. The longer the autocrat has held power, and the more pervasive his personal influence, the more dependent a nation's institutions will be on him. Without him, the organized life of the society will collapse, like an arch from which the keystone has been removed. The blend of qualities that bound the Iranian army to the Shah or the national guard to Somoza is typical of the relationships—personal, hierarchical, non-transferable—that support a traditional autocracy. The speed with which armies collapse, bureaucracies abdicate, and social structures dissolve once the autocrat is removed frequently surprises American policy-makers and journalists accustomed to public institutions based on universalistic norms rather than particularistic relations.

The failure to understand these relations is one source of the failure of U.S. policy in this and previous administrations. There are others. In Iran and Nicaragua (as previously in Vietnam, Cuba, and China) Washington overestimated the political diversity of the opposition—especially the strength of "moderates" and "democrats" in the opposition movement; underestimated the strength and intransigence of radicals in the movement; and misestimated the nature and extent of American influence on both the government and the opposition.

Confusion concerning the character of the opposition, especially its intransigence and will to power, leads regularly to downplaying the amount of force required to counteract its violence. In neither Iran nor Nicaragua did the U.S. adequately appreciate the government's problem in maintaining order in a society confronted with an ideologically extreme opposition. Yet the presence of such groups was well known. The State Department's 1977 report on human rights described an Iran confronted

> with a small number of extreme rightist and leftist terrorists operating within the country. There is evidence that they have received substantial foreign support and training...[and] have been responsible for the murder of Iranian government officials and Americans....

The same report characterized Somoza's opponents in the following terms:

> A guerrilla organization known as the Sandinista National Liberation Front (FSLN) seeks the violent overthrow of the government, and has received limited support from Cuba. The FSLN carried out an operation in Managua in December 1974, killing four people, taking several officials hostage,...since then, it continues to challenge civil authority in certain isolated regions.

In 1978, the State Department's report said that Sandinista violence was continuing—after the state of siege had been lifted by the Somoza government.

When U.S. policy-makers and large portions of the liberal press interpret insurgency as evidence of widespread popular discontent and a will to democracy, the scene is set for disaster. For if civil strife reflects a popular demand for democracy, it follows that a "liberalized" government will be more acceptable to "public opinion."

Thus, in the hope of strengthening a government, U.S. policy-makers are led, mistake after mistake, to impose measures almost certain to weaken its authority. Hurried efforts to force complex and unfamiliar political practices on societies lacking the requisite political culture, tradition, and social structures not only fail to produce desired outcomes; if they are undertaken at a time when the traditional regime is under attack, they actually facilitate the job of the insurgents.

Vietnam presumably taught us that the United States could not serve as the world's policeman; it should also have taught us the dangers of trying to be the world's midwife to democracy when the birth is scheduled to take place under conditions of guerrilla war.

If the administration's actions in Iran and Nicaragua reflect the pervasive and mistaken assumption that one can easily locate and impose democratic alternatives to incumbent autocracies, they also reflect the equally pervasive and equally flawed belief that change *per se* in such autocracies is inevitable, desirable, and in the American interest. It is this belief which induces the Carter administration to participate actively in the toppling of non-Communist autocracies while remaining passive in the face of Communist expansion.

At the time the Carter administration came into office it was widely reported that the President had assembled a team who shared a new approach to foreign policy and a new conception of the national interest. The principal elements of this new approach were said to be two: the conviction that the cold war was over, and the conviction that, this being the case, the U.S. should give priority to North-South problems and help less developed nations achieve their own destiny.

More is involved in these changes than originally meets the eye. For, unlikely as it may seem, the foreign policy of the Carter administration is guided by a relatively full-blown philosophy of history which includes, as philosophies of history always do, a theory of social change, or, as it is currently called, a doctrine of modernization. Like most other philosophies of history that have appeared in the West since the 18th century, the Carter administration's doctrine predicts progress (in the form of modernization for all societies) and a happy ending (in the form of a world community of developed, autonomous nations).

The administration's approach to foreign affairs was clearly foreshadowed in Zbigniew Brzezinski's 1970 book on the U.S. role in the "technetronic era," *Between Two Ages*. In that book, Brzezinski showed that he had the imagination to look beyond the cold war to a brave new world of global politics and interdependence. To deal with that new world a new approach was said to be "evolving," which Brzezinski designated "rational humanism." In the new approach, the "preoccupation" with "national supremacy" would give way to "global" perspectives, and international problems would be viewed as "human issues" rather than as "political confrontations." The traditional intellectual framework for dealing with foreign policy would have to be scrapped:

> Today, the old framework of international politics...with their spheres of influence, military alliances between nation states, the fiction of sovereignty, doctrinal conflicts arising from 19th-century crisis—is clearly no longer compatible with reality.*

* Concerning Latin America, Brzezinski observed: "Latin American nationalism, more and more radical as it widens its popular base, will be directed with increasing animosity against the United States unless the United States rapidly shifts its own posture. Accordingly, it would be wise for the United States to make an explicit move to abandon the Monroe Doctrine and to concede that in the new global age geographic or hemispheric contiguity no longer need be politically decisive. Nothing could be healthier for Pan-American relations than for the United States to place them on the same level as its relations with the rest of the world, confining itself to emphasis on cultural-political affinities (as it does with Western Europe) and economic-social obligations (as it does with less developed countries)."

Only the "delayed development" of the Soviet Union, "an archaic religious community that experiences modernity existentially but not quite yet normatively," prevented wider realization of the fact that the end of ideology was already here. For the U.S., Brzezinski recommended "a great deal of patience," a more detached attitude toward world revolutionary processes, and a less anxious preoccupation with the Soviet Union. Instead of engaging in ancient diplomatic pastimes, we should make "a broader effort to contain the global tendencies toward chaos," while assisting the processes of change that will move the world toward the "community of developed nations."

The central concern of Brzezinski's book, as of the Carter administration's foreign policy, is with the modernization of the Third World. From the beginning, the administration has manifested a special, intense interest in the problems of the so-called Third World. But instead of viewing international developments in terms of the American national interest, as national interest is historically conceived, the architects of administration policy have viewed them in terms of a contemporary version of the same idea of progress that has traumatized Western imaginations since the Enlightenment.

In its current form, the concept of modernization involves more than industrialization, more than "political development" (whatever that is). It is used instead to designate "...the process through which a traditional or pre-technological society passes as it is transformed into a society characterized by machine technology, rational and secular attitudes, and highly differentiated social structures." Condorcet, Comte, Hegel, Marx, and Weber are all present in this view of history as the working out of the idea of modernity.

The crucial elements of the modernization concept have been clearly explicated by Samuel P. Huntington (who, despite a period at the National Security Council, was assuredly not the architect of the administration's policy).

The modernization paradigm, Huntington has observed, postulates an ongoing process of change: complex, because it involves all dimensions of human life in society; systemic, because its elements interact in predictable, necessary ways; global, because all societies will, necessarily, pass through the transition from traditional to modern; lengthy, because time is required to modernize economic and social organization, character, and culture; phased, because each modernizing society must pass through essentially the same stages; homogenizing, because it tends toward the convergence and interdependence of societies; irreversible, because the direction of change is "given" in the relation of the elements of the process; progressive, in the sense that it is desirable, and in the long run provides significant benefits to the affiliated people.

Although the modernization paradigm has proved a sometimes useful as well as influential tool in social science, it has become the object of searching critiques that have challenged one after another of its central assumptions. Its shortcomings as an analytical tool pale, however, when compared to its inadequacies as a framework for thinking about foreign policy, where its principal effects are to encourage the view that events are manifestations of deep historical forces which cannot be controlled and that the best any government can do is to serve as a "midwife" to history, helping events to move where they are already headed.

This perspective on cor emporary events is optimistic in the sense that it foresees continuing human progress; deterministic in the sense that it perceives events as fixed by processes over which persons and policies can have but little influence; moralistic in the sense that it perceives history and U.S. policy as having moral ends; cosmopolitan in the sense that it attempts to view the world not from the perspective of American interests or intentions but from the perspective of the modernizing nation

and the "end" of history. It identifies modernization with both revolution and morality, and U.S. policy with all three.

The idea that it is "forces" rather than people which shape events recurs each time an administration spokesman articulates or explains policy. The President, for example, assured us in February of this year [1979]:

> The revolution in Iran is a product of deep social, political, religious, and economic factors growing out of the history of Iran itself.

And of Asia he said:

> At this moment there is turmoil or change in various countries from one end of the Indian Ocean to the other; some turmoil as in Indochina is the product of age-old enmities, inflamed by rivalries for influence by conflicting forces. Stability in some other countries is being shaken by the process of modernization, the search for national significance, or the desire to fulfill legitimate human hopes and human aspirations.

Harold Saunders, Assistant Secretary for Near Eastern and South Asian Affairs, commenting on "instability" in Iran and the Horn of Africa, states:

> We, of course, recognize that fundamental changes are taking place across this area of western Asia and northeastern Africa—economic modernization, social change, a revival of religion, resurgent nationalism, demands for broader popular participation in the political process. These changes are generated by forces within each country.

Or here is Anthony Lake, chief of the State Department's Policy Planning staff, on South Africa:

> Change will come in South Africa. The welfare of the people there, and American interests, will be profoundly affected by the way in which it comes. The question is whether it will be peaceful or not.

Brzezinski makes the point still clearer. Speaking as chief of the National Security Council, he has assured us that the struggles for power in Asia and Africa are really only incidents along the route to modernization:

> ...all the developing countries in the arc from northeast Asia to southern Africa continue to search for viable forms of government capable of managing the process of modernization.

No matter that the invasions, coups, civil wars, and political struggles of less violent kinds that one sees all around do not *seem* to be incidents in a global personnel search for someone to manage the modernization process. Neither Brzezinski nor anyone else seems bothered by the fact that the political participants in that arc from northeast Asia to southern Africa do not *know* that they are "searching for viable forms of government capable of managing the process of modernization." The motives and intentions of real persons are no more relevant to the modernization paradigm than they are to the Marxist view of history. Viewed from this level of abstraction, it is the "forces" rather than the people that count.

So what if the "deep historical forces" at work in such diverse places as Iran, the Horn of Africa, Southeast Asia, Central America, and the United Nations look a lot like Russians or Cubans? Having moved past what the President calls our "inordinate fear of Communism," identified by him with the cold war, we should, we are told, now be capable of distinguishing Soviet and Cuban "machinations," which anyway exist mainly in the minds of cold warriors and others guilty of oversimplifying the world, from evolutionary changes, which seem to be the only kind that actually occur.

What can a U.S. President faced with such complicated, inexorable, impersonal processes *do?* The answer, offered again and again by the President and his top officials, is, not much. Since events are not caused by human decisions, they cannot be stopped or altered by

them. Brzezinski, for example, has said: "We recognize that the world is changing under the influence of forces no government can control...." And Cyrus Vance has cautioned: "The fact is that we can no more stop change than Canute could still the waters."

The Carter administration's essentially deterministic and apolitical view of contemporary events discourages an active American response and encourages passivity. The American inability to influence events in Iran became the President's theme song:

> Those who argue that the U.S. should *or could* intervene directly to thwart [the revolution in Iran] are wrong about the realities of Iran....We have encouraged *to the limited extent of our own ability* the public support for the Bakhtiar government. ...How long [the Shah] will be out of Iran, we have no way to determine. Future events and his own desires will determine that....It is impossible for anyone to anticipate all future political events. ...Even if we had been able to anticipate events that were going to take place in Iran or in other countries, obviously our ability to determine those events is very limited [emphasis added].

Vance made the same point:

> In Iran our policy throughout the current crisis has been based on the fact that only Iranians can resolve the fundamental political issues which they now confront.

Where once upon a time an American President might have sent Marines to assure the protection of American strategic interests, there is no room for force in this world of progress and self-determination. Force, the President told us at Notre Dame, does not work; that is the lesson he extracted from Vietnam. It offers only "superficial" solutions. Concerning Iran, he said:

> Certainly we have no desire or ability to intrude massive forces into Iran or any other country to determine the outcome of domestic political issues. This is something that we have no intention of ever

doing in another country. We've tried this once in Vietnam. It didn't work, as you well know.

There was nothing unique about Iran. In Nicaragua, the climate and language were different but the "historical forces" and the U.S. response were the same. Military intervention was out of the question. Assistant Secretary of State Viron Vaky described as "unthinkable" the "use of U.S. military power to intervene in the internal affairs of another American republic." Vance provided parallel assurances for Africa, asserting that we would not try to match Cuban and Soviet activities there.

What *is* the function of foreign policy under these conditions? It is to understand the processes of change and then, like Marxists, to align ourselves with history, hoping to contribute a bit of stability along the way. And this, administration spokesmen assure us, is precisely what we are doing. The Carter administration has defined the U.S. national interest in the Third World as identical with the putative end of the modernization process. Vance put this with characteristic candor in a recent statement when he explained that U.S. policy vis-à-vis the Third World is "grounded in the conviction that we best serve our interest there by supporting the efforts of developing nations to advance their economic well-being and preserve their political independence." Our "commitment to the promotion of constructive change worldwide" (Brzezinski's words) has been vouchsafed in every conceivable context.

But there is a problem. The conceivable contexts turn out to be mainly those in which non-Communist autocracies are under pressure from revolutionary guerrillas. Since Moscow is the aggressive, expansionist power today, it is more often than not insurgents, encouraged and armed by the Soviet Union, who challenge the status quo. The American commitment to "change" in the abstract ends up by aligning us tacitly with Soviet clients and irresponsible

extremists like the Ayatollah Khomeini or, in the end, Yasir Arafat.

So far, assisting "change" has not led the Carter administration to undertake the destabilization of a *Communist* country. The principles of self-determination and nonintervention are thus both selectively applied. We seem to accept the status quo in Communist nations (in the name of "diversity" and national autonomy), but not in nations ruled by "right-wing" dictators or white oligarchies. Concerning China, for example, Brzezinski has observed: "We recognize that the PRC and we have different ideologies and economic and political systems.... We harbor neither the hope nor the desire that through extensive contacts with China we can remake that nation into the American image. Indeed, we accept our differences." Of Southeast Asia, the President noted in February [1979]:

> Our interest is to promote peace and the withdrawal of outside forces and not to become embroiled in the conflict among Asian nations. And, in general, our interest is to promote the health and the development of individual societies, not to a pattern cut exactly like ours in the United States but tailored rather to the hopes and the needs and desires of the peoples involved.

But the administration's position shifts sharply when South Africa is discussed. For example, Anthony Lake asserted in late 1978:

> ...We have indicated to South Africa the fact that if it does not make significant progress toward racial equality, its relations with the international community, including the United States, are bound to deteriorate.
>
> Over the years, we have tried through a series of progressive steps to demonstrate that the U.S. cannot and will not be associated with the continued practice of apartheid.

As to Nicaragua, Hodding Carter III said in February 1979:

The unwillingness of the Nicaraguan government to accept the [OAS] group's proposal, the resulting prospects for renewal and polarization, and the human-rights situation in Nicaragua...unavoidably affect the kind of relationships we can maintain with that government....

And Carter commented on Latin American autocracies:

My government will not be deterred from protecting human rights, including economic and social rights, in whatever ways we can. We prefer to take actions that are positive, but where nations persist in serious violations of human rights, we will continue to demonstrate that there are costs to the flagrant disregard of international standards.

Something very odd is going on here. How does an administration that desires to let people work out their own destinies get involved in determined efforts at reform in South Africa, Zaire, Nicaragua, El Salvador, and elsewhere? How can an administration committed to non-intervention in Cambodia and Vietnam announce that it "will not be deterred" from righting wrongs in South Africa? What should be made of an administration that sees the U.S. interest as identical with economic modernization and political independence and yet heedlessly endangers the political independence of Taiwan, a country whose success in economic modernization and egalitarian distribution of wealth is unequaled in Asia? The contrast is as striking as that between the administration's frenzied speed in recognizing the new dictatorship in Nicaragua and its continuing refusal to recognize the elected government of Zimbabwe Rhodesia, or its refusal to maintain any presence in Zimbabwe Rhodesia while staffing a U.S. Information Office in Cuba. Not only are there ideology and a double standard at work here, the ideology neither fits nor explains reality, and the double standard involves the administration in the wholesale contradiction of its own principles.

Inconsistencies are a familiar part of politics in most societies. Usually, however, governments behave hypocritically when their principles conflict with the national interest. What makes the inconsistencies of the Carter administration noteworthy are, first, the administration's moralism—which renders it especially vulnerable to charges of hypocrisy; and, second, the administration's predilection for policies that violate the strategic and economic interests of the United States. The administration's conception of national interest borders on doublethink: it finds friendly powers to be guilty representatives of the status quo and views the triumph of unfriendly groups as beneficial to America's "true interests."

This logic is quite obviously reinforced by the prejudices and preferences of many administration officials. Traditional autocracies are, in general and in their very nature, deeply offensive to modern American sensibilities. The notion that public affairs should be ordered on the basis of kinship, friendship, and other personal relations rather than on the basis of objective "rational" standards violates our conception of justice and efficiency. The preference for stability rather than change is also disturbing to Americans whose whole national experience rests on the principles of change, growth, and progress. The extremes of wealth and poverty characteristic of traditional societies also offend us, the more so since the poor are usually *very* poor and bound to their squalor by a hereditary allocation of role. Moreover, the relative lack of concern of rich, comfortable rulers for the poverty, ignorance, and disease of "their" people is likely to be interpreted by Americans as moral dereliction pure and simple. The truth is that Americans can hardly bear such societies and such rulers. Confronted with them, our vaunted cultural relativism evaporates and we become as censorious as Cotton Mather confronting sin in New England.

But if the politics of traditional and semi-traditional autocracy is nearly antithetical to our own—at both the symbolic and the operational level—the rhetoric of progressive revolutionaries sounds much better to us; their symbols are much more acceptable. One reason that some modern Americans prefer "socialist" to traditional autocracies is that the former have embraced modernity and have adopted modern modes and perspectives, including an instrumental, manipulative, functional orientation toward most social, cultural, and personal affairs; a profession of universalistic norms; an emphasis on reason, science, education, and progress; a deemphasis of the sacred; and "rational," bureaucratic organizations. They speak our language.

Because socialism of the Soviet/Chinese/Cuban variety is an ideology rooted in a version of the same values that sparked the Enlightenment and the democratic revolutions of the 18th century; because it is modern and not traditional; because it postulates goals that appeal to Christian as well as to secular values (brotherhood of man, elimination of power as a mode of human relations), it is highly congenial to many Americans at the symbolic level. Marxist revolutionaries speak the language of a hopeful future while traditional autocrats speak the language of an unattractive past. Because left-wing revolutionaries invoke the symbols and values of democracy—emphasizing egalitarianism rather than hierarchy and privilege, liberty rather than order, activity rather than passivity—they are again and again accepted as partisans in the cause of freedom and democracy.

Nowhere is the affinity of liberalism, Christianity, and Marxist socialism more apparent than among liberals who are "duped" time after time into supporting "liberators" who turn out to be totalitarians, and among Left-leaning clerics whose attraction to a secular style of "redemptive community" is stronger than their outrage at the hostility of socialist regimes to religion. In Jimmy Carter—egalitarian, optimist, liberal, Christian—the tendency to be repelled by

frankly non-democratic rulers and hierarchical societies is almost as strong as the tendency to be attracted to the idea of popular revolution, liberation, and progress. Carter is, *par excellence,* the kind of liberal most likely to confound revolution with idealism, change with progress, optimism with virtue.

Where concern about "socialist encirclement," Soviet expansion, and traditional conceptions of the national interest inoculated his predecessors against such easy equations, Carter's doctrine of national interest and modernization encourages support for all change that takes place in the name of "the people," regardless of its "superficial" Marxist or anti-American content. Any lingering doubt about whether the U.S. should, in case of conflict, support a "tested friend" such as the Shah or a friendly power such as Zimbabwe Rhodesia against an opponent who despises us is resolved by reference to our "true," our "long-range" interests.

Stephen Rosenfeld of the Washington *Post* described the commitment of the Carter administration to this sort of "progressive liberalism":

> The Carter administration came to power, after all, committed precisely to reducing the centrality of strategic competition with Moscow in American foreign policy, and to extending the United States' association with what it was prepared to accept as legitimate wave-of-the-future popular movements around the world—first of all with the victorious movement in Vietnam.
>
> ...Indochina was supposed to be the state on which Americans could demonstrate their "post-Vietnam" intent to come to terms with the progressive popular element that Kissinger, the villain, had denied.

In other words, the Carter administration, Rosenfeld tells us, came to power resolved not to assess international developments in the light of "cold-war" perspectives but to accept at face value the claim of revolutionary groups to

there purly
1962.

represent "popular" aspirations and "progressive" forces—regardless of the ties of these revolutionaries to the Soviet Union. To this end, overtures were made looking to the "normalization" of relations with Vietnam, Cuba, and the Chinese People's Republic, and steps were taken to cool relations with South Korea, South Africa, Nicaragua, the Philippines, and others. These moves followed naturally from the conviction that the U.S. had, as our enemies said, been on the wrong side of history in supporting the status quo and opposing revolution.

One might have thought that this perspective would have been undermined by events in Southeast Asia since the triumph of "progressive" forces there over the "agents of reaction." To cite Rosenfeld again:

> In this administration's time, Vietnam has been transformed for much of American public opinion, from a country wronged by the U.S. to one revealing a brutal essence of its own.
>
> This has been a quiet but major trauma to the Carter people (as to all liberals) scarring their self-confidence and their claim on public trust alike.

Presumably, however, the barbarity of the "progressive" governments in Cambodia and Vietnam has been less traumatic for the President and his chief advisers than for Rosenfeld, since there is little evidence of changed predispositions at crucial levels of the White House and the State Department. The President continues to behave as before—not like a man who abhors autocrats but like one who abhors only right-wing autocrats.

In fact, high officials in the Carter administration understand better than they seem to the aggressive, expansionist character of contemporary Soviet behavior in Africa, the Middle East, Southeast Asia, the Indian Ocean, Central America, and the Caribbean. But although the Soviet/Cuban role in Grenada, Nicaragua, and El Salvador (plus the transfer of MIG-23's

to Cuba) had already prompted resumption of surveillance of Cuba (which in turn confirmed the presence of a Soviet combat brigade), the President's eagerness not to "heat up" the climate of public opinion remains stronger than his commitment to speak the truth to the American people. His statement on Nicaragua clearly reflects these priorities:

> It's a mistake for Americans to assume or to claim that every time an evolutionary change takes place in this hemisphere that somehow it's a result of secret, massive Cuban intervention. The fact in Nicaragua is that the Somoza regime lost the confidence of the people. To bring about an orderly transition there, our effort was to let the people of Nicaragua ultimately make the decision on who would be their leader—what form of government they should have.

This statement, which presumably represents the President's best thinking on the matter, is illuminating. Carter's effort to dismiss concern about military events in this specific country as a manifestation of a national proclivity for seeing "Cuban machinations" under every bed constitutes a shocking effort to falsify reality. There was no question in Nicaragua of "evolutionary change" or of attributing such change to Castro's agents. There was only a question about the appropriate U.S. response to a military struggle in a country whose location gives it strategic importance out of proportion to its size or strength.

But that is not all. The rest of the President's statement graphically illustrates the blinding power of ideology on his interpretation of events. When he says that "the Somoza regime lost the confidence of the people," the President implies that the regime had previously rested on the confidence of "the people," but that the situation had now changed. In fact, the Somoza regime had never rested on popular will (but instead on manipulation, force, and habit), and was not being ousted by it. It was instead succumbing to arms and soldiers. However, the assumption that the armed conflict of Sandinistas and Somozistas was the military equivalent of a national referendum enabled the President to imagine that it could be, and should be, settled by the people of Nicaragua. For this pious sentiment even to seem true the President would have had to be unaware that insurgents were receiving a great many arms from other non-Nicaraguans; and that the U.S. had played a significant role in disarming the Somoza regime.

The President's mistakes and distortions are all fashionable ones. His assumptions are those of people who want badly to be on the progressive side in conflicts between "rightist" autocracy and "leftist" challenges, and to prefer the latter, almost regardless of the probable consequences.

To be sure, neither the President, nor Vance, nor Brzezinski *desires* the proliferation of Soviet supported regimes. Each has asserted his disapproval of Soviet "interference" in the modernization process. But each, nevertheless, remains willing to "destabilize" friendly or neutral autocracies without any assurance that they will not be replaced by reactionary totalitarian theocracies, totalitarian Soviet client states, or worst of all, by murderous fanatics of the Pol Pot variety.

The foreign policy of the Carter administration fails not for lack of good intentions but for lack of realism about the nature of traditional versus revolutionary autocracies and the relation of each to the American national interest. Only intellectual fashion and the tyranny of Right/Left thinking prevent intelligent men of good will from perceiving the *facts* that traditional authoritarian governments are less repressive than revolutionary autocracies, that they are more susceptible of liberalization, and that they are more compatible with U.S. interests. The evidence on all these points is clear enough.

Surely it is now beyond reasonable doubt that the present governments of Vietnam, Cambodia, Laos are much more repressive than those of the despised previous rulers; that the government of the People's Republic of China is more repressive than that of Taiwan, that North Korea is more repressive than South Korea, and so forth. This is the most important lesson of Vietnam and Cambodia. It is not new but it is a gruesome reminder of harsh facts.

From time to time a truly bestial ruler can come to power in either type of autocracy—Idi Amin, Papa Doc Duvalier, Joseph Stalin, Pol Pot are examples—but neither type regularly produces such moral monsters (though democracy regularly prevents their accession to power). There are, however, _systemic_ differences between traditional and revolutionary autocracies that have a predictable effect on their degree of repressiveness. Generally speaking, traditional autocrats tolerate social inequities, brutality, and poverty while revolutionary autocracies create them.

Traditional autocrats leave in place existing allocations of wealth, power, status, and other resources which in most traditional societies favor an affluent few and maintain masses in poverty. But they worship traditional gods and observe traditional taboos. They do not disturb the habitual rhythms of work and leisure, habitual places of residence, habitual patterns of family and personal relations. Because the miseries of traditional life are familiar, they are bearable to ordinary people who, growing up in the society, learn to cope, as children born to untouchables in India acquire the skills and attitudes necessary for survival in the miserable roles they are destined to fill. Such societies create no refugees.

Precisely the opposite is true of revolutionary Communist regimes. They create refugees by the million because they claim jurisdiction over the whole life of the society and make demands for change that so violate internalized values and habits that inhabitants flee by the tens of thousands in the remarkable expectation that their attitudes, values, and goals will "fit" better in a foreign country than in their native land.

The former deputy chairman of Vietnam's National Assembly from 1976 to his defection early in August 1979, Hoang Van Hoan, described recently the impact of Vietnam's ongoing revolution on that country's more than one million Chinese inhabitants:

> They have been expelled from places they have lived in for generations. They have been dispossessed of virtually all possessions—their lands, their houses. They have been driven into areas called new economic zones, but they have not been given any aid.
>
> How can they eke out a living in such conditions by reclaiming new land? They gradually die for a number of reasons—diseases, the hard life. They also die of humiliation.

It is not only the Chinese who have suffered in Southeast Asia since the "liberation," and it is not only in Vietnam that the Chinese suffer. By the end of 1978 more than six million refugees had fled countries ruled by Marxist governments. In spite of walls, fences, guns, and sharks, the steady stream of people fleeing revolutionary utopias continues.

There is a damning contrast between the number of refugees created by Marxist regimes and those created by other autocracies: more than a million Cubans have left their homeland since Castro's rise (one refugee for every nine inhabitants) as compared to about 35,000 each from Argentina, Brazil, and Chile. In Africa more than five times as many refugees have fled Guinea and Guinea Bissau as have left Zimbabwe Rhodesia, suggesting that civil war and racial discrimination are easier for most people to bear than Marxist-style liberation.

Moreover, the history of this century provides no grounds for expecting that radical totalitarian regimes will transform themselves. At the moment there is a far greater likelihood of progressive liberalization and democratization in the governments of Brazil, Argentina, and Chile than in the government of Cuba; in Taiwan than in the People's Republic of China;

in South Korea than in North Korea; in Zaire than in Angola; and so forth.

Since many traditional autocracies permit limited contestation and participation, it is not impossible that U.S. policy could effectively encourage this process of liberalization and democratization, provided that the effort is not made at a time when the incumbent government is fighting for its life against violent adversaries, and that proposed reforms are aimed at producing gradual change rather than perfect democracy overnight. To accomplish this, policymakers are needed who understand how actual democracies have actually come into being. History is a better guide than good intentions.

A realistic policy which aims at protecting our own interest and assisting the capacities for self-determination of less developed nations will need to face the unpleasant fact that, if victorious, violent insurgency headed by Marxist revolutionaries is unlikely to lead to anything but totalitarian tyranny. Armed intellectuals citing Marx and supported by Soviet-bloc arms and advisers will almost surely not turn out to be agrarian reformers, or simple nationalists, or democratic socialists. However incomprehensible it may be to some, Marxist revolutionaries are not contemporary embodiments of the Americans who wrote the Declaration of Independence, and they will not be content with establishing a broad-based coalition in which they have only one voice among many.

It may not always be easy to distinguish between democratic and totalitarian agents of change, but it is also not too difficult. Authentic democratic revolutionaries aim at securing governments based on the consent of the governed and believe that ordinary men are capable of using freedom, knowing their own interest, choosing rulers. They do not, like the current leaders in Nicaragua, assume that it will be necessary to postpone elections for three to five years during which time they can "cure" the false consciousness of almost everyone.

If, moreover, revolutionary leaders describe the United States as the scourge of the 20th century, the enemy of freedom-loving people, the perpetrator of imperialism, racism, colonialism, genocide, war, then they are not authentic democrats or, to put it mildly, friends. Groups which define themselves as enemies should be treated as enemies. The United States is not in fact a racist, colonial power, it does not practice genocide, it does not threaten world peace with expansionist activities. In the last decade especially we have practiced remarkable forbearance everywhere and undertaken the "unilateral restraints on defense spending" recommended by Brzezinski as appropriate for the technetronic era. We have also moved further, faster, in eliminating domestic racism than any multiracial society in the world or in history.

For these reasons and more, a posture of continuous self-abasement and apology vis-à-vis the Third World is neither morally necessary nor politically appropriate. No more is it necessary or appropriate to support vocal enemies of the United States because they invoke the rhetoric of popular liberation. It is not even necessary or appropriate for our leaders to forswear unilaterally the use of military force to counter military force. Liberal idealism need not be identical with masochism, and need not be incompatible with the defense of freedom and the national interest.

An Ideology That Didn't Match Reality

Sidney Blumenthal

The neoconservatives rose to prominence largely on their claims to foreign-policy mastery. In dealing with revolutions that imperil dictators friendly to the United States—revolutions in places like the Philippines—they prescribed a definitive solution: Stand by your strongman.

But as the authoritarian Marcos regime fell, so did the neoconservative theory. Some neoconservatives made a last stand on the op-ed pages, apologetically defending Marcos. But the Reagan administration, confronted with one of its greatest foreign policy crises, eventually followed a strategy that ignored the neoconservatives' formula. Though the neoconservatives offered themselves as the administration's instructors, their influence at the crucial moment proved to be virtually nil.

In 1979, Jeane Kirkpatrick, a scholar whose specialty was Peronist Argentina, presented a full-blown theory, published in *Commentary*

Sidney Blumenthal, "An Ideology That Didn't Match Reality," *Washington Post*, Mar. 2, 1986, p. C2.

magazine, attributing the fall of the Nicaraguan and Iranian autocrats to the Carter administration's "lack of realism." She derided the idea that "deep historical forces," finally beyond the control of American policy-makers, were at work. By failing to support Somoza and the shah, Carter had contributed to the rise of hostile regimes.

Carter's policy fostered instability, Kirkpatrick wrote. She dismissed the "pervasive and mistaken assumption that one can easily locate and impose democratic alternatives" in the Third World and the "equally pervasive and equally flawed belief that change per se in...autocracies is inevitable, desirable and in the American interest." She argued instead for backing "positively friendly" authoritarian rulers. And she insisted that "right wing autocracies," unlike totalitarian ones, "do sometimes evolve into democracies...."

Ronald Reagan was among the readers of Kirkpatrick's article. He was so impressed that he praised it during the 1980 campaign and named its author ambassador to the United Nations after the election.

In the 1984 campaign, during his second debate with Walter Mondale, Reagan reiterated the Kirkpatrick argument point by point. This time, he employed it specifically to describe the situation in the Philippines, asserting that failure to support "our friend" there would result in the triumph of "totalitarianism, pure and simple, as the alternative."

Thus even after Kirkpatrick left the U.N. to become a syndicated columnist, Kirkpatrickism still had the status of a reigning doctrine.

The Philippines crisis, more than any other event of the 1980s, seemed made to order for the neoconservatives. All the elements present in the Philippines were also present in their theory. There was the "positively friendly" authoritarian dictator, the communist insurgency, the moderate "third force," and clear American interests—in the form of gigantic military bases. In this living laboratory, the theory was put to the test.

In December 1985, Kirkpatrick wrote a column ranking Marcos' Philippines in the top third of U.N. members in the good-government category. The unpleasantries uncovered by "American newspapers, newsweeklies and network newscasts" reflected an "obsessive intolerance" with "a nation of great strategic importance." The shah and Somoza and other long-gone dictators were recalled. "The failings of each were magnified by people who played on American political purism...."

The pattern seemed obvious to Kirkpatrick: "Once these rulers had fallen" they were replaced by "more tragically repressive, aggressive dictatorships...." Kirkpatrick suggested that the "campaign against the government of the Philippines" might "produce similar consequences."

Early this month, she prepared another column on the Philippines, at the very moment that its presidential election was taking place. "Amer-

ican liberals," she charged, were orchestrating a "campaign...to suggest the existence of an anti-Marcos 'consensus' inside the United States government." The result was "meddling" and "interference in Philippine politics." She denounced the "American role" as not "edifying" and cast doubt on charges of Marcos' election fraud—"it seems very unlikely."

American policy-makers, she urged, must "cease" their "interference" or we would suffer the fate of the explorer Magellan, who was "hacked to death" by "the Philippine tribes." The Carter nightmare appeared to be recurring, only with Reagan in the White House.

But just as the Reagan administration was edging away from the weakening Philippine strongman, Kirkpatrick began edging away from her previously prepared column. Her line became muddy. As the column was being distributed by her syndicate, she rewrote it and sent out a revised version. In this one, she noted that "charges of fraud destroyed (the) perception" of "a creditable election."

A day after Kirkpatrick's original and altered columns simultaneously appeared in various newspapers, Reagan made the debate muddier. In an interview with the *Washington Post* on Feb. 11, the president praised the emergence of a "two party system" in the Philippines and wondered whether the election fraud was really just "one sided." That evening, Reagan continued his musings at a press conference, at which he suggested "the possibility of fraud...on both sides."

Strangely enough, Reagan's comments had little connection with the policy pursued by his administration. On the morning of his press conference, policy-makers at the White House had issued a statement expressing concern about Marcos' election fraud. The battle on the inside had already been won by those trying to extricate the U.S. from the Filipino dictator.

Most of the neoconservatives, however, were not taking their cue from the real administration position but from Reagan's remarks, which he had repudiated himself. Soon, from the neoconservative columns, came a shower of praise for the new "two party system" now in place in the Philippines.

Something was happening that was "...more important than whether Ferdinand Marcos or Corazon Aquino 'wins,'" wrote Ben Wattenberg, the neoconservative writer, in *The Washington Times*. "...[D]emocracy has won a mighty battle." In this view, the election was more meaningful as an existential act than a political one.

The emergence of a "two party system" seemed to bear out the Kirkpatrick thesis that authoritarian regimes could evolve into democracies. But in fact there were not two parties and it wasn't a system. Marcos' organization was a party in the sense that the Gambino crime family is a party. And Aquino's party was a ramshackle affair, sustained by deep popular yearnings, expressed mainly in the streets.

On Feb. 22, the neoconservatives found themselves in the unlikely and uncomfortable position of having the same line as Tass, the Soviet news agency, which attacked the U.S. for its "attempt to interfere in the internal affairs of the Philippines." To be sure, the conjunction of the neoconservatives and the Soviets as the last apologists for Marcos was a curious event. Certainly, their motives differed. The Soviets' action was a classic demonstration of cynical *realpolitik*. The neoconservatives acted out of ideological conviction. Yet both sought to put aside soft sentimentality about democratic niceties in the service of national interest.

The cardinal liberal sin, according to the neoconservatives, is "moral equivalence"—the equation of American and Russian shortcomings. But in the Philippines crisis, the neoconservatives exhibited a moral equivalence of their own—the equation of authoritarians and democrats. Because authoritarian regimes have been toppled and replaced by democratic

ones—for example, in Greece, Portugal and Argentina—the neoconservatives tend to see every permutation within authoritarianism as a hopeful step toward democracy. The conclusion they draw is that these regimes should be defended as if they were the seed of democracy, not the suffocating lid.

In the heat of the Philippines controversy, no one articulated the neoconservative sensibility better than Owen Harries, the co-editor of *The National Interest*, a neoconservative quarterly intended to tutor the Reagan administration in foreign policy. On Feb. 23, in *The New York Times*, he blamed the crisis on "the well-intentioned efforts of Americans of various political persuasions...." He claimed the mantle of a higher realism: "Moral considerations... cannot be the decisive factors leading to demands for the removal of President Marcos...." And he sketched a scenario in which Aquino's victory fostered "bloody chaos leading to the rapid growth of Communist power...." Marcos, he concluded, must stay.

Blas Ople, Marcos' Minister of Labor, agreed. In the final days, Ople achieved a certain notoriety as Marcos' spokesman on television interview shows. On Feb. 23, he appeared on "This Week With David Brinkley," where he pasted the last fig leaf on his regime: "I would like to paraphrase the distinguished ambassador to the United Nations from the United States, Jeane Kirkpatrick, who warned against a foreign policy of the United States, dedicated to the, literally, to the subjugation of a friendly nation. This is not the business of U.S. foreign policy."

But by the end, even a few neoconservatives seemed to question a theory that seemed to have so little relevance to what happened in the Philippines. Their advice had gone unheeded. They had been overrun by circumstances, unable to adjust, frozen in their past assumptions.

Charles Krauthammer, a *Washington Post* columnist with neoconservative sympathies, concluded this week that "the authoritarian-totalitarian distinction...as a guide for deciding which regime the United States will push toward democracy...has been superseded...." Thus the old neoconservative doctrine was now declared obsolete.

Perhaps the most apposite text on the neoconservatives' current condition is Kirkpatrick's famous *Commentary* essay. The "mistakes and distortions" of the Carter years were "all fashionable," she wrote. The liberals had "good intentions," but they were guilty of "idealism." They allowed the "blinding power of ideology" to govern their "interpretation of events."

11B Are developments in the Philippines that resulted in the toppling of the Marcos regime an exception to the validity of the Kirkpatrick thesis about the use of human rights as a goal of foreign policy?

YES

Jeane Kirkpatrick

Philippine Exception

NO

Sidney Blumenthal

Kirkpatrick and Democracy

Philippine Exception

Jeane Kirkpatrick

"How can Ronald Reagan bring down two right-wing authoritarian governments in a month and escape the criticism heaped on Jimmy Carter?"

"How do the events in the Philippines and Haiti fit into your analysis of authoritarian regimes?" I have been asked these questions a dozen times in recent days.

The reference is to an article I wrote in June 1979 called "Dictatorships and Double Standards," which criticized the Carter administration for bringing down authoritarian governments in Iran and Nicaragua, which were promptly replaced by revolutionary totalitarian governments.

The Carter administration, I argued, had sought to promote moderate democratic governments in Iran and Nicaragua but had instead helped to bring to power the Ayatollah Khomeini and the Ortega brothers. These failures, I suggested, were unnecessary as well as tragic because history provided ample evidence that compared with traditional autocracies, totalitarian governments were more repressive, less susceptible to liberalization and hostile to U.S. strategic interests.

While there were various examples of traditional authoritarian regimes evolving into democracies (Spain, Portugal, Greece, Venezuela), there was not one example of a totalitarian regime becoming a democracy except by war and military occupation. Therefore, no one should imagine that democracy could be achieved by supporting the rise of a Marxist or other extremist revolutionary movement. And U.S. governments concerned with protecting our interests and promoting democracy should take pains to distinguish between democratic

and totalitarian movements and support only the former. "Authentic democratic revolutionaries," I asserted, "aim at securing governments based on consent of the governed and believe that ordinary men are capable of using freedom, of knowing their own interest, and of choosing rulers."

How does that analysis apply to the Philippines? Almost not at all. The political configuration in the Philippines differed in crucial respects from that in Iran and Nicaragua. Philippine politics were not polarized between an entrenched autocrat and a totalitarian movement. Corazon Aquino's movement and her mass electorate far more closely resembled an authentic democratic reform movement than a totalitarian party. Mrs. Aquino rests her claim to legitimacy on the elections just passed. Moreover, she heads a coalition in which extremist groups clearly do not possess a monopoly of force. The Philippines has in addition a substantial experience with democracy and has just conducted broadly free elections. This further strengthened the presumption that a democratic alternative to the governing party existed.

Even in Haiti, which has far less experience with democracy and less democratic infrastructure, there was no polarized, forced choice between Baby Doc Duvalier and a totalitarian movement. The situations in Haiti and the Philippines were not analogous to those in Nicaragua and Iran, and this is the most important reason that the behavior of the Reagan administration is not analogous to that of the Carter team.

There are elements of similarity. It is true that Haiti and the Philippines had governments friendly to the United States. It is widely—almost universally—perceived that the Reagan administration actively helped to bring them down. The administration also may have helped to create instability that could lead eventually to the institutionalization of undemocratic governments that pose strategic problems for the United States. Can such a negative evolution be avoided, especially in the Philippines—where a substantial, brutal communist army already has a territorial base and, one hears, some ties to Mrs. Aquino's circle?

The answer depends on what happens now. The test of the pudding is in the eating. The test of policy is in its consequences. Carter policy failed because of what came after the shah and Somoza. We do not yet know what will come after Marcos and Duvalier.

Mrs. Aquino proved a dynamic and skillful campaigner and catalyst for anti-Marcos feeling. Will she prove equally dedicated and skillful in holding together the broad-based coalition needed to govern that heterogeneous country? Will she be inclusive, open and tolerate opposition? Will she preserve the armed forces that are the only counterforce to the New People's Army? Will she seek experts to rebuild the economy?

These questions are more important in the short run than her attitude toward U.S. bases. In any case, it is time now to rethink our relationship to those bases.

Do we really need them? Should not Japan assume a much larger responsibility for her defense and for the security of the region? After all, the Japanese are technologically sophisticated and enormously successful people. If they are informed now of an American intention to withdraw—not from a strategic role in the Pacific and not from a tactical role, but only from the Philippine bases in 1991—there would be ample time to plan for our replacement.

It makes a lot more sense than the stories of alternative sites being bruited about or permitting concern about the bases to drive our policy toward the Philippines.

Kirkpatrick and Democracy

Sidney Blumenthal

Jeane Kirkpatrick offers herself as a defender of democracy. Yet her defense of it in the Philippines came after the fact. When the dictator, Ferdinand Marcos, still held power, she supported him and scourged his opponents. When his government became shaky, she began to waver. And when he fell, she scurried to call Corazon Aquino the leader of "an authentic democratic reform movement."

Kirkpatrick's commendation, however, was intended more for her own theory than for Aquino. What happened in the Phillipines, she wrote, was an "exception" to the rule that toppling an authoritarian regime can produce a totalitarian one. It was also an exception to her fear that a principled U.S. position on human rights can accelerate the authoritarian's fall, harming the U.S. national interest. Still, Kirkpatrick's approval of Aquino was tempered. "The test of policy is in its consequences," she wrote. "...We do not yet know what will come after Marcos...." Perhaps, if Aquino fell, removing the exception to the rule, Kirkpatrickism would be thoroughly vindicated after all.

Kirkpatrick's agnosticism about democracy in the Philippines indicated her general attitude. In her usage, "democracy" was an almost completely theoretical construct. For Kirkpatrick, the trouble with her theory began when it came to empirical case studies.

Sidney Blumenthal, "Kirkpatrick and Democracy," was written especially for *The Cold War Debated*.

The Iran-Contra arms scandal provided an even more illuminating example of the Kirkpatrick approach than the Philippines "exception." To be fair, Kirkpatrick was apparently unfamiliar with the Philippines, which may have accounted for her uncharacteristic lack of certainty. That could not be said about her greatest cause—the Contras.

In November and December of 1982, according to a source intimately involved in the administration's internal councils, Kirkpatrick pushed President Ronald Reagan hard to make fervent public speeches on behalf of the Nicaraguan rebels. She also urged that the issue be taken out of the hands of the insufficiently ardent State Department. Whatever her influence, which was never great, mostly because of her grating personal style, the National Security Council began to assume more responsibility for the Contra war. And the man designated to run it was Lt. Col. Oliver North. (After the scandal broke, Kirkpatrick told acquaintants that she had not urged the White House to usurp the State Department and that she had never liked North.)

Throughout the 1986 debate in Congress over military aid to the Contras, Kirkpatrick cast it as a battle of democracy versus its enemies. On one side were the Contras and their supporters. "The Contra leadership," she wrote in a March 17 column in the *Washington Post,* "is drawn almost wholly from men who actively opposed Somoza, fought to overthrow him and sought to bring democracy to Nicaragua." As she claimed, the political leaders of the Contras included those who had opposed Somoza. But there was more to the story. They had been initially assembled by the CIA and spent much of their time bickering with each other. They were not only ineffective within Nicaragua, but within the Contra movement itself, where those who wielded the real power were the military commanders, almost exclusively men who had been members of Somoza's National Guard.

The initial training of the Contra army was conducted by the shock forces of the Argentine military dictatorship that practiced a fierce internal terrorism. These strongmen enjoyed the friendship of Kirkpatrick who, on the night Argentina invaded Britain's Falkland Islands, was dining at the Argentine embassy in Washington. The transition from authoritarianism to democracy in Argentina was made possible by the subsequent war.

Kirkpatrick also took a benign attitude toward the Chilean dictatorship. As United Nations ambassador, she traveled to Chile in August 1981. After meeting with strongman Augusto Pinochet, she said that the United States would try to "normalize completely its relations with Chile in order to work together in a pleasant way." When asked about the regime's abuses of human rights, she declined comment. The *Washington Post* reported that "former justice minister Jaime Castillo Velasco, president of the Chilean Commission on Human Rights, had tried unsuccessfully to arrange a meeting with Kirkpatrick to introduce her to representatives of an organization of relatives of the 'disappeared'—600 presumed political prisoners who disappeared after arrest by the Chilean secret police."

In the case of the Contras, Kirkpatrick's argument had a curious twist because of her previous criticism of the Carter administration, which, she wrote, "had sought to promote moderate democratic governments in Iran and Nicaragua but had instead helped to bring to power the Ayatollah Khomeini and the Ortega brothers." But who was she supporting now, at least in her own terms, if not "moderate" democrats? (Of course, Reagan defended his attempt to trade arms for hostages with the Ayatollah as an effort to build bridges to Iranian "moderates.")

Kirkpatrick discounted criticism of the Contras by challenging the motives of their critics. Those who failed to back the cause were in league with nefarious forces. "Opponents of aid,'' she wrote in the *Washington Post* on July 28, ''can be expected to concentrate on the Contras' real and imagined shortcomings, because it has become harder and harder for an American elected official to defend the government of Nicaragua.'' But Kirkpatrick neglected to name names; no official who ''defended'' the regime was cited.

Her villains, it might be said, were guilty by dissociation. Those who did not support the Contras were transformed into supporters of the Sandinistas. But she had not pioneered the method of guilt by dissociation in this debate. In March, in an article in the *Washington Post,* Patrick Buchanan, the very conservative White House communications director, said that the vote on Contra aid ''will reveal whether [the Democratic party] stands with Ronald Reagan and the resistance—or Daniel Ortega and the communists.'' Kirkpatrick's echo of Buchanan extended her theory. Just as she was dubious about an alternative to authoritarianism and totalitarianism emerging in the Third World, she seemed to be dubious about its existence in the United States.

Almost as soon as the exposure of the Reagan administration's covert dealings with Iran—and of the routing of money through Swiss bank accounts to the Contras—Kirkpatrick leaped to the administration's defense. Her justification revealed her fundamental premise that open, democratic government was dangerous in a dangerous world.

''Governments, including those of our best friends,'' she wrote in a November 16 piece in the *Washington Post,*

> normally maintain open channels and working relations with as many other governments as possible. They justify such practices in terms of strategic interests and the geopolitical balance. The belief is that maintaining contact will somehow make things better. When their nationals are held hostage, they try dealing and, on occasion, they try force. Usually they act alone. Often, they say one thing and do another. This is the way the world is.

What needed reforming, in the aftermath of the scandal, was the American mind: ''We are shocked because we are invincibly innocent about the ways governments deal with one another.'' The realpolitik Kirkpatrick advocated might even ''mean paying blackmail.''

As with her remarks about the Marcos administration, Kirkpatrick's views on the scandal were quickly revised. She tried to calm criticism by declaring her position of a week earlier a false alarm. ''...I did not intend to approve, defend or justify the actions of the Reagan administration,'' she wrote on November 24 in the *Washington Post.* And she protested that she was not an enthusiast for a pure realpolitik: ''American foreign policy should reflect our own values and goals at the same time that it seeks to protect our interests.'' But she did not bother to define what these values might be. Instead, she rushed to join the rising chorus of neoconservatives, who were lamenting that an excess of democracy was subverting a worthy foreign policy. ''But as 'politics ain't beanbag,' '' she wrote, ''international affairs are not a moral melodrama.'' The United States, it seemed, was inferior to the Old World because it lacked Europe's knowing cynicism. Kirkpatrick's logic, however, resembled a dog chasing its tail.

In part, Kirkpatrickism is about the debasement of language in the interest of ideology. ''Democracy'' is something Kirkpatrick supports in the abstract. When its messy operation produces an outcome she dislikes, she tends to attack its workings in the name of a higher realpolitik. Through the Carter and Reagan administrations alike, she has always blamed the United States first.

QUESTIONS FOR DISCUSSION

1 How consistent was the Carter administration in its pursuit of human rights in the wider world?
2 Should the United States have done more to support the Shah of Iran?

3 Was it a U.S. interest to prop up the Somoza regime in Nicaragua?

4 Should the United States pursue an identical foreign policy toward all the Marxist regimes in the Third World?

5 Why did the Reagan administration abandon the Marcos regime in the Philippines?

6 Can a consistent distinction be drawn between right-wing and left-wing dictatorships with respect to human rights?

SUGGESTED READINGS

Armacost, Michael H. "Human Rights and U.S.-Soviet Relations," *Department of State Bulletin,* **85** (Nov. 1985), pp. 58–61.

Buckley, William F., Jr. "Death Squads and U.S. Policy," *National Review,* **36** (Feb. 24, 1984), pp. 62–63.

Garthoff, Raymond L. *Detente and Confrontation: American-Soviet Relations from Nixon to Reagan.* Washington, D.C.: Brookings Institution, 1985.

Hoffmann, Stanley. "Reaching for the Most Difficult: Human Rights as a Foreign Policy Goal," *Daedalus,* **112** (Fall 1983), pp. 19–49.

Kessler, Richard J. "Marcos and the Americans," *Foreign Policy,* no. 63 (Summer 1986), pp. 40–57.

Muravchik, Joshua. *The Uncertain Crusade: Jimmy Carter and the Dilemma of Human Rights Policy.* Lanham, Md.: Hamilton Press, 1986.

Plattner, Marc F. (ed.). *Human Rights in Our Time: Essays in Memory of Victor Bares.* Boulder, Colo.: Westview Press, 1984.

Ullman, Richard. "Both National Security and Human Rights Can Be Served Simultaneously," *Center Magazine,* **17** (Mar.–Apr. 1984), pp. 21–29.

Vance, Cyrus R. "The Human Rights Imperative," *Foreign Policy,* **63** (Summer 1986), pp. 3–19.

12 Should the Reagan Doctrine be implemented?

YES

Jack Wheeler

[*In Defense of the Reagan Doctrine*]

NO

Christopher Layne

The Real Conservative Agenda

[In Defense of the Reagan Doctrine]

Jack Wheeler

The term "National Liberation Movement" has long been associated with Third World insurgencies who are anti-Western, Marxist, and backed by the Soviet Union. Today, El Salvador notwithstanding, this association is becoming a relic of the past. What is emerging is what we might call the second stage of post–World War II liberation movements. The first stage was directed at Western colonialism, which Moscow attempted to control, manipulate, and use for its own imperialist ends as much as possible. This strategy has now boomeranged on Moscow, for the majority of guerrillas and guerrilla wars in the world today are viruently anti-Soviet and anti-Marxist.

There are wars of liberation being conducted in eight Soviet colonies on three continents at this moment: in Nicaragua, Angola, Mozambique, Ethiopia, Afghanistan, Laos, Cambodia, and Viet Nam. The emergence of these Democratic Liberation Movements may well signify the end of the expansion of Soviet imperialism and the initiation of its contraction. With the era of Western imperialism over, there is a growing realization throughout the Third World that rather than Soviet Marxism being the road to the future, it is a one-way ticket to oppression and poverty, that Soviet Russia is the last great 19th century imperialist empire.

Of all the democratic insurgencies struggling against the Marxist fascism imposed upon their countries by Moscow, the one closest to outright victory is RENAMO, the Mozambique National Resistance, led by Afonso Dhlakama. Dhlakama's 20,000F guerrillas control upwards of 70% of Mozambique, and are operating on the outskirts of the capital, Maputo. The

From U.S. Cong., Senate, *U.S. Policy toward Anti-Communist Insurgencies,* Hearing before a Subcommittee of the Committee on Appropriations, 99th Cong., 1st Sess., 1985, pp. 78–84.

totalitarian dictatorship of Samora Machel does not possess the oil revenues as does its sister dictatorship in Angola to pay for Cuban mercenaries. It has thus lost its capacity to contain the rebellion.

When I interviewed Afonso Dhlakama in Africa [in 1984], he told me Renamo had two demands: the withdrawal of all foreign troops and advisors from Mozambique, including the Tanzanians, Zimbabweans, East Germans, and especially the Soviets—"the Soviet Union is the world's curse," he said—and the dismantling of the current Marxist-Leninist system, with a democratic, multi-party system and free elections in its place. "We want each Mozambican," Dhlakama said, "to peacefully conduct his life and earn his living as he sees fit—instead of being told his purpose in life is to work for the benefit of the State and of Samora Machel."

Instead of working to achieve these goals, however, the State Department has developed an almost hysterical hostility to Renamo, and is naively boasting how it can "win" Machel, a man responsible for the death and torture of tens of thousands, "over into our camp." One can have nothing but revulsion towards State's equation of cynicism with sophistication in foreign policy, and its rhetoric of "peace and stability" with the consolidation of Marxist tyranny in Mozambique—and in Angola.

The movement of UNITA, with 50,000+ guerrillas led by Dr. Jonas Savimbi, has consolidated control of one-third of Angola, substantial control of another third (that's an area much larger than Texas), and is advancing into the remaining third and upon the capital, Luanda. It takes 35,000 Cuban mercenary soldiers, paid for by Gulf Oil through its concession royalties in Cabinda, Angola, to keep the Soviet-backed Marxist-Leninist regime of the MPLA (led by Eduardo dos Santos) in power. And it is now also taking Chester Crocker and the State Department.

By not calling for "liberty and democracy" (instead of "peace and stability"), for direct talks between dos Santos and Savimbi, and Machel and Dhlakama, to negotiate a cease-fire and hold internationally-supervised elections, and for the democratization of Angola and Mozambique, Crocker and State are prolonging the conflict—and, in terms of practical politics, are backing losers. They are now part of the problem, rather than the solution.

Crocker's policies are a prime example of the piecemeal, fragmented, and inchoate foreign policy of the U.S., and highlight the obsoleteness of the policy of "containment." Some time ago, *The Wall Street Journal* ran an editorial entitled, "Why Not Victory?" The question embodies a perspective that many people at State and others in Washington seem unable to grasp. For far too long have we had a foreign policy limited to containment and defensive reaction—genuinely reactionary. We need to reorient our perspective from a strategic defense to a strategic offense—to develop an activist, forward-looking, dynamic foreign policy with the clear-cut strategic goal of destabilizing the Soviet Empire, forcefully persuading it to disarm and democratize through an energetic and orchestrated exploitation of its vulnerabilities.

The Reagan Administration has indeed made laudable steps in this direction—most especially through its attempts to aid the freedom fighters in Nicaragua, the so-called "Contras." But what the press has dubbed "The Reagan Doctrine" of support for anti-Soviet democratic liberation movements has not been put into practice consistently and coherently. Sadly, this doctrine exists more in presidential rhetoric than in deeds.

What is required is a policy of coordinated material and diplomatic support for *all* these insurgencies across the board, for the entire phenomenon of Democratic Resistance as a whole. Perhaps the best way to effect such a policy would be for the President to appoint a White House Advisor on Democratic Liberation Movements capable of coordinating such a policy and overriding obstacles caused by, e.g., State's affliction of "clientitis," and its insistence on maintaining diplomatic relations with Soviet colonies such as Afghanistan and Nicaragua.

What we must *not* do is look upon these anti-Soviet democratic insurgencies in isolation and piecemeal—but instead as all related parts of a geopolitical phenomenon of immense historical importance: that just as the Third World rejected Western colonialism in the 1950's and '60's, so it is rejecting Soviet colonialism in the 1980's.

What is *vital* for us to understand is that the Contras in Nicaragua are fighting *the same struggle* as the Mujahaddin in Afghanistan, the KPNLF in Cambodia, the ELOL in Laos, Phuc Quoc in Vietnam. Unita in Angola, Renamo in Mozambique, and the EPLF, TPLF, and others in Ethiopia.

Certainly the Soviets are making the connection. The extent of the disaster of the defeat in Congress of aid to the Contras can be seen in how Moscow is using it to weaken support for the Afghan Mujahaddin in Pakistan. Already, the Soviet-infiltrated NDP (National Democratic Party) is arguing for recognition of the Karmal puppet regime in Kabul on the grounds that the U.S. is such an unreliable ally that it is safer to cut a deal with Moscow: if the U.S. can sell out the Contras in Nicaragua, who are resisting Soviet imperialism right on the U.S. doorstep, it can sell out the Mujahaddin as well. America cannot be trusted: that is the message Soviet agents are now spreading in Pakistan and around the world in the wake of Congress' vote.

The Afghan resistance to Soviet colonization remains a national uprising on such a scale that it has no parallel in the 20th century. The

Afghans are simply the bravest people on this earth. We need to encourage the new unity of Mujahaddin groups under the leadership of Moulavi Younis Khalis. Because of our timidity with the Saudis, this unity is being undermined by the Saudis' demanding that their man— Rasul Sayyaf, who is ineffectual and has no followers but is bankrolled by the powerful Wahabi sect in Saudi Arabia—be leader instead.

An overt program of food and other humanitarian supplies should be instituted with flags flying on a Marshall Plan scale if the continued mass slaughter of civilians and an impending Soviet-manufactured famine of Ethiopian proportions is to be avoided. The resistance should receive not merely an increase in the *quantity* of weapons (which has occurred recently), but in the *quality* of weapons, most especially those capable of shutting down the airbases: 80% of all Soviet combat and logistical operations in Afghanistan are airborne.

Should the Soviets respond by stepping up subversion and sabotage in Pakistan (e.g., in Baluchistan, their next imperialist target), then we should respond in turn with a program of subversion among the Moslems of Soviet Central Asia, and encourage the Afghans to carry their Jihad into the Soviets' sanctuary. Soviet Moslems comprise the fifth largest Islamic population in the world, and are the most oppressed of all Islamic peoples. They represent a true Achilles Heel of the Kremlin's: the U.S.S.R. is itself a colonial empire within its own borders, and of all its ethnic minorities, perhaps the Soviet Moslems are the greatest potential threat to its continued existence as an intact political entity.

The Democrats in Congress are to be congratulated for taking the lead in military aid to the non-communist resistance in Cambodia. Only by strengthening the KPNLF will the Cambodian people have a third alternative to their present dilemma of continued Soviet-backed Vietnamese occupation or the nightmare of Pol Pot's Khmer Rouge seizing power again.

I can only hope that Congress would now apply the same logic to other Democratic Liberation Movements, instead of devising contrived distinctions to rationalize treating them differently. I can only hope that the House and the Senate, Democrats and Republicans, would join together with the Administration in a bipartisan committment to forthrightly and proudly assist the most thrilling and hopeful geopolitical development of our time. These Democratic Liberation Movements are on the side of history. History has now passed the Soviet Union and Marxism-Leninism by. The values we cherish, of liberal democracy and individual liberty, are what are inspiring people in the world today.

These heroic people, the Afghans, the Nicaraguans, the Cambodians, the Angolans, and others, know first hand the evil of Soviet Marxism. They are risking their lives, many sacrificing their lives, to fight against Soviet Marxism and to bring freedom to their country. These freedom fighters are on the verge of winning. They are handing us an opportunity to reduce, perhaps permanently, Soviet power and influence in the world—and thus its capacity to be a threat to our country—on a silver platter.

We are now at a real fork in the road of history. Down one path is the possibility that what the Soviets call "the correlation of forces" may turn dramatically against them. Their entire colonial structure is being challenged by the guerrilla wars being waged in eight of their colonies, and may unravel and collapse in the next few years. Down the other path is the possibility that unless we seize the window of opportunity available to us, and go on a strategic offensive against Moscow, then it will digest and consolidate its imperialist gains and soon go on the march again, whether in Central America or Baluchistan and the Saudi oilfields.

The Soviet Union bases its claim to super-power status on military force alone. Brute force is all it has left to offer the world. Only when that force ceases to be capable of achieving the continued expansion of the Soviet Empire, will Moscow turn inward to try and solve its gross economic and demographic difficulties. This is the only hope for genuine and lasting peace, for Afghanistan, for Indochina, for Central America, for Angola, Mozambique, and Ethiopia, and for the entire world.

The Real Conservative Agenda

Christopher Layne

Pushed by a group of neoconservative intellectuals, global containment is making a comeback as the cornerstone of U.S. foreign policy. It could not happen at a worse time. The United States is running enormous budget and trade deficits, economic growth is slowing, and public support for the Reagan military build-up has all but evaporated. Global containment—recast as the Reagan Doctrine—commits the United States to resisting Soviet and Soviet-supported aggression wherever it arises; to building American-style democracies in Third World countries; and to rolling back communism by aiding anticommunist insurgencies. The Reagan Doctrine aims to create an ideologically congenial world, and it assumes that America's security requires nothing less.

It is now clear that no major challenge to this quixotic quest is likely to come from the Democrats in Congress. They are in disarray, split between the "defense Democrats," who offer a "me-too" policy of getting tough with the Soviets, and those whose outlook on national security policy still is shaped by the Vietnam syndrome—reflecting the mistaken belief that the United States can remain a global power while all but ruling out using military force to protect its vital interests abroad.

Christopher Layne, "The Real Conservative Agenda," *Foreign Policy,* no. 61 (Winter 1985–86), pp. 73–93.

Therefore, it is up to the Republican party's real conservatives to offer an alternative to the neoconservative Reagan Doctrine. Because they are not liberals, real conservatives will not subordinate American national interests to the requirements of multilateralist internationalism. Real conservatives do not believe that the United States should sacrifice its political and economic interests to appease Western Europe and Japan. And real conservatives reject the idea that providing development aid, promoting human rights, and supporting international organizations should be major elements of U.S. foreign policy. But because they are not neoconservatives, real conservatives also reject the New Right's crusading ideological internationalism.

Real conservatives represent a tradition deeply rooted in America's political culture and history and associated with figures like Ohio Republican Senator Robert Taft, mid-century America's leading conservative voice, President Dwight Eisenhower, and realist scholar-diplomat George Kennan. As early as the late 1940s these men realized that America's strategic and economic circumstances required the United States to define its interests more realistically than the cold warriors of their day were doing and to reduce the scope of the country's overseas commitments. They knew that the United States has few vital interests in the Third World and that it is futile—and counterproductive—to try to mold the world in America's image. Most of all they knew that the pursuit of global containment imperils important political and economic goals at home not only dear to conservatives, but also vital for America's future: noninflationary growth, lower taxes, and fewer government controls over the private and economic lives of Americans.

The real conservatives' critique of global containment was prescient. But it also was premature. Thus when they challenged the emerging cold war orthodoxy, real conservatives lost the great debate of 1950–1951. They underestimated America's overwhelming military, political, and economic strength during that period, and their warnings about the limits of American power rang hollow. Moreover, their strong aversion to a crusading interventionist foreign policy was overcome by the ideological imperatives of the cold war. Because the real conservatives were intellectually discredited by their defeat in the great debate, the Eisenhower administration—though led by a real conservative president, notwithstanding his earlier military career—trimmed its sails to the political wind and embraced and extended the Truman administration's global containment policy.

But the Taft-Kennan critique of American foreign policy is unusually timely and penetrating today. The geopolitical changes of the last 35 years have finally validated their analysis. Thus the real conservatives of America's successor generation are charged with the task of rediscovering their intellectual antecedents and of building upon them to frame a new foreign-policy synthesis that reconciles a realistic policy of selective containment abroad with the advancement of conservative values at home.

Debates about foreign policy often boil down to clashes of ideas about the nature of international politics. This is especially true of the clash between real conservatives and neoconservatives, which forces Americans once again to examine the fundamental objectives of their foreign policy.

Should America attempt to contain the spread of communist ideology worldwide and try to impose democracy on repressive regimes? Or should it follow a more traditional balance-of-power policy that aims only at containing the expansion of Soviet political influence and military power in regions truly vital to U.S. national security? When should the United States intervene militarily in overseas conflicts? How much can America afford to do in the world and what is the proper balance between the country's goals overseas and its domestic aspirations?

NEOCONSERVATIVES VERSUS REAL CONSERVATIVES

Real conservatives and neoconservatives are especially divided over the questions of what America should do and what it can afford to do. To the extent it seriously addresses these questions at all, the Reagan Doctrine offers simple answers. Its neoconservative authors depict world politics as a Manichaean struggle between democracy and communism. Neoconservatives believe that the primary threat to the United States is ideological and that the balance of power is fragile. When combined, these two assumptions suggest that if America fails to resist the advance of communism worldwide, its allies and neutrals will realign with the U.S.S.R.

According to the Reagan Doctrine, communist ideology per se threatens American security. Neoconservative intellectuals like Norman Podhoretz and Irving Kristol, who have given the Reagan Doctrine its conceptual underpinnings, stress that America is locked in an ideological struggle with communism rather than in a traditional great-power rivalry with the Soviet Union.[1]

Because it equates American security with an ideologically compatible world, the Reagan

[1] See Podhoretz, "The Future Danger," *Commentary* (April 1981).

Doctrine is classically Wilsonian. Thus Secretary of State George Shultz frequently says that America must use its power to preserve an international environment conducive to the survival of its values, and he warns that the defeat of "democracy" by communism anywhere jeopardizes American security everywhere. Like the political scientist Michael Ledeen, writing in the March 1985 issue of Podhoretz's journal, *Commentary,* neoconservatives believe that America's task "is actively to encourage non-democratic governments to democratize and to aid democratic movements that challenge totalitarian and authoritarian regimes." Like all Wilsonians, neoconservatives justify these beliefs by arguing that the world would be peaceful and harmonious if only non-democratic states (which are inherently bad) became democratic states (which are inherently good). This explains Shultz's insistence, in a February 1985 speech, that there is a worldwide "democratic revolution" that America must support in word and deed by standing for "freedom and democracy not only for ourselves but for others."

Superimposed on their ideological view of world politics is the neoconservatives' conviction that the balance of power is precarious and unstable and that America's overseas commitments are interdependent—which explains the fear that any failure of American resolve will erode U.S. credibility and lead to a worldwide stampede to the Soviet camp. The view that states tend to engage in what political scientist Kenneth Waltz of the University of California at Berkeley calls "bandwagoning" behavior lies behind Shultz's April 1984 statement that American credibility is itself a vital national interest that the United States must fight to preserve.

The Reagan Doctrine also holds that the Third World is the critical battleground in the war against communism. It is in Angola, Afghanistan, Cambodia, and Nicaragua that Shultz says America must halt the spread of communism. "It is in the Third World rather than in the United States or Europe," Podhoretz wrote in *Commentary* in 1981, "that Communism remains the greatest ideological menace." Consequently, the Third World is where American neoconservatives are pushing the administration, with some success, to organize an international alliance of "democratic freedom fighters." The president himself declared in February 1985: "We must not break faith with those who are risking their lives—on every continent...to defy Soviet-supported aggression and secure rights which have been ours since birth. Support for freedom fighters is self-defense."

Like the global containment policy of the pre-Vietnam years, the Reagan Doctrine has no obvious limits. Because it does not differentiate between what is vital and what is merely desirable, the doctrine holds that U.S. security is endangered by communism wherever it takes hold. If so, however, the United States must resist communism and defend democracy everywhere. Such a policy will make America ever more dangerously overextended. Although the administration's policies to date have been restrained, words and ideas do have consequences.

The Reagan Doctrine is a throwback to the global containment policy that characterized the cold war liberalism of Presidents Harry Truman, John Kennedy, and Lyndon Johnson. This strategy, and the Manichaean convictions on which it was based, reached its zenith in Kennedy's ringing inaugural vow in 1961 that the United States would "pay any price, bear any burden" to defeat communism around the world, and in then Secretary of State Dean Rusk's assertion that U.S. national security required nothing less than making the total international political environment ideologically safe. But if these goals ever were realistic, they certainly are not today.

Real conservatives should oppose the Reagan Doctrine on three principal grounds: In current and foreseeable circumstances it can bankrupt America; the American people wisely have no stomach for it; and it is based on a fundamental misreading of America's real interests and of the way in which countries behave.

The Reagan Doctrine calls for extending U.S. foreign commitments precisely at a time when circumstances require their reduction. Before Vietnam, U.S. hegemony was based firmly on strategic nuclear superiority and overwhelming economic muscle. Today, the former is gone and the latter is degenerating. To take one indicator, in 1945 the United States accounted for approximately one-half of world manufacturing output, and in 1953 this figure stood at a still formidable 44.7 per cent.[2] It was during this period of economic and political predominance that America assumed the commitments to defend Western Europe, Japan and Korea, and the Mediterranean and the Middle East that have formed the core of its global strategy for the past 35 years.

By 1980, however, the United States accounted for only 31.5 per cent of world manufactures, and this share could fall to 20 per cent by the end of the century. Yet during the last 6 years U.S. commitments abroad actually have increased as America has assumed responsibilities in the Persian Gulf and Central America. As a March 1985 Congressional Research Service report entitled *U.S.-Soviet Military Balance, 1980–1985* states, "Our military force structure is inadequate to meet our formal and informal worldwide military commitments." The Reagan Doctrine, however, suggests that America will incur further obligations in the Third World.

THE POWER-INTERESTS GAP

America can balance its power and commitments in two ways: It can increase its power or

reduce its commitments. The Reagan Doctrine explicitly rejects the notion of curtailing America's obligations. Former Secretary of Defense James Schlesinger told the Senate Foreign Relations Committee in February 1985: "For any great power—and most notably the protecting superpower of the West—to back away from commitments is more easily said than done. In practice, the loss in prestige may actually reduce our power more than the reduced claims on our military resources enhances that power." Therefore, Reagan Doctrine supporters must assume that the power-interests gap can be closed by increasing America's capabilities. This is extremely doubtful.

The Reagan defense program has been denounced vehemently as excessive. The administration's build-up does lack a coherent, realistic, strategic rationale, but by pre-Vietnam standards, the administration's military outlays have not been extravagant. From 1955 to 1970 defense spending stood consistently between 8 per cent and 9 per cent of gross national product (GNP)—only dipping below this range in 1965—and accounted for 40–45 per cent of annual federal outlays. In contrast, the Reagan administration's original fiscal 1986 defense proposal called for spending just under 8 per cent of GNP on the military—about 30 per cent of total federal spending.

Nevertheless, widespread perceptions that the administration's defense budgets are exorbitant and lack an overall strategic design have already killed the chances of congressional or public support for even modest real increases. Yet current spending fails to meet the country's present strategic commitments. Indeed, during Reagan's presidency, despite the administration's military build-up, the power-interests gap has widened. The country shows no signs of wanting to pay for the Reagan Doctrine.

Not only has America's international economic and political power waned, but also its domestic economy by any measure is much less robust than during the period of American

[2] Paul M. Kennedy, "The First World War and the International Power System," *International Security* 9, no. 1 (Summer 1984): 36–39.

hegemony. The persistent and worsening federal deficits of the past 30 years symbolize both America's decline and its current economic predicament. The deficit attests to the country's inability to set priorities and to live within its means. As the political scientist David Calleo and many others have suggested, deficits and strategic overextension really are two sides of the same coin. Taken together, they indicate that America's aspirations at home and abroad have outstripped its ability— or willingness—to pay for them.

The federal deficit endangers America's economic well-being, primarily by raising the risk of renewed runaway inflation. This is why real conservatives in the Senate, such as the majority leader, Robert Dole (R.-Kansas), and California Republican Pete Wilson, have worked so hard to achieve major deficit reductions in fiscal year 1986.

Ronald Reagan was elected in 1980 largely because of a pledge to reverse America's economic decline by cutting taxes to stimulate productivity, reducing government spending to curb inflation, and removing pervasive governmental regulations that stifled initiative and creativity. But budget deficits in the hundreds of billions of dollars now loom "as far as the eye can see" on the economic horizon, and the military build-up required to implement the Reagan Doctrine will only make matters worse. Apparently neoconservatives think that America can afford this no matter what it costs and that the country can embark on foreign-policy crusades without paying for them. Common sense says otherwise. As Senator Barry Goldwater (R.-Arizona) says, "[Y]ou can't keep pumping out money you don't have." Sooner or later America will pay for the Reagan Doctrine's almost limitless appetite for defense outlays, either with higher taxes, inflation, or both. These are not attractive options.

The United States can avoid this choice only with big cuts in government spending. Obviously, the burden of such cuts should not fall on the military budget alone. But like all advanced societies, the United States is to some degree an entitlement society, and beyond a certain point reductions in domestic spending provoke too much opposition for politicians to ignore.

Moreover, America's ability to sustain any level of strategic commitments depends on its economic strength. In a real sense the economy is the fourth branch of the armed forces. Under the Reagan Doctrine, the country would have to come very close to full mobilization to close the gap between its power and its responsibilities. The threat posed by such a policy to America's prosperity and freedoms is incalculable.

Unlike past and present advocates of global containment, real conservatives have always understood this. As Taft once observed, no country "can be constantly prepared to undertake a full-scale war at any moment and still hope to maintain any of the other purposes in which people are interested and for which nations are founded."[3] Few more poignant statements of these concerns can be found than Eisenhower's April 1953 speech to the American Society of Newspaper Editors declaring that "every gun that is made...signifies, in the final sense, a theft from those who hunger and are not fed, and those who are cold and are not clothed."

Real conservatives have recognized that a tension always exists between the needs of an interventionist foreign policy and those of a healthy economy. Taft predicted that global containment would impose "tremendous" economic burdens and threaten the country's prosperity. Eisenhower's Secretary of State John Foster Dulles warned that large defense outlays "unbalance our budget and require taxes so heavy that they discourage incentive. They so cheapen the dollar that savings, pensions, and

[3] *A Foreign Policy for Americans* (Garden City, N.Y.: Doubleday and Co., 1951), 68.

Social Security reserves already have lost most of their value."[4]

It was Eisenhower who put the point in sharp focus. Economic strength, he said, is the foundation of military power. Americans must be careful, Eisenhower warned, that their foreign-policy objectives do not become so ambitious that their pursuit ends up destroying what they seek to defend—the vitality and strength of America's political and economic institutions.[5] These are precisely the institutions that could be threatened by the Reagan Doctrine's version of global containment.

The all-but-evaporated public support for bigger defense budgets is only one signal that the American people want nothing to do with policies like the Reagan Doctrine. The doctrine purports to be a policy of strength and—on the declaratory level—is meant to rally the public behind the administration's defense build-up and U.S. intervention in Central America. But the more neoconservatives talk about a global anticommunist crusade, the more public anxiety they create about a possible superpower confrontation, thereby diminishing support for a policy of strength. Because the doctrine fails to set military and foreign-policy priorities, Americans know only that it will be expensive. They have difficulty seeing how this policy has made them stronger. There is a risk of what is known as mirror-imaging here: The public may become so disillusioned with the Reagan Doctrine's costs that, like the neoconservatives, it may lose the ability to distinguish between those military programs America needs and those it does not.

Moreover, the Reagan Doctrine's interventionist instincts run counter to the public's desire for noninvolvement in the rest of the world—especially in the Third World. Most

Americans view the Third World as an unpleasant place: the home of corrupt regimes and equally nasty revolutionaries. U.S. intervention there, it is felt, will hurt America without helping others. Americans strongly oppose prolonged and costly military involvement in Third World countries and know that there are many more potential Vietnams than potential Grenadas. They understand that not even superpowers are omnipotent, and that the United States lacks the material, psychological, and spiritual resources to remake the world in its own image. And they remember that rhetorical excesses ("pay any price, bear any burden") can easily lead to foreign-policy excesses. Americans will be more likely to support intervention to defend the country's vital interests in Central America if they are reassured that this policy is not simply a prelude to an endless series of entanglements in faraway, insignificant lands, involving people of whom they know little or nothing.

PAYING THE PRICE

If global containment is economically and politically beyond America's reach, how then can the United States accomplish the admittedly vital objective of containing the Soviet Union? First, by taking advantage of the natural dynamics of the international balance of power. Second, by defining its national interests more realistically.

The Reagan Doctrine implicitly assumes that the United States is not doing enough in the world. But the first objective of U.S. policy must be to compel others—namely, Western Europe and Japan—to do much more so that America can do much less.

One leading cause of America's relative decline in power is the increase in West European and Japanese economic power since the end of World War II. Yet the distribution of military responsibilities in Western Europe and Japan still reflects the conditions of 40 years ago.

---

[4] "A Foreign Policy of Boldness," *Life*, 19 May 1952, 146.
[5] Quoted in John Lewis Gaddis, *Strategies of Containment* (New York: Oxford University Press, 1982), 134-136.

Japan, the world's second-ranking economic power, spends a mere 1 per cent of its GNP on defense and depends completely on the United States for its security. Taken as a unit, the economies of NATO's European members compare favorably to America's, but these countries devote considerably less of their individual GNPs to defense. More to the point, a recent Pentagon study indicates that the U.S. commitment to NATO accounts for some 58 per cent of America's own defense budget.[6]

America's early postwar policy aimed to assist Western Europe and Japan in their respective recoveries in the expectation that they could resume some semblance of their traditional international roles and relieve the United States of its global burdens. The U.S. commitment to this reconstruction—and to its corollary, multilateral free trade—made it inevitable that these countries would be strengthened at America's expense. But this was judged an acceptable price to pay because, on balance, the United States would be better off in a world where Western Europe and Japan could protect themselves. Today, America continues to pay the price for its postwar policy but is not reaping any of the benefits.

The United States should complete its historic postwar mission and devolve to Western Europe and Japan full responsibility for their own defense. What Washington needs—and what real conservatives should offer—is a sequel to the Marshall Plan. This far-sighted program helped Europe recover its economic independence. "Marshall Plan II" would build on the economic strength of Western Europe and Japan and allow them to become politically and militarily independent. To avoid leaving these countries out in the cold, the United States should set a firm timetable for a phased, long-term American withdrawal—perhaps over 10 years—coupled with an invitation to Western

Europe and Japan to formulate their own postalliance defense plans. Washington would give them the assistance they needed to implement these plans. But when the transition period ended, U.S. defense commitments would terminate.

Western Europe and Japan unquestionably have the capability to defend themselves. Marshall Plan II would give them the incentive—which they will lack as long as they remain under the American umbrella—to transform their resources into real military power. Marshall Plan II may or may not lead to the pentagonal balance of power of which former President Richard Nixon and his secretary of state, Henry Kissinger, once spoke. But for this new U.S. policy to work these countries need only become strong enough to act as credible regional counterweights to the Soviet Union. This they easily can do.

The older generation of American policymakers—accustomed to U.S. hegemony—is temperamentally unable to contemplate the measures required to balance U.S. commitments and resources. However, because it is the first group of Americans in this century to experience something other than American omnipotence in world politics, the successor generation is more prepared to undertake the major strategic reorientation needed to bring about this balance.

Marshall Plan II also would be opposed on the ground that postalliance Europe would fall under the Kremlin's control. But here American and European Atlanticists join with many neoconservatives in fundamentally misperceiving the nature of world politics. States tend to balance—not to jump on bandwagons. As the Princeton University political scientist Stephen M. Walt wrote in the Spring 1985 issue of *International Security:*

Threatening states will provoke others to align against them. Because those who seek to dominate others will attract widespread opposition,

---

[6] Richard Halloran, "Europe Called Main U.S. Arms Cost," *New York Times,* 20 July 1984, 2.

status quo states can take a relatively sanguine view of threats. Credibility is less important in a balancing world because one's allies will resist threatening states out of their own self-interest, not because they expect others to do it for them. Thus the fear that allies will defect declines. Moreover, if balancing is the norm *and* if statesmen understand this tendency, aggression is discouraged because those who contemplate it will anticipate resistance.

Indeed, history provides many examples of balancing behavior. In the nuclear era, China has balanced against the menacing and proximate power of the Soviet Union by entering into an informal strategic entente with the United States. During the era of U.S. hegemony, Charles de Gaulle's France maximized its independence by moving away from the United States and edging slightly toward the Soviet Union. But in the late 1970s and early 1980s, the shift of the strategic nuclear balance toward Moscow caused Paris to tilt back toward Washington.[7] Benito Mussolini's Italy, in fact, is recent history's only major example of "bandwagoning," and all Europeans know the price his country paid.

West Europeans have strong reasons for exploiting U.S. fears that they will jump on Moscow's bandwagon if America withdraws from the Continent. They find the Atlanticist status quo comfortable. But surely Western Europe's leaders are smart enough to realize that weak states that align themselves with strong states are at the mercy of the stronger powers. Moreover, Europe's diplomatic history is the history of the balance of power. Before World War I, European states balanced against Germany's drive for continental hegemony, and they coalesced against Charles V of the Holy Roman Empire, Louis XIV of France, Napoleon I, and Adolf Hitler. Indeed, the revival of the Western European Union, recent efforts to improve Franco–West German defense cooperation, and various West European proposals for an independent West European nuclear force suggest that Western Europe already is thinking about its strategic posture in a postalliance world.

There is a small risk that Western Europe might choose to join the U.S.S.R.'s bandwagon after a U.S. withdrawal. But the United States runs a much greater risk in refusing to think about life after NATO. Although many leaders choose to deny it, the evidence of NATO's progressive, inevitable decay is overwhelming. Unlike their elders, successor generation real conservatives do not have a romanticized view of the Western alliance. Because geopolitical circumstances change, alliances never last forever. NATO is unraveling because Western Europe and America have very different perceptions of the Soviet threat and because they are divided by major, deepening divergences of their principal political, strategic, and economic interests.

In these circumstances, America's willingness to maintain its commitment to Western Europe is bound to diminish—especially as Americans become more fully aware of the nuclear dangers and economic costs of this commitment. At the same time, Western Europe's restlessness with America's dominance is growing, and West European countries are increasingly asserting their independence from the United States. Paradoxically, the tensions that result from trying to preserve the facade of alliance unity offer Moscow its best chance to permanently damage U.S.–West European relations.[8]

The emergence of a postalliance world can either strengthen or weaken the United States: It all depends on how America gets there. A managed transition like Marshall Plan II will maxi-

---

[7] See Stanley Hoffmann, "Gaullism by Any Other Name," *Foreign Policy* 57 (Winter 1984–85).

[8] These arguments are developed in Christopher Layne, "Toward German Reunification?" *Journal of Contemporary Studies* (Fall 1984), and "Ending the Alliance," *Journal of Contemporary Studies* (Summer 1983).

mize the likelihood of a positive outcome. An ostrich-like policy that lets events run their course on the assumption that NATO will last forever will make the reverse more likely. Wise leadership does not resist the inevitable; it seeks to turn the inevitable to its own advantage.

CRITERIA FOR INTERVENTION

Balancing the ends and means of U.S. policy also requires the United States to define more realistically its goals for the Third World. The United States has few tangible interests in the Third World that compel military or even extensive political involvement. There is no Third World region or country whose loss would decisively tip the superpower balance against America—including the Persian Gulf, whose oil is vital only to Western Europe and Japan, and whose defense would be handled by these countries under Marshall Plan II. The United States is not economically dependent on Third World markets. And its current reliance on Third World raw materials can be minimized by diversifying sources of supply, by stockpiling, by developing synthetic replacements, and by using natural substitutes.

Instead, U.S. involvement in the Third World flows mainly from intangible concerns. Americans often fear that their failure to step into Third World conflicts will lead to Soviet gains. This is the price Americans pay for regarding the world as both politically and ideologically bipolar. This perspective rules out the existence of marginal areas and depicts international politics as a zero-sum game in which a single setback will inevitably have repercussions elsewhere.

The Reagan Doctrine in fact creates a self-fulfilling prophecy by failing to distinguish vital from secondary interests. When Washington says a particular outcome would be a defeat—or that U.S. interests in some part of the world are "vital"—others believe it. Thus the doctrine's rhetoric presents the country with two equally bad alternatives in the Third World: using American power to prevent political changes defined as "unacceptable," or accepting the unacceptable—with consequent damage to U.S. credibility. A wise foreign policy does not paint policymakers into corners like this.

America's avowed ideological interest in containing communism and supporting democracy also motivates U.S. involvement in the Third World. It is unclear whether neoconservatives actually believe—as did Rusk—that the United States can be secure only when its total international environment is safe. But it is clear that they believe—as the University of Maryland political scientist George Quester wrote in *Foreign Policy* 40 (Fall 1980)—that "the politics of Minnesota would also work in Burma or Kenya or Cuba or Algeria." But the question arises: How much are Americans prepared to pay to bring this about?

Any such attempt probably will prove costly and ultimately futile. In a world torn by political, social, and religious upheaval and by Third World nationalism, violence is endemic and conflicts usually intractable. Thus Third World interventions by outside powers recently have run into major troubles: America in Vietnam, the Soviet Union in Afghanistan, the United States and Israel in Lebanon. Both superpowers' inability to influence events in the Persian Gulf war illustrates the same point.

Because nationalism runs so high in the Third World, superpower intervention is resented, and its costs usually exceed the benefits. Although Americans find it difficult to accept, most states want to increase their independence from both superpowers, and an overly active U.S. policy in the Third World may have the perverse effect of pushing developing countries toward Moscow. Regardless of whether the Reagan Doctrine really seeks to impose American values on the Third World, crusading American rhetoric convinces other countries that America intends to do so, and they feel threatened. "Certainly," as Taft observed, "however benevolent we might be, other people simply do not like to be dominated, and we would be in the same position of suppressing rebellions by force in which the British found themselves during the nineteenth century."[9]

Ironically, despite Third World fears of U.S. domination, America exercises virtually no control over "friendly" developing countries or over anti-Soviet "freedom fighters." They may be allies, but they are peculiar allies, because they are no more committed to liberal democratic values than are their Marxist opponents. It is naive to imagine that American political values could flourish in countries that have no indigenous democratic traditions and that lack the social, cultural, and economic institutions upon which the U.S. democratic structure rests. America's continuing search for a "third force" between the totalitarians and authoritarians of the Left and the Right is unavailing. Political pluralism in the Third World is not promoted by America's choosing among equally unsavory groups whose brutality is distinguishable only by whether it is used to hold power or to seize it.

U.S. interests may be threatened by Third World conflicts. But the United States is not threatened by the spread of communism per se. As became apparent when Josip Broz Tito's Yugoslavia broke with the Kremlin, and again when China and the U.S.S.R. split, nationalism can impel even communist governments to follow anti-Soviet policies. It is other countries' foreign policies, not their domestic systems, with which the United States must be concerned. The impact on U.S. interests of communism's advance into a particular place depends, as Kennan noted, on such questions as whether and to what extent a region's loss would augment Soviet strength and shift the

balance of power.[10] Also pertinent is whether America's historical involvement in the threatened area is so deep that a U.S. setback could justifiably damage American credibility; whether U.S. intervention would be necessary to force Moscow to recognize the legitimacy of U.S. geopolitical interests; and how important the threatened area is to the security of the American homeland.

But in his *Memoirs* Kennan also pointed out that the existence of a threat to American interests is "only the beginning, not the end, of the process" of deciding whether to plunge into the Third World. Kennan—and more recently, Secretary of Defense Caspar Weinberger, in a widely noted November 1984 speech to the National Press Club—set out similar criteria on which such a decision must turn. Above all, American troops and resolve should never be used as a substitute for the troops and resolve of others.

THE CENTRAL AMERICA DEBATE

The difference between the neoconservative and the real conservative approaches to America's Third World policy is illustrated by the debate over U.S. Central America policy. Central America is no more hospitable a theater for direct U.S. military involvement than is the rest of the Third World. Yet the United States has a strong interest in maintaining a favorable political and strategic environment in neighboring areas. Moreover, a stable superpower relationship requires each superpower to respect the other's critical sphere of influence. The Soviets are not likely to show such respect, however, unless America so compels them by assertively defending U.S. interests.

Although the loss of Central America would not decisively affect America's core security, America does have important strategic interests in the Caribbean Basin, such as Mexican and

[9] Quoted in Ronald Radosh, *Prophets on the Right* (New York: Simon and Schuster, 1975), 139.

[10] Gaddis, *Strategies of Containment*, 40–42.

Venezuelan oil, the Panama Canal, and the Caribbean sea-lanes. Moreover, America's strategic position obviously would be less comfortable if Mexico turned pro-Soviet. Taken individually, none of these interests is vital enough to justify direct U.S. military involvement. But taken collectively, they are.

Still, Americans must be clear on what does and does not justify U.S. military intervention in Central America. Neoconservatives, until recently at least, have not decided whether the Nicaraguan threat is ideological or geopolitical. If the former, the United States can accept nothing less than the Sandinistas' overthrow, and direct U.S. military intervention is very likely at some point.

Real conservatives see the threat as geopolitical: They insist that the United States cannot allow Nicaragua to become a Soviet satellite or to use force and subversion to export its revolution. But they do not believe that Washington's interests are threatened by the Sandinistas' domestic policies in and of themselves. These policies are odious, but they are the Nicaraguan people's business, not America's. For real conservatives it is not necessarily the case that the United States must overthrow the Sandinistas, because they can envision the possibility of a political accommodation that would exchange an American guarantee of noninterference in Nicaragua's internal affairs for the withdrawal of all Soviet-bloc, Cuban, Libyan, and Palestine Liberation Organization military advisers from Nicaragua; the cessation of Sandinista support for Central American insurgents; and strict quantitative and qualitative limits on Nicaragua's armed forces. These terms will ensure that Nicaragua does not become a Soviet satellite.

Real conservatives recognize that war is a continuation of politics by other means and that U.S. policy must combine force and diplomacy to compel changes in Nicaraguan policies that threaten regional security. Thus the United States must support the anti-Sandinista *contra* forces and exert other forms of military and economic pressure, because, otherwise, the Sandinistas have little incentive to accommodate U.S. wishes.

Central America, however, is a special case for real conservatives. They agree with neoconservatives that Moscow should not have a free ride in the Third World and that, within well-defined limits, the United States should do what it can to make the Soviets pay for their interventions. But real conservatives also know that vital American interests are not engaged in Afghanistan, Angola, Cambodia, and similar Third World hot spots, and they are under no illusions that the anti-Soviet groups in these places are fighting for liberal democracy. Neoconservatives talk as if the contrary is true, and this is one reason that the Reagan Doctrine's implications are so disturbing. By placing so much emphasis on the "worldwide democratic revolution" and on U.S. support for anti-Soviet forces, the Reagan Doctrine may link American prestige and credibility to the outcome of these peripheral conflicts. The Reagan Doctrine forgets that in the real, balancing world there are, in fact, many areas of only marginal importance to America.

But real conservatives are realists. Although today there is nothing in the Third World other than Central America vital enough to compel U.S. military intervention, they know that circumstances can change and that some other region or country could become vitally important to the United States in the future. But before they take the United States down the interventionist road, real conservatives will recall Taft's advice: "Our people...cannot send armies to block a communist advance in every far corner of the world."

America's experience as a world power has been unique because for much of that time its power was unchallenged. Obviously, this no longer is true. Everywhere are the signs of a more plural international system—a system America helped create. Yet American foreign-policymakers still do not understand that the era of American predominance was an anomaly, not the historical norm. The Reagan Doctrine's neoconservative authors in particular seem to be caught in some Spielbergian time warp that has transported them back to the early 1950s. They talk as if the relative decline of American power, and Vietnam, had never occurred. They do not understand that the end of American hegemony was brought about by complex, objective geopolitical factors; it is not something that can be reversed merely by an assertion of national will.

The most critical functions of political leaders in a democratic society are to define the national agenda and to educate the public. The Reagan Doctrine's creators seemingly do not understand what the important issues are. The Republican party stands at the threshold of majority status. But power brings responsibility, and America needs an alternative to the Reagan Doctrine. It falls to real conservatives of America's successor generation to provide it—first by changing the terms of the foreign-policy debate and then by changing U.S. foreign policy itself. The essence of a conservative policy is to preserve national strength, husband resources, and expend them wisely. The successor generation's real conservatives must carry the message that American power is finite and that not even a superpower can impose order on a recalcitrant world. The attempt can lead only to exhaustion, to dangerous overextension, and to lasting damage to the fabric of American society.

QUESTIONS FOR DISCUSSION

1 How far has the Reagan Doctrine been only a matter of rhetoric?
2 Should the United States attach more importance to securing or protecting friendly regimes in Central America than elsewhere?
3 Has the United States too many military commitments in the world?
4 Are U.S. economic problems caused mainly by the existence of overseas commitments?
5 Which, if any, Marxist regimes could be overthrown by U.S.-supported guerrilla groups?

SUGGESTED READINGS

Bode, William R. "The Reagan Doctrine," *Strategic Review,* 14 (Winter 1986), pp. 21–29.
Harries, Owen. "Doctrine Overdose," *New Republic,* 194 (May 5, 1986), pp. 17–18.
"Interventionism: An Exchange," *New Republic,* 194 (Apr. 28, 1986), pp. 20–21.
Kirkpatrick, Jeane J. "Anti-Communist Insurgency and American Policy," *National Interest,* no. 1 (Fall 1985), pp. 91–96.
Krauthammer, Charles. "The Poverty of Realism," *New Republic,* 194 (Feb. 17, 1986), pp. 14–18, 20–22.
Ledeen, Michael. "How to Support the Democratic Revolution," *Commentary,* 79 (Mar. 1985), pp. 43–46.
Liska, George. "The Reagan Doctrine: Monroe and Dulles Reincarnate," *SAIS Review,* 6 (Summer–Fall 1986), pp. 83–98.
Rosenfeld, Stephen S. "The Guns of July," *Foreign Affairs,* 64 (Spring 1986), pp. 698–714.
U.S. Cong., Senate. *U.S. Policy toward Anti-Communist Insurgencies,* Hearing before a Subcommittee of the Committee on Appropriations, 99th Cong., 1st Sess., 1985.

CHAPTER 4

INSTRUMENTS OF POWER

Rarely can analysts say with confidence that a state has clear and unambiguous goals, certain to be pursued with consistency over a protracted period. Even in such cases analysts are not in a position to forecast accurately the unfolding of events. Moreover, sovereign states have a great variety of options when it comes to pursuing such clear goals as they may actually have. These we call instruments of power.

The debates in this chapter are concerned primarily with the use of such instruments rather than with any particular goals that the superpowers may have in view. Such instruments include military, economic, rhetorical, and covert methods.

ECONOMIC LEVERAGE

The United States has a great advantage in the Cold War: its economy is in almost every respect superior to that of the Soviet Union. This superiority has meant that on many occasions the United States has been able to provide economic support for its friends and allies on a scale that the U.S.S.R. has had no possibility of matching. For example, the Soviets give massive assistance to Castro's government in Cuba, but almost certainly they could not multiply that assistance if large numbers of Latin American countries also acquired pro-Soviet regimes and asked for similar support. On the other hand, the United States was able in the postwar years to provide economic assistance to large numbers of countries, not least in war-devastated Western Europe under the terms of the Marshall Plan of 1947. Indeed, the United States has not had to contemplate some military actions because timely economic moves have bolstered friendly regimes that otherwise might have found themselves facing subversion or even civil wars. In contrast, had the Soviet Union been able to give more economic aid to *its* friends, it might have avoided military actions within its much smaller sphere of influence. The need to send tanks into Hungary and Czechoslovakia in 1956 and 1968 respectively might, for example, have been averted.

If economic assistance can sustain friendly regimes, denial of such assistance can be no less important and effective. Here again the United States has the advantage over the Soviet Union. Such measures as the cutting off of U.S. aid or the erection of protective barriers to trade in certain commodities can be highly effective in destabilizing disapproved regimes, as Chile under the quasi-Marxist government of Salvador Allende discovered in the early 1970s. And often the mere threat of such action can have a potent effect on countries that are undecided about the course to follow.

Economic leverage is thus obviously important in the superpower competition for influence in the wider world. Some experts believe, moreover, that it is no less effective in shaping the central superpower relationship itself. This proposition is controversial, however, and it often divides Western "hawks" and "doves" among themselves. Some "hawks" believe that the Soviets are in such dire need of U.S. advanced technology and grain supplies, for example, that they will pay a high political price provided the United States has the sense to demand it and is not undermined by its NATO allies. Others contend that the Soviet tyranny is so rigid and confident that it is unlikely to respond much to either economic threats or economic inducements from Washington.

Western "doves" are likewise divided. Some hold that the Soviet Union can be hurt by sanctions but that in practice it will not, as a world superpower, allow itself to be seen as pushed around. They accordingly counsel against the use of economic leverage to destabilize the Soviet regime or even to try for concessions out of Moscow, courses they consider doomed to be counterproductive and possibly increasing international tensions. Other "doves" are more skeptical about the extent to which the Soviet Union can be said to be truly vulnerable to Western economic pressures. They question their opponents' opinion that the Soviet economy is in unprecedented crisis and believe economic sanctions against Moscow are simply futile.

Given such a multiplicity of possible positions dividing both "hawks" and "doves," it need not surprise us that some commentators do not fall neatly into any particular category. Such is the case with both Bruce W. Jentleson and Edward A. Hewett, whose views constitute our first debate in this chapter. Broadly, however, the latter is more skeptical than the former about the possibilities for applying effective U.S. economic leverage on Moscow.

SPONSORSHIP OF TERRORISM

The superpowers—as well as many other states—have another means of exerting leverage over adversaries. They can engage in acts of violence designed to destabilize or overthrow an unfriendly regime. In common parlance this activity is known as sponsoring terrorism. But the term "terrorism" is pejorative, so if one favors such violence in a particular case one tends to talk of a "freedom struggle." In a very real sense, one person's terrorist is another person's freedom fighter.

In recent years there has been a striking growth in this kind of terrorism (or, to use detached terminology, "substate violence"). Many Western experts believe that the increase is in the main due to the covert activities of the Soviet Union, which has the advantage of a revolutionary rhetoric that appeals ideologically to a large variety of terrorist groups. Nobody claims, of course, that *every* terrorist incident is planned in Moscow. But there are many in Washington, and especially among those close to the Reagan administration, who see the Soviets as responsible for orchestrating a great deal of terrorism—even that which derives from apparently unconnected Islamic terrorist groups. This assessment is, however, controversial, as our next debate illustrates.

The Wall Street Journal, in an editorial dated June 25, 1985, advanced the thesis that sees the Soviets and their allies in the center of a "Terror Network." But a critic of this outlook, Alexander Cockburn, published a refutation in the same newspaper. Not only does he doubt the involvement of the Soviet Union and other Warsaw Pact countries in some actions often attributed to them without proof, but he asks whether the United States has such clean hands given, for example, that it sponsors the so-called Contras in Nicaragua.

BALLISTIC MISSILE DEFENSE

If the superpowers have the option of seeking to exercise leverage over adversaries by sponsoring low-intensity violence by substate actors, they have at the other end of the scale the capability, in the last resort, to threaten unimaginable destruction by means of nuclear weapons.

So far as the superpowers are concerned, this mutual leverage by nuclear threat is usually referred to as "deterrence." But what is often insufficiently appreciated is that there is a fundamental asymmetry in the superpowers' approach to "deterrence." The Soviets appear to see their own nuclear weapons as a deterrent to the initial use of these weapons by the United States (or other potential enemies). Hence, Andrei Gromyko, when Soviet foreign minister, felt able to announce at the United Nations that his country would never be the first to use nuclear weapons. If this declaration is a reflection of real Soviet intentions—and not all Western experts agree that it is—then the Soviets in essence need only an invulnerable second-strike capability. For them, then, a Mutual Assured Destruction (MAD) relationship with the United States may be acceptable.

For the United States, however, nuclear weapons have long had a purpose going far beyond deterring a first Soviet recourse to the nuclear option. Successive administrations since Eisenhower have also seen nuclear weapons as a deterrent to major Soviet *conventional* aggression as well. This approach arose out of the U.S. decision to guarantee, under the NATO arrangements, the security of various Western European allies. Such was—and is—the assured conventional inferiority of NATO vis-à-vis Soviet-led forces that, in the NATO view, this guarantee would have negligible credibility if the United States were not prepared in the last resort to threaten use of nuclear weapons—tactical and/or strategic—against a major act of conventional aggression. It was, of course, relatively easy to make this threat in the early 1950s, when the United States itself was practically invulnerable to Soviet nuclear forces. But by the 1960s the Soviets had begun to catch up, and today they are widely held to have achieved effective nuclear parity.

What is known as "extended deterrence" (i.e., the U.S. nuclear guarantees of Western Europe) is nowadays therefore not nearly so credible as when it was first enunciated. All the same, nobody in the Kremlin can really be certain that the United States would *not* escalate to the nuclear level if its armed forces in Europe were overrun.

There are, however, many Americans who worry about the extent to which this threat to use nuclear weapons first is ceasing to be a convincing deterrent. For some the answer is simply to abandon the threat. They would join the Soviets in declaring that they would never use such weapons except in retaliation; and they would rely for the defense of Western Europe on increased conventional forces (whether to be mainly provided by the United States or by Western Europeans themselves being a matter for dispute). By contrast, other Americans believe that no adequate conventional deterrent could ever be established, and hence they have sought ways to enhance the credibility of the nuclear first-use threat. They have, however, a particular problem in that the most accurate intercontinental missiles, the land-based ICBMs, seem to be increasingly vulnerable to a Soviet first-strike. Hence many experts believe that the first step to enhancing "extended deterrence" is to protect those ICBMs.

Although protecting ICBMs is in theory possible by a number of means, in recent years attention has focused mainly on the possible deployment of either land-based or space-based defensive technology. This issue has been at the center of discussion since Reagan made his famous "Star Wars" speech in March 1983. In some respects the speech was confusing, for Reagan appeared to hold out the hope that defenses could be made so perfect that nuclear weapons would be rendered "impotent and obsolete." Now if what he appeared to envisage—namely the creation of leak-proof shields over both superpowers—could be achieved, then the present form of "extended deter- rence" would at a stroke be rendered impossible, as the Soviet Union would cease to be vulnerable to a first use of nuclear weapons and there would be no shield over West Europe. No doubt fears on this score led most Western European states to react without enthusiasm to the "Star Wars" speech.

Increasingly, however, almost everyone interested in this subject, with the possible exception of Reagan and some of his advisers, has come to accept that perfect defenses are a pipe dream. So the *real* debate has focused on whether limited defenses would serve U.S. interests and, above all, whether they would serve to give the United States increased leverage vis-à-vis the Soviet Union in any crisis involving Europe.

The controversy about the wisdom of the United States's seeking to deploy antiballistic missile defenses is, of course, multifaceted. But a fair impression of what is at stake can be gleaned from our debate between John C. Toomay and Jack Mendelsohn. Both accept the premise that deterrence of Soviet aggression is desirable. But their reading of the technological possibilities and their assessment of the possible political repercussions diverge fundamentally.

LINKAGE

The superpowers' relationship since the advent of approximate nuclear parity between them has been compared to two scorpions in a bottle. They are adversaries but behave with prudence toward each other lest they precipitate mutual mass destruction.

What is less clear is whether measures to limit or reduce the means of inflicting such mass destruction is of such paramount importance that they should be pursued in isolation from other apparently less vital matters. The issue has been debated in the United States since at least 1969, the year which saw the inauguration of serious superpower negotiations on nuclear arms control. Throughout the SALT process, which lasted until 1979, and in the various continuations of that process during the Reagan presidency, some Americans have held that nothing else has comparable importance and hence that progress in the talks should not be made conditional on good or even less bad behavior by the adversary in other respects. They particularly regretted the U.S. refusal to ratify the SALT II Accords as a response to the Soviet invasion of Afghanistan in 1979. In other words, what is called "linkage" is to be deplored and avoided. That is essentially the line taken by John A. Hamilton, a foreign service officer, in his contribution to our next debate.

Prof. Richard Pipes of Harvard University is strongly in the other camp on this issue. To be sure, he believes the decision not to ratify the SALT II Accords should not have turned on punishing the Soviets for isolated misdeeds. But he does not see nuclear arms competition as being the only or even the most important issue of our era. For him strategic nuclear weapons cannot be seen other than in the broad context of the superpower relationship, which he deems based on a fundamental hostility deriving from Soviet global ambitions. He believes, moreover, that the Soviets in a certain sense share his perspective. "In the Soviet view," he writes, "strategic weapons are integrated into a comprehensive ideology of conflict in which military matters constitute discrete elements of a broad spectrum of coercive instrumentalities."

U.S. LEVERAGE ON NATO ALLIES

The superpowers have, as we have seen, a great many ways of bringing pressure to bear on one another. They are also able, and on occasion willing, to use some instruments of power to influence allies as well. These actions they no doubt believe essential in the wider context of the Cold War struggle.

There are some obvious asymmetries between the two major alliance systems. Probably the most important derives from the fact that none of the sixteen member governments of NATO is at present a dictatorship, and hence all must be presumed to have the consent of their people for their participation. And certainly any country that sees fit to withdraw would not be prevented from doing so by a U.S. military intervention. In the case of the Warsaw Pact, however, no member state has free pluralistic elections, and hence it may well be that in at least some cases the governments concerned do not represent a popular desire for membership. In fact the Soviet Union has twice invaded its supposed allies to enforce continued loyalty to Moscow—in Hungary in 1956 and Czechoslovakia in 1968. To be sure, Albania has been permitted to opt out of the Warsaw Pact, and Rumania, while remaining a member, has shown considerable independence. All the same, it is clear that the U.S.S.R. is willing in some circumstances to use armed force to keep its European camp in order, whereas the United States is not.

This does not mean, however, that the United States has no leverage at its disposal when differences arise. In particular, the presence of more than 300,000 U.S. troops in Western Europe is of central importance. If these troops were withdrawn, Western European governments would feel extremely vulnerable to Soviet pressure or even attack—notwithstanding the U.S. nuclear "guarantee" whose credibility is, as we have seen, no longer what it was.

Successive U.S. administrations have never threatened to withdraw some or all U.S. forces over trivial matters. But there is one issue on which the U.S. Senate has come to feel strongly enough at least to contemplate executing such a threat. This relates to the contribution that Western Europeans themselves make to collective conventional defense. Since 1952 successive U.S. administrations have insisted that the allies spend more on conventional forces, and this demand has become ever more strident as the credibility of nuclear first-use threat (discussed above) has been to some degree undermined by Soviet advances at the nuclear level. To be sure, Western Europeans have made repeated pledges to mend their ways, but their efforts have usually fallen short of what was promised.

In these circumstances some members of Congress have thought it desirable to threaten withdrawal of U.S. troops if Western Europeans do not increase their NATO contributions. Those legislators willing to engage in this kind of leverage have, of course, been a minority, but they can make common cause with another minority, namely those members of Congress who would like to see some or all U.S. forces brought home from Europe no matter what part Western Europeans play in NATO. (The latter group has roots going back to 1951, when in the so-called Great Debate Sen. Robert Taft led a number of Republicans in opposition to the original permanent deployment of U.S. troops in Europe under NATO arrangements. In the ensuing years the torch of opposition passed from Republican hands into those of Democrats led by Sen.

Mike Mansfield. At no time, however, not even at the height of the trauma caused by the Vietnamese war, did support for outright withdrawal carry the day.)

In the final debate in this chapter we have Sen. Sam Nunn of Georgia arguing, in 1984, the case for those who genuinely wish to retain U.S. forces in Europe but only if the NATO allies cooperate. We reproduce his argument in favor of cutting U.S. forces by up to 30,000 a year if Western Europeans for their part fail to reach appropriate targets. Nunn was opposed by Sen. Richard Lugar of Indiana, who judged that this kind of public pressure on Western Europe might be counterproductive. In 1984 Lugar's view was shared by the Reagan administration, and the Senate eventually accepted it, too. This acceptance did not mean, of course, that the administration was not able to draw the attention of NATO allies to the kind of movement Nunn was leading, and hence it no doubt exercised some private leverage that over time may yield the desired responses. If not, further overt Senate pressures on Western Europe may be confidently expected.

13 Can the United States use economic inducements to achieve political concessions from the Soviet Union?

YES

Bruce W. Jentleson

The Political Basis for Trade in U.S.-Soviet Relations

NO

Edward A. Hewett

[Economic Leverage in U.S.-Soviet Relations]

The Political Basis for Trade in U.S.-Soviet Relations

Bruce W. Jentleson

Is there a political basis for trade in American-Soviet relations?[1] Or will American exports to the Soviet Union only fulfill Lenin's prophecy that eventually the capitalists would sell the communists the rope for their own hanging?[2] These questions are especially relevant in the 1980s. American economic sanctions have had little economic impact and even less political influence on the Soviet Union.[3] The purpose of this article is to consider the possibilities of economic inducement as an alternative strategy. I will do this in four steps. First, I will offer a critique of the major historical and theoretical arguments that have been made against an economic inducement strategy. Second, I shall assess the experience of the

Nixon administration's application of this strategy to American-Soviet relations. Third, I examine the economic evidence pointing to the increasing internationalisation of the Soviet economy in the 1980s. Finally, I will propose some directions for a future American policy of trading with the Soviet Union.

QUESTIONING OLD ASSUMPTIONS

The usual indictment against economic inducement is based on two principal arguments. First is the critique of what can be called the "naive theory of interdependence."[4] Albert Hirschman traces the idea that international commerce can foster international peace back to Montesquieu and John Stuart Mill. Montesquieu wrote of "the natural effect" of international trade as being "to bring about peace." Mill went even further in seeing the expansion of international trade in the mid-nineteenth century as "rapidly rendering war obsolete."[5] On the very eve of the First World War, Sir Norman Angell, foremost successor to this tradition, diagnosed war as "a failure of understanding" that could be corrected by the kind of mutual understanding bred by international commerce.[6] Given such extraordinary claims, the fact that war broke out in 1914 despite the high levels of economic interdependence that existed at the time (for example, Germany was Britain's second leading trade partner) has been

Bruce W. Jentleson, "The Political Basis for Trade in U.S.-Soviet Relations," *Millennium: Journal of International Studies,* **15** (Spring 1986), pp. 27–47. The author gratefully acknowledges the financial support of the University of California, Institute on Global Conflict and Cooperation and the Committee on Research of the University of California, Davis. An earlier version of this paper was delivered at the 1984 Annual Meeting of the American Political Science Association.

[1] I intentionally pose the question in terms of "political basis" and "American-Soviet" relations. My reasons are to isolate the political arguments in favour of American-Soviet trade from the economic, and also to isolate those factors that pertain directly to the relationship of the two superpowers from those which might be more relevant to bloc relations as seen from a West European perspective. The two sets of considerations are obviously interrelated, but for both analytic and prescriptive purposes it also is important to separate them.

[2] One source for attributing this statement to Lenin is a speech given to the AFL-CIO by Alexander Solzhenitsyn on 30 June 1975 and cited in Carl Gershman, "Selling Them the Rope: Business and the Soviets," *Commentary* (Vol. 67, No. 4, April 1979), p. 35.

[3] See my arguments in the following: "Khrushchev's Oil and Brezhnev's Natural Gas Pipelines," in Robert J. Lieber (ed.), *Will Europe Fight for Oil? Energy Relations in the Atlantic Area* (New York: Praeger, 1983), pp. 33-69; "From Consensus to Conflict: The Domestic Political Economy of East-West Energy Trade," *International Organization* (Vol. 36, No. 4, Autumn 1984), pp. 625-60; and *Pipeline Politics: The Complex Political Economy of East-West Energy Trade* (Ithaca, NY: Cornell University Press, 1986).

[4] This parallels Johan Galtung's critique of "naive theories of economic warfare." See "On the Effects of International Economic Sanctions, with Examples from the Case of Rhodesia," *World Politics* (Vol. 19, No. 3, April 1967), pp. 378-416.

[5] Albert O. Hirschman, *National Power and the Structure of Foreign Trade,* expanded edition (Berkeley, CA: University of California Press, 1980), p. 10.

[6] E.H. Carr, *The Twenty Years' Crisis, 1919-1939* (New York: Harper and Row, 1964), pp. 25-6.

taken as the ultimate refutation of the peace-building potential of international commerce.

Such a conclusion, however, has its own logical fallacies. We know from the numerous studies that have been conducted over the years that the causes of the First World War were exceedingly complex.[7] Failures of diplomacy, military doctrine, demographic and economic trends, domestic politics and many other factors contributed to the breaking of the peace. Clearly, it would be naive to think that somehow economic interdependence could override these other sources of conflict and instability. Yet it is equally disingenuous to conclude that because economic interdependence was not a sufficient condition to prevent war, it therefore had absolutely no value as a force for peace. That it did not guarantee the peace in 1914 does not mean that it had no effect; the only certainty is that it did not have a sufficient effect. Nor does it mean that in a different international scenario economic interdependence might not have more of a stabilising effect on political relations between nations. In particular, it leaves open the question of whether trade is a necessary condition for improving relations between adversaries.

In questioning this first assumption, it should be further noted that while the limits of trade as a force for peace can be established, we know much less about their possible scope. Empirical cases are hard to find because there are very few historical instances of relations between adversaries improving dramatically without a war first being fought. Furthermore, there is the lack of a theoretical framework with which to approach the question of co-operation between

adversaries. Almost 15 years ago David Baldwin raised the issue of how little research and theorising had been done on the use of "positive sanctions" (meaning promises and rewards for co-operative behaviour, not limited to but including the expansion of trade) as distinct from "negative sanctions" (trade embargoes, among other threats and punishments). Political scientists, Baldwin rightly pointed out, tend "to assume a priori that negative sanctions work better than positive ones."[8] A few years later the same point was made in a more applied context by Alexander George and Richard Smoke who saw the pressing need for deterrence theory "to be supplemented with what might be called "inducement theory."[9] The need still remains to this day. To the extent that there have been significant contributions to the development of theories of co-operation, they have tended to apply only to situations in which, as Robert Keohane suggests in his own recent book, "the existence of mutual interests" can be taken "as given"—a qualification that excludes East-West relationships.[10]

The openness of the question, however, should not mean rejection of the very hypothesis that there can be such a thing as economic inducement. If the scientific tradition of political inquiry is to be taken seriously, the question should remain open, the hypothesis should be tested, the theoretical analysis should be developed; that is, unless one believes that the possibility of economic inducement in relations with the Soviet Union should be summarily rejected. This assumption relies on what Daniel Yergin calls the "Riga axioms," a view of the Soviet Union as "a world revolutionary state, commit-

[7] For example, Nazli Choucri and Robert C. North, *Nations in Conflict: National Growth and International Violence* (San Francisco, CA: W.H. Freeman, 1975); A.F.K. Organski, *World Politics* (New York: Knopf, 1958), especially Chapter 14; F.H. Hinsley, *Power and the Pursuit of Peace* (Cambridge: Cambridge University Press, 1963), especially Chapter 13; and George H. Quester, *Offense and Defense in the International System* (New York: John Wiley and Sons, 1977).

[8] David A. Baldwin, "The Power of Positive Sanctions," *World Politics* (Vol. 24, No. 1, October 1971), p. 35.

[9] Alexander L. George and Richard Smoke, *Deterrence in American Foreign Policy: Theory and Practice* (New York: Columbia University Press, 1974), p. 606.

[10] Robert O. Keohane, *After Hegemony: Cooperation and Discord in the World Political Economy* (Princeton, NJ: Princeton University Press, 1984), p. 6.

ted to unrelenting ideological warfare, powered by a messianic drive for world mastery."[11] From this perspective the attempt to use trade to induce the Soviet Union into more co-operative political relations makes little sense. Even if Soviet leaders make some initial concessions and otherwise elicit a cooperative attitude, by definition these are to be dismissed as attempts to lull and deceive. For, as William Zimmerman so aptly characterises what he terms the "essentialist" view of the Soviet Union, "this is not what the country [the Soviet Union] does...but what it is which is the source of conflict."[12]

This assumption fares equally poorly under analysis. First of all, there is no consensus in the Sovietology literature on the nature of the Soviet threat. Yergin counterpoints the Riga with the "Yalta" axioms, and Zimmerman the essentialist with the "mechanistic" and "cybernetic" views.[13] Second, there is a certain amount of empirical evidence which suggests that the Soviet Union has been more responsive to mixed strategies combining positive inducements with negative sanctions than to the more strictly negative approach confined solely to threats and punishments.[14] Finally, there is the growing theoretical work on what can be called the interactive nature of international conflict. Jervis' historically-based studies of perception and misperception, Axelrod's game-theoretic analysis of the prevalence of tit-for-tat patterns, and Kaplowitz's psychopolitical analysis of reciprocity in conflict strategies all run counter to

the Riga/essentialist Soviet-centric assessment of the causes of East-West tensions.[15]

The appropriate conclusion, therefore, is that there are neither theoretical nor empirical bases for precluding, *a priori,* the plausibility of economic inducement in U.S.-Soviet relations. The next task is to assess the experience of the 1970s, in particular, the Nixon-Ford-Kissinger period when economic inducement was an integral part of the overall American detente strategy.

LESSONS OF THE 1970s

The Nixon administration had two principal objectives in liberalising trade with the Soviet Union. Most immediate was the calculation that trade would have instrumental utility as a bargaining tool in the initial stage of negotiations over nuclear arms, Vietnam and other political and strategic issues high on the American agenda. Henry Kissinger recounts in his memoirs how the administration opposed Congressional moves in 1969 to liberalise export controls unilaterally and without any linkage to superpower politics. It was not that Kissinger wanted the linkage to be explicit. But if the Kremlin wanted access to the economic benefits of trade with the United States it first "would have to show restraint in its international conduct and arrange for progress on key foreign policy issues." Economic concessions would be offered only "after the Soviet Union cooperated with us in the political field."[16]

Less direct and less immediate, but potentially more comprehensive and more enduring, was the second objective of structural influ-

[11] Daniel Yergin, *Shattered Peace: The Origins of the Cold War and the National Security State* (Boston, MA: Houghton Mifflin, 1977), p. 11.

[12] William Zimmerman, "Choices in the Postwar World: Containment and the Soviet Union," in Charles Gati (ed.), *Caging the Bear: Containment and the Cold War* (Indianapolis, IN, and New York: Bobbs-Merrill, 1979), p. 91.

[13] See also William Welch, *American Images of Soviet Foreign Policy: An Inquiry into Recent Appraisals from the Academic Community* (New Haven, CT: Yale University Press, 1970).

[14] Russell J. Leng, "Reagan and the Russians: Crisis Bargaining Beliefs and the Historical Record," *American Political Science Review* (Vol. 78, No. 2, March 1984), pp. 338-55.

[15] Robert Jervis, *Perception and Misperception in International Politics* (Princeton, NJ: Princeton University Press, 1976); Robert Axelrod, *The Evolution of Cooperation* (New York: Basic Books, 1984); Noel Kaplowitz, "Psychopolitical Dimensions of International Relations: The Reciprocal Effects of Conflicts Strategies," *International Studies Quarterly* (Vol. 28, No. 4, December 1984), pp. 373-406.

[16] Henry A. Kissinger, *White House Years* (Boston, MA: Little, Brown, 1979), p. 155.

ence, of building what Nixon and Kissinger liked to call "the structure of peace." Expanded economic relations, a major policy statement asserted, would build

> in both countries a vested interest in the maintenance of a harmonious and enduring relationship. A nation's security is affected not only by its adversary's military capabilities but by the price which attends the use of those capabilities. If we can create a situation in which the use of military force would jeopardize a mutually profitable relationship, I think it can be argued that our security will have been enhanced.[17]

In a certain sense this amounted to a change of means more so than ends. The objective still was to contain Soviet power and influence. But now, as John Lewis Gaddis later put it, the "new combination of pressures and inducements ...would, if successful, convince the Russians that it was in their own best interests to be 'contained.' "[18] That is, their economic stakes in a stable relationship with the United States were expected to affect Soviet calculations of the relative costs and benefits of confrontational action. Consequently, while trade could not be an absolute prophylactic against conflict, the "gradual association of the Soviet economy with the world economy" would "foster a degree of interdependence that adds an element of stability to the political equation."[19]

What made both the instrumental bargaining and structural influence objectives seem feasible was that by the 24th Party Congress (1971) and the Ninth Five Year Plan (1971-75), trade with the capitalist West was becoming institutionalised in Soviet policy and planning. No longer were Soviet leaders content to rely exclusively on the regional integrative, semi-autarkic economic strategy embodied in the Council for Mutual Economic Assistance (CMEA). Nor was there any more blustering about economically burying the West. Instead, officials such as Minister of Foreign Trade Nikolai Patrolichev sounded more like David Ricardo than Karl Marx in stressing how trade with the West allows the Soviet Union

> to make fuller and more rational use of its own resources and possibilities, and at the same time to acquire, by way of commercial exchange, goods of other countries that are not produced in our country or whose production would cost more than it does to import them.[20]

This perspective, while not unanimously held in the Kremlin, did have the critical support of Premier Alexei Kosygin and especially General Secretary Leonid Brezhnev, whose internal power was then on the rise. "We have entered a stage of economic development," Brezhnev declared in 1970, "that no longer allows us to work in the old way but calls for new methods and new solutions."[21] One of the new methods Brezhnev had in mind was to increase imports of Western capital goods and technology to stimulate the Soviets' own lagging commercial technological base. Another, and even more pressing problem in the wake of the disastrous 1971-72 grain harvest, was to provide emergency food relief by increasing grain imports.

[17] Peter G. Peterson, *US-Soviet Commercial Relations in a New Era* (Washington, DC: Government Printing Office, 1972), pp. 3-4.

[18] John Lewis Gaddis, *Strategies of Containment* (New York: Oxford University Press, 1982), p. 289.

[19] Testimony to Senate Foreign Relations Committee, 19 September 1974, included in Henry A. Kissinger, *American Foreign Policy* (New York: W.W. Norton, 1977), pp. 158-59.

[20] Cited in Herbert S. Levine, "Soviet Economic Development, Technological Transfer and Foreign Policy," in Seweryn Bialer (ed.), *The Domestic Context of Soviet Foreign Policy* (Boulder, CO: Westview Press, 1981), p. 190.

[21] Cited in M. Elizabeth Denton, "Soviet Perceptions of Economic Prospects," in U.S. Congress, Joint Economic Committee, *Soviet Economy in the 1980's: Problems and Prospects* (Washington DC: Joint Committee Print, Vol. 1, 97th Congress, 2nd Session), p. 32. Raymond Garthoff takes this further, citing a Brezhnev speech on West German television in 1973 in which he explicitly repudiated autarky and stated that Soviet economic policy "proceeds from the premise" of growing economic relations with the West: *Detente and Confrontation: American-Soviet Relations from Nixon to Reagan* (Washington, DC: Brookings Institution, 1985), p. 88.

For both of these economic objectives, trade with the United States was of key importance. While industrial technology also could be (and was) imported from Western Europe and Japan, "for both real and imaginary reasons," as economist Herbert Levine put it, the Soviets continued to "have a high regard for the high level of American technology."[22] And, of course, no country grew grain in the quantity that the United States did.

In their official pronouncements Soviet leaders repeatedly and staunchly opposed both the bargaining tool and structural goals of political-economic linkages.[23] But on three key issues on which progress was made in the 1971-73 period—SALT I, a Vietnam peace treaty and emigration by Soviet Jews—there is some evidence that trade inducements were an effective bargaining tool. Seymour Hersh contends that it was a promise by the Nixon administration to liberalise existing controls on grain exports that led, in May 1971, to the key breakthrough in the SALT negotiations in which the Soviets abandoned their insistence that an ABM treaty precede any agreement to limit offensive strategic missiles.[24] While Kissinger does not mention such a linkage, he does acknowledge that only three weeks after the Soviet concessions on SALT, an executive order was issued liberalising grain exports.[25]

Shortly thereafter, the Soviets signed contracts for three million tons of American grain, valued at $136 million. When the longshoremen and maritime unions then refused to load the grain,[26] Hersh quotes Charles Colson as saying he received a call directly from the President telling him to work on the unions because "SALT depends on it." Soviet Ambassador Anatoly Dobrynin reportedly had informed the White House "that there would be no SALT agreement unless the grain deal was worked out."[27] To avert this prospect, the Nixon administration not only used the route of Colson's pressure but also promised the unions a major new subsidy programme for the maritime industry.

Trade inducements also contributed to progress made before and at the May 1972 summit on another top American priority, the Vietnam War. When Nixon went ahead with the bombing and mining operations against North Vietnam on the eve of the summit, Kissinger and other foreign policy experts were convinced that, as with the 1960 U-2 incident, the Soviets would cite American aggression as the reason for cancelling the summit. The fact that they did not, like the proverbial dog that didn't bark, said a great deal. The American journalist Stanley Karnow recounts being enlisted by a Soviet embassy official to deliver the message to Washington that "we've done a lot

[22] U.S. Congress, Senate Committee on Foreign Relations, *Detente* (Hearings, 93rd Congress, 2nd Session, 1974), p. 33.

[23] Adam B. Ulam, *Dangerous Relations: The Soviet Union in World Politics, 1970-1982* (New York: Oxford University Press, 1983), p. 59; Franklyn D. Holzman and Robert Legvold, "The Economics and Politics of East-West Relations," *International Organization* (Vol. 29, No. 1, Winter 1975), pp. 295-96.

[24] Seymour M. Hersh, *The Price of Power: Kissinger in the Nixon White House* (New York: Summit Books, 1983), pp. 334-49.

[25] Kissinger does mention the 10 June executive order de-controlling gear-cutting machinery ordered by the Soviets for the $1 billion Kama River truck foundry then under construction; Henry Kissinger, *White House Years, op. cit.,* p. 840. The liberalisation of grain exports involved two actions. One removed the requirement that grain exports to

communist countries first receive a special licence from the Commerce Department. The other rescinded the requirement that 50 per cent of all grain shipments to communist countries be carried on American flag vessels. Back in 1963-64 when the Kennedy and Johnson administrations made the first grain deal with the Soviets, the longshoremen and maritime unions went on strike until Congress added the 50 per cent shipping requirement. But because American shipping was as much as 30 per cent more expensive than other flags, the Soviets did not buy any more American grain. To bring them back into the American market, the Nixon administration needed to make American grain more price competitive by lifting the 50 per cent shipping requirement.

[26] Not only were the unions retaliating against the lifting of the 50 per cent shipping requirement, they were also long a bastion of virulent anti-communism.

[27] Seymour Hersh, *op. cit.,* p. 347.

for those Vietnamese, but we're not going to let them spoil our relations with the United States."[28] Not only did the Soviets tolerate the American bombing of their ally, but according to Kissinger, they also agreed "to help us" conclude a treaty that would allow American disengagement.[29] Soon after the summit President Nikolai Podgorny went to Hanoi. While precisely what transpired is not known, Kissinger was said to have "observed a distinct change in the tone of Le Duc Tho" when the Paris negotiations reconvened in July. In August, American intelligence reported a slowdown in the delivery of Soviet supplies to North Vietnam.[30] That same month an editorial appeared in *Nhan Dan,* Hanoi's official newspaper, criticising the "terrible pressure" coming from Moscow for compromise.[31] This pressure undoubtedly was not the only reason the North Vietnamese finally agreed five months later to the Paris Peace Treaty, but it was an important one. And while, from the American perspective, much would go wrong later, Nixon was sufficiently pleased to join with Brezhnev in a joint communiqué at the June 1973 summit in which "the two sides expressed their deep satisfaction" with the Paris Peace Treaty.[32]

The most graphic testimony of the connection to Soviet interest in American trade comes from a story reported in *The Wall Street Journal.* Soviet Trade Minister Patrolichev was said to have been at the home of Commerce Secretary Peter Peterson when Nixon's speech announcing the mining and bombing operations came on television.

After hearing Mr. Nixon's tough words, he [Patrolichev] turned to his host [Peterson] and said: "Well, let's get back to business." And a couple of days later he posed happily with the President, a clear signal to Hanoi that Moscow put its own interests first.[33]

The same point was also made by Marshall Goldman, who in a report to the U.S. Congress stated that "in the Soviet scheme of things, the toleration of the escalation of U.S. violence in Vietnam was an unfortunate part of the price the Soviet Union was prepared to pay to obtain the American imports it needed."[34] Adam Ulam also concurs with this assessment, pointing out that by May 1972 the Soviets were already aware of the severity of their harvest failure and therefore had American grain very much on their minds when they agreed to go ahead with the summit.[35]

The surprising influence achieved in 1972-73 on another issue, Soviet Jewish emigration, was even stronger evidence of a political basis for trade.[36] The Soviet Jewry issue reached the linkage agenda despite the Nixon administration's own reluctance to include it. Even before the bilateral trade treaty promising the Soviets most-favoured-nation (MFN) status and substantial export credits was signed in October 1972, Senator Henry Jackson had introduced a bill in Congress making MFN conditional on increased Soviet Jewish emigration. (This became known as the Jackson-Vanik amendment, after Senator Jackson and his principal co-sponsor, Representative Charles Vanik.) The administration's preferred

[28] Stanley Karnow, *Vietnam: A History* (New York: Viking Press, 1983), p. 646.

[29] Tad Szulc, "Behind the Vietnam Cease-Fire Agreement," *Foreign Policy* (No. 15, Summer 1974), p. 44. See also Garthoff, *op. cit.,* p. 314.

[30] Joseph L. Nogee and Robert H. Donaldson, *Soviet Foreign Policy Since World War II* (New York: Pergamon Press, 1984), pp. 260-61.

[31] Cited in Raymond Garthoff, *op. cit.,* p. 259.

[32] *Ibid.,* p. 332.

[33] Robert Keatley, "The Truce: China and Russia's Role," *The Wall Street Journal,* 30 October 1972.

[34] Marshall I. Goldman, "Interaction of Politics and Trade: Soviet-Western Interaction," in Joint Economic Committee, *op. cit.,* p. 121.

[35] Adam Ulam, *op. cit.,* p. 90.

[36] An excellent and detailed study of this issue in particular is Paula Stern, *Water's Edge: Domestic Politics and the Making of American Foreign Policy* (Westport, CT: Greenwood Press, 1979). See also Kissinger's account in *Years of Upheaval* (Boston, MA: Little, Brown, 1982), pp. 985-98.

position was reflected in Kissinger's private remark during the Moscow summit: "How would it be if Brezhnev comes to the United States with a petition about the Negroes in Mississippi?"[37] Publicly his opposition was framed in less biting language. "The balance cannot be struck," he warned a Senate committee, "on each issue every day, but only over the whole range of relations and over a period of time." Such a position, he contended, was not "moral callousness" but rather a recognition of the 'limits of our ability to produce internal changes in foreign countries."[38]

This, too, was the official Soviet position. "Questions of sovereignty and of our internal affairs," President Nikolai Podgorny protested, "have never been and will never be a matter for political bargaining."[39] As on SALT and Vietnam, however, Soviet actions somewhat belied their words. For at the same time as stepping up their anti-linkage rhetoric, the number of exit visas issued also increased from 13,020 in 1971 to 31,681 in 1972 and almost 35,000 in 1973.[40] The 60,000 quota insisted on by Senator Jackson was not reached; the very idea of a quota decreed by the United States was patently unacceptable, irrespective of the number attached to it. But President Gerald Ford recounts that Dobrynin privately gave him an oral guarantee of 55,000.[41] Here was another demonstration that the Soviets wanted American trade badly enough to bargain with political issues which, while less than the original demands, were substantially more than any previous Soviet government had been willing to concede.

Yet, as became all too clear, there were definite limits to how far economic incentives would push the Brezhnev leadership. The 1972-73 increases in Jewish emigration were intended to send a signal to the American Congress that tying MFN to Jewish emigration was unnecessary, that the Soviets already were co-operating. When the Congress went ahead anyway, with the House passing Jackson-Vanik in December 1973 and there being little doubt that Senate passage would follow, it was no longer possible for the Soviets to give ground and hide it. The choice was narrowed to overt compliance or blatant non-compliance. The Soviets chose the latter. During 1974, as a very different signal to an American Congress on the verge of going too far, the Soviets slashed the number of exit visas issued to a level (20,628) 41 per cent lower than 1973. When the Senate gave the Jackson-Vanik amendment final passage, rather than accept the new conditionality, the Soviets renounced the 1972 bilateral trade treaty and Jewish emigration fell to 13,221 in 1975.

Thus, one of the lessons of the Jackson-Vanik amendment was that in wielding trade as a bargaining instrument, tactics matter. It showed that there is a point of diminishing returns beyond which pressure becomes counter-productive even if the reward for co-operation is a valued one. The Soviets did prove susceptible to instrumental influence on the issue of Jewish emigration, but only up to a point. When American tactics became too overt and "loud," they became self-defeating.[42]

---

[37] William Safire, *Before the Fall* (New York: Doubleday, 1975), p. 454.

[38] Henry Kissinger, *American Foreign Policy, op. cit.,* p. 145.

[39] Cited in Raymond Garthoff, *op. cit.,* p. 466.

[40] Robert O. Freedman (ed.), *Soviet Jewry in the Decisive Decade* (Durham, NC: Duke University Press, 1984), Annex 1.

[41] Gerald R. Ford, *A Time to Heal: The Autobiography of Gerald Ford* (New York: Harper and Row, 1979), pp. 138-9.

[42] Nor, it should be pointed out, are such parameters of pressure peculiar to the Soviet Union. Numerous studies of economic coercion involving other nations have shown that the more overt the tactics, the less likely they have been to succeed in bringing a coercer state political influence over its target state. Johan Galtung, *op. cit.;* Richard Stuart Olson, "Economic Coercion in World Politics: With a Focus on North-South Relations," *World Politics* (Vol. 21, No. 4, July 1979), pp. 471-4; and Jerrold D. Green, "Strategies for Evading Economic Sanctions," in Miroslav Nincic and Peter Wallensteen, *Dilemmas of Economic Coercion: Sanctions in World Politics* (New York: Praeger, 1983), pp. 61-85.cion: Sanctions in World Politics (New York: Praeger, 1983), pp. 61-85.

At the same time that it passed the Jackson-Vanik amendment, Congress also enacted a series of measures limiting official export credits to the Soviet Union. A lucrative line of credit had been the other major pledge (along with MFN status) made to the Soviets in the 1972 bilateral trade treaty. Up until this point the Nixon administration had been making good on this pledge. The Soviets had received $750 million in Commodity Credit Corporation (CCC) financing for their grain purchases and $476 million from the Export-Import Bank for industrial equipment and technology exports. Now, however, Congress moved to close the lending window. It imposed a $300 million ceiling on total new Eximbank credits to the Soviet Union. It gave itself veto authority over any single credit greater than $50 million. It set a $40 million sub-ceiling on credits for energy research and exploration. And it banned outright any lending related to energy production, processing and distribution.

Whereas the Jackson-Vanik amendment boomeranged against American bargaining power on the particular issue of Jewish emigration, the credit restrictions had the even more sweeping effect of undermining the broader structural influence strategy. If there was to be any prospect of building a structure of peace, the economic benefits the Soviets stood to gain had to be sufficiently ample. Not having MFN status was not that great an economic loss; the Soviets did not expect to be able to export all that much to the American market. Having their access to credit cut back, however, was of major economic importance.[43] Without an open credit line there could be little infusion of American technology. Contract negotiations with American corporate consortia for the de-

velopment of the vast natural gas reserves of Siberia were now moot. Furthermore, having to pay cash for American grain would eat up, whatever hard currency the Soviets had.

Thus, in terms of inducing an adversary into an enduring co-operative relationship, the American Congress had managed to put together the worst possible combination of adding to the disincentives by bringing Soviet domestic policy into the linkage while reducing the incentives by cutting back the potential economic benefits to be gained. It is interesting and important to note that a number of authors who otherwise disagree on the causes of the failure of detente concur on the damage done by the Jackson-Vanik amendment and Eximbank credit restrictions. Harry Gelman cites them as "the central cause" of Soviet disillusionment with detente, a "watershed" in the deterioration of Soviet-American relations. Alexander George singles them out as "a major blow to the further development of detente." Raymond Garthoff notes the particular embarrassment they caused Brezhnev, who "personally accepted and pushed more vigorously than any other top leader, the policy of maximizing East-West trade." Finally, as Adam Ulam remarks, even "if the Kremlin had been ready to swallow its injured national pride" after the Jackson-Vanik amendment, "it certainly would not do so for a paltry" few million dollars.[44]

One, therefore, must be wary of arguments which point to the unravelling of detente in the second half of the 1970s—Angola, the Horn of Africa, Solzhenitsyn and Sakharov, the Soviet military build-up, Afghanistan—as "evidence" refuting the economic inducement strategy. That detente unravelled is not open to dispute, but the

---

[43] Marshall Goldman confirms this, based on his discussions with Soviet officials. See his "The Evolution and Possible Direction of U.S. Policy on East-West Trade," in Abraham S. Becker (ed.), *Economic Relations with the U.S.S.R.* (Lexington, MA: D.C. Heath, 1983), pp. 164-5.

[44] Harry Gelman, *The Brezhnev Politburo and the Decline of Detente* (Ithaca, NY: Cornell University Press, 1984), pp. 122-3, 148-51; Alexander L. George, "Detente: The Search for a 'Constructive' Relationship," in his *Managing U.S.-Soviet Rivalry: Problems of Crisis Prevention* (Boulder, CO: Westview Press, 1983), p. 22; Raymond Garthoff, *op. cit.*, p. 88; and Adam Ulam, *op. cit.*, p. 123.

attribution of causality is. Most of the actions and events cited occurred *after* the economic inducements had been stripped away. Thus, Gelman, while sceptical about the likelihood that the Kremlin would have been induced "even if this legislation has not been passed," acknowledges that "the issue was never put to the test." The same conclusion is reached by Gaddis, in almost the same words and without the qualifying scepticism: "the abortive congressional attempt at 'linkage'... made it impossible to test Kissinger's theory that economic interdependence would give the Russians an incentive to exercise political restraint." Samuel Pisar, a longtime advocate of East-West trade and a key figure in the policy of the 1970s, goes even further in arguing that economic inducement could have succeeded except that "the tissue of relations that they would find too costly to sunder had never been built."[45]

In summary, then, it is my argument that: (1) Soviet interest in trade did bring the United States some limited but significant instrumental bargaining influence in the early 1970s, and (2) the demise of detente does not disprove the economic inducement theory because for the most part it occurred after the economic inducements had been substantially reduced. This is not to go so far as to arrive at the opposite conclusion, that the detente experience authoritatively proves the efficacy of economic inducement. Economic motivations were not the only, or sufficient, condition for Soviet policy on SALT, Vietnam or Jewish emigration. The Soviet Union is not the glaring exception to Morgenthauian principles. Nor is there any guarantee that had the economic pillar been left intact, the structure of peace would not have collapsed under the weight of some of the other tensions and conflicts. Here, too, there were too many other variables to speak definitively. My primary purpose is to demonstrate that just as there are serious logical and historical fallacies in the theoretical assumptions that preclude the possibility of economic inducement in American-Soviet relations, based on the experience of the 1970s there is also little empirical substantiation. On the contrary, although within the qualifications I have noted, the detente experience supports the conclusion that from the American perspective there can be a political basis for trading with the Soviet Union.

INTERNATIONALISATION OF THE SOVIET ECONOMY

By the early 1980s the Soviet economy had sunk to its lowest levels since the Second World War. The rates of growth in industrial output, productivity, technological innovation and oil production all hit post-war lows. Grain imports hit an all-time high. Kremlin leaders competed with each other in calling for reversal of these trends. There were even semi-official criticisms of the Soviet economic system, the most notable being the scathing critique made by economists of the Novosibirsk branch of the Soviet Academy of Sciences.[46]

As both cause and consequence of these economic problems, Soviet leaders were going through their own disillusionment with Western trade. Minister of Trade Patrolichev, for example, now argued that

> stricter attention should be paid to our ability to manufacture certain goods and equipment, so as to avoid spending foreign exchange on purchases of those foreign-made goods and technologies that can be developed and produced in the Soviet Union.[47]

Reflecting such sentiments, new orders for Western machinery and equipment dropped to $2.6 billion in 1980, only 43 per cent of their 1976 level of $6 billion. Part of the reason for

[45] Harry Gelman, *op. cit.,* p. 151; John Lewis Gaddis, *op. cit.,* p. 315; and Samuel Pisar, *Of Blood and Hope* (Boston, MA: Little, Brown, 1979), p. 269.

[46] *The New York Times,* 5 August 1983, p. 1.
[47] Cited in Gordon B. Smith, "The Impact of Western Technology Transfer on the Soviet Union," Paper presented to Conference on Technology Transfer in the Modern World, Georgia Institute of Technology, April 1984, p. 22.

this was the realisation that the actual economic benefits of Western technology imports had proven less than expected. Absorption and application of Western technology had been handicapped by organisational disincentives, inadequate infrastructure, shortages of spare parts and other factors internal to the Soviet economy.[48] Stories were rife of rusting machinery by the roadside and brand new factories in which the key was never turned. In another respect, though, the drop in imports of Western industrial technology was less the result of intentional policy than the consequence of the crunch on Soviet purchasing power. The combination of the rising costs of grain imports, the levelling off of hard currency earnings from their energy exports as a result of their own stagnating oil production and falling world oil prices, and the drying up of new loans from Western banks in reaction to the Polish debt crisis, was forcing the Soviets to cut back wherever possible on hard currency imports.

The question that Western governments, scholars and policy analysts were left with was whether this economic turn inwards would continue through the rest of the 1980s. While there still is a great deal of debate, I would argue that the strongest indications are that it will not. My primary reason for arguing this position is that the Soviet economy *needs* to trade with the West. I use the verb "need" intentionally, but also carefully. I do not mean "need" in the Reagan-Weinberger economic warfare sense that the Soviet economy faces imminent collapse without Western trade.[49] The Soviet Union has before and

could again survive without trading with the West. Nor, on the other hand, do I mean that trade with the West is a cure-all for the complex problems plaguing the Soviet economy. What I do mean is that the Soviet economy has become deeply and fundamentally interrelated with the international economy, more internationalised than ever before. Trade with the West has come to perform three key functions for the Soviet economy which, given the nature of its problems, are integral parts of an optimal policy of economic reform, growth and development.

The first of these functions is the infusion of industrial technology. Here the lessons of the 1970s were mixed. For while the actual industrial productivity gains achieved through Western technology imports were less than expected, in most sectors imported technologies still had a much better relative productivity record than Soviet domestic technologies. Herbert Levine suggests a 3:1 ratio in favour of imported machinery.[50] Microeconomic studies of the chemical industry attribute disproportionate shares of fertiliser, plastic and textile production to imported plants. Similar conclusions have been reached for machine tools, computers, automobiles, oil and natural gas.[51] Thus, as George Holliday concludes, "while assimilative difficulties will not disappear, Soviet needs for Western technology are likely to persist.... Indeed, increasing scarcities of labor, capital and materials are likely to make the rationale even more compelling in the mid and late 1980s."[52]

cumulative obsolescence.... Thus, the West helps preserve the Soviet Union as a totalitarian dictatorship." *Annual Report to the Congress of the Secretary of Defense, FY 1983* (Washington, DC: U.S. Government Printing Office, 1982), Section 1, pp. 22-3, and Section 2, pp. 26-32.

[50] Herbert Levine, *op. cit.,* pp. 187-8.

[51] U.S. Congress, Office of Technology Assessment, *Technology and East-West Trade* (Washington, DC: Government Printing Office, 1979), pp. 228-42; Organisation for Economic Co-operation and Development (OECD), *East-West Technology Transfer* (Paris: OECD, 1984); Philip Hanson, *Trade and Technology in Soviet-Western Relations* (New York: Columbia University Press, 1981).

[52] Joint Economic Committee, *op. cit.,* pp. 529-30.

[48] Joint Economic Committee, *op. cit.,* Section 2; Smith, *op. cit.,* pp. 14-18; Robert W. Campbell, "The Economy," in Robert F. Byrnes (ed.), *After Brezhnev* (Bloomington, IN: Indiana University Press, 1983), pp. 68-124; Abram Bergson, "Technological Progress," in Abram Bergson and Herbert S. Levine (eds.), *The Soviet Economy: Toward the Year 2000* (London: George Allen and Unwin, 1983), pp. 34-78.

[49] "Without constant infusion of advanced technology from the West," Secretary of Defense Caspar Weinberger has written, "the Soviet industrial base would experience a

Such statistical findings and policy conclusions by Western analysts are not inconsistent with what thus far appears to be the basic approach of Soviet leader Mikhail Gorbachev. Gorbachev's speeches and actions have been marked by an awareness of the complexities of Soviet economic problems. He has continued the workplace discipline campaign initiated by Yuri Andropov. He has also expanded the number of ministries included in the experiment with decentralised planning from five to 20.[53] But fundamentally, his approach has stressed "technology, technology, technology."[54] This has not meant a technology buying spree *á la* early 1970s. Gorbachev has been prominent among the critics of the buy-the-best-but-use-it-poorly technology-importing practices of the Brezhnev era. Nor has it meant importing Western technology to the exclusion of Soviet domestic technological development. In June 1985 Gorbachev rejected the draft of the new Twelfth Five Year Plan precisely because the goals set and resources allocated for domestic technological development were too low. But this heightened emphasis on domestic technologies has been in addition to, rather than instead of, Western imports. For example, new trade agreements signed with France and Italy call for more than 200 per cent increases in Soviet machinery and equipment imports. And in July 1985 a highly publicised contract was signed with Japanese firms for microcomputer imports. This is expected to be followed by additional computer contracts and perhaps also an even bigger contract for the building of a microcomputer factory in the Soviet Union. There have also been any number of reports in the press of discussions with Western governments, exporters and lenders on other potentially major export and technology transfer deals.

The second key function performed for the Soviet economy by trade with the West is the food relief provided by massive grain imports. Despite the long-term priority given to agriculture—the sector received 26 per cent of total economic investment in the Ninth Five Year Plan, 27 per cent in the Tenth Five Year Plan—the need for Western grain imports has not abated. Net agricultural output grew by only 1.8 per cent annually in the 1970s, well below the 3 per cent and 4.8 per cent growth rates for the 1960s and 1950s, respectively. Even at current nutritional levels, minimum requirements for feeding the growing Soviet population are a 10 per cent increase in farm output by 1990 and another 5 per cent between 1990 and the year 2000. Approaching the long-standing promises made to Soviet consumers for improvements in their diet, in particular for more meat, would require even greater increases. As of 1978, for example, Soviet per capita meat consumption was nearly 50 per cent below the East European average.[55] Recent events in Poland and sporadic reports of food riots in some Soviet cities have underlined the problem.

Most Western economists give the Soviets little chance of achieving the necessary increases in grain and other agricultural production.[56] An improved harvest in 1982-83 had raised some hopes of progress, but the 1984-85 harvest was the second worst of the past decade. The U.S. Department of Agriculture estimated it at only 170 million metric tons. This compares to the original Eleventh Five Year Plan goal of 238–243

[53] Thomas H. Naylor, "Changing the Economic Mechanism in the Soviet Union," Fugua School of Business, Duke University (mimeo).

[54] Jerry F. Hough, "Gorbachev's Strategy," *Foreign Affairs* (Vol. 64, No. 1, Fall 1985), p. 40. See also Gorbachev's speech of 12 June 1985 to the CPSU Central Committee, *Current Digest of the Soviet Press* (Vol. 37, No. 23, 3 July 1985).

[55] Karl-Eugen Wadekin, "Soviet Agriculture's Dependence on the West," *Foreign Affairs* (Vol. 60, No. 4, Summer 1982), p. 894; Douglas B. Diamond, Lee W. Bettis and Robert E. Ramsson, "Agricultural Production," in Abram Bergson and Herbert Levine, *op. cit.*, pp. 143-77.

[56] Karl-Eugen Wadekin, *op. cit.*, and D. Gale Johnson and Karen McConnell Brooks, *Prospects for Soviet Agriculture in the 1980s* (Bloomington, IN: Indiana University Press, 1983).

million metric tons, a 28–30 per cent production shortfall. It also caused imports to reach a record high of 55 million metric tons.

The third and most significant way in which the Soviet economy has grown inextricably inter-related with the world economy is in the energy sector. In 1984 oil and natural gas exports accounted for over 80 per cent of total Soviet hard currency earnings, with oil alone accounting for 64 per cent. Especially given the continuing tightness of export credits, these energy exports must almost single-handedly finance the grain and industrial technology imports from the West. Yet increasingly over the past few years the hard currency earning potential of Soviet energy exports has been strained. Oil production growth rates, stagnated for a number of years and then in 1984, for the first time since the Second World War, oil production actually declined. At the same time world oil prices, which had rocketed in the 1970s, plummeted. The Soviets were forced to cut their price from its peak of $36.53 per barrel in 1981 to under $15.00 per barrel in early 1986. Consequently, whereas in the late 1970s they were able to export less oil to the West but earn more hard currency (e.g., in 1979 oil exports were 9 per cent smaller in volume but with 68 per cent greater earnings), between 1982 and 1984 they had to increase the volume of their crude oil exports to OECD countries by 34.8 per cent to yield a 20 per cent increase in hard currency earnings.

One factor which facilitated these increased export earnings was the arms-for-oil barter arrangements with Iraq and Libya.[57] Another factor was the cut in Soviet domestic oil consumption achieved through new strict conser-vation measures and through natural gas conversion programmes.[58] A third factor, the most problematic, was the cutbacks imposed on oil exported to Eastern Europe. In the short term these cuts have succeeded in their objective of adding to the oil available for hard currency earning purposes. However, given the links between economic problems and political instability which have characterised Eastern Europe under Soviet dominance, and which most recently were a central cause of the near revolution in Poland, oil supply cutbacks run considerable political risks.[59]

Similarly, increased exports of natural gas have partially countered the squeeze on oil earnings but will also be more problematic in the future. Unlike the oil sector with its recurring shortfalls, Soviet natural gas production consistently has been at or over Plan targets. In the wake of the 1979 OPEC oil crisis, Western Europe was keenly interested in Soviet gas as a means of decreasing its dependence on OPEC oil. This combination of abundant supply and strong demand made for an almost 300 per cent increase in Soviet hard currency earnings from natural gas exports, from $1.4 billion in 1979 to $4 billion in 1980. Since then, however, while Soviet production has continued to grow at impressive rates, West European demand for natural gas has levelled off as a consequence both of recession-induced slower GNP growth rates and of the renewed attractiveness of once again cheap(er) oil. The consensus among gov-

---

[57] Jochen Bethkenhagen estimates a 300 per cent increase in Soviet oil imports from Iraq and Libya from 3.5 million metric tons per year in 1980 to 10.5 million in 1984. Total Soviet oil imports are estimated at 5.5 million metric tons for 1980 and 20 million tons for 1984. "Soviet Energy: Oil Exports Stabilise Thanks to Increased Natural Gas Production," *Economic Bulletin* (Vol. 22, No. 7, September 1985), German Institute for Economic Research (DIW), p. 11.

[58] Jochen Bethkenhagen, *op. cit.,* p. 9, puts Soviet domestic oil consumption for 1984 at 34.9 million tons coal equivalent, an 8.9 per cent reduction from 1980 consumption of 38.3 million. Domestic natural gas consumption, in contrast, increased 22.4 per cent during the same period. Total energy consumption increased 12.3 per cent.

[59] After averaging 7.6 per cent in the first half of the 1970s and 3.6 per cent for 1976-80, the aggregate average economic growth rate for Eastern Europe in 1981-83 sunk to 0.8 per cent. An "energy squeeze," as *The Economist* put it, "will be a big obstacle to improving growth rates, in the rest of the 1980s and the 1990s." *The Economist,* 20 April 1985, Survey 12.

ernment and industry analysts is that Soviet natural gas exports to Western Europe will continue to increase under existing contracts until at least 1995, but the rate of increase will be less than originally anticipated.[60] The compensating effect on the oil price production squeeze therefore will only be a limited one.

Looking to the future, then, the Soviets will be left with the trade dilemma of hard currency purchasing power increasing more slowly than hard currency import needs. One way out, of course, would be to increase oil production. Western demand is there, especially if the Soviets continue their strategy of undercutting OPEC prices.[61] The key problem, though, is the technological constraint of the most promising oil reserves—*e.g.,* Western Siberia, Eastern Siberia, the Barents Sea—being the most technologically difficult to extract. Without overstating Soviet technological inferiority one must also not underestimate the gap between Western and Soviet energy technologies. In terms of quantity, Soviet industry has historically produced most of its own energy equipment. They consistently have relied qualitatively on Western equipment and technology imports for key functions at virtually every key stage of the energy production process: computers for exploration, deep-well and diamond rock drill bits for Siberian well-drilling, rigs for off-shore wells, turn-key plants for refining, and wide-

diameter pipe, turbines and compressors for natural gas pipelines.[62] And as one major recent study concluded, "(energy) equipment manufacture and supply comprise a major area in which the Soviets are facing great difficulties—both presently and in the future."[63]

It would be an overestimation of Soviet technological deficiencies to draw the conclusion that without Western imports oil production increases would be impossible for the Soviet Union. That is not my point. Nor is it my wish to imply that the Soviet Union could be forced into an energy crisis by a Western embargo. My point is rather that significant production increases are much less likely without Western energy technology imports, and my implication therefore is that the optimal economic policy for the Soviet Union is to import energy technology from the West.

Thus, the energy sector brings us full circle. It is, as Thane Gustafson has put it, "not merely a part of the growing internationalization of the Soviet economy, it is the essential center of it."[64] It is both exemplary of the more general pattern of the growing interdependence of the Soviet economy with the international economy, and the central cog in that more general pattern. The Soviet Union needs and will continue to need to import large quantities of grain to feed its people. It also needs and will continue to need to import Western industrial equipment and technology. But its capacity to

---

[60] When Italy finally signed its new contract for Soviet natural gas in May 1984, the volume was only about 60 per cent of what had been set in a preliminary agreement back in October 1981. Then in 1985 the Soviets were pressured into renegotiating existing contracts with Gaz de France and Ruhrgas for lower prices and stretched-out delivery periods for the agreed volumes. This assessment is also based on extensive interviews conducted by the author in Europe during June and July, 1985.

[61] Nor are there the same security-related constraints as with natural gas on imports from the Soviet Union. The current Soviet share of the West European oil market is only about 15 per cent, roughly half its share of natural gas markets. Moreover, the spot market nature of most oil sales makes them less sensitive to the fears of supply interruption characteristic of the less flexible natural gas infrastructure.

[62] U.S. Congress, Office of Technology Assessment, *Technology and Soviet Energy Availability* (Washington, DC: U.S. Government Printing Office, 1981), pp. 35-37, 46-48, 53-55, 62-64, 67-70. See also Robert W. Campbell, *Soviet Energy Technologies* (Bloomington, IN: Indiana University Press, 1981).

[63] Robert G. Jensen, Theodore Shabad and Arthur W. Wright (eds.), *Soviet Natural Resources in the World Economy* (Chicago, IL: University of Chicago Press, 1983), pp. 316 and 316-23.

[64] Thane Gustafson, "Energy and U.S.-Soviet Relations: The Question of Eastern Europe," in Donald J. Goldstein (ed.), *Energy and National Security: Proceedings for a Special Conference* (National Defense University Press, 1981), p. 148 (emphasis added).

import depends on its ability to export enough oil and natural gas to earn enough hard currency. And the prospects for increasing energy exports will be enhanced by importing key energy equipment and technologies from the West.

This is not the profile of an autarkic economy. It is rather the profile of an economy for which turning inwards still remains an option, while the economic costs of doing so have become rather substantial. Having said this, however, the distinction between an internationalised and dependent Soviet economy needs to be underlined. Useful in this regard is the general theoretical differentiation made by Keohane and Nye between the sensitivity and vulnerability aspects of international economic interdependence.[65] Sensitivity refers to the initial costs that can be imposed on a nation's economy by sanctions or other external disruptions. Generally speaking, the more internationalised a nation's economy, the greater these initial costs will be. Vulnerability, however, is a temporal concept that takes into account the continuing costs that a nation suffers because of external events or actions. It is determined less by the level of sensitivity than by state capacity to take actions over time to reduce the costs of disruption. The greater a state's capacity to take such vulnerability-reducing actions, the less likely is the internationalisation of its economy to develop into economic dependence.

There are two main reasons why Soviet vulnerability remains low despite an increase in sensitivity. One is that its own vast resources and endowments, as well as those available to it through its imperial dominance of Eastern Europe, give the Soviet Union a useful base on which to draw in time of need. Regional autarky may not be an optimal policy any longer, but if

necessary it can still be a policy option. The second reason for the Soviet Union's limited vulnerability has more to do with the international market place. Even in the case of the 1980 American grain embargo, in which the United States held back a 77.6 per cent share of Soviet grain imports, there emerged alternative suppliers to whom the Soviet Union could turn.[66] The initial disruption of grain supplies by the American grain embargo did impose some costs, as did the premiums added on to their prices by Argentina and other commercially opportunistic grain exporters. But while these testified of Soviet sensitivity to the American grain embargo, far more important in the broader politico-strategic picture was the fact that alternative suppliers were available and vulnerability thus reduced.

As far as industrial technology is concerned, given the mere 3 per cent American share of total Soviet machinery imports from the West, the United States is in an even weaker position for converting Soviet economic internationalisation into economic dependence. The United States embargoed its exports of equipment for construction of the West Siberian natural gas pipeline, but the Soviets still could turn to Western Europe.[67] When the Reagan administration then tried to coerce its allies into supporting the sanctions, it ended up setting off such an intense intra-alliance imbroglio that within a few months it had to retreat. If the Soviets had not been able to import the turbine power-compressor station from Western Europe, completion of the pipeline would have been complicated. It is in this respect that the Soviet economy is internationalised. But they were able to import what they needed—it is in this sense that their economy is not dependent.

[65] Robert O. Keohane and Joseph S. Nye, Jr., *Power and Interdependence* (Boston, MA: Little, Brown, 1977), pp. 11-19.

[66] Robert L. Pearlberg, *Food, Trade and Foreign Policy: India, the Soviet Union and the United States* (Ithaca, NY: Cornell University Press, 1985), p. 197 and generally.
[67] Bruce Jentleson, *Pipeline Politics, op. cit.,* Chapter 6.

CONCLUSION: THE POLITICAL POSSIBILITIES OF ECONOMIC INDUCEMENT IN THE 1980s

My case as presented thus far rests on three central arguments. First is that the two cardinal assumptions on the basis of which the possibility of economic inducement is rejected, the naive theory of interdependence and the Riga-essentialist conception of the Soviet threat, themselves are to be rejected. Second, the 1970s detente case was shown to provide some empirical substantiation of political influence achieved through economic inducement. Moreover, given the trade restricting actions taken by the American Congress, questions were raised about indicting the economic inducement strategy on the basis of its failure to avert the collapse of detente. And, third, because of the increased internationalisation of the Soviet economy a stable and growing trade relationship with the West has come to be of greater value to the Soviet economy in the 1980s than ever before.

To be sure, these arguments also have their qualifications. The rejection of the old anti-inducement assumptions stops well short of either claiming that expanded trade relations will automatically improve political relations between adversaries, or of embracing an overly benign view of the Soviet Union. With respect to the case of detente, the complexity of Soviet motivations was stressed both as part of the explanation of the influence that was achieved and in not implying any certainty that detente would have succeeded except for the restrictions imposed on trade. Finally, it was acknowledged that no deterministic claim can be made about the political consequences of the internationalisation of the Soviet economy.

Such qualifications notwithstanding, these arguments do open up the question of the political possibilities of economic inducement in the late 1980s. The case made compares favourably to the limits and drawbacks of the economic sanctions strategy, as demonstrated by the outcomes of the 1980 grain embargo and the 1982 natural gas pipeline sanctions. In nei-ther case were substantial economic costs imposed on the Soviet economy. Nor can any claim to political influence be made. As to the contention that breaking with business as usual reinforced the overall credibility of the American deterrence posture, at best this is a non-falsifiable proposition. More likely, given the fact that first the grain embargo was lifted without even a token Soviet political *quid pro quo,* and then the natural gas sanctions were softened without Soviet concessions, American credibility was left worse rather than better off.

If either or both of these cases could be written off as aberrations, then perhaps prospects could still be held out for anti-Soviet sanctions to be effective in the future. However, on the contrary, the politics of these cases have become the rule, not the exception. For, as Hirschman writes, if

> a country menaced with an interruption of trade with a given country has the alternative of diverting its trade to a third country...it evades more or less completely the damaging consequences of the stoppage of its trade with one particular country. The stoppage or the threat of it would thus lose all its force.[68]

Moreover, there has come to be significant domestic opposition within the United States to sanctions. This was especially graphic in the grain embargo case but also influential in the natural gas pipeline case. This has created the additional constraint of what, drawing on Bruce Russett and Harvey Starr, can be called "the bluffer's dilemma."

> If societal support is lacking and prevents a government from pursuing certain policies or using certain capabilities, the credibility of the government declines in the eyes of other states. Its ability to influence them shrinks as its reputation as a "bluffer" grows.[69]

[68] Albert Hirschman, *op. cit.,* p. 29.
[69] Bruce Russett and Harvey Starr, *World Politics: The Menu for Choice* (San Francisco, CA: W.H. Freeman, 1981), pp. 237-8.

The case for a renewed attempt at an economic inducement strategy therefore rests both on the positive reasoning of its own possibilities as well as on the negative reasoning of the probability of continued inefficacy of economic sanctions. The Soviet Union is no more likely to be compelled to change its foreign policy by economic sanctions than it has been in the past. This is even more true of Jewish emigration, Soviet dissidents or other Soviet domestic policy issues. Here the paradox the United States faces is what Samuel Pisar called the mind versus the heart. "My heart," Pisar wrote in reconsidering his 1974 testimony to a Congressional committee, "ordered me to say nothing that could give comfort to those in the Soviet Union who were suppressing freedom and stopping Jews from emigrating to the land of their choice." But "my mind told me that nothing was more important to the solution of some of the world's most critical problems than a real expansion of U.S.-Soviet contacts, human and commercial."[70]

Strobe Talbott captures this dilemma as the tension between doing good in normative terms and doing well in pragmatic terms. The Soviets are not impervious to pressure on human rights issues. They did open their exit doors wider in 1972-73, in large part because of their interest in American trade. When in 1978-79 the Carter administration and the Congress indicated willingness to reconsider the Jackson-Vanik amendment's restrictions, the Soviets again allowed significant increases in Jewish emigration (e.g., from 16,736 in 1977 to 51,320 in 1978).[71] In both instances, though, as soon as more overt linkage tactics were resorted to (the Jackson-Vanik amendment's passage in 1974, its repeal removed from the agenda by Afghanistan in 1980), the exit doors were closed.

Talbott extends the point of the diminishing returns argument more generally to the liberalisation of Soviet society and applies it also to periods other than the 1970s. He concludes that "only at those moments when they have felt less threatened by their external enemies have the Soviet leaders decided that they could be more lenient towards potential and imagined enemies within."[72] It would run contrary to the American character to suggest that American foreign policy suddenly and somehow drain itself of its idealistic tradition. But a pragmatic approach would be to maintain a degree of human rights pressure on the Soviet Union, but conscious of the point of diminishing returns (which, it bears repeating, is a general characteristic of overt economic coercion in international relations), refrain from explicit linkages to trade.

Some other types of linkages may be possible as part of the initial instrumental bargaining over the re-opening of relations if the issues are chosen carefully and overt manoeuvring avoided. This is what Nixon and Kissinger did in the 1971-73 period and could be attempted again. But priority should be given to the more long-term structural influence objective of developing mutual interests which will add an element of stability to American-Soviet relations. This will mean resisting the quasi-behaviouralist impulse to resort to the carrot-and-stick approach explicitly and directly rewarding prescribed behaviour and punishing proscribed behaviour.[73] It will also mean avoiding the temptation to over-sell the policy as part of electioneering. One of the fatal flaws of the Nixon-Kissinger policy was the gap between what the American public expected and what had actually been achieved. A weary public's expectation that all conflicts between the United States and the Soviet Union were now things of the past was consciously cultivated by an administration

---

[70] Samuel Pisar, op. cit., p. 281.
[71] Strobe Talbott, "Social Issues," in Joseph S. Nye, Jr. (ed.), The Making of America's Soviet Policy (New Haven, CT: Yale University Press, 1984), pp. 183-205; Jewish emigration data from Robert O. Freedman, op. cit., Annex 1.

[72] Strobe Talbott, op. cit., p. 205.
[73] This was the Carter administration approach. See Samuel P. Huntington, "Trade, Technology and Leverage: Economic Diplomacy," Foreign Policy (No. 32, Fall 1978), pp. 63-80.

worried about its re-election prospects. Now that we were selling them our grain and technology, the presumption went, they will be good world citizens. But while the Soviets did do some political trading in the bargaining process (as noted in the earlier discussion), overall superpower global competition for influence had by no means been adjourned.

Domestic support also requires that trade be conducted on sound commercial terms so that there not be another "great grain robbery" debacle. In 1972 the Soviets got all the grain they needed and at subsidised prices, while the resulting short supply situation fed American inflation. Nothing could have been more of an affront to the American consumer than a foreigner, especially a Soviet, getting lower interest rates and grain prices than (s)he could get at the local bank or shop. The only possible compensation would have been political concessions of a magnitude far greater than those possible. It was a profound and damaging irony that the gains from trade ended up so maldistributed as to be a source of opposition.[74]

It is also important that while allowing trade to expand in most sectors, appropriately defined national security export controls should be maintained. National security controls are those based on the nature of the exports themselves, as distinct from foreign policy controls which are based on the nature of the American-Soviet relationship at a particular moment. Clearly it is not in the United States' interest even when relations are on the upswing to export products or technologies which directly and significantly enhance Soviet military capabilities. The line defining how much and what kind of military significance is permissible is not always easily drawn, especially when technologies which potentially have dual uses or products which embody such technologies are involved. But by appropriately defined national

security controls, I mean avoiding the kind of infinite elasticity of what constitutes military significance that, as Khrushchev once caricaturised it, leads to embargoes on zippers because without them soldiers would have to use their hands to hold up their trousers instead of to carry guns.[75]

Even more to the point were the Reagan controls on the natural gas pipeline compressors. When, as in this case, the United States opts for too broad an interpretation of military significance, it runs into the same international and domestic forces that constrain foreign policy embargoes. As noted earlier, the nations of Western Europe always have, still do and undoubtedly will continue to favour a narrower interpretation of "military significance." Consequently, as Marshall Goldman and Raymond Vernon have observed, "as long as the United States pursues highly restrictive policies...the prospects of finding a working consensus with the Europeans on this basic subject seems close to zero. And without the support of Europe, a US effort...is almost meaningless."[76]

A similar differentiation has marked American domestic politics.[77] Battles are still fought, especially over dual-use cases and, as over the past few years, between the Commerce and Defense Departments over departmental jurisdiction and the discretion that comes with being the leading agency. Congressional Democrats are in general also more inclined to err on the side of a narrow interpretation than are their Republican colleagues (with notable exceptions within both parties). But compared to the major

---

[74] Raymond Vernon, "Apparatchiks and Entrepreneurs: U.S.-Soviet Economic Relations," *Foreign Affairs* (January 1974), pp. 249-62.

[75] The Khrushchev anecdote is included in Angela Stent, *From Embargo to Ostpolitik: The Political Economy of West German–Soviet Relations* (New York: Cambridge University Press, 1981), p. 93.

[76] Marshall Goldman and Raymond Vernon, "Economic Relations," in Joseph S. Nye, Jr., *op. cit.,* p. 168; see also William A. Root, "Trade Controls That Work," *Foreign Policy,* (No. 56, Fall 1984), pp. 61-80 and Ellen L. Frost and Angela E. Stent, "NATO's Troubles with East-West Trade," *International Security* (No. 8, Summer 1983), pp. 179-200.

[77] Bruce Jentleson, *Pipeline Politics, op. cit.,* Chapter 7.

conflicts over foreign policy controls, these-battles have been both less intense and less extensive. There continues to be an operative domestic consensus on the necessity for national security controls. Consequently, it is possible as well as desirable to restrict trade in the most militarily relevant sectors as a defensive measure while allowing it to expand in other sectors as a positive initiative.

Finally, it must be recognised that trade is a necessary but not a sufficient condition for improved political relations. It is necessary as a means for introducing mutuality into a relationship in which it has been sorely lacking. Next to the mutual interest in avoiding nuclear war, economic relations hold the greatest prospect of providing a basis for American-Soviet co-operation. This cannot be a sufficient basis for a new detente, however, because given the anarchic nature of international relations economic incentives are always a relative calculation. On the one hand they are relative to other indicators of intentions to improve relations, and are more likely to be inducing if there is reason to believe that continued, real and lasting progress towards a

more stable and co-operative relationship is possible. On the other hand they are relative to the benefits that could be achieved by reverting to a more competitive relationship. It is in this latter respect that economic inducement has to be pursued as a complement to, not as a substitute for, sustained political and military deterrence.

My contention therefore is not that of the straw men with which anti-trade critics often respond, of predictions of Soviet society being consumerised, or the Soviet political system being liberalised, or the Soviet economy being "capitalismised". Nor is it that there are any guarantees. And there are potential risks. There is nothing automatic about accommodation between political systems which boast such antagonistic ideologies, have experienced so many years of antipathy and possess as many conflicting interests as do the United States and the Soviet Union. All too often, though, intellectually as well as politically, policies for seeking accommodation are treated as guilty until proven innocent, while those premised on the Cold War's immutability are allowed the more traditional status of innocent until proven guilty.

[Economic Leverage in U.S.-Soviet Relations]
Edward A. Hewett

The Reagan Administration is convinced that the Soviet economy is vulnerable to economic pressures exerted through East-West economic relations, and that Soviet leaders will respond to those pressures in a predictable way which will serve U.S. policy interests. Europeans are skeptical on both counts, which is how close allies who share revulsion for events in Afghanistan and Poland can find themselves in such profound disagreement over what to do about

From U.S. Cong., Senate, *Economic Relations with the Soviet Union,* Hearings before the Subcommittee on International Economic Policy and the Committee on Foreign Relations, 97th cong., 2d Sess., 1982, pp. 128–131.

it. All of our European allies are unwilling to join the Reagan Administration in embargoing equipment for the gas pipeline because they fear that the very substantial costs they will incur now (lost exports of at least $5 billion, lost gas imports later, and considerable irritation on the part of the Soviets) will bring forth no obvious benefits by changing the trend of events in Poland or Afghanistan. On a more general, but related, level the Reagan Administration has implied that it is a good idea to exert economic pressure on the Soviet Union in order to force Soviet leaders to choose between increases in defense expenditures and increases in living standards, the supposition being that they must bow to increasingly insistent consumer demands, and therefore reduce the growth of Soviet military power.

These are very serious matters indeed which touch on the foundations of NATO, in particular those regarding the nature of the Soviet threat and the best way to deal with it. The Reagan Administration is isolated, yet apparently adamant, in its views. For both reasons it is important that we as Americans do all we can to explore the validity in the fundamental tenets of this policy, exposing weaknesses where they exist. This testimony, while too brief and general to do justice to that task, nevertheless does endeavor to ask some important questions and suggest what the answers might be.

Those who seek to use East-West economic relations to influence Soviet foreign policy implicitly assume that: (1) If western countries act in unison, then they can impose significant costs on the Soviet economy by manipulating East-West trade and financial flows; (2) Soviet leaders will be forced to respond to those increased costs by shifting resources from the military to the civilian sector, all other options being closed by political or technical restraints; and (3) Soviet leaders will become much more wary of foreign adventures, much less capable of shoring up regimes in Eastern Europe, and that therefore Soviet foreign policy will change in directions favored by the West.

The first point is the subject of other testimony at these hearings, and will not be discussed here in any detail. I would only note in passing that right now the United States and Europe are so deeply divided on the appropriateness of sanctions against the Soviet Union, that the only practical question is whether the United States alone can impose any long-term costs on the Soviet economy through embargoes which Europe and Japan ignore, and on this matter I am quite pessimistic.

Setting that aside, I turn now to the other two propositions. What are Soviet leaders' op-tions should the United States succeed in "penetrating their economic defenses" and imposing on the economic system significant economic costs? And, as they choose among those options is it inevitable, or even likely, that they will feel compelled to change Soviet foreign policy either in order to avoid further costs, or because military capabilities are not sufficient to support their foreign policy goals?

In any discussion concerning how western countries can use East-West economic relations to influence Soviet economic performance it is important to realize that western policies regarding commerce with the U.S.S.R. are a relatively unimportant determinant of the level and growth rate of Soviet GNP. The Soviet economy is a huge, complex mechanism, which in 1980 had a GNP of approximately $1.4 trillion (about ½ U.S. GNP for that year). The system is enormously well endowed with natural and human resources, and it is organized through a political system which—albeit very inflexible—has nevertheless been up to the task of making the U.S.S.R. one of the major military powers in the world.

The major determinants of the level of economic activity in this system are internal, having to do with (1) how well or poorly Soviet leaders organize the economic system and set policies to guide the operation of the system; (2) factors out of the control of any leadership such as demographic trends, weather and world economic developments. In the last 3 years, for example, the major shock to the Soviet economy has not been two U.S. administrations' increasingly severe restrictions on East-West trade, but rather the very poor weather which has affected agricultural output, and therefore GNP.

Throughout the postwar period the Soviet economy has experienced a generally steady decline in growth rates of GNP reflecting unfavorable trends in the basic factors determining Soviet economic performance. (GNP growth rates averaged 5 percent in the 1960's and 3 percent in the 1970's. They are unlikely to surpass 2 percent in the 1980's.) The major problems here are: (a) low and declining growth rates in the labor force, with all new additions coming in the least industrialized areas of the U.S.S.R.; (b) a fall in productivity growth rates; (c) increasing economic difficulties in Eastern Europe, Cuba, and Vietnam, all of whom depend in varying degrees on Soviet largesse for maintaining living standards; (d) increasing costs of extracting and transporting raw materials and energy; and (e) an aging leadership with only a loose grip on a rigid bureaucracy, seemingly incapable of assessing and dealing with the fundamental causes of Soviet economic problems.

Some of these trends are out of the control of Soviet planners, but others could conceivably be reversed over time. For example, a new Soviet leadership could introduce radical economic reforms and as a consequence reduce trends in labor productivity growth rates, which would be an important step in reversing the downward decline in GNP growth rates. But there is no indication that the current leadership is inclined to take the necessary steps, and a new leadership would find it very difficult to do so until it had been in office for several years. Therefore the Soviet economy is in for a very grim decade indeed, no matter what policies Western governments pursue regarding East-West economic relations.

As a result Soviet leaders shall have to make, indeed are already making, some very unpleasant choices among competing claims from consumers, investors, the military, and Soviet client states (most notably Eastern Europe and Cuba). One, and probably two of these groups, will have to accept at least stagnation, and probably a drop in their real income from Soviet GNP.

The Reagan Administration is quite clear, in fact probably somewhat overly impressed, concerning the dismal economic prospects facing the Soviet economy. But for them this is apparently not enough. They seek to add to Soviet economic problems an unfavorable climate in East-West trade and finance, in order to hasten the decline of Soviet economic performance. Implicitly the theory is that the Soviets shall have to adjust to deteriorating economic performance by reducing the growth rate of military expenditures and support for client states. Consumers are regarded as adamant in their zeal to protect and improve their living standards, and investment demands shall have to rise if the economy is even to stand still.

However the current debate between Europe and the United States may come out concerning President Reagan's economic sanctions, the net impact on the Soviet economy from these sanctions is likely to be relatively minor in comparison to all of the other negative trends discussed above. Therefore the basic question we must ask is how Soviet leaders are likely to adjust to continuing economic difficulties, and in particular what impact these difficulties will have on military expenditures. A second and now very important issue is if U.S. economic policy succeeds in contributing to Soviet economic difficulties, can we be sure that Soviet planners will choose the same types of adjustment policies they would choose if the problems had primarily internal causes?

On the first point I would suggest that Soviet options are considerably broader than the Reagan Administration might suppose. It is certainly true that the political inclinations of Soviet planners will lead them to protect living standards as best they can, even to increase them by some modest amount, in order to avoid further dissatisfaction in any form resembling that which propelled the Polish regime to catastrophe. And indeed in the period since 1979 when GNP growth rates have averaged under 2 percent there is ample evidence that Soviet leaders are doing their best to insulate consumers from much (although not all) of the required adjustment.

Secondly it is also true that Soviet client states, in particular those in Eastern Europe, can expect to see subsidies from the U.S.S.R. fall somewhat. How far they fall depends on how far the Soviets think they can push individual East European countries without precipitating a serious economic/political crisis. Throughout this decade those subsidies shall probably have to remain fairly substantial, and therefore they will provide little relief in the event of persistent low growth rates.

Assuming that consumption continues to enjoy protection, that leaves investment and the military, and here it seems quite likely that Soviet planners will try first to freeze investment levels. Investment in the Soviet economy is currently 33 percent of GNP, easily 10 percentage points above investment rates in Europe, and double that of the United States. There is probably a good deal of slack in those figures, and Soviet leaders are virtually certain to look there before turning to a final and very hard choice between military and consumer needs. Indeed that seems to be the strategy in this 5-year plan (for 1981-85) where annual growth rates for investment are planned at about 1 percent, well below projected GNP growth rates.

If investment cannot provide the needed slack for adjusting to lower growth rates, and if therefore the choice is back to military or consumption, then I see three options for Soviet leaders: (1) to go ahead and cut the growth rate of military spending below its recent historical rate of 4 percent per annum, (2) to maintain that rate but cut the growth rate of consumption to below that of GNP, and (3) to introduce serious economic reforms which would boost labor force productivity and GNP growth rates, and which would therefore allow the Soviets to avoid the hard choices they otherwise would face.

In a world where United States-Soviet relations were characterized by some form of détente, Soviet leaders might be inclined to pursue the first option, simply because the other two options hold so many political uncertainties

for them. But as long as the United States persists in its current policy of thinly veiled economic warfare against the Soviet Union and rapid increases in military spending, then the first alternative is out of the question for any Soviet leadership which wishes to stay in power. To choose such a path would be obvious capitulation in the face of U.S. coercion, and the Soviet economic situation is not nearly so desperate as to force that unpleasant task on the current leadership.

Although in a period of détente the second option (cutting consumption) would be politically quite risky for Soviet leaders, the current international climate increases considerably their latitude (and inclination) to impose austerity. U.S. administration policies give Soviet leaders ample ammunition to sell the Soviet population an economic policy which pursues high growth rates for the military and low consumption growth rates as a patriotic response to an external threat. In fact U.S. policy could well serve as a convenient scapegoat for poor Soviet economic performance, which in reality reflects weaknesses in the Soviet economic system. As a short-term policy, say through the mid 1980's, that might work rather well. As a longer term policy it would surely have its limits, in particular since the next U.S. election could well bring a shift away from open U.S. hostility to the Soviets, and to East-West relations.

That is why as a long-term policy the third option seems to be the likely one for the Soviet leaders to pursue. The rigidity of Soviet economic institutions imposes tremendous costs on Soviet economic performance. And if Soviet leaders are forced into economic reform as the only viable way to maintain the legitimacy of their regimes, they will probably find that serious reforms will unleash considerable creative forces, stimulating economic performance. The inefficiency of the Soviet economy is at once its greatest weakness and its greatest potential strength. Political leaders in the U.S.S.R. will not willingly choose to attack the fundamental source of inefficiency, in part because of the unforeseeable political consequences. But in the process of a leadership succession, and in the context of declining economic performance (possibly associated in part with U.S. policy), it is radical economic reform, rather than reduced military spending, to which Soviet leaders are likely to gravitate.

If this analysis of Soviet options is at all close to the mark, then the Reagan Administration's policy towards the U.S.S.R. is very strange indeed. The Administration is risking important relationships with Europe in order to impose costs on the Soviet economy which will only in a marginal way further aggravate an already deteriorating economic situation. By pursuing that path openly, and by enunciating other policies designed to impress the Soviets with U.S. determination to reattain military superiority, the United States will force Soviet leaders to do what otherwise might be hard or impossible for them to accomplish: tax consumers for high military expenditures in the short run, and introduce radical economic reforms in the medium term. Furthermore such a policy virtually guarantees an intensification of Soviet economic pressure in Eastern Europe with consequences which are not easily predictable. There is, as far as I can see, little thought given in this Administration to how Eastern Europe will fare in an economic war with the Soviet Union.

Certainly there is little prospect that current Reagan Administration policies will force the Soviet leaders to change any important aspects of their foreign policies in areas of fundamental importance to them, such as Afghanistan or Poland. In the first place it is unlikely, for reasons discussed above, that U.S. economic pressure can exert any perceptible influence on Soviet military expenditures. Even if we do manage to impose through our policies costs on the Soviet economy, it is consumers, investors, Soviet clients, and possibly even Soviet economic institutions which will take the brunt of the adjustment. If military expenditures are adjusted, it will be for far more fundamental reasons than a response to U.S. sanctions or U.S. displeasure with Soviet behavior.

It is even less likely that the Soviets will change their foreign policy in response to the threat of U.S. sanctions. This Administration is dangerously schizophrenic about the Soviet Union. On the one hand they contend that the U.S.S.R. is superior to the United States as a military power. Yet at the same time they contend that the economy is so fragile that the military power means nothing and that the threat of economic sanctions will so frighten the Soviets that they will change important aspects of their foreign policy. Such a proposition would be ridiculous were it not for the sad fact that it underlies current U.S. policy.

Although I am not myself trained in military matters, I presume it is regarded as the most elementary of principles that in warfare one should fully appreciate, if not over-appreciate, the capabilities of his adversary. And indeed when this Administration is arguing for defense expenditures it seems to follow that tenet with some zeal in its depiction of Soviet military capabilities. And yet when this same Administration argues for economic warfare it persists in underestimating its adversary. The economic system is painted in incredibly simplified terms best described as a caricature of the actual Soviet economic system. Soviet leaders are depicted as having few, if any, options and the system is seen to be in dire straits. It is this caricature, rather than careful analysis, which allows policy makers to delude themselves that policies costly to the Atlantic Alliance also carry potentially high benefits.

It is time for the Reagan Administration to move beyond caricatures of the Soviet economy to an understanding of the far richer reality of the real system. The Soviet economy has a long history of economic difficulties, and an equally long history of economic successes. Throughout the last 20 years when Soviet specialists were carefully (and accurately) describing how cumbersome the system was, it still managed to produce real GNP, military spending, and consumption growth rates quite respectable by world standards. And while the decade ahead will hardly be a good one for the Soviet economy; that could be said of many countries. There is little the United States can do objectively to make the situation better or worse. And what we can do to make it worse may damage the Atlantic Alliance and push Soviet leaders away from the very policies we should like to see them pursue.

QUESTIONS FOR DISCUSSION

1 Is the Soviet economy in a condition of acute crisis? If so, is the regime itself potentially vulnerable to a counterrevolution?

2 Should the United States seek to influence Soviet foreign policy by either inducements or sanctions in the economic sphere?

3 Would such inducements or sanctions be likely to be effective?

4 Have Western European members of NATO behaved disloyally to the United States in developing economic ties with the Soviet Union?

5 Should U.S. economic leverage on the Soviet Union, if feasible, be used solely to seek improved Soviet international conduct, or should human rights issues within the domestic jurisdiction of the Soviet Union also be raised?

SUGGESTED READINGS

Bartlett, Bruce. "What's Wrong with Economic Sanctions?" *USA Today Magazine,* **114** (May 1986), pp. 22–25.

Becker, Abraham S. *Economic Leverage on the Soviet Union in the 1980s.* Santa Monica, Calif.: Rand, 1984.

Bernstam, Mikhail, and Seymour Martin Lipset. "Punishing Russia: Reagan Was Wrong about the Embargo," *New Republic,* **193** (Aug. 5, 1985), pp. 11–12.

Buchan, David. *Western Security and Economic Strategy Towards the East.* Adelphi Paper no. 192. London: International Institute for Strategic Studies, 1984.

Feldman, Jan. "Trade Policy and Foreign Policy," *Washington Quarterly,* **8** (Winter 1985), pp. 65–75.

Fossedal, Gregory A. "Sanctions for Beginners: When They Work and When They Don't," *New Republic,* **193** (Oct. 21, 1985), pp. 18–21.

Melvern, Linda, Nick Anning, and David Hebditch. *Techno-Bandits: How the Soviets Are Stealing America's High-Tech Future.* New York: Houghton Mifflin, 1984.

Parrott, Bruce (ed.). *Trade, Technology, and Soviet-American Relations.* Bloomington, Ind.: Indiana Univ. Press, for the Center for Strategic and International Studies, 1985.

Roeder, Philip G. "The Ties That Bind: Aid, Trade, and Political Compliance in Soviet-Third World Relations," *International Studies Quarterly,* **29** (June 1985), pp. 191–216.

Roosa, Robert, Armin Gutowski, and Michiya Matsukawa. *East-West Trade at a Crossroads: Economic Relations with the Soviet Union and Eastern Europe: A Task Force Report to the Trilateral Commission.* New York: New York Univ. Press, 1982.

Suzman, Helen. "What America Should Do about South Africa," *New York Times Magazine,* **135** (Aug. 3, 1986), pp. 14–17.

14 Do most terrorists serve as instruments of Soviet foreign policy?

YES

Wall Street Journal

Bombing the West

NO

Alexander Cockburn

A Connected Terrorist under Every Bed

Bombing the West

Wall Street Journal

The Free World has now endured more than a decade of relentless, spectacularly destructive bombing. Had some of these bombs been dropped in the traditional manner from airplanes onto cities or villages, some of the Free World's nations would most surely have launched a warlike response against their attackers in whichever countries they reside. But because wired clocks explode bombs today, the citizens of the Free World are merely dying.

Throughout this period the dominant attitude in the West has been that because no known means exists to decisively defeat terrorism, we should accept it as a fateful condition of modern life. Some urge that we seek to understand the roots of its grievances, while others hope at best to contain it at acceptable levels. But forbearance has earned the West primarily an accumulation of debris and the death of innocents.

The latest bomb blew up Sunday morning. The 329 men, women and children on Air-India Flight 182 fell 31,000 feet into the sea. About the same time, a bomb blew apart baggage coming off a Canadian airliner in Tokyo, killing two Japanese men.

Yesterday Israel released 31 of its Shiite detainees. To this, Lebanese Minister of Justice Nabih Berri replied that only all 766 would do, and he added (inevitably) to his list of demands that U.S. ships off Lebanon depart. And over the weekend, TV viewers had to absorb the image of President Reagan meeting the coffins of four Marines who had been machine-gunned by El Salvador's guerrilla movement while sitting in a cafe in San Salvador. Last Wednesday a suitcase bomb blew up in Frankfurt, West Germany's airport, and a woman and two small Australian children died. Also that day, a bomb blew up a candy shop in Tripoli, Lebanon, and 33 Moslems died.

These latest incidents have marked an active two weeks of terror, but are merely the latest in an active era of political terror. Last October, a bomb blew up a resort hotel in Brighton, England, killing or crippling several members of the British government or its Conservative Party. Precisely one year earlier, a bomb went off in Rangoon, Burma, killing four members of South Korea's cabinet and two valued presidential advisers.

On April 18, 1983, a bomb blew up the U.S. Embassy in Beirut and 46 men and women died. That October, a bomb blew up the Marine barracks in Beirut and some 240 men serving as American soldiers died beneath the rubble.

In December 1983, a bomb blew up in Harrods department store in London, killing six and injuring 91 shoppers. In August 1980, a bomb blew up in a train station in Bologna, Italy, and 84 people died.

Other events: the attack on Pope John Paul II, the Munich Olympics massacre, Aldo Moro, KAL Flight 007, the Armenian assassination of Turkish diplomats, the assassination of Lord Mountbatten, the "yellow rain" attacks against the unsubjugated Hmong people of Laos. And so many other exploded bombs and innocent deaths across Europe, the Middle East and Asia that the news records them with the efficiency of a police official—location, number of victims, device used, group claiming responsibility.

As this terrorist wave has been building these past years, a small number of writers and analysts have begun telling people in the West that it is wrong to react to terrorism with numbed helplessness. Foremost among these has been Claire Sterling, a free-lance Ameri-

Wall Street Journal (editorial), "Bombing the West," *Wall Street Journal*, June 25, 1985, p. 30. Reprinted with permission of *The Wall Street Journal*. Copyright © Dow Jones & Company, Inc. All rights reserved.

can writer living in Italy who in 1981 produced a book titled "The Terror Network." The book's achievement was that it refuted the popularized notion that terror was randomized violence by lunatics. It should be seen instead as a paramilitary tactic with political ends.

The world has always been full of historical ethnic grievances and irredentist movements. What emerged in the 1970s, however, was the realization that one could recruit people from within these groups and teach them the logistics and technology of terror. That training took place in East Germany, Czechoslovakia, Bulgaria, Libya, Cuba, South Yemen, North Korea, Middle East fedayeen camps, Vietnam and the Soviet Union.

The graduates of these schools now commit bombings and assassinations in places like Ireland, Spain, Belgium, West Germany and Latin America. Just this past March 3, the *Miami Herald* published an enormously detailed description by reporter Juan Tomayo of the extent to which Managua, Nicaragua, has now become a hostelry for terrorists for whom arrest warrants have been issued throughout the West. The Soviets and their allies do not plan every bombing that takes place, of course, but their nurturing of terrorism has clearly done much to set the fashion.

Up to now, political elites have managed to successfully ridicule or dismiss reporting like that of Ms. Sterling and Mr. Tomayo. With this wave of terror over the past two weeks, our sense is that an awareness is sinking more deeply into the public mind that terrorism is intent on eliminating Western values and replacing them with the political values of the Warsaw Pact's most closed nations. Many more people are coming to believe that the West must fight back.

This means above all defeating terrorism as a political tactic, raising its cost and reducing its rewards. It means imposing costs on identifiable terrorists like the Lebanon hijackers. It means defeating the Salvadoran rebels. It means building rather than destroying our intelligence capabilities, even at the risk they will sometime make mistakes.

All of this starts, though, with a few basic recognitions by Western publics and Western leaders: That the price of doing nothing is becoming too great. That with inaction, terror will increase in incidence and scale. That the terror we are facing today is not always or even often the work of madmen, but of coldly rational political calculators sensitive to changes in risks and benefits. That terrorism is not simply our fate, that the answer lies not in our stars but in our will.

A Connected Terrorist under Every Bed

Alexander Cockburn

"The Free World has now endured more than a decade of relentless, spectacularly destructive bombing." This was the suitably apocalyptic start to a *Wall Street Journal* editorial on June 25, and as the writer pounded away at his keyboard, anger drove sense and syntax out of the computer till we were left with mere notations of the paranoid world view that has come to be associated with these pages: "Other events: the attack on Pope John Paul II, the Munich Olympics massacre, Aldo Moro, KAL Flight 007, the Armenian assassination of Turkish diplomats, the assassination of Lord Mountbatten, the

Alexander Cockburn, "A Connected Terrorist under Every Bed," *Wall Street Journal,* July 11, 1985, p. 25. Reprinted with permission of Alexander Cockburn.

'yellow rain' attacks against the unsubjugated Hmong people of Laos.''

The mechanism of paranoia links discrete phenomena and perceives in them a conspiracy against the paranoid victim. A man once called me to say that planes circling over his house were filled with secret agents broadcasting unsettling messages to him via the fillings in his mouth. It turns out that he had bad teeth and lived near LaGuardia Airport. What pattern is there in the list of violent acts spluttered out in the *WSJ's* editorial? Are we somehow to assume, to take three of them, that the IRA splinter group that blew up Lord Mountbatten is in league with the Armenians and that both are in some way connected with ''yellow rain,'' which itself no longer attracts much credence as a toxic substance outside of its most enthusiastic sponsors in the *WSJ's* editorial offices?

The pattern apparently inferred by the *WSJ* editorial writer and, to judge by his speech to the American Bar Association Monday, at least one loyal reader in the form of President Reagan, is that these violent acts enjoy common sponsorship by socialist-bloc countries and ultimately and most particularly by the Soviet Union. The *WSJ* editorial did generously concede that not every bombing in the world is planned by the Soviet Union and its allies, but this concession came as a *pro forma* addendum to the central thesis of a ''Terror Network.''

The words ''Terror Network'' bring us to a great heroine of the *WSJ* editorial writers and probably of the president, too, in the form of Claire Sterling. She is a free-lance American writer living in Italy and, as the *WSJ* editorial gratefully recognized, has been an enthusiastic exponent of the notion of a Terror Network sourced in Moscow. Her most celebrated illustration of the workings of this same network has been the so-called ''Bulgarian Connection'' (Paranoid Plots always look better if they begin with capital letters), which supposes that Ali Agca, the Turkish would-be killer of the pope,

was prompted to his assassination bid by the KGB, working through its Bulgarian ''proxy.''

Though she is perhaps the best known of the Bulgarian Connecters, Ms. Sterling has not worked alone. Other assiduous Connecters have been Paul Henze, Arnaud de Borchgrave, Marvin Kalb of NBC and Michael Ledeen. For the better part of the past three years they've had the run of the airwaves and of both the news and editorial pages in major U.S. newspapers such as *The Wall Street Journal* and *The New York Times* to make their charges and often to insinuate (a traditional part of the paranoid vision) that nonbelievers in the Connection are therefore by definition part of the Connection themselves. And as the months and years have rolled by since the Connection was first suggested to an American audience on this page by Paul Henze in October 1981 (eight months before Agca thought of it himself, a year after his arrest), these advocates of the Connection have been the ubiquitous ''experts,'' ex-officio members of the prosecution of Sergei Antonov, the unfortunate Bulgarian, a political prisoner actually, who has been in jail or under house arrest in Rome, without trial, since Nov. 25, 1982.

Anyone who took the trouble to examine the case for a Bulgarian Connection rapidly found it to be riddled with absurdities. The imputed Soviet/Bulgarian motive for killing the pope was his support for the Polish Solidarity movement. But the Agca-Bulgarian Connection was supposedly made in July 1980, at least a month before the proclamation of Solidarity in August of that year. Agca first threatened to kill the pope (as a Christian Threat to The Moslem World) in 1979, during John Paul II's visit to Turkey. Aside from endless inconsistencies of this nature, no witness or material fact has, to this day, been produced to support any of Agca's allegations of a Bulgarian Connection.

None of this bothered the Connecters, nor dampened their benign reception in the U.S. mass media (with the honorable exception of the *Washington Post's* Michael Dobbs) until the trial of Agca's alleged accomplices began in Rome on May 27. Since that day a profound and embarrassed silence has overtaken the Connecters. Ms. Sterling's byline suddenly disappeared from reports of the trial filed by *The New York Times's* Rome bureau. Other Connecters appear to be lying low. The reason is not hard to find. As anyone who has studied his "testimony" down the years knows well, Agca is not proving to be a very reliable or convincing witness. But this time his antics are being observed by a large press corps and a vigorous judge. Hardly had the trial begun before Agca declared he was Jesus Christ. Later he offered to resurrect a "scientifically dead person" in the presence of Ronald Reagan. On June 25, near the end of a month in court, the Italian prosecutor said of his main witness, "If he wanted to destroy his own credibility he has succeeded magnificently," and Agca said despondently that "I cannot invent anything more," perhaps in response to Judge Severino Santiapichi's angry remark to him that "you can't come out with a new truth every time you open your mouth."

Along with Agca's collapse has come some interesting testimony in a separate Italian Mafia trial suggesting that Agca may well have been coached into his allegations of a Bulgarian Connection by agents of SISMI, the Italian agency for military intelligence. SISMI had in fact anticipated Agca's Connection, claiming a mere six days after the assassination attempt that it had been ordered by the late Soviet defense minister Dmitri Ustinov.

In other words, Exhibit A in the Terror Network is in a very sorry state right now and its collapse should act as a warning of how delusive paranoid visions can be, and how useless they are as a guide to how the U.S. should comport itself in the world today. For one thing, the paranoid vision is monocular. The *WSJ* editorialist who writes about the "relentless, spectacularly destructive bomb-ing" of the Free World apparently forgets that the most destructive bombing in the Western Hemisphere in the last decade is being achieved with U.S. supplied bombs, planes and supervision by President Duarte's air force in El Salvador, with thousands dead in consequence. An honor roll of terrorism that excludes South Africa—as does both the WSJ editorialist and President Reagan—looks somewhat lopsided to many people in the world. The bombs detonated in Nicaragua by the contras are not supplied by Bulgarians or the KGB.

Above all the paranoid vision eschews facts in favor of fantasy, sees international politics mostly in terms of plots by the dark hand of Moscow. The result is a paranoid foreign policy that provokes ridicule or hatred in much of the rest of the world, neither of which emotions are in the best interests of the U.S.

QUESTIONS FOR DISCUSSION

1 Can most state-sponsored terrorism be traced back to Moscow?
2 Are the Soviets justified in claims that the United States sponsors terrorism in Central America?
3 How should the United States respond to any proven cases of Soviet sponsorship of terrorism?
4 Is state sponsorship of terrorism always morally wrong?
5 Is state-sponsored terrorism by the Soviet Union likely to increase in intensity?

SUGGESTED READINGS

Alexander, Yonah, David Carlton, and Paul Wilkinson (eds.). *Terrorism: Theory and Practice*. Boulder, Colo.: Westview Press, 1979.

Carlton, David, and Carlo Schaerf (eds.). *Contemporary Terror: Studies in Sub-State Violence*. New York: St. Martin's Press, 1981.

Cline, Ray S., and Yonah Alexander. *Terrorism: The Soviet Connection*. New York: Crane, Russak, with the Center for Strategic and International Studies, Georgetown Univ., 1984.

Francis, Samuel T. *The Soviet Strategy of Terror.* Rev. ed. Washington, D.C.: Heritage Foundation, 1985.

Goren, Roberta. *The Soviet Union and Terrorism.* Winchester, Mass.: Allen and Unwin, 1984.

Henze, Paul B. "Coping with Terrorism," *Fletcher Forum,* 9 (Summer 1985), pp. 306–323.

Herman, Edward S. *The Real Terror Network.* Boston, Mass.: South End Press, 1982.

Shultz, George. "Terrorism: The Challenge to the Democracies," *Department of State Bulletin,* **84** (Aug. 1984), pp. 31–34.

Sterling, Claire. *The Terror Network: The Secret War of International Terrorism.* New York: Holt, Rinehart and Winston, 1981.

U.S. Cong., Senate. *Historical Antecedents of Soviet Terrorism.* Hearings before the Subcommittee on Security and Terrorism of the Committee on the Judiciary, 97th Cong., 1st Sess., 1981.

U.S. Cong., Senate. *Role of Cuba in International Terrorism and Subversion,* Hearings before the Subcommittee on Security and Terrorism of the Committee on the Judiciary, 97th Cong., 2d Sess., 1982.

U.S. Cong., Senate. *Terrorism: Origins, Direction and Support,* Hearing before the Subcommittee on Security and Terrorism of the Committee on the Judiciary, 97th Cong., 1st Sess., 1981.

U.S. Cong., Senate. *Terrorism: The Role of Moscow and Its Subcontractors,* Hearing before the Subcommittee on Security and Terrorism of the Committee on the Judiciary, 97th Cong., 1st Sess., 1981.

15 Is it a U.S. interest to develop and deploy ballistic missile defenses?

YES

John C. Toomay

The Case for Ballistic Missile Defense

NO

Jack Mendelsohn

Five Fallacies of SDI

The Case for Ballistic Missile Defense

John C. Toomay

With his strategic defense initiative, President Reagan has called on American scientists and engineers to devise a defense against nuclear ballistic missiles. In proposing that the United States switch from an offense-oriented to a defense-oriented strategic policy, the president has sparked a lively public debate about the merits of such a policy. As he noted in his March 1983 address, our current strategic policy is to deter aggression through the promise of retaliation. Deterrence has worked, and we have averted a nuclear exchange of any kind, for over forty years. But I believe we cannot afford to be complacent about changes that have occurred in the strategic balance over these years. As a member of the Defensive Technologies Study Team (Fletcher panel) that advised the president, I am persuaded that an increased effort to develop ballistic missile defenses is a wise course for the United States.

THE DETERRENCE EQUATION

Deterrence has become a complex and subtle matter. The fine points of how to maintain deterrence in peacetime, in crisis, even during war, have been the subject of much discussion. But the basic concept of deterrence is relatively simple. The word itself comes from the Latin, meaning "from fear": deterrence is the state of not acting for fear of the consequences. Gen. Russell Dougherty, former head of the Strategic Air Command, has described it as the product of military capability and the will to use it.[1] In the case of nuclear deterrence, we must pay far more attention to our opponent's capabilities— the weapons and the means of using them—

than to his will. We cannot gamble that he might be lacking in will, when the consequences of being wrong are so grave. Therefore, our current strategic posture is based substantially on the power of our offensive forces. It emphasizes the *capabilities* of the Soviets rather than their intent. We do not question that the Soviets have the will to act; instead, we make conservative estimates of the capabilities of Soviet strategic forces and assume they will use them in the way most destructive to our interests.

Our deterrence equation must also take into account our estimate of what the Soviets believe is unacceptable damage to their country. Because we have little confidence in our abilities to probe the psyches of Soviet leaders, our estimate is again very conservative. Our strategic force requirements are determined by working backward from the level of potential damage that we are confident will ensure deterrence. We believe we can deter the Soviets if their calculations always show that we are capable of inflicting unacceptable damage on them in retaliation, even after they have executed an all-out surprise attack against us.

Our ability to gauge what deters the Soviets has been sufficient to avert a nuclear exchange of any kind for over forty years. I assert that this is evidence that deterrence has worked. We seem to accept these decades of deterrence quite casually, even complacently, for two reasons. The first is manifest: human nature comes to accept the status quo as natural. The second is vital: until recently, the margin of our advantage over the Soviets in strategic forces has been wide. Even very large errors in our estimates of Soviet intent or Soviet capability would not have significantly changed the equation.

Today, however, the situation is less sanguine: the relation is one that some call "rough parity." There is much debate over the signifi-

John C. Toomay, "The Case for Ballistic Missile Defense," *Daedalus*, **114** (Summer 1985), pp. 219–237.
[1] Gen. Russell E. Dougherty, "Capability × Will = Deterrence," *Air Force Magazine*, June 1984, pp. 7–8.

cance of this shifted balance. Devotees of minimum deterrence argue that when both superpowers have thousands of nuclear weapons only a few hundred of which are capable of inflicting massive damage, an increase in numbers, no matter how asymmetrical the result, is irrelevant and therefore cannot jeopardize deterrence. Advocates of stronger strategic forces, on the other hand, warn that any imbalance encourages Soviet intransigence and adventurism, and a gross imbalance might invite a limited nuclear attack, which could easily escalate into a massive exchange.

We have no way of knowing, before the fact, which of these two interpretations is correct. Yet we can reflect on the experiences we have had. The Cuban Missile Crisis of 1962 is often cited as an example of Soviet accommodation to our nuclear superiority; in contrast, Soviet stubbornness during the intermediate nuclear force (INF) negotiations of 1981–83 is seen as an example of Soviet implacability in our present world of ''parity.'' Such evidence is anecdotal and hence not altogether convincing. Perhaps we need to address the matter in a different way: what have we gained by letting our strategic superiority erode, and what have we risked? The benefits have presumably included reduced expenditures on strategic forces, reduced numbers of nuclear weapons, and an international reputation as a peace-seeking nation. The world has not been made a safer place, however, nor has nuclear war been made less likely by such erosion. The potential risks from an eroded strategic posture are far more onerous. They include new wars of national liberation, major incursions into, for example, Europe, or actual nuclear exchanges and loss of sovereignty and freedom.

We have tried various stratagems since the mid-1960s to sustain our strategic position. At first, we sought to preserve superiority; this was followed by ''balance''; then came, in rapid succession, ''essential equivalence'' and ''counter-

vailing forces''—all euphemisms for a declining strategic margin. During much of the 1960s and 1970s, we cut the budget for nuclear forces almost every year. We have made some efforts to bolster our strategic forces, though with mixed results. The B-1 bomber, at first cancelled, has been revived, though in drastically reduced numbers. The MX has been approved, though again in reduced numbers. Minuteman's accuracy and hardening have been improved, cruise missiles are being deployed on bombers, and Trident submarines are operational.

Nevertheless, our efforts pale beside those of the Soviets, whose massive buildups have now spanned over twenty years and have brought them parity in numbers of strategic warheads and superiority in total explosive power. Moreover, the Soviets have devoted themselves to the full range of strategic forces, including defenses. They have maintained and are now improving their ABM system around Moscow; their air defense network is extensive; Soviet civil defense preparations are vastly greater than our own; and they are pressing ahead with advanced ballistic missile defense technologies.

The United States has also tried detente and arms control as methods of stabilizing the strategic balance. The SALT negotiations may have diverted, but they did not halt, the Soviet buildup of forces; our efforts at limiting strategic arms by negotiations have proved disappointing. As things now stand, we are frustrated in our dealings with the Soviets, we have no consensus at home about what our policy should be, and our media's recent focus on the horrors of nuclear war has unsettled us. What we are in need of is a new approach, one that might allow us to escape our current dilemmas while still preserving viable strategic forces. The addition of strategic defenses to our national policy serves just this function.

To discuss the promise of ballistic missile defense, we must first consider what the Strategic Defense Initiative refers to as ''intermedi ate capabilities.''[2] I will begin by examining those types of defense that raise relatively clear issues—defense of valuable hard targets, local area defense, and light area defense—and move gradually to consider full, ''perfect'' defense of the nation, the most contentious issue. (It will be useful, throughout the discussion, to bear in mind that these defenses could also be useful for our allies and in some cases would demand deployment by them.) We will trace how these defenses would carry us from the offense-oriented deterrence we now know to a potentially more powerful, but certainly less familiar, defense-oriented strategy.

HARD-POINT DEFENSE

One dimension of the Soviet strategic buildup that must concern us is the increase in their number of highly accurate, high-yield ICBM warheads appropriate for attacking U.S. deterrence forces and other hardened military targets. Carrying out such an attack would by no means be an easy task, as the Scowcroft Commission has pointed out. Yet when the Soviets devote so much effort and resources to acquiring a military capability, we must take seriously the potential threat that it poses. While hard-point defenses of our retaliatory forces were not explicitly addressed by the Fletcher panel (they had, after all, been studied almost continuously since the early 1960s), the possibility was examined by the Hoffman panel, which came out in support of such a policy.

Hard-point defenses would complement deterrence in a straightforward manner. Our present retaliatory forces achieve survivability in many ways: bombers are launched on warning (mobility); submarines patrol under the oceans (mobility and concealment); and land-based ICBMs are deployed in silos (hardening).

[2] Texts of the Fletcher and Hoffman reports, as well as the Defense Secretary's summary report, can be found in ''Strategic Defense and Anti-Satellite Weapons,'' Senate Committee on Foreign Relations, 98th Cong., 2nd sess., April 25, 1984, pp. 94–175.

As the accuracy of Soviet ICBMs has improved, however, the ability of our hardened silos to withstand attack has become a matter of acute concern. Of the several ways to preserve or reestablish the survivability of our ICBMs, defense shows considerable promise. Hard-point defenses are an alternative to deploying more offensive forces in order to maintain the strategic balance. Instead of installing an offensive missile in yet another silo, a defensive interceptor could be deployed to destroy an attacking warhead before it reaches the silo. Conceptually, either of these methods increases the survivability of our retaliatory forces. The choice a country makes would depend on the cost-effectiveness of offensive versus defensive systems and their political and diplomatic ramifications. Three factors so far seem to have prevented the United States from deploying hard-point defenses: the existence of the ABM treaty, uncertainties about the importance of ICBM ''vulnerability,'' and disagreements about what should be done to rectify it.

It is difficult for most people to grasp that the time to act on the survivability of our land-based ICBMs is while their effectiveness is still intact. This point deserves emphasis. If we wait until the threat to our retaliatory forces is unambiguously clear, we will have plunged ourselves into a situation of great strategic instability. Since it takes a decade or more to design, develop, and deploy any major weapons innovation, the time to begin improving our forces is long before the danger actually confronts us.

In our past calculations of what we needed for effective deterrence, we have always presumed that the Soviets would make a massive attack against our Minuteman ICBMs—as well as many other targets—and that only a fraction of them would survive. The role of active defenses would be to assure survival of at least this fraction in the face of an increasing Soviet threat. One tactic available to us is preferential defense. In preferential defense, the defender marshals his resources (in this case BMD interceptors) to defend only a limited number of points he has secretly selected. If the defender concentrates his defense effort to protect a few targets, the attacker must also increase the size of his attack on those targets if he wishes to destroy them. But if the attacker does not know in advance which targets will be defended, he must increase the magnitude of his attack on *all* targets. Just a few BMD interceptors on the part of the defense, therefore, forces the offense to multiply his forces manyfold—or develop a wholly new tactic.[3] To be effective, a preferential defense system must be able both to defend itself and to give the *appearance* of being able to defend an area much wider than the few targets actually selected.

Some systems being considered for defense of future land-based ICBM systems would have even greater leverage. For example, a system could combine defense with deceptive missile basing, which would move a relatively small number of ICBMs among a very large number of shelters. Because the location of each missile would be kept secret, the enemy would be compelled to attack all the shelters to be sure of destroying the missiles hidden within some of them. One defensive interceptor accompanying each ICBM would approximately double the number of warheads required to destroy all the missiles. If there were two hundred ICBMs and four thousand shelters, for instance, the enemy might consider an attack with four thousand warheads to be adequate. But if each ICBM were protected by an interceptor, the enemy would have to target *two* warheads on each shelter—or eight thousand warheads in all—in order to be successful.[4]

The small, hard-mobile ICBM—or Midgetman—system that is recommended by the president's Commission on Strategic Forces has some inherent suitability for such high-leverage defense. In this system, the missiles would be moved randomly on mobile launchers over government land in the Southwest. Since the Soviets would not know where each launcher was at any moment, but would presumably know the bounds of the overall deployment area, they would have to barrage the entire area with warheads to destroy the missiles. A mobile launcher is inherently a softer target than a silo and may potentially be damaged even by warheads that explode a considerable distance away, thus making it harder for a limited defense to protect the missile. Still, if an interceptor (and its associated equipment) accompanied each missile and shot only at those warheads that would destroy the missile, the warhead requirements for the Soviets would be doubled.

There is little doubt of the cost-effectiveness of such defenses. The Soviets would be hard-pressed to add, say, four thousand warheads to their strategic arsenal for every two hundred interceptors and associated equipment we deploy. The marginal cost to the attacker of adding another warhead to his missile force and modifying his post-boost vehicles seems to be about $3 million apiece—or $12 billion for four thousand additional warheads. A modern BMD interceptor would cost somewhat less than $3 million, although the two hundred small radars and the complex system integration equipment would be expensive, perhaps $10 million per missile—or $2 to $3 billion for the whole system. These ratios favor the defense by about five to one. Adding a second round of interceptors would increase the leverage even more.

---

[3] One such tactic is shoot-look-shoot, in which the attacker fires a first wave of missiles, watches to see which sites are defended successfully, and then fires a second wave concentrated on those targets. In the time required for shoot-look-shoot, however, the defender may retaliate with his surviving forces.

[4] See Harold Brown, *Thinking about National Security: Defense and Foreign Policy in a Dangerous World* (Boul-

der, Colo.: Westview Press, 1983), p. 71. Brown describes the concept of preferential defense for ICBMs, but notes that unless the ICBMs are deployed in deceptive basing, adding ballistic missile defenses will not have a significant effect on ICBM vulnerability.

Hard-site defenses also have very favorable attributes from the perspective of strategic arms control. They add to deterrence because they protect retaliatory forces while leaving urban-industrial targets unprotected, and they add to stability because they do not threaten either the cities or the forces of the other side. They have the additional advantage of providing the command authority with more time to make crucial decisions. Of course, the ABM treaty, as amended, allows each side to defend either an area containing missile silos, or its national capital. The forces permitted by the treaty (only one hundred interceptors) are insufficient for creating an effective overall defense, however. Thus, even a defense that is almost wholly in accord with the principles of strategic arms control would require renegotiation of the ABM treaty for deployment. Verification of limitations on such defenses would be feasible in several ways, although on-site inspection would probably be required.

It is inappropriate to leave off discussion of these high-leverage defense systems without noting their technical difficulties. Unless the ICBM launchers or shelters can be made as hard as their advocates claim, and the exact location of the missiles at any moment kept secret, preferential defense will lose its effectiveness. And unless the defense radars (or other sensors) are as hardened as the missiles they are protecting, or are rapidly replaceable if damaged, an attacker could degrade or nullify the defense by attacking its weakest part. The offense might try other clever tactics: shoot-look-shoot, nuclear blackout of the defense radars, or maneuvering warheads. Shoot-look-shoot entails risks, because while the attacker is looking, we could be retaliating with the ICBMs that survived the first strike. Nuclear blackout is not so effective against a preferential defense that is able to intercept warheads in the last seconds of flight. And maneuvering vehicles lose velocity and accuracy very rapidly when making hard turns at low altitudes. All these

countermeasures deserve further investigation as part of a BMD program.

In sum, there are important factors favoring ballistic missile defense of our land-based ICBMs. Furthermore, we foresee no apparent detrimental effects if the Soviets should also deploy such defenses, within reasonable constraints. The technical and political problems do not seem insurmountable; it is rather an inchoate public suspicion of defense, and apprehensions about tampering with the ABM treaty, that are the obstacles to be overcome.

LOCAL AREA DEFENSES

Another "intermediate" defense option would be defense of valuable, but not necessarily hardened, targets or clumps of targets such as air bases, command-and-control centers, and seaports. This was addressed explicitly by the Hoffman study and implicitly by the Fletcher panel and so is a legitimate option within the SDI.

The merits of defense for such local area targets are not so easy to state as for land-based ICBM forces. Many of these targets are in or near cities and most are soft. The technical problems of defense are greater because incoming warheads have to be intercepted much farther away. And where such targets are few in number and the survival of each quite important, preferential defense may not be feasible—any or all of them might be destroyed by a concentrated attack. Given these target characteristics, it would usually be more cost effective as a first step to try more conventional means of protection: proliferation, mobility, secrecy, hardening, or some combination of these.

Over the years, studies have been made of ballistic missile defense for some valuable targets such as strategic bomber bases. Currently, we ensure that a significant fraction of our bombers will survive attack by putting them on twenty-four-hour alert, ready to take off on warning of attack. During crises, the fraction on alert can be raised and the bombers dispersed to other bases. Defending bomber bases arguably offers two advantages over these procedures: it would also protect that portion of the bomber force not on alert, and it would increase the survivability of airfields after a nuclear exchange. Yet defending the bases would probably be the most expensive way of guaranteeing the survival of bombers. A full defense of airfields would have to intercept large numbers of SLBMs, ICBMs, and cruise missiles—all of which the Soviets could place on target almost at their leisure, because once our alert forces have departed, the remaining planes are slow to respond. Moreover, defense of bomber bases presumes nuclear war-fighting and protracted nuclear war. It thus raises the question whether money spent on defending air bases might be better spent on forces that would increase deterrence and prevent nuclear exchanges in the first place.

As for command-and-control centers, increasing their numbers seems a more efficient way to ensure continued operations. Suggestions that we defend them seem to stem more from a sense that it would be easier to obtain funding for defense than for adequate command-and-control facilities themselves. But if we think of the national command authority (NCA) as people, rather than facilities, the issue is more easily resolved. The whereabouts of the president and secretary of defense at the start of an attack can never be anticipated, so their safety can never be fully guaranteed. Short of an almost leak-proof whole-country defense, the most effective tactic for preserving command authorities is to equip and train the NCA hierarchy and staff.

For similar reasons, defense of seaports probably does not make sense. The number of major seaports is small, they are soft targets, and they tend to be far apart. The Soviets could simply overwhelm the defenses if they choose to make a large enough attack. More important, however, seaports are more of a military con-

venience than a necessity. The Soviets could not stop the flow of goods to our allies by attacking seaports. There are far too many ways to transport material of all kinds: over the beaches; by air; through improvised ports; or through the small ports, marinas, and piers that dot our 23,000 miles of coastline.

Defending various valuable but soft targets with local area defenses, then, does not seem promising.

LIGHT AREA DEFENSES

So-called "light area defenses" would be a step beyond local area defenses. They would protect the country as a whole from a light attack, that is, a level of nuclear attack substantially less than what would be expected in a major nuclear exchange. The United States started to deploy a light area defense, the Sentinel system, in the 1960s. In 1968, Sentinel's name was changed to Safeguard, its mission was changed to protecting Minuteman ICBMs, and its light area defense role was markedly reduced. After the ABM treaty was signed, the few sites that had been built were dismantled. Studies of light area defenses continued, however, on the assumption that the United States would eventually need them. One rationale was that we needed to raise the threshold of any small nuclear attacks made on us by the Soviets. It cannot be denied that as the commitment of weapons required by an attacker increases, and the intensity of probable responses therefore becomes larger, the likelihood of his engaging in impulsive acts declines dramatically. It was further argued that the whole country needs protection—with increasing urgency as nuclear weapons proliferate—from attacks by nations with small nuclear arsenals, from accidental or unauthorized attacks by any source, and from attacks by terrorist groups. Supporters of light area defense reason that although such attacks may be unlikely, there is a finite probability that one or more will eventually occur.

Until recently, light area defenses had to rely on strings of radars along the coasts, as ground-based radars could not survey beyond the horizon. Short-range surveillance begat numerous (and expensive) short-range missile sites. Several developments since the early 1970s have altered that situation. Air- and space-based surveillance of huge areas is now feasible. Small, accurate, hypervelocity BMD warheads are practical, making the interceptors that carry them much faster given the same overall weight. The huge signal and data processing requirements of a central site can probably be accommodated now because of vast improvements in computers. Space-based directed-energy weapons could provide light area protection even if they could not achieve whole-country ballistic missile defense.

Light area defenses would also have growth potential as the threat became more sophisticated or the potential number of attacking warheads increased; more interceptors could simply be added. The sensors and computers are the key components for upgrading; they need higher capacities and improved software to solve the complex problem of finding warheads among a variety of penetration aids. As this upgrading is achieved, the light area defense could gradually become the terminal portion of a whole-country defense.

An upgraded light area defense system deployed overseas might also provide a dense defense against attacks on NATO by Soviet theater nuclear forces. Our European friends might be comforted by the realization that the United States would no longer be constrained in its diplomatic support by the concern that the Soviets might engage in nuclear adventurism against Europe as a response. If the Soviets also deployed a defense, it might neutralize the retaliatory forces of both Great Britain and France, but both could field sophisticated penetration aids that would add to the Soviet Union's uncertainties about its defense effectiveness. Of course, with the nuclear threshold raised on both sides by the presence of defenses, NATO readiness at the conventional level would become even more important than it is now.[5]

While effective light area defenses would require modification of the ABM treaty if we decided to deploy them, they seem to violate none of the precepts of strategic arms-control theory. They would simply force the Soviets to increase the scale and risk of a successful nuclear attack, thereby deterring an attack and increasing stability. Small numbers of interceptors would not significantly undermine assured destruction. They would not increase the level of nuclear weapons in the world. Even if they drove the Soviets to counter with an increase in offensive weapons, that increase would presumably be nullified by the number of weapons that would be intercepted and rendered useless. The world should be a somewhat safer place with light area defenses, particularly since they could evolve to meet an increasing threat.

In the cases of hard-point and local area defenses, it was noted that alternatives to defense could be used to achieve the same objectives, sometimes at lower costs. There are no alternatives, though, to light area defense, so we must think quite differently about the costs involved. Cost comparisons must be tied to the damage that expenditures on light area defense could prevent, including the loss of human life. Tens of thousands of human deaths and billions of dollars of property damage would be a tragic price to pay when they could be avoided by deploying an efficient light area defense.

One point should not be forgotten, however: none of these hard-point, local area, or light area defenses against ballistic missiles can provide effective protection unless augmented by air defenses against bombers and cruise missiles. Although BMD systems have substantial

---

[5] Colin S. Gray, *Nuclear Strategy and Strategic Planning* (Philadelphia: Foreign Policy Research Institute, 1984), pp. 86–92, provides a point-by-point discussion of the effects that BMD might have on the NATO alliance.

capability against airborne threats, they are insufficient. Air defense would also be required for whole-country BMD systems.

WHOLE-COUNTRY DEFENSE

Whole-country defense is the subject of greatest contention in discussions of ballistic missile defense. President Reagan's March 1983 speech set the protection of all Americans from the threat of all nuclear weapons as the ultimate goal. The Fletcher panel also focused on defense-in-depth of the whole nation as the heart of its study, acknowledging lesser deployments as potentially useful components of the whole.

When ICBMs first appeared in 1957, whole-country defense was an immediate concern. But in the following decade, the outlook for a successful city defense became bleaker. When a 1968 Defense Department study showed that even a very expensive city defense system would not reduce the casualties sustained in a heavy attack, the major funding for city defense R&D was cut back and substantial funds were diverted to hard-point defense.

What were the technical deficiencies that spelled the demise of city defense? Boost-phase defenses had been examined in the early 1960s and found impractical—surveillance requirements could not be met with existing technology, and interceptor velocities (even from a space platform) were too slow to allow a sensible system design. The effectiveness of penetration aids in space, where the drag of the atmosphere is not a factor, made an effective mid-course defense unlikely. Although atmospheric drag would separate warheads from decoys during the terminal phase, the altitudes at which this occurred were too low for city defense. And the capacities of computers required to handle an intense attack were far beyond the state of the art.

But if whole-country defense was laid to rest in the late 1960s, why resurrect it now? Tech-

nological advancements have occurred that promise order-of-magnitude improvements in every area previously deficient. Multi-spectral infrared sensor technology allows surveillance of the whole earth from deep in space; computer processing capacity has increased a thousandfold. The most exciting new technologies are speed-of-light weapons, which could substitute for slower interceptors and make space-based boost-phase intercept feasible. Regardless of current criticisms, such weapons might prove cost-effective. After all, the chemical energy equivalent of ten kilograms of fuel would be sufficient to kill a hardened Soviet missile weighing hundreds of thousands of kilograms. Furthermore, protection and survivability of space platforms can in principle be enhanced, so there is some prospect that they can win a long-term offense-defense competition.

There are still a good number of problems to be addressed. Intercepts occurring earlier in the ICBM's trajectory (as early as the boost-phase, in fact) must cope with a panoply of penetration aids, and it is important to determine whether new technologies will meet that requirement. It is also important to assess whether the systems that emerge will be lethal enough to perform the mission, and robust enough to survive a massive effort by the Soviets to nullify or counter them.

POSSIBLE SOVIET ACTIONS AND REACTIONS

The Soviets will doubtless regard the various tiers of a BMD system differently, reacting more strongly to space-based weapons systems than to the more familiar terminal or mid-course systems. How, then, might the Soviets respond to our deployment of a broad-coverage, terminal/mid-course ballistic missile defense that contained airborne and space-based sensors, but no space-based weapons?

First, the Soviets would have to assess the overall current and potential effectiveness of our defense and build up their offensive forces accordingly. In order to attack those targets they believe are critical, they would have to take into account that our defense can range over a large area, and they would therefore have to use large multiples of the actual number of targets. In a democracy, preferential defense of regions is obviously inappropriate. Yet if an attack occurs, our defenses, although deployed for broad protection, must surely first be employed to protect those sites critical to our survival as a nation. The worst aspect for the Soviets will be uncertainty; not knowing which targets we are determined to save, they cannot be confident that their attack will succeed. To counter the obstacles posed to a successful preemptive strike by the survivability of our retaliatory forces and the existence of our defenses, the Soviets will be driven to building defenses of their own. To be uncertain of their capabilities against us, while certain that we could annihilate them should be intolerable for the Soviets.

The result would be a world in which both superpowers have deployed offensive *and* defensive strategic systems. Would such a situation merely reestablish, but at a greater cost to both sides, the status quo?[6] The answer is no, because of two new, key factors. Defenses will have raised the threshold for effective attacks so high that only major nuclear strikes would have an effect, and the uncertainty of outcomes would be great. Thus, the likelihood of a nuclear exchange would be substantially reduced, the spectrum of conditions under which it might occur greatly narrowed, and both sides would have means of protection against accidental launches and third party attacks.

The Soviets may react more vigorously to a

U.S. defense system if it is deployed in space. Since space-based weapons have to be deployed gradually, on orbital paths the Soviets can readily predict, we should expect that the Soviets, fully aware of the threat such weapons pose, would make every effort to destroy them. The Soviets may calculate that speed-of-light weapons in space would grant global hegemony to the first country that deploys them successfully. They may reason that once either side gets a space-based system in place, its survivability may depend on preventing the other side from undertaking unauthorized launches into space. They might also reason that even if *both* sides deployed space defenses, the copresence in space of Soviet and U.S. directed energy weapons of approximately equal capability might be extremely destabilizing, as an attack by either side on the other's defense could grant a country global hegemony in a matter of minutes. Motivated by such fears, the Soviets may consider attacking our defense satellites and launch pads.

Accommodating such extreme possibilities would require heroic measures. Our launch sites might be hardened against all but nuclear attacks, they might be defended, or their security might be part of a negotiated arrangement with the Soviets covering defenses. As for security in orbit, defensive satellites (DSATs) could be launched into orbit with each directed energy battle station.

Because of its obvious expense and complexity, a space-based defense will probably not be deployed unless it is a low-leakage system. How would such BMD further affect the strategic balance set by terminal/mid-course defenses? First, it would remove us from the era of deterrence by mutual assured destruction. An all-out Soviet attack may still wreak havoc on our country, but it could not annihilate us. Second, it would place increased demands on the Soviet defense system, which would be driven to achieve balance with our own. Our inability to destroy each other would establish a

[6] In the late 1960s, when the United States first considered deploying a ballistic missile defense, Secretary of Defense Robert McNamara argued, for instance, that "all we would accomplish by deploying ABM systems against one another would be to increase greatly our respective defense expenditures without any gain in real security for either side." *Department of Defense Annual Report, FY 1968* (Washington, D.C.: Government Printing Office, 1967), p. 40.

new deterrence, one based not on the terror of offensive forces, but on respect for defensive systems. This situation has been characterized by some as a move from assured vulnerability to assured survivability. This is not exactly the case, since no imaginable set of defenses can prevent a determined and resourceful enemy from detonating nuclear weapons in our country. But the attacker's certainty that his objectives (other than naked terrorism) cannot be achieved, provides a quantum change in strategic perspective.

How does whole-country defense fit in with strategic arms-control theory? It would certainly be consistent with important goals of arms control. It would improve stability by raising the nuclear threshold and introducing a greater measure of uncertainty into an attacker's plan. There are those who disagree with this: they argue that defense is *de*stabilizing because deployment of defenses may alarm the other side by signaling a changing strategic balance, thereby encouraging a preemptive nuclear attack; and that defenses, known to be imperfect, will only be used by the *attacker*— against his opponent's ragged response to a massive first strike. The first of these objections would be sound only if there existed a huge imbalance in superpower forces—which is not at all the case today. The second objection would be valid only if it were the case that reducing the number of attacking warheads would allow poor defenses to become nearly perfect. But a defense of acknowledged mediocrity can be penetrated in a variety of ways by forces whose survival from an all-out first strike can be assured. A ragged retaliatory strike, therefore, is inexcusable militarily; neither side should allow the balance or the quality of offensive forces to become so degraded.

Arms control would still have an important role in a world of whole-country defenses. Even though the defense systems may themselves be non-nuclear, the total number of nuclear weapons in the world would be increased if the Soviets responded to our defense deployments (or we respond to theirs) by deploying a larger number of offensive forces. Moreover, in the absence of mutual restraints, either country may feel compelled to continue augmenting its offensive forces without limit, even if cost-exchange ratios favor defenses. That a truly massive effort in offensive deployment could overcome any defense is a certainty. Thus, even in a defense-oriented world, agreements on acceptable levels of offensive nuclear arms would be imperative.

Whole-country BMD does violate one of the precepts of current strategic arms-control theory: it renders retaliatory forces less effective. But a defense orientation would rely on a different form of deterrence: the would-be aggressor would be dissuaded not by the fear of annihilation so much as by the recognition of futility. Particularly if the cost-exchange ratios favor defense, the motivation would be to negotiate. In the end, the level of nuclear weapons required by the superpowers should become just sufficient so as to maintain an adequate margin over any combination of forces of lesser nuclear powers.

NEAR-TERM COST ESTIMATES

The last question to ask about the move toward a BMD-oriented world might be whether the amount of money earmarked for the president's Strategic Defense Initiative is too much. The plan was to spend about $26 billion over the first five years (1984–89), then to decide in the early 1990s which technologies are suitable for incorporation into systems. This would give future administrations the option to proceed with engineering development of those technologies and to deploy them—if feasible—in the first decade of the twenty-first century. Some technologies, and therefore some systems, can be ready for engineering development (building of prototypes) before 1993 and deployment before 2000. But the $26 billion SDI estimate includes no full-scale engineering development for these systems, and does not provide funds beyond 1989.

Estimated expenditures for the SDI through the 1980s average around $5 billion per year. Historically, the Pentagon has allotted about 10 percent of its budget to research and development of all kinds. The current amount is about $30 billion per year. By 1989, the SDI will require about 17 percent of the Pentagon's R&D budget—not insignificant, but certainly affordable. Government officials have estimated that $15 to $20 billion of the projected $26 billion would have been spent anyway in research and development on projects that are technologically similar to potential defense systems, on work to prevent technological surprise, or on efforts to keep penetration-aids technology at the state of the art.[7] The whole SDI budget will amount to far less than what Americans will spend on cigarettes or cosmetics during the same period.

The costs of possible future systems development can only be guessed at. Major systems such as submarine-launched ballistic missiles and bombers cost several billion of today's dollars to develop. A complete BMD system might consist of as many as ten separate systems, costing perhaps $40 billion for full engineering development. Estimates of the full-scale engineering development costs, like the ultimate systems costs, should be given little attention and still less credence now, especially since they seem to be within the broad bounds of affordability.

In considering these costs, we need to take a broader view than is usual in the formulation of public policy. Both the promise and the problems of the new defense technologies being investigated in the SDI will require a long time to clarify. This urges us to seek a new perspective on our long-term strategic posture. Because we elect our politicians to terms of two, four, and six years, and make five-year guid-

[7] "SDI Hearings Focus on Financial Aspects," *Aerospace Daily,* May 10, 1984, pp. 57–58.

ance plans for the Defense Department, we find it hard to think in terms of the twenty-, fifty-, or one hundred-year future. But the challenge we face is a massive one: averting nuclear holocaust for centuries. Our ambitions to create an effective whole-country defense using futuristic weapons should be viewed in that light. And the costs of developing such a defense should be considered in those terms as well.

THE SDI AND ARMS CONTROL

Perhaps the most delicate issue raised by the SDI concerns the coordination of defense research with the development of a rational strategy for strategic arms reductions. As I noted above, arms control will remain important even in a defense-oriented world. Therefore, we must not blunder into situations that would be disastrous to our prospects for strategic arms reductions. Neither do we wish to cling to tenets of arms control that are flawed or outdated. Each defense discussed above would require renegotiation of the ABM treaty before its deployment, and testing many of the components in the ABM mode might also require treaty modifications. Our existing treaties are the product of honest and diligent efforts, and reflect the views, ideals, and technologies of the time. Nevertheless, they should not be viewed as sacrosanct. These treaties were all originally devised for security purposes, and if those purposes can be shown to be better served in new ways, the treaties should be adapted to changing circumstances.

As I have argued above, there are a variety of defense systems beneficial to American security that appear consistent with arms-control goals implicitly endorsed by the Soviets in their signing of past agreements. In many instances, the Soviets came to accept arms-control measures they initially condemned—the ABM treaty is an excellent example of this change in Soviet posture. We should not be surprised if the Soviets react to the SDI in much the same way.

SUMMARY

I have argued that many new technologies show promise of making a spectrum of BMD systems practical; that a strategic posture based on defense can contribute to deterrence, increase stability, and reduce—and perhaps eventually eliminate—the threat of nuclear extermination; and that we ought to support a vigorous development of BMD technologies to discover their true potential.

In saying these new technologies show promise, I am not assuming, or offering a guarantee of, success. The Fletcher panel concluded only that the technologies were sufficiently understood for us to sketch out broad systems concepts for a multilayered defense. The crucial technological issues will take years of research, engineering, and analysis to resolve; they certainly cannot be resolved now by polemics. Yet in our open society, any large and technically ambitious initiative like the SDI is subject to immediate and widespread attention from the media and the citizenry. Temptations are irresistible for intellectuals, who deal in words rather than hardware, to attack broad system concepts as if they were actual system designs, and to predict confidently the outcome of decades of research. Any broad-based technology program such as the Strategic Defense Initiative must be guided by a set of conceptual systems that is admittedly incomplete and imperfect. Unless the public is discriminating, it may find itself unable to distinguish issues from quibbles in the debates over the direction of the SDI. Thus, the seeds of good ideas may be lost before any facts can be determined. For now, the question should not be whether conceptual systems will work, but whether the technology is worth pursuing to find out what can be achieved: let us stick to that question.

Five Fallacies of SDI

Jack Mendelsohn

It is difficult to imagine a more disruptive issue in U.S.-Soviet relations than the Strategic Defense Initiative. SDI has paralyzed arms control discussions, buffeted U.S.-Allied relations, mobilized the Soviet military and propaganda apparatus, and jeopardized the already slim chances for improving bilateral relations between the superpowers.

It is also difficult to determine which aspect of SDI is the most disruptive: the falsely-placed hopes for a leak-proof astrodome defense; the hype surrounding the abolition of nuclear weapons; the waste involved in a "top-down" driven

Jack Mendelsohn, "Five Fallacies of SDI," Speech delivered at the Virginia Military Institute Spring Symposium, April 7, 1986, Lexington, Va. Reprinted by permission of Westview Press from *Perspectives on Strategic Defense*, eds. Stephen W. Guerrier and Wayne C. Thompson. © 1987 by Westview Press, Boulder, Colorado.

technology hunt; the futility of attempting to delegislate mutual deterrence; or the lack of logic which envelops the entire program. While SDI certainly provides a vast field for critical comment, this paper will concentrate on five major fallacies of SDI and their impact on U.S.-Soviet relations.

SDI is predicated on five major fallacies which have affected the U.S.-Soviet relationship: the cooperative fallacy; the technological fallacy; the exhaustion fallacy; the last-move fallacy; and the strategic fallacy.

THE COOPERATIVE FALLACY

In response to the knotty problem of how to assure the Soviet Union of the basically benign intent of the SDI program and how to restrain the Soviet Union from any rash acts before SDI comes on line, the president has several times stated that the U.S. would share its SDI technology with the Soviet Union. Most recently, in an interview before the Geneva summit conference with a group of Soviet journalists, the president said: "If such a weapon is possible, and our research reveals that, then our move would be to say to all the world, 'here, it is available.'...And we make that offer now. It will be available for the Soviet Union, as well as ourselves."[1]

In addition, when faced with the problem of how to untangle the Soviets from their devotion to the existing offensive-dominated world of mutual deterrence, Paul Nitze, speaking for the administration, has described the need for a "cooperative" shift to a defense-dominated world. In a speech celebrated for at last creating a coherent rationale for SDI, Nitze noted that "what we have in mind is a jointly managed transition, one in which the U.S. and the Soviet Union would together phase in new defenses in a controlled manner while continuing to reduce offensive nuclear arms. We recognize that the transition period...could be tricky. We would have to avoid a mix of offensive and defensive systems that, in a crisis, would give one side or the other incentives to strike first. That is exactly why we would seek to make the transition a cooperative endeavor with the Soviets."[2]

As regards the first cooperative proposal, is it conceivable that the U.S. would consider transferring its most advanced technology to the Soviet Union and thereby aiding an adversary either to obtain or defeat our own defenses? Unless the Soviet leadership has totally changed their spots, handing over U.S. defense plans and technol-

ogy—which, incidentally, we are not prepared to do with even our closest allies—is an ultimate folly. As a recent Office of Technology Assessment (OTA) study on ballistic missile defense (BMD) notes: "If BMD plans or devices are transferred, potential adversaries might be able to study them to discover vulnerabilities, enabling them to circumvent or destroy our own such components.... Furthermore, many BMD-relevant technologies have applications in other military areas that we may not want to help the Soviets develop."[3]

As for the second cooperative aspect, why should the U.S. have any reason whatsoever to trust or expect the Soviets to cooperate in the implementation of a transition to a defense-dominated world? Everything this administration and critics of the Soviet Union have said about the "evil empire" would lead one to just the opposite conclusion: that the Soviet Union would do everything within its power *not* to cooperate with the United States. And everything we intuitively believe about how nations interact, whether correct or not, would lead one to conclude that the Soviet Union, as a major adversary, cannot be trusted to cooperate.

A much more realistic assessment of SDI's impact on U.S.-Soviet relations is that it will trigger a reaction in the Soviet Union, the general outlines if not the exact details of which are clear:

- the Soviet Union will assume that the U.S. has no intention of cooperating in the development and implementation of SDI;[4]
- the Soviets will resist or respond to any effort to overturn offense-dominated deterrence;
- the Soviets will attempt to develop and obtain SDI technology, both overtly and clan-

---

[1] President Reagan, interview with Soviet journalists, October 31, 1985.

[2] Paul Nitze, address to the North Atlantic Assembly, October 15, 1985. General James Abrahamson has said the same thing: We "would hope the Soviets would recognize the inevitability of the emergence of defensive systems and cooperate in the establishment of mutual deployment arrangements and mutual offensive force reductions."

[3] Office of Technology Assessment, *Ballistic Missile Defense Technologies,* September 1985.

[4] Administration spokesmen (e.g., General Abrahamson) have already made it quite clear that "it is imperative that we have a much more effective defense than they have," *New York Times,* December 17, 1985.

destinely, and to subvert U.S. efforts to develop a workable system; and

• the Soviets will exploit any changes or
instabilities in the strategic balance created by
SDI.

THE TECHNOLOGICAL FALLACY

This fallacy also has two aspects to it. One aspect
is the notion that since the U.S. is technologically
advanced it will somehow humble the Soviet
Union in the race to develop SDI. Former Science Advisor George Keyworth put it this way:
"I see this shift [from offensive to defensive
weapons] as a decided advantage to the West in
maintaining a stable peace. The reason stems
from the superiority we and other Western countries have over the Eastern bloc in terms of
industrial capacity and industrial base....[The
Soviets] have to play catch up when it comes to
advanced technology....In that way, by the ex-
pedient of always staying several steps ahead, we
can thwart even the most aggressive attempts by
our adversaries to keep up."[5]

Secondly, and conversely, the case is also
made that the Soviets are so far ahead of the
U.S. in SDI-type research that we are compelled to catch up with them. For example, the
administration has made clear its concern about
a ground-based laser facility at the Sary Shagan
test site, and President Reagan has said that the
Soviets have "been conducting research in this
sort of thing for a long time. And they already
have far beyond anything we have."[6] Secretary
of Defense Caspar Weinberger has recently
reported that "the Soviets [are] ahead of us
today in the development and deployment of
strategic defenses."[7]

But Donald A. Hicks, the undersecretary of
defense for research and development, notes in
his annual technical report to Congress that the
U.S. leads the Soviet Union in fourteen basic
technologies and trails in none, with the two
nations about even in six areas. The Soviet
Union has worked hard to redress the balance,
the report adds, but with little success. As a
matter of fact, this same report shows that since
1982 the relative U.S. position in basic technologies vis-à-vis the Soviet Union has improved,
from two areas where the Soviets were superior
to the U.S. and five where they were equal to
none where they are superior and six where
they are equal.[8]

The fact of the matter is that U.S. technology
in those areas likely to be critical to SDI is five
to ten years ahead of comparable Soviet programs. For example, in target acquisition and
computer technologies, the Soviets are six to
ten years behind the U.S. And Soviet infrared
tracking and homing tests have failed thirteen
out of thirteen times. Even so, it is a fundamental mistake to attribute to a Soviet SDI program, or to a Soviet response to a U.S. SDI
program, the requirement that it reach the comparable U.S. technological level. It probably
will not do so, nor does it need to.[9]

The simplest and most immediate Soviet
response to a high-tech SDI program may be a
low-tech offense (proliferation and deception)
and mid-tech counter-measures (hardening and
antisatellite [ASAT] systems). Coupled with
this is the fact that the technology to produce an
effective ASAT weapon (for use against space-
based defenses) in most instances is less stressing than the technology to produce an effective
ABM weapon. This means that the demands on
Soviet technology to defeat SDI will actually be
less than those on the U.S. to develop it. As

---

[5] *Science,* July 1, 1983. General Abrahamson agrees
with this: "In the key technologies needed for a broader
defense—such as data processing and computer software—
we are far, far ahead."

[6] Remarks to the Committee for the Free World, London, March 19, 1985.

[7] Department of Defense, Annual Report, Fiscal Year
1987.

[8] Undersecretary of Defense, Research and Engineering, Annual Report, Fiscal Year 1987. Radar sensors have
moved from U.S.-U.S.S.R. equal to U.S. superior.

[9] Council on Economic Priorities Newsletter, December
1985.

Harold Brown has noted, "everything that works well as a defense also works somewhat better as a defense suppressor."[10]

But the Soviet Union cannot allow itself to be perceived as technologically inferior to the United States. Therefore, we can expect some sort of parallel effort to whatever the U.S. undertakes in the area of SDI. The obvious mid-term Soviet response will, of course, be to develop those aspects of SDI which they can successfully master, for example ground- or space-based laser systems. Additionally, Soviet scientists claim that certain SDI counter-measures are already "on-the-shelf" and will be put on-line as the exact nature of the American SDI threat becomes clearer. And while there is no question that the complexity and "sweetness" of American SDI technology will by far outshine that of the Soviets, if they are not running, a Mercedes affords no better transportation than a Pontiac.

THE EXHAUSTION FALLACY

This fallacy maintains that the U.S. can, through its technological dominance, use SDI to race the Soviet Union into the ground economically, if not militarily. Again, it is unclear why those who distrust the intentions of the Soviet Union or who see the Soviets as engaged in the largest military build-up in history, refuse to heed Soviet leaders when they declare that "all attempts at achieving military superiority over the U.S.S.R. are futile. The Soviet Union will never allow them to succeed. It will never be caught defenseless by any threat. Let there be no mistake about this in Washington."[11]

The Soviet nation is accustomed to making the economic sacrifices needed to meet a real or even imagined challenge, perhaps even more so than is the U.S. Even Secretary of Defense Weinberger,

in the recent edition of *Soviet Military Power (SMP),* admits that "the Soviet leadership can devote a large percentage of the national income to defense programs—a cost no Western nation is willing to pay nor need incur in times of peace."[12] Moreover, external security threats are a mobilizing factor to the Soviet leadership. The American SDI program—which the Soviets characterize as an offensive threat—gives the Soviet leadership a convenient excuse to demand further sacrifices from its citizens while exhorting them to produce even more to meet the threat of U.S. "aggression."

In other ways, "exhausting" the Soviet Union economically has a certain ring of unreality to it: the Soviet Union has the world's second largest economy, a large and skilled work force and an enormous resource base. Administration claims notwithstanding, there is no evidence that the Soviet Union is in any danger of economic collapse or even of being paupered by the sacrifices required in its pursuit of strategic defense. The Central Intelligence Agency and the Defense Intelligence Agency, in a recent report to the Joint Economic Committee, point out that since the mid-1970s, major investments in defense industrial facilities have resulted in a substantial expansion and upgrading of the Soviet defense industry. "As a consequence, most Soviet weapons expected to be delivered to the Soviet forces through 1990 will be manufactured in plants already built and operating."[13] Moreover, the Defense Department claims that the Soviet Union already has made, and continues to make, substantial investments in the strategic defense sector—the Soviet laser weapons program alone would cost roughly $1 billion per year in the U.S. according to *SMP.*[14] If this is true, then marginal shifts in resource allocation—and not large-scale new investment—are

[10] "Is SDI Technically Feasible?" *Foreign Affairs, America and the World, 1985.*

[11] Andropov, *Pravda,* March 27, 1983.

[12] *Soviet Military Power,* p. 3.

[13] CIA-DIA, "The Soviet Economy under a New Leader," March 19, 1986.

[14] *Soviet Military Power,* p. 46.

all that will be required for the Soviet Union to undertake short- and mid-term responses to SDI.

Even so, as a recent Council on Economic Priorities Newsletter notes, "U.S. efforts to force the Soviet Union into an accelerated SDI race-...may, in the long run, backfire." At issue "is the question of how a strategic defense effort might influence and change the Soviet scientific community." This is admittedly speculative, but "should SDI become a high priority," the newsletter continues, "such a program might lead to a greater emphasis on the building of the Soviet scientific infra-structure. Strategic defense relies heavily on computers and sensing technologies. The Soviets may, in turn, pursue these programs more aggressively and choose to accord higher priority to the coordination and efficient control of its research and development efforts. Thus, pressuring the Soviet Union toward this policy change may not be in the best long-term interests of the U.S." and, rather than leading to an "exhaustion" of the Soviet economy, may very well serve to reinvigorate it.[15]

There is no question but that SDI represents a technological challenge to the Soviet Union which it would rather not undertake. But the Soviet leadership will meet that challenge if forced to; this is the record of the last fifty years of Soviet behavior, and there is no sign on the horizon that Soviet determination to "keep up with the Joneses" will change.

THE FALLACY OF THE LAST MOVE

Hope springs eternal, it seems, especially when dealing with technology or the Soviet Union. The latest manifestation of this is the president's call for science to create defensive systems to render nuclear weapons "impotent and obsolete." This belief in the ability of science to solve what are essentially political problems is often linked with the fourth fallacy, that of the "last move"—the belief that somehow the next great technological breakthrough will knock out our adversary, put an end to the nuclear threat, and/or return strategic superiority to the United States.

In the U.S., at least, it is quite difficult to be rid of this extraordinary belief both in the ability of science to save us from our political follies or in the irrepressible fallacy of the last technological move. But as one of the scientists (David Parnas) engaged to review the computing demands of SDI put it, "it is our duty, as scientists and engineers, to reply that we have no technological magic that will accomplish that [i.e., making nuclear weapons impotent and obsolete]. The President and the public should know that."[16]

As for the fallacy of the last move, Senator James Exon (D-Neb.) observed: "I think it should be clear to all if there is one thing we have learned, although we may not have learned it well, [it] is that for every action there is a counteraction, and certainly if we proceed in this area, the Soviet Union is not going to sit idly by. So, I guess while we must build up our defenses from a deterrent standpoint, I suggest that we never will find the ultimate weapon because whatever we do, the other side is going to take countermeasures."[17]

History gives us good reason to believe that, as in the past, the U.S.S.R. will respond to new strategic threats. "Their reaction inescapably will be to match us in a defensive systems race, to increase their nuclear missiles and nuclear warheads and to develop decoys, chaff and other techniques to make sure that they can overwhelm any U.S. defense."[18]

---

[15] Council on Economic Priorities Newsletter, December 1985. John Kiser (in *Foreign Policy,* No. 60) says that "in the long run the threat posed by the SDI may actually strengthen the Soviets, pushing them more quickly into a broad-based computer culture and leading them to develop their own defenses ahead of the United States."

[16] *Los Angeles Times,* September 22, 1985.

[17] Testimony before the House Foreign Affairs Committee, May 1, 1985.

[18] Clark Clifford, testimony before the House Foreign Affairs Committee, May 1, 1985.

More fundamentally, the Soviet Union sees SDI as a direct threat to the U.S.-Soviet strategic relationship, which is uneasy, but currently not critically fragile. As such, this threat must be met and mastered and the previous terms of the relationship reestablished. Most likely, the Soviet Union will attempt the latter: reestablishing the strategic relationship—that is, offense-dominated deterrence—by instituting a wide range of counter-threats and countermeasures to SDI. This is a predictable and endless cycle in which both sides have engaged since the beginning of the nuclear competition. A partial listing of the SDI counter-options available to the Soviets includes:

anti-satellite weapons	ground-based lasers
electronic	X-ray lasers
countermeasures	pellets in orbit
space mines	weapons proliferation
paramilitary forces	clustering ICBM
depressed trajectories	launches
booster hardening,	fast-burn boosters
spinning	maneuvering
quick PBV release	penetration aids
salvage fusing	anti-simulation
decoys	saturation attack[19]
masked warheads	

These and other changes in the Soviet strategic force, such as greater Soviet reliance on air- and sea-launched long-range cruise missiles, could be initiated and put in place in a comparatively short time—that is, compared to any substantial deployment of SDI hardware. Ironically, as in the economic sector, these changes in Soviet hardware and strategy could lead to a situation where the Soviet Union actually improves its relative standing vis-à-vis the U.S. as a result of the stimulus of an SDI program that the U.S. might

not actually deploy. Thus, rather than being the "last move," SDI is likely to trigger a massive series of intermediate moves and countermoves on both sides with unpredictable and—with one exception—uncertain outcomes. The one certain outcome is that neither side will permit the other to improve its relative strategic position over the long term.

THE STRATEGIC FALLACY

For a number of socio-psycho-political reasons—including an attachment to an offense-dominated strategy, traditional adversarial distrust, and an ineradicable knowledge of weapons technology—it is not likely that the present strategic relationship based on offense-dominated nuclear deterrence will be abandoned. Deterrence based on the capability to "punish" is not a strategy of choice; it is a "condition" rooted in man's socio-political behavior. It is, as Hans Bethe has said, "not a policy or a doctrine but rather a fact of life."[20]

If that is true, and I firmly believe that it is, then the U.S. cannot simply "delegislate" mutual deterrence and transition from an offense-dominated to a defense-dominated world. It is partly this realization which led the administration to propose a discussion of a "cooperative transition" touched upon earlier. But even if we wished to declare mutual deterrence outmoded, no one knows how to proceed to the next stage. The recent comprehensive OTA study of BMD had this to say about an arms control agreement intended to phase in BMD:

> It would have to establish acceptable levels and types of offensive and defensive capabilities for each side and means for verifying them adequately. It would have to specify offensive system limitations that prevented either side from obtaining a superior capability to penetrate the other's defenses. It would have to specify the BMD

[19] *SDI: Progress and Challenges,* Staff Report Submitted to Senators Proxmire, Johnston, and Chiles, March 17, 1986.

[20] *Scientific American,* October 1984.

system designs for each side that would not exceed the BMD capabilities agreed to. *It is important to note, however, that no one has yet specified in any detail just how such an arms control agreement could be formulated.*[21] [Emphasis added]

And no one can, from either within or without the administration!

I think it worthwhile to continue to quote from the OTA study on this matter:

OTA was unable to find anyone who could propose a plausible agreement for offensive arms reductions and a cooperative transition.... Without such agreement on the nature and timing of a build-up of defensive forces, it would be a radical departure from previous policies for either side to make massive reductions in its offensive forces in the face of the risk that the other side's defenses might become highly effective against the reduced offenses before one's own defenses were ready.

Although this is the last of the "fallacies" I have chosen to discuss, it is the most basic one. The U.S., much as it may wish to, cannot single-handedly move out from under the umbrella—or threat—of mutual deterrence. It may not be a comfortable position, but it is a realistic one and one which can be better managed but not overthrown. This is where SDI comes up against its most demanding challenge: no one can satisfactorily explain how SDI will accomplish anything except provoke a spiral of offense-based deterrence to higher levels.

IMPLICATIONS FOR THE FUTURE OF U.S.-SOVIET RELATIONS

What are the implications of these five fallacies for the future of United States–Soviet relations?

In regard to the first or "cooperative" fallacy, despite the call—even the reliance—on cooperation to effect a move to a defense-dominated environment, there is no chance the Soviet Union will see the U.S. strategic defense program as a cooperative opportunity to improve U.S.-Soviet relations. Rather, the Soviet Union will continue to view SDI as a threat to the very basis of the existing strategic relationship, and as a challenge to the technological "manhood" of the Soviet industrial establishment. So instead of cooperation, we will have increased tension between the superpowers and an intensified—not diminished—adversarial relationship.

As for the second or "technological" fallacy, we are likely to find that rather than pushing the Soviet Union to the technological edge, we will have provided it with a mobilizing factor for the next decade or two. Also, quite unintentionally, we might force it to organize and forge ahead in just those areas where it is weakest and where it would be to U.S. advantage to leave it so. Without question the Soviet Union is having difficulty in adjusting to the computer-driven, information-processing revolution. As Loren Graham observed in an article two years ago in the *Washington Post,* "if we can gain time by controlling the military technology that can so easily destroy us all, the civilian computer technology that is now penetrating to the lowest level of society—the individual—will give a real advantage to societies that do not try to control information."[22] A vigorous U.S. SDI program risks doing exactly the opposite.

As for the third or "exhaustion" fallacy, even Secretary Weinberger admits that Moscow shows no indication of reducing the percentage of resources dedicated to the Soviet armed forces. In brief, it is very unlikely that SDI will cause the "evil empire" to throw in the strategic towel. Marshal [Sergei F.] Akhromeyev has made it very clear that "if this process goes on we will have nothing to do but to take up retaliatory measures in the field of both offensive and defensive weapons."[23] There is

[21] Office of Technology Assessment, *Ballistic Missile Defense Technologies*, September 1985.

[22] March 11, 1984, Outlook Section.
[23] *New York Times*, December 17, 1985.

no reason not to believe the Soviets on this issue, and there is no indication they will not make every sacrifice to assure the resources are available for whatever effort they may undertake to counter SDI.

If the Soviet Union is forced to mobilize in order to respond to SDI, then it is likely that the U.S. will become more useful as a whipping boy than as a partner. This will make it almost axiomatic that the hard-liners in foreign and domestic policy will dominate deliberations in Moscow and that diversionary challenges to the U.S. in the Third World and elsewhere will become even more attractive to the Soviet leadership than they are at present.

As for the fourth fallacy, that of the "last move," rather than bringing about the end to nuclear weapons, we are more likely to see SDI stimulate a very vigorous and broad-gauge offensive response. The most direct Soviet response to SDI will be to proliferate, harden, and decoy offensive systems. Secondly, the response will focus on defensive countermeasures to SDI, including ASAT systems and ground-based laser threats. Thirdly, the Soviets will work on their own version of SDI. It may not be an elegant system, but as Stephen Meyer has noted, "the innovation and development philosophy that allowed the U.S.S.R. to deploy the first ICBM, ABM system, and SSB ('don't make it fancy, don't worry if it doesn't quite work initially, and let people run it') may triumph again."[24]

Another result of striving for the ultimate technological "fix" of SDI is likely to be the destruction of arms control as we have understood it for the past fifteen years. This is not meant as a value judgment, but it is unclear what, if anything, will substitute for the loss of this process. For good reason, the U.S. military has favored retaining what little arms control is still in place: it places predictable constraints on the Soviets; it simplifies U.S. force planning; and it conserves resources. All of these advantages would be lost without arms control: SDI would provoke an unpredictable series of reactions from the Soviets; it would enormously complicate U.S. force planning, both offensively and defensively; and it would represent an intolerable drain on the budget.

The last of our fallacies, the strategic one, has the most serious implications for U.S.-Soviet relations. An effort by the U.S. to move away from offense-dominated deterrence is doomed to failure, and the development and deployment of strategic defenses will be viewed by the Soviet Union as both provocative and destabilizing. At a minimum it increases fears that the actual goal of an imperfect strategic defense is to protect against a ragged retaliation after a first-strike by the side with the defensive systems. We can expect a vigorous quantitative and qualitative response from Moscow, one that—together with the demise of traditional arms control—will revise the nature, if not the terms, of the strategic relationship. Specifically, we will stimulate the growth of strategic arsenals on both sides, waste untold billions on deploying useless defensive systems, increase tension, and decrease stability. And after all this, mutual deterrence will still be with us as the primary means of keeping the uneasy peace.

In short, our five fallacies lead to the following five implications for the future of our relations with the Soviet Union:

- rather than cooperation we will have tension;
- rather than decreasing our technological edge we may well dissipate it;
- rather than exhausting the Soviet Union we will mobilize it;
- rather than making the "last move" we will trigger another arms cycle; and
- rather than abandoning an offense-dominated strategy we will reinforce it at higher and less stable levels.

---

[24] *Survival,* November-December 1985.

It is difficult to conceive of a more serious, threatening, and negative set of implications for the future of U.S.-Soviet relations.

QUESTIONS FOR DISCUSSION

1 In what circumstances, if any, should the United States be prepared to use or threaten to use nuclear weapons?
2 How far is President Reagan's program laid down in March 1983 technologically achievable, and in what time frame?
3 Should the United States seek to defend its ICBMs with antiballistic missiles based either on land or in space?
4 Is there a good chance that the United States and the Soviet Union will cooperate to provide any form of defenses against nuclear attack?
5 Is the Soviet Union ahead of the United States in the race to construct nuclear defenses? If so, will the United States be able to catch up or overtake the Soviet Union?

SUGGESTED READINGS

Drell, Sidney D., and Wolfgang K. H. Panofsky. "The Case against Strategic Defense: Technical and Strategic Realities," *Issues in Science and Technology,* **1** (Fall 1984), pp. 45–65.

Fossedal, Gregory A. "S.D.I. Deployment and History," *American Spectator,* **19** (Dec. 1986), pp. 30–31.

Gray, Colin S. "Strategic Defences: A Case for Strategic Defence," *Survival* (London), **27** (Mar.–Apr. 1985), pp. 50–55.

Hartung, William. "Star Wars Pork Barrel," *Bulletin of the Atomic Scientists,* **42** (Jan. 1986), pp. 20–24.

Lehrman, Lewis E. "The Case for Strategic Defense," *Policy Review,* no. 31 (Winter 1985), pp. 42–46.

Lellouche, Pierre. "SDI and the Atlantic Alliance," *SAIS Review,* **5** (Summer–Fall 1985), pp. 67–80.

Meyer, Stephen M. "Soviet Strategic Programmes and the U.S. SDI," *Survival* (London), **27** (Nov.–Dec. 1985), pp. 274–92.

Payne, Keith B. *Strategic Defense: "Star Wars" in Perspective.* Lanham, Md.: Hamilton Press, 1986.

Rothschild, Matthew, and Keenen Peck. "Star Wars: The Final Solution," *Progressive,* **49** (July 1985), pp. 20–26.

Stares, Paul B. *The Militarization of Space: U.S. Policy,* 1945–1984. Ithaca, N.Y.: Cornell Univ. Press, 1985.

Union of Concerned Scientists. *The Fallacy of Star Wars: Why Space Weapons Can't Protect Us.* New York: Random House, 1984.

U.S. Cong., House of Representatives. *Implications of the President's Strategic Defense Initiative and Antisatellite Weapons Policy,* Hearings before the Subcommittee on Arms Control, International Security and Science of the Committee on Foreign Affairs, 99th Cong., 1st Sess., 1985.

Wieseltier, Leon. "Madder Than MAD," *New Republic,* **194** (May 12, 1986), pp. 18–22.

16 Are superpower nuclear arms control agreements so vital that the United States should avoid using the negotiations to introduce linkages to other issues?

YES

John A. Hamilton

To Link or Not to Link

NO

Richard Pipes

[Linkage]

To Link or Not to Link

John A. Hamilton

At a White House news conference nine days after his inauguration, President Reagan told reporters: "You can't sit down at a table and just negotiate unless you take into account—in consideration at that table—all the other things that are going on.... In other words, I believe in linkage."

It is still too early to tell exactly how Reagan will use linkage in his foreign policy. But the prominence accorded the concept in the foreign policies of recent U.S. administrations sets a precedent for broad use of linkage in both public and private diplomacy. The press is already full of speculation about whether Reagan is using linkage in dealing with immediate issues such as F-16 fighter-bomber shipments to Israel or long-range issues such as SALT.

Linkage is not a new idea. As early as the fifth century B.C., Herodotus filled his *Persian Wars* with discussions of the diplomatic linkages practiced by Greek city-states in forming alliances to resist the Persian onslaught. Then, as now, linkage was the practice of tying a concession by one party to a concession by the other. One party could, for example, make an offer of military assistance contingent upon a reciprocal offer of economic assistance.

The heyday of linkage occurred in the early nineteenth century, when the foreign ministers of Britain, France, Prussia, Austria, and Russia—the great powers of the Concert of Europe—employed the tactic as the cornerstone of their international relations. Former Secretary of State Henry Kissinger in 1957 analyzed the prerequisites of effective use of what is now known as linkage diplomacy in *A World Restored: Metternich, Castlereagh and the Problems of Peace 1812-1822*. He implied that the

concert's success depended on three conditions: rough parity between the issues under negotiation, involvement of several countries of appreciable geopolitical status, and fluid or potentially fluid alliances.

Without parity, no bargain could exist. When one country believed its advantage to be greater than anything the other country could offer in return, it would work to retain that advantage, precluding genuine negotiation. Even with parity, bargains were sometimes difficult to conclude unless a third country entered the negotiations to push the two sides to a settlement; negotiations between two governments of approximately equal strength could founder on some minor impediment. Moreover, without fluid alliances even a system encompassing many states could become inflexible, no government of a smaller state being willing to break off its relationship with its sheltering superpower to serve as potential mediator or to tip the balance of power.

In succeeding decades, linkage played an important role in relations between nations. But in the last dozen years, use of the tactic has taken a new turn. In essence, this cornerstone of quiet diplomacy has been transformed into a political tool. Government officials now offer linkage for public consumption in a way that would have puzzled some of its most gifted practitioners. Austrian statesman Metternich, for example, would have insisted that linkage worked best when it was least obvious.

Democratic processes and institutions are partly responsible for the rise of public linkage. In the late 1960s, Americans and their elected legislators, jolted by events in Vietnam, were beginning a decade-long assault on the executive branch's monopoly of foreign policy. Linkage served as a political tool—a way of explaining U.S. actions in the world to an increasingly

John A. Hamilton, "To Link or Not to Link," *Foreign Policy*, no. 44 (Fall 1981), pp. 127–144.

informed and demanding domestic constituency. Unfortunately, this democratically inspired use of public linkage often clashed with the real need for confidentiality in diplomacy.

Moreover, the growing importance of the media whetted the public's appetite for the reasons behind government actions. The clamor of the press and Congress for greater openness transformed the televised presidential address from an occasional event into a prerequisite for political survival. At a time when the American public feared weakness, linkage rhetoric seemed to embody the sense of strength—and the Madison Avenue touch—that officials sought in responding to the opportunities and burdens of increased visibility and vulnerability. Americans were outspoken. They wanted their country to be the number one diplomatic and military power in a world in which that status had become hard to achieve. At the same time, many were increasingly less willing to make the effort necessary to maintain power. Media diplomacy was a temporary solution for the beleaguered public official.

The well-publicized linkages under Nixon and Carter, for example, boiled down to an attempt to maintain public morale by demonstrating that the United States could still be tough with the Russians. Ultimately, the strategy represented a bid for political survival. Members of Congress joined the campaign, initiating many linkages over the next few years, including the 1974 Jackson-Vanik amendment, linking emigration of Soviet Jews to the Soviet Union's receipt of most-favored-nation trade benefits, and numerous amendments to foreign assistance bills tying aid to a nation's respect for human rights.

Executive officials did not always handle this new phenomenon skillfully. In many cases, they outdid their critics in touting the virtues of openness, discovering in linkage an instrument for making U.S. foreign policy seem to reflect the nation's democratic values. They sometimes used linkage for their own personal ben-

efit. But most often, they failed to think through the consequences of making public what should have remained private.

THE RISKS OF PUBLIC LINKAGE

It was naive to expect that an administration could accomplish through public statements what it might conceivably have achieved in private diplomatic negotiations. The experience of the Carter administration made this lesson clear when former Secretary of State Cyrus Vance, following Carter's lead, publicly established improvement of human rights as a precondition for aid. The United States lost much of its influence in several countries as a result. Uruguay, for example, rejected any U.S. assistance linked to human rights. The diplomatic moral seemed inescapable: A sovereign nation cannot publicly yield to another except under rare circumstances. Governments must maintain the respect of not only the people they serve, but also other nations in order to remain effective in preserving their international interests. They lose that respect if other nations can cow them openly. Making a diplomatic demand or linkage public forces the other nation, almost inexorably, to assume a public posture of defiance, thereby rendering a diplomatic solution impossible.

Yet linkage in one form or another always has been and always will be the essence of bargaining and the stock in trade of diplomats. International relations comprise a vast, complex system of barter in which nations use their strengths to make up for their weaknesses. In a society of nominal equals, there is really no arbiter, no supranational authority to decide who will cede what in case of conflict.

In such transactions, governments would prefer to bargain with one another privately rather than publicly. Inevitable oversimplifications and misinterpretations occur when negotiations take place in the public arena. The limitations of the news media result in the public's receiving only bits of the logic behind negotiating positions. Constituencies evolve around these simplified versions of government policy. As a result, when engaging in public linkage, a nation's leaders risk not only undermining their bargaining power internationally, but also provoking domestic protests that they bowed to another government.

The recent U.S. negotiations with Morocco provide a good example of an effective use of private linkage. In 1976 armed conflict broke out between Morocco and the Polisario Front, which desired an independent state in the western Sahara. One of the major objectives of U.S. diplomacy in North Africa has been to promote a negotiated settlement of the conflict. Moroccan interest in American armaments created the basis of an understanding. Although never publicly articulated, linkage appears to have guided the negotiations. Angier Biddle Duke, former U.S. ambassador to Morocco, offered the following testimony before a joint hearing of two House Foreign Affairs subcommittees in March 1981:

> Morocco has taken several steps in the direction of a negotiated solution to the war....I believe that our views influenced this evolution and that such influence would not have been possible without a continuation of a measured and carefully considered but stable program of military assistance.

Later in his testimony, Duke discussed the application of linkage:

> ...Even confining ourselves to the single issue of ending the war, our policy is more likely to promote a negotiated solution if it is implicit, because an explicit link courts a Moroccan reaction and it is, moreover, impossible to synchronize with evolving events.

As Duke took pains to point out, linkage works best when it is merely intimated.

Public linkage increasingly has acquired a purpose, but one very different from that of private linkage. Political leaders can use public linkage to awaken citizens and other nations to a particular danger or point of view or to recruit political support, at home and abroad, for major changes in policy. Sometimes public linkage works to forestall a foreign nation from committing a particular act, but the inherent need to save face in international relations generally prevents success in compelling another country to reverse an act once it has been committed. Public linkage can change the atmosphere surrounding a country's relations with other nations, but it cannot reasonably be expected to yield concrete achievements.

Carter's embargo on the sale of U.S. grain to the Soviet Union and his boycott of the 1980 Moscow Olympic games in retaliation for the 1979 Soviet invasion of Afghanistan are examples of the correct use of public linkage—even if they failed to produce the intended result. The Carter administration exacted a political and economic price for the Soviet military activity. Carter did not appear to expect that his use of public linkage would force the Soviets out of Afghanistan. Rather, he wanted to recruit support at home and abroad for taking a harder line toward Moscow. Ironically, his success in accomplishing this end helped undermine his own electoral position, creating support not for his own campaign but for that of his opponent, who seemed more genuinely tough minded in his approach to the Soviets.

Even the proper use of public linkage can generate unacceptable risks to long-term interests. Public linkages easily acquire lives of their own that are difficult for even the skilled politician to manage. For example, Carter's Afghanistan linkage generated expectations—most notably for the withdrawal of the Soviets—that the tactic itself and Carter's policy in general were unable to meet. Any number of interest groups at home were ready to take up administration pronouncements, fortify them with their own interpretations, turn them into general policy ultimatums, and throw them back at the officials later. Public linkage cannot be fine tuned.

A graver danger unique to public linkage is the possibility that a policy based on such a tie will degenerate into propaganda and demagogy. An administration can bemuse its constituents with public linkages that sound like policy but are mere substitutes for negotiating difficult private linkages or for taking other steps to check problems requiring linkage.

Both dangers can be limited by qualifying the nature of the public response. A government can simply state that it will retaliate against another government's actions in a particular way for a limited period of time, without challenging the other government to reverse itself. This qualified linkage minimizes expectations at home that the foreign government will yield and leaves room for behind-the-scenes maneuvering between the two governments during that period. Thus, the Carter administration should have stipulated that in protest of the Soviet intervention in Afghanistan the United States would impose a one- or two-year grain embargo. It would not then have been forced to attempt the impossible and impose an embargo of unlimited duration. Furthermore, Carter's successor could have avoided the difficult circumstances surrounding a decision to end the arrangement.

EVERYMAN'S BAILIWICK

Kissinger brought the term linkage into vogue in 1969. In February of that year, he drafted a memorandum from the president to the secretaries of state and defense and the director of the Central Intelligence Agency linking U.S. willingness to negotiate the SALT treaty to Soviet assistance in ending the Vietnam war and in stabilizing the situation in the Middle East. At a press conference, he spoke of "the linkage between the political and the strategic environment." Kissinger played down the term after SALT I was ratified and he became secretary of state, but linkage continued to play an

important role in his diplomacy. Indeed, it underlay his whole approach to détente: America would link its willingness to trade with and transfer technology to the Soviet Union to Moscow's political and military restraint outside Soviet borders.

However effective such a linkage might have been if employed in private, Kissinger's public linking of SALT I to other matters weakened the Nixon administration politically and hence diplomatically. In the eyes of a country increasingly opposed to the war in Vietnam, linkage made the administration, rather than Moscow, appear to be the chief obstacle to a treaty. The administration's prime blunder was to assume that it could manage a public linkage to its advantage domestically. Making linkage public was supposed to put pressure for concessions on the Soviet Union; instead, it generated domestic pressure for concessions by the United States.

Kissinger himself admits in the *White House Years* that Soviet Premier Aleksei Kosygin was "probably emboldened by American domestic criticism of our linkage concept." Under the circumstances, the administration could probably not have avoided criticism from an increasingly assertive Congress and media, but Kissinger provided critics a public target.

The Carter administration initially threw overboard the previous administration's notion of linkage. Carter desired to distance himself as much as possible from Kissinger's realpolitik; he considered strategic arms control too important to mortgage to other foreign policy concerns. His administration viewed linkage as a provocative tactic that did not bring out the Soviets' most cooperative side. Vance was the spokesman for these views within the administration and vindicated them to an extent by negotiating the SALT II treaty to completion.

The treaty was already endangered in the Senate, however, probably because of a general loss of confidence in the Carter administration's overall sense of direction, particularly in security matters and in dealings with the Soviet Union. Carter's protestations that SALT should be considered strictly on its own merits—in isolation from other foreign policy issues—seemed to betray a blindness to the realities of politics. The administration should have realized that it faced a Congress and a press even more inclined to assert themselves in the formulation of foreign policy during the late 1970s than in the earlier part of the decade when linkage had created problems during the debate on SALT I. Whether the Carter administration liked it or not, the public would inevitably link SALT II to overall Soviet conduct and to the general state of U.S. defenses. Under these conditions, the administration should have eschewed public mention of linkage because raising the issue would only arm the administration's enemies.

But for a few fateful months in 1978, the Carter administration did the opposite. It reversed its earlier policy of "delinking" SALT II and began flirting with the notion of linkage, a serious error for two reasons. First, Carter's seeming support for linkage in 1978 contradicted his earlier policy. This apparent confusion undermined his credibility as a strategist and as a politician. Second, the president's resuscitation of the term linkage provided a rallying point for opponents of the SALT treaty.

In the early months of 1978, after a year of outspoken delinkage, Carter began to muddy the political waters by hinting at linkage of the SALT treaty to Soviet activities on other fronts. Zbigniew Brzezinski, national security adviser, urged the president to intimate that the treaty negotiations could not proceed smoothly until the Soviets ceased their meddling in the Horn of Africa. Brzezinski went several steps further, threatening the Russians openly. Vance continued to espouse delinkage in public; but Brzezinski appeared to speak for the president.

Brzezinski's opening salvo came in February. He asserted that Soviet behavior in the Horn of Africa might affect both "the negotiating process" and "any ratification that would follow the successful conclusion of the [SALT] negotiations." He went on to invoke the dread word, linkage. Shortly afterward, Carter echoed Brzezinski's double-barreled threat at a press conference, laying particular emphasis on the notion that Soviet activities in Africa jeopardized congressional approval of any eventual SALT treaty. "The two [Soviet actions in Africa and difficulties in completing SALT II] are linked," he stated, "because of actions by the Soviets. We don't initiate the linkage."

Perhaps without realizing it, the Carter administration had made a mistake Kissinger had always avoided. Kissinger had put the Russians on notice that their adventurism jeopardized negotiation of a SALT treaty by threatening U.S. interests. But Carter and Brzezinski went further and warned Moscow that its actions compromised not only negotiation of a treaty, but also Senate ratification. Kissinger had wisely refrained from going this far in public, probably because he realized that by stressing the dangers to ratification he would allow initiative for this crucial element of security policy to slip from the executive to the Congress. That in fact happened in 1978.

The Carter administration's public linkage of ratification of the treaty to Soviet behavior strengthened the hand of SALT's hard-line opponents in the Senate, who, led by Senator Henry Jackson (D.-Washington), opposed both the treaty and Soviet activities in the Horn of Africa. The administration bestowed on the group the added authority that comes from receiving the endorsement of a former opponent. Certain liberal senators whose support of the treaty was expected followed suit and opposed SALT II in protest of the political trials of the Soviet dissidents Anatoly Shcharansky and Alexandr Ginzburg. In August 1978 Senator Frank Church (D.-Idaho), chairman of the Foreign Relations Committee, commented that the President, himself, may have opened the door to this kind of linkage, when he suggested that the successful conclusion of SALT II could be jeopardized by Soviet and Cuban activities in Africa. Once the concept of linkage between strategic arms negotiations and other extraneous political developments had been legitimized, it is inevitable that this same principle will be invoked by others to argue in favor of suspending the arms control talks for a myriad of other reasons.

Thus, a heterogeneous anti-SALT coalition began to develop in the Senate even before negotiations were completed. The passage of initiative to the Senate became most apparent after the Soviet invasion of Afghanistan in December 1979. Congressional predication of ratification upon Soviet withdrawal so undermined support for the treaty that Carter requested that the Senate majority leader suspend consideration of the document. But as early as August 1979, Church himself stated that progress in overall U.S.-Soviet relations was contingent upon removal of the Soviet brigade from Cuba. Other senators had seconded him by drafting formal resolutions to that effect. Thus, after Brzezinski's melodramatic coyness in early 1978, public linkage became everyone's bailiwick, especially the senators', spelling trouble if not death for SALT II.

The popularity of linkage at this time had its roots not only in the Carter administration's susceptibility to such rhetoric, but also—and more fundamentally—in a loss of faith in the administration's security policy. Many suspected that the administration had obscured the decisions that had to be made instead of framing foreign policy choices and finding appropriate responses. The disproportion in linking SALT to Soviet activities in Africa seemed to imply basic imbalances in the overall posture of U.S. defense.

The Carter administration did not seem to understand that linkage applies in the United States as well as internationally. It did not appear to appreciate that the SALT treaty was always, necessarily, a part of the larger issue of defense. Early in his tenure, Carter made a series of decisions that raised doubts about his competence in handling military matters and gave away leverage he might have had on hawkish opponents of SALT. Considering the issues in isolation from the overall U.S. military stance, he decided to cancel production of the B-1 bomber and deployment of the neutron bomb. But he failed to bargain for a symmetrical concession from the Soviets. At the time, critics berated him for giving away leverage with relation to the Soviet Union. In retrospect, the leverage he gave away to the Senate was perhaps even more fateful.

By 1978, when Carter first put linkage into action, the United States had allowed the strategic balance to deteriorate for a decade. In the wake of the Vietnam war and the social struggles of the 1960s, the United States had neglected its armed forces and placed constraints upon its ability to counter meddling in the underdeveloped world by the Soviets and their proxies. Congress had muzzled the CIA, placed legislative constraints on the president's use of arms sales as a tool of foreign policy, and curtailed, in various ways, the range and flexibility of presidential options in foreign relations. These initiatives sprang from a Congress that thought it was correcting not only abuses of U.S. foreign policy but also misuse of presidential power by asserting itself in foreign policy more vigorously than it had at any time since World War II. As a result of these measures, the United States became less prepared to counter Soviet adventurism in kind, if and when action became necessary.

Linking a treaty supposedly defensible on its own merits and crucial for national security to anything else contained an inherent contradiction. The Carter administration had claimed that the treaty was as strategically advantageous for the United States as it was for the Soviets. But the U.S. attempt to use SALT as a bargaining chip to get the Soviets out of the

Horn of Africa cast doubt on these claims. Unless both Moscow and Washington believed the treaty bestowed more advantages on the Soviets than it gave the Americans, the basis for the deal implied in the linkage would not have existed, and Carter would have had to offer the Soviets something more than the treaty in return for their leaving Africa.

Linkage thus contradicted the premises upon which the administration had been trying to sell SALT to the American public: that the treaty supported the interests of both parties equally because both had made equal strategic concessions. It also stirred doubt in the United States about the technical merits of the treaty and the coherence of the administration's positions on defense. The Carter team eventually came to understand that it had blundered and quietly tried to shelve linkage. But its confusion compromised its credibility and, more important, the confusion permitted exploitation.

A BUREAUCRATIC CREDO

Recent administrations, then, attempted to use linkage diplomacy to accomplish specific ends, misunderstood the preconditions for its successful employment, and displayed a naive blindness to its potential political repercussions at home. Although some of the confusion was inadvertent, all too often officials sought to avert criticism from themselves by using linkage as a public narcotic.

High officials were ensnared in a double bind. On the one hand, the United States has limited leverage on Soviet behavior. Although the Soviet Union must import advanced technology and food, the nations of Western Europe and the developing world increasingly can and probably will undercut any economic sanctions the United States might apply. Nuclear weapons may be Washington's sole means for severely punishing Moscow, as Kissinger and Brzezinski must have quickly realized. But nuclear attack is an unthinkable response to all but the most major transgressions imaginable.

On the other hand, these high officials faced sometimes virulent criticism from the people, the press, and Congress. Carter had risen to power in 1977 on a wave of faith in good intentions and openness. But when the Soviets and their proxies began overrunning the Horn of Africa, the public began to call for the president to take harsher moves against the Soviets. The Carter administration was caught in a cruel dilemma: Unless the United States quickly reversed its priorities and allowed itself to develop capabilities it had recently repudiated, little could be done to halt Soviet interference in Africa, at least in the immediate future. Short of outright acquiescence, linkage was the only option left to the administration.

Carter would not have had to play this card if he had held a stronger hand originally. Linkage concealed the systematic impoverishment of U.S. policy options during the preceding years. It served as a smoke screen for confused priorities and a pretext for ignoring strategic weaknesses.

Making firm decisions to pursue one or two policies at the expense of others inherently detracts from the power of those who invested themselves in the discarded policies. Linkage permitted key officials to avoid making enemies in the press, the Congress, and the bureaucracy, all of whom had varying degrees of allegiance to programs past their prime. It allowed the administration to avoid difficult choices by letting the Soviets set U.S. priorities or at least to exonerate the government from having any of its own. The use of linkage rationalized an abnegation of policy in the interest of harmony at home. But as an attempt to counter Soviet adventurism without paying economic, political, or military prices, it was a bluff—and the rest of the world increasingly perceived it as such. For a time, however, the intellectual shallowness of public linkage as policy was obscured—or overshadowed—by the bureaucratic and personal purposes it fulfilled.

Kissinger and Brzezinski were the most zealous advocates of linkage in the administrations in which they served. Perhaps their own foreign roots gave them a keener sense of history than most Americans possess, and with it a sense that the barter involved in traditional diplomacy—linkage—has now become more important for the United States. Accustomed to overwhelming power and influence in almost every aspect of foreign relations since World War II, Americans are not used to bartering for their achievements abroad. But during the past two decades, U.S. economic, military, and diplomatic power has diminished relative to other countries. This decline has not affected all spheres equally, so that the United States still has overwhelming advantages in some areas, if fewer in others. Understandably, U.S. foreign policy makers now try to use these advantages more aggressively than they have in the past in order to compensate for new American weaknesses. Kissinger and Brzezinski enhanced the thinking of U.S. policy makers by increasing awareness of linkage as a tactic essential— when used in private—to the maintenance of American power.

But both national security advisers also applied the concept in a manner that seemed excessively public and self-serving. Both owed a large part of their prominence to the media: Linkage served their purposes because it seemed to place them in the center of the action.

The supposed existence of a master plan linking all of the nation's foreign policy concerns magnifies the role of the national security adviser. He alone, with the president, is supposed to make the ultimate policy tradeoffs, serving as the master linker. Linkage is his bureaucratic credo, a job description in the guise of policy. The assistant imposes essential coordination on the various agencies handling foreign policy matters, and linkage endows him with the mystique that enables him to play his part effectively.

The two advisers also seemed to invoke linkage in order to demonstrate that U.S. foreign policy possessed intellectual respectability, to forestall the frequent criticism that it lacked a vision of the whole. Kissinger was particularly sensitive to this view. "The major weakness of United States diplomacy has been the insufficient attention given to the symbolic aspect of foreign policy," he wrote in *Nuclear Weapons and Foreign Policy*. In much of his later writing and public service, Kissinger was apparently trying to remedy this admittedly crucial handicap in ideological and diplomatic competition with the Soviet Union.

In the *White House Years,* Kissinger stressed the importance of having a vision of the whole:

> Linkage, however, is not a natural concept for Americans, who have traditionally perceived foreign policy as an episodic enterprise. Our bureaucratic organizations, divided into regional and functional bureaus, and indeed our academic tradition of specialization, compound the tendency to compartmentalize. American pragmatism produces a penchant for examining issues separately: to solve problems on their merits, without a sense of time or context or of the seamless web of reality. And the American legal tradition encourages rigid attention to the "facts of the case," a distrust of abstractions.
>
> Yet in foreign policy there is no escaping the need for an integrating conceptual framework. ...The most difficult challenge for a policymaker in foreign affairs is to establish priorities.

Kissinger seems to intimate that linkage can provide "integrating conceptual framework."

Yet this approach is nothing more than a vain attempt to raise a tactic to the level of strategy. Linkage, after all, has form but no content. It can never take the place of an ideology in shaping policy, inspiring people and countries, or underpinning diplomacy. Ideology is necessary to confer a basic sense of purpose. The values ideology embodies point out general directions and provide the ultimate arbiters of choice in decisions that characteristically require policy makers to rely on uncertain or limited information. Kissinger, and Brzezinski after him, intoned linkage in an attempt to head off the common criticism that U.S. foreign policy lacks coherence, that it champions style over substance. Yet their attempts, ironically, confirmed the criticism.

THE BLUFF WEARS THIN

In assessing the role that linkage diplomacy will play in its own foreign policy, the Reagan administration will find that in some cases the grounds for sound and successful linkage will exist. In other instances, however, the tactic will prove inappropriate and potentially damaging, whether employed in public or in private. Tying nuclear security policy to any other specific issue is just such a case.

Avoiding, or at least minimizing, a nuclear war is an objective without equal. In the traditional 18th- and 19th-century European world—the acme of linkage diplomacy—no priority held such superiority. War was not the ultimate option it is today for the nuclear superpowers. Countries frequently fought one another. Conquest by a foreign government was rarely total or irrevocable. Victory or defeat sometimes brought only minimal disruption of daily life. More important, war generally risked the lives of only a small minority of citizens in the armed forces or of mercenaries. In some cases, avoiding war was no more important than avoiding a tariff, and a ruler could trade one for the other without incurring the risk of further danger to his subjects or territory. But linking strategic arms control to other specific issues violates the first condition for successful linkage: There must be rough parity between the issues under negotiation.

In the area of conventional weapons, a rough parity between economic and military issues can still exist. U.S. military-base agreements are often built on such broad linkages. The American right to use facilities in Spain and Turkey is more or less linked to packages of military and economic aid to those countries. But it is difficult to imagine a nuclear analogy. Assisting Spain and Turkey in developing nuclear weapons in exchange for bases is out of the question. Correspondingly, neither of the countries could offer the United States any concession that might induce it to reduce the U.S. nuclear arsenal.

Even in dealing with Moscow, the possibilities of linkage outside the immediate SALT framework are remote. A bipolar balance of power currently dominates international security relations and presents a formidable impediment to the successful use of linkage to resolve an issue such as nuclear arms control. There is little room for diplomatic maneuver because only the United States and the Soviet Union are of commensurate geopolitical importance. Particularly in the field of strategic arms policy, they stand alone, for other countries—even countries such as China and France—have relatively little to offer them or to threaten them with. Both superpowers have indigenous energy resources, food supplies, and technological skills. It is difficult to imagine a third country being crucial to the superpowers' strategic arms policies under these conditions.

Moreover, unless alliances are potentially fluid, effective linkage diplomacy cannot take place. While the world was polarized from 1945 until the Sino-Soviet rift in 1960, neither the United States nor the Soviet Union could enlist the help of any major countries to break their cold war deadlock. Ideology froze everyone in place. A more fluid situation such as that obtaining in 18th-century Europe would have permitted more genuine use of linkage diplomacy during the 20 or 30 years subsequent to World War II, but it would not have broken the strategic arms deadlock between the United States and the Soviet Union or halted their arms race. It would not have affected those two countries' solitary pre-eminence in nuclear power, which is the root of the impasse. Kissinger's celebrated opening to China, which was intended to restore some flexibility to modern U.S. diplomacy, does not change the fact of that pre-eminence. Even the emergence of a non-aligned Third World bloc would mean little because of the unique nature of the stakes involved. Fluid alliances have little significance in this instance unless the third parties involved have comparable nuclear capabilities.

There is a final factor militating against the successful linkage of SALT to anything else. Diplomatic linkage can work to the extent that the power of decision is vested in a single entity that can make ultimate policy tradeoffs—perhaps the reason why linkage diplomacy reached its zenith during the period of the strong monarchies of Europe. Government in many large 20th-century states, particularly the United States, has largely devolved on many relatively decentralized, specialized bureaucracies and legislative committees. This development precludes the flexibility required for linkage: Specialized units of power generally do not respond

well to the lure of a net gain when that gain might result in some loss within their particular spheres. Linkage diplomacy has therefore grown more difficult to employ in U.S.-Soviet relations. And nowhere has linkage become so delicate an internal matter as in the area of arms control because the issue cuts across so many centers of intergovernmental—and extragovernmental—power.

Strategic arms negotiations with the Soviet Union must thus be pursued in isolation. To drag other matters into the negotiations is to underestimate the importance of a strategic arms treaty and overestimate diplomatic virtuosity. Any SALT treaty will have to stand and be defended on its own merits.

The requirements of diplomacy differ from those of politics, however. Sensing an erosion of U.S. pre-eminence during the past decade, the public sought reassurance. Public officials' evocations of linkage, no matter how cynical and confused, long seemed to answer the political need to appear resolute. But the bluff is wearing thin. Only a real upgrading of the U.S. defense posture will convince the country to allow its leaders to conclude a strategic arms treaty.

[Linkage]

Richard Pipes

One of the more controversial aspects of SALT II involves the issue known as linkage. The controversy is over the question whether negotiations for strategic arms control ought to proceed on their own separate track, oblivious of the broader context of American-Soviet relations or, on the contary, ought to be re-

From U.S. Cong., Senate, *Military Implications of the Treaty on the Limitation of Strategic Offensive Arms and Protocol Thereto,* Hearings before the Committee on Armed Services, 96th Cong., 1st Sess., 1979, pt. 3, pp. 1305–1308.

lated to the overall pattern of Soviet behavior toward us and the rest of the non-Communist world.

The proponents of the treaty argue that the cause of arms limitation is so singularly important that the SALT process, complicated enough as it is, ought not to be burdened by other considerations; whatever else we and the Russians may disagree over, we have an equal stake in the survival of humanity and must seek to arrive at strategic arms limitation treaties without allowing extraneous factors to intrude.

This argument, unfortunately, does not withstand closer analysis either in its premises or its applications. Such force as it possesses derives in part from ill-considered views of the military utility of nuclear weapons and in part from the emotional appeal exerted on many persons by every theory or pseudotheory which seems to hold out the promise of banishing the specter of nuclear disaster.

Linkage, in my opinion, is essential, though not in its trivialized form. SALT II ought not to be ratified as a reward to the Soviet government for its good behavior, nor ought the treaty be rejected as a means of punishing the Russians for such noxious actions as placing a combat brigade in Cuba.

The Russians are not children and we are not their teachers. A meaningful linkage approach calls for an assessment of the entire spectrum of Soviet policies; furthermore, it does not assume a priori that strategic weapons ought to be isolated from all other kinds of weapons.

There is a deeply held conviction in this country, due in large measure to the memory of Hiroshima and Nagasaki, that nuclear weapons are unique not only because they can cause unprecedented destructiveness but also because no defenses exist against them; the aggressor in this instance suffers the same punishment as his victim.

This view, originally articulated in the influential symposium, "The Absolute Weapon," published in 1946, has dominated American thinking for a long time and to this day underpins the theory of arms limitations. It provides the intellectual and psychological support of the opposition to linkage, for if strategic weapons are unique then they clearly ought to be treated in a unique manner.

Now, there are at least three flaws in this reasoning. Those who regard nuclear weapons as absolute weapons ignore, for the purpose of their argument, the possibility of limited strategic options, uses which could fall short of all-out destructiveness. They also unduly deprecate various defensive measures, including the possibility of new technology someday devising effective means of neutralizing offensive strategic weapons.

Last, but not least, they leave out of consideration the political leverage that inheres in nuclear superiority and that may enable the superior party to secure submission to its will without recourse to violence, this despite the fact that we have benefited politically from just such a preponderance in the Korean war and the Cuban crisis of 1962. In other words, the alternative—arms limitation–Armageddon—is palpably false, for it leaves out of view a great variety of intermediate possibilities.

More grievous yet is the failure of the proponents of this line of argument to take into account that strategic thinking by its very nature involves at least two parties, for which reason it is not enough to develop a strategy suitable for oneself; one must adjust it to that of one's potential adversary.

Unfortunately, most of American strategic thinking since World War II has been carried out in a political vacuum from which the Soviet Union has been eliminated, except as a weapons system. The notion that there can be two diverse strategies based on the same weaponry apparently strikes many of our civilian experts to be as absurd as the idea that there can be two different sciences of physics.

In fact, however, anyone who addresses himself to Soviet military literature on the subject will quickly discover that over the past 20 years the Soviet leadership has formulated a very different theory of the nature and utility of strategic weapons from ours. Whether this view is sound or not is not at issue here. What matters is that they hold it, implement it, and in case of conflict are likely to act on it.

We can ignore this disparity of views only at the gravest risk to our national security. The differences between our essentially defensive nuclear strategy and the Soviet overwhelmingly offensive one stand in as sharp a contrast as the perceptions of armored warfare held, respectively, by the German and the Allied high commands before World War II, with consequences that are all too familiar. I believe it was the lasting contribution of so-called team B, which I had the honor to chair, to have addressed itself to these questions 3 years ago, and to have provided alternative explanations which, unorthodox as they may have seemed then, have been borne out by subsequent events.

SOVIET VIEW OF LINKAGE

In the Soviet view, strategic weapons are integrated into a comprehensive ideology of conflict in which military weapons constitute discrete elements of a broad spectrum of coercive instrumentalities.

The place of nuclear weapons in this ideology can be elucidated by a sequence of related propositions:

One, in a world in which there exists private ownership of the means of production and, derived from it, antagonistic social classes, class conflict is both inevitable and progressive.

Two, since October 1917, when the Soviet state came into being as the first Socialist country in the world, all international conflicts pitting the Soviet Union against the capitalist world, headed by the United States, assume the character of class conflict.

Three, the inevitable outcome of the competition between the Socialist and the capitalist camps will be the triumph of the former and the disappearance of the latter, following which class and international conflicts will cease.

Four, the competition between the two camps goes on all the time, on all levels, but ultimately it must result in war. The more positions the Socialist camp can secure peacefully, the easier and less painful will be the attainment of final victory, the most important point least appreciated in this country.

Five, strategic nuclear weapons have not upset the traditional principles of military science, but they have revolutionized their application, in that they make it possible to attain the ultimate strategic objective of all war—disarming the enemy, directly, in a matter of hours, instead of by a sequence of prolonged operations.

Six, should general war become unavoidable, that side will gain victory which will boldly strike in a preemptive attack. This strategy calls for a preponderant strategic force with vast strategic reserves and defensive preparations to limit damage.

In this chain of reasoning it will be noted that nuclear weapons are seen not as absolute weapons, endowed with some magic qualities that make them *sui generis,* but as a particularly effective means of exercising military coercion, which is itself part of an historic conflict.

Soviet thinking is imbedded in a network of linkages connecting history, economics, politics, ideology, and military hardware. The very idea that one can separate nuclear weapons from the broad range of political-military instrumentalities, and the latter from the historic conflict between socialism and capitalism, would appall any person even superficially versed in the theories of Marxism-Leninism.

SOVIET VIEW OF SALT

If, nevertheless, the Soviet Union engages in negotiations on strategic arms limitations that in fact posit the uniqueness of strategic weapons, it is because—well aware of our view of this matter—they see ample opportunities to exploit it to their advantage.

If I may quote myself on this subject:

In Soviet calculations SALT is not a vehicle for general disarmament, as it is with us, but a device to inhibit the United States response to Soviet long-term strategic programs.

In the Soviet view, SALT, on the most elementary level, fixes the number of United States systems and thereby facilitates the task of estimating what is required to render them harmless.

On a higher level, SALT alleviates the Soviet Union's recurrent nightmare that an American technological achievement, such as ABM or the cruise missile have been in the past, should suddenly neutralize the ponderous and incremental Soviet buildup.

Last but not least, in the Soviet outlook SALT serves to create in the United States a political atmosphere obstructive to defense expenditures. SALT persuades much of the American public that any improvements in strategic forces are "destabilizing." SALT inhibits the U.S. Government from funding weapons programs presumptively subject to becoming limited or even prohibited in later negotiations. ["Why the Soviet Union Wants SALT II"— Committee on the Present Danger, Washington, D.C., 1979.]

Should SALT be linked to Soviet global behavior? It most emphatically should. After all, we practice a sort of positive linkage in regard to Great Britain and France, both of which possess enough strategic weapons to destroy much of the United States, but neither of which is perceived as threatening our way of life, for which reason their strategic capabilities give us no anxiety.

In the case of the Soviet Union, the threat resides not so much in the destructive power of its strategic arsenal as in its intentions toward us, as manifested in word and deed. If the Russians view nuclear weapons as an intrinsic element of a broad spectrum of coercive instrumentalities, it behooves us in our dealings with them to relate nuclear weapons to Soviet overall behavior.

The utility of SALT II has to be measured against a large range of indicators of Soviet intentions and actions. It must be placed against the background of relentless Soviet anti-American hate propaganda inside the Soviet Union and in the Third World, against Soviet armed interventions in Afghanistan, Ethiopia, Vietnam and, more recently, the Caribbean, against Soviet support of terrorism all over the globe, against Soviet encroachments on Norwegian territory and the militarization of the Kuriles, against the building of military highways and railroads in eastern Europe.

None of these actions in and of itself can be said to threaten the United States. Seen in their totality, they suggest a most ominous pattern of threatening hostility.

Surely, it would be imprudent to treat the nuclear balance in isolation from Soviet thinking and Soviet behavior. Linkage means that until and unless the Soviet Union radically modifies its thinking and external policies, we cannot count on SALT enhancing our security and diminishing the probability of war. These ends can be better attained by building up our strength to the point where the Soviet leadership can no longer hope to attain its global ambitions and is forced to turn inward.

QUESTIONS FOR DISCUSSION

1 Should nuclear weapons be seen as "absolute weapons"?
2 Can and should controlling the nuclear arms race be treated in isolation from other issues in the superpower relationship?
3 In what sense, if any, do the Soviets believe in linkage?
4 Compare the linkage policies of the Nixon, Carter, and Reagan administrations.

SUGGESTED READINGS

Crozier, Brian. "Of Linkage and All That," *National Review,* **37** (Dec. 13, 1985), p. 22.
Johnson, Paul G. "Arms Control and Managing Linkage," *Survival,* **28** (Sept.–Oct. 1986), pp. 431–444.

Kissinger, Henry. *Years of Upheaval.* Boston, Mass.: Little, Brown, 1982.

Nixon, Richard M. *RN, The Memoirs of Richard Nixon.* New York Grosset and Dunlap, 1978.

U.S. Cong., House of Representatives *Fundamentals of Nuclear Arms Control,* Pt. 8: *Linkage: Nuclear Arms Control in the Broader Context of United States–Soviet Relations,* Report prepared for the Subcommittee on Arms Control, International Security and Science of the Committee on Foreign Affairs by the Congressional Research Service, Library of Congress, 99th Cong., 2d Sess., Jan. 1986.

17 Is it wise for the United States to threaten its NATO allies with possible reduction in U.S. troops in Europe if the allies do not live up to their alliance commitments?

YES

Sam Nunn

[*The Nunn Amendment*]

NO

Richard Lugar

[*The Nunn Amendment*]

[The Nunn Amendment]

Sam Nunn

Mr. President, this amendment has as its goal major collective improvements in NATO's conventional defense capabilities. I am hoping that this amendment will become known as the "NATO Conventional Defense Improvements Amendment" and not the "NATO Troop Withdrawal Amendment."

Let me begin by quoting an assessment by Gen. Bernard Rogers, NATO's Supreme Allied Commander Europe, of the state of conventional defenses in Europe:

> Allied Command Europe's current conventional posture does not provide our nations with adequate deterrence and it leaves the nuclear threshold at a disturbingly low level.
>
> Thus, NATO's deterrence is jeopardized by our current heavy reliance on the early use of nuclear weapons to stop a non-nuclear attack. The remedy is for NATO to strengthen its conventional forces which will also raise the nuclear threshold.
>
> There are a number of shortcomings in NATO's nonnuclear forces that put us in the predicament I describe. However, the fundamental cause is a low level of sustainability. ACE is simply unable to sustain its conventional forces in combat for long with manpower, ammunition and war reserve material to replace losses and expenditures on the battlefield.[1]

Mr. President, we cannot continue to paper over such serious and dangerous military problems in NATO. Here we have the highest military leader of the alliance stating bluntly that NATO's current conventional posture is little more than a delayed tripwire for early resort to nuclear escalation. The alliance has spent hundreds of billions of dollars for the common defense to this point.

During the decade of the 1980's and beyond we need more than a military posture that, to quote General Rogers again, would require:

> The release of nuclear weapons fairly quickly after a conventional attack. And I'm talking about in terms of days, not in terms of weeks or months.

The citizens of both this nation and Europe will, and should, question why their hundreds of billions in defense investment buys such a limited conventional defense that NATO must rely on the untenable military strategy of early resort to nuclear weapons.

Some would argue that the Europeans want it this way; they do not want more robust conventional defenses and are content to rest deterrence of Warsaw Pact conventional attack on the threat of rapid nuclear escalation.

Others would suggest that it is a matter of economics, that while a nuclear tripwire may be less than desirable, it is the best that can be obtained for the funds that the Europeans are willing to spend on defense.

Still others suggest the Europeans have merely recognized a soft touch, that they know the United States will continue to "cover their gaps" by spending the money for all our forces in NATO, for six POMCUS division sets, for many hundreds of tactical aircraft, for airlift and aerial tankers to move these assets to Europe in a crisis, and for munition stocks substantially above those of most allies. They figure that as long as the United States will spend over 30 percent of our annual budget—$90 billion—in support of NATO, why should they spend more? I ask unanimous consent that a DOD chart showing the range of U.S. cost in supporting NATO be entered in the record.

From *Congressional Record*, 98th Cong., 2d Sess., June 20, 1984, pp. S778–S7782.

[1] Testimony before House Armed Services Committee, March 6, 1984.

There being no objection, the material was ordered to be printed in the *Record,* as follows:

The Range of Nato Costs[2]

The Range of NATO Costs—As noted in the preceding section, estimates of the cost of the United States' commitment to NATO can vary widely, depending on the categories of forces and the types of expenditures being evaluated. The following examples illustrate a range of possible estimates (expressed as total obligational authority for fiscal year 1985), along with the assumptions that were made in developing them:

(a) the incremental operating costs incurred by stationing U.S. forces in Europe rather than in the United States (about $2 billion);

(b) the incremental operating costs associated with maintaining European-deployed U.S. forces in the active force structure (about $15 billion);

(c) the total cost of European-deployed U.S. forces (about $55 billion);

(d) the total cost of European-deployed U.S. forces and those U.S.-based forces that we have pledged to contribute as NATO reinforcements in the early stages of a conflict (about $90 billion);

(e) the total cost of European-deployed U.S. forces and all of the U.S.-based forces that we have pledged to contribute as NATO reinforcements over the course of a conflict (about $177 billion);

(f) the total cost of all U.S. conventional forces (about $227 billion); and

(g) the total cost of all U.S. forces (about $306 billion).

Mr. President, I do not know which reason or combination of reasons can explain the current situation but I do know that it is high time—indeed past time—to put the issue of European intentions to a reasonable and responsible test. Our Ambassador to NATO, David Abshire, believes that European intentions are changing for the better. I hope he is correct. We must

---

[2] The following is a verbatim transcript from page 9 of the June 1984 Secretary of Defense's Report to Congress on "United States Expenditures in Support of NATO."

begin, however, to measure programmatic progress and not just intentions. If the allies are not prepared to make more modest efforts to improve conventional defenses in the remainder of this decade, while the United States plans to spend many hundreds of billions of dollars on our NATO commitment—if the allies really want, or will continue to settle for, a nuclear tripwire, then I believe the United States should recognize this and adjust our own military commitment and our defense priorities. We can provide for a nuclear tripwire—or even what some call an extended tripwire—with far fewer conventional forces and personnel than the United States currently has stationed in NATO. And, I might add, without the expense of massive reinforcements, all at significantly less cost than we now incur.

Mr. President, I consider myself a longstanding and strong supporter of the NATO alliance. I have written three reports to the Senate on the subject, have sponsored various legislation over the years to improve NATO's defense capabilities and was a leader in the floor fights in the mid-1970's to defeat the Mansfield amendments to cut U.S. forces in NATO unilaterally. I want to emphasize one point at the outset. Although my amendment calls for sizable troop reductions in the late 1980's if our European Allies do not show a willingness to improve conventional defense capabilities, this amendment is not intended either as blackmail or as punishment. I am hopeful that no troops will ever be withdrawn by reason of this amendment. It is merely a recognition that continued, even redoubled, U.S. sacrifices to improve conventional defenses and to raise the nuclear threshold in Europe are to no avail without similar allied efforts. We must move forward and improve the alliance in tandem. We must head for these goals on a bicycle built for two—the United States can have the front seat but it takes someone pedaling behind as well.

In an era of well-recognized NATO disadvantage in theater nuclear weapons, at a time of rough strategic nuclear parity between the United States and the Soviet Union, it is, in my view, unrealistic and dangerous to rest the fate of the alliance on a strategy of deliberate, early nuclear escalation. Yet what General Rogers has described in clear testimony is a situation in which, in the event of a major Warsaw Pact conventional attack on NATO, the alliance leaders would be faced with choosing "in terms of days, not weeks" between capitulation or NATO being the first to use nuclear weapons. Even if the Soviets limit their attack to conventional means, NATO will be forced to escalate the conflict into a nuclear exchange, an area of alliance disadvantage. We cannot continue this posture.

Mr. President, the United States is pledged to ship to Europe, within the first 10 days of such a war, a total of six Army divisions and 20 tactical fighter wings as early reinforcements to the fourth divisions and seven wings we already have over there. Yet if this huge early reinforcement nonetheless leads only to "days, not weeks" before nuclear weapons are used, I question the soundness of the basic plan under which we in America are spending hundreds of billions of dollars.

If NATO is going to have to surrender, then six more U.S. divisions added to the four already there more than doubles our "Dunkirk problem." If instead, NATO is going to resort to early nuclear escalation, our additional divisions will be irrelevant by the time they arrive there.

Indeed, Mr. President, General Rogers addressed this situation, too:

> Because of the failure to meet commitments in the conventional area by all nations and through trying to buy alliance defense on the cheap by relying on nuclear weapons, we have mortgaged our defense to the nuclear response.

To his considerable credit, General Rogers has done everything in his power to correct this military untenable situation. Now the U.S. Senate must lend a helping hand. We cannot permit

the bulwark of Western defense—NATO—to continue this situation endlessly into the future. If it does, the alliance has no real future.

Mr. President, we can debate why we are in this untenable military trap today, and there are many sides to this argument. However, two things are clear—first, we must improve conventional defenses; and second, NATO is not currently planning to make these improvements. This is the case despite alliance agreements in principle year after year, starting in the late 1970's, to implement specific measures to improve NATO's conventional defense capability.

From a major set of alliance meetings in 1977 and 1978 emerged the following agreed goals which are still in effect today:

The pledge to increase defense spending in each country by at least 3 percent per year in real terms; the pledge to acquire a 30-day supply of conventional munitions within 5 years in the center region; and the agreement on what ultimately became the rapid reinforcement plan.

These goals have been agreed to in NATO Ministerial Guidance and have been reaffirmed at their annual meetings. The rapid reinforcement plan constitutes the commitment by the United States to move a total of six Army divisions and roughly 20 tactical fighter wings from the United States to Europe within 10 days to reinforce our forces already there.

Now, Mr. President, as noted, the United States has been spending many billions of dollars on Army combat equipment to go into the six prepositioned overseas material configurated in unit sets [POMCUS] sites, so that we can fly only the troops from the United States to Europe and have them match up over there with their equipment. This means we have to buy two sets of equipment—one here to train with, one there to fight with. We have been spending many more billions to acquire the 20 wings of tactical aircraft for rapid deployment. We have been spending still more billions of dollars on airlift and tanker support, in order to carry out these time-urgent deployment plans. We have been spending billions for U.S. stocks of munitions in Europe, which are well above the 30-day NATO goal and climbing. We plan to spend $52 billion on munitions for our NATO forces over the next 5 years to increase this sustainability level even higher.

In return for all this, the allies agreed to do two things. First they agreed to provide "host-nation support" in wartime, the provision of some of their reservists and equipment and to provide rear area support for our reinforcing combat divisions. To give our allies their due there has been some progress in this wartime host nation support area. The chairman of the Armed Services Committee and I have led the fight in Congress to back up these agreements. Second, the allies also agreed to fund critical facilities and aircraft shelters for our reinforcing aircraft.

Finally, we have carried out our 3-percent pledge every year in the process of implementing all of these activities. The Secretary of Defense has just reported to Congress that we have exceeded our 3 percent goal every year since 1979 and that the total cost of European-deployed U.S. forces and those U.S. based forces that we have pledged to contribute to a NATO reinforcement in the early stages of a conflict is "about $90 billion" of the fiscal year 1985 budget, or over 30 percent of the entire budget. The Secretary's report also indicates that the total cost of all the U.S. NATO deployed forces and reinforcements planned over the course of a NATO conflict is $177 billion in this year's budget.

Now, Mr. President, let me briefly recount what our allies have done to meet their commitments:

They have not achieved the goal of a 3-percent increase after inflation, on average, in any year since the pledge was made; indeed the size of their increases has gotten smaller each year. For fiscal year 1983, DOD estimates that the average allied increase will be 1.9 to 2.1 percent; for fiscal year 1984, 1.2 to 1.7 percent. The United States, however, has met the goal every year and continues defense spending that is substantially above 3 percent real growth. Starting with 1980, our increases have ranged from 4.9 to 9 percent.

No allied country has reached the agreed goal of a 30-day supply of munitions. Allied sustainability is uneven at best; some kinds of munitions are close to the goal but others are in critically short supply, measured in days, not weeks. Most allies have indicated that they plan little or no progress toward the 30-day goal in their current 5-year projections. During the same period, the United States will be spending $52 billion to increase its stocks which are already substantially larger.

Secretary Weinberger has summarized this situation well in his May 1984 report to Congress on "Improving NATO's Conventional Capability." He stated:

> The lack of adequate capability to sustain combat operations for long with...munitions...is one of NATO's most critical and persistent shortfalls. In war, such shortages would force commanders to curtail operations to avoid running out...and the price of such rationing would be measurable directly in lives and kilometers lost.

Secretary Weinberger added,

> History records that of all the reasons given for military defeat, running out of ammunition ranks near if not at the top.

The Secretary also stated:

> The current situation is sufficiently serious that the need to increase munitions stocks is important enough to give that effort a higher priority than other national force improvements.

The situation is not much better in terms of the facilities and shelters the allies are to provide on their air bases for U.S. reinforcing tactical aircraft. Our own United States main operating bases in Europe are so crowded with our seven wings already there that most of the roughly 20 U.S. reinforcing wings will be scattered across many European air bases operated by other NATO countries. Those bases are called colocated operating bases, or COB's; they have enough space to accept our arriving aircraft. However, these COB's do not have extra minimum essential facilities, such as fuel and ammunition storage adequate for 7 days operations, extra emergency operating facilities such as control towers and maintenance facilities and extra semi-hardened aircraft shelters to protect our reinforcing aircraft. Without these facilities and shelters that the Allies have agreed to provide, the arriving $50 billion worth of U.S. aircraft are unlikely to survive, let alone be able to operate effectively. Where are we specifically in terms of the facilities and shelters to support our early reinforcement aircraft?

Today—6 years after the agreement—there are minimum essential facilities in place for less than 20 percent of our reinforcing aircraft. There still are virtually no hardened aircraft shelters for any of these reinforcing aircraft. In other words, only a relatively few aircraft will have fuel and ammunition available and they will be unsheltered, in the open, in the middle of world war III. Now, we learned as long ago as the 1973 Middle East war that unsheltered aircraft really are sitting ducks. Yet, year after year, we renew in the "Defense Planning Questionnaire" our commitment to deploy over $50 billion worth of the finest and most modern U.S. fighters to become sitting ducks. These aircraft have little chance to survive since our NATO allies have been unwilling to provide the roughly $1 billion extra to fuel, arm and protect these aircraft. That is right—the total cost to the allies to provide minimum essential facilities, emergency operations facilities, and hardened shelters for our 50 billion dollars' worth of aircraft is about $1 billion more. It is incomprehensible that $50 billion of sophisticated aircraft would be virtually useless because our allies

refuse to provide an additional $1 billion to house them.

Mr. President, we could continue this sorry tale. Let me give only one more pertinent example. The NATO force goals, which are developed every 2 years by the NATO military commanders and cover 6 years, are considered an expression of the forces and facilities necessary for the accomplishment of NATO military commanders' assigned missions. These goals are designed to challenge each nation to meet these critical missions.

It should be no surprise to anyone that the performance toward these goals has been less than satisfactory for the most part.

In fact, General Rogers recently said that NATO was running in the wrong direction in terms of the force goals:

> When we figured out the force goals—not the one we just approved earlier this month but the previous one approved in 1982—we figured that they would require a 4 percent real increase in defense spending per year, per nation for each of the 6 years from 1983 to 1988 to fully meet those force goals. New force goals have just been approved for the years 1985 to 1990. Now we calculate that to meet those force goals fully, it's only going to cost a little over 3 percent. So you see we're running in the wrong direction. We're going down to 3 percent to meet those force goals. Those force goals, even if fully implemented, won't give us the kind of conventional capability that I've talked about.

General Rogers is pessimistic that the NATO allies will even meet these lower force goals:

> When you ask the question do I think it's logical that they're going to be able to meet it, the answer is no.

Mr. President, it is my belief that it is time to challenge our European allies to begin to make good on longstanding commitments like those I have described. Without achieving these goals, a more robust conventional defense of Europe is virtually impossible. It is time to turn our attention to raising the nuclear threshold by improving NATO's collective conventional defenses.

It is time to put to a reasonable and responsible test the proposition of whether the Europeans want to continue a nuclear tripwire posture or seriously want to improve conventional capability. It is shape up or ship out time for NATO.

Let me briefly describe how my amendment is designed to test this proposition. The test will be comprised of two optional paths: one based on input goals; the other based on output goals.

First, the amendment extends and makes permanent the troop ceiling on U.S. ground forces stationed in NATO at a level of 326,414. This is a cap at exactly the level DOD has requested for the end of fiscal year 1985. The Department does plan over the next 5 years to request additional increases. Given the current situation and the lack of any major indication that the allies are moving forward, it makes no sense for us to increase our forces beyond the fiscal year 1985 level at this time. Since 1977 U.S. forces in NATO have increased by almost 45,000 personnel while allied force levels have remained essentially static. Interestingly enough, 1977 was the year the United States began to have serious discussions with our allies on improving conventional defenses.

Second, the intent of the amendment is to establish a 5-year period during which the NATO allies will be expected to meet certain goals related to improving conventional defense. All of these goals have been formally agreed to by the alliance, but the allies may need a year to discover America is finally ready to fish or cut bait on conventional improvements.

The amendment works as follows: The allies would have 1 year to get ready—1985, plus the balance of 1984—and then 3 years of performance would be measured—1986, 1987, 1988. Serious deficiences would be corrected at a rate

of 20 percent a year in those 3 years. By requiring performance over only the 3 of the 5 years needed to make up 100 percent of the deficiencies in the designated areas, Congress will have an opportunity for a mid-term review and to make adjustments should unforeseen circumstances arise.

The amendment ties future U.S. troop strength in NATO to progress—or lack of it—by the allies in improving conventional defense capabilities in certain specified areas.

The input oriented test is the NATO agreed target of a 3-percent average increase in defense spending, after inflation, by the non-U.S. NATO allies. This goal, first established in 1979, has just been reaffirmed by the NATO Ministers. If the non-U.S. allies reach this goal, no troop reductions are required. As indicated, this would be adequate for the allies to achieve the current force goals.

However, if in any year the allies fail to meet the 3-percent test in any year, the amendment offers an output oriented path for the allies to forestall the U.S. troop reductions, by meeting a set of three other goals in specific areas of longstanding deficiency. Each could be considered a war stopper in its own right.

What we are essentially asking the allies to do is either meet the longstanding three percent increase pledge; or

First, to increase systematically over 5 years their munitions sustainability to reach the 30-day goal, at the rate of 20 percent of the shortfall each year. These increases would require the six Center Region allies collectively to spend less than $1 billion per year. While these allies together would have to spend about a billion a year more to get to 30 days, the United States is spending $6.2 billion this year on our NATO munitions, and plans to spend $52 billion over the next 5 years to increase our stocks which are already substantially higher than theirs.

Second, to commit to an infrastructure funding level adequate to provide over 5 years the roughly $1 billion extra needed from the allies to build the facilities and shelters to give the $50 billion we have invested in U.S. reinforcing tactical aircraft a fighting chance; the needed facilities and shelters also must be committed to construction at the rate of 20 percent of the shortfall per year. To meet this test, the allies would have to agree to contribute about $600 million more to the NATO infrastructure fund during the 3-year measuring period; $1 billion is needed to completely close the gap.

Third, to make significant progress in lengthening the interval between onset of a conventional attack by the Warsaw Pact and the time at which nuclear release would have to be requested, as determined and certified to the U.S. Secretary of Defense by the SACEUR, General Rogers.

If, upon reflection and with 2 years in which to plan and begin responses, the allies are nonetheless unwilling to make these essential and agreed-upon improvements, the United States will have a clear indication of allied intent. It will be evident that the allies are content with nothing more than a tripwire, and we can begin to reduce the number of our forces stationed in NATO and also begin to reduce our related NATO expenditures.

Let me now describe the reductions. If the allies do not make the first path of 3 percent, and also fail to meet any of the three goals under path two, then the ceiling will be reduced by 30,000 per year. If, however, the allies meet one of the three goals under path two, the ceiling would be reduced by only 20,000; if 2 out of 3 under path two, by 10,000, and if they meet all three, or if they meet the 3 percent there would be no reduction.

I repeat, either of the compliance paths offered, the 3-percent growth path or the specific goals path, is both realistic and affordable. Moreover, for the second path the spending is entirely in Europe on European goods and services, and produced by European labor. Indeed, in the case of facilities and aircraft shelters at European bases, the United States will also pay more than one-fourth of the total bill as its share of common infrastructure funding. Moreover, Mr. President, nothing in this amendment forces the allies to do anything that has not been agreed to previously—indeed, agreed, and agreed again. All that has been missing is performance on the agreements.

Thus, Mr. President, if NATO's de facto strategy really is a conventional tripwire with early resort to nuclear weapons, the last thing the United States should be planning is to send six more divisions and about 1,500 more tactical aircraft into Europe just as the alliance is ready to escalate to nuclear weapons.

Indeed, if that is the strategy the Europeans want, I believe that a far smaller commitment of U.S. stationed forces than those we now maintain in peacetime would be called for. That is why I regard as wholly appropriate the troop reductions called for in this amendment, if the allies are not serious about improving conventional capability.

Mr. President, this amendment also requires the Secretary of Defense to submit an annual report outlining U.S. defense expenditures in support of NATO. This report would provide a direct link between our defense spending and our formal commitment to NATO as reflected in the NATO "Defense Planning Questionnaire Response." This is an annual document in which the member nations commit forces to NATO. We will be able, using this report, to determine just what this commitment costs.

This reporting will also include an assessment of allied performance in meeting the following:

Increasing overall defense spending;
Increasing sustainability as well as support for U.S. reinforcing tactical aircraft;

Improving airbase defenses;

Meeting NATO force goals;

Increasing NATO infrastructure funding;

Increasing trained manpower levels, particularly reserves;

Increasing war reserve material;

Improving initial defense capability;

Improving NATO's ability to neutralize enemy follow-on forces, particularly through the use of emerging technologies;

Improving mine/counter mine capability;

Improving offensive counter air capability.

With this assessment, Congress will be able to look at U.S. expenditures in support of NATO and how the allies are performing in certain key areas. Congress can then make judgments on whether or not the U.S. expenditures should be approved in the annual authorization process or whether they should be reduced.

In my judgment, this is an appropriate way to link allied performance to our own commitment to NATO. If the Europeans simply shift their priorities and resources to meet these formal tests, abandoning other agreed goals, we will soon recognize this shift.

Finally, Mr. President, I must note one area where the U.S. has clearly not done enough over the years—making the two-way street in armaments cooperation work. The chairman and I have been strong supporters of the emerging technology initiative in NATO, and I welcome the recent tangible progess in this area. Nonetheless, our European allies spend a great deal more on U.S. weapons systems and components than we do in acquiring European-developed systems. While some of that can legitimately be justified on the grounds that our worldwide commitments sometimes impose requirements beyond those typically considered by European manufacturers, I am inclined to believe that much more of that stems from U.S. industry and service reluctance to buy somebody else's product rather than being involved from the very beginning.

However, Mr. President, I say that if we are ever to get to the point where NATO's resource inputs, which are larger than those of the Warsaw Pact, are efficiently transformed into a larger defense output, it must be because we have done a better job of mutual planning, cooperative development, and equitable sharing of production. Therefore, I have included in the amendment a provision to encourage the side-by-side testing, by the Secretary of Defense's Office of Test and Evaluation, not by the services themselves, of systems and subsystems of European manufacture against those developed by our military establishment. This is but a small step toward greater transatlantic cooperation in armaments, but I hope it will mark an important new start, and help persuade European governments that we do not want troop cuts, we want more effective conventional defenses, and we are willing to look closely at what they have to offer.

In summary, the United States cannot continue to expend billions and billions to prepare for the conventional war that our allies are not prepared to fight. These precious resources are better applied for other purposes, to meet our other worldwide interests and commitments.

I am under no illusions about the ability of the legislative branch of one nation to influence the actions of other nations. Also I am under no illusions about the many obstacles to improved conventional defense capabilities that would remain even if the allies fully comply with the goals of the amendment.

It is not a panacea but it is a beginning—a modest test of whether the vitality of the alliance is still capable of being energized. If such movement is begun, the amendment has a significance beyond its modest scope.

In my judgment, the citizens of the Western democracies will not long sustain nor support large defense establishments that can only provide a military posture that has as its end result either capitulation or resort to early use of nuclear weapons. In an era of pronounced NATO theater nuclear disadvantage and rough strategic nuclear parity between the United States and U.S.S.R., this makes no sense.

I urge my colleagues to send a strong signal that we want this to change—we want NATO to improve its conventional capability—over a 5-year period—within defense spending levels that are readily achievable.

[The Nunn Amendment]

Richard Lugar

Mr. President, I have learned much from Senator Nunn's contributions over the years to Senate debates on national security matters and issues of strategy. I think I understand the intent of this amendment, and I share with him some of the frustrations and concerns in achieving a more equitable sharing of the defense burden by our NATO allies.

I fully recognize the strong imperative for increasing NATO's conventional capabilities in order to have a true flexible response, with no semblance of an extended tripwire. The issue is: Will this amendment in its present form, and particularly because of its timing, have its intended effects if enacted now? Or, will enactment of this amendment now have precisely the opposite effects?

There are several factors that enter into my judgment that enactment of this amendment at this time will produce consequences that would be totally at odds with the intention of the amendment's sponsor.

First, our European allies are still contending with the fallout from the INF deployment decision. The Soviet Union engineered and is still pursuing a massive campaign of intimidation against the deploying countries. Yet, all basing nations with one exception have stayed with the 1979 INF deployment schedule. These deployments indeed constitute a major ongoing effort to redress the middle leg of the triad of flexible

From *Congressional Record,* 98th Cong., 2d Sess., June 20, 1984, pp. S7736–S7738.

response which has been of concern to Members of this body. Our European allies have met the test of sharing the burden in the deployment of these systems. These deployments in the face of Soviet intimidation efforts and massive demonstrations in the streets are a reflection of the willingness of European governments to buttress the NATO deterrent.

Equally important, the emergence of the alliance from a major test case of its vitality and cohesion has been accompanied by attitudinal changes and a growing conviction that more must be done to improve the conventional leg of the triad. The last two meetings of the NATO Defense Ministers are testimony to the fact that the alliance has begun to shift the focus of its attention from the now successful improvements of NATO's theater nuclear posture to means of enhancing the alliance's conventional posture. There has emerged from those meetings an impressive consensus on the need for better conventional defense through such measures as improved sustainability and exploitation of emerging technologies. These are measures long supported by Senator Nunn.

European support for such measures is reflective of conclusions drawn from debates in Europe over the dangers of reliance on any kind of extended tripwire. Discussions of NATO strategy—either its alteration or the development of capabilities to meet the current one—are to be encouraged.

Mr. President, there are three essential prerequisites to a stronger NATO conventional option: First, a broad alliance consensus regarding the threat; second, a similar consensus that deterrence of this threat requires enhanced conventional defense; and third, a widespread belief that this can be generated at a cost politically acceptable to free societies. The feasibility of any NATO conventional option will depend critically on these prerequisites being met. However, enactment of this amendment is unlikely to contribute to a more enlightened debate on NATO strategy, nor to an alliance willingness to draw the appropriate conclusions from such a review of strategy.

It is worth remarking that the prospects for enhancing the conventional defense posture seem greater than at any previous time in NATO's 35 years. While deterrence remains NATO's overriding aim, the advent of nuclear stalemate has engendered a growing recognition that nuclear deterrence-on-the-cheap—even cheaper for the Europeans—is eroding in credibility. The result has been a renaissance of interest in conventional deterrence in both Europe and the United States, particularly since the gap between Warsaw Pact and NATO conventional capabilities is far wider than in nuclear capabilities. This is not to suggest that nuclear deterrence has been robbed of all credibility, but only that the NATO nuclear deterrent is no longer to be relied upon as heavily as in past decades. In effect, NATO is in a period of strategic transition from primary reliance on nuclear deterrence toward a more balanced flexible response posture which its strategy has long called for but which the alliance has never adequately funded in practice.

The fact of the matter is that NATO is already buying and paying for the great bulk of the capabilities required to develop a credible conventional defense—at least in the crucial central region. With European NATO already spending over $100 billion per annum—(1982 figure)—on defense, an approximately 25 percent real increase over the level of a decade ago, and the United States spending even more, NATO is already within shooting distance of this goal. Yes, it may seem strange that, when they are already spending so much, the Allies have seemed unwilling to fund the relatively modest additions necessary to maximize the deterrent value of the huge sums that they already collectively invest.

Nonetheless, it has been a political fact of life that, with economic recession throttling much of Europe, even modest increases on the order of 3 to 4 percent in real defense spending per annum could not be funded by NATO parliaments. Under these circumstances, the only viable solution has appeared to be efforts to impose stricter priorities, focus as much as possible on low-cost measures, seek realistic phasing, stress more rational burden sharing, and seek offsets and tradeoffs within existing defense program levels.

Third, the Department of Defense has laid before the Senate a report on improved conventional defense, a report containing some 30 recommendations. The Senate displayed concern and imagination in requesting this report. However, all parties concerned need some time to digest these recommendations and to arrive at considered judgments with respect to priorities for implementation. I would expect the Senate to take a lead in attempting to translate these recommendations into action programs. In short, the United States and its allies are becoming more specific on how the allies can do more in the conventional sphere. But we— the Senate, the Department of Defense, and the allies—need some time to react. Enactment of this amendment could well derail, if not scuttle, efforts to implement many of these recommendations.

Further, Mr. President, I would note that in a few days time Lord Carrington will take over as the new Secretary General of NATO. Lord Carrington is not only well acquainted with congressional concerns about more equitable burden sharing within the alliance; he has also made known the priority he will attach to enhancing the alliance's conventional force posture upon his assumption of office. Lord Carrington will need positive support from Washington as he undertakes this task, support that could be seriously eroded if this amendment is enacted.

Moreover, Mr. President, in the aftermath of the "Euro-missile" debate and at a time of chilled Soviet-American relations, political harmony and cohesion within the alliance are a prerequisite to improved East-West relations. After a period of Soviet intransigence with respect to all Western efforts to revive the East-West negotiating process, and with the recent calls by the President to the Soviet leadership to sit down with us to discuss East-West issues, we may be seeing some light at the end of the cold East-West tunnel.

Yes, this amendment may be intended to send a signal to our allies. But it would also send a very unhelpful signal to the Soviet Union, a signal that could constitute an open invitation to Moscow to redouble its efforts to drive a wedge between Europe and North America. And yes, it could lessen rather than encourage Soviet interest in dealing seriously with the United States on a variety of strategic and global issues. We must not do by legislation what the Soviets have failed to do with threats and intimidation. During the months ahead, as we seek to revive the East-West dialog, unity is particularly important between and within the NATO countries.

Mr. President, the issue as well is how to move forward with conventional improvements at a time when European economic recovery lags behind the U.S. recovery. First, we have to make better use of existing NATO resources. Second, we need to increase the contribution of defense resources by all NATO partners.

Senator Nunn has been in the lead of encouraging NATO planners to develop a more effective resources strategy. In particular, efforts have to be undertaken to promote more effective armaments cooperation, both transatlantic and within Western Europe, and further, we must move forward with the sound application of new technologies. The more effective use of resources through improved NATO planning will in turn strengthen the political support in allied countries so necessary for increased NATO contributions.

An increase in the amount of resources devoted to defense—that is, a greater burden sharing on the part of our allies—cannot be exacted through threats. Such increases can only flow from a European appreciation of the fact that European security is enhanced by improvements in the conventional leg of the triad. From my travels in Europe and from conversations with European officials, I am convinced that European governments, despite relatively poor economic conditions at present, want and will move in this direction.

In sum, Mr. President, concerns expressed in this body in the past over the need for more equitable burden sharing on the part of our allies have had an impact in Europe. We are beginning to see the allies move in the direction that we have long advocated. However, an amendment of the kind that we are currently debating, despite its constructive intent, can only be misinterpreted in Europe and will pull the rug out from under recent efforts and advances to enhance our conventional force posture. Such an amendment, if enacted, would prove especially harmful and dispiriting to those European governments and parties who have painfully held the line against opponents during the INF debates and sought to move publics in the direction of improved conventional defense.

We cannot allow our commitment to and interests in NATO to become hostage to the politics of the day. Moreover, we should take no comfort from the fact that any reductions proposed in the amendment, if certain conditions are not met by our allies, would only take effect at the end of 1987. Passage of this amendment in its present form will invite immediate reaction in Europe which could interrupt precisely those efforts of the day by our allies that are leading in the direction of an improved conventional capability.

If the proponents of this amendment are primarily interested in shaping the terms of reference for the policy debate on this issue, I applaud this intention. And the debate currently underway in this body will go a long way in that direction. However, passage of this amendment would destroy the prospects for a meaningful debate with our allies and derail current and planned efforts to work toward an improved conventional deterrent.

Mr. President, we are asking the American people to make sacrifices in the interest of a strong national defense. We can do no less in urging our NATO partners and European publics to make equally painful sacrifices in the interest of Western security. Without burden sharing, there can be no collective defense. The views of the Congress, and the Senate in particular, must be heard on this issue. There should be no doubt in the mind of any European ally that this body stands for a strong alliance, a credible strategy, and the capabilities to meet the strategy. However, I do not believe that those objectives are furthered by enactment of this amendment. I, too, pledge that the concerns of this body will be transmitted to our allies at every opportunity. The message of the need to make better use of existing NATO resources in defense and to increase the contribution of defense resources by our European partners will be delivered loudly and clearly.

Mr. President, I would urge my colleagues to work with our allies in improving the Alliance's conventional force posture. For that reason, Mr. President, I would also urge my colleagues to reject the Nunn amendment.

QUESTIONS FOR DISCUSSION

1 Is the continued presence of more than 300,000 U.S. troops in Europe essential to maintain the independence of Western European countries?
2 Are Western Europeans letting NATO down by failing to spend more on conventional defenses?
3 If so, what steps, if any, should the United States take to try to secure an improvement? How successful would such steps be likely to be?
4 Will U.S. troops be in Europe in the twenty-first century?
5 Is the level of U.S. forces in Western Europe an issue appropriate and desirable for the U.S. Senate to determine?

SUGGESTED READINGS

Bowie, Robert H. "Nunn Amendment: NATO Must Do More on Conventional Arms," *Christian Science Monitor,* June 29, 1984, p. 14.

Cohen, Eliot A. "Do We Still Need Europe?" *Commentary,* **81** (Jan. 1986), pp. 28–35.

"Controversy over NATO Cost-Sharing: Pro and Con," *Congressional Digest* (Aug.–Sept. 1984), pp. 193–224.

Golden, James R., Asa A. Clark, and Bruce E. Arlinghaus (eds.). *Conventional Deterrence: Alternatives for European Defense.* Lexington, Mass.: Lexington Books, 1984.

Huntington, Samuel P. "Conventional Deterrence and Conventional Retaliation in Europe," *International Security,* **8** (Winter 1983–84), pp. 32–56.

Joffe, Josef. "Europe's American Pacifier," *Foreign Policy,* no. 54 (Spring 1984), pp. 64–82.

Krauss, Melvyn. *How NATO Weakens the West.* New York: Simon and Schuster, 1986.

Radway, Laurence. "U.S. Forces in Europe: The Case for Cautious Contraction," *SAIS Review,* **8** (Winter–Spring 1985), pp. 227–242.

Ravenal, Earl C. "Europe without America: The Erosion of NATO," *Foreign Affairs,* **63** (Summer 1985), pp. 1020–1035.

Schwartz, Charles. "Mansfieldism Revisited," *SAIS Review,* **4** (Winter–Spring 1984), pp. 145–159.

Sloan, Stanley R. *NATO's Future: Toward a New Transatlantic Bargain*. London: Macmillan, 1986.

Treverton, Gregory F. *Making the Alliance Work: The United States and Western Europe*. Ithaca, N.Y.: Cornell Univ. Press, 1985.

Williams, Phil. "The Nunn Amendment, Burden-sharing and U.S. Troops in Europe," *Survival* (London), **27** (Jan.–Feb. 1985), pp. 2–10.

———. *The Senate and U.S. Troops in Europe*. New York: St. Martin's Press, 1985.

CHAPTER 5

FORMAL CONSTRAINTS ON CONFLICT

The modern international system has always been based unambiguously on the primacy of sovereign states. But the terrible carnage caused by warfare during the twentieth century has led many people, from philosophers to political activists, to argue that the sovereign state now needs to be superseded or at least placed under mutually agreed and binding constraints.

Early in this century global agitations to this end reached a peak. In the United States the most powerful movement for ending or at least modifying the "international anarchy" came to be associated with Woodrow Wilson, president from 1913 to 1921. An internationalist eager to make World War I the "war to end war," Wilson was the principal architect of the League of Nations and hoped that that body would inaugurate an era of collective security, universal respect for international law, and all-round disarmament by international treaty.

Wilson was unable to secure Senate approval for his visionary approach, and the United States accordingly entered upon an era of so-called isolationism. But many of Wilson's ideals enjoyed a renaissance after the United States became involved in World War II. In varying degrees Presidents Roosevelt, Truman, Eisenhower, Kennedy, and Johnson could all be said to have pursued policies based on "liberal internationalism" (or "bourgeois internationalism," as the Soviets contemptuously call it).

U.S. "liberal internationalists" have come in many varieties—some having been supporters and others opponents of traditional U.S. Cold War policies. They have included those who have been out-and-out world government advocates; those who have sought to strengthen the League of Nations and/or the United Nations; those who have striven for greater respect for international law; those who have sought the control or destruction by treaty of armaments both conventional and nuclear; and those who have desired to see the United States lead a resolute coalition of like-minded nations willing if necessary to wage war to counter expansionist, authoritarian adversaries of Wilsonian values. In this final chapter we consider some of the arguments of adherents of two of these groups, together with the case presented by those with a more skeptical outlook.

THE WORLD COURT

One important concern of U.S. internationalists, with roots going back into the nineteenth century, has been to strengthen the place of international law in world affairs. Many U.S. liberals have advocated the international arbitration or adjudication of disputes involving their own country.

The most important global center for the administration of international law is the International Court of Justice at The Hague in the Netherlands, established in its present form in 1945. The United States committed itself to support the Court in 1946—though with reservations about the extent to which the nation was obliged to accept the Court's jurisdiction in any particular case.

In recent years, however, U.S. conservatives have become increasingly unhappy with the character of the Court. Some have stressed that it is a hollow sham, rarely effective on issues of importance. Other U.S. conservatives have attacked the Court as having fallen increasingly under the influence of anti-U.S. forces similar to those now in the majority in the United Nations General Assembly. These conservatives have been particularly enraged at the efforts of Nicaragua to put the United States literally in the dock—a development that led the Reagan administration to give notice in 1985 that it did not consider itself bound by the World Court's jurisdiction.

Most U.S. liberals, however, continue to see merit in the work of the Court and have no desire to see the United States abandon its links with it. They see the United States as a country with both practical and idealistic reasons for wishing to be considered a standard-bearer of global rule-of-law aspirations.

In our first debate, Richard N. Gardner, a professor of law at Columbia University and a former U.S. ambassador to Italy, defends continued U.S. loyalty to the Court. Burton Yale Pines of the Heritage Foundation, the Washington-based conservative "think tank," takes essentially the opposite line and welcomes the Reagan administration's decision to distance itself from the Court.

ARMS CONTROL

A strong component in the Wilsonian approach to international politics has been concern about armaments and arms races. At the end of World War I President Wilson and his followers were inclined to hold the pre-1914 European arms race as to a considerable degree responsible for the catastrophe that had ensued. Hence, at the Paris Peace Conference in 1919 the great powers committed themselves to negotiate a reduction in armaments down to "the lowest level consistent with national safety." These negotiations continued intermittently throughout the 1920s and culminated in the World Disarmament Conference in 1932–1935. The United States, though otherwise largely turning its back on Wilsonian policies, took a full part in these negotiations. Despite some partial achievements in limiting naval armaments, however, the interwar quest for arms control and disarmament was destined to collapse in failure.

In the post-1945 Cold War era, under the shadow of nuclear weapons, negotiations for arms control and disarmament have continued without intermission in a variety of forums. But at first the superpowers appear to have engaged in mere polemics rather than in serious negotiations. Hence, in the first two postwar decades the only agreement of first-rank importance was the signing by the United States, the Soviet Union, and Great Britain of the Partial Test Ban Treaty of 1963. In 1969, however, superpower arms control discussions suddenly assumed great seriousness with the beginning of the Strategic Arms Limitation Talks (SALT), which led to a number of celebrated agreements. This process has continued (lately under different labels) until the present. The irony is that this process began at a time when Wilsonian idealism in the United States was in most other respects beginning to wane. The explanation for the timing probably lies in the fact that the Soviet Union had at last achieved effective nuclear parity with the United States. Until then the Soviets would not agree to be bound by treaty to a state of inferiority, and the United States would not grant by treaty an equality the Soviets had not in practice achieved.

But how important are negotiations and treaties in respect to nuclear arms control and disarmament? Many Americans in the Wilsonian tradition, as well as some like Kissinger who are not, are inclined to see them as a vital development that may play a part in significantly reducing the risk of global war. But many other Americans—and not only conservatives—consider that armaments are really only of marginal importance in preventing or causing wars. Hence, they believe analysts and policy makers who give excessive attention to the arms race are conceivably neglecting to give appropriate consideration to the more pressing dangers and risks we may face. In our final debate these matters are among those considered. Wolfgang K. H. Panofsky is an enthusiast for arms control, whereas William A. Schwartz and Charles Derber are skeptics about what they consider to be a "misplaced focus."

18 Should the United States acknowledge the jurisdiction of the World Court?

YES

Richard N. Gardner

[*The United States and the World Court*]

NO

Burton Yale Pines

Should the United States Acknowledge the Jurisdiction of the World Court?

[The United States and the World Court]

Richard N. Gardner

Last month [the Reagan] Administration terminated a forty year old commitment by our country, entered into with the overwhelming support of the Senate, to submit legal disputes to the International Court of Justice at the request of any other country accepting the same obligation. This commitment was terminated without the full consultation and discussion with the Senate that I believe was necessary and appropriate, considering the Senate's direct involvement in the shaping of that commitment.

I also believe the Administration's decision was contrary to the national interest. That interest would have been served better by modifying the terms of our acceptance of compulsory jurisdiction in ways that I shall shortly explain and which are illustrated at the conclusion of my testimony. I hope the Committee will consider urging the Administration to file a new declaration accepting compulsory jurisdiction along these or similar lines.

Our commitment to accept the compulsory jurisdiction of the World Court was taken by the Truman Administration in 1946 and was maintained by the Administrations of Presidents Eisenhower, Kennedy, Johnson, Nixon, Ford and Carter. A reading of the statements by these Administrations on this subject suggests that they were influenced by a number of considerations, some moral and some very practical. These Administrations believed

- that the United States should be a leader in promoting the rule of law in the world;
- that as a law-abiding nation we should be willing to hold ourselves accountable for our

From U.S. Cong., House of Representatives, *U.S. Decision to Withdraw from the International Court of Justice,* Hearing before the Subcommittee on Human Rights and International Organizations of the Committee on Foreign Affairs, 99th Cong., 1st Sess., 1985, pp. 110–122.

actions before an international tribunal upon the request of other countries prepared to do the same;

- that our national security is best served by building up international institutions to promote stability, order and justice in international relations;
- that the International Court of Justice can advance these goals by applying rules of international law in the peaceful settlement of disputes;
- that international law as applied by the Court will, in most cases, be consistent with our interests;
- and that, since our Constitution and laws offer rights and remedies to foreign citizens and corporations greater than most other countries grant to our citizens and corporations, we will have more occasion to go before the Court as plaintiff than as defendant.

I believe these reasons made sense then and that they make sense now.

In support of its decision to terminate our acceptance of the Court's compulsory jurisdiction this Administration and those who support its decision have advanced a number of arguments. I do not believe they are persuasive.

First, it is argued that more than two-thirds of the members of the United Nations have not accepted compulsory jurisdiction. But that is no reason why a minority of countries including the United States should not accept compulsory jurisdiction in disputes among themselves if it serves their interests to do so. The United States and like-minded members of a "law bloc" could also work to encourage others to accept compulsory jurisdiction, something we have made no effort to do in recent years.

Second, it is argued that it is unjust for judges whose countries have not accepted the

Court's compulsory jurisdiction to decide cases involving countries who do. But the judges of the Court serve in their individual capacities. If they are jurists of ability, integrity and independence, as most of the judges are, the failure of their countries to accept compulsory jurisdiction should not disqualify them.

Third, it is argued that we have never been able to use our acceptance of compulsory jurisdiction to bring other countries before the Court. But this is our own fault. The Connally reservation to our acceptance of compulsory jurisdiction made an exception for matters within our domestic jurisdiction as determined by ourselves.

We could have employed this self-judging reservation to bar Nicaragua's suit against us in the World Court, but did not do so because we were ashamed to argue that mining another country's harbors and supporting insurgents seeking to overthrow its government was a matter within our domestic jurisdiction. Yet under the reciprocity clause in the Court's statute, the reservation can be and has been invoked against us as an absolute bar to litigation by countries using it in good or bad faith. The remedy for this self-inflicted injury is not to terminate our acceptance of compulsory jurisdiction but to eliminate the self-judging reservation that effectively denies us the benefits we thought we were getting when we took the original commitment. The proposed reservations at the close of this testimony include a change in the Connally reservation to accomplish this.

Fourth, it is argued that the Court overstepped its powers and thus demonstrated its lack of responsibility in taking jurisdiction in the case Nicaragua has brought against us, because this case is a "political" matter and therefore inadmissible. This is exactly the argument which the Khomeini government of Iran asserted against us in the hostages case and that both we and the Court rightly rejected.

The fact is that many controversies before the Court are both legal and political. There is nothing in the Statute of the Court or in the United Nations Charter that prevents the Court from deciding such cases provided it confines itself to adjudicating the legal issues. Indeed, Article 36(3) of the U.N. Charter which deals with disputes that endanger international peace and security, provides that "legal disputes should as a general rule be referred by the parties to the International Court of Justice." It is therefore not surprising that our argument on the inadmissibility of Nicaragua's claim was rejected by every one of the judges of the Court, including Judge Schwebel of the United States.

Fifth, it is argued that the Court exceeded its powers in the Nicaraguan case by taking jurisdiction in a controversy involving armed conflict and the rights of a country to individual and collective self-defense. But here again, there is nothing in the Court's Statute or in the U.N. Charter to support this claim, nor is there any support in the practice of the Court and of the United States itself. Since 1945 thirteen cases have been brought before the Court involving the use of armed force, eight of them by the United States, three by the United Kingdom, and one by Israel. Nicaragua's was the thirteenth.

Nevertheless, though the Court has the power to decide such cases, it must be recognized that where armed conflict is continuing it may be difficult or impossible to determine the facts. Moreover, international law concerning aggression and self-defense and intervention in civil war situations is so controversial, and the national security interests of states so paramount, that it is simply not realistic in the present state of international relations to expect nations to accept decisions of an international tribunal on the legality of their behavior in armed conflicts in which they are or have been involved. Reservation (d) at the end of my statement therefore makes an exception for such cases, while preserving the rights of nations to bring other cases to the Court arising out of individual acts of terrorism or violence such as the occupation of our Embassy in Teheran. I concede that this reservation carves out a big exception to compulsory jurisdiction, but it still leaves a vast area where compulsory jurisdiction can be effective.

Finally, it is argued that the judges of the Court are not impartial and independent jurists but that a majority of them are politically biased against the United States.

On this subject it is necessary to speak with care and precision. The World Court does not behave like the U.N. General Assembly. It is composed in the main of respected jurists and its opinions are based on careful reasoning and scholarship. Seven of its judges come from countries allied to the United States (four from NATO countries, one from Japan, two from Latin America). These judges are all friendly to our country and perform their judicial functions with competence and independence. Together with the outstanding American judge, Stephen Schwebel, they account for a majority of eight members in a Court of fifteen.

On the other hand, the independence of the Soviet judge is certainly open to question, and it would be naive to expect him not to take the Soviet view when Soviet and American interests are in conflict. National pressures also weigh heavily upon the judges from Poland and Algeria. The two judges from Africa, the Indian judge, and the new judge from China are eminent jurists, though their views on international law may diverge from our own more frequently than those from the Western nations and Japan.

All in all, it is a less than perfect tribunal from our point of view, as any truly international court representative of the world's main legal systems is bound to be. But I do not believe that the record of the Court so far indicates that it is biased against us or that its interpretations of international law are unreasonable.

If in the future the behavior of some of the judges were found to tilt the balance of the court in ways that are adverse to our interests—a conclusion I do not believe to be justified at this time—there is a better remedy than rejecting the Court's compulsory jurisdiction. We could condition our acceptance of compulsory jurisdiction on our right to have any case to which we are a party decided by a chamber of the Court composed of judges acceptable to ourselves. But before we try this remedy we should recognize that under the reciprocity provision an unwilling defendant country against whom we are bringing a case could claim the same right and could defeat the Court's jurisdiction by declining to accept any combination of judges acceptable to us. There is also the possibility that the Court would hold such a reservation to be incompatible with the acceptance of compulsory jurisdiction, although I believe this is unlikely. For these reasons, I have included a reservation on chambers at the end of this testimony only as a possibility for the future, not as a remedy to be adopted now.

The other proposed reservations which are set out below cover more technical matters. I have proposed that we be in a position to terminate our acceptance of compulsory jurisdiction immediately, without any notice requirement. To assure that we are not subject to "hit and run" actions by countries who accept the Court's jurisdiction only for the purpose of suing us, I have included a reservation modelled on one adopted by the United Kingdom some years ago. I have also dropped the so-called "Vandenberg reservation" because its meaning is unclear and because the Court's own Statute and rules provide adequate opportunity for other parties to multilateral treaties to intervene in disputes to which they are also parties involving the interpretation of such treaties.

Taken together, I believe the proposed reservations would adequately protect our national interest as a defendant before the Court, while still permitting us to use the Court to vindicate our rights and to benefit from the contributions—admittedly long-term—that the Court can make to a more just and stable world order.

In the last analysis, our conclusions about the desirability of accepting the Court's compulsory jurisdiction must result from a realistic calculation of the balance of benefits and risks. I do not accept the view that our adherence to the Court's compulsory jurisdiction could endanger our national security. This argument is based on the wholly unrealistic assumption that some future Administration would refrain from taking an action that it considered essential to the national security because of an adverse decision by the World Court. We all know that no nation, including our own, behaves that way.

In situations of crisis, our action will almost always take place before the Court's procedures allow it to reach a decision. Moreover, if the decision is unacceptable to us in a vital national security matter we will ignore it, and our veto in the Security Council protects us from any U.N. effort to enforce it.

Of course, I am not suggesting that we should be in the habit of ignoring decisions of the International Court. I am simply saying that in the remote contingency that the Court decides against us on a vital national security matter (armed conflicts having already been reserved), the political cost of disobeying that decision would be less than that of denying ourselves completely the possibility of invoking the Court's compulsory jurisdiction against other countries.

To sum up, I believe there is a way for our country to reap the benefits of compulsory jurisdiction—benefits that all previous Administrations have found substantial—without jeopardizing any important national interest. I hope these hearings will help develop a consensus on the best way to achieve this important objective.

PROPOSED RESERVATIONS TO A NEW DECLARATION OF U.S. ACCEPTANCE OF THE COMPULSORY JURISDICTION OF THE INTERNATIONAL COURT OF JUSTICE

Provided, that this declaration shall not apply to

(a) disputes the solution of which the parties shall entrust to other tribunals by virtue of agreements already in existence or which may be concluded in the future; or

(b) disputes with regard to matters that by international law fall within the domestic jurisdiction of the United States of America; or

(c) disputes in respect of which any other party to the dispute has accepted the compulsory jurisdiction of the International Court of Justice only in relation to or for the purpose of the dispute or where the acceptance of the Court's jurisdiction by another party to the dispute was deposited or ratified less than twelve months prior to the filing of the application bringing the dispute before the Court; or

(d) disputes relating to international or internal armed conflicts or to actions taken by the United States in the exercise of individual or collective self-defense or in accordance with decisions of regional organizations; provided, however, that this reservation shall not be deemed to cover actions not justified by military necessity against ships and aircraft, diplomatic and governmental agents and government property, or private citizens and their property; and

Provided further, that this declaration shall remain in force until notice may be given to terminate or amend this declaration.

Possible Additional Reservation

Provided further, that any case brought by any party against the United States of America on the basis of compulsory jurisdiction in accordance with this declaration shall be decided by a chamber of the International Court of Justice composed in accordance with Article 26 of the Statute whose membership is acceptable to the United States.

Should the United States Acknowledge the Jurisdiction of the World Court?

Burton Yale Pines

When we attempt to evaluate the World Court, we confront the dilemma of idealistic image versus sober reality. This is clear from the Court's formal name—the International Court of Justice. This evokes images of magisterial solemnity—a bench of internationally trusted Solomons resolving the thorny disputes that divide nations. Yet the Court's gritty reality differs vastly from its lofty image. For good reason, therefore, has the Reagan Administration decided to deny the tribunal automatic jurisdiction over United States actions regarding Nicaragua and other political matters. This decision ought to be reassuring to those Americans determined to base foreign policy on reality and concerned with preserving their nation's sovereignty.

To start with, no one denies Washington's right to tell the Court to keep its nose out of America's business. The Court's own by-laws unambiguously specify that the Court has jurisdiction only when parties to a dispute grant it such jurisdiction. A defendant state cannot be brought before the international tribunal nor can a default judgment be given against the state unless it has so consented.

Indeed, the world's nations typically have told the Court to butt out. West Germany, Italy, Ireland, China, India, Iceland, France, the Soviet Union, all Soviet-bloc nations and scores of other countries have rejected the Court's jurisdiction. Some examples:

In 1973, Pakistan tried to take India to the Court for refusing to repatriate Pakistani prisoners captured during the war over East Pa-

From U.S. Cong., House of Representatives, *U.S. Decision to Withdraw from the International Court of Justice,* Hearing before the Subcommittee on Human Rights and International Organizations of the Committee on Foreign Affairs, 99th Cong., 1st Sess., 1985, pp. 49–53.

kistan's secession; India refused to participate in the proceedings.

That same year, Paris insisted that the Court lacked competence when Australia and New Zealand tried to take France to the Court on charges that its nuclear testing in the South Pacific violated international laws.

Nearly two decades earlier, Moscow ridiculed the notion of appearing before the Court when the U.S. tried on several occasions to press charges that the Soviet Union, in various aircraft incidents, had violated the law. Similarly, Moscow to this date ignores the 1962 Court ruling that the U.S.S.R must pay its assessed share of United Nations' costs for the Congo operation. The fact is that neither the Soviet Union nor any of its East Bloc satellites ever have accepted the Court's jurisdiction.

Of the United Nations' 159 members, only 45 have granted the Court automatic jurisdiction. (Such jurisdiction is granted by Switzerland and Lichtenstein, which are not U.N. members.) The U.S., therefore, is hardly alone—indeed, not even in a minority—by the action of the Reagan Administration.

It is no wonder that the Court's fifteen judges are probably the world's most underworked jurists. Between the Court's founding in 1945 and 1981, it handled a meager 42 contentious cases and gave advisory opinions on an additional 17 cases. And from 1966 to 1981, the Court was given only six new cases and handed down only five advisory opinions. Just one case was filed between 1976 and 1981. On average, since its founding, the Court has rendered fewer than two judgments per year—a number which has been decreasing.

Those few cases which the Court does hear almost all concern rather tame matters and only rarely deal with even minor differences between nations. The bulk of the Court's calendar has been filled by disputes concerning fishing rights, delimitation of continental shelves, minor boundary disputes and such burning questions as whether the World Health Organization had the right to move its regional office out of Alexandria, Egypt.

In short, the World Court, despite its pretensions and grand quarters at The Hague, is a hollow and rather useless institution to which hardly any nation ever turns for settling hardly any dispute. It is a relic of an earlier age whose internationalism and simplistic idealism are now discredited. For this reason alone, the Reagan Administration is wise to deny the Court jurisdiction.

It is wise also because the Court resembles no tribunal familiar to the Anglo-Saxon tradition of jurisprudence. The Court is as highly politicized and as biased as the U.N. General Assembly. Indeed the Court's 15 judges are elected by the General Assembly and Security Council. Sitting on the bench are such impartial champions of international justice as Algeria, the Soviet Union, Poland, Senegal and Nigeria. We would be naive to expect justice from such a group.

There is a more compelling reason for the Administration's action. The World Court now, as at its inception, threatens the very concept of sovereignty upon which the nation-state rests. By what right or for what good reason should a body of international jurists don robes, judge the action of the U.S. and render a decision binding the U.S.? Such a fundamental transfer of sovereignty has been resisted since the American Republic's earliest days—from George Washington's injunction against foreign alliances to the Senate's repudiation of League of Nations membership. Even the NATO treaty, the most solemn declaration of international commitment ever made by the U.S., falls short of automatically binding the U.S. to any action. If America's European allies are attacked, for instance, the U.S. does not automatically find

itself at war but merely is obliged to regard that attack as an attack on the U.S.

When the Senate in 1946 ratified U.S. membership in the World Court, it pointedly insisted that an integral part of the ratification was the statement, called the Connally Amendment (named after its sponsor, Thomas Connally of Texas), that the U.S. reserved the right to determine the Court's jurisdiction as it affected the U.S. The U.S. Senate thus anticipated wisely the situation in which the U.S. in recent years has found itself at the World Court.

The Reagan Administration's refusal to grant jurisdiction to the World Court is a reaffirmation of America's two-century old vigorous defense of its sovereignty. It is this reaffirmation of sovereignty and independence from international bodies—at a time when the United Nations, UNESCO and almost every other international organization has been turned into an anti-American and anti-West lynch mob— which deserves the support of Congress and the American people.

QUESTIONS FOR DISCUSSION

1 Should sovereign states accept the constraints of international law in all circumstances?
2 Can the United States expect justice from the International Court of Justice as presently constituted?
3 Do the Soviet Union and the United States have fundamentally different approaches to international law?
4 Could increased respect for international law by both superpowers help significantly in diminishing Cold War tensions?

SUGGESTED READINGS

Beres, Rene. "Becoming an Outlaw: United States Foreign Policy and Central America," *International Journal,* **40** (Summer 1985), pp. 510–529.
Boyle, Francis Anthony. *World Politics and International Law.* Durham, N.C.: Duke Univ. Press, 1985.

Chomsky, Noam. "Law and Imperialism in the Central American Conflict," *Journal of Contemporary Studies,* **8** (Spring–Summer 1985), pp. 25–46.

Cutler, Lloyd N. "The Right to Intervene," *Foreign Affairs,* **64** (Fall 1985), pp. 96–112.

Dore, Isaak. *International Law and the Superpowers: Normative Order in a Divided World.* New Brunswick, N.J.: Rutgers Univ. Press, 1984.

Lewis, Anthony. "Against the Law," *New York Times,* Apr. 12, 1984, p. A27.

Moore, John Norton. "Legal Issues in the Central American Conflict," *Journal of Contemporary Studies,* **8** (Winter–Spring 1985), pp. 93–109.

Morrison, Fred L. "Reconsidering United States Acceptance of the Compulsory Jurisdiction of the International Court of Justice," *World Affairs,* **148** (Summer 1985), pp. 63–70.

Owens, Mackubin Thomas. "Grenada, Nicaragua, and International Law," *This World,* no. 9 (Fall 1984), pp. 3–14.

U.S. Cong., House of Representatives. *U.S. Decision to Withdraw from the International Court of Justice,* Hearing before the Subcommittee on Human Rights and International Organizations of the Committee on Foreign Affairs, 99th Cong., 1st Sess., 1985.

19 Do U.S.-Soviet arms control agreements enhance the prospects for peace between the superpowers?

YES

Wolfgang K. H. Panofsky

Arms Control: Necessary Process

NO

William A. Schwartz and Charles Derber

Arms Control: Misplaced Focus

Arms Control: Necessary Process

Wolfgang K. H. Panofsky

It has become fashionable to attack the arms control process not only for those protagonists who envision that the United States with its technological superiority could prevail in an arms race with the Soviet Union, but also for those critics who would like to see more drastic measures in place to terminate the arms race. The "doves" in the latter category measure the past achievements of arms control against self-set standards of achievement which have not been met. Yet, as figure 1 shows, the achievements of negotiated arms control since the end of World War II have not at all been negligible and have certainly demonstrated that agreements in this field are possible among nations whose interests are greatly at variance in other areas. Still, there must be more if the arms race is to be stopped and reversed.

Before dealing with this crossfire between the right and the left, let me make some remarks on the nature of arms control itself. The goal of arms control is to manage the competition among nations in order to lessen the dangers and burdens of armament. Arms control results in contracts between or among sovereign nation-states that have many diverse, and frequently conflicting, interests on this globe. Such contracts are arrived at by negotiation. As in any other negotiating process, an agreed contract will only result if all sides concur that it is more to their advantage to sign than not to sign. Arguing about who has gained and who has lost in an arms control agreement is futile; all sides must agree that their national security is enhanced. It is more than futile and in fact

highly destructive to abuse the arms control process in the interest of achieving a substantial advantage for one side or the other. Needless to say, this does not preclude hard bargaining with the goal kept firmly in mind of achieving greater national security at lesser risks and burdens of weaponry for all parties.

Naturally, any product of such negotiations can and in fact is expected to be subject to criticism. As a homely example, if agreement has been reached between seller and buyer on the cost of transferring title to a house, then the buyer's friends can reasonably argue that he should have gotten the house for less, while the seller's friends can argue that he should have sold it for more. Yet both parties have agreed that the transfer of title served their interests at the particular price. It is thus much too easy for a presidential candidate to criticize the SALT II agreement as "fatally flawed" on grounds that, for instance, it permitted the Soviets to retain over 300 large ballistic missiles while the United States was not permitted (nor had ever desired) to build matching devices. Such criticism, however, ignores the basic bargain that was reached early in the SALT negotiations: the Soviets were willing to forego inclusion of the U.S. "forward based systems" located in Europe under U.S. control which threatened the Soviet homeland—and were therefore strategic by the Soviet definition—in exchange for U.S. agreement to continue the imbalance in very large missiles.

One should be reminded that arms control, like any other piece of binding legislation or agreement, only draws a line between what is allowed and what is forbidden. One should not fault an agreement for not having constrained what is allowed. Yet many critics ignore this elementary fact.

Wolfgang K. H. Panofsky, "Arms Control: Necessary Process," *Bulletin of the Atomic Scientists*, **42** (Mar. 1986), pp. 35–38. Reprinted by permission of the *Bulletin of the Atomic Scientists*, a magazine of science and world affairs. Copyright © 1986 by the Educational Foundation for Nuclear Science.

FIGURE 1   PRINCIPAL ACHIEVEMENTS IN ARMS CONTROL
(Italicized treaties are not in force)

	Signed	U.S. ratified
Antarctic Treaty	1959	1960
"Hot Line" (modernized 1971 and 1984)	1963	Not needed
Limited Nuclear Test Ban Treaty (LTBT)	1963	1963
Outer Space Treaty	1967	1967
Latin America Nuclear Free Zone (amended)	1967	1971*
Nuclear Non-Proliferation Treaty (NPT)	1968	1969
Seabed	1971	1972
Biological Convention	1972	1975
ABM Treaty	1972	1972
Salt I Interim Agreement	1972	Not needed
Threshold Test Ban Treaty/Peaceful Nuclear Explosion Treaty (TTBT/PNET)	1974/6	
SALT II	1979	
Environmental Modification	1977	1979

* Applicable to first protocol only.

Figures 1 and 3 are based on the author's compilation and analysis. Figure 1 includes information from the Arms Control and Disarmament Agency, *Arms Control and Disarmament Agreements* (Washington, D.C.: ACDA, 1985). The listings in Figure 4 are adapted from the Arms Control Association, *Countdown on SALT II* (Washington, D.C.: ACA and Plowshares Fund, 1985).

The criticism of the arms control experience to date from those who would like to see more dramatic limitations is varied:

• *Past arms control measures have not stopped the arms race.* Nor has anything else. Yet, one should recognize that in the absence of the arms control agreements tabulated in figure 1 the arms race might well have accelerated much faster. One can argue persuasively that in the absence of the 1972 ABM Treaty both defensive and offensive buildups would have been larger and that in the absence of the Non-Proliferation Treaty more than the current six states would have joined the nuclear club. Figure 2 shows the expected growth of Soviet strategic weapons by 1990, depending on whether or not both sides continue not to undercut SALT II.

• *Arms control has not solved the problem of the vulnerability of fixed land-based missiles.* True, but again, nor has anything else, including the many technological fixes that have been

proposed. Increasing accuracy and the multiplicity of MIRVs have left fixed land-based missiles vulnerable. The only remedy can be either elimination of such fixed systems in favor of mobility or rebasing such systems away from land altogether. Alternatively, one can increase the number of inexpensive aim points relative to the number of attacking warheads to a sufficient extent to make preemptive attack against land-based missiles unproductive. These approaches remain objectives of arms control.

• *Arms control has overemphasized raw numbers.* Since in the arms control process the parties have negotiated about, and to a certain extent have agreed to, numerical limits on many categories of deployments, such numbers have acquired a political importance which their military and technical significance does not deserve. Thus, public discourse tends to give prominence to discussing who is ahead and who is behind. Yet, with the vast numbers of nuclear weapons now deployed and the many political, geographic, and economic asymmetries between the Soviet Union

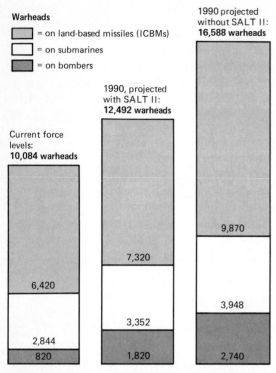

Warheads

■ = on land-based missiles (ICBMs)
□ = on submarines
■ = on bombers

Current force levels:
10,084 warheads

6,420

2,844

820

1990, projected with SALT II:
12,492 warheads

7,320

3,352

1,820

1990 projected without SALT II:
16,588 warheads

9,870

3,948

2,740

The warhead numbers assume the Soviets will use as many warheads per weapon as possible, within the SALT guidelines

FIGURE 2. HOW SALT II AFFECTS THE SOVIET ARSENAL (*Source:* Central Intelligence Agency)

and the United States, such numerical comparisons have hardly any relation to the outcome of a potential nuclear conflict.

This criticism has some merit. Clearly, a few hundred more or less out of 2,300 strategic delivery systems cannot be a predictably significant military factor. Yet one should recognize that in contracts in civilian life—for example, the price of a house referred to above—a specific figure has to be arrived at in order to reach agreement at all. Much civilian legislation involves somewhat arbitrary numbers such as speed limits, maximum permissible concentrations of pollutants, and so forth. Such limits do slow down the average traffic and lower the toxic exposure of the public, even if individual violations occur.

• *Arms control has legitimized the arms race by explicitly permitting certain activities.* Yes, this interpretation can be given, but the alternative is to prohibit all or permit all—clearly a prescription preventing any progress.

• *The purpose of arms control agreements can be bypassed by new technological developments.* Arms control agreements apply constraints to known or reasonably projected military systems and their deployments. It is difficult to constrain what has not been invented or does not yet exist, but one can try. The ABM Treaty of 1972, as restricted further in 1974, includes both specific and generic restraints. Such generic restraints are incorporated in the now controversial Article V banning development and testing of ABM systems and components not located at fixed permitted sites. The Treaty defines ABM by the ABM *mission*, not by then existing ABM technology. The Reagan Administration's recent attempt to deny this interpretation, which had been accepted by all parties since 1972, has rightfully drawn the ire of those familiar with the negotiating history that led to the formulation of such generic constraints.

There is no infallible way to prevent new technology from eventually making old arms control agreements obsolete, as there is no fundamental way to prevent new technology from making old laws and regulations obsolete in the civilian sector. Yet much can be done to forestall such technological obsolescence. For instance, arms control agreements could be negotiated to apply overall constraints on the resources which fuel the arms race or which can increase confidence that bypass of an agreement is not likely to be attempted or will not be successful. Cases in point are such agreements as cutoff of the production of fissionable material for military purposes which has been proposed by several U.S. administrations since President Eisenhower's and which recently has been endorsed at least in part by the Soviet Union. Such a resource constraint would at least impede the mushrooming of new nuclear weapons systems unconstrained by previous arms control treaties. The bypass processes, even where possible and legal, require a long time and could be dealt with by future measures facing the changing technological situation.

Defense protagonists—that is, "hawks"—criticize arms control agreements in terms of their specific provisions, as well as in respect to the following general concerns:

• *Verification.* Arms control negotiations between the United States and the Soviet Union are affected by the asymmetries between the two societies. Thus, as a practical matter verification is of less concern to the Soviet Union than it is to the United States. Moreover, the Soviets, stemming from centuries-old tradition, are more sensitive to intrusive inspection measures than is the United States, although the United States is by no means immune to such concerns. As a result, negotiation of verification provisions beyond national technical means presents problems vis-à-vis the Soviets, and this in turn is interpreted by critics as a signal of Soviet intent to cheat.

The issue essentially is one of the standards required for verification to be adequate. Verification need not be an absolute yes-or-no proposition, although any confirmed violation undermines confidence in a treaty. The eminently reasonable standard that verification is to prevent evasions that would vitiate the basic purpose of the agreement and entail dangers to the national security is considered inadequate to some critics, who tend to flag any possibility of evasion as a fatal flaw in a potential agreement. Yet, in respect to civilian legislation or regulation, complete enforceability is rarely if ever made a condition for enactment of new law.

Recently, critics, including those within the Administration, have tended to handle treaty compliance issues by looking at alleged evasions rather than at the overall record of compliance. For instance, comparison of the military impact of the much heralded evasions (figure 3) alleged to have been incurred vis-à-vis the provisions of SALT I and II with the impressive list of actual restraints on Soviet actions (figure 4) and of accomplished dismantlement of systems in response to these treaties, reveals an impressive net positive effect on U.S. security.

Inadequate verification—long the recurrent basis for opposition from the right to the enactment of a comprehensive nuclear test ban treaty—has recently been replaced by more candid U.S. statements maintaining that such a treaty would simply not be "in the national interest." In general, verification issues should not be a stumbling block to enactment of far-reaching arms control agreements, with the possible exception of agreements intended to lead to reductions to such small residual forces that relatively small violations would have profound military consequences.

• *Interference with national plans.* Any effective arms control agreement will naturally interfere with all parties' military programs, either those in being or those in preparation. Defense partisans tend to demand that somehow arms control measures should control only the other side's weapons but have minimum impact on their own programs. The result of such concerns has been that arms control agreements frequently prove non-negotiable within the U.S. government unless they constrain only the generation after next of military systems, but leave current programs intact. For example, it proved unacceptable for the United States to introduce a "zero ABM" option during the SALT I process since construction of a Safeguard site was already in progress.

We must learn that arms control will have little future unless we are willing to accept the

FIGURE 3   A LOOK AT ALLEGED TREATY VIOLATIONS

	Action	Treaty	Basis of violation	Possible military impact
Soviet Union	SS-25	SALT II (unratified)	May violate "one new type" rule, or be a legal "modernization"	Minor; may be stabilizing
	Encryption	SALT II	Ambiguous language	Possibly significant
	Krasnoyarsk radar	ABM Treaty	Location illegal, early warning function legal	Minor
	Explosions over 150 kilotons	Threshold Test Ban Treaty	Technical interpretation of seismic data is highly debatable.	Very minor
	"Sverdlovsk incident"	Biological convention	At least procedural noncompliance	Minor
United States	Minuteman covers	SALT II	Definite	None
	Thule/Fylingdales radars	ABM Treaty	Arguable	Minor
	Homing overlay experiment	ABM Treaty	Arguable	Minor
	Unwillingness to negotiate CTBT	Non-Proliferation Treaty; Limited Test Ban Treaty	Failure to pursue preambles' call for a comprehensive test ban	Indefinite
Both countries	Nuclear test venting	Limited Test Ban Treaty	Technical violation	None

impact of agreements on national programs. Arms control provisions must be evaluated under a net assessment which weighs the impact on national and international security of limits on both sides' programs. A problem is that under such an assessment the impact of a potential agreement on U.S. military systems is relatively easy to evaluate while the potential impact on Soviet systems can be subject to considerable uncertainties. Nevertheless, a negative impact on one's own systems viewed in isolation should not be, but in practice often is, a reason for opposition to arms control.

• *False confidence.* Right-wing critics of arms control agreements often express the view that the agreement under consideration would inspire "false confidence" and thus detract from the national will to provide adequately for the national defense. Such a fear basically leads to opposition to any arms control agreements and expresses lack of confidence that the democratic processes of this country can lead to wise security policy decisions. The false confidence argument leads to the conclusion that the

arms competition among nations can never be managed in any manner other than by unbridled competition. One could with greater merit argue that false expectations generated by the premise that specific new weapons systems will buy real security are much more dangerous than false expectations generated by arms control. In particular the expectation generated by the premise that Star Wars may provide a technological fix to the threat of nuclear weapons is dangerous at best and detracts from the pressure to attack the nuclear arms race at its roots: through reductions and other negotiated arms control limitations.

Arms control is an important aspect of national security. The premise that national security necessarily increases with an increasing level of armament is patently false: since the end of World War II, the risk of the lives of our citizens from war has increased as the levels of armaments have increased. Thus, the decision-making mechanisms in Washington must confront the different components of national security—military preparedness, foreign relations,

FIGURE 4   HAVE THE SALT AGREEMENTS
AFFECTED SOVIET PLANS FOR DEPLOYING
OFFENSIVE WEAPONS?

Since SALT II (1979), the Soviet Union:
  • has never exceeded the SALT I limit on ballistic
missile launchers or violated its commitment not to
undercut the SALT II limits on total strategic
nuclear warheads and MIRVed ballistic missiles;
    • has not constructed a single new fixed ICBM silo;
    • has not tested a new "heavy" ICBM;
    • has not tested or deployed a mobile "heavy" ICMB;
    • has not increased the number of warheads on
existing ICBMs;
    • has not developed or tested ballistic missiles for
installation on surface ships or emplacement on the
ocean floor;
    • has provided advance notification of tests involving
multiple missile launches and extraterritorial test flights;
    • has produced 30 or fewer Backfire bombers per
year, and has removed refueling probes from Backfire
bombers to reduce their potential utility as "strategic"
intercontinental bombers;
    • has not deployed the Backfire with long-range
cruise missiles which would give it intercontinental
capability and thus require that it be counted under SALT
II limits;
    • has not tested an ICBM that released more than 10
"reentry vehicles" (representing warheads), or tested an
SLBM that released more than 14, in compliance with
SALT II's "fractionation" restrictions. No more than nine
mock warheads have ever been released during a Soviet
SLBM test. In addition, under the SALT I and SALT II
accords the Soviets have removed 1,007 ICBMs, 233
SLBMs, and 13 "Yankee"-class nuclear-missile-carrying
submarines.

economic and political strength, and arms control. Although all these factors target a single
goal—national security—they at times necessarily will lead to conflicting requirements.

Progress in arms control thus demands that the
interests of national security through military
strength, national security through well-
managed foreign relations, and national security through arms control each be inde-
pendently championed and reconciled only at
the highest level. Making the formulation of
arms control policy subservient to any one of
the other components of national security is
destructive. This realization was the origin of
the establishment of the Arms Control and
Disarmament Agency and the General Advisory Committee in 1961. It is essential that the
erosion during recent administrations of these
institutions, which provide such independent
policy inputs, be reversed.

In the near term, arms control is the only
intermediate means at hand between the extremes of unilateral steps toward arms reductions and unfettered arms competition. In many
respects the arms controllers are the realists
while both the unilateral disarmers and the
military hardware enthusiasts are visionaries. It
is no less visionary to propose that a new
generation of technology will make nuclear
weapons impotent and obsolete than it is to
propose that a new international order that
would obviate the need for such weapons be
established. We must have arms control before
either vision can conceivably lead to reality.

Arms Control: Misplaced Focus

William A. Schwartz and Charles Derber

Almost everyone takes for granted the importance of the nuclear arms race. Right, center, and left fiercely disagree about whether the United States should try to win it, end it, or maintain a stalemate, but underneath lies a hidden consensus that its outcome is the key to nuclear war and peace. Most of the nuclear debate consists of arguments about which weapons systems should be built, controlled, cancelled, frozen, or retired.

Short of virtually complete, multilateral nuclear disarmament, however, no change in the pace, balance, or even the direction of the arms race can make much difference in the risk of nuclear war, the damage should one occur, or the division of international political power. This includes Star Wars, the nuclear freeze, and even large cuts in or stabilization of offensive nuclear arsenals.

A better starting point for nuclear politics would be the insight that nuclear weapons have completely changed the logic of power as it has been handed down through the ages. Military force, perfected to its highest level, has invalidated itself—for in a nuclearized world, any resort to force by a nuclear power risks escalation to its ultimate level, and thus to oblivion for all. Trying to rationalize and control the ultimate force is far less realistic and important than limiting the provocation of conflict and the use of force at lower, non-nuclear levels—by the United States, its clients, and, to the extent possible, its adversaries.

Without doubt, the existence of nuclear weapons per se and their possession by particular nations matters a great deal. The fallacy lies in attributing great significance to the size and characteristics of the superpowers' nuclear stockpiles, and especially to the margins of each arsenal: incremental additions to or subtractions from the current force, such as the building of 100 MX missiles or the removal of cruise missiles from Europe.

With conventional military technology, such concerns—what political scientist Samuel Huntington has called "weaponitis"[1]—do make some sense, because conventional wars are largely processes of attrition. One side's weapons and soldiers must gradually neutralize those of the enemy before a threat of destruction can be posed to the enemy's inner society. The side with more or better weapons does not always win, because other factors may intervene, but it enjoys a definite edge.

The immense power of an individual atomic weapon, especially the later hydrogen weapon, changed this. A nation's armed forces do not have to be defeated before its society can be credibly threatened by such weapons, since only a single one must penetrate to destroy a city. General war was no longer to be a process of military attrition, but one of outright, mutual social devastation. After both superpowers accumulated enough nuclear weapons to destroy the other—perhaps as early as 1955, and certainly by the early 1960s—increasing the number or quality of such weapons could add little to military potential or risks.

William A. Schwartz and Charles Derber, "Arms Control: Misplaced Focus," *Bulletin of the Atomic Scientists,* **42** (Mar. 1986), pp. 39–44. Reprinted by permission of the *Bulletin of the Atomic Scientists,* a magazine of science and world affairs. Copyright © 1986 by the Educational Foundation for Nuclear Science. An expanded version of the article will be published in 1988 by the University of California Press.

[1] Speech at Boston College Graduate Student Association symposium on the arms race and nuclear war, Oct. 12, 1983. See William Schwartz, "U.S. Nuclear Policies Increase Threat of War," Boston College Heights, Oct. 17, 1983.

Even the massive "overkill" in modern nuclear arsenals might not have rendered the arms race irrelevant if it had proved possible either to build effective defenses against these great arsenals, or to keep a nuclear exchange limited to a very small fraction of available warheads. But precisely because of the great power of the individual hydrogen weapon, neither can be achieved with any confidence. A meaningful defense of cities against such weapons would have to be near-perfect, which no military technology can achieve, and even small numbers of nuclear weapons could do unthinkable damage to rural areas, to the underlying ecological, economic, and social infrastructures that support human life, and perhaps even to the planetary temperature-regulation system.

Moreover, in its diverse physical effects—blast, heat, radiation, electromagnetic pulse—this weapon not only kills people and destroys property, but also disrupts the complex pathways of authority, communication, transportation, coordination, and technology that permit a society and its military system to function. After its use on anything but the most limited scale, there could be no predicting or rational planning for what will happen after hostilities break out. To assume that cities may be spared or that only a small number of missiles will be used is to presuppose a level of control that probably will not exist. All-out escalation is not inevitable, but its possibility is inherently present, and its probability is unknown.

Very simply, then, developments in the arms race do not much affect the risk of nuclear war because they cannot change the basic situation faced by national leaders: if nuclear weapons are ever again used in war, whatever the sizes and characteristics of the arsenals, this will necessarily precipitate a substantial but unknown chance of mutual annihilation.

Many who understand this continue to worry about the arms race, partly because of an understandable gut-level fear that since nuclear weapons are bad, more of them must be worse. A more sophisticated concern, felt equally on both sides of the political spectrum, is that the emergence of "first strike" weapons may undermine this condition of mutual vulnerability upon which stability is thought to depend. Some fear the Soviet SS-18 and SS-19, while others think the Pentagon is seeking its own first-strike arsenal, with MX, Pershing II, Trident II, and Star Wars.

The concern is that one side may develop the ability to rob the other of its retaliatory capability and thus wage nuclear war without risking its own destruction. The "superior" side will supposedly be tempted to launch a disarming premeditated attack. And the vulnerable side will supposedly feel that it must "use or lose" its own weapons, believing that a preemptive first strike of its own, though very hazardous, is preferable to being disarmed. If, as many argue, both powers are building first-strike arsenals, then the situation is even more alarming, for both will feel the war incentives of the superior as well as the inferior position.

Despite all the worry, the simple fact remains that hydrogen warheads are too powerful, and nuclear weapons platforms too diverse and well-defended, for any existing or anticipated technology to permit one side to rob the other of its retaliatory capability. This would require the emergence of an overwhelming, near-simultaneous threat to the survivability of virtually all nuclear delivery vehicles, including submarines at sea, or even less plausibly, to warheads after launch. Even a single surviving ballistic-missile submarine or several dozen ICBMs or strategic bombers would sustain the essential risk—destruction of the attacking nation. Even were such a wildly implausible threat to become possible in principle, it could never preclude retaliation with confidence, because of the risk of malfunctions and miscalculations associated with all complex human/machine systems, especially untestable ones.

Even those who accept this view often continue, strangely, to decry the dangers of first-strike weapons. In the peace movement, for example, many insist that nuclear war cannot be won, no matter who strikes first, yet worry that these new weapons will destabilize the arms balance precisely because they may give one side the ability to strike first. The two positions are inconsistent.

Consider the most common image: some future Soviet premier is confronted with horrifying blips on a radar screen during a crisis. He could, as feared, preempt, using his missiles out of fear of losing them—thus seriously risking an exchange producing unacceptable damage to the Soviet Union, whether or not a real U.S. attack was in progress.

Or he could wait to see for certain if the suspected attack is real. If it is, the Soviet Union is destroyed, and a retaliatory blow will fall on the United States—a smaller one than if he had launched before absorbing the attack, but probably enough to destroy the United States. Preempting, then, is tantamount to suicide, while *not* preempting holds out a chance of survival: the very real chance that the radar blips are a false alarm. The strength of incentives to preempt is questionable, no matter how many first-strike weapons the United States has. The premier's goal is not, after all, to save missiles. It is to save the Soviet Union.

In any case, from the premier's standpoint the most worrisome threat is not that the blips are new counterforce missiles coming at his missile silos. Rather, it is that they are missiles, counterforce or not, coming at his nuclear command and control network—which, like its U.S. counterpart, has been at risk since the 1960s and could be easily neutralized by current offensive weapons. After such "decapitation," Moscow would probably lose the ability to choose, order, and coordinate a retaliatory response. Some form of spasmodic, uncoordinated retaliation would probably occur anyway on the initiative of local commanders, but the Soviet state would have lost any capability to conduct the war in a planned way with specific goals. The ability to control whatever weapons survive, and thus to use them to advance Soviet goals, is far more important than the number that survive, which will always be sufficient for retaliation.

While the importance of the first-strike scenario has been highly exaggerated relative to others, such as incremental escalation from a conventional war, there is at least one circumstance in which it could become the most likely path to nuclear war—when a leader is virtually certain that the other side is about to push the button. Once war is assumed to be inevitable, a preemptive first strike may seem to offer the best chance of disrupting enemy attacks, thereby somewhat limiting damage and holding out some small chance of eliminating retaliation entirely through decapitation.

What must be avoided, then, are the extreme *political* conditions in which a Soviet or U.S. leader could actually believe that his counterpart had decided to launch World War III. The desperate feeling that the axe is about to fall one way or the other, not the size, accuracy, or speed of the axe, is the key factor. To the extent that first strike and preemption are worrisome possibilities, avoiding them depends much more upon the prevention and defusing of military confrontations and the reduction of war hysteria than either the construction or obstruction of new weapons.

Preventing a nuclear attack might also depend upon countering any misperception of the facts as we have described them. Weapons might matter, some argue, if only because people think they do. Leaders might mistakenly believe they could win a war on the strength of their new systems, or that they had to preempt because of the other side's new systems. Or short of this, one side might gain major political advantages on the strength of a nuclear arsenal perceived by others to be superior.

It is true that leaders on both sides decry the dangers of the opponent's nuclear weapons and constantly seek new systems of their own. In the peacetime budgetary and domestic political processes, weapons certainly matter to them. But this does not mean that leaders also *act* in the international arena on the basis of these same exaggerations of the importance of weapons.

Historical experience suggests, instead, that military and political leadership on both sides have a self-contradictory philosophy of nuclear weapons. While they do attach great importance to the weapons balance in the planning and procurement process, in real foreign policy decisions and in the handling of real crises their behavior is not substantially affected by which weapons each side has built. This does not mean that they are unwilling to run substantial risks of nuclear war— they are—but only that when they do, the details of the nuclear balance do not influence them.

In the Cuban missile crisis, for example, according to President Kennedy's senior advisers: "American nuclear superiority was not...a critical factor, for the fundamental and controlling reason that nuclear war, already in 1962, would have been an unexampled catastrophe for both sides....No one of us ever reviewed the nuclear balance for comfort in those hard weeks."[2] A recent study of newly released documents adds: "There is no evidence that President Kennedy and his advisers counted missiles, bombers, and warheads, and decided on that basis to take a tough line....No one discussed what American counterforce capabilities were—that is, how well the United States might be able to 'limit damage' in the event of an all-out war. It was as though all the key concepts associated with the administration's formal nuclear strategy...in the final analysis counted for very little."[3]

Similarly, nowhere in President Nixon's extensive memoirs can one find any reference to consideration of the nuclear weapons balance in his decision to alert U.S. nuclear forces during the Middle East superpower crisis of October 1973—despite Nixon's deep concern with weapons systems in domestic politics both before and afterward. Nixon apparently had no doubt that the Soviets saw things as he did.[4]

Other crises and foreign policy initiatives have shown the same pattern. As McGeorge Bundy has said, "There has been no Soviet action anywhere that can be plausibly attributed to the so-called window of vulnerability."[5] And no one has demonstrated that U.S. power anywhere in the world has concretely benefited since the mid-1950s from an American strategic edge. Bundy was probably correct, as well, when he said that in none of the great Suez, Berlin, and Cuban crises "would the final result have been different if the relative strategic positions of the Soviet Union and the United States had been reversed....A stalemate is a stalemate either way around."[6]

In their more honest moments outside the budgetary process, military leaders on both sides have agreed that weapons hardware does not affect the basic military realities. Marshal Ogarkov, the Warsaw Pact commander in chief, said in a May 1984 interview in the Soviet press: "The deployment of U.S. intermediate-range missiles in Western Europe did not increase the possibility of a 'first strike' against the Soviet

---

[2] Dean Rusk, et al., "The Lessons of the Cuban Missile Crisis," *Time* (Sept. 27, 1982), p. 85.

[3] Marc Trachtenberg, "The Influence of Nuclear Weapons in the Cuban Missile Crisis," *International Security,* vol. 10, no. 1 (Summer 1985), pp. 137–63. Supporting documents are in the same journal, pp. 164–203.

[4] Richard Nixon, *RN: The Memoirs of Richard Nixon* (New York: Grosset and Dunlap, 1978).

[5] McGeorge Bundy, "The Unimpressive Record of Atomic Diplomacy," in Gwyn Prins, ed., *The Nuclear Crisis Reader* (New York: Vintage, 1984), p. 51.

[6] Bundy, "To Cap the Volcano," *Foreign Affairs,* vol. 48, no. 1 (Oct. 1969), p. 11.

Union. Both sides fully recognize the inevitability of a retaliatory strike."[7] General David Jones, former chairman of the Joint Chiefs of Staff, has agreed: "I don't know any American officer, or any Soviet officer, who really believes either superpower can achieve a true first-strike capability, that one side could ever so disarm the other as to leave it without the ability to retaliate.... [Both] strongly agree that neither side can win a nuclear war in any meaningful sense."[8] Such men might well advise a leader to begin World War III someday, but not because they misperceive the importance of figures on a nuclear weapons balance sheet.

Besides, even if some consequential misperceptions about weapons do exist, we still would doubt the wisdom of pretending that weapons matter in order to assuage the fears of those who think they do. This inevitably involves one in a twisted logic that ends up reinforcing the very misperceptions one is trying to counter. Hawks frequently argue for new U.S. weapons to counter Soviet misperceptions that we have become strategically inferior. But to justify the expense to Congress and the public, they must decry glaring weaknesses in the U.S. force posture. This only adds to the undeserved image of weakness that was the reason for concern in the first place, as psychologist Steven Kull has brilliantly shown.[9] Similarly, when the peace movement works to stop "destabilizing" weapons, partly to prevent any misperception that the United States is acquiring a knock-out first-strike capability, it must urgently decry the dangers of first-strike weapons. It thus, unwittingly, adds legitimacy to the erroneous idea that in nuclear war it matters who strikes first— reinforcing the very fears it is trying to allay.

Questions must be raised, then, about the weapons-focused political agendas of right, center, and left—respectively, rearmament, arms control, and disarmament. In each case, the attention to hardware betrays a serious misunderstanding of the nuclear problem. But for each, "weaponitis" also serves narrower political interests by deflecting attention from the difficult political questions that a more rational nuclear debate would inevitably raise.

While U.S. military power cannot be significantly boosted by nuclear rearmament, focusing the debate on nuclear hardware helps the political right to safely channel opposition away from its more important international agenda: massive conventional military buildup, and the political and ideological shifts that will permit use of the military in emerging Third World conflicts. Similarly, nuclear arms control can do very little to prevent nuclear war, but it does provide middle-of-the-road politicians with a popular and risk-free program for addressing the nuclear problem.

As veteran arms-controller George Rathjens of the Massachusetts Institute of Technology has said, arms control "is deceptive to the point of almost being a gigantic fraud: there is the implicit suggestion that controls on weapons of the kind that have been tried will solve the problem—or at least make a big difference— when there is no real reason for so believing. ...The negotiations have been predicated on a belief that numbers and detailed performance characteristics of weapons are important," and as a result "the importance of differences in capabilities have been exaggerated to the point where political leaders and the public have been led to believe that such differences could be exploited militarily, when almost certainly they could not be."[10]

Although mainstream arms-controllers rarely advocate this, reductions to less than

[7] Dusko Doder, "A Comeback by Ex-Soviet Military Chief," *Boston Globe*, July 18, 1985, p. 13.

[8] David Jones, "Is Arms Control Obsolete?," *Harper's*, vol. 271, no. 1622 (July 1985), p. 44.

[9] Steven Kull, "Nuclear Nonsense," *Foreign Policy*, no. 58 (Spring 1985), pp. 28–52.

[10] George Rathjens, "First Thoughts," unpublished manuscript, pp. 8–9.

one-tenth of current stockpiles might somewhat reduce the damage of a nuclear exchange. But under current political conditions it is unclear whether such reductions would increase or decrease the likelihood of an exchange, and it is unrealistic to think that they will follow naturally from the incremental reductions now being discussed. In the absence of long-term political change, near-total nuclear disarmament would pose qualitatively new and perhaps insurmountable political difficulties and verification problems.

The peace movement's strategy of opposing weapons, and even viewing progress toward disarmament as the guiding program, must also be challenged. As difficult as it may be for activists to accept, stopping the MX, killing Star Wars, or even negotiating a comprehensive nuclear weapons freeze would probably not improve the risks or consequences of nuclear war by more than a small amount. This "weapons strategy" has, however, permitted the peace movement to mobilize large segments of the population, the media, and the Congress, for it is a way to be active on the nuclear issue without confronting the more radical and divisive issue of the links between nuclear war and U.S. foreign policy.

Activists often respond that even if working to stop the arms race cannot much reduce the risk of nuclear war, it has other virtues, such as saving the billions of dollars wasted on new systems and limiting other social and psychological costs of the arms race. These benefits may be real, and may in fact constitute the best reasons for opposing the arms race, but they should not be confused with direct progress in preventing nuclear war. It is also conceivable, as some argue, that the purely symbolic benefits of ending the nuclear arms race might improve superpower relations to the point of affecting the risk of war between them. But such benefits are speculative, do not square with the very short-lived aftereffects of past arms control agreements, and are probably small compared with the potential benefits of direct assault on the more significant causes of bad superpower relations: for example, on their mutual use of a largely mythical threat from the other to justify violent actions to maintain control within their own empires.

Activists also respond that the arms race, even if not important in itself, is an excellent vehicle for mobilizing populations around the nuclear danger generally. Once recruited to the nuclear issue by the nuclear freeze or other antiweapons campaigns, people can and often do move on to confront more important matters, such as the legitimacy of nuclear diplomacy as a tool of state.

The peace movement has done incalculable good by educating people about the consequences and danger of nuclear war. But using the "weapons strategy" to do this is questionable, for it requires giving the public misinformation: that the race in weapons is the problem and stopping the arms race is the solution, or at least a major step along the way. The main reason that the weapons themselves carry such great mobilizing power is precisely that much of the public has been led to believe that halting their accumulation can materially reduce the chances that they and their families will die in a nuclear war. If activists came to accept the marginal strategic significance of the nuclear arms race and still continued this strategy, they would then be engaged in a calculated misrepresentation of the issue to the movement rank-and-file and the general public—something no democratic movement should tolerate, and no activists would support.

Nor is it obvious that the weapons strategy even works as a mobilizer in the long run. If the arms race is successfully portrayed as the problem, then a major movement victory such as the freeze—literally the end of the arms race—could well destroy public concern through complacency, even though the risk of nuclear war would be unchanged. If, more likely, major antiweapons campaigns continue to fail, the movement risks demobilization through despair, as we have recently seen in the European peace movement after the deployment of the euromissiles, and the American one after the failure to achieve the bilateral freeze or to defeat even a single new weapons system.

The nuclear debate must break free from the technicism and insularity of a primarily *nuclear* discourse focused on weapons. It must, instead, highlight the endemic *conventional* violence of the world, from which nuclear war can always escalate, and the sources of this violence in domestic and international social structures, political systems, cultures, and ideologies. It must therefore be a socio-political debate which acknowledges the futility of seeking technical solutions to the deeply social problems of war and peace.

The central task must be to avert armed confrontation involving one or more nuclear-armed powers. This logically requires two steps: restricting the spread of nuclear weapons to states and organizations that do not now possess them, and avoiding political and military facedowns between those that do. In both cases the essential problem is the pervasive conventional militarism that has brought bloody domestic and interstate conflict to virtually every region of the world since World War II.

Like the more general nuclear debate, proliferation has traditionally been couched as a technical problem—of denying non-nuclear powers the strategic materials, technology, and knowledge to build bombs. Undoubtedly, the massive spread of nuclear technology, under the guises of the "peaceful atom" and the Non-Proliferation Treaty, have scandalously increased the dangers, and tighter controls are essential. But this process has now advanced so far that it can only be a matter of time before the capacity to make or steal nuclear warheads becomes available to any nation or major organization that seeks it.

As long as nations and other organized international groups feel threatened by aggression, or suffer grievous disenfranchisement or oppression, some will seek the ultimate weapon as a way out. This largely explains the patterns of nuclear proliferation to date, with technically advanced but nonmilitarist countries such as Switzerland, Canada, Australia, Austria, Belgium, and Yugoslavia avoiding nuclear weapons for lack of motive, while others seek them because they are embroiled in conflict.

Focusing on sources of conflict and the militarism they produce is equally the best strategy for averting confrontations involving those powers that have already built nuclear stockpiles—which, barring outright accidental launches on a large scale, will be the immediate cause of any new world war. As Noam Chomsky has sensibly put it: "If we are concerned to avert nuclear war, our primary concern should be to lessen tensions and conflicts at the points where war engaging the superpowers is likely to erupt."[11] Europe has traditionally received the most attention, especially around the possible escalation of an uprising in Eastern Europe. But despite recent Administration "rollback" rhetoric, Europe remains far more stable and controllable than many points in the Third World. Conflicts there—especially those involving our own nation, whose policies Americans stand the most chance of affecting and have the most responsibility for monitoring—must therefore assume a central role.

Technical approaches such as crisis management, while not without value, are inadequate. Keeping major crises limited is extremely difficult and uncertain at best. Making basic changes in the foreign policies which enflame regional conflicts and bring about crises in the first place is much more important.

---

[11] Noam Chomsky, "Interventionism and Nuclear War," in Michael Albert and David Dellinger, eds., *Beyond Survival: New Directions for the Disarmament Movement* (Boston: South End Press, 1983), p. 259.

Adding an antimilitarist plank to the highly developed campaigns around weapons—as debated periodically by the nuclear freeze movement—is not an adequate response. The former is far more important than the latter, and the two are not linked in the ways that some theorists of the "deadly connection" contend.[12] That is, stopping new U.S. nuclear weapons systems is unlikely to demilitarize conventional U.S. foreign policy by curtailing interventionism or support for aggressive client states. U.S. leaders may well purchase both strategic and tactical nuclear weapons in part because they *hope* that these will increase their capacity to project power. But in practice, nuclear force balances have little military import, and, as we have said, political leaders do not consider them in making real politico-military decisions.

Interventions, whether in Grenada, Afghanistan, Lebanon, or Poland, are almost certainly undertaken, rather, on the basis of perceived interests and opportunities specific to each situation, within the broad context of each superpower's global ambitions. Preventing the deployment of MX, for example, would have little if any direct effect on the United States' hazardous Middle East policies. These can be altered only through a specific effort aimed at those policies themselves.

A frontal effort must be launched, then, against conventional state violence, which not incidentally causes massive human suffering among the victims and should be opposed on that basis alone. This, and the politics which breeds it, should constitute the overwhelming focus of efforts to prevent nuclear war.

Some would say that this is self-evident and has long been accepted. But while everyone sees political dimensions to the nuclear problem, the overwhelming attention given to the weapons themselves by all sides to the debate cannot be denied. Despite the *Bulletin's* significant coverage of conventional militarism, for example, in recent years a large number of articles, including almost half its cover stories, have focused on nuclear hardware, primarily new weapons systems and arms control. In addition, five of the eight changes in the hands of the *Bulletin's* "doomsday clock" since the Cuban missile crisis were in large measure responses to developments in weapons technology or arms treaty negotiations. The hands moved to their most hopeful setting ever (12 minutes to midnight) because of the SALT I treaty in 1972; they advanced to their most frightening position since the invention of the hydrogen bomb (three minutes to midnight) two years ago, largely in response to the "accelerating nuclear arms race" and the suspension of arms control negotiations.[13] The editorial of the recent fortieth-anniversary issue approvingly notes that "the need to end the arms race has become widely recognized as the overriding issue of our time."

Other critics counter that while militarism and the conflicts underlying it may in fact be far more important than the arms race, these are so deeply engrained that their elimination is a very long-term if not completely hopeless task, and certainly a poor way to deal with the pressing problem of nuclear war. A comparable argument would be that eliminating nuclear weapons is almost certainly impossible over anything but the longest run, and therefore that it should be abandoned as an anti-nuclear-war strategy. In fact, definite short-term steps are possible both to limit conventional state violence and to limit nuclear stockpiles, although neither can be fully accomplished over a short period and without major socio-political change. Since, as we have argued, incremental changes in hardware stockpiles are almost meaningless, it is only logical to seek whatever brakes on militarism are practical at the present time.

---

[12] See *The Deadly Connection: Nuclear War and U.S. Intervention* (Philadelphia: New Society Publishers, 1986).

[13] *The Freeze Focus,* vol. 4, no. 3 (April 1980), p. 19.

While underlying causes of international violence—such as the nation-state system, the imperialisms of East and West, ethnic hatred, and mass poverty—can be addressed only gradually, decisive action can be taken now to limit many volitional acts of state aggression and repression. Some of the required changes in foreign policy can be advanced through bilateral negotiations with the Soviets about political arrangements and the use of conventional force in the rest of the world. For example, an agreement to ban direct superpower military intervention in the Middle East, along with commitments by both to restrain their clients from offensive use of the massive conventional military hardware they have supplied, would substantially reduce the likelihood of another superpower crisis in that region.

The 1982 Israeli invasion and subsequent occupation of Lebanon clearly illustrate the dangers of current policy, with U.S.-backed Israeli troops and Soviet-backed Syrian troops actively engaged. U.S. intervention in the war through extensive naval shelling and bombardment raised even graver possibilities. Going deeper into the political origins of Middle East conflict, the superpowers could agree to condition further aid upon sincere efforts by all parties to reach a fair agreement concerning the underlying political conflicts, such as the rights of Israelis, Palestinians, and other Arabs to secure coexistence on the basis of national sovereignty.

Even more important, for Americans, is action to change the role of this country in:

- sponsoring or supporting regimes that murder, repress, and starve their people, and that must ultimately use great violence to remain in power, or those that aggress against other peoples;
- sustaining regional conflicts and blocking peace efforts in order to advance U.S. corporate or state "interests";

- armed interventions to prop up friendly governments or overthrow unfriendly ones; and
- other actions which enflame conflict, produce large-scale political violence, and draw the superpowers into unnecessary conflict. Most of these have nothing to do with any concrete Soviet threat. They must be addressed through political action here at home, and not just concerning South Africa and Central America, where current peace efforts are most developed.

One small step in the required educational effort might be the invention of "nuclear war impact statements," to expose for the public the depth of the now invisible connections between U.S. foreign policy and the nuclear threat. Policy for each region could be evaluated for its likely effect on local tensions and conflicts, the likelihood that these could erupt into a head-on confrontation between the superpowers or other nuclear powers, and less hazardous alternatives for regional policy. Other practical steps will be possible as well once we acknowledge that controls on nuclear weapons must be decisively subordinated to the limitation of state violence generally, and the resolution of the grievances that often produce it.

The disarmament movement cannot accomplish such things. This is a job for a full-fledged peace movement.

QUESTIONS FOR DISCUSSION

1 Do arms races cause wars?
2 Do both superpowers genuinely desire nuclear arms control and/or disarmament?
3 Should the achievement and/or preservation of approximate nuclear parity be the principal aim in superpower arms control negotiations?
4 Can both superpowers be relied upon not to cheat on arms control agreements?
5 What would be the impact on countries other than the superpowers if the superpowers significantly reduced their armaments?

SUGGESTED READINGS

Adelman, Kenneth. "Arms Control With and Without Agreements," *Foreign Affairs,* **63** (Winter 1984–85), pp. 240–263.

Committee on International Security and Arms Control, National Academy of Sciences. *Nuclear Arms Control: Background and Issues.* Washington, D.C.: National Academy Press, 1985.

Greb, G. Allen, and Gerald W. Johnson. "A History of Strategic Arms Limitations," *Bulletin of the Atomic Scientists,* **40** (Jan. 1984), pp. 30–37.

Levine, Herbert M., and David Carlton (eds.). *The Nuclear Arms Race Debated.* New York: McGraw-Hill, 1986.

Miller, Steven E. "The Viability of Nuclear Arms Control: U.S. Domestic and Bilateral Factors, " *Bulletin of Peace Proposals,* **16**, no. 3 (1985), pp. 263–276.

Perle, Richard. "The Soviet Record on Arms Control," *National Interest,* no. 1 (Fall 1985), pp. 97–101.

Schell, Jonathan. *The Abolition.* New York: Knopf, 1984.

Schelling, Thomas C. "What Went Wrong with Arms Control?" *Foreign Affairs,* **64** (Winter 1985–86), pp. 219–233.

Staar, Richard F. (ed.). *Arms Control: Myth and Reality.* Stanford, Calif.: Hoover Institution Press, 1984.

Talbott, Strobe. *Deadly Gambits.* New York: Knopf, 1984.